SOCIALISM
OR YOUR MONEY BACK

ARTICLES FROM

THE SOCIALIST STANDARD

1904-2004

THE SOCIALIST PARTY
2004

Published in 2004 by
The Socialist Party of Great Britain

ISBN 0 9544733 1 0

Design and layout by Jayne Clementson

Printed in the European Union by
Legoprint S.r.l., Turin, Italy

CONTENTS

FOREWORD

T he first issue of the *Socialist Standard* appeared in September 1904 as the "official organ of the Socialist Party of Great Britain". The Socialist Party, or SPGB, had been founded in June of the same year by ex-members of the Social Democratic Federation dissatisfied with its lack of internal democracy and with its policy of pursuing reforms of capitalism instead of concentrating on campaigning for socialism.

For them, the sole aim of a socialist party ought to be socialism, defined as a system of society based on the common ownership and democratic control of the means of production and distribution by and in the interest of the whole community. They took the view that such a society could only be brought into being through the political action of the working class – as the class of those compelled by economic necessity to sell their mental and physical energies for a wage or salary – when a majority of them had come to realise that they were living in an exploitative, class-divided society and that their interest lay, as the exploited class, in converting the means of production into the common property of society under the democratic control of all the people.

With this approach, and knowing that a majority of their fellow workers were not class conscious in this sense, the members of the new party saw their main task as to propagate socialist ideas amongst their fellow workers. To this end they ran street corner meetings, held public lectures, organised education classes, debated against other parties, contested elections, handed out leaflets, sold pamphlets – and produced the *Socialist Standard*.

The *Socialist Standard* has appeared every month since September 1904, analysing contemporary political, economic and social events and expounding aspects of socialist theory such as Marxian economics and the materialist conception of history. As such its back numbers are an invaluable source of historical material about the period in which they appeared. They also provide a running commentary from a socialist point of view on the key events of the twentieth century as they happened.

Because the *Socialist Standard* was aimed at the average literate working man and woman – for most of its existence its main outlet was sales at public meetings – it was written in an accessible style that has been compared to popular science writing. In fact, this was essentially how its writers – all of them writing in their free time out of conviction – saw what they were doing. The articles were signed, but discreetly, as the writers were regarded as expressing the view of the Party not a personal view.

To mark the centenary of its foundation and of its monthly journal, the Socialist Party is publishing this selection of articles from the *Socialist Standard* over the last hundred years. Only seventy of the well over ten thousand that must have appeared over the period have been chosen. A choice of what type of article to include had to be made and it was decided that the articles should concentrate on what the *Socialist Standard* said at the time about the key events in the century that most people will have heard of – such as the sinking of the Titanic, the First World War, the Russian Revolution, the first Labour Government, the General Strike, to go only as far as the 1920s. The articles have been grouped by period, with a short modern introduction.

Inevitably, other types of article had to be omitted, such as basic statements of the case against capitalism or for socialism (interesting as it would have been to compare how this was expressed over the decades) and theoretical articles on aspects of socialist theory (which could have provided material for a separate book – the *Socialist Standard* had plenty to say on the ideas of Marx, Engels, Kautsky, Plekhanov, Rosa Luxemburg, Daniel De Leon, Lenin, Trotsky, etc., as well as on anarchism and syndicalism).

Also omitted are all but two of the articles, which began to appear with increasing regularity from the 1970s onward, dealing with some of the practical

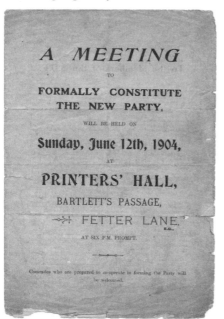

aspects of how a socialist society – as a democratic society and one with no buying and selling or money – could function and orient the production and distribution of wealth to meet people's needs. Excluding such articles was a difficult decision, especially as the Socialist Party is particularly proud of the fact that one of the things we have succeeded in doing over the past hundred years has been to keep alive the original idea of what a socialist society was to be – a classless, stateless, frontierless, wageless, moneyless society, to define it somewhat negatively, or, more positively, a world community in which the natural and industrial resources of the planet will have become the common heritage of all

First Party Conference, 1905

humanity, a democratic society in which free and equal men and women co-operate to produce the things they need to live and enjoy life and to which they have free access in accordance with the principle 'from each according to their ability, to each according to their needs'.

A hundred years ago, when the Socialist Party was formed, there was widespread agreement that this was what socialism meant, despite disagreements as to how to get there. Unfortunately, as a result of the failure in the intervening period of both gradualist reformism and Leninist dictatorship this is no longer the case. Reformists, who believed that capitalism could be gradually transformed through a series of social reform measures into a better society, themselves ended up being transformed into routine managers of the capitalist system. The Bolsheviks, who seized power as a minority under Lenin and Trotsky in Russia in 1917, ended up developing capitalism there in the form of a state-run capitalism under a one-party dictatorship. Both failures have given socialism a quite different – and unattractive – meaning: state ownership and control, even state dictatorship, which is what, as the *Socialist Standard* was pointing out even before both policies were tried, is more properly called state capitalism.

This has been represented as the 'failure of socialism'. But socialism in its original sense has never been tried. If those who are committed to the interest of the majority class of wage and salary earners and who want a better society to replace capitalism are not to make the same mistakes of reformism and minority revolution that dominated radical thinking and action in the twentieth century, they need to return to the original idea of socialism and to the understanding that the quickest way to get there is to campaign for socialism directly and as a matter of urgency. This book is aimed at contributing to that understanding.

THE SOCIALIST PARTY
May 2004

EDWARDIAN TIMES

The first edition of the *Socialist Standard* appeared nearly three months after the formation of the Party, being dated "London, September, 1904" and costing one penny. It was eight pages of dense type and small headlines (in that sense very much the style of the time) but noticeably larger than the current A4 page size. The first editorial promised "we shall give a fair hearing to all sides on any question, and trust that our correspondence columns will be freely used," a promise that has been upheld ever since by both sides.

The first edition included an editorial outlining the Party's hopes (in some ways over-optimistic) for the development of the *Standard* and the movement for socialism in general, but for reference we include in this section an article from this first issue simply entitled 'The Socialist Party of Great Britain'. This is because it explains, from the standpoint of the founder members, the basic political positions of the Socialist Party in distinction to those held by the growing number of other organisations claiming the title 'socialist' at the time.

The *Standard* during this pre-First World War period mainly tended to comprise original articles from Party members on topical issues of the time plus theoretical articles expounding aspects of the materialist conception of history and Marxian economics, some written by Party members themselves but many reprints or translations of the writings of some of the 'greats' of the Second International period like Kautsky, Bebel, Lafargue, Guesde and Morris. Perhaps belying the somewhat staid physical appearance of the *Standard*, the topical articles written by members tended to be lively and polemical, using rhetorical devices in a way the Party's outdoor orators often did. The article about the official appearance of the Labour Party on the British political scene in Westminster ('The New 'Force' in Politics') is as good as an example of this an any, though some of the later articles we have included in this section certainly run it close for tightly-argued political invective.

Politically, the Socialist Party nailed its colours to the mast on the nation or class issue at the outset and the article included here on the rise of Sinn Fein in Ireland is a stinging attack on the idea that 'national liberation' movements against established imperialist powers are in some way progressive and worthy of working class support. The stark class division identified as being at the heart of capitalism's social relations by the Party's Declaration of Principles was reflected in many other articles of the time too. Indeed, many modern readers may be surprised at the vehemence with which the early Party opposed the Suffragette movement on class grounds, identifying the Suffragettes as – at best – an irrelevant movement of propertied women falsely claiming to represent the interests of female workers.

The naked working class anger at the iniquities of capitalism to be found in the pages of the *Standard* in its early years is understandable given the conditions of the time and it is exemplified no better than in the articles on the brutal suppression of the miners' strike in South Wales by the Liberal government and the piece written on the sinking of the luxury liner, the Titanic. Both are fine examples of a particular style of political prose in the small revolutionary milieu in Britain at the beginning of the twentieth century and of the application of a class-based analysis to contemporary issues. But contrast these with the more elegant – even quaint – piece on the 'motor car problem', specifically as it affected post-Victorian London where the majority of Socialist Party members at the time were based.

Lest this particular piece lull any readers into labelling the Party 'backward-looking' in its attitudes to developing social issues during this period, the article expounding 'The Case For Free Love' should dispel any such myths. It manages to put an eloquent and considered case on the subject long before it was fashionable to do so in radical circles, let alone in the mainstream press.

The Socialist Party of Great Britain

The greatest problem awaiting solution in the world today is the existence in every commercial country of extreme poverty side by side with extreme wealth. In every land where, in the natural development of society, the capitalist method of producing and distributing wealth has been introduced, this problem presses itself upon us. Not only so but the greater the grip which capitalism has on industry the more intense is the poverty of the many and the more marked are the riches of the few.

In observing the conditions of this problem, the fact is quickly forced under our notice that it is the producer of wealth who is poor, the non-producer who is rich. How comes it that the men and women who till the soil, who dig the mine, who manipulate the machine, who build the factory and the home, and, in a word, who create the whole of the wealth, receive only sufficient to maintain themselves and their families on the border line of bare physical efficiency, while those who do not aid in production – the employing class – obtain more than is enough to supply their every necessity, comfort, and luxury?

To find a solution to this problem is the task to which the Socialist applies himself. He sees clearly that only by studying the economics of wealth-production and distribution can he understand the anomalies of present-day society. He sees, further, that having gained a knowledge of the economic causes of social inequality, he must apply this knowledge through political action – through the building up of a Socialist organisation for the capture of Parliament and the conquest of the powers of government.

To every sober observer of social facts it is patent that the life condition of the workers is one of penury and of misery. The only saleable commodity they possess – their power of working – they are compelled to take to the labour market and sell for a bare subsistence wage. The food they eat, the clothing they wear, the houses in which they live are of the shoddiest kind, and these together with the mockery of an education which their children receive, primarily determine the purchasing price of their labour-power. By organising in their various trades they may force their wage a little above this normal value, but taken on the average they are bound to sell their activity – physical, mental and moral – for the bare cost of their subsistence. In return for this wage they create, by the conversion of raw material into manufactured products or by other means, a value far in excess of the value paid them as wages. The difference between these two values is taken by the employing class, and constitutes the source of profit, interest, and rent. These three forms of exploitation are the result of the unpaid labour of the working class.

So long as this lasts – and it will last as long as the capitalist system of society it will not be possible for the workers by any Trades Union organisation to more than slightly modify their condition, and their power in this direction is becoming every day more limited by the combinations among employers to defeat the aims of the working class.

Then, too, the magnitude of industrial operations, ever tending to increase by the inherent tendency under free competition of the large producer to crush out his smaller trade rivals – the joint stock company takes the place of the large individual capitalist, the trust the place of the joint stock company. The worker is thus brought face to face with an ever greater foe.

The Socialist can calmly view this struggle, knowing that ultimately the victory is with him. In the meantime, however, he has to show the workers that while their organisation in trades will prove an invaluable aid in the transformation of society by facilitating industrial reorganisation, yet at present they can best help to emancipate themselves from the thraldom of wage-slavery by recognising that in their class struggle with their exploiters they can be most certain of success in the political sphere of action.

Such political action will, however, be quite futile unless carried on by a class-conscious party with definite aims. Such a party must recognise that in the class-war they are waging there must be no truce. They must adopt as their basis of action the Socialist position, for in no other way can their ills be redressed.

To neither of the two historic parties can we look with any hope. The Liberal Party, like the Conservative Party, is interested in maintaining the present class society, and cannot, therefore, be expected to help in its transformation from capitalism to Socialism.

The National Democratic League and the Labour Representation Committee are also to be avoided. The former has a programme of purely political measures, each of which is found in the constitutions of France and the United States of America without the working class being in any way benefited. The latter organisation has no programme whatsoever, and its members possess no principles in common save the name 'Labour'. As soon as any question of constructive legislation is brought before it its component elements will break apart, being unable to agree among themselves. Unity is only possible among those who possess common principles. Unity can not, therefore, be secured for any length of time by the members of the Labour Representation Committee, but even if it could, the body is not based upon Socialist principles and should not receive the adhesion of working men.

We, as Socialists, venture to assert that the party which is ultimately to secure the support of the rank and file of the working class must be a Socialist party. Such a party must be ever prepared to further the realisation of a Socialist Society. It must proclaim the fact that this realisation can be achieved by the members of the working class using their political power to return to Parliament and other public bodies only those who are members of The Socialist Party.

In the past two bodies of men have put forward the claim to be Socialist parties, *viz.*, the Independent Labour Party and Social Democratic Federation. We who have for many years taken a share in the work of the latter organisation and who have watched the progress of the former from its initiation, have been forced to the conclusion that through neither of them can the Social Revolution at which we aim be achieved, and that from neither of them can the working class secure redress from the ills they suffer.

The Independent Labour Party, founded for the ostensible reason of forming a half-way house to Socialism, was fated to meet with the reward of every party founded upon a compromise. With a membership of those who were sympathetic with Socialism, but who were not Socialists, they were bound to drift nearer and nearer to the Liberal Party. Having neither the courage to proclaim themselves Socialists nor to disavow Socialism, they are today coquetting with that working class wing of the Liberal Party – the Labour Representation Committee. When the question of Socialism was raised on the committee, their chief representative declared that it was neither the time nor the place for such discussion. With a party of this kind, which, in the words of their president, "is independent to support, independent to oppose" the two historic political parties, the working class should have nothing to do.

The Social Democratic Federation formed to further the cause of Socialism in Great Britain, has, during the last few years, been steadily following the compromising policy adopted from the first by the Independent Labour Party. So much is this the case that today, for all purposes of effective Socialist propaganda they have ceased to exist, and are surely developing into a mere reform party, seeking to obtain the provision of Free Maintenance for school children.

Those Socialists who, within its ranks, sought to withstand this policy, have found the task to be an impossible one, and have consequently seceded and formed themselves into the Socialist Party of Great Britain – a party determined to use its every effort in the furtherance of Socialist ideas and Socialist principles

The Socialist Party of Great Britain is convinced that by laying down a clearly defined body of principles in accord with essential economic truths, and by consistently advocating them, swerving neither to the right nor to the left, but marching uncompromisingly on toward their goal, they will ultimately gain the confidence and the support of the working class of this country. Once this is secured it is a small step to the organisation of a Socialist Parliamentary party. When this is accomplished all is gained.

The first duty of The Socialist Party is the teaching of its principles and the organisation of a political party on a Socialist basis. The party becoming strong will capture parliamentary and other governmental powers. When these powers – legislative, administrative, and judicial, are wrested from their present class holders, the way is clear for the building up of the industries of the country upon the principle of collective production and collective distribution, and for the establishment of the Socialist Republic.

Men and women of the working class, it is to you we appeal! Today we are a small party, strong only in the truth of our principles, the sincerity of our motives, and the determination and enthusiasm of our members. Tomorrow we shall be strong in our numbers, for the economic development of capitalist society fights for us, and as, through the merging of free competition in monopoly and the simplification of industry, the personal capitalist gives place to the impersonal trust as your employer, you will be forced to see that the welfare of the people can best be guaranteed by the holding of all material wealth in common.

We ask you, therefore, to study the principles upon which our party is based, to find out for yourselves what Socialism is and how Socialism and Socialism alone can abolish class society and establish in its stead a society based upon social equality. When you have done this we know that you will come with us and, by enrolling yourself a member of The Socialist Party of Great Britain, help to speed the time when we shall herald in for ourselves and for our children, a brighter, a happier and a nobler society than any the world has yet witnessed.

(September 1904)

The New 'Force' in Politics

So! We are, it seems, to rejoice in the advent of a new force in English politics. We are to observe "the descent of a bolt out of the blue" and be happy. We are to note that 'Labour' no longer sits on the 'doorstep' but is inside the House of Commons and will do things. We are even to accept the fact as a sign of victory for – Socialism! Well! This is interesting. Because in our ignorance we thought this sort of 'Labour' force descended from the blue, or, to be more accurate, ascended from the black, very many moons since. We seemed to have recollected even of a 'Labour' minister in a Liberal administration before Mr Burns. It is true these old-time 'Labour' representatives received the support of the Liberal Party. True also that the Rt. Hon. Thomas Burt was for very good reasons *persona grata* with Liberalism. But then so also was and is Mr Burns, the chairman of the "Labour" group in the last parliament. And is it not the indisputable fact that with few exceptions, the present 'Labour' members were the unofficial candidates of the Liberal Party and were backed by most of the local Liberal associations? Then why should we rejoice?

Weighed in the balance

What if this sort of 'Labour' representation *has* got inside the House of Commons in rather larger force than usual (which we suppose is what our enthusiastic exhorters mean when they have called upon us to be glad) – what then? Have they some greater power behind them by which they will be capable of performing greater deeds than their predecessors? What power? Are they not the nominees of an organisation whose members have not reached the stage of political development wherein they can dissociate their interests from the interests of the capitalist political factions? Are not these 'Labour' members' wages therefore dependent upon the manner in which they approach the measures introduced by the capitalist parties? Can they freely attack these measures and the parties introducing them and be sure that their action will not be misunderstood by those who pay the piper? If so, what becomes of the argument in favour of the strict independence of the LRC candidates on the ground that if they were associated with the Liberal Party (for example) the Tory members of the LRC would break away? If not, are they not obliged to give their support to capitalist legislation (unless, of course, that legislation is so glaringly anti-Labour that even the members of the LRC could appreciate it) for fear the contrary action would be misunderstood? Are they not for the same reason forced to proceed with exceeding circumspection in their endeavours to induce the capitalist government to adopt measures they (the capitalist government) do not desire to adopt?

Found Wanting

Is it not the fact that the majority of these 'Labour' representatives are themselves, in everything but name, Liberals, and, not understanding the reason for the position of the working class, cannot act as champions of working class interests? And is it not undeniable that those who *do* profess to understand, and who at other times are prepared to call themselves Socialists, have repeatedly obscured their Socialism in order to secure the position (as when they stood for election) and confused the minds of those whose intellectual clarity they are supposed to desire, by associating themselves with the representatives of capitalism for capitalist objects? Then what can be expected from these more than their predecessors? What is the use of their separate party and separate whips? The fact is that nine out of ten of them have been elected in alliance with the Liberals; they are by education and sympathy Liberals; they are paid by an organisation overwhelmingly Liberal, and they may be expected to act, as Crooks and Shackleton and Henderson, and in a slightly modified manner, Hardie, have all along acted – Liberal. The man who expects more from them is likely to be disappointed; the man who regards their return as a victory for Socialism simply doesn't know what he is talking about.

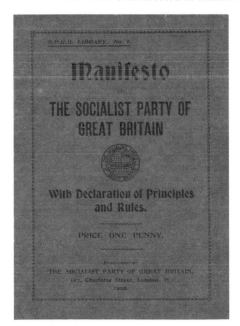

Why the 'Labour' men will not do

Our position is that these men, whatever their intentions, are actually retarding the development of the only organisation of the working class that can enter into effective conflict with the forces of capitalism, because they obscure the fact that this conflict exists *always* in industrial affairs, and do not insist that it must be waged upon the political plane also. By association with capitalist representatives in both political and economic affairs they induce the idea (which capitalism does everything possible to foster) that the hostility does not exist, yet until that fact is grappled with and clearly understood there can be no material improvement in the workers' condition. It is unfortunate, of course, that the workers do not understand. It makes the task of those who are concerned with the overthrow of capitalism, and the emancipation of the working class from wage-slavery, very difficult. The results of their work seem so very slow a-coming. And some of them tire and drop out of the movement, and others – the Irvings and the McNabs of the SDF, for example – curse the stupidity of the working class, while others again – the Hyndmans and Quelches and Hardies and the rest – weary of the work, endeavour to secure some immediate consolation by pandering to the ignorance they once may have thought to dispel, and so simply increase the difficulties in the way.

The irreconcilable few
Only the few remain in the forefront of the fight, waging unceasing battle for their class. These are they who, belonging themselves to the working class, have been at pains to obtain information as to the causes of the ignorance of their fellows; who have seen how, for generation after generation they have been oppressed and misled, sent off upon a barren quest by one set of supposed friends, confused by the actions and instruction of another set; now buoyed up with the hope of happiness, now plunged into the apathy of disappointment and despair. Knowing these things the few set out with no delusions upon the score of the reception their propaganda will receive at the hands of their class, and are not downcast and peevish when the results desired fail to materialise as quickly as they wish.

We of The Socialist Party of Great Britain are of this few. Our mission is simple. We have to proceed with our educational propaganda until the working class have understood the fundamental facts of their position – the facts that because they do not own the means by which they live they are commodities on the market, never bought unless the buyers (the owners of the means of life) can see a profit to themselves in the transaction, always sold when the opportunity offers because in that way only can the necessaries of life be obtained. We have to emphasise the fact that no appreciable change is possible in the working class condition while they remain commodities, and that the only method by which the alteration can be wrought is by the working class taking the means of life out of the hands of those who at present hold them, and whose private ownership is the cause of the trouble. Before this can occur the workers will have to understand the inevitable opposition of interests between them and the capitalist class, who, because of their ownership of the means of life, are able to exploit them, so that they will not make the mistake of voting into power, as they have always done hitherto, the representatives of the interests of those owning the means of life, because those who dominate political power dominate also the armed forces that keep the working class in subjection.

The justification of hostility

Therefore are we in opposition to all other political parties, holding on irrefutable evidence, that these other parties are confusing what must be clear to working class minds before a change can be effected. This is our mission, and we shall conduct it with all the energy we have at our command. We know that the row we have to hoe is likely to be a long one. That does not affright us – because we know that were the row twice as long it would have to be hoed. There is no dodging the duty. There are no short cuts. Naturally, however, we wish the work to be covered as soon as possible, and that is why we oppose and expose those gentlemen who, sometimes with the best of intentions, blur the issue that must be kept unblurred, and so prolong our labours.

That is our position. If it contains flaws we shall be glad to hear of them. Meanwhile we regret that the entrance of the 'Labour' men into the best club in Europe is not a Socialist victory and cannot be a Labour triumph. Labour only triumphs where Socialism wins. Meanwhile also, those who thought that the entrance of Burns into ministerial position would result in administration to the advantage of the unemployed should note that the Local Government Board has refused to sanction that portion of the loan applied for from Tottenham which was intended to meet the difference between the cost of work performed by a contractor and its cost if executed by the local unemployed. And those who thought that the advent of a new Liberal administration implied a large-hearted and sympathetic Labour policy should observe that sixty men have been sent to prison for five days each, and fifteen to one month each, for taking up collections in the street during unemployed demonstrations.

(February 1906)

The Sinn Fein Policy

The Policy Foreshadowed

"I had come to the conclusion that the whole system ought to be met with resistance at every point; and the means for this would be extremely simple: a combination amongst the people to obstruct and render impossible the transport and shipment of Irish provisions; to refuse all aid in its removal; to destroy the highways; to prevent everyone, by intimidation, from daring to bid for grain or cattle if brought to auction under distress (a method of obstruction that had put an end to church tithes before); in short, to offer a passive resistance universally, but occasionally, when opportunity served, to try the steel."

The above lines were written by John Mitchell in 1847 when the Irish Confederation refused to endorse his policy of immediate resistance to the collection of rents, rates, and taxes. The portion relating to the transport and shipment of Irish goods referred to the exportation of Irish produce in a time when the country was devastated by famine and thousands were dying of starvation.

Parnell's proposition to the Nationalist members, "to withdraw from the British House of Commons and organise the people in Ireland to resist English rule at every point" was defeated on a vote of the party.

The idea of carrying on a campaign of passive resistance to British rule in Ireland is therefore not by any means new, but the Sinn Fein Party is the first party that has attempted to organise the people for this object. It has already succeeded in winning over the youngest and most ardent of the Irish race; it has converted four of the official Nationalist members of Parliament including one of their whips, Sir T.G. Esmonde. At a meeting of the Nationalist Party in the House of Commons it was proposed and seconded that the Party adopt the Sinn Fein policy and withdraw from Westminster. In North Leitrim the member, Mr Dolan, having embraced the new doctrine, is about to contest the seat against the official Nationalist candidate.

The Movement Realised

The Sinn Fein Party claim to have a majority in favour of their policy in the County and District Councils in the country, and Mr Sweetman, chairman of the Meath County Council, at the meeting of councillors from various counties proposed and caused to be discussed at length a resolution to this effect: "that we refuse to collect any more rates or taxes". Thus we see that the Sinn Fein policy will probably in the future be the method adopted throughout Ireland to resist and if possible destroy the domination of "the thrice accursed British Empire".

What is the nature and origin of the Sinn Fein movement? The words Sinn Fein mean 'ourselves alone', and those who are acquainted with Ireland know that within the last ten years a movement was set on foot for the restoration of the Irish language, customs, industries, music and art; started and organised by the Gaelic League it was at first strictly non-political and non-sectarian, its ultimate object was an Irish Ireland, everything in language, clothing, manner and sport which was not originally Irish was banned and ridiculed, and the offenders were termed 'Shoneens', 'Flunkeys', and 'West Britons'. The Gaelic League was a decided success and it did not exist long before it had a political party formed independent of all others and having for its object 'Ireland a Nation', not in the sense of a British colony, but independent of all external authority. This party was formed on the same basis as Wolfe Tone a century ago formed the 'United Irishmen', and like Tone it wanted "to unite Catholic, Protestant, and Dissenter under the common name of Irishman." "Our independence must be had at all hazards; if the men of property will not support us they must fall; we can support ourselves by the aid of that numerous and respectable class of the community, the men of no property". Thus we see the Sinn Fein Party is the child of the Irish education movement, and is alluded to by the Parliamentarians as the 'crowd of intellectuals', 'armchair agitators', etc.

It sees the Futility of Compromise

The Sinn Fein Party is now possessed of several weekly journals that voice its views. It has also published a large number of pamphlets that have aided considerably in bringing the Party to its present position. In their weekly journals the Sinn Feiners riddle the arguments of the Parliamentarians, they point to the fact that in 1847 the population of Ireland was nine millions, while today it is about four millions after over half a century of labour on the "flure of the House". That the Land Acts were fraudulent and did not even touch the question of the poverty problem, that a Liberal Government is now in office but not officially pledged to Home Rule; in short, that the Nationalist Party is ineffective as a weapon against British misrule in Ireland.

The Sinn Fein Party propose the immediate withdrawal from Westminster of the 82 Irish members and that the £30,000 now annually spent in maintaining this useless weapon be spent in sending consuls to foreign countries to open up markets for Irish goods. That all monies invested in the banks of Ireland at the present time be withdrawn and a People's Bank be formed to lend money and transact all business at interest to cover only the cost of management. That a National Stock Exchange be formed in Dublin. That the people refuse to pay rent, rates, or taxes, and that the County Councils and other such bodies responsible refuse to collect same. That, if possible, no articles from which the British Government derives a revenue be consumed by the people. That the money saved in rent, rates, and administration be used in fixing machinery and starting the disused mills and factories, to revive dying industries and introduce new ones. That, in short, by common consent, by means of duly elected members or a general council of the County and District Councils the people of Ireland will refuse to recognise English law, authorities, or customs, and that henceforth Ireland shall be ruled only by the will of the people of Ireland.

Some of the chief spokesmen of this movement are large land owners and capitalists. Mr John Sweetman owns a large tract of land in C. Meath, is a county councillor, railway director, etc. Edward Martyn is a landowner of County Galway, a J.P. and is the exact reflex of the English capitalist. Sir T.G. Esmonde, Bart, M.P., is a bank director, railway director, and landlord. These and many others connected with the Sinn Fein movement give as their principal reason for supporting it the insecurity of their stock, the railways are not making any profit worth speaking of, the canals are idle, and so on.

But is itself Futile

From this it is quite evident that if the Sinn Fein movement succeeds profits are intended to rise at the expense of the Irish worker. The Irish capitalist class is still to remain the proud possessor of the land, factories, mills, railways, etc., and readers of this journal know what that means for the poor wretches employed.

The proud boast of the Sinn Fein Party is that Hungary was placed in much the same position as under Austria as Ireland is under England, and that when Hungary established her independence in exactly the same manner as the Sinn Fein movement proposes Ireland should, her trade increased by leaps and bounds, her population increased and new industries were developed, yet we know that today the Magyar is as much a slave as ever, and that there are in Hungary workhouses, prisons, asylums, unemployed, and all the other characteristics of the capitalist system. We know that the trade of Great Britain was greater last year than ever before, and that last year was nevertheless for the workers a year of great unemployment, poverty and privation. Even regarding the present success of the Sinn Fein movement it may be pointed out that the prospect differs vitally from that of Hungary in the important fact that Hungary was almost the equal in population and strength of Austria, and so was able to command political success. Hungary was also helped by the important tactical position it occupied as a barrier against Russian and Turkish advance. But as far as the condition of the people is concerned the Hungarian worker is not one whit better off than the Irish worker, whilst emigrants from Hungary may be counted by the hundred thousand, by whom, it is evident, the foreign exploiters are found at least no worse than the Hungarian masters from whom they flee.

For only Socialism can help the Workers

In view of these facts it is our duty to warn our fellow-workers in Ireland of the futility of the Sinn Fein policy as far as they are concerned. There can be no relief for the oppressed Irishman in changing an English robber for an Irish one. The person of the robber does not matter – it is the fact of the robbery that spells misery. National divisions are a hindrance to working class unity and action, and national jealousies and differences are fostered by the capitalists for their own ends.

The crowd of hungry 'intellectuals' clamouring for jobs both within and without the Irish parliamentary party do not represent the interests of the working class in Ireland. They do not, indeed, profess to favour other than capitalist interests, provided that the landlord or capitalist be Irish, but the Irish capitalist is in no wise more merciful than the English exploiter. The national sentiment and perennial enthusiasm of the Irishmen are being exploited by the so-called leaders in the interests of Irish capitalism, and the workers are being used to fight the battles of their oppressors. The Irish capitalist rebels against the English capitalist only because the latter stands in the way of a more thorough exploitation of the Irish workers by Irish capital. Let the thieves fight their own battles! For the worker in Ireland there is but one hope. It is to join the Irish wing of the international Socialist working class and to make common cause with the Socialist workers of all countries for the end of all forms of exploitation; saying to both English and Irish capitalists: "A plague on both your houses". For the true battle-cry of the working class is broader, more significant and more inspiring than mere nationalism, and that rally cry is: THE WORLD FOR THE WORKERS!

(September 1907)

Suffragette Humbug

Not long ago the hoardings of London startled the man in the street with ugly black and white posters asserting that women were poor, that women were sweated, that women walked the streets, and that misery and vice stalked in our midst, all because women had not the vote. Those statements, issued by the Suffragettes, were and are unblushing falsehoods, unsustained and unsustainable by any shred of evidence.

The Socialist is in no quandary as to why the many are poor. It is not because propertied women have not the vote, nor even because women in general are not electors – it is because the many are robbed. And the stopping of this robbery depends not upon a mere all round increase in the number of votes, but upon the intelligence of the workers and the correct use of the vote in their hands.

Democracy is not an end in itself, but a means to an end; and for us that end is Socialism. And were the workers to understand rightly their position and their policy, the political freedom they now possess would enable them to achieve their emancipation irrespective of sex.

It is, moreover, not a sex war that exists in Society but a class war, but the Suffragettes endeavour to blur this class issue by screeching qualifications.

What are the facts regarding the Suffragettes? Under the pretence of sex equality they are buttressing class privilege. Under the guise of democracy they are endeavouring to strengthen the political power of property. They plausibly propose that women be admitted to the franchise on the same terms as men, and since all Socialists want sex equality this looks attractive. But wait. What does it really mean? Men vote at present under the £10 franchise. The suffrage is thus upon a property basis with plural voting for the wealthy. Therefore, according to the proposals of the women Suffragists, only those women having the necessary property qualifications are to be allowed to vote. This excludes not only all those single working women unable to qualify because of their poverty, but it also bars practically the whole of the married women of the working class who have no property qualifications apart from their husbands'. Further, it increases enormously the voting power of the well-to-do, since the head of the wealthy household can always impart the necessary qualifications to all the women of his house, while the working-man, through his poverty, is entirely unable to do so.

The limited suffrage movement is consequently only a means of providing votes for the propertied women of the middle class, and faggot votes for the wealthy; possibly tipping the balance of votes against the workers – men and women. Yet the Suffragettes pretend that this is a movement for the benefit of working women! The huge sums spent in this agitation prove that it is not a workers' movement. It is a movement by women of the wealthy and middle class to open up for themselves more fully careers of exploitation, and to share in the flesh-pots of political office, to get sinecures, position and emoluments among the governing caste.

In their cry for 'equality' do not their methods betray them? Every move on their part is an appeal not to sex equality but to sex fetishism. Their tactics rely upon and appeal to the worship of sex. They know that their sex gives them privileges before the magistrate and protects them from the usual police brutality, and that any strong measures against them would immediately raise a storm in their favour amongst the sex worshippers. Hence their peculiar tactics, which have no other explanation. Let anyone compare mentally the treatment that would be meted out to working men did they pursue a similar policy to these Suffragettes. Let them compare the way the suffragist invasions of Downing Street or the House of Commons were dealt with, with that which would follow persistent forcible entries of the Commons by bands of unemployed. Broken heads, bullets, and long terms of imprisonment – and not in the second division – would be their lot, and instead of hysteric sympathy being created for the ill-treated unemployed, horror at their audacity and a determination to repress them brutally would take its place. And the middle class examples of sex arrogance rely upon this very woman worship and sex inequality to further their demands.

The Suffragette movement is upon all counts but a bulwark of capitalism. It is directly opposed to the interests of the working class – women as well as men, and the Independent Labour Party shows its capitalistic nature when it supports that movement in strengthening the political power of the propertied against the propertyless.

Both sexes of the workers are exploited and suffer. Both are victims of those who live by the ownership of the means of life. Therefore the salvation of working class women lies in the emancipation of their *class* from this wage-slavery. Their interests are identical with those of working men, and the women of the middle class do but attempt to lure them with false phrases to desert their fellows and to aid the propertied enemies of their class.

The duty of working women is to refuse to allow themselves to be used as catspaws of the wealthy, and to join with their fellows in The Socialist Party, the organisation of their class; thus working for the emancipation of the toilers as a whole, irrespective of sex. Sex-equality cannot be the fruit of the Suffragette humbug, it can only come through economic equality – and economic equality is impossible except through Socialism.

(June 1908)

Remember Tonypandy!

Some weeks back a strike occurred in the Moabit quarter of Berlin, during which the workers were brutally assaulted by the police and soldiers. The London Liberal Press saw in that outbreak the dire effects of Tariff Reform and an anti-Liberal Government! But recent events in South Wales, where under Free Trade and Liberal rule, the striking miners have been treated with barbarity before which the Berlin horrors pale, have exploded this idea. Moreover, the chief owner concerned is a prominent member of the Liberal Party, and so greatly is he esteemed by them that they propose to raise him to the Peerage now that he has retired from the House of Commons. Wales, too, is such a stronghold of Liberalism that the events there show up Liberalism in no uncertain light.

It will be remembered that for years past the South Wales miners have been trying to get an eight hours Bill passed. But – manifestation of the fraud of capitalist reform – ever since this 'Great Charter of the Miners' has been law they have been striking against its effects. The employees of the Cambrian Combine in the Rhondda Valley, and of the Powell Duffryn Co. in the Aberdare district, have been driven to desperation by the harassing conditions imposed by the great Liberal mine owners. Tremendous profits have been made – the Cambrian Trust have made a million pounds profit in the last dozen years with a capital only half that sum – yet the companies have added device to device in order to increase their spoliation, until thousands of miners can make no more than two shillings per day. And now the owners refuse to allow the men to take home firewood – a privilege they have had for half a century.

Altogether 20,000 miners are out, and in order to induce others to join them they have held demonstrations and appointed pickets, and the pickets have been attacked by the police. But the climax came on the 8th November, at Tonypandy. Prior to this the mine-owners became alarmed for the safety of their property, and determined to cow the strikers into submission by sheer force of arms. In the words of the *Daily Chronicle* (8th November) "the Company, as a precautionary measure, had wired for a detachment of cavalry to protect the pits."

Although "every available constable from the surrounding country had been summoned," the Home Secretary sent over 1,000 metropolitan police – many of them being mounted and armed with swords – besides which about 1,500 soldiers, including many cavalry, were despatched. The hypocrisy of Churchill was shown by the statement he issued on 8th November, declaring that he had sent police *instead* of soldiers, whereas he had already ordered the 18th Hussars, North Lancashire Regiment, and the North Lancashire Fusiliers to Wales (from Tidworth, Salisbury Plain), and they arrived at Pontypridd next morning.

Boiling water was directed upon the strikers and live wires were put around the vicinity of mines, but notwithstanding all their savagery the Companies could not break the strike.

The night of the 8th saw the most bloodthirsty attack upon the workers that has been recorded throughout the strike. Men and women were bludgeoned, kicked and maltreated so terribly that hundreds were maimed and wounded beyond description. Even little children did not escape, and many are disabled for life. Samuel Royce, a miner, was murdered by the police that night; he had joined the Territorials some time ago to defend 'his' country. What a tragic commentary!

For evidence of police brutality let us quote the Liberal MP for Merthyr. Speaking in the House of Commons on 15th November, Mr E. Jones, "referring to the conduct of the police and soldiers at Aberdare, said the people were bludgeoned a quarter of a mile from the mines, absolutely innocent people being savagely attacked. It was openly stated in that district that the policemen in this case were under the influence of drink, and many incidents pointed to the fact that the police had altogether lost their heads." (*Daily Chronicle*, 16th November 1910).

Although the soldiers have not been in action yet, they are being kept on the spot in case the police fail to satisfy the requirements of the colliery owners. In his official statement of Nov. 10th the Home Secretary said that he will not hesitate to use the military, and in the House of Commons (15th November) he stated that "the Central Government has acted more directly than is usual or usually desirable," and further said "I take full responsibility for all that has been done."

In face of these admissions of the murderous nature of capitalist government, the workers should note the despicable conduct of those who claim to represent them in the House of Commons. That prominent member of the Labour Party, Mr W. Abraham ('Mabon') in the House of Commons on 15th November said that "he declined to take any part in condemning the Home Office or the Government for the part they took at the commencement of the sad affair". His attitude is that of all the other members of that wing of the Liberal Party. For the sake of securing their seats and their salaries they are now engaged in supporting Liberals all over the country. In Dundee, for instance, the workers are being told to vote for the two 'progressives', who are Mr Alex Willie and – the assassin Churchill! Elsewhere – at Bow and Bromley and at Deptford for example – the Liberals are carrying out their share of the bargain by telling their supporters to vote for the 'Labour' candidates.

Mr Keir Hardie is anxious for the Government to appoint a Committee of enquiry. Of course – many of those on strike are his constituents. But how childish to ask the capitalists to appoint a committee to enquire into their own conduct! It will be remembered that on the occasion of the Featherstone massacre the Liberal Government gave way (!) to public demand and appointed a Committee of enquiry. Here are the miners' names: Lord Bowen, Sir A.K. Rollit, and Mr Haldane. The result could only be the whitewashing of butcher Asquith. The traitorous Labour Party were dumb when the workers were slaughtered at Belfast in 1907 by order of the Liberal Minister Birrel. And Keir Hardie absented himself time after time in 1893 although Asquith challenged him to be present and accuse him inside the House.

Notice the impartiality of our capitalist masters. See what a sham the party divisions of Liberal and Tory are, when the issue is between the workers and the capitalists. When the Tory mine-owner, Lord Masham, appealed for soldiers to protect the Acton Hall Colliery, the Liberal Asquith immediately drafted troops to the spot, with the result that Gibbs and Duggan were murdered. Now when the Liberal mine-owner D.A. Thomas applies for military aid he receives it. The Tory Party are in the same boat. When Penrhyn sought military assistance to subdue the starving quarrymen ten years ago it was readily afforded him. And in 1887 they sent armed mounted police to Trafalgar Square to disperse the unemployed – and poor Linnell was done to death.

The working class have many things to remember concerning the history of both political parties. The fact stands out clear that both political fractions have used every agency at their command to keep the working class in subjection. The

hypocritical Liberal cries out against the Tory: 'Remember Michaelstown!' what time he overlooks those landmarks in the class struggle – Featherstone, Belfast, and now Tonypandy.

The lessons of Tonypandy should be remembered by the toilers and driven home whenever support is asked for for the capitalist candidates. Capitalism stands for murder, whether direct as at Tonypandy or indirect as at Whitehaven, West Stanley, or at the Maypole Colliery – murder, whether in the enforced starvation recorded daily in the papers, or in the suicide of those unable to bear the burden of misery any longer.

The race for profits by our masters is a race that means misery, starvation and premature death for its victims the workers. Therefore our policy must be one of unceasing hostility to capitalism, whether 'reformed' or not. Unceasing hostility to all is upholders, whether they label themselves Liberal, Tory, Labourite or Social-Democrat.

We cannot ever ally ourselves with that class whose hands are stained with the blood of our fellow toilers. We can never forget that in the struggle between the workers and the capitalists there can be no truce, no quarter, no compromise! The South Wales horrors have once again demonstrated this fact with the tragic emphasis of blood. It is for us to point again the lesson that the armed forces of the State – nay, the whole machinery of the State – exists but to conserve the interests of the ruling class. The capture of this State machinery must then be the object of our endeavours. Vengeance and our emancipation are one and the same thing, and must both be sought on the political field. If the miners learnt this lesson the masters would have cause to Remember Tonypandy!

(December 1910)

The Class Struggle Aboard the 'Titanic'

Once again humanity has been staggered by an appalling catastrophe, in which hundreds of human lives have been thrown away, and hundreds of homes plunged into grief and despair. Once again the wild cry of horror has vibrated through the world, and the multitude have been not only shocked, but astounded, as if the unexpected had happened. Once again the newspapers have been slobbering sentimental platitudes and unctuous hypocrisy as though this were not the best thing that has happened for them for many a long day. Once again the machinery of bogus inquiries and sanctimonious 'charity' has been set in motion in order to hide awkward and incriminating facts. And finally, once again have the flouted working class, on whom the brunt of this stupendous sacrifice to Mammon has fallen, begun to forget all about it.

Well, there is nothing at all unusual in that. The workers have proverbially short memories. They have forgotten Featherstone; they have forgotten Whitehaven, they have forgotten Bolston, and in a few short days they will have forgotten the 'Titanic'.

Murder of workers is so common; the workers are so used to it, that they cannot even recognise it for what it is. When the murderous rifles of the soldiery shoot unarmed workers down, it is only the operation of the Law, and there's an end on't. When mine-owners neglect to keep their mines ventilated, and blow hundreds of miners into eternity, or brick them up in the pit to be burnt alive, it's a lamentable occurrence but quite an accident, and again there's an end on't. And now that the vast 'unsinkable', the floating city, has carried its full living cargo to the bottom of the Atlantic, the workers arouse themselves in horror of it for a day or two, note with approval that the Royal Family have donated about one day's income to the relief fund, and then slip quietly back into their sleeping sickness.

And, of course, they are to be helped to do this by a sham enquiry which will start out with the set purpose of fixing the blame on the iceberg, or at most on the dead officers who were supposed to have control of the ship. But this enquiry is a mere blind, a cunning attempt to cloak the real position and to screen from blame the real culprit.

The enquiry in America, for all its seeming fierce determination to get to the bottom of the matter, and for all the awkward evidence it has elicited, was only embarked on for the purpose of skating on the surface. If they could fix the blame on the White Star people, then so much the better for the American shipping interests. But beyond this they did not go; beyond this they never intended to go; beyond this they dared not go. All their virtuous indignation is of a piece with the 'patriotism' of their grandfathers, who poisoned Washington's soldiers with villainous provisions with an unscrupulousness even modern Chicago fails to beat.

To those who understand modern conditions no enquiry is necessary in order to apportion the blame. The starting point of this enquiry will, of course, be the hour immediately preceding the collision. They will go on the worn-out assumption that the captain had the command of the ship. No one will ask why was the 'Titanic' built. No one will dream of making the designing of the ship the starting-point of the enquiry. No one will dare to suggest that the captain and his officers had not the command of the vessel.

Yet this way lies the truth. In the very designing of the 'Titanic' is the first word of the tragic story, in keeping with which is every jot and tittle of evidence to the end. In the luxurious furnishings – the swimming baths, the flower gardens, the racquets courts – read the secret of the catastrophe. The ship was built to carry rich passengers across the herring-pond.

Almost the first comment that was made by the newspapers when the fatal news came to hand was that among the first class passengers aboard the vessel were millionaires who were collectively worth £30,000,000. This in itself is significant.

The fares of those six hundred first and second class passengers must have totalled an enormous sum, compared with which the passage money of the steerage was a negligible quantity. The 'Titanic', then, was essentially built for rich passengers upon whom the White Star Company depended to enable their vessel to 'earn' a dividend.

The course is clear from this. The ship was on her maiden voyage; it was necessary to convince the wealthy, whose time is so extremely valuable, that she was a fast boat. So, as it is admitted, there was a general order to "smash all records" – which was duly done.

This explains why the lookout men had glasses until they reached Queenstown, but not afterwards – record smashing on the Western voyage commences at

Queenstown. When records are to be smashed it is very inconvenient to have the lookout seeing too much – especially when the ship is an 'unsinkable' and well-insured. It also explains why the vessel was on a wrong course at a wrong speed, and why no notice was taken of the lookout's warning.

Much will be made of these latter facts, no doubt, and the dead officers will be blamed. It must not be forgotten, however, that capitalist companies invariably choose for responsible positions those men to do what they are paid to do. It is all moonshine to talk of the captain being in command. They command who hold his livelihood in their hands. If he will not take risks and get the speed they want, then he must give place to one who will.

So at the bottom it is the greed for profit and the insatiable desire for speed on the part of the rich that is responsible for the disaster, whatever conclusion the Committee of Enquiry may come to. Of course, they will not give any such verdict as that, for that would be to indict the capitalist system.

The actual details of the wreck afford a further opportunity of pressing home a lesson. The evidence of the survivors and the evidence of the official figures of the saved, show that even on the decks of the sinking liner, and to the very end, the class struggle was on. Those who had clamoured for speed were the first to monopolise the boats, and the way was kept open for them by the officers' revolvers. Even the capitalist newspapers are compelled to admit the significance of the figures. Of the first class men 34% were saved; of the steerage men only 12%. Figures like those are eloquent enough without the evidence of the officer who admitted that he kept steerage passengers from a half-filled boat with shots from his revolver.

Much has been made of the fact that the cry 'Women and children first' was raised, and it is not necessary to cast aspersions on the courage of any man who survives. The salient fact is that it was not a question of courage but of class. 'Women and children' meant women and children of the wealthy class. Of first class women and children practically all were saved, some even with their pet dogs. Of the steerage women and children more than half perished. The 'chivalry' of the ruling class does not, save in very rare instances, extend itself to the class beneath them.

We are not of those who expect any great results from this ocean tragedy. Working class lives are very cheap, and the age that abolishes the Plimsoll Line at the demand of those greedy for profit is hardly likely to insist upon the provision of proper means of life-saving or the careful navigation of passenger vessels. Murder by wholesale may be committed without doing violence to 'law and order', so long as it is committed by the capitalist class in the 'legitimate' scramble for profits. The law only moves against the Crippens and the Seddons, but the murders quite commonly committed by the capitalist class are not one whit less foul, for all nobody is hanged for them.

(May 1912)

The Balkan Conspiracy

To arms! To arms! Thus once again is the 'Eastern Question' answered. Turk and Bulgarian, Mohammedan and Christian, are at one another's throats in a frenzy of bloodlust. The clash of arms and the roar of guns once more shake the hills and mountains of the near East, and the cries of wounded and dying men fill fair valleys with horror.

What does it all mean? What has it got to do with us of the working class?

Although some say it is no affair of ours, we emphatically hold otherwise. Before almost all else we Socialists are internationalists. We belong to the international working class. Our grievance is international; our only hope is international, and our enemy is international also. Hence we are interested in every activity that hurts, hinders, or helps our fellow workers anywhere and everywhere.

The Press, the politicians and the parsons are quite certain the war is the fight of Christian martyrs against the infamies of the Turk! We hear from them much of the gross barbarities, the murders and the miseries, inflicted upon helpless Macedonia by the Terrible Turk. But we are unconvinced. It may all be true. The Christian may be as meek and mild as he is usually painted. All the provocation may be on the side of the unspeakable Turk. But the information is suspect. Black and bad as the crimes of the Turks may be, criticism comes with little grace from Russia, reeking with the blood of butchered workmen, or from Spain, dank yet with her blood-feast of Barcelona, or from Italy, washing her hands after her callous inhumanities in Tripoli, or from France or Germany where as late as this year even, peaceful gatherings of unarmed workers have been ruthlessly crushed with the sword, or from Belgium with her Congo record, or from Britain whose capital has almost blotted a people out in the Putomayo district of Peru, with every fiendish cruelty that could be cheaply inflicted.

To mouth the horrors of Armenia, to point to the infamies of the Sultan in Macedonia, as do those who are trying to find excuses for this stupendous waste of working class life, it is quite obvious, is nothing but the sheerest humbug. Why, then, this war?

Montenegro was the first with its declaration of war – a country with under 250,000 inhabitants – not, in that respect, the equal of the London suburb, West Ham – and as poor as the oft-quoted church mouse. Where did she get her armaments? Bulgaria, Servia, Greece, every one of them poor – who backed them and why?

Why did Russia take up the Montenegrin war loan? Why did 'The Powers' take up the Bulgarian loan? Were they moved to do so by the promptings of humanity? Read the cynical answer in the story of past wars.

Japan fought Russia for the forests of Manchuria. Korea helped Japan – now Korea belongs to Japan. The United States fought Spain ostensibly on the ground of the Cuban 'horrors', and the Yankee Eagle has his beak in the hearts of the Cubans and the Phillipinos.

The English Government "sought neither gold nor territory" in South Africa, but the Transvaal and the Orange Free State went the way of Zululand and the Basutos' country – and it was the wrongs of the Uitlanders, who hadn't got the vote, that justified the war!

Every brutal and bloody gang of rulers, sitting armed on the backs of their groaning, bleeding and starving multitudes, have sobbed and slobbered and shed crocodile's tears over the suffering subjects of the Sultan. Austria was so shocked by the miseries of the poor people of Bosnia and Herzegovina that she had to soothe her feelings by 'annexing' both these countries. Britain also has been sorely troubled over the horrors perpetrated in the Ottoman Empire, so the Cross relieved the Crescent of Egypt and Cyprus. Russia wrung her hands in agony, and then laid them on Bessarabia. That monument to Garibaldi's genius, a United Italy, itched to stop the villainies of the Porte, so she seized Tripoli at the admitted cost of 9,000 Italian workers' lives, and goodness knows what cost to 'the enemy', if we are to believe the Italian boasts of slaughter.

Have we answered the question of why this war? It is the old story of Grab! The monopolists of the means of life are out for plunder. Already the *Daily News and Leader* has published a possible division list of the spoils – of the division of Macedonia – the filching of Turkish territory.

The world's financiers, the world's brigands, are seeking wider fields for exploitation. The owners of the New World are grasping at the old. Bulgarian peasants, Servian toilers, Grecian slaves, are to sacrifice their lives to provide plunder for the moneyed tyrannies of Europe. Women of our class are to be widowed, children to be orphaned, homes to be desolated, to make a masters' holiday. Hence the war fever is aroused, religious rivalries stirred up, racial hatreds and jealousies fanned to fury by judicious but unscrupulous lying – and all that Macedonia may go the way of Persia.

We counsel our toiling brothers of the Balkans, be their religion what it may, to seriously ask themselves who really is to benefit by this war. The 'Powers', who so applaud their 'heroism', who affect such pained surprise at each new enormity of the Porte, could have prevented those enormities, could have prevented this war, if they had been in agreement upon anything else than the desire for plunder. But they were not. For a generation they have been sitting like vultures on the mountain tops waiting for a beakful of carrion. For a generation they have carefully treasured every discordant element that could possibly engender strife and evolve into 'atrocity' because they knew that out of that strife and 'atrocity', sooner or later, would come the dismemberment of the Turkish Empire, and the attendant rich pickings for whoever was strong enough to take them.

Make no mistake about it – the 'Powers' wanted war. Just as the Christian religion has been the stalking horse of European diplomacy for the last half century, preserving ever fresh the excuse of 'Turkish misrule', so now the Balkan States are the stalking horse of that same callous diplomacy. If that diplomacy has not entirely overreached itself; if it has not set up in this Balkan League a power it is afraid to tackle; if the fruits of its machinations have not developed into something beyond its control, then the plums of the Turkish cake will find their way into the insatiable maws of the 'Powers' at last.

The lesson of it all for the workers is that nothing in the world is sacred that stands in the way of capitalist aggrandisement – which is spelt: 'Profits'. In pursuit of profits no crime is too stupendous to be undertaken. We have examples of this everywhere, from the supplying of poisonous provisions to American troops by American contractors during the War of Independence to the deliberate raising of the load line of ships by the present British Government.

Some years ago a novel was published, the essence of which was the situation of a man who had a great fortune within his reach if he would, by the mere pressure of an electric button, slay an unknown man many thousands of miles away. The book created something of a sensation – which shows how very ignorant are the average man and woman of the obvious facts of the world about them. The situation depicted by the author presented nothing new. It just reduced to the private individual the situation groups of the dominant section of society are always finding themselves in, with, of course, different details – the situation they use all their diplomatic forces to place themselves in. In the pursuit of this end every known means is exploited without compunction. Religion, patriotism, greed – any human emotion will serve. Hence the Jameson raid as a prelude to the South African War – it roused the 'patriotic' fervour of the 'bulldog breed' to frenzy. Hence religious strife has been fostered in the Near East by the great European powers, in order to provide the excuse that it was the Cross against the Crescent.

It doesn't need the inducement of a great fortune for the button of murder to be pressed in our modern civilisation. We have just been told the price English capital sets upon human life. The silk hats of Throgmorton Street have manipulated the button which sent a Peruvian native to death for – guess what – two hundredweight of rubber! In the Congo human beings were much cheaper. Every fourteen pounds of Congo rubber produced under the auspices of that moral turpitude, the late King of Belgium, cost one human life.

For the mines of Morocco hundreds of French soldiers went to their doom. The armies of Russia and Japan died on account of forest concessions in Manchuria in the hands of a few Russian nobles. An English court of enquiry has just found that 23 British seamen were sacrificed for the freightage of 160 tons of overload cargo. The chairman of the Consolidated Mines spoke volumes when he told his shareholders some thirteen years ago that a victory for the British arms in the war then raging (South Africa) would mean £4,000,000 a year in extra profits.

Workers of the world, it is necessary for you to understand these things in order that you may penetrate the curtain of excuses behind which it is endeavoured to hide the real reasons for this new butchery. You see from the above how much value the rulers anywhere set on the lives of the workers. What, then, think you, are the sufferings of Macedonian Christians to them? They would press the murder button on the lot for the sake of a concession to run a railway over their corpses.

The working class of the world has only one enemy – the master class. We call earnestly upon all working men and women to join with us for the overthrow of that enemy.

To arms!

(November 1912)

The Pace That Kills: the modern street traffic problem discussed

A philosophy in a nutshell

'Hurry on, please!' is the catch phrase of the day. It expresses the salient characteristic – with or without the please – of every modern industrial centre, just as 'Get on or get out!' sums up its brutal philosophy. In the roaring traffic of the highway, indeed, we have a vivid yet typical example of this 'non-stop' age.

Take modern road traffic, then, as a case in point. It illustrates the rapid yet enormous changes forced upon society by economic development, and it shows unmistakably how little the hireling worker profits by the wonderful mechanical progress his physical and mental labour has made possible.

The ubiquitous motor has made the dweller in the most distant hamlet familiar with its dust and dangers, but in London's streets the 'motor peril' now reaches its apotheosis. Truly the motor is everywhere, but on the crowded roads of the metropolis its presence and speed have raised a problem for which the multitudinous highway authorities seek in vain a solution.

The streets are turned into slaughter yards, and it is no crime in the eyes of those who administer the law, for the motorist to slay the harmless passer-by. It is by far the cheapest form of murder, for it is scarcely too strong a statement to say that the motorist has practically been granted the right to slaughter any who dare to cross his path.

At inquests the motorist is almost always exonerated from blame – particularly if it is pointed out that he was sober. And even in those rare cases where this does not happen the penalty is a puerile censure, or a punishment ludicrously disproportionate to that which is inflicted when the murder is done other than with the aid of a motor.

Way for the road hog!

Above all the conflicting and hysterical statements anent the modern highways problem one thing is clear: that high speed is the chief bugbear. "It's the pace that kills." *Exceeding the speed that is safe in the particular circumstances* is the cause of most of the maiming and slaughter. Indeed, the law, ass though it is, nominally establishes a speed limit. Yet motorists habitually exceed that limit. In fact, travelling at the legal limit is stigmatised as a 'mere crawl'. Moreover, it is not for the safety of the public that corners are rounded and roads widened and strengthened, but simply to allow greater speeds to be attained – with the inevitable consequence of a longer casualty list.

It is, further, an understood thing that the police never prosecute for exceeding the speed limit unless it is exceeded by over five miles, and very rarely even then. The car owner's most frequent boast is of the speed at which his motor travels, and the rare fine is regarded as a certificate to the quality of his engine, and is a tribute to his childish vanity.

Despite the fact that most of those killed and maimed on the highways would still be safe and sound if a rational speed in the circumstances had been adhered to, representatives of motor associations fatuously assert that not high, but 'low' speeds, are the concomitants of accident! And as though to support this risible doctrine, almost every motorist in the courts, contemptuous of the law relating to perjury, states his speed to have been at the time of the smash, between five and twelve miles an hour! That is the homage that vice pays to virtue!

Motoring magistrates are ever ready to condone the recklessness of the motorist, and sometimes even lecture pedestrians and cyclists on the nuisance and danger their existence on the road presents for the man behind the 'petrol gun'! They reserve the vials of their wrath, however, for the urchin on a bicycle, whose crime was in enjoying an innocent 'coast' down an incline at little more than half the legal speed limit for motors!

The hog's grunt translated

To such a pass have things come that the attitude of the average motorist is practically that the roads are his property, and that all others are trespassers, to be hooted off. 'Get off the earth or I'll push you off!' is the sentiment expressed in the imperious howl of the motor syren.

Besides being the capitalist's instrument of profit, the motor is now his chief toy – or at least it runs his 'blonde' or his 'brune' very close for pride of place in this connection – and to the arrogance engendered by the possession of the most powerful and speedy thing on the road is added the arrogance of wealth and class. The result is a growing contempt and intolerance on the part of the motorist toward the weaker users of the road, mitigated only faintly by spasmodic reprisals and agitations on the part of the latter.

But why go on? It is neither necessary nor advisable to recount at length the manifold abuses of the motor vehicle – the simplest statement of fact suffices.

Yet the petrol engine is a marvellously efficient instrument, and in its further development its *possibilities* are great for humanity. The simple question to be emphasised then arises – why should an undoubted mechanical advance spell greater discomfort, toil, and danger to the workers?

It would be quixotic, or worse, to attempt to stop the development of motor traffic, and it would be equally futile to drag the red herring of the individual 'reckless driver' and the exceptional 'road hog' across the trail. The trouble has deeper roots. The chauffeur, for example, must obey his master or be supplanted by a more obedient servant. The taxi driver must keep up the earnings of his cab or lose his livelihood. The employee of the motor-bus trust must keep carefully to his schedule times and maintain the earnings of his vehicle – indeed his wage depends on the number of miles he can run. Thus it is that other road users suffer who are too weak to cope with the powerful motor.

Inciting to murder

Among the weakest of road users is the cyclist, and, it so happens that the cycle is, above all others, the workers' vehicle; and those who employ it as a means of getting to and from their daily toil, know full well how the danger grows. But the bus driver, held by the trust to an inelastic time table, with his livelihood endangered if the takings of his vehicle and its daily mileage fall, is economically compelled to make unscrupulous use of the power his motor gives him, to the detriment of others. Self-preservation makes him regard the slowly moving cyclist and pedestrian as obstacles to his livelihood, hindrances to the keeping of his time schedule, impediments to his speed in getting first to paying points on the route.

The type of mind engendered by such an economic position may be gauged from the complaint of a motor-bus driver, at a South London inquest on a victim, with regard to cyclists, that "he *frequently had to give way to them*".

Not always, evidently. Indeed, when pedestrian or cyclist is killed, well, 'accidents will happen', and there is an obstacle less on the road, while after all, coroners are indulgent. If a cyclist is scared off, he becomes a passenger the more for the bus, and another source of profit for the trust – a trust which, by the way, has the sublime effrontery to pose, in an official letter to the Press, as jealous of its "*reputation as the guardian of the public safety*". Gordelpus!

Of course, if every human being killed or injured by their agency was made to cause such a heavy monetary loss to the transport companies that it outweighed the profitableness of high speed and reckless driving, then the massacre would cease. But is anyone so simple as to believe this will be done? Can thugs be relied upon to prohibit murder? It is motor owners who legislate. What avails human life when put in the scales against dividends. Indeed, the attempt to make human life of more account than profits would be howled down as a dastardly, senseless, revolutionary attack upon the sacred rights of property.

A profitable 'remedy'

No. Whatever 'reforms' may be inaugurated will not diminish, but may increase, profits. A limitation of further bus licences is already semi-officially foreshadowed, and worked for. This would mean the granting of a permanent monopoly against the public to the existing trust, and the exclusion of fresh competition, without any guarantee for public safety or convenience.

But is this question of the killing and maiming by motors the only one, or even the most important? Obviously it is not; and it is only dealt with here because it is but a symptom. It is true that nearly 150 persons have been killed outright by the motor-bus trust in the metropolitan area alone during the past year. That is terrible enough; but have not equal numbers of workers being sacrificed at one fell swoop in preventable colliery disasters – not this year alone but every year? And should we have heard so much about the motor-bus slaughter had it not suited the purpose of a set of office-hunters to make political capital out of it, on behalf of that cheerless piece of humbug, 'the people's trams'?

There is, however, no need to belittle in any way the facts relating to the motor peril. They are appalling. But the rest is more terrible still. The one is but the manifestation of the greater evil, for the sinister result of modern traffic conditions has a deeper meaning than is realised or expressed by commentators in the Press. It signifies the growing pace and intensity of industrial life, the universal acceleration of production, and the decreasing value of the life of the worker when put in the balance against the pleasure or the profit of the class that owns the country. The huge and increasing size of industrial centres, and the greater distances between the workers' home and the factory, the need for more quickly transferring labour, the greed of the rack-renter of the central districts, the knowledge that the workers' 'time is money' to the capitalist, the rush for profits of a transport trust, and the all-pervading atmosphere of hustle, recklessness, and speed that is engendered by capitalist greed and the ever-increasing worldwide competition – all these are symptoms of the deep-lying social malady.

It is not very long ago that miners were entombed in a burning mine by bricking up the mouth of the pit in order to save the property! No! the sacrifice of human life on the road is not an isolated phenomenon. The drowning of seamen for the sake of a few extra tons of cargo consequent on the raising of the load-line by a Liberal Board of Trade; the killing and maiming of an enormous and increasing number of workers in mine and factory for the sake of extra output and extra profit; and the toll of life taken on the highways for the sake of the profit or pleasure of accelerated transport, are all phases of the same fact. Men are the slaves of the machines they have created.

Modern machines, in their marvellous precision, complexity, and swiftness, bring with them the possibility, the material groundwork, of greater leisure, and the provision of the good things of life in ever-increasing abundance. Yet the only reward of those who toil is more intense labour, a less secure position, greater hardships and dangers, and a shortened life. Out of good cometh evil? Why? Because those who work are hirelings, while those who toil do not own. The machine supplants the hireling, makes him redundant, and starves him instead of feeding him. The new machines and higher speeds only increase the wealth of the parasitic owner, enabling him to discharge more wage-labourers, reduce wages, and intensify toil. Thus it is that instruments capable of dispensing wealth and leisure to all, impoverish and overwork the many. Thus it is that the triumphant advance of technology has only carried our class on to ever more painful labours. We are victims of the machine only because we are the hirelings of the class that owns it. The evolution of industry leads us on, and we struggle painfully to adapt ourselves to its steps. Hitherto the workers have neglected the one needful step – the democratic ownership and control of all industrial machinery.

Speed and concentration are the order of the day. But the London transport trust, while it provides the example of the disease, hints at the only remedy. Industry after industry has developed to the trust stage, and has shown us plainly that since those who produce now run the machinery and organise industry – for absentee shareholders – they are demonstrably capable of running production for themselves! Surely the time when they will do so is near at hand! The need, the possibility, and the economic foundation of Socialism are manifestly present.

Industrial advance places the means of socialised production within the workers' reach, and their daily trials and difficulties must open their eyes to the supreme need of realising that possibility, and of wresting the power to control from those who now usurp it. Then they will resume control of their means of life, becoming the masters of the tool of production instead of remaining enslaved; and will for the first time be able to utilise technical progress humanly and intelligently, to provide more leisure and a completer life for all.

But so long as class ownership remains, for just so long will the long list of killed and maimed continue to grow, and all remediable measures fail to keep pace with the breakneck speeding up of our daily tasks. Already we are becoming inured to the motor murders as to the butchery in other spheres of industry. The sudden development of the road motor 'within the memory of a schoolboy' has struck the popular imagination, leaving scarce heeded other and more deadly fields. But soon this too will pall, and the great problem as a whole will only press more surely for solution.

Hustle and worry, then, will continue to be the worker's lot; danger, suffering, and want dog his footsteps ever more closely, until, in the fullness of time, the scales shall fall from his eyes and he shall see how frail his fetters are. And when he feels his mighty strength, and at long last sees its obvious use, woe betide the parasites who have battened on his sweat and blood in the long night of his blindness and ignorance!

(January 1913)

The Case for Free Love: some capitalist hypocrisies exposed

Some social idiocies

To the Revolutionist it is almost an axiom that modern society is rotten – rotten to the root! The production of wealth – the first essential form of human activity – is carried on, not for the purpose of satisfying the physical needs of the workers, but with the motive of accumulating wealth in the shape of capital. The means of production are exalted above the producer. These supplementary organs of society are owned and controlled by a small percentage of the race, and the rest of mankind exist merely to augment them for the benefit of the few. Every human faculty capable of serving the interests of these exploiters has to be surrendered by those who possess nought else in return for the wherewithal to purchase the bare means of subsistence. It thus becomes perverted and deteriorates as a consequence. Cash dominates all social relationships and vitiates them.

Sexual relations form no exception to the general rule. The natural purpose for which men and women should mate is the perpetuation of the race and the incidental satisfaction of the sexual instinct. This motive, however, has about the least weight of any in determining the conditions of sexual intercourse at the present day.

The great majority of women, as of men, are dependent on the capitalist class for bread, and being by nature inferior to men as wealth producers, are compelled to turn their sexual attractions to account in order to balance the handicap which sex itself imposes upon them in the competition for employment. Just as the poet, the artist, the physician and the lawyer, to say nothing of the parson and the politician, regard their special abilities as the means of 'making a career', so women generally look upon their natural endowment as an economic asset. On the other hand men have come to regard women as existing mainly, if not wholly, for the satisfaction of their own sexual desires, which tend to degenerate as a natural result into lust unredeemed by any regard for the will or the affection of women.

Wedded blis-ter pricked

In ordinary public prostitution the divorce of the sex relation from its true motive is too obvious to need special comment. Marriage, however, is in reality similar in nature. Stripped of all the sentiment with which an essentially false conventionalism has surrounded it, the legal contract, like all others, consists of an exchange of commodities. In return for the guarantee of economic maintenance the woman surrenders her body to the man, who thereby acquires the 'marital right' to force maternity upon her whenever he chooses, irrespective of her own desires.

It is true that wives are also useful as household drudges, but considering only the sexual aspect of the relationship, the only difference between marriage and so-called immorality for cash is that the former is purchase, with the terms legally recognised and enforceable while the latter is hire. The monetary damages awarded in breach of promise and divorce cases serve to illustrate this. The loss of prospective maintenance by the woman, or the loss of the conjugal monopoly by the man, as the case may be, is estimated at so much in cash. Need more be said to show that the sex-nature in woman has been reduced by capitalism to the level of a commodity?

Children may be said to be the incidental bye-products of marriage rather than its fundamental object. They also become the property of the husband who, like any other slave owner, is responsible for their maintenance.

The advantages of this arrangement to the parent, however, depends upon his own economic status. The capitalist can exploit the 'expectations' of his heirs by making their inheritance depend upon the subservience of their activities to his commercial interests. It is considered a matter of honour for both sons and daughters to make matches with a view to enhancing the stability of the family fortunes.

The workingman's 'quiverful'

On the other hand, the working man with a precarious income is compelled to drive his 'brats' to the factory, the workshop, or the office in order to enable him to barely fulfil his legal responsibilities toward them. Indeed, large numbers are compelled to rely on similar aid from their wives. Even these measures tend to cut the ground from under the feet of the working men themselves, for the entrance of women and children into the labour market necessarily results in keener competition for jobs hitherto performed by men, with a resulting lowering of the rate of wages and an increased inability to maintain a family on their part.

Verily, modern machinery under capitalism is the sword promised by the Prince of Peace to set parents against children and vice versa, and to make a man's foes 'those of his own household'.

Marriage and family, for the working class, are to the extent that they survive, mere legal devices to prevent encroachment upon the pockets of the ratepayers. For society as a whole they are the means of maintaining and augmenting private property. We come back, then, to our starting point, that human relations are dominated by this necessity. Let us consider its effect on the quality of sex.

These are tricks in every trade

In all phases of the competitive supply of human requirements, their quality is determined by the power of the purse. The economic resources of the great mass of the people consist of subsistence wages. Consequently cheapness is the first consideration, and quality naturally deteriorates. Sex is affected in the same manner as all other commodities. Supply tending to exceed demand in this as in all other markets, all manner of tricks to ensure a ready sale are resorted to. Sham attractions are set in competition with real ones. The adulteration of food stuffs, clothing, etc., in such a manner as to tickle the palate and catch the eye, is here paralleled by the substitution of paint on the cheeks for the glow of health, and the use of perfumes for preventing the detection of the symptoms of indigestion. Constricted waists and artificially exaggerated figures seek to excite male passions, while in order that these same passions may be cheaply indulged, various methods for the prevention of conception are commonly resorted to. Finally, the excessive and promiscuous intercourse, which the legal contract can neither prevent nor completely hide, gives rise to various diseases, which form a source of profit for innumerable purveyors of patent medicines, appliances, and systems, which, like most palliatives (political ones included), make bad worse.

The fancied security offered by marriage from the necessity of entering the labour market or adopting life on the streets leads women to give little consideration to the physical fitness of the first male person who is in a position to offer marriage and does so. Consequently matrimonial misfits, temperamental and physiological, tend to become the rule rather than the exception, and it is not to be wondered at that the children of such unions are degenerate. Add to this the myriad forms of 'literary', 'artistic', and 'theatrical' enterprise devoted to the stimulation and exploitation of vicious imaginations, and the 'problems' arising from the possession of the same, and it becomes questionable whether the limit has not been reached in the commercialisation and degradation of sex.

The gentle art of mugging

Above this welter of misery the employers of cheap feminine labour, the financiers of the white slave traffic and all the gold barons who directly or indirectly levy toll on the vice and its effects, idle away useless, harmful, albeit 'philanthropic' lives amid the luxury heaped up by their degenerate slaves; while, hanging on to their purse strings with the tenacity of limpets, the parsons and moralists, 'physicians' and 'reformers' of every description, pretend to be clearing up the mess – incidentally appearing to enjoy the job the more the longer it lasts and increases in extent – and in the market squares and recreation grounds crowds of debilitated and anaemic wage-slaves listen with bated breath and simulate the pious shudders of the 'intellectual' gents of the Anti-Socialist Union as they describe the orgy of bestiality which they assure their audiences will be inaugurated by the advent of

Socialism. "Community of Women!! Universal Prostitution and Promiscuity!!" they cry, endeavouring to frighten their hearers with the shadow in order to divert their attention from the reality, and the economic system on which it is based and which these same paid hacks are out to defend.

Years ago Marx and Engels (unlike the Fabian Society, the ILP, and all the other pseudo-Socialist crowd who allow this misrepresentation of free love), challenged these gentry with the facts in terms that are worth quoting. In the *Communist Manifesto*, section II, dealing with numerous objections to Communism, they say:

"The bourgeois (capitalist) sees in his wife a mere instrument of production. He hears that the means of production are to become common property, and naturally can only think that the lot of becoming common property will likewise fall to women.

"He never suspects that the real point aimed at is to do away with the position of women as mere instruments of production.

"For the rest, nothing is more ridiculous than the virtuous horror of our bourgeois at the community of women which he pretends will be officially established by the Communists ...

"The members of our bourgeoisie, not content with having the wives and daughters of their proletarians at their disposal, not to speak of common prostitutes, take special delight in mutually seducing each other's wives.

"Bourgeois marriage is in reality community of wives. The Communists could at most be accused of wishing to replace a hypocritically concealed community of women by an official and open community of women. For the rest, it is evident that with the abolition of the present system of production will disappear also the community of women resulting from it, i.e., public prostitution."

And so it is.

The degradation of women as a sex is but a special aspect of the general degradation of humanity. The cause of this degradation is, as we have shown, the private ownership of society's means of subsistence. To remove the cause is the task of the great mass of society – the working class. Only by converting the instruments of production into common property can they emancipate themselves from the necessity of prostituting their faculties to the foul service of the capitalist class, which, like an octopus, sucks the blood of every part of the social body.

With this freedom established, all human activities will depend upon their desirability and usefulness to those who perform them. Consequently our faculties will be devoted, unhampered by economic considerations, to their true purpose. When women have free access, as members of the community, to a sufficiency of those things necessary to a healthy and happy life, their genuine sex-nature will assert itself. When children are born with a similar birthright, the need for avoiding them or exploiting them for private ends will disappear also. They will be born and reared for their own sake, as they should be. Therefore between man and woman, parents and children, affection will be the only tie. Modern marriage and the present so-called family life, like all other legal institutions, with their sordid monetary and proprietary bases, will be relegated to the limbo of the forgotten past. Where love exists chains are unnecessary; where it does not they are undesirable to those who would be free. But to expect sexual love, parental love, or fraternal love to flourish under a social order based on competition, greed, and hatred is akin to looking for figs on thistles.

To sweep away the foul conditions of producing and distributing the material wants of mankind, which today render these latter qualities essential to existence, thus preventing the development of human love, we call our fellow-workers to arise.

There is a sordid system to be overthrown, a class battening thereon to be fought. And as the power of this class, to which it ferociously clings, consists of the control of the political allegiance of the workers themselves, our course is obvious. We must organise as a class, wrest from our masters the forces of coercion directed by the machinery of government, and having thus removed the only obstacle, take possession of the indispensable resources of nature and of society – the land, the machines, and all those things necessary for the production and distribution of wealth. Such is the programme of the Socialist Party. We do not flinch from any of its implications.

"The Communists disdain to conceal their views and aims ... The proletarians have nothing to lose but their chains: they have a world to win".

(December 1913)

THE FIRST WORLD WAR

When war broke out in August 1914, the *Socialist Standard* expressed the position of the Socialist Party of Great Britain at the first opportunity. The September issue carried a front page declaration denouncing the war as a 'business war' over "questions of the control of trade routes and the world's markets" and stating that there were therefore no interests at stake justifying "the shedding of a single drop of working class blood". It ended "The World for the Workers".

This internationalist, anti-war position was maintained throughout the war. Socialist Party members refused to go and kill their fellow-workers and were either jailed or went 'on the run' from the authorities.

The *Socialist Standard* itself was not subject to censorship, though it was banned by the War Office from being sent overseas. Perhaps ironically, the only article during the war which was subject to censorship was prevented from appearing because of objections from the typesetting firm contracted to produce each monthly issue. This was an article on 'Lloyd George and the Clyde Workers' in February 1916, which was replaced by a short explanation and otherwise blank columns where the article should have been.

Censorship did, however, have an effect in terms of the amount of information available as to what exactly was going on in the world at large. It was because the censors did not allow too much to leak out that the *Socialist Standard* had very little to say about the events in Dublin over Easter 1916 and that the article on the Bolshevik seizure of power in November 1917 had to be devoted to setting out the theoretical reasons why, whatever had happened, it could not have been a socialist revolution.

During these years the main concern of socialists, both in Britain and on the Continent, was, apart from renewing international links, simply to stop the slaughter of workers. Thus the *Socialist Standard*, besides exposing the economic causes of the war and countering pro-war propaganda, repeatedly called for an immediate and unconditional end to the war. This was expressed not only in declarations sent to various conferences of workers' organisations from different countries but also in reprinting anti-war appeals from such organisations in other countries, including one from Rosa Luxemburg in Germany and another, in 1915, from the Bolshevik wing of the Russian Social Democratic Labour Party.

When the Bolshevik government did try to take Russia unilaterally out of the war and stop the slaughter on the Eastern Front this earned it the praise of the *Socialist*

Standard despite reservations about the Bolsheviks' claims to have started establishing socialism in Russia. In a war situation, with workers dying for causes that were not theirs, stopping this slaughter was regarded as the priority for any organisation or publication committed to the working class interest, and this is reflected in the articles reprinted in this section.

The War and You

As we went to Press with our last issue, but too late for us to deal with the events in our pages, the great capitalist States of Europe were flinging declarations of war at each other and rushing in frenzied haste to the long-expected and carefully prepared for Armageddon.

When we say that this mad conflict has been long expected and well-prepared for we make a statement which is almost trite. However much the masters of Europe may have tried to hide the underlying causes and objects of their military preparations, they have never taken any pains to conceal the fact that they were arming against 'the day', and that 'the day' was inevitable. Miles of paper and tons of printing ink have been used in the various countries in order to disseminate among the 'common' people – i.e. the working class – explanations calculated to fix the blame on other shoulders. In each country voluminous 'exposures' have been made of the villainous machinations of the 'foreigner', always in such deep contrast to the Christian innocence of the exposers. But so far have any of the chief parties ever been from disguising the inevitability of the event they have been arming for, that they have used these very 'exposures' to obtain the assent of public opinion to the race for armaments and the preparations for wholesale slaughter.

On the Continent they speak of British hypocrisy. The truth is that there is, among the rulers of every capitalist country, hypocrisy enough and to spare, and the attitude of British Statesmen toward neutrals and the working class at home reeks with characteristic hypocrisy. In spite of the fact that nowadays very few even of their working class dupes really believe in the 'altruistic' humbug regarding the maintenance of the 'independence of small nations', or attach any importance to Asquith, Grey & Co's drivel about the 'honour of Britain', it is on those canting grounds that our masters seek to justify their plunge into the red vortex of war.

However hard our masters may try to cover their actions with the tattered and slimy cloak of 'national honour' like slobbering and sentimental frauds, and however a politically and economically ignorant working class may applaud and echo these sentiments as if in an effort to hide from themselves brutal facts of which they are conscious and ashamed, there remains the obstinate truth, obvious to anyone who will go out into the streets and listen to what is there said, that even the working class realise that the motive for the war is in the last resort an economic one. Behind the covering screen of cant about British honour and German perfidy is the consciousness, frequently voiced, that it is a question, not of German perfidy but of German trade; not of British honour, but of wider markets for the disposal of British surplus products.

Let us, then, clear away from our minds the befogging folds of cant and humbug in order that we may see the facts naked and understand them, and face the situation as it really is.

We must understand, first of all, that it is essentially the character of the modern system of wealth production to bring into existence a tremendous amount of surplus wealth. This surplus wealth is that portion which the workers produce but do not receive; the portion which goes to the employers and other sections of the ruling class in the shape of Rent, Interest and Profit.

There are two things peculiar about this surplus: 1). Production cannot continue unless it is produced, because the landlord only lets his premises in order to get his rent, the investor only lends his money in order to get interest, and the employer only employs to get profit; and 2). Production can only continue whilst this product can be sold, because the proceeds of the sale pay the landlord his rent, the investor his interest, and to realise for himself that profit which is his sole incentive to engage in industrial enterprise.

The result of these two features of modern production is very simple. They have brought the master class of every capitalist country face to face with the problem of finding a market for the disposal of their surplus products. And this problem becomes every day more pressing for the following reason.

The wealth produced by the workers is divided into two portions – the portion which they receive (wages) and the portion which is retained by the masters. The portion they receive is just sufficient to enable them to reproduce their strength and efficiency, and is therefore nearly stationary. But as the means and

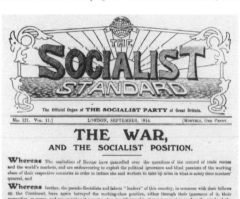

methods by which they produce are improved, the total of their product increases. Hence, since their share remains practically constant, what remains – the surplus or master's share – increases in proportion as the machinery of production improves. Therefore, since this machinery improves at a prodigious rate, the surplus which the masters have to find a market for becomes larger every day.

As the rate of surplus wealth produced increases, it becomes more impossible for the inhabitants of the country in which it is produced – inhabitants of both classes – to use it up. The consumption of the working class is limited to that which their wages will buy, and therefore cannot encroach upon the surplus which is just that portion of their product their wages will *not* buy back. The consumption of the master class is limited on the one hand by their physical capacity, and on the other hand by their necessity for ever increasing their capital. Hence an outlet for it must be found in foreign markets.

Every reader will go with us so far, of course. Every British working man feels that behind all the cant and slobber about honour and the rest of it, is the solid, practical consideration that the successful issue of the war will cripple a great trade rival and provide increased opportunity of work for British workers – and so far our theory does not conflict with this. That the conception is false, however, we shall see when we return to it, as we shall later.

Military history of the past fifty years has been based upon this fact. Britain has gained control of the sea trade routes, and has seized most of the best markets of the world. At the same time it has been the policy of her statesmen to take up a repressive attitude towards the aspirations of all possible rivals. Hence the Crimea was fought in order to prevent Russia establishing herself on the trade routes to the East. Since then every endeavour has been made to prevent Russia getting an outlet to the sea through a port free from the ice grip in winter, and from the oppression of commanding forts of rival nations. This antagonism continued until the Japanese put a stopper on Russian hopes in the East, and other jealous eyes were watching her nearer home.

Now took place a change of policy – or rather, a change in the direction of the old policy. A new rival had come to ripeness. And here we come to the drivel about national 'honour'.

First, a treaty with Japan releases the larger part of the British Naval forces in the Far East. Then an arrangement with France transfers the French Fleet to the Mediterranean, and clears the way for the concentration of the British Fleet in Home waters.

Now these facts are matters of history, and allow of no dispute. Therefore it is quite plain that so far was it from being any question of honour which impelled the British Government to range themselves on the side of France, that they had deliberately planned the present situation years ago.

Therefore when Sir Edward Grey came before the British House of Commons and declared that it was simply a point of honour for the British Fleet to defend the Northern coast of France he spoke with his tongue in his cheek. It was not honour but just cut and dried policy. A man so completely versed in these matters as is Sir Edward Grey must have known that there could have been no such qualified neutrality as this. In the face of such an attitude as this not only was the Northern coast of France protected from German attack, but her Southern shore and her Fleet in the Mediterranean also; for the German Fleet dared not put to sea for fear of being cut off by the British ships and caught in a trap. Meanwhile German shipping was to be at the mercy of the French and the latter left to transport troops from their African colonies without a care in the world.

As far as effecting the course of the war goes England could do very little more. If Germany was to be strangled at sea by a 'neutral' nation who could not strike very hard on land, then Germany had but little more to fear from flouting that nation's 'love' for Belgium. And this is so very obvious that it must have been plain to those who entered into the arrangement with France by which the defence of the French coasts was shouldered by the British Navy.

That arrangement was no secret to Germany, and its purpose and object must have been perfectly clear to them. It meant that, under the guise of neutrality, perhaps, the British naval force was to be thrown into the scale against Germany. How would this affect the situation of Belgium? The very foundation of the treaty to respect the independence of Belgium was the assumption that when either France or Germany should attempt to use Belgium as a jumping-off ground against the other, it would be at the cost of arraigning Britain on the opposing side.

But years before the war broke out the British Fleet was placed at the disposal of France, under a cunning arrangement that could not possibly deceive those against whom it was directed, and on whom the responsibility of meeting it fell. All they had to consider, then, in making their plans, was whether the British Naval force against them, and the rapidity of action more than ever necessary by reason of their strangulation at sea, the employment of the British Expeditionary force against them was too dear a price to pay for the advantages of a passage through Belgium. Whether the German military authorities blundered or not, they decided to take the risk.

There is no escaping, then, from the conclusion that British statesmen deliberately planned some years ago to place the country in such a position that the outbreak of the war must inevitably have involved both the participation of Britain and the invasion of Belgium. So much, then, for the canting reference to honour and the preservation of the independence of small nations – such as the Boers, for instance!

It is not for us to say that there is anything to be ashamed of in admitting that the war has an economic basis. It is certainly more honest than throwing it back upon such humbug as the 'honour of the British nation'. But it has this disadvantage in the eyes of the ruling class – it leaves this clear issue facing the working class (who are to do the fighting): what economic advantage are *they* going to gather as the reward of the blood they spill, the lives they sacrifice, and the miseries they endure through this most ghastly of all ghastly wars?

To this question their masters have but one reply, and that is based on an economic fallacy. They say that as a result of humbling Germany British trade will expand and there will be plenty of work for everybody. Only so long as the ruling class can maintain the belief in this fallacy among the working class can they hope to get working class support for their wars. The old 'bulldog breed' brand of 'patriotism' is nearly dead – as the War Office recognised when, in their great recruiting campaign of a few months ago, they abandoned their time-worn policy of trying to convince the worker that he has a 'glorious heritage' to fight for, and appealed to him on the ground that civil life had such poor prospects to offer him that he would be better off in the Army.

The contention that the crushing of Germany would lead to the extension of British trade and plenty of work for the British worker is plausible and perhaps partly true. British trade may certainly expand, but then the curious thing is that expansion is its normal condition, yet unemployment accompanies the unceasing growth of 'Britain's prosperity'.

Extracts from two Government publications will knock the bottom clean out of the argument that the expansion of British trade necessarily means less unemployment for British workers.

The 55th No. of the Statistical Abstract (Cd. 4258) published in 1908, gives the following information (page 69):

	1897	1907
Total exports of the United Kingdom	£234,219,708	£426,035,083
Proportion per head of population	£5 17s 2d.	£9 13s 3d.

(The figures refer to the produce of the United Kingdom only.)

In ten years, it will be seen, the total exports of home produce almost doubled, and even as regards proportion to population, jumped up from £29 5s 10d. to £48 6s 3d. per family of five people. Now what was the result upon unemployment? Has this gigantic increase in the national exports provided 'plenty of work'?

The Local Government Board's Statistical Memoranda Cd 4671 tells us that the average unemployment among Trade Unions making returns was in 1897, 3.65; in 1907, 4.3.

So we arrive at the result, fatal to the argument that the seizure of Germany's trade must mean "plenty of work for the British worker," that this vast increase of exports which took place in a single decade, was actually accompanied by an increase of unemployment. The reason for this is very simple. It is due to that unceasing improvement in machinery which is constantly making human productive energy more fertile and enabling each worker to produce more wealth in a given time.

Now what would be the effect of Great Britain capturing a large portion of Germany's export trade? The capitalist economists say that it would result in the absorption of the unemployed. Suppose we accept that, even then what is the position?

One of the first effects of a decrease in unemployment is the rise of wages, as is indicated from the Local Government's Board's Cd. 4671 (page 44):

Year	Unemployment	Wages
1897	3.65	162.3
1898	3.15	166.5
1899	2.40	170.4
1900	2.85	178.7
1901	3.80	177.0
1902	4.60	174.7
1903	5.30	173.7
1904	6.8	172.8
1905	5.6	173.3
1906	4.1	175.7

It will be noticed that there is a fall, a rise, and a second fall of unemployment recorded in the above table, and in agreement therewith, a rise, a fall, and a second rise in wages.

Wages are the price of labour power. Labour power, like other commodities, cannot be sold in the face of cheaper and efficient competitors. It has one such competitor – machinery.

Think what the general nature of the pressure of machinery upon labour power is. It is not that this pressure is only asserted when and where some new invention has appeared. No, on the contrary there are many labour saving devices which are anything but new which still have not altogether displaced the means which were in use before them, though they are conquering fresh ground every day. The steam plough is an example in farming, the morticing machinery in joinery, and the Linotype Composing Machine in printing.

In almost every field of industry the workers know that what they are doing by hand can be done quicker with machinery, and what they are doing with machinery can be done still quicker with more efficient machinery. Take the cylinder machine in printing. First a worker is necessary to 'lay on' the sheets of paper and another to 'take off'. Then the invention of 'flyers' knocked out the latter, and the perfection of a pneumatic appliance made the 'layer-on' redundant.

Yet today there are probably far more machines in operation without flyers than there are with the 'laying on' apparatus.

So it is in every branch of industry. At every point operations are being performed by the means that are cheapest today, but at every point also other and more highly developed means are trying to oust the old. They can only advance by cheapening the productive process, that is, by economising the labour cost.

It is clear from this that a rise in wages, desirable as this is, is after all a handicap on labour power. At a given price it offers a given resistance to the advance of its competitor, machinery; but a rise in that price (a rise in wages) at once encourages the introduction of machinery which will enable the work to be done by fewer men.

For instance, suppose ten men with horse ploughs can plough a field at the same cost as three men with a steam plough outfit. If all their wages go up five shillings the steam plough at once becomes the cheaper means, because the advance of wages is only fifteen shillings on three men, while in the other case the rise affects ten men, and amounts to fifty shillings.

So it is seen that the inevitable result of the capturing of German trade must be after a little that machinery would advance and, by displacing workers, provide a new unemployed army. This indeed always happens with the expansion of trade. The exports of British products increased by over £50,000,000 in the single year 1906-7, yet so easily did machinery absorb the 'shock' that, instead of there being 'plenty of work', unemployment rose from 4.1 to 4.3!

So much, then, for the economic fallacy with which the masters, with their tales of their preparations for capturing German trade, try to make the workers think they are interested in the issue of the war. The workers are wage-slaves, and as such they are and always must be subject to economic laws which govern the wages system. An unemployed army suitable to the capitalist requirements of the time is one of the constant provisions of the operation of those laws – working through the development of machinery. No matter how trade may expand, or whether the German masters rule the country or the English masters continue to do so, this unemployed army will continue to be produced, and will determine the main conditions of working class existence.

In addition, to take a job from a German in order to give it to a Briton still leaves unemployment in the working class, and the unemployed German simply follows the job to this country, and thus unemployment is again in our midst.

The question for the working class, then, is not that of British or German victory, since either event will leave them wage-slaves living upon wages. Under German rule those wages cannot be reduced lower than under British, for every British workingman knows that the masters who are shouting so loudly today for us to go and die in defence of our shackles and their shekels, have left no stone unturned to force wages to the lowest possible limits. The question, then, before the workers, is the abolition of the whole social system of which war and unemployment are integral parts, and the establishment of society upon the basis of common ownership of the means of production – the establishment, that is, of SOCIALISM.

(September 1914)

The Call of the 'Patriot'

Fellow workers – During the last three months there has been staring at you from every hoarding, from trams, 'buses, and stations, from vans, warehouse walls, and notice boards on churches, from the pages of the newspapers and every other available space, the statement that: "*Your King and Country need* you."

This statement, showing, if you will but think, how important and vitally necessary you are to the ruling class, has been reiterated again and again, with innumerable variations, from countless pulpits and platforms up and down the country. Urgent appeals by the hundred thousand have been made to all 'fit' men to enlist; every device and every weapon that the 'liberty-loving' masters could invent, from the call of a sham patriotism to the wholesale backing of employers; from lying to bribery; from silent coercion to the insults of the white feather brigade, and from this to the deliberate suppression of hostile opinion, have been used either to entice or drive you into the ranks. For *you*, fellow workers, are today, as you *always* are, indispensable to the bosses, both for the production of profits in the 'piping times of peace' (!) and for cannon fodder and the slaughter of the 'enemy' in times of war.

Without *you* the masters are helpless; without *you* the State collapses and the rulers of the one country cannot hope to win in their struggle against the rulers of another country; and knowing this, and recognising *your* supreme importance, the bosses have been moving heaven and earth, spending money like water, lying like Christians, combining cajolery with economic pressure, and ringing the changes on every form of cant, from 'stirring' appeals to your manhood to virulent denunciation of your indifference or backwardness, in order to make *you* go and fight battles from which you will receive the usual rewards of empty honour, broken health, wounded bodies, or the eternal silence of the grave.

The reasons advanced why you and the working men of Europe should fight each other have been many, and we could fill a column with the contradictions of the politicians, the black coats, and the 'intellectuals' on this matter. Any excuse has been good enough as long as it has had the effect of making you and the German working men defend your respectïve masters. From the violation of treaties by Germany to deliberate provocation on the part of England; from Russian Court intrigue to the capture of international trade; from the rottenness of secret diplomacy to the enthronement of Atheism; from the policy of 'blood and iron' to the jealousy and hatred of the Allies: each and every excuse in its turn, according to whether the apologist was pro-British or pro-German, has been offered as justification for the infamy now going on, and as a reason why you should take part in it.

In England it is declared to be a war for 'liberty, righteousness, democracy', and other bunkum – although the bosses occasionally give the game away by stating, as the *Sunday Chronicle* of 30th August, that "the men in the trenches are fighting on behalf of the manufacturer, the millowner, and the shopkeeper." In Germany it is declared to be a conflict in which the ruling class of England, Russia, and Japan have combined to reduce her to the level of a fifth-rate power, and to render her politically, militarily, and above all economically, impotent for ever. And each side, using every possible device, has dragged you and your fellow-workers abroad into the arena.

You had neither lot, voice, nor counsel in the events leading to the conflict; *your* place while it lasts is that of automata, conscious only to obey blindly and, if need be, to suffer; and your lot after it is over will be the usual lot of your class, the lot of the poor, the downtrodden and the oppressed everywhere.

Of the forces now engaged not more than 5% come from the ranks of the well-to-do; *you* furnish the remaining 95%. *You* have to bear the infinitely greater proportion of the deaths, the disease, the permanent injury and the awful strain, while those who goad you on with sweet words or threats, rest securely and comfortably in their easy chairs in club or office, killing the enemy every day with their mouths, but taking particular care, in the vast majority of instances, never to risk their precious carcases within a hundred miles of the actual conflict.

We Socialists would therefore ask you to put on your considering caps and think for yourselves, instead of allowing the capitalist Press, Tory, Liberal, and sham Labour, to think for you.

When the war is over, and you are tramping the country, as you will be in many cases; when you and those near and dear to you hunger and thirst; when you feel the whip of semi-starvation and the gaunt spectre of want is your daily companion, will your 'King and Country' need you then? Does not your daily experience teach you that you have no country, that you are landless and propertyless? Does it not show you that here, as in Germany, the land and its fatness belong to the masters, your portion being a mean tenement in a mean street, with the bare means of existence, and then only if you are lucky enough to get work?

When the bosses ask you to fight – to offer your lives for 'democracy and liberty against militarism'; when they pose as the defenders of oppressed people, and express themselves deeply concerned to uphold justice, humanity, and right, ask them why it is that they have so long practised in England – practise to this day – the tyranny and oppression they now denounce abroad.

The present British Government, the 'champions of liberty', through their then Home Secretary, Churchill, prepared, previous to the railway workers going on strike, and turned out at the request of the railway magnates, no less than 58,000 troops, crushing by militarism the attempt of those workers to slightly improve their admittedly rotten conditions of existence.

This Government, 'the apostle of humanity', during the last London Dock strike – when the men merely asked that agreements previously entered into by the Government itself should be honoured – placed at the disposal of the capitalist Devonport and the gang around him, an unlimited supply of police and military, and deliberately starved the women and children, in some cases to death, in order to break the resistance of the men.

This Government, the 'defender of freedom, the upholder of justice, and right', endorsed martial law, the denial of all liberty and the firing on defenceless crowds in South Africa; it batoned 700 men in Dublin, turned out the military against *you* at Belfast, Llanelly, Leith, the Rhondda valley and elsewhere; it has callously refused to give underfed children sufficient food; it mocks with pretty words, but cynical, brutal inaction, the condition of the ever-growing army of unemployed; it has sanctioned wholesale imprisonment, exile and butchery, in India, Persia, Egypt, and the New Hebrides, and allied itself with the infamies perpetrated in Russia and Japan: in a word, it reeks with lying pretence and self-satisfied Pharisaism, for in very truth, it is the ever-willing tool of autocracy, capitalism, and class rule and the deadly enemy of the working class everywhere.

Ask this or any capitalistic Government for their credentials, examine their records, and you will learn that, beyond all dispute, whether it be England or Russia, France or Belgium, Germany or Japan, there is, so far as *you* are concerned, no difference between them whatever. They are all made in the same mould, filled with the same lust – the lust of exploiting *you*. When it suits them they flatter you; but when you ask them for a little of the justice they now prate about, then they insult, imprison and often murder you. Today they want you badly, for they are at war with each other and want *you* to do *their* dirty work; but remember that whoever wins or loses, your lot will be the same; the politician will still soft-soap you ; the industrial machine will still grind you, and poverty and all that it means will still enchain you.

If, therefore, you are wise, if you are men, if you are really anxious for freedom from slavery, then look around you here, and you will soon learn the truth, that it is your class which is denied this freedom, and denied it by the very class who now call upon you to act. One law for the rich and one for the poor. Adulation, servility and the world's wealth for the rich; grinding toil, insecurity and eternal hardship for the poor – these are the commonplace of every day life. Is it not so?

Your duty, then, is to fight against this, and the only way you can fight successfully is by understanding your position in society, realising that wars and hate, malice and theft, oppression and greed, class rule and the travail of the workers the world over, are today born of capitalism. *This is the root evil*; it is this you have to war against if you would be free, for all else is futile; and when you do this, *but not before*, then liberty will be with you as your possession; there will be no oppressed peoples, for the might of the working class, organised consciously for the overthrow of the modern octopus, will have conquered, and the international commonwealth will be here.

(November 1914)

Strikes for Peace

Signs are steadily growing that the working class of Europe are becoming weary of the war, with its endless slaughter, its lack of decisions making for peace, and the increased privation and misery that result from its continuance.

Enthusiastic at first for the war, with an enthusiasm inflamed and fed by the Press and the preachers – religious and political – of the master class, the workers of the various belligerent countries rushed to the fray, to the cry of 'On to Berlin!' 'Paris in a week!' and the like. Three and a half years of appalling slaughter have intervened, with immense improvements and developments in the instruments of torture and destruction, but the belligerents are no nearer a military decision now, on either side, than they were in 1914.

Food is becoming short, not only because millions of men have been called to the armies and navies, but also because millions more have been taken from the production of the necessaries of life and put to making instruments and articles for its destruction. And this second army has to be fed along with the first.

This food shortage is further aggravated by the favouritism that is rampant all round. Working-class women may wait for hours in queues for meat or margarine, and then fail to obtain any, but wealthy novelists, paunchy parsons, triple chinned quondam 'white-feather' ticklers, and prosperous 'patriots' in general, can easily obtain hundreds of pounds weight of good things to nourish their determination to sacrifice and strengthen their 'will to victory'. Shops in working class neighbourhoods are often shut for days because of the lack of supplies, but there is no shortage of first class meat, genuine butter, choicest tea, and so on at the big hotels and clubs of the West End of London, and of certain fashionable resorts. The wives of the capitalists *never* stand in queues for anything except a view of the latest extravagance in expensive fashions.

Although the news published here of things that are happening on the Continent has to be taken with a certain amount of caution, as we must remember that the Censor will only allow the publication of items that suit the interest of the master class, it seems fairly certain that disaffection is growing there and strikes are increasing. In many cases the avowed object of the strikes in Germany and Austria is the securing of food, but nearly always accompanying this demand, and in some cases forming the sole object, is the call upon the governments to declare an armistice and enter into negotiations for peace.

In this country a similar movement is spreading and strikes are not only in progress, but more are threatened. This movement has received a great impetus from the introduction by the Government of a measure for extending the power of Conscription by the military authorities, usually referred to under the misleading but catchy title of the 'Man Power Bill'. In the Press the greatest prominence has been given to the attitude taken up by the Amalgamated Society of Engineers, though this society is not the only, or even the most important, section affected by the Bill. The reason for singling out the ASE has been the refusal of the Executive of that body to take part in a joint conference with the other trades and Sir Auckland Geddes, on the details of applying the Bill. The ASE Executive claim that, as they have a separate agreement with the Government on this question, they should be consulted separately on the withdrawal of that agreement.

While this Government have a complete answer to this objection, it is significant that, so far, they have not attempted to bring that answer forward. Sir Auckland Geddes or Mr Lloyd George (whose title will no doubt arrive later on) could easily have answered the ASE Executive somewhat as follows: "It is true we made that agreement with you, but what of it? Did we not point out at the time that there was no guarantee that we would keep it? Did not Mr Henderson answer your question on this point by telling you point-blank that no such guarantee would be given? And, far more important than this, is it not a fact that we have made various promises, pledges, and agreements, several of them embodied in Acts of Parliament, not only to sections, but to the whole working class? Even now your protest is not on behalf of the working class, but a claim that a small section – the members of the ASE – should not be placed in the Army until the 'dilutees' have been taken. Surely if you did not complain when we smashed agreements and pledges given to the whole working class it is illogical to complain now when a section of that class is being similarly treated."

This latter fact is the fatally weak point in the ASE case, and is being used effectively by the capitalist Press and spokesmen against them.

While such narrow, short-sighted views are held by sections of the working class the master class have an easy task in keeping alive the jealousies and divisions that are so useful to them in their fights with the workers.

Sir Auckland Geddes was quite successful in urging the other trade union leaders whom he met in conference to accept his proposals and to promise to persuade their followers to accept them without trouble or friction. One reason why the ASE officials were not so ready to follow their old methods on this occasion is the growth of the 'Shop Stewards' movement up and down the country. This movement has helped to undermine the influence of the 'official' cliques in the trade unions, as shown by the numerous 'unauthorised' strikes, and with the loss of this influence over the rank and file the officials realised that their chance of bargaining for jobs with the master class would be gone.

Apparently some of the Shop Stewards, however, are merely rivals for the 'official' positions and refuse to move far outside the beaten track. According to the *Daily Telegraph* for 30th January 1918, the National Administrative Council of Shop Stewards passed the following resolution: "That they are not the body to deal with the technical grievances arising out of the cancellation of occupational exemptions from military service embodied in the Man Power Bill, and must, therefore, leave such grievances to be dealt with by the official organisations concerned."

Most of the 'official organisations' are swallowing the 'grievances' whole.

It would be a big mistake to suppose that these strikes and threats to strike indicate an acceptance of the principles of Socialism, or even a general awakening to the fact that they are slaves to the master class, on the part of those engaged in this movement. In some cases there may be some suspicion as to the good faith of certain Ministers and the War Cabinet, but even this suspicion is only of a faint type, as is shown by several of the resolutions passed at various meetings. According to Press reports resolutions of similar character have been passed (up to the time of writing) at meetings held at Woolwich, Albert Hall (London), Barrow, etc., in the following terms: "That the British Government should enter into immediate negotiations with the other belligerent Powers for an armistice on all fronts, with a view to a general peace on the basis of self-determination of all nations and no annexations and no indemnities. Should such action demonstrate that German Imperialism was the only obstacle to peace they would co-operate in the prosecution of the war until the objects mentioned in the first part of the resolution were achieved. Failing this they would continue their opposition to the man-power proposals" (*Daily News*, 28th January 1918).

These resolutions show the confused mental condition of the workers concerned. Does their claim for 'self-determination' apply to Ireland, India and Egypt? If so, do they really imagine the British capitalist Government will agree to such application? Certainly they must be simple if they believe a threat to strike would bring such a result.

A resolution moved at Glasgow at a meeting where Sir A. Geddes was present struck a firmer note in the following terms: "That having heard the case of the Government, as stated by Sir Auckland Geddes, this meeting pledges itself to oppose to the very uttermost the Government in its call for more men. We insist and pledge ourselves to take action to enforce the declaration of an immediate armistice on all fronts; and that the expressed opinion of the workers of Glasgow is that from now on, and so far as this business is concerned our attitude all the time and every time is to do nothing in support of carrying on the war, but to bring the war to a conclusion."

The supporters of the war could of course point out that, as far as the workers are concerned, there is as much – and as little – reason for carrying on the war now as ever there was. Better late than never, however, and if the Clyde workers realise even at this late date that they have nothing to gain but a good deal to lose by the continuance of the war it is a point to the good.

Of course the Government soon arranged for a counterblast to these resolutions, and the Press gives somewhat vague and rather circumstantial accounts of meetings where resolutions of support of the Government were supposed to be passed. But this action itself is a proof of how widespread, if not deep, is the movement.

It would be folly, or worse, for the workers to fail to recognise the forces that can be employed against them by the Government if it chooses. Already in certain cases where men have refused to work in a particular factory or on a particular job the protection cards have been withdrawn, the men called to the colours, and then ordered back to the factory or job at ordinary soldier's pay. With its present powers and without troubling to pass the 'Man Power' Bill at all the Government could withdraw the protection cards and exemption certificates of the engineers and others concerned, call these men to the colours, and then draft them back into the shops and shipyards under military orders and discipline and on army pay.

The messages, more or less reliable, purporting to show that this action is also taking place in Germany against certain of the strikers there may merely be the newspaper preparation for an extension of such action here.

It is true that, to the outsider, signs of another sort are not wanting. The sudden calling of the Labour Party Conference to formulate what it called its 'Peace Aims' without even taking time to consult its constituent bodies was undoubtedly the work of the Government to prepare for a "climb down" on their previous bombastic claims. The contemptuous treatment of Mr Havelock Wilson at the Conference shows how readily the capitalists throw aside their tools when they have served their purpose. Mr Lloyd George's speech a few days later was practically a withdrawal of almost every claim, from Constantinople to Alsace-Lorraine, previously put forward. Of course the game of bluff will not be dropped all at once; but how transparent it is becoming is shown by the official statement of the Inter-Allied War Conference published on 4th February, 1918: "The Allies are united in heart and will, not by any hidden designs, but by their open resolve to defend civilisation against an unscrupulous and brutal attempt at domination" (*Daily Telegraph*).

To draw up such a statement during the very week that the question as to whether the war was to be continued till the objects of the secret treaty with Italy were attained was being raised in the British Parliament was certainly an exhibition of irony.

Rumours have been floating round that the Bill was introduced with the object of raising disturbances so as to give grounds for a further abatement of claims on the part of the Government, and whether these rumours have any foundation in fact or not, it is certainly curious that a Bill should be introduced to give the Army authorities power they already possess in substance if not in method. The excuse that the matter is too pressing to allow the time necessary for the present procedure, while valid, hardly seems strong enough for the introduction of such a trouble-raising measure.

By far the greatest danger to the workers lies in another direction. The ablest representative of the master class today on the public Press is Mr A.G. Gardiner, of the *Daily News*. Not only has he a firm grasp of the situation from the masters' side, but he is easily the cleverest of their agents at the game of misleading the workers by using a style of seeming honesty and openness to cover up a substance of slimy deceit. A good example of this was his 'Open Letter to the Clyde Workers' (*Daily News*, 19th January 1918). His articles, while appearing to condemn the Government, are strenuous attempts to defend the existence and maintenance of capitalism. Another instance of danger from this direction is the employment of Mr Henderson as a decoy duck to lure the workers into dangerous waters. Despite his unceremonious and contemptuous dismissal at a moment's notice from his position in the Cabinet, he is again engaged on dirty work for the masters in the statement he issued to the Press on 1st February. In that screed he urges the workers to realise the gravity of their threatened action because it "... may precipitate a crisis which in the interests of the whole international working class movement we must do all in our power to avert" (*Daily Telegraph*, 1st February 1918).

The cant and humbug of talking about an 'international working class movement', that has no existence, while the capitalist governments refuse to allow even a meeting of international delegates, is characteristic of one who has done all in his power to urge the workers to slaughter each other for the *national* interests of the capitalist class.

But these statements, along with those of Mr Gardiner, sound plausible. Their purpose is to persuade the workers to still leave in the hands of the masters' agents the manipulation and direction of affairs. And there is a great danger that the workers, so long used to following this course, so long in the habit of following 'leaders' will succumb once more to this influence. Some of them not daring to trust themselves to manage affairs, will believe it better to leave the management to these 'experts'. If only half of the blunders and appalling crimes of this war should be brought into the light of day, these timid workers will have a rude shock concerning the ability of those 'experts'. Even such reports as have leaked through up to now show what a gigantic hypocrisy is their claim. The revelations that have been published in regard to Mesopotamia should convince every worker that they simply could not themselves manage matters worse, while the contempt they are held in by both the master class and its agents may be illustrated by a small incident from one of the war fronts.

A certain road on a portion of the line is used to bring up munitions and food to the men in the trenches. The 'enemy' knows the position – and use – of this road quite well. It is therefore watched during the light hours, and swept with shell and machine-gun fire during the night. The transport vans are stopped just outside the area of fire to save the mules (four legged ones) and the supplies are then carried through the shot-swept zone by the men.

As the working class begin to understand the position they occupy in modern society; as they begin to take a hand in settling affairs of social importance, they will make many blunders and mistakes. In the main, however, these will be easily recognised and corrected. But the biggest danger that confronts them – the biggest mistake they can make – is to place power in the hands of 'leaders' under any pretext whatever. It is at once putting those 'leaders' in a position to bargain with the master class for the purpose of selling out the workers. It allows the master class to retain control of the political machinery which is the essential instrument for governing Society. All the other blunders and mistakes the workers may make will be as dust in the balance compared with this one, and not until they realise this fact will they be on the road to Socialism.

(February 1918)

Peace (!)

Peace, we are told, has now been made. On 28th June, 1919, the representatives of the Allied powers and Germany signed a 'Peace treaty', officially terminating the 'Great War', which it had claimed would "end all war" and "make the world safe for democracy."

To achieve the great result millions of the working class lie in war graves, millions are maimed, crippled, or disfigured for life, millions more, with constitutions shattered, are wondering what the future holds for them.

Alongside this enormous waste of human life and limb, the destruction of wealth that has taken place seems trivial. Yet here the quantities are staggering. Numberless houses, factories and works, numerous mines, roads, railways and canals, thousands of ships with their cargoes, millions of tons of munitions, and extensive crops, forests, and the like, have been destroyed in this welter of war. And even now we are not at the end of the waste and destruction, for Mr Bonar Law, speaking at a 'Victory Loan' meeting, stated that there were still 23 other wars in progress.

But the 'Great War' has ended. And almost immediately, in every country throughout the capitalist world, strikes and struggles between masters and workers blaze up. In the countries of the conquerors and the conquered alike, in neutral States and border zones, overriding all the artificial divisions of territory and race, the antagonism between the working class and the master class gains greater prominence, with fiercer fights, than ever before. These fights, necessary for immediate purposes as many of them are, provide no solution for the fundamental problem facing the working class.

To the capitalist class a solution is impossible. They cannot abolish the antagonism except by abolishing themselves.

The 'League of Nations', claimed by its supporters to be the greatest safeguard of future peace that has resulted from the war, is cynically exposed by the military treaties between England, France, and America, to be a combination of the stronger Powers to enforce methods and conditions suitable to their own interests upon the weaker nations.

What other arrangements or undertakings have been made we do not at present know, but the refusal of China, one of the Allies, to sign the 'Peace' Treaty is significant. One reason for China's action that has leaked out is the practical handing over of Chinese territory – the Shantung Peninsular – to Japan. As this action threatens to at least restrain, if not to shut out, American trade in that part of China, because of the important seaports on the Shantung coast, it is raising a pretty quarrel between America and Japan, whose trade rivalry is already intense.

Such portions of the 'Peace' Treaty with Germany as have been published further support our case. Large areas are to be taken from Germany and handed over to France, Belgium, Poland, and Denmark. In some cases a plebiscite of the inhabitants of certain areas may be taken later on, but this is entirely within the discretion of the 'League', who may withhold such plebiscite if they wish. It is, of course, quite an accident that so many of these areas contain rich coal and ore deposits. In addition the Allies are to enjoy the "most favoured nation" treatment in commerce, to have unrestricted freedom of transit for their goods, and no Tariff discrimination for five years. While children are starving in Germany over 100,000 milch cows are to be taken by the Allies.

In the *Socialist Standard* for September 1914, in our Manifesto on the War, we stated: "The Capitalists of Europe have quarrelled over the questions of the control of trade routes and the world's markets, and are endeavouring to exploit the political ignorance and blind passions of the working class of their respective countries in order to induce the said workers to take up arms in what is solely their masters' quarrel."

Alone of all parties in this country we took our stand upon the Socialist position. So-called Socialist parties that supported the war then, are now in many cases pretending to be opposed to such wars, and are urging the workers to demonstrate and strike against British soldiers being used against Russian workers. Too ignorant or cowardly in those days to stand for the interests of the working class, they now try to achieve a popularity and reputation by urging soldiers to refuse to fire on Russian workers, while they applauded or were silent when the same soldiers were shooting down German, Austrian, or Hungarian soldiers.

Nay, even when these soldiers were used against workers at home – in Dublin, Hull, Tonypandy, and Glasgow – they accepted the right claimed by the capitalists to use such forces for their own interests, without any call for a strike.

In the manifesto mentioned above we said: "The machinery of government, including the armed forces of the nation, exists only to conserve the monopoly by the capitalist class of the wealth taken from the workers. These armed forces, therefore, will only be set in motion to further the interests of the class who control them – the master class."

As far as Russia is concerned, there are signs that 'intervention' is nearing its end – not because of the demonstrations (those called for 21st July were a ghastly failure), but because of a division of interests in the capitalist camp.

While the British and French capitalists who have invested large amounts of capital in developing Russian industry, desire intervention for the purpose of seizing control of the productive forces, either for themselves or in combination with the Russian master class, the other capitalists are quietly but effectively protesting against the scheme. Those who manufacture at home and seek markets abroad, note with anxiety how Japan and America are preparing to take hold of the Russian market. According to some reports, German merchants are already trading in Russia. On the other hand the Bolshevik Government has repeatedly announced its readiness to make 'economic' and 'industrial' concessions to foreign capitalists in exchange for seeds, machinery, and tools. The acceptance of these 'concessions' can have but one result – the running of the main industries of Russia on capitalist lines.

The backward economic conditions of Russia compel the Bolsheviks to make these offers that are in flat contradiction to their theories, and they can no more resist successfully the force of these circumstances than they could avoid signing the peace treaty of Brest-Litovsk.

Hence that section of the capitalist class who wish to open trade with Russia favour the withdrawal of Allied support of all kinds from Kolchak and Dennikin, and the making of a commercial agreement with the Bolshevik Government. Their need for haste is increased by the open campaign of jingoism that arose again after the Armistice and which has been epitomised by Sir Douglas Haig when receiving the Freedom of the City of London on the 12th June 1919. Speaking of his experience of the war he said: "My message to you, and through you to the Empire, is to urge you, now that the war has given you at once the reason and the opportunity to do so, to set up forthwith the organisation of a strong citizen Army on Territorial lines – an organisation which shall ensure that every able-bodied citizen shall come forward when the next crisis comes, not as a willing, patriotic, but militarily ignorant volunteer, but as a trained man." (*Daily News*, 13th June 1919).

Here, even before the 'Peace' treaty was signed, was the exposure of the foul lies of the capitalist class that this war was 'to end all war'.

While competition between capitalist groups for routes, markets, and control of raw material exists, the cause of war remains. The amalgamation of some of these groups into 'leagues' or 'associations', while it may put off the evil day for a while, only makes the struggle the greater when it does arise. But even if the whole of the greater capitalists of the world were to unite for the control of the globe, there would still remain the greatest of all wars to be fought out – the Class War for the freedom of Mankind.

During the 'Great War' the capitalist class on both sides broke down many of the old national and racial barriers that still existed between various sections of slaves under their control. Black chattel slaves fought alongside yellow contract workers. Irish Home Rulers stood by jingo Englishmen, French Syndicalists by Japanese Imperialists.

Clearer than ever before stands out the great fact that there is no hope for real peace in the world until these various sections of workers recognise the common fundamental character of their slavery and set to work to remove it, thus ending the enslavement of the human race by the establishment of Socialism.

As in September 1914, so now we say: "Having no quarrel with the working class of any country, we extend to our fellow workers of all lands the expression of our good will and Socialist fraternity, and pledge ourselves to work for the overthrow of capitalism and the establishment of Socialism."

(August 1919)

THE INTER-WAR YEARS

The period between the First and Second World Wars saw the emergence of a physically more compact but no less combative *Socialist Standard*. The political changes of the time gave it some new targets to aim at and it didn't shirk the challenge. Its pages were lively and typically filled with polemics against emergent political rivals vying for the support of the working class together with attacks on the 'unsound' theories they promoted, from vanguardism to currency crankism.

Politically, the period saw Labour come to displace the Liberals as the second party and alternative government to the Tories. In the 1924 general election the Tories lost their overall majority and for the first time a Labour government, even if a minority one supported by the votes of Liberal MPs, came into office under Ramsay MacDonald. It didn't last long and didn't achieve much except to demonstrate to the Establishment that Labour was 'fit to govern' the British Empire. The same situation occurred again in 1929, only this time it ended in disaster for Labour as the government collapsed under the impact of the slump, and Ramsay MacDonald left to be Prime Minister in a Tory-dominated government.

Throughout the 1920s and 1930s the working class was on the defensive as employers, faced with increased competition from abroad and in the 1930s with shrinking markets, tried to protect their profits by pushing down wages. It was evident as early as 1922 that things were heading for a show-down. Interestingly, the *Socialist Standard* pointed out that the only way of testing the relative strengths of the two sides of industry would be a general strike. The employers and the government made the same calculation and the test came in May 1926 with the General Strike, which the workers lost.

Then came the Wall Street Crash of 1929 and yet another 'Great Depression'. Although employment held up in the new industries of the Midlands and the South East, in the old industrial heartlands of the North, Scotland and Wales surviving on the dole became a major concern. Here, too, the government sought to make economies, introducing in 1934 the notorious household Means Test which left a bitter memory amongst workers for years to come, as chronicled in an article from the *Socialist Standard* of the time.

Abroad, the period opened with the fall of the German and Austro-Hungarian empires and the appeal of the Bolshevik government in Russia to workers elsewhere to come to their aid. A significant minority of workers did come to regard the Bolshevik regime as socialist and so as worthy of support. Thus, the working class political scene saw the appearance of Communist Parties alongside the openly reformist Labour and Social Democratic parties. The *Socialist Standard* was not impressed either with the claim that Russia was socialist (the SPGB pioneered the view in the English-speaking world that what was being developed in Russia was state capitalism) nor with the activities of the British Communist Party whose policies were increasingly dictated from Moscow and ranged from calling for a Labour government to urging the unemployed to fight the police.

In 1933 Hitler came to power in Germany, marking the end of political democracy there. Political democracy was under threat in other countries too, culminating in the Spanish Civil War that broke out in 1936. Many continued to see the main danger as being another world war but many others now saw the issue as having become democracy versus fascism. This view was encouraged by the Communist Party, especially following a change in Russian foreign policy in 1935, but this only muddied the issue as state-capitalist Russia was just as much a political dictatorship as Nazi Germany. The Socialist Party was not taken in, though most Leftwing intellectuals were. In the 'Civil War in Spain', the *Socialist Standard* – while emphasising the importance of political democracy for the working class – rejected both a united front with pro-capitalist parties and war (which everyone knew would mean another world war) as a means to defend it.

A Socialist View of Bolshevist Policy

Where we stand

Ever since the Bolshevik minority seized the control of affairs in Russia we have been told that their 'success' had completely changed Socialist policy. These 'Communists' declare that the policy of Marx and Engels is out of date. Lenin and Trotsky are worshipped as the pathfinders of a shorter and easier road to Communism.

Unfortunately for these 'Bolsheviks', no evidence has yet been supplied to show wherein the policy of Marx and Engels is no longer useful, and until that evidence comes the Socialist Party of Great Britain will continue to advocate the same Marxian policy as before. We will continue to expose and oppose the present system and all its defenders and apologists. We shall insist upon the necessity of the working class understanding Socialism and organising within a political party to obtain it.

Socialism far off in Russia

When we are told that Socialism has been obtained in Russia without the long, hard and tedious work of educating the mass of workers in Socialism we not only deny it but refer our critics to Lenin's own confessions. His statements prove that even though a vigorous and small minority may be able to seize power for a time, they can only hold it by modifying their plans to suit the ignorant majority. The minority in power in an economically backward country are forced to adapt their program to the undeveloped conditions and make continual concessions to the capitalist world around them. Offers to pay war debts to the Allies, to establish a Constituent Assembly, to compensate capitalists for losses, to cease propaganda in other countries, and to grant exploitation rights throughout Russia to the Western capitalists all show how far along the capitalist road they have had to travel and how badly they need the economic help of other countries. It shows above all that their loud and defiant challenge to the capitalist world has been silenced by their own internal and external weaknesses as we have so often predicted in these pages.

Lenin's Confessions

The folly of adopting Bolshevik methods here is admitted by Lenin in his pamphlet *The Chief Tasks of Our Times* (page 10): "A backward country can revolt quicker, because its opponent is rotten to the core, its middle class is not organised; but in order to continue the revolution a backward country will require immediately more circumspection, prudence, and endurance. In Western Europe it will be quite different; there it is much more difficult to begin, but it will be much easier to go on. This cannot be otherwise because there the proletariat is better organised and more closely united."

Those who say 'Russia can fight the world', are answered by Lenin: "Only a madman can imagine that the task of dethroning International Imperialism can be fulfilled by Russia alone."

Lenin admits that "France and England have been learning for centuries what we have only learnt since 1905. Every class-conscious worker knows that the revolution grows but slowly amongst the free institutions of a united bourgeoisie, and that we shall only be able to fight against such forces when we are able to do so in conjunction with the revolutionary proletariat of Germany, France, and England. Till then, sad and contrary to revolutionary traditions as it may be, our only possible policy is to wait, to tack, and to retreat."

State Capitalism for Russia

We have often stated that because of a large anti-Socialist peasantry and vast untrained population, Russia was a long way from Socialism. Lenin has now to admit this by saying: "Reality says that State Capitalism would be a step forward for us; if we were able to bring about State Capitalism in a short time it would be a victory for us. How could they be so blind as not to see that our enemy is the small capitalist, the small owner? How could they see the chief enemy in State Capitalism? In the transition period from Capitalism to Socialism our chief enemy is the small bourgeoisie, with its economic customs, habits and position" (page 11).

This reply of Lenin to the Communists of the Left (Bucharin and others) contains the further statement that, "to bring about State Capitalism at the present time means to establish the control and order formerly achieved by the propertied classes. We have in Germany an example of State Capitalism, and we know she proved our superior. If you would only give a little thought to what the security of such State Socialism would mean in Russia, a Soviet Russia, you would recognise that only madmen whose heads are full of formulas and doctrines can deny that State Socialism is our salvation. If we possessed it in Russia the transition to complete Socialism would be easy, because State Socialism is centralisation control, socialisation – in fact, everything that we lack. The greatest menace to us is the small bourgeoisie, which, owing to the history and economics of Russia, is the best organised class, and which prevents us from taking the step, on which depends the success of Socialism."

Here we have plain admissions of the unripeness of the great mass of Russian people for Socialism and the small scale of Russian production.

If we are to copy Bolshevist policy in other countries we should have to demand State Capitalism, which is not a step to Socialism in advanced capitalist countries. The fact remains, as Lenin is driven to confess, that we do not have to learn from Russia, but Russia has to learn from lands where large scale production is dominant.

Lenin and the Trusts

"My statement that in order to properly understand one's task one should learn socialism from the promoters of Trusts aroused the indignation of the Communists of the Left. Yes, we do not want to teach the Trusts; on the contrary, we want to learn from them" (page 12). Thus Lenin speaks to his critics. Owing to the untrained character of the workers and their failure to grasp the necessity of discipline and order in large scale production, Lenin has to employ 'capitalist' experts to run the factories. He tells us: "We know all about Socialism, but we do not know how to organise on a large scale, how to manage distribution, and so on. The old Bolshevik leaders have not taught us these things, and this is not to the credit of our party. We have yet to go through this course and we say: Even if a man is a scoundrel of the deepest dye, if he is a merchant, experienced in organising production and distribution on a large scale, we must learn from him; if we do not learn from these people, we shall never achieve Socialism, and the revolution will never get beyond the present stage. Socialism can only be reached by the development of State Capitalism, the careful organisation of finance, control and discipline among the workers. Without this there is no Socialism." (page 12).

That Socialism can only be reached through State Capitalism is untrue. Socialism depends upon large-scale production, whether organised by Trusts or

Governments. State capitalism may be the method used in Russia, but only because the Bolshevik Government find their theories of doing without capitalist development unworkable – hence they are forced to retreat along the capitalist road.

The Internal Conflict

Lenin goes on: "The workers who base their activities on the principles of State Socialism are the most successful. It is so in the tanning, textile, and sugar industries, where the workers, knowing their industry, and wishing to preserve and to develop it, recognise with proletarian common sense that they are unable at present to cope with such a task, and therefore allot one third of the places to the capitalists in order to learn from them."

This concession is another example of the conflict between Bolshevik theory and practice, for the very argument of Lenin against Kautsky and others was that in Russia they could go right ahead without needing the capitalist development such as it exists in other countries.

The whole speech of Lenin is directed against the growing body of workers in Russia who took Lenin at his word. These people fondly imagined that after throwing over Kerensky they could usher in freedom and ignore the capitalist world around them. They thought that factory discipline, Socialist education, and intelligent skilled supervision were simply pedantic ideas.

A further quotation from Lenin will make this clear: "Naturally the difficulties of organisation are enormous, but I do not see the least reason for despair and despondency in the fact that the Russian Revolution, having first solved the easier task – the overthrow of the landowners and the bourgeoisie – is now faced with the more difficult Socialist task of organising national finance and control, a task which is the initial stage of Socialism, and is inevitable, as is fully understood by the majority of class-conscious workers."

He also says: "It is time to remonstrate when some people have worked themselves up to a state in which they consider the introduction of discipline into the ranks of the workers as a step backwards." And he points out that "by the overthrow of the bourgeoisie and landowners we have cleared the way, we have not erected the structure of Socialism."

How far they have cleared the capitalists out of the way is uncertain, as they are a long way from self-reliance. The long road ahead is admitted by Lenin in these words: "Until the workers have learned to organise on a large scale they are not Socialists, nor builders of a Socialist structure of society, and will not acquire the necessary knowledge for the establishment of the new world order. The path of organisation is a long one, and the tasks of Socialist constructive work require strenuous and continuous effort, with a corresponding knowledge which we do not sufficiently possess. It is hardly to be expected that the even more developed following generation will accomplish a complete transition into Socialism." (page 13).

The rule of the minority

The denunciation of democracy by the Bolshevik leaders is quite understandable if we realise that only the minority in Russia are Communists. Lenin therefore denies control of affairs to the majority, but he cannot escape from the compromise involved in ruling with a minority. Not only is control of Russian affairs out of the hands of the Soviets as a whole, but not even all the members of the Communist Party are allowed to vote. Zinoviev, a leading Commissar, in his report to the First Congress of the Third International said: "Our Central Committee has decided to deprive certain categories of party *members* of the right to vote at the Congress of the party. Certainly it is unheard of to limit the right voting within the party, but the *entire party has approved* this measure, which is to assure the homogenous unity of the Communists. So that in fact, we have 500,000 members who manage the entire State machine from top to bottom." (*The Socialist*, 29th April 1920. Italics not ours.)

So half a million members of the Communist Party (counting even those who are refused a vote within the party) control a society of 180 million members. It is quite plain why other parties' papers were suppressed: obviously they could influence the great majority outside the Communist Party. The maintenance of power was assured by the Bolshevik minority through its control of political power and the armed forces.

(July 1920)

Ireland, the Labour Party and the Empire

After a long and bitter struggle, there is at last the prospect of peace in Ireland. The workers of Ulster and the South have fought with a fervour only equalled by the frenzy of the late world war, and are now to be able to see what it really was they fought for. If they hope for anything better than the fate common to ex-soldiers in all the countries of Europe – victors and vanquished alike – then disappointment awaits them.

Sinn Fein, behind a screen of fine sounding no-surrender proclamations, appears to be preparing to forego the demand for full recognition of Ireland's status as an independent Republic; while the English Government, under the pressure of a variety of political and financial factors, considers the cost of continued refusal of concessions prohibitive, and offers a form of Dominion Home Rule. The chief, the economic, causes of the dispute are not far to seek. The northern Capitalists, whose prosperity lies in their easy access to markets within or protected by the British Empire, could never submit to being cut off from the source of their wealth. Similarly, the numerically strong body of farmers and traders in the South, plundered and thwarted for centuries by successive English Governments, and seeing themselves, for the benefit of their competitors, denied the right of freely developing commercial relations abroad, looked to the victory of Sinn Fein as the precursor of a new era of expansion for their trade. Add to this the hopes of the younger generation for satisfaction of their hunger for land, hitherto inaccessible to them owing to foreign ownership and profitable use for non-agricultural purposes, and we have some idea of the material basis for the Irish war.

The workers were called upon to take up arms for objects far enough removed from these, 'Protestantism and the Flag' or 'Catholicism and Liberty', as geographical accident ordained: it was always the trade of the politician to provide plausible excuses. They responded with the usual disastrous results for themselves. Under the pretext of the necessity for presenting a united front to the external enemy, robbed and robbers, workers and employers, closed up their ranks to the manifest advantage of the latter.

Trade Union organisation was wrecked by internal dissension, or rendered innocuous in the larger interest of patriotism, that is, of the employers, whether Belfast shipbuilders or Southern farmers. Now, with the coming of peace, the class struggle will once more be forced to the front, and whether the wage-earners are in a position to resist attempts to lower their standard of living or not, they can at least learn the lesson of their recent folly. In Erin, no more than in this or any other Capitalist country, do war slogans or the sentiments of national brotherhood weight heavily where they conflict with profit-making.

The cessation of guerrilla warfare and the raising of martial law will provide a welcome removal of political and mental obstacles to our propaganda, but it must always be remembered that the form, the time, and the terms of the peace are in the hands of the Ruling Class. Theirs is the political control, and the accompanying military power enables them to give or withhold, and to bargain as they think fit. On neither side have the workers the deciding voice.

As might be expected, the Labour Party, which has long put at the forefront of its programme the solution of the Irish problem, has something to say at this juncture which incidentally is of interest to us. The Labour Party, as also might have been expected by those who know that body, puts the case for the English Capitalist Class.

At the height of the conflict, when there was no sign of a weakening on either side, of or any kind of rapprochement, the Labour Party, somewhat vaguely it is true, stood for Ireland's right to Independence with but two qualifications: guarantees for the protection of minorities and against the possibility of future military or naval menace to this country. Now, however, that changed circumstances or changed feeling in the constituencies lead the Government to negotiate, the Labour Party withdraws from the attitude it had taken up. When war is the order of the day, it is useful but harmless in bye-election tactics to promise Independence, but when Capital decides to have peace and the actual terms are to

Seventeenth Annual Conference, 25th March 1921

be settled, the Labour Party is called to heel and must follow its masters.

Thus we have Mr J.H. Thomas declaring (*Daily Herald*, 2nd September) that "no political party in England can hold out any hope of an Irish Republic." The *Herald* commented adversely on this "astounding" remark, and dismissed it as a private opinion only, not representative of the Labour Party.

Curiously enough, a week before H.N. Brailsford has written in the *Herald* under the title 'Ireland and Sea-Power', expressing the same opinion in even more vigorous language, and it is with this that I propose to deal. The *Daily Herald* did not comment on Brailsford's article!

Brailsford is a Labour candidate, and in the *Labour Daily* which in this instance claims that it represents the real attitude of the Labour Party, he writes as follows (August 30th): "The British Government (with the nation behind it) is, I believe, sincere in its readiness to yield everything except naval control ... In plain words the issue for the British people is our world power. That is the only issue for which we ever fight ... but it is an issue for which we always fight, and will fight. It was the issue in the world war; first, because the German navy challenged ours, and, secondly, because a German occupation of the Belgian coast must have interfered with our control of Dover Straits ... For sea-power is the instrument of our economic expansion. Upon it rests our possession of half Africa and all India, and our ability to expand at will in China or elsewhere."

This is somewhat staggering, and one cannot help wondering whether the hundreds of thousands of out-of-work ex-soldiers are fully appreciative of the advantages that accrue to them through their "possession" of "half Africa and all India." To continue with the quotation:

"No instinct is so deeply rooted in us all (the exceptions are negligible) as the instinct which teaches us without talk or exhortation, or reflection, to guard our naval ascendancy against any risk. None even of the sincerest advocates of the

League of Nations (not even Lord Robert Cecil) had a word to say in support of Mr Wilson's proposals for the freedom of the seas. No one criticises (I except the eccentrics) the virtual British seizure of Constantinople.

"One may feel sure in advance that while we may accept, or even propose at Washington, a limitation in shipbuilding, we shall not agree to abate by a single vital concession our unlimited and uncontrolled right to blockade."

Incidentally this throws an interesting light on the bona-fides of the League of Nations and on the use to the workers of it and its Labour Party backers. We notice, too, that the 'eccentrics' are excluded from those the Labour Party claims to represent. For my part, I must confess to being one of them: the deep-rooted instinct of guarding 'our naval ascendancy' seems to have passed me by, and I simply never froth at the mouth at the mention of this bloody old Empire.

"We are ready to concede much … but we will no more give up our naval stations on the Irish coast than we will give up Gibraltar or Malta or the Suez Canal. To do so would be to begin to give up world-power.

"On the ordinary level of thought (Tolstoyans, Quakers and Communists are the only exceptions) we are acting rationally. An independent Ireland would be a danger. Our next enemy at sea would assuredly occupy, or try to occupy, it. Belgium was not the only violated neutral in the last war. China, Greece, Persia and Albania were all used or overrun. There will be no yielding here … and Irishmen who expect us to yield eventually will have to wait till our Empire is overthrown and our sea-power vanished like Germany's."

Have you grasped the full import of this frank statement of what the Labour Party stands for? The class privileges of the Capitalists are in question, and the Labour Party is forced into the open to defend them.

Of course, the Ruling Class will not allow the Empire to be endangered by an independent Ireland. The Empire is theirs, and they won't see their private property damaged, unless superior force compels. That is simple enough. They have the power, and use it to protect and further their interests against opposition from workers and other States alike. But what is the Labour Party doing in this?

They offer themselves as an alternative to the Coalition and are in great hopes of early success. We consider them worthy of condemnation for their past record alone, but are told we should give them a chance, and wait and judge by results. Well, here is their own promise of their intentions. The fulfilment may be worse; it can hardly be better. Not only Ireland is touched upon: "The (Washington) Conference may then be futile, and, over the issue of Imperialist exploitation in the Far East, the naval rivalry will begin in earnest, and ultimately we may find ourselves involved even in war."

What does this mean in brief? Just this: The wealth of the Empire, built up by the toil and sacrifice of generations of British workers, is to remain what it now is, the exclusive possession of our exploiters, and for their acquiescence in this the Labour

Party is to be graciously permitted to take over the Government. Only nominally in power, they will be, in reality, as helpless as the Labour Governments in Australia, and will serve, as they are intended to serve, as the last defence of the Capitalist system.

Hoodwinked by a repetition from the mouths of their leaders, of the old fiction of the alleged community of interest between themselves and the employers, the workers are again to be privileged to defend the country they do not own, against all comers, from the Capitalists of the USA to the Irish Republicans. Their reward will be the reward the unemployed are reaping now.

Did the last war concern the workers, or will the next? Does it matter to them that 'our' naval supremacy should remain intact, any more than it matters whether Sinn Fein colours or the Union Jack fly over Dublin, or whether the German Black, Red and Gold, or the flag of Poland mocks their poverty in Silesia?

While the Capitalist Class dominates the civilised world, and owns and controls all the means of wealth production, the disposal of nations in this or that empire or sphere of economic interest is not the business of the Working Class. If you think the choice of war ministers as between, say, Churchill and Col. Will Thorne, to direct you to the slaughter-house, is worthy worrying about, then, of course, you will select your respective champions in the Coalition or the Labour Party.

If you don't, and if you consider it time that any fighting the workers may have to do, be done for their own emancipation from the system which makes wars inevitable, you will be well repaid for the devotion of a few hours to the study of Socialism. There is urgent need for you inside The Socialist Party.

(December 1921)

Fake Labour Government: the puppet show

The workers, the producers of wealth, are poor because they are robbed; they are robbed because they may not use the machinery of wealth production except on terms dictated by the owners, the propertied class. The remedy for working class poverty and other social ills is the transfer of ownership of these means of production from the Capitalist Class to society. That, in a few words, is the case for Socialism.

The work of rebuilding society on this new basis cannot be started until power is in the hands of a Socialist working class, and that cannot be until many millions have been convinced of the need for change and are broadly agreed on the way to set to work to bring it about.

It is just here that the Socialist meets with an objection which is in appearance reasonable enough. Many who would accept the foregoing remarks can go with us no further.

Is it not better, they say, in view of the certainty that Socialism cannot be introduced at once, to devote much, if not all, our energy to making the best of Capitalism, and getting 'something now'? By 'something now' they mean higher wages, increased State protection against destitution through illness or unemployment, and other like proposals. It may then come as a surprise to them that we also believe in getting something now. We differ in that we are not willing to subordinate Socialist propaganda to the demand for reforms of Capitalism, and in that we strongly hold that the best way to get these things is by the revolutionary activity of an organisation of revolutionaries. In other words, the quickest and easiest method of getting reforms from the ruling class is to let them see that it will endanger their position to refuse.

While we recognise that Socialism is the only permanent solution, we are not among those who consider that the Capitalists are simply unable to afford better conditions for the workers. A comparison between the total income from property, and the petty cost of doles and relief, shows the falsity of that somewhat common notion. On the one hand the workers would, if they ceased to struggle, soon find that there is still room for a worsening of their conditions, and on the other hand were they free from the mental blindness which prevents them from striking a blow when and where it would be most damaging, they might, even within Capitalism, raise their standard of living and diminish their insecurity. Unfortunately they do not yet see the brutal facts of the class struggle, and too often allow themselves to be paralysed in action by their belief in the supposed community of interest between them and their exploiters, by their response to every deceitful appeal in the name of patriotism, and by their lack of confidence in their own powers and intelligence. They will put up a straight fight against their employers, but they have not yet seen through the more subtle hostility of the newspapers, the politicians, and all the other defenders of the employing class who pose as neutrals because it makes their influence more deadly. The employers and their hired defenders know well enough that your gain is often their loss, and they therefore have good reason to persuade you not to seize the opportunities that offer of raising your wages or reducing your hours. But many who talk about the beauties of an "advanced programme of social reforms" seem not to have realised that if such things are to be of any worth to you they necessitate at first the dipping into the profits of the other class. Various well-meaning persons may preach arbitration and conciliation, but you know well enough that sweet words do not, as a rule, charm employers into giving higher wages. They will not give up any part of what they hold except under pressure. One kind of pressure is fear; the fear that refusal to spend *part* of their wealth on reforms will encourage revolutionary agitation for the seizure of the *whole*. There is supposed to be another way of getting 'something now'. It is to assist into office a non-revolutionary party like the Labour Party.

It is pleaded at the moment on that Party's behalf that it is "in office but not in power," and that its weaknesses arise from that one fact due to causes beyond its control. Within limits this is true, but why in such circumstances was office accepted? It can hardly be questioned that an official opposition, 192 strong, bent on hampering the Government could have influenced legislation not less than when actually in office. In fact, however, the Labour Party was not free to choose. It dared not refuse office; it dare not while in office attack the roots of Capitalist privilege, and had it continued in opposition to Baldwin's Government it would not have dared to obstruct as a means of compelling the granting of concessions. The reasons for its impotence in each of these situations are the same. Its programme and policy, its supporters, the basis of its organisation, and the ground upon which it chose to fight elections all combined to commit it to the administering of Capitalism as distinct from treating the present opportunity merely as a prelude to the fight for Socialism.

From the circumstance that the bulk of the members of the Labour Party do not accept Socialism as a present political issue, but at best only as a hope for the future, it would be plainly suicidal for them to talk of throwing down a challenge to the Capitalist Class. The only alternative is to do as the Labour Party are trying to do. They are trying to run the Capitalist system better than the older parties have done.

We can we can readily concede that as administrators the Labour men will prove themselves no less intelligent and capable than their predecessors, and probably more receptive of new ideas and methods than the men who made and mismanaged the war.

But the essence of our opposition to this policy is that except in quite minor respects there is only one way of administering Capitalism – the Capitalist way. Ultimately it is the economic organisation of society which dictates the broad lines of policy and breaks those who ignore them. The problems which present themselves for settlement, such as war, unemployment, poverty, arise from the very nature of the present social system. They may be dealt with in more than one way, but they cannot be treated in a manner satisfactory to the workers without first destroying Capitalism.

Support of the unemployed at comparatively trifling cost is, from the Capitalist viewpoint, a solution of the unemployment problem. *Their* problem is to avoid the risk of riot and revolt and their policy succeeds. War is but an extension of ordinary commercial competition, and poverty is both the effect and the necessary condition of capitalist wealth and monopoly.

Even where a Labour Government is able to introduce certain alleviations, these must be paid for in the sacrifice of political independence. The removal of the 'Gap' is the price of consent to plans of the Conservative majority for the Navy and Air Force. To argue that these objectionable measures would have been carried through by the last or any other Capitalist Government misses the point of our criticism. Capitalism produces certain evils. These evils, have, by their persistence, discredited three Governments since 1918. A Labour Government which seeks to carry on is certain not to be able to remove the evils, and under the added embarrassment of having roused high hopes, will be discredited, too, and the unhappy sequel will be that those who openly defend the present system will with some show of reason instance the failure of the Labour Party as proof that there is no solution, and many of the Labour men will drift or be forced into offering the same defence themselves.

It is to the general situation and not to the weakness or cowardice of individuals that we must look for an explanation of the actions of the Labour Government, many of which have already given obvious displeasure to their more advanced supporters.

Their term began with a strike of locomotive men, who, despite their solidarity, were compelled to accept wage reductions. So far from intervening to obtain 'something now' for the strikers, Mr MacDonald appointed as Colonial Secretary Mr J.H. Thomas, who quite openly condemned them and hoped and intrigued for their defeat.

The miners, too, are putting forward a demand that their wages be raised to the 1914 standard, but the Editor of the *Labour Magazine* (January, 1924), an official Labour Party organ, can offer them no better assistance than an appeal in the following terms: "We are sure that the miners will not embarrass the first Labour Government by pressing untimely demands ..."

It would appear at least reasonable for the miners to receive slightly more than a starvation wage before the non-producers who own the mines should be allowed to draw their millions of pounds of profits. Even if the Labour Party, like MacDonald, are definitely committed to retaining the profit-making system, it cannot be doubted that they would, if they conveniently could, raise the miners wages; but because they are 'administering capitalism' such a demand is of necessity an 'untimely' one. What the miners get, even if it be given legislative endorsement, will be the result of their own organisation and action.

When the Dockers came out on strike for increases which were generally admitted even by some of the Dock employers to be long overdue, the Government had mails unloaded by Naval ratings and had made all preparations for unloading foodstuffs, etc., had the strike continued. This does not necessarily imply on their part a positive wish to break the strike. What it does mean is that this is one of the duties inevitably forced upon those, whatever their beliefs, who would undertake to administer Capitalism.

The strike had to be ended or countered. If the Labour Government had refused to act it would have forfeited the right to govern. Through Mr Shaw, therefore, pressure was brought to bear on the Dockers' representatives to accept certain terms which were actually slightly worse than those finally granted by the employers.

"It was stated yesterday that the settlement terms follow the 'private suggestion' made by the Minister of Labour last week, with the exception that July instead of June was first proposed for the operation of the second shilling increase." (*Daily News*, 22nd February, 1924.)

As for the nature of the 'private suggestion' referred to, the *Worker* (1st March) quotes as follows from Mr Bevin's speech to the delegates: "The Government is responsible for the moving of the mails. They have refrained from using soldiers, naval ratings, blacklegs or force of any kind. But they are being driven up against it, and soon will have to take the choice of exercising their powers or going out of office. That was the choice, and there is no need to beat about the bush. We discussed the position with the Government ... I want you to see the influence on our judgment in the course of the developments that have gone on."

With regard to the unemployed, Mr MacDonald, in his opening speech on policy in the House of Commons, made it quite plain that he is not going to assist them at the expense of the propertied class. "We are not going to diminish industrial capital in order to provide relief" (*Daily Herald*, 13th February). This was received with "renewed cheers."

That attitude is explained by an interview MacDonald gave to an unemployed deputation in Edinburgh, at which he is reported as saying: "The possibility of financial panic was also a factor to be taken into account ... For the immediate future good administration was requisite to win the confidence of the financial groups and ensure stability." (*Worker*, 9th February.)

It is evident that to gain and keep the "confidence of the financial groups" rules out all measures aimed at depriving the Capitalist Class of any part of what they hold, except on terms pleasing to them.

Dr Salter, in the *New Leader*, lays down a general principle on the wage question: "It is quite certain that under present world circumstances and in view of the competition in outside markets, no new and higher rates of wages in any industry or in any locality should be imposed by law without careful preliminary expert investigation" (7th March, 1924).

It would doubtless be 'untimely' and 'embarrassing' to suggest careful enquiry into the need for supporting an idle class of property owners out of the product of industry.

But the question of armaments has shown up in its most glaring aspect the weakness of the Labour Government, its complete dependence on those who pull the strings, and the truth of the Socialist contention that those who accept office on such terms can be no more than caretakers of the Capitalist system. In the first place it was no accident that anti-working class imperialists like Lord Chelmsford and Brigadier-General Thompson should have gone to the Admiralty and the Air Ministry respectively. Labour members may be allowed to prattle about the Sermon on the Mount, provided they keep the fighting forces up to the level require by the international situation. Thus we have Mr "Pacifist" Ammon at the Admiralty announcing the intention of laying down five new cruisers and two destroyers, and MacDonald actually defending it as a means of providing employment. Of the whole batch of Labour men only one, the Rev. H. Dunnico, voted against the Government; 161 voted with them, and the rest abstained. Some of the latter will perhaps follow Dunnico on the next occasion. The internal anarchy of the ILP is well illustrated by their inability to control the MPs. A message of congratulation to Dunnico was passed unanimously by the 55 delegates attending the half-yearly conference of the Northern Counties Divisional Council of the ILP. It conveyed to him "Heartiest congratulations on being the only M.P. who stood loyally to the principles which our party hold" (*Daily News*, 27th February). It was left to Liberals like Kenworthy to protest.

The Government which will not "diminish industrial capital in order to provide relief" for the unemployed has also agreed to "a big scheme of Air Defence," involving an additional expenditure of £2,500,000 for 1924-25, and with the promise that "the total of air Estimates may be expected to rise for some years" (Lord Thompson, *Daily Herald*, 8th March).

The *Herald* uses the word 'Defence' on its front page, yet in its editorial of the same day it endorses MacDonald's view, supported by numerous 'experts', that no aircraft building can really provide any security whatever against hostile raids.

Much has been made by Labour Party apologists (e.g. *New Leader*, 14th March) of the fact that the gross expenditure on the three services is less than last year, but as Lansbury points out, this is merely due to the changing technique of warfare: "It is said we are to spend less on armaments as a whole; it is true, because the more deadly weapons, such as bombs, gas, aeroplanes and submarines, are cheaper and yet more deadly than the obsolete Dreadnoughts and other costly weapons" (*Daily Herald*, 15 March).

Lansbury's further reply to those who pretend to see something different in the Labour Party's attitude to armaments is equally forcible. "But far more important is it to realise that exactly the same kind of speeches as are being made today from the Government benches in defence of armaments, were made during the years 1906-14 by Sir E. Grey, Lord Haldane, Mr Winston Churchill, and Mr Lloyd George." (*Ibid.*)

The belief, which is now the bedrock of the Labour Party's policy, that peace can be ensured by preparing for war, is not new, and it has not exactly been confirmed by history.

The truth is that competition in disposing of the surplus products of each Capitalist country in the world's markets, and rivalry in the struggle for possession of raw materials and trade routes, lead inevitably to war. The Labour Government are now busy considering schemes for reducing the cost of production in the Empire's staple export industries. In a capitalist world that means more embittered competition, and a consequently increased probability of early war with those who feel themselves being throttled in the commercial struggle. Those who have taken on the administration of Capitalism must also face the responsibility of preparing for the conflicts that are the product of Capitalism.

The true cause of modern wars was bluntly exposed by a French General, Marshal Lyauty, speaking at a Banquet of the National Congress of Councillors of Foreign Trade at Marseilles in October, 1922 (*Star*, 31st October 1922). "French soldiers are fighting in Morocco to acquire territory in which rise rivers capable of supplying power for electrification schemes which will prove of great advantage to French trade. When we have acquired the last zone of cultivatable territory, when we have nothing but mountains in front of us, we shall stop. Our object is commercial and economic. The military expedition in Morocco is a means, not an end. Our object is the extension of foreign trade."

Without foreign markets capitalist industry in Great Britain perishes. Without protection by dominant armaments those markets are prizes to be had for the asking. Those Labour men who believe that they can promote capitalist trade without needing to arm in order to hold what they gain, are living in a fool's paradise. They have to build cruisers and bombing planes to overawe and if need be to shatter the forces and cities of whatever States come into conflict with Great Britain.

We Socialists see that wars are unavoidable if the interests of the Capitalist Class are to be protected, but we are not concerned in protecting them. We recognise that under Capitalism the workers have nothing to lose in war except their lives and nothing to gain, and so we urge them not to support Capitalist wars or the preparation for them.

Our aim as Socialists is the destruction of the Capitalist system of society, and we are therefore unalterably hostile to all political parties which seek to gain control of Parliament for any other purpose than the establishment of Socialism. The Labour Party is such a party; it has gone into office in the custody of the Liberal Party; its so-called Socialists are puppets dancing on the strings of the industrial and financial capitalists behind the scenes; its Pacifists are merely decoys who will allay suspicion while the militarists prepare for war; its wild men are a convenient buffer to receive the blows of the workers so soon as they tire of waiting for something to be done to relieve their misery. As has been well said, the Labour Party has taken over a bankrupt concern; not, however, to wind it up, but to carry it on. As well as the troubles of previous administrations, the present Cabinet is threatened with a promising crop of revolts. The men of peace grown suddenly stiff-necked and high-handed in office will surely come into early conflict with those of their late 'comrades' who were too honest to desire or too insignificant to be offered posts in the Government. The genuine disapproval of the former and the ill-concealed venom of some of the others are likely to make for turbulence rather than tranquillity. So that even if our first Labour Government is only a Puppet Show, it should merit the distinction conceded by one observer, of being the best show in London.

(April 1924)

The General Strike Fiasco: its causes and effects

The long anticipated month of May has come and nearly gone, and with it have evaporated both the fantastic hopes of the hot-heads of the Communist Party and the baseless fears of the nervous old women of both sexes who run the Primrose League and kindred organisations. Mr A. J. Cook has repeatedly promised us "the end of capitalism" if the mineworkers attempted to force the miners' wages still further down; but in spite of the fact that the attempt is being made, with many prospects of success, the 'revolution' obstinately refuses to materialise. In its place we have witnessed what looks suspiciously like the dying kick of Trades Unionism in its present form.

Four years ago (in our issue for April, 1922, to be precise) we definitely advocated combined action by the workers to resist the wholesale onslaught by the masters upon wages and working conditions. We did not promise a sweeping victory nor encouraged illusions regarding the ever-downward tendency of the standard of life of the workers under capitalism, but we did lay stress upon the necessity for making the best, instead of the worst, of a bad job, by means of an organised test of strength along class lines.

Experience had repeatedly shown that the old sectional mode of industrial warfare was obsolete; that, while the development of industry had united the masters into giant combinations, with interests ramifying in every direction, supported at every point by the forces of the State, representing the entire capitalist class, the division among the workers, according to their occupations, led automatically to their steady defeat in detail. The only hope, even for the limited purpose of restricting the extent of the defeat, lay, therefore, in class combination.

The *Socialist Standard* has only a small circulation, and our words passed unheeded by the mass of the workers, doped both by the organs of capital and the counsels of their own leaders. They were too absorbed in the petty details of their sectional struggles to perceive the general conditions governing those struggles. They could not see the wood for the trees; or they saw it only in the blurred form visible through the spectacles provided for them by the Labour Party. Those of their number who looked to 'nationalisation', piecemeal or wholesale, to solve their problems and end the class conflict, considered themselves 'advanced'; and their duly sceptical fellows were regarded as reactionary and hopeless. Thus, economic and political ignorance kept the workers divided and the defeats went on.

Yet even worms will turn, and rats forced into corners will fight; and it would, indeed, have been nothing less than supernatural if at length the steadily increasing pressure of their backs against the wall had not forced the hard truth into the workers' enslaved minds. There is a limit even to the stupidity of sheep; and not all the smooth-tongued eloquence of their shepherds could prevent the flock from realising that they may as well hang together as hang separately.

The first official indication of this changing outlook occurred last July when the threat of a further attack upon the slave-rations of the miners led the TUC to intervene. The modesty of the workers' aspirations was proved by the ease with which their representatives were satisfied. The granting of a subsidy to the mineowners (in order to gain time and enable the Government and the master class as a whole to prepare for the wider struggle) was hailed by the entire Labour Press as a 'great victory'. Subsequent events have shown the absurd hollowness of that claim.

When the miners were working through the winter increasing the stocks to enable their bosses to lock them out, their leaders wasted precious time and money in futile negotiations with those employers. While the Government proceeded coolly and leisurely with its scheme for maintaining essential services and breaking the resistance of the workers, the General Council of the TUC took no step to similarly organise the efforts of the working class. Practically every section of any size (miners, engineers, railwaymen, transport workers), all had grounds for demanding *increases* in wages; yet instead of co-ordinating these demands in a common plan and thus giving a solid basis for united action, sectional negotiations were proceeded with, in honour of that capitalist shibboleth, the 'sanctity of contract'. The enemy was allowed, not merely choice of ground and weapons, but the opportunity to get in the first blow.

Much ink has been spent on discussing the responsibility for the breakdown of negotiations, yet it was plain for months that war was inevitable. Mr Baldwin had made it plain that "all wages must come down", and that position, in practice, is still adhered to by the class which he represents. So far as the rank and file of trade unionists were concerned, the renewed attack on the miners was merely the commencement of a series of further attacks all round; and this fact, not some belated 'sense of justice', explains their ready response to the signal for the general stoppage. Lacking any clear insight into their class position in society, however, they were guided by feeling rather than by reason, and blindly left the conduct of the struggle to the executives of the unions and the General Council.

The weakness of the leaders in the face of the common foe, their abject "begging and pleading for peace" (in the words of J.H. Thomas), merely expressed the disorganised condition of the movement as a whole. No such weakness characterised either the Government or the mineowners.

The lock-out notices were posted at the time appointed and the terms for their withdrawal were laid down. Having allowed themselves to be bluffed and held off by months of diplomatic confab, the General Council were forced, relentlessly, to act or abdicate. Yet to the last their irresolution was apparent.

Mr A. Pugh in a statement to give 'the *real* truth' in the *British Worker* of 11th May, said: "From the moment the mineowners issued lock-out notices to their workpeople, the question at issue, so far as the General Council was concerned, was the withdrawal of those notices as a condition preliminary to the conduct of negotiations. From that we have never receded."

Yet according to the same statement, they continued negotiations right up to the evening of Sunday, the 2nd of May, two days after the lock-out notices were actually operating! They waited for the Government to give them the final ignominious kick, and this was duly administered on the pretext that the printers of the *Daily Mail* had more determination than their 'leaders'.

Once the stoppage commenced, however, these same leaders assumed all the airs of omniscient military generals. Pompous exhortations to the rank and file to "hold fast" and "remain calm and dignified" were issued in their official *Strike Bulletin* what time they were already succumbing to the siren-like blandishments of that 'friend' of the workers, Sir Herbert Samuel.

Not once had the leaders any cause to complain of lack of support. On all hands they admitted that the workers were solid behind them. In the issue already quoted they announced: "The number of strikers has not diminished, it is increasing. There are more workers out today than there have been at any moment since the strike began." Further, "the engineering shops and shipyards are to stop tonight ... The men have awaited the instructions impatiently, and all over the country they received their marching orders with enthusiasm and a sense of relief."

As an expression of working class solidarity the response of the rank and file was unquestionably unprecedented; but the long months, nay, years of delay found effect in the official confusion between 'essential' and non-essential occupations, the handling of goods by some unions which

were banned by others and the issuing of permits one day which had to be withdrawn the next. Just prior to the strike the railwaymen were working overtime providing the companies with the coal to run their blackleg trains. Afterwards they refused to handle any traffic at all while the transport workers tried to pick and choose. The lack of practical unity with which to give expression to the sentiment and secure the end in view justifies, up to the hilt, our long-standing criticism of Trade Unions upon their present base.

The confusion on the industrial field was reflected in the political sphere. In spite of the obvious fact that they were involved in a *class* struggle and that the machinery of government was being brought to bear at every point, the Council fatuously endeavoured to represent the issue as purely industrial. They endeavoured to confine the efforts of a class to the point at stake in one industry. They thus denied the very basis of their own existence, i.e. class interests; but if they were blind to the logic of the conflict, the Government were not. They brazenly declared the whole affair to be an attack upon the Constitution and Parliamentary methods. In order to obscure the class character of their own acts, they invoked the mildewed pillars of the 'nation'. According to their spokesmen, the Council with whom they had been negotiating had suddenly become "an alternative government". With unerring judgement they saw in the manifestation of working class solidarity the latent possibility of revolution.

The only objective of a social revolution, however, is Socialism. The very facts, that the Government were in power, that millions of workers had supported them less than two years ago at the polls and that those who did not were, in the main, far from understanding Socialism, rendered any *immediate* question of revolution ridiculous. It was the *ultimate* outcome of the ceaseless struggle to which their apprehensions gave expression.

The role played by the Labour Party corresponded with that of the General Council. While disclaiming any desire to see the Government defeated by the strikers, they nevertheless proclaimed from their platforms that the Government were responsible for the 'trouble'. "Had the Labour Party been in office", men were told, "such a situation could not have arisen." They relied upon the short memories of their followers who omitted to remind them of the loco' and transport strikes during Labour's term of office, and the application of the Emergency Powers Act by these false 'friends'. In their eyes the Government's chief crime lay not in its support of the mineowners, but in its breaking off of negotiations with the General Council. The lock-out and the strike were secondary matters compared with their being shut out from the counsels of their beloved friends, the bosses.

True to their sham romantic outlook, the Communists covered themselves with 'glory' by circulating wild rumours as to disaffection among the troops. They performed the worst possible service to the workers by trying to persuade them that the soldiery would not fire if called upon. Fortunately few people took them seriously, and in the main, the only sufferers from their advice were themselves. The importance of possessing political power was brought well to the front in repression of anything in the nature of incitement, and the bulk of the workers showed their keen appreciation of the fact in their orderly behaviour.

A sinister secrecy surrounds the capitulation of the General Council on 12th May. At the time of writing they have yet to give an account of their action to their constituents, the TUC. Their cool contempt for the intelligence of their followers easily gauged by the correspondence between themselves and Sir H. Samuel, which they had the audacity to publish in the *British Worker* of the 13th.

The emissary of 'peace' frankly stated that he "acted entirely on his own initiative, had received no authority from the Government and could give no assurances on their behalf". Yet on the strength of this diplomat's unofficial memorandum (rejected on the 12th by the miners' officials) the General Council "terminated the strike assuming that the subsidy would be renewed and the lock-out notices would be immediately withdrawn."

We are not prepared to state in what exact proportion the ingredients of treachery and cowardice were mingled in the composition of the General Council. Suffice it that the miners remain locked-out and that, thanks to the capitalist terms of peace, even the rank and file are not deceived as to what actually happened. Union after union has signed a treaty of surrender which leaves the workers worse off than ever. In addition to this the unemployed army on the Exchange books has swollen to the tune of half a-million, thus giving the employers an unparalleled opportunity for further inroads upon wages and working conditions. The height of enthusiasm reached by the workers during the strike is now matched by the depth of demoralisation of the leaders everywhere apparent.

The outlook before the workers is black, indeed, but not hopeless, if they will but learn the lessons of this greatest of all disasters. 'Trust your leaders!' we were adjured in the Press and from the platforms of the Labour Party, and the folly of such sheep-like trust is now glaring. The workers must learn to trust only in themselves. They must themselves realise their position and decide the line of action to be taken. They must elect their officials to *take* orders, not to *give* them!

Most important of all, however, they must change the object of their organisation. Even in the now unlikely event of the miners gaining the day over the wages question, how much will the necessary sacrifice avail them? The reorganisation of the industry, to which they have agreed, will, on the admissions of its promoters, spell more unemployment among the miners! Are they prepared in face of recent experience to trust any capitalist promise such as is contained in the suggestions of the Samuel memorandum? At the very best they will but be marking time.

On every hand it is evident that the downward pressure upon the slave-class will continue until they unite to end their slave-status. The sentiment of solidarity must be embodied in practical organisation based, not upon the mere transient necessity for wage adjustments, but upon the permanent need of the workers for the abolition of the wages system.

That can be secured only through the establishment of Socialism by the conversion of the means of living into the common property of the whole people.

To that end the workers must organise as a class, not merely industrially, for the capture of supreme power as represented by the political machine. For this purpose neither the Labour Party nor the Communist Party is of any value. The former is hopelessly compromised with the ruling class, while the latter ignores the basis of political power. It is useless for the workers either to 'trust' leaders or to 'change' them. The entire institution of leadership must be swept by the board.

The one thing necessary is a full recognition by the workers themselves of the hostility of interests between themselves and their masters. Organised on that basis, refusing to be tricked and bluffed by promises or stampeded into violence by threats, they will emergence victorious from the age-long struggle. Win Political Power! That is the first step.

(June 1926)

The Cause of the Crisis

In the two preceding articles [March and April 1932] it was shown that the fundamental cause of the crisis is not to be found in the defects of the world's monetary systems, and that the collapse of the gold standard, in this and other countries, was not responsible for the chapter of accidents but merely one of the features of the economic collapse. The real cause of that collapse has now to be determined. In discussing the depression in which the trade of the world has been floundering since the end of 1929, it is usual to relate the sequence of dismal events since then to the sharp break in general gold prices that occurred at that date. Thus Sir Henry Strakosch, in a Memorandum on the Crisis (Supplement to the *Economist*, January 9th, 1932) writes that, "Today it is difficult to imagine that, even among the uninstructed, there is anyone who does not regard the fall of commodity prices as the root cause of the present crisis." A discussion of the cause of the crisis can therefore fairly take as its starting point the sharp fall in prices that has occurred during the last eighteen months.

The answer to the question, 'Why did prices collapse in 1929?' contains the explanation of the causes of the crisis. It can be affirmed straight away that such factors as reparations and war debts, tariffs, maldistribution of gold, failure on the part of creditor countries to lend unlimited amounts to debtor countries, etc., were not the cause of the fall in prices, although they may have helped to intensify the decline. The price structure crumbled in 1929 because then a number of factors, such as those just mentioned, combined to reveal the unsound position that had been built up in the preceding years.

After the break that occurred in 1921, the general level of gold prices remained comparatively steady up to 1929, although there was a slight downward tendency from 1925. This steadiness in the general price level is of importance, because it occurred at a time when production of all commodities was expanding rapidly. The expansion was due to a variety of causes. In industrial production the extension of capital equipment, the simplification of processes, new inventions affecting technique, rationalisation, etc., were characteristic of the period preceding 1929. The truth of this statement is so obvious and well known that it is hardly necessary to elaborate the point. Nevertheless, it is perhaps worth while to refer to the following statements taken from the *Commerce Year Book for 1930* (US Department of Commerce). While they only relate to American conditions, they are indicative of world trends: "For 1929 the index (of industrial production) stood 18% above the average for the base period from which it is computed (1923-1925) ... On account of the increasing efficiency of manufacturing industry, resulting in greater output per man employed, the number of workers in factory industries has shown no such upward movement during post-War years as is shown in the production statistics. There was, in fact, some decrease in the number between 1923 and 1927, the latest year for which complete census data are available ... In the factories each wage earner on the average is aided by engines and other prime movers of a capacity of 4.7 horse power: in 1899 the average was 2.1."

In all branches of mining the opening of new areas, for example, the new copper fields in Central Africa, estimated to be capable of satisfying, by themselves, the whole world's requirements (see *Manchester Guardian Commercial,* 7th March 1929), and new methods such as those that have permitted gold to be mined at greater depths and that raised the percentage of refined petroleum recoverable from crude oil from 26.8% in 1920 to 44% in 1929, added to productive capacity.

The same tendency manifested itself in agriculture. As an example wheat can be taken. The production of wheat (excluding Russia and China), which was about 368 million quarters a year before the War and averaged 391 million quarters in the four years immediately after the War, rose to 480 million quarters in the bumper crop year of 1928, and averaged 447 million quarters for the four year period 1927-30. For all practical purposes it can be taken that the increase in production has been accompanied by a nearly equivalent increase in acreage, although notable increases in the yield per acre have occurred in some areas. The higher yields in these parts, however, have been offset by the low yields in some of the newer areas, where production has not yet been fully developed. The increase in acreage is attributable to the expansion that took place during the War, when belligerent Governments were prepared to pay high prices for foodstuffs for their armies, and to biological and mechanical discoveries. For instance, Canadian acreage is now two-and-a-half times what it was before the War. The introduction of the Marquis variety of wheat alone permitted the cultivation of areas which had formerly been unsuitable, for climatic reasons, for wheat. It was stated in the *Report of the Imperial Economic Committee on Wheat* (1931) that, "The striking result of these biological developments has been to extend very greatly the area within which wheat can be grown. By sowing these newer types, wheat is now cultivated fifty to a hundred miles further north than was possible ten years ago" (page 29). In the same report the opinion is expressed that "the most significant change (in wheat cultivation during the post-War period) has been the rapid increase in the application of mechanical aids to the farm in the principal wheat producing and exporting countries."

Later the following facts are quoted to show the extent to which mechanisation has proceeded: "In the United States in 1916 only some 30,000 tractors were manufactured. In 1928 it is estimated that some 850,000 were in use. In 1914 the total number (of combined Harvester-Threshers) manufactured in the United States was 270; ten years later, in 1924, it was 5,828; two years later, in 1926, it had more than doubled to 11,760; in another two years, in 1928, it has again doubled to 25,392; and in the next year, in 1929, it had increased once more by very nearly 50% to 36,957 ... In regard to Australia the 'combine' or its equivalent is now 'universally used'; other harvesting machines, including the 'stripper thresher' and the 'header harvester'; are also widely used ... In Argentina over 30% of the total wheat area is now harvested by means of the 'combine'."

Before proceeding with the main argument it is interesting to look for a moment at some of the effects of this mechanisation. Four of these are of particular importance. These are the reduction in production costs, the reduced demand for farm labour, the 'decasualisation' of harvest labour, and the decline in the number of horses used in farming, which has meant a decrease in the acreage required to provide their food. On these points the Report, already referred to, makes, together with many others, the following statements: "A combined harvester-thresher usually harvests and threshes wheat at a cost of from 3 to 5 cents a bushel while the cost of threshing alone, when the header or binder is used, usually amounts to more than 10 cents per bushel ... The total working cost of harvesting per acre with different types of machinery is:

10-foot combine	1.47 dollars per acre
12-foot header	3.56 dollars per acre
7-foot binder	4.22 dollars per acre

Canadian official estimates (of costs) show a reduction from 17 cents to 9-1/3 cents per bushel harvested. Figures from Argentina also show a similar result ...

"In 1928 the largest Canadian crop ever recorded was estimated to have been harvested by 16,500 fewer men than would have been necessary if some 4,000 combines had not been in operation. In 1929 the considerably smaller crop was harvested with the aid of some 7,500 combines without a single harvest excursion being run from Eastern Canada. It is now considered that the day of the harvester excursion is over ... In the United States for agriculture as a whole the output per agriculture worker during the decade following the war is estimated to have increased on an average 25% – during which time, however, more than three million people left the land.

"Mechanisation in harvesting has 'decasualised' harvest labour where casual labour has been employed; it has smoothed the traditional peak in the labour curve and has thereby greatly reduced labour costs ... Next to harvest, the time of severest strain on the labour staff is at ploughing and sowing. Here again mechanisation is producing a fundamental change. It is stated that in the United States one person with a large tractor-drawn drill can sow from 70 to 80 acres a day, while one man using at 50 h.p. tractor can plough as much as 18 acres a day. According to the United States Secretary for Agriculture it is possible, when conditions are suitable, to farm as much as 1,600 acres per day, by using improved cultivators instead of ploughs.

"Technical advances in the methods of wheat production of (these) magnitudes carry with them the implication of a continuous pressure of wheat on the world's markets, as an inevitable accompaniment of the spread of the new technique. The extension of the use of the tractor on the farm and of the motor on the farm and in the towns has led to a reduction of the number of horses, and therefore to a decline in the acreage required to provide their food ... Between 1918 and 1928 the arable land thus released in the United States amounted to not less than 18 million acres."

After this digression we can return to the point, already made, that the period preceding the crash was one of the great increase in capacity over the whole field of production. Although consumption of nearly all commodities was expanding, it was not keeping pace with the increase in productive capacity. This disequilibrium, however, was masked in some industries by the shutting down of excess capacity. In others where it was found to be impossible to apply this method and stocks accumulated, recourse was had to schemes of artificial price control. In a memorandum (*Stocks of Staple Commodities*) published by the Royal Economic Society in October 1930, it was stated, "When all factors are weighed together – production, consumption and prices – it is now quite clear that there was a definite lack of equilibrium in tin, rubber, sugar, coffee and petroleum: with copper lead, spelter, nitrate and cotton conditions were somewhat less out of line ... Conditions of free production and marketing existed last summer only in cotton, tin, rubber and tea out of the twelve commodities (cotton, copper, tin, lead, spelter, rubber, sugar, tea, coffee, petroleum, nitrate)." This memorandum dealt with only twelve commodities, but the list of articles subject to artificial control, of one kind or another, could be extended indefinitely and would include finished products as well as raw materials. Now schemes of artificial control, if they are to enjoy even a temporary success, require financing. A large volume of credit was in fact utilised for the purpose of maintaining, and in some instances raising, the prices of commodities. A few instances must suffice. Between 1925 and 1928 the world's production of coffee doubled, mainly as a consequence of an immense increase in Brazilian production due to better methods of cultivation, a greater use of fertilizers and an extension of planting. During the same period consumption rose by only about 10%. As a consequence world stocks rose to an amount nearly equal to a year's consumption (today stocks are nearly 30 months' consumption). Despite this manifest disequilibrium, the price of coffee did not decline, as Brazil stored the excess supply and so kept it off the market. This she was only able to do because of the large amounts borrowed abroad both for long and short periods. In 1927-28, for example, £13¾ million was borrowed in London for the acknowledged purpose of financing coffee. When finally prices crashed in 1929 a further £17 million was borrowed in order to prevent a complete disaster for the Brazilian producers and those who had provided the periods loans. (On this, see *Studies in the Artificial Control of Raw Material Supplies*, No. 3, by J.W.F. Rowe: Royal Economic Society.)

The position in wheat was very similar. Apart from direct Government assistance to producers in Europe through tariffs, quotas, etc., the formation of the Federal Farm Board in USA in 1929 and the action of the Canadian and Australian 'pools' in keeping supplies off the market were directed to maintaining prices, unjustified by the relationship between supply and demand. At the end of the 1931 crop year the Federal Farm Board was holding 265 million bushels of wheat which it had taken off the market, and it had also made loans to wheat co-operatives. Funds for these operations were obtained from the Treasury. "The increase of holdings (of wheat) in the USA was largely the result of official efforts to support prices by means of loans to growers and actual buying and hoarding by the Government. The larger Canadian stocks were mainly furnished by the big crop of 1928, which the West Growers' Pool refused to sell at competitive prices. There is no doubt that the action of the Pool in this matter received Government approval, and, eventually, Canadian Provincial Governments guaranteed the loans which banks had made to finance the wheat." (*The World's Staples: Wheat*, by G.J.S. Broomhall, published in the *Index*, April, 1931, the official organ of the Svenska Handelsbanken, Stockholm.) Instances of the dependence of price stability on restriction of supply, itself dependent on the provision of finance by banks, governments or other lenders, could be multiplied indefinitely. These two, however, will suffice to show what a crazy structure had been built up prior to 1929, and how it was inevitable that the whole edifice would crash if anything occurred to restrict the supply of credit available for holding up of supplies. When the time came there was no lack of factors capable of toppling everything over. The crash in Wall Street in October, 1929, which led from stock liquidation to forced selling of commodities, and to the calling in of loans by banks and a cessation of new lending, ushered in the deluge; but in any event the game could not have been played much longer. With the increasing disequilibrium between production and consumption of all kinds of commodities, it was inevitable that sooner or later it would become impossible to obtain finance for the stock accumulated, or to enable a sufficiently large capacity to be shut down.

We have now got so far behind the fall in prices as to be able to trace it to the persistent disequilibrium between production and consumption that resulted from the increase in the world's productive capacity. This has already been affirmed in several quarters. Thus Prof. Bonn writes: "The crisis was ultimately due to the misuse of capital. The savings which productive surplus had yielded, or was expected to yield, had been spent in the construction of newer productive plants of constantly increasing capacity in the hope that the consumers on whose behalf this vast apparatus was to operate would grow up automatically."

To pass from this stage to the statement that the crisis was the result of over-production is not to solve the problem, but merely restate it. The question at once arises, "Why was there over-production?"

In the first place it is clear that over-production, in the absolute sense, never has existed and is hardly likely to exist. At no stage in history, and certainly at no time in recent years, has the supply of goods and services been more than sufficient to satisfy the needs of the people of the world. No one would venture to assert that there is, or has been, over-production relative to needs in view of the fact that in this country alone, even during the years of prosperity, unemployment for no length of time fell below a million. Today world unemployment is over twenty million, and it is estimated that, including dependants, "over 40,000,000 persons are now living below the minimum standard of health" in America alone (*Manchester Guardian*, 17th March 1932). But there is still over-production. It is patent that the term can only have a relative application. By over-production is meant production in excess of the demands of purchasers. This leads back to the purpose of production today. Under capitalism, with the means of production privately owned and controlled, the purpose of production is the sale of goods at a profit. The making of profits is the aim and object of all production, not the supplying of wants, although of course a producer, having to sell his goods before he can realise his profit, will endeavour to produce commodities that satisfy a want. Not only is production organised for sale at a profit, but it is carried on by the exploitation of legally free workers, working for wages. The consumption of the workers is limited to the amount they receive in wages. This is only a part of the amount produced by their labour, as otherwise there would be no surplus available to constitute the profits of the capitalists. Out of the profits the capitalist takes the amount required for his personal needs. The rest is reinvested in further means of production. Thus fresh means of production are constantly being provided that turn out goods far in excess of the effective demand for them. This is the inherent contradiction in the capitalist method of production which cannot be overcome while that method prevails. As at this moment there must always be a piling up of commodities for which profitable markets cannot be found, owing to the workers being denied access to the production of their labour. And when such accumulations occur, the only way out of the difficulty under Capitalism, short of a destruction of stocks, is an economic crisis, which by causing a slowing up of future production will allow stocks to be reduced, and so prepare the way for another burst of prosperity, which in turn will dissolve into a crisis. This painful corrective of the defects of Capitalism means for the workers unemployment, reduced standards of living, in many instances starvation, acute want and misery. And while Capitalism endures this must always be their lot. Only when, by using their votes to gain political power, they abolish the capitalistic system, and substitute for its anarchy a system of production based, not on profit-making, but on the satisfaction of needs will they benefit materially instead of suffering from man's increased powers of production. Only then will economic crises cease to occur.

(May, 1932)

The Rise of Hitler: a warning to the workers

The rise of Hitler to power in Germany is an event which the workers of all countries should study with care. It is not an isolated phenomenon, but part of a worldwide overflowing of discontent. It is not a coincidence that the three years since the oncoming of the crisis late in 1929 have witnessed the abrupt and sometimes violent overthrow of governments in different parts of the capitalist world. 'National' Governments in the United Kingdom and many of the British Dominions; the advent of De Valera in the Irish Free State; the colossal defeat of 'Prosperity' Hoover in the USA; repeated cabinet crises in France; political revolutions and counter-revolutions in South America; the Republic in Spain; political crises in Scandinavia; expulsions of leaders and reversals of policy in Russia; no country has escaped the economic consequences of a capitalist world which is seriously out of joint.

Each country has witnessed the consequent political stresses and strains of new discontents, and new slogans, which had generally brought about new political groupings and new figureheads. The universal insurgency expresses itself in different ways according to the traditions, experience and constitutions of the various countries. A century ago such economic crises brought to a head deep underlying social conflicts and produced the revolutions of '30 and '48, with their violent overthrow of kings and absolutist constitutions. Nowadays the more advanced countries have developed systems which permit easier adjustment to new pressures, avoiding the disturbance and expenses of the appeal to violence. Countries which have not travelled so far along the road of capitalist democratic government still resort to the old method of the bomb, the rifle, and the machine gun, the mass demonstration, the barricade, and the organisation of insurrection in the armed forces.

In a broad way the cause and the effect are the same everywhere. Everywhere capitalist private ownership reigns. Everywhere the rulers must serve the interests of the capitalist class, but everywhere it is an overriding condition of social life that rulers cannot ignore the active discontent of the mass of the population. The discontent, even the open rebellion, of individuals and minorities can be bludgeoned into acquiescence, but when great masses of the population are driven by intolerable conditions into organising for common action then the rulers must sooner or later provide a safety valve; placate the movement or find means of dividing it; turn it into new directions or harness it directly to the capitalist state. In no other way can capitalism maintain itself.

Long before the war the British ruling class learned how to incorporate radical politicians and labour leaders in the parties of capitalism. The German capitalists in 1918 jettisoned the Kaiser for a similar end. Fifty per cent of the German voters had registered their disillusionment and war-weariness by voting for the reform programme of the Social Democratic Party. German capitalism thereupon 'digested' the SDP and watched it stabilise German capitalism in the troubled post-war years. The military and civil associates of the Imperial Kaiser humbled themselves to the 'upstart' labour leaders because they had to have someone who could control the workers and keep them loyal to the fundamentals of capitalism. So for fourteen years the Social Democrats, either in coalitions or in 'friendly opposition', worked out their policy of bargaining for reforms as price of their support. The outcome was inevitable. They have shared the fate that has always overtaken 'Labour' politicians and parties when they accept responsibility for the administration of capitalism. Discontent with the effects of capitalism cannot for ever be stifled by Labour promises of better times or apologetic assurances that things might be worse. The membership and influence of the German SDP declined year by year until it had shrunk to a third of its former size. Part of the loss was picked up by the Communist Party, but in the meantime a new group had arisen, led by Hitler. At the election on 5th March he received 17,266,000 votes (43.9%) and his allies, the Nationalists, received 3,132,000 (8%), giving him a clear majority. The Social Democrats received 7,176,000 (18.3%) and the Communists 4,845,000 (12.1%).

In one important respect Hitler's Nazis are just like the Social Democrats and the Communists; they are all parties of discontent. Hitler promises work for the workless; secure government jobs in the police, the Army or the Civil service for

100,000 of his members; higher prices for agricultural products to help the peasants; and protection for the small investor and little shopkeeper squeezed by the big stores and the banks.

Immediately on taking office Hitler imposed fresh taxes on the big departmental stores and chain stores with the professed object of helping the small shopkeepers. He promised also to find posts for out-of-work professional men (doctors, lawyers and others), and it is because a relatively large number of bankers, proprietors of big stores and the more successful professional men are Jews that the party has taken on a violently anti-Jewish character. Every Jewish doctor driven out of practice, every Jewish lawyer barred from the courts, every Jewish schoolmaster and civil servant dismissed, makes another vacancy for one of his members. He was supplied with funds by German heavy industry, by armament manufacturers both in Germany and in France, and by American and other business men and financiers who had investments in Germany for which they needed protection. With the help of these funds Hitler's party has known how to rally all kinds of discontent into a great movement representing half the electorate of Germany. Therefore Hitler has had to be 'digested' as fourteen years ago were the Social Democrats. The stately and imperious Hindenburg and the aristocratic Von Papen, representing the military caste and big landowners, have had to receive on terms of equality the Austrian house-painter Adolf Hitler. Dr Hugenberg and the Nationalist Party, representing big industrial capitalists, have had to enter into coalition with him. Hitler will now have to administer capitalism. He will have to curb the demands of his followers, disappoint them, and ultimately lose many of them to new political adventurers, whereupon the capitalists and landlords who now use him will scrap him and use his successor.

The great lesson to be learned from the decline of the Social Democrats is the sterility of the policy of reforms and of reform parties. The day on which a reform party reaches power is the day on which the evil effects of capitalism begin to sap and undermine the strength of the party, turning the members' blind loyalty first into bewilderment and then into dissatisfaction, causing them to drift into new parties.

The depths of mental bankruptcy of the reformists are shown by the comment of the Fabian *New Statesman* (London, 11th March 1933). After explaining that Hitler scored because he appealed, with banners and uniforms and parades, to the electorate's love of glamour, the German correspondent of the *New Statesman* says that the Social Democrats should have done the same, and should have given more prominence to pageantry and less prominence to social reforms. In other words, the workers are to be enticed, not even by the old plan of 'bread and circuses', but by circuses without the bread! This is what forty years of Fabian reformism has brought to the working class movement!

The second lesson is one which has been entirely missed by the Labour Press in Great Britain, that is the evidence given by the Hitler episode of the overwhelming importance of controlling the political machinery. Six months ago, although the largest party in Germany, Hitler was not in control of the German Parliament and the machinery of government. He was ridiculed and derided by the members of the Government, and insulted by President Hindenburg. His party officials were hauled into court on charges of treason, and thrown into prison. Others were forced to flee the country. His newspapers were suppressed, his offices were raided by the police, his troops were forbidden to parade or wear uniforms in the street. When they attempted defiance they were driven off just like the Communists.

Now, having become possessed of the political machine and confirmed in power by the electors, he is able to turn the tables on his former opponents. He has removed the Governments of all the States of Germany. Former Cabinet Ministers have been arrested, beaten and made to suffer many indignities. Newspapers have been suppressed and their offices raided – from Conservative Catholic newspapers at one end of the scale to Social Democratic and Communist newspapers at the other. The Communists, in spite of their 5,000,000 voters and their year-long boasting of their belief in 'mass action' and military revolt, have been cowed into complete submission without offering any real resistance whatever. Events are proving to them what they refused to learn. The organised political majority which controls the political machinery of the modern State is in a position to dominate, and can enforce submission on minorities. There is no road to Socialism except through the control of the machinery of government by a politically organised majority of Socialists.

(April 1933)

Can the Means Test be Abolished?

Ever since 1931, when a large number of unemployed were brought under what is known as the 'Means Test', this has been a burning question in British politics. All of the opposition candidates at the November General Election promised, in more or less guarded fashion, to abolish the test, although we are entitled to wonder whether their promises mean quite what the electors thought they meant.

Before going into that question further, it will be useful to explain what is the means test – or rather, what are the several means tests applied by the Government in connection with unemployment pay, Public Assistance, and Old Age Non-contributory pensions.

The Poor Law Means Test 300 years old

First, in point of time, is the Poor Law or Public Assistance Means Test. This has a very ancient history and has been the model on which other tests have been based. The group of Poor Laws which concern us here are those passed in the sixteenth and seventeenth centuries. By that time, recognising that they were faced permanently with the problem of workless and homeless men and women, then deprived of a main source of help by the abolition of the monasteries, the Governments abandoned the effort to torture the starving into quiet submission and arranged to provide some sort of maintenance for them. Several Acts passed during the sixteenth century, culminating in the Acts of 1597 and 1601, appointed collectors in each parish whose duty it was to levy householders and use the proceeds – flax, hemp, wool, thread, iron and other materials – to provide work for the poor. Pauper children were sent out as apprentices and alms-houses were built for the aged. Needless to say, the provision was niggardly and hedged about with callous restrictions, although some of the most inhuman of the earlier provisions had to be dropped because those responsible would not work them. (See *Social Administration, including the Poor Laws*, by John J. Clarke, M.A. Pitman & Sons, Ltd; 1922; page 25). What particularly concerns us is the principle of family responsibility. Already in 1601 it was laid down that the destitute must be kept by their relatives if the latter had the means. Under the Act of that year it was provided that grandparents must maintain their grandchildren, parents their children, husbands their wives (and the children of their wives by another father, up to age sixteen), and finally, children had to maintain their parents. (See Clarke, page 29.) This principle has been retained through many changes of Poor Law Administration, and we find it in the Poor Law Act, 1930, with little alteration. Section 14 of the 1930 Act lays it down that "it shall be the duty of the father, grandfather, mother, grandmother, husband or child, of a poor, old, blind, lame or impotent person, or other person not able to work, if possessed of sufficient means, to relieve and maintain that person." Under this clause the authorities may, and do, force relatives to contribute.

The mother of an illegitimate child, so long as she is unmarried or a widow, is bound to maintain the child until age sixteen. A man who marries a woman who has a child, whether legitimate or illegitimate, is responsible for the child till age sixteen.

One interesting addition is that a married woman, with property of her own, now has responsibilities similar to those of the husband.

It will be seen that the ruling class do not show to the destitute wealth-producers and their dependants even a crumb of the open-handed generosity with which they reward dud Generals and Admirals. Yet although the applicant for relief has to satisfy the above conditions, and many others, we find that, on the last Saturday in September, 1935, Poor Relief was granted to no fewer than 1,280,942 persons, equivalent to 3.17% of the population, double the number in 1913 (611,448).

The old age pension means test
One development of the Poor Law has been the smaller use of workhouses and the greater extent to which relief is paid to the applicant in his own home. Provided

that the authorities maintain a tight check – as, of course, they do – they have found the latter method cheaper. According to the *Fourteenth Annual Report of the Ministry of Health* (page 199) the average cost of relief in general Poor Law Institutions in 1932-33 was about 24 shillings a week, while the average expenditure on relief per head of the "ordinary outdoor poor" (i.e. excluding persons ordinarily employed) was 6s. 1d. a week.

An extension of this method of relieving the destitute in their own homes was the grant under various Acts from 1908 to 1924 of non-contributory old age pensions at age seventy. There are at present something like 760,000 persons in receipt of old age non-contributory pensions of 10s. a week or less. This system has now been copied in the USA, and, there, also, one of the arguments used in support of it is that of cheapness. As Mary T. Norton, a Congresswoman from New Jersey, USA, declared last year, "old age pensions are cheaper than poor houses" (*New Militant*, New York, November 30th, 1935).

The non-contributory pensions are not given to all persons over seventy years of age, but are subject to the condition that the applicant's income from all sources, including gifts, is below a specified low level, savings also being taken into account. The 'means test', however, only concerns the income of the applicant, not that of his relatives as well. It differs, therefore, from the 'family means test'.

The unemployment pay means test

We now come to the question which has so much occupied the Opposition parties in recent years, the 'family means test' applied to some of the unemployed. In 1931 the Law was altered by the National Government so that unemployed persons who had exhausted their right to benefit (by reason of the fact that they had received benefit for six months in a benefit year), and persons who could not show thirty stamps for the two years preceding their application for benefit, were declared eligible for 'transitional' payments only. Before this change there was no limit to the period an unemployed person could draw ordinary benefit, provided he or she satisfied the various other conditions.

The difference between ordinary unemployment benefit and 'transitional' benefit was that the latter was only payable provided that the Public Assistance authority satisfied itself that the claimant was *in need of assistance*. In other words, when an unemployed man came under the transitional benefit regulations his claim became subject to the 'family means test', the kind of test applied from 1600 onwards.

The applicant had to provide information regarding the earnings of *all members* of the household, also Army and Navy pensions, blind pensions, etc., income from Workmen's Compensation, Friendly Society benefits, assistance from relatives not living at home, savings, etc., etc.

These provisions were embodied, with modifications, in the Unemployment Act, 1934. Section 38 provides that unemployed persons who run out of benefit, instead of having transitional benefit shall come under the newly-created Unemployment Assistance Board and be entitled to an allowance dependent on needs, the need being determined by taking into account the resources of all members of the household. The 1934 Act ruled out, however, from the family income which is taken into account, part of the benefit from a Friendly Society and from National Health Insurance, the first £1 of a disability pension and half of any weekly payment by way of Workmen's Compensation.

That is the Law as it stands at present, but the Unemployment Assistance Board's activities promptly led to further outcry and the Government is still considering the question of the allowances. The Means Test will still apply. Eventually the Unemployment Assistance Board is to have control, not only over the unemployed who have fallen out of benefit, but also other able-bodied unemployed (including those not insured at all), who are now under the control of the Public Assistance authorities.

The Labour government's poor defence

The application of the family Means Test to the unemployed was an innovation of importance affecting hundreds of thousands directly, and likely to affect others if they remained unemployed for over six months. All the same, the extent and violence of the outcry surprised not only the National Government but even the Labour Party. The reasons why the question has taken on such importance in elections is not far to seek. It meant that the unemployed found even the security of unemployment pay taken from them and also the parents and children of anyone unemployed or likely to become unemployed found themselves involved. They resented the obligation to contribute to the support of their unemployed relatives out of their own inadequate earnings, and resented having to provide information. The interest of the unemployed and their relatives is understandable enough, but the indignation of the Labour Party leaders is not so easy to understand.

It is true that the National Government was responsible for applying the family Means Test to the unemployed after twenty-six weeks on benefit, but the two Labour Governments had applied the test under the Poor Law and appear never to have contemplated its abolition.

Moreover, the Labour Government, in 1931, just before its resignation, had already agreed to economies which included the application of a Means Test to those of the unemployed who had been long out of work. What they deny having agreed to was a *family* Means Test.

Mr J.H. Thomas recently infuriated some of the Labour MPs by saying – as he has often said before – "there is no leader sitting on that Front Bench who was a member of the Labour Government with me who dares to say that he opposed the Means Test" (*Hansard*, 9th December 1935, col. 688).

Mr George Lansbury thereupon intervened to explain exactly what happened in

1931 and what was the attitude of the Labour Government. He said: "While it is true, as I have said several times, that we were in favour of a Means Test, we were definitely and emphatically against putting the unemployed under the Poor Law and thus bringing them within the Poor Law Means Test ... The unemployed who were receiving transitional payments never came under the Means Test until after the Economy Act, brought in by Lord Snowden, was passed by this House ... The able-bodied poor who came to the Poor Law were always under the Means Test ..." (col. 696).

In order that there may be no doubt about the attitude of the Labour Government in 1931, we may refer also to other authoritative statements. Speaking in the House of Commons on 13th November 1931 (*Hansard*, 13th November, col. 446), Mr Lansbury said: "As to the Means Test, the hon. Member knows as well as I do what is our attitude on the subject. I am not prepared to give people money year after year without knowing what is their own personal position; that is to say, if a person has gone out of ordinary benefit and has means of his own to maintain himself. I am not prepared to pay him State money."

In keeping with this policy of favouring a Means Test, but not one based on family income, an *amendment* moved by Mr Kirkwood, at the Scarborough Conference of the Labour Party, 1931 (see Report, pages 206-209), which would have entirely abolished the Means Test for workers on transitional benefit, was defeated. The resolution which was carried was moved by Sir Stafford Cripps. It merely committed the Labour Party to the abolition of the 'Poor Law tests', leaving the way open for a non-family Means Test.

The Labour Party's Election Address, 1935, cautiously promises to sweep away "the humiliating Means Test imposed by the National Government", but does not promise to abolish all means tests, either for Poor Law or for Unemployment pay.

A vital question for capitalism

It does not require much examination to see why the question of Means Tests is a vital one for capitalism. Capitalism cannot exist without something which will drive the workers to submit themselves to exploitation for the benefit of the propertied class. That something is poverty and the threat of starvation. The capitalists must have always at their disposal the millions of wage-earners ready to be exploited in order to live. Once allow the able-bodied (i.e. profit-producing) workers to have free access even to the most frugal necessities of life and capitalism is ended. For reasons of stability and security of property the rulers must provide something for those workers whose services are not at the moment required, but it must be so hedged about by restrictions that it does not enable workers to receive from all sources more than will barely keep them alive. So the working class must not receive unemployment pay indefinitely without fathers and children being made to meet part of the cost; they must not be able to get Public Assistance while they or their relatives have the means to keep them. Mrs Sidney Webb in her useful lecture on *The English Poor Law* (Oxford University Press, 1928), gives an apt quotation from Patrick Colquhoun. He was living in the early nineteenth century, but the relative position of capitalists and workers, has not changed since then: "Without a proportion of poverty there could be no riches, since riches are the offspring of labour, while labour can exist only from a state of poverty ... Poverty is, therefore, a most necessary and indispensable ingredient in society, without which nations and communities could not exist in a state of civilisation."

If we remember that for Mr Colquhoun 'civilisation' meant 'capitalism', his statement is a good description of the facts; and, in passing, it is interesting to recall how Mr Colquhoun proposed to enforce poverty. Mrs Webb calls him "the inventor of the modern system of preventive police", and one of the chief original purposes of the police system was to smash up workers' demonstrations without loss of life and without incurring the criticism which the use of troops always aroused (see *British History in the Nineteenth Century*, G.M. Trevelyan, Longmans; 1922; page 199). The police came in useful when the starving agricultural labourers and textile operatives demonstrated against the effects of the Poor Law Act of 1834, which brought to an end the practice of subsidising low wages by Poor Relief.

Coming back to the present problem of the Means Test, it is conceivable that the Government could achieve the same purpose – that of compelling the workers to submit themselves to exploitation – without any kind of Means Test, family or otherwise, by applying much more harshly the remaining restrictions. The present method, however, has the advantage from their point of view that an unemployed man's relatives can usually be relied on to goad him into accepting any work, however ill-paid and uncongenial. How much more satisfactory that is to the Government than that the Government itself should be accused of driving unemployed into accepting work at all costs!

Only Socialism will abolish means tests

One thing is absolutely certain. Any political party which administers capitalism has got to find some means of *compelling* the workers to produce profits for the capitalists. Nothing but the alternative of starvation will do it. No appeal, whether in the name of patriotism, religion, social duty or anything else will serve the purpose. Capitalism is supported by force and will collapse if the force is withdrawn.

That explains why we can be sure that no Government, Liberal, Labour, Conservative, or any other, *which administers capitalism*, will abolish the Means Test without reintroducing it under another name or something of similar effect and equally obnoxious. That explains why the Labour Party and its spokesmen in the House of Commons do not undertake to abolish all Means Tests, but only to abolish the 'family' Means Test, and even that they do not promise to abolish in relation to Public Assistance.

They may have the best intentions, but capitalism is based on class ownership, class antagonism. The effort to keep the basis but humanise the administration may decrease somewhat the amount of human misery, but cannot solve the problem. It also increases the opposition of those who say that the workers abuse every concession made to them, and that, therefore, progress and Socialism are impossible.

Only Socialists have a solution. Society must get rid of the class basis and the system of wage-labour. It must be so organised that people are no longer offered the alternatives of being exploited or of striving to retain or become an exploiter. Wealth must be produced only for use and without the wealth producers being driven to their uncongenial tasks by the whip of starvation wielded by the ruling class and their governments.

The incentive must be the common appreciation that work, in which all will co-operate, will be for the good of all. Access to the necessaries and comforts of life must be free. There will be no need for 'means tests' for anyone. All will be members of society without privilege one over the other.

(January 1936)

The Civil War in Spain

The civil war, which began with the revolt of 18th July, is, at the time of writing, still dragging on without either side having gained decisive victory. What the outcome will be it is still impossible to say, for the issue depends to a great extent on the assistance given to the rebels by foreign governments. Before examining the struggle from the Socialist standpoint, we may pay tribute to the conduct of the Spanish workers. Believing that a vital principle was at stake, they rallied to the Government against a powerful revolt backed by the greater part of the armed forces. Workers, with little or no military training, stood up to trained and experienced soldiers. On the one side was all the advantage of organisation and equipment, and on the other the enthusiasm and voluntary discipline of a popular movement. It is true that large sections of the military forces remained loyal to the Government, but even these were hampered by treason and sabotage among the officers. Only the untrained volunteer militias were thoroughly dependable. The Madrid correspondent of the *Economist* (London, 15th August 1936) was moved to admiration and wrote: "The splendid way in which the citizens of Madrid rushed to arms was a fine page in the history of democracy."

He pointed out something else deserving of notice: "As far as Madrid is concerned, discipline has been excellent. In the early days, when almost every working man in Madrid had a rifle in hand, the jewellers' shops were open as usual, with their windows full of valuables, without the slightest attempt at theft being registered."

If the workers attacked churches, "that was", he said, "because of the close political connection between the clericals and the Conservatives."

So much for the conduct of the Spanish workers. What of the wisdom of their action in rallying to a purely capitalist government in order to defend it against a military, aristocratic and clerical rebellion?

The need for democracy

It has always been recognised by Socialists that it is necessary for the workers to gain the vote, so that they may be able to place themselves democratically in control of the machinery of government. Marx was one who recognised this.

At first sight the Spanish struggle appears to be simply a struggle of this kind, and many people have indeed represented it to be. When, however, all the facts are taken into account, the position is by no means simple and straightforward.

The recent political history of Spain dates from 1931, when the Monarchical Government was overthrown, undermined by its own corruption and decay. At the first democratic election the Spanish Labourites (the so-called Socialist Party) obtained 117 seats out of 470, and three of their representatives entered the first provisional Government in coalition with various other parties. The Government introduced a number of important pieces of legislation providing for the division of the big landed estates among the land-workers and peasants, the disestablishment of the Catholic Church, divorce laws, an educational system to remove the appalling illiteracy, and the grant of a wide measure of autonomy to Catalonia. The last-named law is to be explained largely by the fact that Catalonia contains (in and around Barcelona) a big share of Spain's industrial concerns, the owners of which have interests opposed to those of the landowners, the Catholic organisations, the military cliques and the Conservative traders of Seville and elsewhere. The aim of the Republican Government, in brief, was to change the constitution and governmental system of Spain in the direction of capitalist development. From the first they faced the wealthy, powerful and ruthless opposition both of the representatives of the old order, who are able to appeal to the ignorance of the priest-ridden sections of the population, 60% of which is rural, and also of new groups preaching some kind of Fascism, who can attract quite a number of idealistic young people with promises of the rebirth of a unified powerful Spain.

The Coalition Government did not last for long. The Monarchists and military groups recovered their courage, and, at the same time, dissension arose between the Labourites and other workers' groups, and the frankly capitalist parties. The latter felt that they no longer had need to rely on the organised workers and pay a certain price for their support.

At the General Election in November, 1933, the Labourites lost heavily and came back with only 61 seats.

The next development was an abortive military coup by workers' organisations and Catalan separatists in October 1934, in answer to the inclusion of three Catholics of Fascist sympathies in the Cabinet. As was inevitable, the revolt was crushed by the Government without difficulty, but with great brutality. Some 30,000 workers were imprisoned and held there throughout 1935. Indeed they were not released until the victory of the 'Popular Front' at the election in February 1936, the indignation caused by their imprisonment and ill-treatment being one of the factors which helped the Popular Front to win.

The Popular Front at the General Election, February 1936

The reasons for the electoral victory of the Popular Front were many, but outstanding among them were the following. First, dissatisfaction with the results of two years of Conservative Catholic rule, and the disclosure of financial scandals affecting members of the Government. Then the fact that the reforms begun by the first Republican administration were not only not carried through but had been largely undone. Most important of all, however, was the electoral pact between a number of organisations hitherto bitterly hostile to each other. The Popular Front consisted of the following large or fair-sized parties, together with several smaller ones (the figures are the seats won at the election in February 1936): Labourites (about 96), Left Republicans (80), Republican Union (32), Esquerra (Catalonian Party: 20), Communists (16). Above all, this was the first time that the Syndicalists, who normally oppose all political action, had voted at an election. Another contributory cause for the Popular Front victory was the shocking poverty of the land-workers, aggravated by wage reductions enforced under the former Government. The Popular Front undertook to raise wages if they got power.

The outcome was that the Popular Front obtained a total of about 265 seats, to 148 for the Right group and 55 for the Centre group. Even so the total votes obtained by Popular Front candidates were slightly fewer than those given to the candidates of the Right and Centre together – 4,357,000 to 4,571,000 (*Daily Herald*, 27th February 1936).

The new Government was entirely a capitalist-Republican one, under Señor Azana of the Left Republican Party. It took office pledged to introduce certain reforms, but without any suggestion of trying or even desiring to help Socialism. As Senor Azana constantly said in his election speeches, "I am not a Socialist and I am not a socialisator" (*Manchester Guardian*, 27th February).

The Government contained not one Labourite, Communist, Syndicalist, Anarchist or Trotskyite. All its members were avowed supporters of capitalism. In addition to being pledged to carry through the reforms introduced by the first

Republican Government, the Azana Government proposed to introduce an income tax and to bring the banking system under Government control.

The government faces revolt

No sooner did the Government take office than it received due warning that the military-clerical-Fascist groups would not accept their electoral defeat as in any way binding on them. They do not pretend to have any time for democracy and majority rule, as was admitted by General Franco, leader of the present revolt, to a *News Chronicle* representative on 28th July. When asked "What about the February elections? Didn't they represent the national will?" Franco's contemptuous reply was, "Elections never do" (*News Chronicle*, 29th July 1936).

Thus it was that General Franco and General Godet (the latter was executed in Barcelona on 11th August for his part in the new revolt) staged an unsuccessful rising in February, immediately the election results were known. The revolt was crushed, but the Government, either through negligence or fear, allowed these and other known rebels to continue to occupy influential officials positions in Majorca, Morocco and elsewhere, positions which they used to prepare a more powerful rising.

In the five months after taking office, the Azana Government was faced with individual acts of terrorism by military and semi-Fascist organisations, which were replied to in a similar way by those workers' organisations which have long preached and practised violence – the Syndicalists and Anarchists. Two culminating incidents were the assassination of Senor Costillo, Lieutenant of the Shock Police, by Fascists, and the counter-assassination of Calvo Sotelo, self-styled future dictator and rebel leader. It is believed that the rebellion was planned for 25th July, but was brought forward a week owing to the assassination of Sotelo.

The rebels took with them the greater part of the army – officered largely by men belonging to the landed aristocracy – and part of the navy. The Government kept the support of most of the air force, part of the navy, some of the rank and file of the army, and the greater part of the Civil Guard (a military police force). The rebels had the backing of the landowners and the Catholic Church, itself the biggest landowner of all, and also the backing (probably in advance of the event) of the German and Italian governments, interested in the promise of naval bases in Morocco, the Canary Islands, and Majorca, if Franco won. The *Daily Telegraph* (supporting the rebels) reported that General Franco was building up a new air force during the first weeks of August with "modern German and Italian 'planes and personnel", and the latest types of German anti-aircraft guns. (*Daily Telegraph*, August 13th, 1936.) The Government in Barcelona unearthed in the headquarters of the German Nazi organisation there evidence of a widespread Nazi organisation in Spain (*News Chronicle*, 19th and 20th August).

As regards the objects of the rebels, the rebellion can be described in the main as a landed-class revolt against the agrarian reforms (splitting up of their estates among the land-workers), aided by the Catholic Church, military group, and by organisations with a more or less Fascist outlook. The last-named are, however, at present probably the least important. The rebel movement, as a whole, and even its Fascist wing, bears little resemblance to Italian Fascism and German Nazism, with their popular appeal, fake-Socialist phraseology, and considerable working class support.

The dictatorships in Germany and Italy – and especially Portugal – have other reasons for being interested in the future Government of Spain. Undoubtedly the revival of workers' confidence and activity in the French stay-in strikes, the Popular Fronts, and the Spanish militias, are having repercussions in Portugal, and even Italy and Germany. It is probably not a coincidence that extensive wage increases are being granted by Mussolini's Government just now.

Spain's divided working class

If the rebels represent more than one point of view, the Popular Front militias are an example of the temporary unity of very divergent forces. Catalonian capitalist-Republicans and Catholic-Conservative Basque nationalists join hands with Labourites, who stand for democratic government, constitutional action and social reform, and with Anarchists and Syndicalists who reject political action and the need to capture the State-machine, oppose centralised organisation and favour local self-governing 'Communes', and whose traditional methods are sabotage, insurrection by strikes, and gunman tactics. In addition there are Communists and Trotskyites, bitterly opposed to each other but agreed in favouring a strong centralised State based on dictatorship.

As regards the relative strengths of the workers' groups, the General Union of Workers (UGT), which supports the Labourites, has about 1 1/2 million adherents, and is the strongest trade union organisation everywhere, except in Barcelona. Their political reflection, the Labourites (themselves divided into 'Left' and 'Right' Wings), are the strongest party in Parliament, with about 96 members. (The next largest was the CEDA, led by the Conservative Gil Robles.)

The Anarcho-Syndicalist National Confederation of Labour (CNT) has about 500,000 members. Although it has recently grown, it is far below its former strength. Its great stronghold is Barcelona.

The Communists and Trotskyites each have perhaps 50,000 members. The Anarchists, especially in Catalonia, have their own organisation with a large following.

These fundamental divergences of aim and method naturally have serious consequences. In the first place, their very existence was a factor which emboldened the rebels and encouraged them to launch their attack. They calculated, not without reason, that such a mixed Popular Front would soon show signs of disintegration. Dissensions have indeed occurred. The Syndicalists, while reluctantly supporting the 'Front' at the elections, and joining the militias, still declined to collaborate with capitalist bodies in the government of Catalonia (*Manchester Guardian*, 8th August). Also, being strongly opposed to the idea of dictatorship, they mistrust and are hostile to the Communists and Trotskyites. Even in the midst of the civil war the leader of the dockers in the General Workers' Union at Barcelona was assassinated with two of his colleagues. As they were Labour Party sympathisers, and had a long-standing quarrel with the Anarcho-Syndicalist CNT, it was taken for granted that the latter were settling old scores (*Manchester Guardian*, 7th August). The past history of the murderous antagonisms between these bodies would make such an action by no means surprising. The Labour Unions protested and were met with the threats of violence. It may be mentioned that the Anarcho Syndicalists have no reason to love the so-called 'Socialist' Party, which coquetted with the dictator Primo de Rivera when he was suppressing them ten years ago.

(In passing, it is interesting to notice the remark of a *Times* correspondent that the customary discipline of the Labourites and Communists in the militias made them more effective as fighting men than the Syndicalists and Anarchists, whose disbelief in organisation resulted in their suffering great losses in action – *The Times*, 6th August).

The Trotskyites continued to deride Parliament, criticise the Government and demand a dictatorship.

The disunity of method, organisation and object of the Spanish workers are important from another point of view. We may readily grant, with Marx, that workers *seeking democracy* have an interest in striving, as well as the capitalists, to overthrow military, Monarchical or autocratic Government, but Marx certainly never envisaged a situation in which not only were the workers' groups bitterly hostile to each other, but many of them (in Spain possibly a majority) are not aiming at democracy at all, having no inclination for it. Should the Communists or Trotskyites gain power they would, as in Russia, promptly and ruthlessly suppress democracy, and along with it the Labourites, Syndicalists and Anarchists. The latter two groups, whatever Government is in power, will continue to do their utmost by strikes, sabotage, and even assassination, to destroy it, even at the cost of producing chaos.

The truth is – and the Spanish workers have got to learn it before they can hope to make progress in organising for the conquest of power for Socialism – that Socialism is at present absolutely out of the question, and that their only present hope is for the right to organise and carry on Socialist propaganda under capitalist democracy. Trying to go beyond this (or in the case of the Anarcho Syndicalists, trying to go backwards) by means of armed revolts, and so on, will gain nothing except disillusionment, and will not help the working class or the Socialist movement.

Things to be remembered

For reasons of space, it is impossible to deal at length with many important aspects of the struggle, but certain points and certain facts deserve to be touched upon or recorded.

First, there were the atrocity stories and the outrageous misrepresentations of sections of the English Press, notably the Rothermere organs, and *The Times* and *Daily Telegraph.*

Lord Rothermere's journals openly sided with the rebels, whom they described as patriots and Christians. His *Evening News* (4th August) actually charged the 'Reds' with being responsible for plunging Spain into a 'blood bath'. By the 'Reds' it meant the Spanish capitalist-Republican Government, but the Rothermere press consistently hid the facts of that Government's composition. The same paper (3rd August) demanded a Fascist victory as the only way of 'saving' Spain and justified the rebellion on the extraordinary plea that the Government's defensive measures against the rebels ("orgy of slaughter and rapine") would have been launched "whether there had been a Fascist rising or not".

Needing to hide the fact that the rebels were largely dependent on Mohammedan Moors in the Foreign Legion and Riff regiments, trained in savage fighting methods, in order to bolster up the claim that the rebels represented Christianity the *Evening News* (8th August) avoided disclosing that they were Moors. Instead they were described as Franco's "men from Morocco".

The Times, with typical craft, dodged standing frankly as the supporter of rebels against a democratically elected Government by maintaining – without any evidence – that the conflict was bound to result in "a despotism either of the Left or of the Right" and that the Government side was becoming "violently Marxist" (*Times*, 29th July); this in spite of the fact that its own correspondent was well enough informed to know, as everybody else knows, that the Anarcho Syndicalists are anti-Marxists (11th August), and in spite of *The Times*'s own admission (29th July) that "Perhaps a majority" of the Government's armed supporters were neither Labourites nor Anarcho Syndicalists, but "members of less extreme groups", i.e. capitalist-Republicans, Catholic Nationalists, or pure and simple democrats.

Another *Times* trick was to describe the rebels as "anti-Government troops", and the Government troops as "an armed mob" (see *Times*, 1st August).

Such misrepresentation, extending in the Rothermere Press to unashamed lying, is what the workers may always expect from some at least of the organs of capitalist interests.

Two important points which emerge from the struggle relate to the importance of having control of the machinery of Government, which has been consistently stressed by the SPGB. In Vienna in February, 1934, and in Spain in October, 1934, workers' armed revolts against the Government were easily crushed. In

Spain, even if the Government is eventually defeated owing to the intervention of Italy and Germany, enough has happened to show that control of the machinery of Government would have gained the day against the rebels, even though they were backed by a large part of the military forces.

The second point is that we can see from Spain how easy it would have been to crush Fascism in Italy in 1922 if the Italian Government at that time had wanted to – which, of course, it did not. Mussolini's rabble could have been dispersed in a few hours, as the military authorities there said at the time.

The dependence of the Spanish rebels on outside aid and the inability of the international working class to give any effective assistance to the Government is worth noting. Collections of money (insignificant in amount except that arranged in Russia by the Government) can make little difference in such a case.

This brings us to the utter futility of the Communist Party of Great Britain. Aware, in spite of themselves, of their impotence, all they could do, apart from making collections, was to appeal for the summoning of Parliament, which they so often declared to be useless (*Daily Worker*, 8th August); appeal for the sending of a co-operative food ship, which the Co-operative Societies refused to do; appeal to the Tory Government to help the Spanish Government (they called it "demanding and resolving to enforce our will that the National Government shall give to the elected People's Government of Spain the help it needs" (*Daily Worker*, 10th August); and to demand "a mighty campaign everywhere in Britain. Meetings, meetings, meetings, in streets and halls and schools … resolutions, protests, collections for the Spanish people … writing to the local Press, to the local Council, to the local MPs" (*Daily Worker*, 11th August). In other words no action of any moment, but simply endless varieties of talk. What we witnessed here was a repetition of the Communist Party's futile gestures of help for Abyssinia. Perhaps the crowning absurdity of the Communists, in view of the League fiasco over Abyssinia, was that they proposed calling the League in to 'help' Spain!

Atrocity-mongering

It is impossible to deny that cruelties, apart from the destruction of the war itself, occurred on both sides. In view, however, of the one-sided or lying reports in many organs of the English Press the following statements are worth recording. It cannot be doubted that the rebels deliberately perpetrated far more ghastly atrocities than anything the Government militia's were guilty of as acts of revenge or reprisal.

When Moorish troops captured Badajoz they slaughtered 2,000 Government troops in cold blood, or, as their commander, Colonel Yaque, said: "Perhaps not quite as many as that" (*News Chronicle*, 17th August).

The *Daily Telegraph* (15th August) reported from their own correspondent that the rebels at the Montana barracks, in Madrid, three times showed the white flag of surrender and each time opened fire under cover of it on the Government forces which came to accept the surrender.

Reuters' correspondent (*Daily Herald*, 28th July) was told by a rebel legionary that they had "been strictly instructed not to take any prisoners but to cut off the heads of all Communists."

Jay Allen, *News Chronicle* correspondent (12th August), stated that the rebel Foreign Legion "are leaving a trail of blood and villages in ruin behind them."

The Times correspondent at Malaga reported (8th August) that 900 Royalist and other rebel prisoners there "are not only safe but in tolerable comfort". Only some five or six, after summary trial, were shot.

On 14th August the British colony in Madrid sent a telegram to the English Foreign Office indignantly repudiating "hysterical stories published in the British Press by refugees from here". The telegram was signed by six business men, and said that none of the British colony had ever been in the slightest danger. Reuters' Madrid correspondent reported (*Manchester Guardian*, 15th August): "there have been, as far as anyone knows, no atrocities here." The same, according to the *Manchester Guardian*, was true of Malaga. The BBC had repeated refugee stories, alleging numerous atrocities at Malaga, but when the *Guardian*'s special correspondent in Andalusia investigated he "found them to be untrue".

One incident deserves to be recorded. Mr Winston Churchill wrote an article on Spain in the *Evening Standard* on 10th August. In it he made the interesting admission that in his view a constitutional, parliamentary Government is only deserving of allegiance if it "prove itself capable of preserving law and order, and protecting life, freedom and *property*" (italics ours).

We think we are not misrepresenting this capitalist politician's outlook when we read into it that he claims the right to stage a pro-capitalism rebellion when a Socialist majority have obtained control of Parliament in a constitutional way. Socialists will remember this.

Regarding the future of Spain it can be said with certainty that whichever side wins the present civil war, the matter will not end at once. The defeated will be awaiting a further opportunity of appealing to arms. Also it may be taken for granted that whether the Government forces or the rebels come out on top they will seek to disarm the workers.

It need hardly be added that the only ultimate solution for class-conflict and unrest in Spain, as elsewhere, lies in Socialism.

(September 1936)

THE SECOND WORLD WAR

The Second World War finally broke out in September 1939 when Britain and France declared war on Germany after Germany had invaded Poland – as part of a carve-up deal with state-capitalist Russia – so threatening British and French markets in the rest of eastern Europe. In a very real sense this was a continuation of the First World War whose outcome had not resolved German capitalism's problem as a leading industrial country without access either to protected markets or to secure sources of raw materials.

The Socialist Party had no hesitation in taking up the same internationalist, anti-war stand as it had 25 years earlier. Not democracy, but the defence of the British empire and markets in eastern Europe was why Britain had declared war, an issue which, once again, did not justify the shedding of a single drop of working class blood and early pieces from the *Socialist Standard* of the time, such as those reproduced here, are a testament to the Party's anti-war stand.

The Defence Regulations brought in during May 1940 were concerned with printed matter that promoted opposition to the conflict and the penalties for transgression were severe. This had a noticeable impact on the composition of the *Standard*. From this point on, it was unable to print articles which explicitly opposed the war. The gap was filled with pieces on Marxism, economics and history, as well as some carefully worded topical pieces.

At the start of the war, Britain and France had not even bothered to claim that the war was simply one of democracy versus fascism but openly admitted that their aim was to dismantle the autarkic trading arrangements Germany had installed as well as protecting their empires. Later, as the war dragged on, the British government decided to present it as a "people's war", a propaganda campaign in which the Communist Party enthusiastically joined – but only after the German invasion of Russia in June 1941. Promises were made of a better future for all after the war had been won. Thus, Sir William Beveridge's 1943 Report promised a whole range of social reforms from family allowances to national insurance against unemployment, sickness and old age. There was talk of a national health service. As the articles here demonstrate, the Socialist Party was not impressed. Beveridge's plan was analysed as an attempt to "reorganise poverty" by redistributing total working class income more rationally from a capitalist point of view, taking from the unmarried and the childless to give to those married with children or from the employed to maintain the unemployed till the next boom came.

The war ended with the worst famine in history in Bengal and with the testing of the atomic bomb on real, live populations in Hiroshima and Nagasaki. Russia conquered half of Europe and installed dictatorial regimes in the countries that fell under its domination. The Western Powers set about restoring multilateral trade via new institutions such as the IMF, the World Bank and GATT (General Agreement on Tariffs and Trade). Colonial wars broke out in Africa and South East Asia. The various Allies had achieved their respective war aims. Then they fell out, and began rearming for the next war.

How Can Hitlerism be Destroyed?

That the Nazi Government, or what has come to be known as Hitlerism, is a menace to the peace of the world, is a fact as much recognised by Socialists as by all those who support the war. No Socialist will deny that all the Hitler regime stands for is repugnant and revolting to every *ideal* which he strives to establish.

The suppression of free expression of opinion, the concentration camp, the *racial* persecution and exiling of all people arbitrarily deemed out of sympathy with Nazism, the public and private burning of a vast literature on Socialist and scientific subjects, the untold number of outrages committed by the Gestapo, are things indicative of a form of social life (pardon the phrase) which must befoul the finer feelings of all those worthy to be classed as really human.

Intellectual development cannot be where such conditions are prevalent. And where intellectual forces are stifled, real social material well-being is impossible of attainment. There must be no mistake that Socialists hate Hitlerism in a manner beyond question. It stands out to us calling aloud for destruction. But when we have said all this we have but touched the fringe of the problem presented by the existence of the present German Government. That Government, like that of any other throughout the world, owes its origin and maintenance to definite historical and social causes, in which we include such mass ideology as that upon which all governments largely depend for their existence.

Let us begin at the beginning.

The basic condition for the rivalry between modern states is the quest for profit on the part of those who own the means of living, the land, mines, railways and all such resources of the earth as the whole of mankind needs in order to live. The people who own these vital forces of human life are, in broad outline, represented by those who are in control of the machinery of government. Whether such government be *democratic* or dictatorship in form, the above statement applies with equal force. It cannot be too often stated that the method of government in all capitalist countries is a sort of by-product of the same general mode of wealth production and distribution. We leave aside for the moment whether the *democratic* or dictatorship form of the state in capitalist countries is more favourable for working class expression and development. One point here is, that in democratic Britain, France and America, as in dictatorship Germany and Italy, wealth is produced primarily for profit. Therein is to be found the secret of the world situation in modern times. Profit represents — is, in fact – the unpaid labour of the workers. Every worker must realise that after he has spent his energy in producing things for the capitalist, and after all materials and other items have been provided for, there is a surplus above the amount he gets in wages. When this surplus fails to materialise, capitalist production normally ceases. We describe the surplus wealth taken by the capitalist as surplus-value. The worker labours for the capitalist (when he is permitted to do so) for wages, and the capitalist puts him to work to realise the difference between the wages paid and the value of the worker's product of labour. "It is this sort of exchange", says Marx, "between capital and labour upon which capitalistic production, or the wages system, is founded, and which must constantly result in reproducing the working man as working man and the capitalist as capitalist."

The perpetuation and expansion of the capitalist's pursuit of surplus-value gave rise to the imperialism underlying modern war. For capital to grow to maturity it must break down national boundaries and seek the world for its sphere of activity and gratification. Hence the conflicts between national groups of capitalists represented by their respective governments backed by armed force.

The phrase, 'the workshop of the world', at one time so aptly applied to this country, indicates an ideological landmark, not merely in the economic history and development of England, but also in that of the other leading capitalist powers. Those who were once the customers of 'the world's workshop' became, in the very nature of the capitalist process, its competitors for

THE
SOCIALIST
STANDARD

OFFICIAL ORGAN OF THE SOCIALIST PARTY OF GREAT BRITAIN

"Everywhere we are stared down on by Wealth and Respectability, while crammed away in retired lanes and dark, damp alleys Poverty dwells with her rags and her tears."
HEINRICH HEINE ("The Wonder of London.")

MAY DAY IN BEDLAM

NATIONAL SERVICE OR
INTERNATIONAL SOCIALISM?

CLASHING INTERESTS IN THE
MEDITERRANEAN

THE HISTORICAL
BACKGROUND
OF HITLERISM

markets, trade routes, spheres of influence, and the occupation of strategic positions, or the acquisition of raw materials.

Thus arose the intense rivalry of Britain and Germany, which culminated in the war of 1914-1918. The defeat of Germany in that conflict and the imposing of the Treaty of Versailles upon her paved the way for the war in which we are once more engaged.

One of the chief architects of the Versailles Treaty, Mr Lloyd George, has said of his own part-handiwork: "I am one of the four upon whom devolved the onerous task of drafting the treaties of 1919 ... The conditions that were imposed upon Germany were ruthlessly applied to the limit of her endurance. She paid £2,000,000,000 in reparations. We experienced insuperable difficulties in paying £1,000,000,000 to America – and we are a much richer country than Germany. We stripped her of all her colonies, confiscating her equipment in those vast territories. We deprived her of part of her home provinces, some of which she had possessed for over 200 years. We took her great fleet away from her. We reduced her army of millions to 100,000 men. We dismantled her fortresses and we deprived her of artillery, tanks, airplanes, broke up all the machinery she possessed for re-equipping herself."

It is no part of our Socialist work to shed tears over the demilitarising of Germany or any other capitalist state. But as we look back from the time of the termination of the last war, up to date, we are forced to observe the economic and political consequences which called forth the author of *Mein Kampf* and his gang as the heads of a great State. Hardly had the Versailles Treaty been signed than the then German Government began to plot and scheme to defeat it. Hemmed in as Germany was by strong powers like England and France, there is little cause for surprise that, to quote Mr Lloyd George again: "When communities are deprived of the protection of law by selfish and unscrupulous interests they generally find refuge in taking the law into their own hands."

That the thrusting of the Versailles Treaty upon Germany was in principle no worse than the German or Prussian Treaty imposed upon France in 1871, than that imposed upon Roumania at Bucharest, or that on Russia at Brest-Litovsk, is but begging the question. The real point is that capitalist treaty-making is not only no safeguard against wars, but is a sort of storehouse for their recurrence. And so is Europe, perhaps the whole world, once more on the verge of a gigantic slaughter, blinding and maiming; the approximate end to the whole butchery and destruction being beyond reasonable forecast.

The British Government again drags the workers of this country and its colonies into the battlefields on the plea of resisting aggression, as it did in the last 'war to end war'. This time we are to smash Hitlerism, as we were in 1914 incited to destroy the Kaiser and his military caste.

But it is not the Nazi form of government as such that the British ruling class seeks to end, but the policy of Hitler's regime in aiming at the interests of those who own and control the British Empire. Hitler and his murderous thugs might have raped and persecuted, imprisoned and tortured indefinitely, without as much as a stir from the 'Mother of Parliaments'. The sacking and slaughter of Abyssinia, the overrunning of Austria and Czechoslovakia, were as much undisputed acts of aggression as that of Poland, but they evoked the British Government to acts of *accommodation* rather than conflict. Not until it was certain that Hitler had designs on the dismemberment of the British Empire were the forces of slaughter released by Great Britain and her ally, France.

If the present war is allowed to run its course until one or other of the combatants is crushed, are we likely to witness, if we are still alive, the downfall of the Nazi form of government in Germany, the restoration of some form of democratic social life in Germany, and the maintenance of what democratic means of expression remain in Europe today? If Chamberlain, Daladier and Company are the spokesmen in setting the seal of defeat on Germany, will they invite the 'leaders' of the working class movement to secure that the German workers be permitted to voice their political and social views, whatever they may be? We know from experience they will do nothing of the kind; it is not a matter in which they are the least bit interested. Therefore, the backing of the 'Labour Movement' given to the British and French governments is preposterous.

The working class movement of Europe, even that part of it which claims the war to be one of Democracy *versus* Nazi Dictatorship, is no more likely to be consulted at the 'funeral' of Hitler than they will be granted their emancipation from wage-slavery by the international capitalist class. The real issue before the working class of the world is one of ending its exploitation and all that such entails.

The present war is most likely to bring in its trail, unless it is stopped by working class action meanwhile, greater misery than the last war, greater and more intensified exploitation, less *freedom* to achieve our purpose than we now possess, whichever side is triumphant in the struggle.

The German workers must, it seems, be the means of effecting the downfall of the Nazi system of government.

For ourselves we, as Socialists, would render them any service which would assist in their accomplishing the overthrow of their despotic ruling gang, if only to gain for them the immediate means of being able to give expression to their social and political aspirations without fear of being murdered or placed in a concentration camp.

Until the working class movement in Germany or anywhere else can gain the means of emerging from underground into the daylight, their chances of finally freeing themselves from capitalism through Socialism are well-nigh hopeless. To assist in the war against Germany is not the way by which this can be accomplished, we should be slaughtering the very people we desire to *liberate* from the Nazi yoke. Moreover, our action then would assist Hitler and Co. to bury still deeper the opposition to his rule. He would point to the unanimity of feeling here to secure it in Germany. We find no valid reason for the support of this war, as we found none for the last war, which left us, of the Socialist Party, more isolated in our opposition than we are today.

When the war of 1914-1918 was at its worst, when the bloodbath was full to overflowing, we said then: "Every Socialist must, therefore, wish to see peace established at once to save further maiming and slaughter of our fellow-workers. All those who, on any pretext, or for any supposed reason, wish the war to continue, at once stamp themselves as anti-Socialist, anti-working class, and pro-capitalist" (*Socialist Standard*, July 1917).

Quite frankly, facing the matter realistically, we see no immediate prospect of the workers becoming Socialists in sufficient numbers to come to real grips with the capitalist class in a challenge to the latter's political power. The talk of a Socialist peace, although supremely desirable and necessary, would therefore seem to be Utopian at the moment. If the working class becomes alive to the realities of the war issue they will see that their first task is to stop the blood-letting, and finally to gain political power for themselves and establish Socialism throughout the world and thus end all wars.

(February 1940)

In the Front Line

Tucked securely into the valleys that cut a deep line between the range of mountains lying in —— , somewhere in England, are a number of small towns and villages once included among the distressed or 'special' areas.

Until three years ago, industrial activity around this neighbourhood was practically at a standstill and it was the exception rather than the rule to find a working class household whose adult males were not on the dole.

The standard of living, poor at the best of times, had sunk to an incredibly low level. Tuberculosis and kindred ailments, directly due to malnutrition, were accepted as an inevitable scourge alongside all the other evils commonly associated with extreme poverty.

But about three years ago the stillness of the surrounding countryside was broken by the clanging sound of hammer upon steel, the staccato of the mechanical drill – builders at work.

The men idling at the street corners sniffed the air like dogs picking up a fresh scent – they smelled work.

And they were right. Far-seeing industrialists, certain of the war to come, were looking for places to build factories to accommodate the needs of capitalism at war, districts comparatively safe from air attacks – not to forget a plentiful supply of cheap labour close at hand. And here they believed they had found both.

Happy mortals, to be able to look the landlord straight in the eye when the grim individual calls for rent on Monday morning, not to slouch into the grocery shop with that hangdog look in your face, because last week's account was still unpaid; no wonder the people's misgivings at the unmistakable signs of coming war – the coat of camouflage paint upon the factory roofs and walls – were stilled and forgotten in the growing realisation that at last work had come again to the idle valley.

The factories have now been in full swing for a considerable time. Textiles, aircraft, paint, sweets – an odd and varying assortment of commodities are being turned out in huge quantities every day. The idlers have gone from the streets, a solitary clerk does duty at the once crowded local labour exchange.

True, the men are not getting the wages they hoped for, but they do not grumble much, for spells of unemployment lasting for ten years or more are not conducive to working class militancy.

Besides, the womenfolk, particularly the younger section, are all working and contributing to the household exchequer.

On Saturdays the shopping centres are literally mobbed with working people. They are charged high prices for shoddy goods, the shops always getting a fat picking out of an industrial boom.

After that there is very little left in the wage packet when the rent and other weekly payments are put by.

The working class table is still short of many of the vital necessities of life. Fresh milk is rare, instead, tins of condensed milk, which are cheaper and save the use of sugar, expensive at present, do duty.

The price of good fruit is prohibitive for the same reason, meat and eggs make only rare appearances.

Because of the terrific strain and worry of work under war conditions, both men and women are heavy smokers, and the outlay on the now so expensive cigarettes makes another deep hole in working class pockets. Still – there's work again on Monday and another wage packet at the end of the week.

Let me take you into one of these factories so that you can see for yourself how working class brawn and brains are swelling Britain's war efforts and the profits of the British capitalist class.

This one is engaged on the manufacture of textiles, and the first thing that amazes you is the overwhelming preponderance of young persons, mostly girls. Large numbers of them are between the ages of fourteen and sixteen and they look what they are – children. They work a forty eight hour week for mere pittances, sums as low as eight and sixpence per week.

Inevitably, with so much unskilled labour, much of the finished material is faulty and then the stern-faced supervisors, all of them elderly and unprepossessing spinsters who stand most of the day with folded arms watching the youngsters like hawks, rate the unfortunate miscreant soundly.

The construction and machinery are of the most modern type, and it seems anomalous for such frail, young bodies to be pitted against the giant structure and faultless precision of the machine tool they operate. Accidents occur and young fingers and hands are badly smashed or ripped, but for the most part young and flexible hands and brains quickly gain control over the intricate mechanism.

The walls are liberally adorned with posters bearing slogans such as 'Go To It', 'Keep At It', and so on, *ad nauseam*; even the lavatories are not immune from these harrying catch-cries.

Evidently the owners are deeply patriotic, and so they should be, for is not their whole existence bound up with the preservation of the British Empire? In this particular instance the factory is engaged on Government contracts, and the young sons of the proprietor have been excused from military service on the grounds that they are 'directors' of work of National importance. What their directing consists of is not quite clear; they live some hundreds of miles away and are only seen when they arrive by car to make a brief tour of inspection.

This takes place once a month and then they are shown around the place by the manager in a manner reminiscent of royalty.

In conformity with the truly enlightened outlook of the modern capitalist, the welfare side of the employees has not been forgotten. There is a canteen which serves badly cooked and microscopic midday meals for sixpence, and there is also a radio, for which all workers are docked a penny a week from their pay.

This instrument is in constant competition with the deafening roar of machinery, but somehow manages to make itself heard above the din now and again.

Modern tunes set everyone singing lustily in accompaniment, but at present everyone is earnestly concentrating on their particular task, whilst a deep, baritone voice is booming out a song about 'Ye Yeomen and Freemen of England', or words to that effect.

Air raid warnings are a frequent occurrence, but no one takes any notice of them, certainly not the management, who would not dream of stopping work for the duration of the 'Alerts'.

Indeed, it would be interesting to know why air raid warnings are sounded at all, since no provision for shelter has been made in the whole neighbourhood.

Nothing much has happened during the warnings – yet. If something did happen, well that would be 'hard lines', bound up with the risk of being in the front line – at the age of fifteen at eight and sixpence per week.

Then you would be informed in the usual BBC singsong that "there were a few casualties, some of which were fatal".

Overtime is compulsory for all the older employees, and the discipline that prevails is that of the barrack room.

If you show any independence of spirit at all and 'answer back' to the humiliating bark of the supervisors or managers you are discharged forthwith.

No concern in the district will entertain direct application for employment – these must be made through the local labour exchange, which transmits particulars of your last employment and reasons for leaving to your prospective employer should the latter require them. This should be sufficient to discourage any sort of defiance in a people already cowed by many years of hunger, and besides, there are always the schools, disgorging hundreds of boys and girls from time to time who can quickly be trained to perform all but the key operations essential to the smooth running of these highly rationalised productive machines.

There is constant pinching of precious minutes from the workers' mealtimes; these are already finely cut: three-quarters of an hour for dinner, and a quarter of an hour for tea in the afternoon. There is no break during the morning, when the workers, including the very youngest, have to slave four hours without a break. The manager and the forewomen, of course, are not included among the 'rabble' – they must have a 'snack' as a relief from their arduous task of watching others work.

Do not make the mistake of thinking that what I am describing are exceptional conditions laid down and carried out contrary to regulations imposed by law or frowned on by Trade Unions.

In fact, all the female employees at least are members of a Trade Union, although the men, to the best of my knowledge, are not allowed by the management to be organised in the same way. In any case, there is no shop steward, and the local Union official, who lives many miles away, is never seen.

And are not the signatures of our big Trade Union bosses on the Government posters, exhorting us to work faster, not to make any trouble, and, above all, DON'T STRIKE! So there is no help to be expected from that quarter.

Some of the older people who remember the last war and the terrific slump that followed are apprehensive. Sometimes, they cannot make up their minds whether they would like the war to end or not. They do not seem to believe the promises of 'a new world', 'a better heritage', and the rest. They are afraid that when the 'piping times of peace' return these factories will be dismantled and the human fodder cast adrift upon the streets and the dole.

And they may be right, unless ...

Perhaps this war will end as neither side has planned. Perhaps even workers as meek and humble as those about which I have been writing will assert themselves as HUMAN BEINGS and, joining hands with their fellows all over the globe, will put an end to this nightmare existence of poverty, tyranny and despair which the rule of capitalism has imposed upon the masses of workers.

Does that day seem far away to you? Then you do not realise the growing force for social change gathering within the present world catastrophe.

(November 1940)

Some Socialist Points on the Beveridge Report

Time does not allow a thorough examination of the Beveridge Report in this issue, but a few preliminary remarks may be made on aspects of particular interest to Socialists.

First we may ask why all this fuss about proposals which even *The Times* – not remarkable for its generosity towards social reforms – admits are "moderate enough to disarm any charge of indulgence" (*Times*, 2nd December). The spokesmen of capitalism are already preening themselves on the score that the Report shows what a generous and progressive country this is. They might pause to notice Beveridge's claim that everything he proposes could and should have been done decades ago. All that time they have been boasting of the numerous reform measures they have introduced, yet the sum total of them all is so niggardly and displeasing in the eyes of its beneficiaries, the workers, that the latter can be impressed by the seemingly important advance the Beveridge scheme represents by contrast with the evil condition of today.

Even so the scheme should be viewed in proper perspective. *The Times* reads into the Report the "confident assurance that the poor need not always be with us", but this is merely a misuse of terms, and one incidentally for which Beveridge appears not to be responsible. He talks all the time of abolishing 'want', by which he avowedly means something quite different from abolishing poverty. By want he means the condition into which the workers fall when their wages stop, not the condition in which they are always because they always are carrying the capitalist class on their backs. Beveridge is quite clear about the distinction and says so. Did he not make a statement on 1st December (reported in the BBC news broadcasts but apparently not in the Press) that it had always been his view that want could be abolished within the ranks of the wage-earners without any inroads into the wealth of the rich? He is saying in effect in his Report that want could be abolished without interfering with capitalism, but neither he nor the *Times* want to abolish poverty. But for the poverty of the poor there could be no riches for the rich – a state which he and they find quite acceptable.

The Report has had a good Press, and already it is claimed that the Liberals and half the Conservative Party view it with favour. A characteristic and intelligible capitalist comment was reported in the *Daily Worker* (3rd December 1942) from Captain Somerset de Chair, who is a Conservative MP. He is reported as follows: "I welcome it as a comprehensive plan to remove insecurity without resorting to the uncertain hazards of social reconstruction," he said. "This plan promises what we young Conservatives have always demanded – a square deal for the working man within the existing social and economic framework, instead of some utopia on the further side of an economic torrent."

The Report is mistakenly referred to as a measure of insurance for the workers against the evils of capitalism. It would be more accurate to see it as a measure of insurance for the capitalists against the (for them) desperate evil of working class discontent with capitalism. Better by far to give something away in time than to risk losing all.

The Report has been criticised by the Insurance Companies whose profits would be affected by the proposal to hand over their industrial assurance work to a Government Board. This was to be expected, but it gives rise to some interesting speculations. The Insurance Companies, with their enormous investments in all kinds of industrial and commercial enterprises, wield great influence, not excluding influence in Parliament and the Press. Fifteen or twenty years ago it was common in so-called Labour papers to see bitter attacks on the Prudential and other companies. What has happened to change all this, so that nowadays the clamour against them has almost disappeared? The *Daily Express* (28th November) has a curious little reference to this in an article on a book by the late Sir Arnold Wilson in which he attacked the insurance companies. According to the writer of the article, Sir Arnold was struck by the way in which the economists had ignored the problem presented by the "concentration of financial power in the hands of the companies." "The oracles," he found, "were strangely dumb ... He searched libraries. He found little. He consulted the experts. And chief among them was Sir William Beveridge, *who explained why the London School of Economics, on the grounds of expediency, had ignored the subject*" (*Daily Express*, 28th November. Italics ours.)

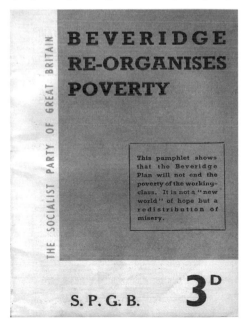

Sir William is, of course, no longer with the London School of Economics, and perhaps finds his hands less tied.

In one fundamental respect, the scheme is a gamble, and Socialists can be certain that the gamble will be a losing one, for it is based on the expectation that unemployment will be less than it was before. If this optimistic assumption proves wrong, then the whole of the financial provisions are undermined and either the benefits would have to be reduced, or the high contributions raised still more or a large further deficit made up from taxation. This optimism of Sir William Beveridge is too much for the City Editor of the *Times*. He points out (3rd

December) that Beveridge assumes that unemployment will not exceed an average of $8^1/2$% of the insured workers, but "only in one year, 1927, in the fourteen years before the war was the average below 10%; in 1932 it was over 22%. It is right to hope ... that unemployment can be reduced to below $8^1/2$% ... But it is clear that a corollary of the social security plan must be a plan for full and efficient employment. Without it the social budget will be thrown out of gear."

The Labour Party who gaily went into office in 1929 with a pledge to deal with unemployment and a hope that things "were on the up grade" should not need to be reminded that what happened to them (unemployment soon mounting to three millions) may well happen again even in the best of all possible capitalist worlds.

The Labour Party might also like to reflect on another incident in their experience. When the crisis occurred in 1931 it was a common theme with them that capitalism was for ever bankrupt and never again could there be any question of trying to make capitalism palatable to the workers by offering social reforms. Capitalism, they said, would never again be able to afford reforms. Socialists pointed out the absurdity of this belief that capitalism, choked with its own surplus products, could not afford to surrender some of them to alleviate the workers' miseries. What have the Labour Party to say now that they are hailing Beveridge and allowing themselves to be manoeuvred into defending his scheme?

One of the major purposes of the Report has already been served, its use as war propaganda. Both from the point of view of offering the workers at home some more or less concrete hope of benefits to come and from the point of view of offsetting Nazi propaganda for a new European Order the Report can be described as an instant success for the Government.

(December 1942)

The Black Hole of Calcutta

What might be termed the sequel to the historical incident we know by the above term has been, and is being written in the blood of thousands of starving, pestilence-stricken Indian workers and peasants of Bengal. Daily references in the newspapers to the famine in India have provided grim evidence of the ghastly scenes enacted on the streets of Calcutta by actors unable to choose the part they wish to play. Stories have been related of children being sold for a handful of rice, and of skeletons of men and women feeding on jungle roots and leaves. Figures of the death rate show it to have increased to nearly four times the normal average. The whole tragedy is graphically epitomised by the Calcutta *Statesman* which said: "Thousands of emaciated destitutes still roam the streets in the ceaseless quest for food, scouring dustbins and devouring rotten remains of castaway food and fruit. Rickety children clutching imploringly the tattered garments barely covering the bones of their mothers are seen in all quarters of the city" (Quoted in *Manchester Guardian Weekly*, 15th October 1943).

Famine has always been a factor to reckon with in the economy of India, and has usually meant suffering for large sections of the population. It is commonly understood that a famine means a shortage of food owing to the natural failure of crops, but what is not generally recognised is that the character of the famine, and the way in which it affects the people, varies with the type of society in which it occurs. To the middle of the nineteenth century famines in India were localized in the area in which there was a shortage of crop, and meant an appalling lack of food in that area and of employment. Even if one had money there was no food to be brought, and the general solution was to migrate to areas where food was available. From about 1850, however, capitalism, under the tutelage of the British, became superimposed on the old Indian feudal economy at an ever quickening rate, with an ever greater intensity.

With the spreading of capitalism the growth of industrialisation, the development of the plantation and factory system, the production of goods for sale came more and more into evidence. Concurrently with this development the means of transport and communication were vastly increased and extended. Hence, in the latter half of the nineteenth century, it became relatively easy to shift quantities of foodstuffs into famine-stricken areas, and a change in the general character of Indian famines took place. They now meant, not so much an appalling lack of food as high scarcity prices and lack of employment, and whilst the growth of the means of communication lessened the danger of local famines, it tended to widen the area where high prices would prevail.

Thus the famine, from being a calamity of the natural order, turned into a calamity of the social order, aggravating the sufferings inflicted on the poorer sections of the population, notably the peasants, the landless day-labourer, and the growing urban working class.

It is true that in the area most affected by the recent famine, Bengal, Bombay, and Madras, there has been some destruction of crops due to natural causes, but at the same time there have been good crops in other provinces. In the reports that have arrived in this country there is a general insistence that the catastrophe has not come about because of any basic natural shortage, but because such deficits in supply as did exist have been taken advantage of by hoarders and speculators. The loss of the Burma rice crop, excessive inflation, and general economic dislocation (all factors arising out of the war), and natural shortages in certain districts, all tended to encourage the farmers and merchants to hold on to their stocks in order to get still higher prices and greater profits when they did at last decide to sell.

This was the position as early as 15th January 1943, when in the *Manchester Guardian Weekly* it was reported that "price control has never been rigorously enforced, except against small retailers. The impression is widespread that there are considerable stocks which would be brought out if price control was removed and this would relieve the shortage until next harvest." The same issue of the paper also stated that black markets flourished everywhere.

After seven months had elapsed the same paper wrote as follows (13th August 1943): "The Government of India's Food Member did not deny last week the allegation that men in authority have obstructed the Government's measures to bring relief to the masses. The Food Secretary on Sunday admitted that Sind had made enormous profits through the sale of surplus wheat and rice. Lack of foresight, the toleration of profiteers, and the fear of alienating certain favoured sections like the landlords, have created the food crisis."

Whilst we learn on the one hand of the fear of alienating certain favoured sections of the property owning class, we learn that there was no such fear during the period of alienating those sections of the population with little or no property. Side by side with the blackest of black markets, dealing in the very lifeblood of the poverty-stricken masses, there were "long queues of hungry workers waiting all night outside Government controlled grain shops in places like Bombay" (*Manchester Guardian Weekly*, 15th January 1943).

Investigations conducted by Calcutta University have revealed that 50% of the families of destitutes have been broken up, and that 47% are landless labourers, 25% small cultivators, 6% town beggars, and the remainder unclassified.

Such evidence as this throws into bold relief the fact that it is the propertyless who suffer and die, whilst the propertied reap excess profits and get all they want in the black markets.

The Indian scene, in normal times, is a picture of a vast mass of humanity living in the grip of abysmal poverty. Utter destitution resulting in a prolonged death through starvation, or a quicker death through malnutritional diseases such as tuberculosis, cholera and typhoid, is the lot of Indian workers and peasants. What then must be their lot when the price of the food they require for a bare existence soars far and away above their means? What can they do but wait for death to claim them, their bony hands held out imploringly for food, on the pavements of the second largest and one of the "most prosperous" cities in the British Empire! In other parts of the same empire the granaries of Australia and Canada are full to overflowing with the wheat that would bring succour to those in need. The problem, however, according to Mr Amery (Secretary for India), speaking in the House of Commons, 12th October 1943, was "entirely one of shipping, and has to be judged in the light of all the other urgent needs of the Allied Nations." Yet the Allied Nations are producing ships faster than they have ever been produced before in the history of mankind, and the USA is able to boast of a production of 15,000 naval ships of all dimensions in the past three years.

Well might the reader at this point exclaim, 'This is madness!'

No, reader, this is not madness – simply another example of the ever present anarchy in CAPITALISM, the economic system of society that holds the world enslaved.

An economic system that is based on the ownership of the means of life by the few, and the exclusion of the means of life from the many. Only under capitalism is it possible for conditions to arise where hoarders, speculators, and black marketeers of every nationality can flourish on the one hand, and be the social complement of starvation, unemployment, squalor, disease and poverty on the other.

Only with the abolition of this private property basis of society and its replacement by the ownership of the means of wealth production and distribution by the whole of humanity, can humanity solve the evils with which it is confronted.

This is the job, the only worthwhile job, of the working class. Not only the working class of this country, but of the working class of the world acting in unison. No longer must they acquiesce in the retention of a system which condemns great numbers of men and women to exist like a seething mass of gentles beneath a rotten, stinking piece of meat. Just as the meat is a condition of existence of the gentles, so is capitalism a condition of existence of the working class. It must be removed, and with it will go all class divisions.

This can only be done by a working class conscious of the cause of its troubles, desirous of solving them, and with knowledge of the solution. Even in the case of the Indian working class the solution to their problems is the same as ours. It does not lie in the substitution of one kind of capitalism for another. It does not lie in the substitution of a native Indian master class in place of the British Raj; their fellow countrymen are among their most ruthless exploiters. In common with the rest of the workers of the world, their solution lies in the establishment of a system of society based upon the common ownership and democratic control of the means of life – the establishment of SOCIALISM. Along this road alone, however tiresome may be the journey and however many pitfalls may be on the way, lies the emancipation of all mankind without distinction of race or sex.

(December 1943)

Concerning 'A National Health Service'

The White Paper issued in February 1944 dilates on proposals for a National Health Service. This is the result of discussions with various bodies including the British Medical Association (which may be termed the doctors' trade union), the Royal Colleges, Voluntary and Municipal Hospital representatives. In the words of the report: "The Government ... want to ensure that in future every man and woman and child can rely on getting all the advice and treatment and care which they may need in matters of personal health; that what they get shall be the best medical and other facilities available; that their getting these shall not depend on whether they can pay for them, or on any other factor irrelevant to the real need – the real need being to bring the country's full resources to bear upon reducing ill-health and promoting good health in all its citizens."

As Socialists we are not impressed by this show of goodwill; we give due regard to the capitalist need for healthy workers, and to the date of publication – viz., during a period of something very like war weariness, when accounts of Jap atrocities are needed to pep up morale.

We will digress for a moment to examine the state of medicine at this time in relation to the working class.

Ideas regarding a State medical service for all, not just for insured workers as prevails at the present time, are by no means new, but in their previous forms they have met with opposition from both the British and American Medical Associations. In their organ, the *British Medical Journal*, the BMA have expressed fear that the present 'free' choice of doctor will cease. The freedom of the present choice will be apparent to most workers, but should any retain illusions, they may be quickly dispelled. A worker may not choose a Harley Street specialist, but most have a general practitioner engaged in panel practice, unless he is prepared to spend his meagre earnings on doctor's fees. The doctor chosen is usually the nearest, in order to save time. Frequently nothing is known of his or her qualifications, letters after the name conveying no more than would hieroglyphics. When the choice is made, unless the worker is extremely ill, he attends an overcrowded surgery, perhaps being allowed five minutes of the doctor's time. He may, however, not get this, for it has long been the custom for doctors with large panel practices to employ assistants – e.g. newly qualified doctors. The assistant sees the panel patients whilst the doctor attends his fee-paying patients. (This practice is in abeyance during war time, due to the calling up of young doctors, so the poor panel patient gets less time than ever.)

In these days of specialisation, the general practitioner cannot completely attend to all his patients' requirements. Equipment and the services of dispensers and secretaries are costly. The White Paper recognises this fact and proposes Health Centres in which a group of doctors could practise with staff and equipment provided. The private patients also suffer under the present system. Their own doctor may administer palliatives inserted of sending them to the appropriate specialist for radical treatment.

The BMA have also feared they may find their members working in the guise of civil servants subject to control, which they state would stifle initiative and responsibility towards those sacred trusts, their patients. The American counterpart went so far as to remove from membership any doctor taking part in salaried practice, until prevented from so doing by an order of the Supreme Court in 1942.

Much of the opposition to a National Health Service arises from the inability of doctors to regard themselves as members of the working class. They are, in their own opinion, a class apart, members of the highest profession, rendering selfless service to mankind. No doubt many start with the highest ideals, but few keep them. This is not intended to portray doctors as battening ghoulishly on the lay public, but like all others, they are caught in the cleft stick of capitalism. The doctor is an expensive product; he must keep up certain appearances, and bring up his children in like manner. To be successful he cannot escape the sordid struggle for life under capitalism. He must sell his labour power in order to live, as does his meanest panel patient. These facts are not readily appreciated by the BMA, who, however, by their resistance to salaried schemes, have compelled the doctor to sell in the open market.

Nevertheless, the views of the BMA have not been wholly representative of opinion here or in America. In a leading article, *The Lancet* (22nd January 1944), anticipating the proposals in the White Paper, commented on the advantages to the patient of co-operation between local authorities, hospitals and the doctor, now inadequate, and states that hitherto most attention has been paid to the convenience of the doctors concerned. Unpopularity of central control may be the reason for this outburst. "Enough of this bureaucratic planning; give me my own show and let me get on with it." The article continues: "The answer to him has already been given. 'The needs of the sick are endlessly variable; the resources of medicine are multifarious; and only a large adaptable, sensitive, smooth running organisation will fit one to the other in the largest number of cases'."

Similarly the attitude in the USA, where there is no National Health Insurance, is changing. Reviewing *Kaiser Wakes the Doctors*, by Paul De Kruif, New York (a work demonstrating the success of shipbuilder Kaiser's medical scheme for workers in the mushroom ship yards of the Pacific coast, employing 60 salaried doctors), *The Lancet* of February 19th, 1944, quotes De Kruif's confession. Hitherto, he had "remained content with official medical explanations that this prepaid medicine was unethical; 100,000 doctors could not be wrong." It now appears that they could. At the present state of development it is uneconomic for the doctors to sell their labour power in the open market, as the worker cannot afford to buy it, and his health suffers in consequence. The needs of wartime industry here and in the States require workers to receive expert medical attention in every sphere, in order to return to work rapidly and make the wheels of capitalism spin. Note the recent accent on 'rehabilitation'. In times of slump the breakdown of a few workers is immaterial when others can be drawn from the reserve army of the unemployed. The present arrangements, in which the general practitioner works alone, are not conducive to the production of efficient, healthy workers. 'Accident proneness' is inevitable in sub-healthy states. Also the fact that the worker's wife has no panel doctor has come to be realised as an anomaly overdue for remedy. As she must be a fee-paying patient, she often fails to seek necessary advice, and comes to accept ill-health as part of her life.

The widespread influence of the BMA compelled the Government to accept its offices in the recent discussions. The White Paper is throughout a sop to the BMA, reiterating again and again that "the patient should choose his own doctor". The suggested arrangements for the entire population to be covered by insurance has the advantage of simplicity, but not so the arrangement of general practitioners. The Health Centres proposed will be used by a group of doctors who will see their patients there instead of at their surgeries. A salary or equivalent will be paid to them but – and what a large 'but' it is – the doctor may still have private fee-paying patients. The report states, however, that no one must be given "reason to believe that he can obtain more skilled treatment by obtaining it privately than by seeking it within the new source."

Socialists may suppress a smile at so naive a hope. What reason is there to suppose that a doctor now giving greater attention to his private patients than his panel will not continue to do so under the new scheme? It is not hard to visualise a doctor seeing his erstwhile panel patients at the Health Centre, receiving his salary for so doing, and then rushing off to see his private patients. True, the better equipment provided at the Health Centre may even be an inducement to persons of means to attend, so that private practice declines and the doctor ceases to sell his labour power in the open market, but what then?

Will the doctor's salaried position enable him to see his true place in society? Time will show, but under neither this proposed scheme nor any other will the worker get the requisite attention. Under any scheme in capitalist society expenditure is resisted at every step, as has been the case with housing for the workers (not their masters), sanitation, education and the like. Even the Beveridge scheme for health insurance requires that large scale unemployment shall not obtain; such statements serve to demonstrate the hollowness of capitalistic schemes, for it is powerless to prevent unemployment, which is inherent in its constitution. Only under Socialism, where the wages system will no longer exist, and where the workers will enjoy the fruits of their labour under ideal conditions without exploitation, can doctors truly serve their fellow-workers, and a real health service for all be established.

(June 1944)

Hiroshima and After!

Another date has been added to history's gruesome chronology of horror. Hiroshima, August 5th 1945, marks the application of a new technique in the sordid science of slaughter. In one catastrophic flash a city has been destroyed and "all life seared to death". While the monument of dust still towered above the ruins, the news was released upon a world almost satiated with carnage.

Yet it is significant to observe that although the use of the atomic bomb hastened the end of the war in the East, the announcement was received with little popular enthusiasm.

Before 1939 it was comparatively easy for the ruling class to convince the workers of the need for a large navy, army, and air force. Armaments, they maintained would ward off would-be aggressors and thereby ensure peace. Their solicitude for our safety seemed almost genuine. Years of grim experience, however, have proved the Socialists' contention that armaments are no insurance against war. New methods of persuasion will be needed next time to herd the population into the future shoddy equivalents of Anderson shelters, particularly since we are told by the US War Department that "an atomic bomb could be made 1,000 times more powerful than the type used on Japan" (*Sunday Despatch*, 12th August 1945). There will be very few near miss stories!

The reaction of the military mind is summed up by General Ismay, who in 1941 stated on behalf of the Chiefs of Staff Committee, "although personally, I am quite content with the existing explosives, I feel we must not stand in the path of improvement" (*Times*, 7th August 1945).

Let there be no mistake! The disastrous effect of this latest device to uplift humanity will in no way prevent its use. In fact because of the power of destruction, it becomes obvious that the element of surprise will be a major advantage in war. It may well be that a matter of hours will decide which group of capitalists will emerge victorious from the next edition, which gang will be jet-propelled on the next Crooks Tour, to sit at the fleshpots of some future Potsdam Conference.

Unfortunately for the British and American capitalistic class it will be impossible to monopolise the development of nuclear power. Sir James Chadwick, chief scientific advisor to the British members of the Combined Allied Policy Committee in Washington, has admitted that any nation with reasonable industrial facilities could start now and produce an atom bomb in five years' time, without assistance from Britain and the USA. Its antecedents are the past ages of patient research. From the 1890s when the Curies conducted experiments in radio-activity, up to the recent perverted achievement, the efforts of such scientists as Professor Rutherford of Manchester, Niels Bohr of Copenhagen, Dr Lawrence of California University, Professor Joliot of France, and others in Germany, Japan, Russia and elsewhere, prove indisputably that in the modern world production is a social function. In brief, as reported by the US War Department the bomb was created "not by the devilish inspiration of some warped genius, but by the arduous labour of thousands of normal men and women" (*Sunday Despatch*, 12th August 1945), i.e. members of the working class.

Needless to remark the news has produced a spate of advice, comments, explanations, warnings, and prophecies from people qualified and otherwise. Among the latter, Mr G.B. Shaw, in the *Sunday Express*, 12th August 1945, unable to explain, yet urged to say something reverts to hollow flippancies, and reminiscences of childhood days. Dr Joad, emulating Churchill thanks God, "for one of the innumerable dispensations of Providence by which this country has been preserved", and asks querulously, "Will nobody stop these damned scientists, put them in a bag, and tie them up! Or into a lethal chamber?" (*Sunday Despatch*, 12th August 1945). Although goaded to repeat the question when we see such waste of print, or hear his brain storms distorting the ether waves, we know that the fault lies not with the scientists, but with the system of society which corrupts their discoveries.

General Fuller in the *Sunday Pictorial*, commenting on the cause of war, says "there are several ... but in the economic age in which we live, the one which seems to me to tower above all others, is the 'profit motive'." To socialists the profit motive is the only explanation of war in the modern world.

As long as Capitalism remains, there will be no slackening of research for even 'better and more beautiful' methods of destruction, no tightening of the purse-strings which have already disgorged £500,000,000. Meanwhile the producers of wealth will be sampling the elusive fruits of rationed victory amid Portal shanty towns and unemployment queues.

There is no need to enlarge on the physical results of atomic warfare. Combined with jet-propulsion, mass-murder is possible by remote control.

It is, however, relevant to examine a few of its effects on the current political fallacies of the defenders of 'private enterprise'.

The USA is now as vulnerable to attack as the rest of the world. Geographical situation offers no advantage, and in consequence the last crumbling bastion of isolationism is breached. This is clearly demonstrated by her policy of expansion especially in the Pacific.

All ideas of warfare are obsolete, or at least require drastic revision, and already, at the end of the worst war in history, the spectre of the next conflict haunts the celebrations of peace.

Sooner than we realize nuclear power may be harnessed to industry. In the inevitable scramble for production and profit gluts, slumps and unemployment figures will reach new levels and defy solution by the obsolete plans of the Beveridge type.

These are just a few of the problems of Capitalism: that Hydra-headed system which the Labour Party now administers in Great Britain; but will never control. Many supporters of the Labour Party are still deluded by the idea that Nationalisation is a major step in a policy of gradualism which will 'reform capitalism out of existence'. The sledgehammer blows of events will nail this tragic error!

Wars are inherent in the private property system itself, and are likely to wipe millions of workers out of existence, while the futile pinpricks of reform leave its structure untouched.

Who can now suggest that the policy of the Socialist Party of Great Britain, though correct in theory, is one for application only in some remote future? Who would question the practicability of our case?

There is no time for complacency! Let us face the fact that time is on our side only if we seize it by the forelock and use it to our advantage.

Socialism, the only solution to the problems which confront us, is the need not of the century, but of the hour!

Sympathisers, men and women of the working class, we urge you to join with us in the struggle for emancipation.

You have but two alternatives! Either the poverty, servitude and degradation of Capitalism, culminating in war, or Socialism in which the inventive genius of man will be used for the welfare of all society.

Your choice is as simple as it is vital! On it rests the future of humanity!

(October 1945)

THE POST-WAR YEARS

For many reasons, the post-war period from 1945 was an important time. It was a time when, after all the miseries of war, a great surge of hope was evident and people looked forward to a new and better world. Expectations were high. There was a determination that the pre-war world of poverty and privilege would not be allowed to return. In Britain, these hopes were placed in the Labour Party which against most forecasts in view of the popularity of Winston Churchill, the war leader, was swept to power with a massive parliamentary majority. It had campaigned on a programme of reform that included a National Health Service, large-scale nationalisation, and management of the economy. The promise was to curb class privilege, sustain economic expansion and rising living standards, to overcome poverty and unemployment and to create a new society.

The spirit of optimism was international. Also in 1945, delegations from most countries met in San Francisco to sign the United Nations Charter. This was more than an undertaking to settle disputes by peaceful means; it was hoped that "nations could plan together so that everyone would have a fair share of the good things of life."

At the time, as the articles in this section show, the members of the Socialist Party were not just sceptical; they were convinced that in the circumstances the popular will for change could not be realised. They understood the limitations of political action under the capitalist system and, in the pages of the *Socialist Standard*, set out the reasons why the policies of reformist governments were bound to fail. The entire period in the *Standard* was characterised by a number of insightful theoretical pieces on these lines, alongside topical commentaries and an increasing number of reviews, particularly book reviews. There was also a special 50th anniversary edition of the *Standard* to mark the Party's half century, filled with reflective pieces about the SPGB's history and analyses of the changing political climate since 1904.

The principal socialist criticism in this period was that, regardless of its intentions, the Labour government would be compelled to work within the economic forces of capitalism and that this would mean upholding the capitalist system and confrontation with the working class. Indeed, the Labour government was soon in conflict with many sections of the workforce including a most bitter dispute with dockers in 1948 in which the military were used against the strikers. Nationalisation was certainly no remedy for industrial strife, as the article from

1947 on the striking miners of Grimethorpe showed. Referring to the National Coal Board the *Standard* said, "the miners have indeed exchanged one hard master for another."

The Labour government had inherited a crippling war debt, mainly to America, that was known as the 'dollar gap'. The intention was to repay this debt through dollar earnings but with a downturn in the American economy there was a sharp fall in export earnings and a severe balance of payments crisis. In September 1949, the pound was devalued and the government introduced 'austerity budgets'. Except on 'defence' its spending was slashed, social services were cut, the housing budget was reduced by £35million, prescription charges were introduced together with charges for spectacles and dentures. A wage freeze brought it into further confrontation with striking workers.

In retrospect, the main outcome of the 1945 Labour government was to steer British capitalism through its post-war difficulties and prepare the ground for its expansion. In doing this it absorbed the popular demand for social change that had brought it to office and made it politically sterile. By 1951, the electorate had gone back to the Tories and voted them back into power for the next thirteen years.

Capitalism in Britain then launched into the boom years of the 1950s. With relatively full employment, there was a massive extension of credit to workers through hire purchase and a strong demand for the household consumer goods that came on to the market. One of these was television which also brought a change in social habits. The preoccupation with consumer culture under the slogan 'live now, pay later', perhaps aided by disillusion with the Labour Party and a need for entertainment following the dreary years of the 1940s, resulted in deepening political apathy. As our article 'Jamaican Journeymen' shows, one noticeable and important change to city scenes was the appearance of many black faces with immigrants from Jamaica and other places.

But the system could not stave off further crises. In 1956, in collusion with France and Israel, Britain invaded the Suez Canal zone. The withdrawal of British troops and the resignation of Anthony Eden, Churchill's successor as Prime Minister, confirmed the emergence of the United States as the strongest Western power. At the same time Russian tanks invaded Hungary to quell a popular rebellion and a demand for democratic rights. This action and the execution of Imre Nagy destroyed any lingering illusions that state-capitalist Russia was anything other than an oppressive occupying power. One political cost was the damage done to the British Communist Party from which it never fully recovered.

Britain's Third Labour Government

"This time there can be no alibis."

For the third time Great Britain witnesses the spectacle of capitalism being administered by a Labour Government – though this time with a difference. The Labour Governments which entered office in January 1924 (for eleven months) and in June 1929 (for two years) had only minority representation in the House of Commons, and were dependent on the support of Members of Parliament belonging to the Liberal Party. This time the Liberal Party is almost wiped out (only twelve MPs in a House of 640), and the Labour Party has an overwhelming majority. There are 390 Labour MPs, and with the support of three ILP MPs, two Communists and some Independents and Liberals it can count on well over 400 votes as against about 210 Conservative MPs and others who will vote Conservative. As one of the Labour MPs writes: "Labour has no alibi left. If it fails to produce the goods – full employment, all-round national prosperity, international concord, health, homes and happiness for the whole people – it can fall back on no excuse" (Garry Allighan MP, *Daily Mail*, 31st July).

This time the Labour leaders have given away in advance the 'alibis' they used in 1931 when they pleaded that their failure, and the secession of their leaders to form a National Government, was the result of an 'economic blizzard' – the world industrial crisis – and of a 'Bankers' ramp'. They are going to nationalise the Bank of England and are naively confident that through a National Investment Board they can eliminate the normal capitalist trade cycle of expansion and depression. Nationalising the Bank merely means bringing this country into line with the rest of the capitalist world. As the *Manchester Guardian* points out "Great Britain is almost the only country in the world to have a privately owned central bank" (2nd August).

In an Election broadcast Mr Herbert Morrison, who occupies one of the most important Cabinet posts in the Labour Government, declared that the Employment Policy accepted by the late Government (in which, of course, the Labour Party was strongly represented), "has quite a fair chance of smoothing out booms and slumps. The idea is very simple. It is one of Labour's basic ideas. It is to make sure there is enough spending power to buy enough goods to keep everyone at work making them. The thing can be done. Whether it will be done depends on how firm a grip the Government intends to keep on the spending policies of the great private industries" (*Daily Herald*, 30th June 1945).

The experiment now being embarked upon is that of trying to run the capitalist system as if it were not a capitalist system. A Labour Government is going to try to straddle the class struggle and to represent at one and the same time the interests of the owning class, and of the class exploited by the owning class! Labour supporters expectantly and hopefully await the outcome. Socialists do not need to wait to prophesy failure.

After experiencing Labour attempts to run capitalism in Great Britain the workers will discover that Labour administrators cannot make capitalism function in any but the accustomed way.

The reasons for the Labour victory are many, though it must be admitted that hardly any observers expected the turnover of votes to be so large. Working class mistrust of the Tories, who had been dominant since 1931 in all the National Governments; the discontent and impatience with slow demobilisation of men in the Armed Forces, most of whom voted Labour; the usual desire of many electors to have a change; the feeling that the very acute housing shortage would best be tackled by a Labour Government – here are some of the factors.

How have the Capitalists taken the advent of 'Socialism'? Their attitude may, perhaps, be described as one of waiting on events, worried but not seriously alarmed. The avowedly Capitalist Press is disposed to assume that the cautious Labour leaders will prevent any very drastic demands of the rank and file from being pressed. This is illustrated by the attitude of the Conservative *Daily Mail* (2nd August), which urges the Labour Government to take steps to let the Press and public in the USA know that their "ludicrous and dangerous doubts and fears" of the Labour Government are needless and misplaced. The *Times* (30th July) accepts that the Labour Government may nationalise coal, at least part of the transport industry, and possibly electricity and gas supply, and is not greatly perturbed. It points out that "to bring public utilities under direct public control and possibly even outright public ownership is not wholly revolutionary; and coal is politically a special case." The *Times* goes on to plead that "with steel, or with manufacturing industries of any kind, the case is rather different", and takes comfort in the view that "the responsible leaders were more hesitant" than the rank and file on nationalisation, and that they may seek a further mandate from the electors before converting any *manufacturing* industry into a State monopoly.

The Liberal *Manchester Guardian* (27th July) declared that "Banking opinion expects the Bank of England to be 'nationalised' but does not turn a hair at the thought." Mr Herbert Morrison recalled during the Election campaign (*Daily Express*, 18th June), that in 1932 the Tory Lord Beaverbrook was advocating nationalisation of the Bank of England in his Daily Express, and likewise it was Mr Morrison who stated in a speech on 11th February 1944 "that more Socialism" (meaning State Capitalism) "was done by the Conservative Party, which opposed it, than by the Labour Party which was in favour of it" (*Times*, 12th February 1944). Mr Morrison had in mind, of course, the nationalisation of Telegraphs and Telephones and setting up of Public Utility Boards (which are the model the Labour Party will follow in its nationalisation schemes) such as the Metropolitan Water Board, the British Broadcasting Corporation and the London Passenger Transport Board. The last named was initiated by Mr Morrison and completed by the succeeding Tory Government.

A factor of importance from the capitalist standpoint is that the Labour Party is wholly committed when taking over industries to do so "on a basis of fair compensation" (*Let Us Face the Future*, Labour Party, 1945, page 7). Some capitalists – those in declining industries – can welcome a change which guarantees their investments against further depreciation since they may receive Bonds with a Government guarantee in place of shares dependent on the ups and downs of fortune of a private company; which recalls a curious comment made by the *Times* (19th September 1942), in an article which urged its readers that "we must beware of the people who advocate Socialism in order to make the world safe for capitalists".

Doubtless the Labour Government will do away with the restrictive clauses on trade unions introduced by the Tories in their Trade Union Act of 1927. This in itself may have little direct effect in the direction of encouraging strikes, but it is certain that the rule of the Labour Government will be accompanied by many and large industrial disputes. A Tory Government at this time would be faced with much industrial unrest, but with a Labour Government there is no doubt that the trade unions will feel encouraged to make large demands for higher wages and shorter hours. This was doubtless foreseen by Mr Ernest Bevin, Minister of Labour in the Churchill Government, who has now become Foreign Secretary instead. The *Daily Express* (28th July), published the following report from Stockholm of a statement made some time ago to a Swedish trade unionist. Mr Bevin is reported to have doubted a Labour Victory and to have said "Even if we win we shall have hard times before us. To convert industry to peace production with lower wages as a result will be an enormous problem." Like other governments in this dilemma the Labour Government may be tempted to make the adjustment by allowing prices to rise instead of lowering wages.

In one field the Labour Government will be tackling a problem that many leading capitalists and capitalist politicians are agreed has to be tackled, in order to prevent the interests of the whole capitalist class from being damaged, that is the problem of monopolies. Here the language of the Tory *Times* and of Mr Churchill in his calmer pre-election frame of mind, is identical with the views advocated by Mr Herbert Morrison in a series of speeches in recent years. Mr Churchill in a broadcast in 1943 said: "There is a broadening field for State ownership and enterprise, especially in relation to monopolies of all kinds (*Manchester Guardian*, 5th Apri 1943). And the *Times* put its view in words every one of which could have been lifted from one of Mr Morrison's speeches: "It is a sound principle that, whenever competition is ousted by monopoly, the monopoly must come under Government control – though certainly not under Government management – either through a public utility corporation or by other means appropriate to the differing circumstances of different businesses" (*Times* Editorial, 19th September 1942).

On Foreign Affairs Mr Bevin hastened to declare "British foreign policy will not be altered in any way under the Labour Government" (*Evening News*, 26th July). In this sphere and in handling India, Egypt, Palestine, etc., the Labour Government will be faced with many knotty problems, not of their own making or to any extent under their control, but arising inevitably out of the normal trade rivalry between the Powers. Here in a most glaring form is demonstrated the childishness of the Labour Party's belief that Labour Governments, by exercising goodwill, can keep capitalism and yet suppress its tigerish propensities.

To conclude we may repeat the words published in the *Socialist Standard* in June 1929, when the last Labour Government entered office: "We deal elsewhere in this issue with the failure of Labour Government in Queensland. We prophesied that failure, and with absolute confidence we prophesy the similar failure of Labour Government here. No matter how able, how sincere, and how sympathetic the Labour men and women may be who undertake to administer Capitalism, Capitalism will bring their undertaking to disaster. As in Queensland, those who administer Capitalism will find themselves, sooner or later, brought into conflict with the working class. Like their Australian colleagues, the Labour Party here will find themselves in a cleft stick. Having no mandate to replace Capitalism by Socialism, they have pledged themselves to solve problems which cannot be solved except by doing the one thing for which they have no mandate."

There is no need to add anything to that. It still stands, as those who have voted Labour will discover.

(September 1945)

Lord Keynes – Economist of Capitalism in Decline

In the sickness of its declining years capitalism is being nursed by the Labour Party. Lord Keynes, who died on 21st April, was the doctor who prescribed the treatment. His theories, on which rest the belief in the possibility of 'full employment' under capitalism, have come to be widely accepted not because of intrinsic merit or originality, but because capitalists and the Labour politicians alike have dire need of a panacea that will, they hope, make capitalism work or at least persuade workers that it will. Faced with mounting unemployment and the political discontent that it causes, many Tory and Liberal politicians had lost confidence in their ability to save capitalism. Lord Keynes promised them another lease of life. The Labour Party, new to power, never had much confidence in its own ability, and the 'economic blizzard' of 1931 that wrecked the Labour Government destroyed even what it had; so Keynes was their hope, too.

He believed that investment and price trends could be made subject to governmental control and thereby booms and slumps could be ironed out and approximately full employment secured. His views found expression in the National Government's *White Paper on Unemployment Policy* (1944), in which the Government accepted "as one of their primary aims and responsibilities the maintenance of a high and stable level of employment after the war." The Labour Government has endorsed this White Paper. Keynes directly influenced the Liberal and Labour programmes.

"It was mainly through his personal influence," says the *Times* (22nd April), "that the Liberal Party adopted as their platform in the election of 1929 the proposal to conquer unemployment by a policy of public works and monetary expansion". The section of the Labour Party that opposed the MacDonald-Snowden economy cuts in 1931 quoted Keynes in support of their view. The Labour Party's report on 'Full Employment and Financial Policy' (1944) largely rests on Keynes's theories. It declares that "the best cure for bad trade is to increase purchasing power and to speed up development." It looks to loans, "compulsory if necessary," from the Banks to "help the Chancellor to find the purchasing power required for full employment ... If bad trade and general unemployment threaten, this means that total purchasing power is falling too low ... We should give the people more money, and not less, to spend."

Socialists have no hesitation in saying that if the Labour Government attempts anything of the kind – it may, of course, get cold feet and scurry to the safety of 'orthodox' financial policies, as did Snowden and MacDonald – it will not succeed in avoiding unemployment and crises. Capitalism depends for its relatively smooth functioning on the capitalists' confidence in their prospect of selling their goods at a profit. By the time that bad trade threatens the capitalists will already be apprehensive and the proposed government policy would sap their confidence still more. It is one thing to propose to increase the workers' purchasing power but the capitalists (including the Government itself in State industries) are at all times forced by competition to seek to reduce the purchasing power of the working class in relation to the mass of goods produced for the market. This they do, if not directly, by wage cuts, then indirectly by installing labour-displacing machinery to increase output and lower costs of production.

Always the workers can buy only part of the commodities they produce (but which belong to the owners of the means of production), the part represented by their wages. Keynes and the Labour Party ignored these basic facts of private ownership and the wages system and looked to financial schemes to relieve the disequilibrium when, periodically, it had produced a crisis of bad trade and unemployment. Events will show that unemployment cannot be abolished under capitalism, even though its growth may for a time be masked by war, war preparations and totalitarian controls.

The extent and nature of the dependence of capitalists and the Labour Party on Keynes's theories was shown by the estimates of his work published by the *Herald* and the *Times* on 22nd April. The *Herald*, under the heading 'The Great Lord Keynes', by a Labour MP, Mr Evan Durbin, said that Keynes "more than anyone else ... bridged the gap between Liberalism and Socialism." The *Times* developed the same idea at length: "The Keynesian approach offered a bridge between the academic economists on the side and 'the brave army of heretics' Mandeville, Malthus, Marx, Gesell and Hobson (to name only a few) on the other. This may yet prove to have been Lord Keynes's most valuable achievement."

Marx is here put in curious company, but the *Times'* inclusion of him had a reason. The *Times* thinks that Keynes had found the way to cure unemployment and thus save capitalism from the challenge of Socialists. It quotes him as defending his policy of full employment through State control of investment "both as the only practicable means of avoiding the destruction of existing economic forms in their entirety and as the condition for the successful functioning of individual initiative."

The *Times* went on to claim that Keynes had shown how to bring about reconciliation between the orthodox political parties and the "growing army of deeply discontented reformers and revolutionaries." The claim is certainly true of the Labour Party, but woe betide that Party when Keynes's full employment policy fails them and the bridge he built collapses. Let it therefore be clearly understood that neither Keynes nor anyone else has reconciled the Socialist demand for the abolition of capitalism with the despairing attempt to make the system tolerable by trying to cure unemployment within its framework.

(June 1946)

The Nationalisation of the Railways

Railway nationalisation has a long and varied history. In comparatively recent times it has occupied a prominent place in the Labour Party programmes, has been backed by railway unions, and has been made an urgent problem for Governments because of the rise of competing motor traffic. Yet the first Act of Parliament giving the British Government power to take over the railways was passed over 100 years ago, more than half a century before the petrol motor was invented or the Labour Party was born. The Railway Regulation Act was passed in 1844 under Sir Robert Peel's Conservative Government and was introduced into the House of Commons by Gladstone, at that time a Conservative Free Trader and President of the Board of Trade. The immediate purpose of the Act was to force the railways to reduce charges in the interests of the whole body of capitalist manufacturers and traders, by holding over their heads the threat of nationalisation. The power was never used, but the threat remained a useful weapon. It is an odd commentary on the broad continuity of policy under different governments that if the compensation terms of that Act had been applied before the recent War (25 times the annual profits based on a three-year average) the compensation would have been very near to the £900 millions that the Labour Government now offers. (If applied to the past three years when traffic and revenue were swollen by abnormal war conditions, the compensation would have been more.)

The Labour Government's Transport Bill provides for the nationalisation of Railways, Road Haulage (except short-distance local carriers), Canals and Buses and Trams. London Passenger Transport Board will be included in the scheme, and power will be given to take over harbours. The present owners will be bought out. The whole organisation, employing nearly 1,000,000 workers will be managed by Boards set up by the Government. When the Bill becomes law British capitalism will have entered on a new stage in the organisation and control of inland transport, nearly a century after railway nationalisation began in some European countries. In Britain it has been a story of continuous conflict, between the sectional groups of capitalists who owned the various means of transport and the whole body of capitalists who depended on them. The former were out to get maximum profits; the latter wanted cheap and efficient service. The owners of the transport services also competed with each other. Proprietors of horse-drawn coaches on the eighteenth and early nineteenth century Turnpike roads were at war with the Turnpike Trusts over the tolls the latter charged for passage on the roads. With the first canal in 1761 an era of competition began between road and canal; followed after 1825 by the entry of a new competitor, the railways. The manufacturers needed the railways, but the canal and road vehicle proprietors used every effort in Parliament to protect their own investments by preventing the railways from being built. In due course the railways triumphed, then fought each other for traffic, then went in for amalgamation to protect themselves against wasteful competition.

At this stage a long battle was waged by traders to get the State to exercise more and more control over railway fares and charges. In the present century the petrol motor brought the roads back into the picture and it was now the turn of the railways to use their influence in Parliament against their road rivals. Already before 1914, many observers had become convinced that British capitalists' problem of underselling the new great trading powers, Germany, America, Japan, etc., in the markets of the world required unification of inland transport with State ownership, or at least close State control, so that the whole body of manufacturers would get cheaper transport for their goods. Their chief argument was that national unification would eliminate wasteful competition and overlapping, and permit charges to be reduced. Supporters of the movement for nationalisation were the Fabian, Mr Emil Davies, the Liberal, Sir Leo Chiozza Money, and other Liberal and Labour politicians, as well as manufacturers and traders. It was, however, road competition that gave the movement new life, and in 1919 the Tory-Liberal

Coalition Government declared its intention of nationalising, though it then drew back and contented itself with the compulsory amalgamation of the numerous large and small railways into the four existing companies.

It was Mr Lloyd George who, in March 1918, told a TUC deputation on nationalisation of railways and canals that "he was in complete sympathy with the general character of the proposals put forward"; and Mr Churchill, who said at Dundee, 4th December 1918, "that the Government policy was the nationalisation of the railways" (*Times*, 5th December 1918). It has remained for the Labour Government to complete what the Coalition Government in 1918 hesitated to do. Truly, as the *Daily Herald* remarks (19th November 1946): "the co-ordination of transport has been advocated by people who are far from Socialist in outlook."

The reactions of the capitalists to the present Bill reflect their various sectional interests. The *Manchester Guardian* and the *Times* are much concerned with the new organisation that is to be set up, wanting to be satisfied that it will provide cheap and efficient transportation.

While most newspapers maintain that the compensation terms are harsh, one exception is the Beaverbrook *Evening Standard* (19th November 1946), which suggests that the shareholders have little to complain about and that it is the "taxpayer" to whom the deal "by no means represents a bargain".

The *Economist* (7th December 1946) takes a cautious view. It starts off from the proposition that the railways and the road transport industry together are much more than is needed to carry the traffic. In fact, as the recent war showed, the railway system "is still about large enough to carry the whole burden". Consequently it would be possible to divide the traffic between railways and road transport in such a way that each handled the kind of traffic it could deal with most efficiently and most cheaply. The railways could handle long-distance traffic and the road industry could act as 'feeder' to the railways. The important point to notice is that this unification would enable both industries to dispense with a great deal of their present equipment (including railway branch lines) and reduce the number of workers employed, these economies being the chief object aimed at." Why the *Economist* hesitates about endorsing nationalisation is that it considers further inquiry is necessary to make sure that these economies can actually be achieved and that the structure proposed in the Bill is likely to produce them.

The Liberal Party issued a statement supporting the nationalisation of the railways (as it had also done at the General election, 1945), but opposing nationalisation of the general road transport industry. The Liberal view is that nationalisation will only give 'cheapness and efficiency' if competition is retained. In their view there should be nationalisation of the railways, canals and docks, and also of the road transport services owned by the railways, but the rest of road transport should be left to compete with the nationalised concern. The Liberal Party also considers that the compensation arrangements are unsatisfactory

(*Manchester Guardian*, 11th December 1946).

Naturally the shareholders clamour for higher compensation. Their special grievance is that, unlike the Bank of England shareholders, they are not being guaranteed the same income as they were getting during or before the war. In effect, they are to receive a State-guaranteed income of about £22,500,000 a year in place of a larger but uncertain sum they received as shareholders in concerns the profitability of which had been rendered precarious by road competition. How the shareholders must regret not having jumped at Nationalisation on the much better terms they would have got in 1919, when profits and share values were higher!

So much for the shareholders. What of the workers? The workers merely change one employer for another; little else is changed, for the State undertaking, as the *Daily Herald* specially emphasises (19th November 1946), has got to pay its way. The *Evening Standard* remarks that nationalisation cannot bring any possible benefit to the railway worker "for him it can mean neither higher wages nor shorter hours" (19th November 1946). And the *Observer*, in like vein, says, "It ... leaves the transport workers and the consumers to wonder what difference it can make to them except for the worse" (1st December 1946). The sudden solicitude of these two journals for the worker is naturally suspect, but 'Critic' writing in the Labour *New Statesman* (30th November 1946), also confesses that "nationalisation of the railways ... really doesn't much matter to anyone except the shareholders, who seem likely to make an uncommonly good thing out of it." This deserves notice, coming as it does from a year-long supporter of nationalisation.

Another journal which has had a sudden flash of enlightenment is the *News Chronicle*. Writing on the trade union 'closed shop', and the danger it involves that if for any reason a man forfeits his union membership "he becomes an economic outlaw and may be unable to get a job at all in his trade," the *News Chronicle* (21st November 1946) goes on to discover that "an even worse danger threatens in a society which is moving steadily towards ever wider nationalisation", the danger that a worker will have to belong to one "monopoly union", that union tending more and more to co-operate with the employer – the State – rather than represent the interests of the men. It will no doubt surprise the *News Chronicle* to be told that the Socialist Party of Great Britain at its formation 42 years ago was pointing out to the workers that nationalisation of an industry would put the worker even more at the mercy of the employer, the State. With competing concerns a worker sacked from one may seek employment in another, but the worker who earns the displeasure of the State monopoly and loses his job is effectively barred from the whole industry.

The other problem affecting the workers is that of redundancy. Nationalisation, by eliminating overlapping will lead to the displacement of many workers, and even if some compensation is provided and they manage to get other jobs, it is bound to mean a worsened position for many of them. It was always the complaint of railwaymen, when the railways were being amalgamated, that a railwayman's specialised training is largely useless for other occupations. The advocates of nationalisation have not been blind to the certainty that it would mean the displacement of many workers: it has, in fact, been one of their main arguments in its favour that it would eliminate waste. Mr Emil Davies in the Fabian pamphlet *State Purchase of Railways* (1910, page 19), suggested that railway nationalisation ought therefore to be introduced gradually in order not to throw too many men out of work at once.

The Labour Government has kept its pledge to nationalise transport, but for the workers it is all sound and fury, signifying nothing. Nationalisation is State capitalism and leaves untouched the real problem of the working class of emancipating themselves from capitalist exploitation.

(January 1947)

The Grimethorpe Miners

For those who have eyes to see there are lots of valuable lessons to be learned from the strike of the Grimethorpe miners against the efforts of the National Coal Board and the Union to make them do more work. The mines were nationalised only on January 1st, 1947, but within a few months the determined resistance of a few hundred men backed by thousands of other Yorkshire miners who struck in sympathy, showed the hollowness of the claim that Nationalisation and Labour Government can solve the problems of the workers. When Nationalisation took place Labour Party supporters welcomed it as a new era of industrial peace and the death of private profit, but socialists warned the workers not to be deceived into thinking that wage-slavery in the mines would be altered in any way. It has not taken long to reveal in the clearest fashion that the difference between private and state capitalism is not worth the workers' votes.

In May of this year the National Union of Mineworkers made an agreement with the National Coal Board for a changeover to a five-day week, without loss of pay, on the understanding that the Union would co-operate with the employers, the Coal Board, to "promote every possible and reasonable means of ensuring that the maximum output of coal is produced". The Union specifically pledged itself to co-operate with the management in persuading the workers to accept reassessments of work which would mean in many cases cutting down the number of men required for a particular piece of work. The Union undertook that it would "not countenance any restriction of effort by workmen resulting in failure to perform the work so assessed" (the full agreement was published in the *Ministry of Labour Gazette*, May, 1947).

The dangers of an agreement which binds the union to help the employers bring pressure on its own members are obvious. If the members of the NUM understood and approved of this the responsibility rests on them and not only on their Communist General Secretary and the other officials who signed the agreement. There is, however, much evidence to show that the members went into it without realising what they were accepting. This may be partly due to a temporary lack of contact between the members and the executive, resulting from the recent changeover from a federation of county associations to a centralised national union. In addition it is certainly due to the close tie-up between the national officials of the Union and the Government, which results in the former imagining that it is their job to give orders to their members rather than take them. The comment of the *Manchester Guardian* is to the point: "The Union leaders took a great risk in giving the Government the assurances they did without being sure that the miners were really willing to attend regularly and to do a full shift's work. It will not do to put the blame on a minority of 'bad' miners. A little slacking has to be taken into account in any calculation. Either the union officials misjudged the temper of their men or they did not do as much as they knew to be necessary to explain what the five-day week meant. This failure is not surprising. The NUM's constant concern with the handling of national policy in Downing Street and Whitehall has left its leaders with too little time for the details of affairs in the pits ... The Union will have to make a bold effort now to regain the full confidence of the miners. Like the National Coal Board it will not do that unless it can restore the close touch with local problems that has to some extent been lost by its conversion to a centralised organisation" (*Manchester Guardian*, 9th September 1947).

The amazing situation developed of the miners' officials denouncing their own members in terms that the former coal owners could not have exceeded for arrogance.

Mr Lawther, President of the Union, told the strikers they were "acting as criminals at this time of the nation's peril." He actually invited the Coal Board to prosecute: "Let them issue summonses against these men, no matter how many there may be. I would say that even though there were 100,000 on strike"(*Daily Mail*, 29th August 1947).

The Communist General Secretary, Mr Arthur Horner, was nearly as bad. In a statement to the Press (*Daily Herald*, 28th August 1947). Mr Horner said that the strikers "must be regarded as an alien force and treated as an enemy of the true interests of the majority of the miners of this country." What some of the miners think of these swollen-headed gentlemen may be judged by the words 'Burn Will Lawther' painted up at the entrance to the Grimethorpe colliery and by the comment made by a miner to a representative of the *Star* (9th September 1947): "Mr Horner seems to have forgotten that he is our servant and is acting as if he were our lord and master. We pay him to fight our battles and not to fight against us."

This miner was right and the sooner all workers take steps to bring their would-be dictators into line the better for the trade union movement.

One aspect of this must not be forgotten. Years ago the Communist Party popularised the slogan 'Watch Your Leaders'. If ever it was necessary to do so it certainly is now when Communists like Mr Horner have reached positions of eminence in the unions. A letter published by the *Daily Worker* (13th September 1947) pointed out how closely Horner's phrases resembled those for which the Communists used to denounce Mr J.H. Thomas. Not that the idea behind the slogan is a sound one. Against the Communist idea that what the workers need is 'better leaders' (who all turn out to be just like their predecessors) the Socialist urges the need to get rid of leadership.

The bitter experience of the Grimethorpe miners brings out clearly that nationalisation has changed nothing, except perhaps that it is harder for men to fight the National Coal Board than it was to fight the local mineowners. The following statement by a *Daily Herald* reporter was published on 30th August: "The real point of their grievance seems to be that in the general reorganisation of work underground involved by the change, men may be put on to other jobs at which they earn less money. A joint committee of miner's delegates and representatives of the Coal Board decided on the increased stint. The Grimethorpe men complain now that they had no representatives on this joint committee, and that the decision to increase the stint came as a bombshell ... They also complain that the divisional Coal Board officials are the same officials they had before the Government took over."

Those foolish optimists who fancied that the bitterness of the class struggle, if not the struggle itself, disappears when the employer is the State might note the remarks of a *Daily Mirror* representative. He wrote (6th September 1947): "How they hate the Divisional Officers of the Board! Big salaries, big cars, big offices, big titles – but they don't go down the mines."

One miner remarked "What do these ____ know about it? They couldn't get themselves enough coal to boil an egg."

The National Coal Board's attitude to the workers was expressed by one of the Board's spokesmen: "This is the test case of our authority. It is the first real test we have had, and at such an early stage in our career we cannot afford to have our prestige shaken by withdrawing the extra stint order" (*Evening Standard*, 4th September 1947).

The miners have indeed exchanged one hard master for another.

Another illusion cherished by Labourites is that when an industry is nationalised human aspects and the well-being of the workers no longer have to take second place to financial considerations. Since the mines have got to pay their way, including the necessity of meeting the cost of compensating the former owners, it is obvious that this cannot be. It remained for the Communist General Secretary of the Miners' Union to dot the i's and cross the t's of this fact. In his statement denouncing unofficial strikes and urging increased production he disclosed that at a secret session of miners' delegates in July he told them that "the Coal Board is at the present time losing money in a very serious fashion" (*Daily Herald*, 28th August 1947). There was a time when miners' officials would have told employers that the finance of the industry was their affair or would, as in 1926, have told the owners to go to the Conservative Government for a subsidy if they couldn't manage otherwise. Now, under a Labour Government, this Communist conveys the employing Board's lament to the workers, and instead of demanding a five-day week unconditionally urges the workers in effect to work harder to put the Board's finances on a profitable basis.

Whatever else may come out of the Grimethorpe strike it should teach some miners at least not to put their trust in Nationalisation, or in Labour administration of capitalism, or in leaders, Communists included.

(October 1947)

What is a Spiv?

In these days, when everybody is becoming Spiv-conscious, to ask what is a Spiv might seem to border on the fatuous. The purpose of this article will merely be to attempt to show that as a comprehensive definition of idler, drone and parasite the word Spiv leaves much to be desired.

Undoubtedly high-powered publicity has focussed the Spiv in constant if dubious limelight. For some he may yet come to acquire something of the symbolical status his more sinister counterpart, the American gangster, possesses for a generation of filmgoers.

Shortages, Rationing, The Black Market, as some of capitalism's present evils, have provided the conditions and opportunities for making England much more a land fit for Spivs to live in than it ever was: or likely to be it seems. For if the statements of certain Government spokesmen are to be taken at their face value, the Spiv is already on his way out. The Government in their efforts to ease the embarrassing, even if temporary, 'labour shortage' for contemporary capitalism, have ear-marked the Spiv as a source of potential labour-power. For this Government of planners the unplanned existence of the Spiv (unplanned that is for the existing requirements of Capitalism) becomes at least a little irksome.

The Spiv thus finds himself the subject of Governmental interest and the object of weighty political pronouncements. The word is officially recognised now and is considered normal to the vocabulary of Cabinet Ministers.

Even in the rarefied atmosphere of The House of Lords the word has made its debut. Lord Pakenham replying to Lord Amwell (formerly Mr Fred Montague, MP) on the direction of idleness, said, "Lord Amwell no doubt referred to the gentlemen known as spivs and drones. He agreed that however wide his definition we had no use for slackers at this time" (*Daily Telegraph*, 7th August 1947). No doubt an interpretation of slackers in the sense of "a wide definition" might have found room for a broader and perhaps more embarrassing inclusion than that permitted by the more restrictive nature of the word Spiv. Doubtless comprehensive definitions of terms, while admirable in theory, are not necessarily politic in practice.

Mr Attlee in the House of Commons the same day said, "We shall take all action open to us against the Spivs and other drones." Like Lord Pakenham Mr Attlee did not attempt a definition of terms. To have done so might have held awkward implications for the consideration of the members present. It might conceivably have led to the reading of 'The Riot Act' in the 'Mother of Parliaments'. A political flashback, nevertheless, recalls the coupling of drones with 'idle rich', in the classic days of Labour Party propaganda.

Nevertheless, Mr Shinwell speaking on the question of appointments to the Electricity Board, did say "We have no regard for those persons who perform no useful service at all ... They have been described as parasites, idlers, drones and rentiers." He added, "I don't intend to appoint them to any Board for which I am responsible" (*Daily Telegraph*, 24th June 1947). Whether this constitutes one of Mr Shinwell's noted lapses into indiscretion or a momentary glimpse of a more fundamental aspect of drones and parasites, we venture no opinion. No threat of work direction for these gentlemen, however, only non-appointment to various Boards.

Mr Isaacs, Minister of Labour, has said, that "Spivs are not so numerous as some people think." But at the trade union Conference he spoke of using full Governmental powers of direction in regard to them (*Daily Telegraph*, 3rd September 1947). He also told us that there are people who toil not and depend on the dividends earned by other workers. Had he said a wealthy section live on dividends and profits produced solely by the workers, he would have obtained full marks. Mr Isaacs is, however, not a person inclined to indiscretions.

Mr Tom Williams, MP, also spoke on direction of labour. He suggested if there are Spivs and drones or *anyone else* (italics ours) who refused to accept occupations, Unemployment Benefit should be stopped, adding that starving men and women into work is the highest penalty which ought to be tried in the first six or twelve months. (*Evening News*, 2nd September 1947). Coupon clippers, rentiers and other profit-participants are, however, debarred from drawing Unemployment Benefit. Moreover, as their level of incomes have no more relevance to 'The Poverty Line' than it has to 'The Plimsoll Line', Mr Williams' dire threats to people refusing direction of work will doubtless be met by them with calm and studied contempt.

The Spiv assumes then the role of the Labour Government's whipping boy. In the past the hard-faced business man and the treble-chinned plutocrat could be pilloried in the political stocks for Capitalism's shortcomings. Called upon to administer capitalism the Labour Party must perforce – vide Morrison – ask for their co-operation and even enthusiasm for 'Labour's' New Social Order. The Spiv will be pleased or perturbed to discover that it is he and not the private ownership of the means of wealth production which now constitutes the basic contradiction of capitalism.

The Spiv, however, is not merely a post-war product or the illegitimate child of a Labour Government. His prototype has for many decades alternatively flourished and decayed in capitalist society. He is generally a big city product. Born mostly in city slums or near slums he early experiences the drab life and sordid surroundings of those who, like himself, dwell there and toil for others. When the opportunity occurs for doing a bit on the side or fiddling, he seizes it as a more lucrative and more colourful occupation than the monotony of the daily grind. He is often, however, compelled to devote more time and energy to his peculiar calling than is customary for him to admit. Neither can the Spiv for the most part wholly emancipate himself from his working class status. 'In bad times' he is often reluctantly forced back into workshop or factory. For the Spiv, however, the age-long habit of work engrained in his fellow-toilers has been seriously undermined.

It has been said that the Spiv is at least a rebel. Some people have even sentimentalised him as a kind of revolt against the conditions imposed by the nature of capitalist exploitation. The Spiv's own anti-Government and anti-authoritarian outlook might seem to lend colour to this view. The Spiv, however, generally lacks the class loyalty and class sentiment that goes to the making of the class-conscious social revolutionary. The zeal and selfless devotion of the socialist, with his illimitable vista of a world based on production for use and the Brotherhood of Man, lights no fires in the mind and imagination of the Spiv. A good time and plenty of fun at the expense of others gravely limits his social horizon. Pleasure and 'the easy way' becomes basic to his existence. His mode of life constitutes a form of social parasitism which conflicts with the healthy social instincts of the vast majority of workers.

Also the Spiv evolves a standard of values that make for unconscious subservience to wealth and luxury. He thus tends to view present society as the natural order of things. He is consequently, however insignificant, a factor making for its perpetuation. At his best he is a politically unreliable element. At his worst he can become the strike-breaking instrument of the employing class or a tool for political reaction. In a socialist society where all able-bodied people will engage in productive activity and where the principle prevails – From each according to his ability, to each according to his need – the Spiv, as such, can have no place.

The social solidarity of a system such as the present one is cleft by its basic class antagonism. With the decay of its own outworn economic functions goes the decay of its outworn ethical creeds. The ideological veneer of its so-called public opinion merely hides the subversion of its traditional moral tenets to private forms of hypocrisy and cynicism. The wealth and luxury of present society then breeds its own type of social parasitism with its individual greed and unscrupulousness and its inevitable anti-social consequences. It is this which sets the individual against society and, as in the case of the Spiv, who attempts to imitate and emulate the ruling section, society against the individual. It is hardly to be wondered that the putrefying effects of such a social cesspool as Capitalism, fail to secure for the population at large a 100% immunity from contamination. Given capitalist society the Spiv must flourish like a green bay tree. Changing circumstances may decimate his ranks, but as an inevitable product of existing social conditions, he can hardly cease to exist.

True that the padded shoulders, the diagonally woven suit, the spear-pointed collar and dazzle tie have given the Spiv a sartorial significance and setting. If, however, for a double-breasted camel coat we substitute a faultlessly cut dress suit, the four bob jive for the dance floors of expensive clubs and exclusive hotels, the cheap billiard hall and garish saloon for Monte Carlo and other fashionable gambling resorts; the significance attached to the word Spiv becomes vague and even blurred.

It may be said that the Spiv, by devious methods of obtaining goods in short supply and selling at extortionate prices, is guilty of anti-social practices. Nevertheless he has the time-honoured methods of 'Rings', 'Market Corners' and their inevitable outcome, Trusts and Combines, to set him a precedent. Again, if he plies a doubtful trade, the long existence of nefarious company-promoters and Bucket Shop sponsors shows that in the matter of shady transactions the Spiv is no path-breaking pioneer. That the Spiv lives by the dubious exercise of his wits may also be true. Yet while a section of the community live on the unpaid labour of others well might the Spiv-kettle, in the matter of social parasitism, retort 'Why call me black, brother pot?'

Nevertheless the word is accepted now. From a slang term of doubtful pedigree it is on its way to an assured place in the English dictionary. Henceforth it will be synonymous with idler, drone and parasite. As a definition it will obscure rather than enlighten. Its emphasis will be on those who live by their wits and doubtful practices and not on those whose social parasitism is the outcome of the exploitation of the vast majority through the medium of class-ownership of the means of wealth production. All of which might suggest that there is a form of intellectual Spivery in addition to a social one. Concluding, may we repeat – What is a Spiv?

(October 1947)

Divide and Rule in India

The British invaders of India did not create Moslem-Hindu rivalry but they certainly made use of what they found. A divided India was a weak India. Although communal riots were troublesome for the Police and costly to traders it was possible for the alien rulers to view them somewhat philosophically. British capitalists were holding down India because they made big profits out of it and they no more thought of getting out of India because of Hindu-Moslem riots than they would have thought of giving up the profits of capitalism at home because of occasional conflicts with the workers.

The enthusiasts for Indian independence, particularly the members of the predominately Hindu Congress Party, built up their propaganda on a foundation provided by two charming myths. One was that if only British capitalism would get out Moslems, Hindus and the adherents of other religious systems would forget their traditional differences and live peaceably together. The other was that India is a 'nation', all its 400 million inhabitants yearning to be united under their own Indian government. Events during the past year have shattered both. British rule has ended but the largely Hindu India and the largely Moslem Pakistan refused to unite. They are two separate States facing each other in an atmosphere of tension bordering on war. Many tens of thousands of Moslems in India and Hindus in Pakistan have been brutally murdered in communal disturbances that dwarf anything that has happened for years. Hundreds of thousands of refugees now live in misery and fear.

It may be asked, in view of what has happened, have the leaders of the Indian parties failed in their object? Were they mistaken in their myths and have their eyes now been opened? By no means. Myths are made by leaders for the deception of their followers, not for the leaders' own consumption. The masses may now be suffering pangs of disillusionment, but not the leaders – except perhaps some curious figures like Gandhi and his circle.

Gandhi's despair was exposed in a speech he made late in September: "If there is no other way of securing justice from Pakistan and if Pakistan persistently refuses to see its proved error and continues to minimize it the Indian Union Government would have to go to war against it. As for myself, my way is different. I worship God which is Truth and non-violence. There was a time when India listened to me. Today I am a back number. I have no place in the new order where they want an army, a navy, and an air force and what not. I can never be a party to all that" (*Times*, 29th September 1947).

No, the propertied classes, the Princes, landowners, and thrusting capitalists with their expanding textile steel and engineering plants have not failed in their object, which was the same as that of the British capitalists in India, the object of preserving their privileged position as exploiters of the masses. Compared with a matter of such paramount importance words about religious and national union are of no account. It is possible some day that India and Pakistan, faced with a menacing threat from some more powerful state may unite for mutual protection, but at present they are rivals, quarrelling about the division of the arms of the former British-controlled army, and manoeuvring for control of areas rich in natural resources or of strategic importance.

So capitalism runs true to form whether under the banner of Christianity, Hinduism or Mohammedanism.

The conflict between Pakistan and India and their religions is being made to serve the interests of the respective ruling class groups just as British capitalism made use of communal rivalry. What could be more useful to the Pakistan ruling class in persuading peasants and workers to be content with their lot than to be able to distract their attention away from bread and butter questions towards the iniquities of Hindus and the greed and aggression of the Indian Government? And how convenient for the latter to be able to rally the masses to the need for patriotism and to defend the country against Pakistan cruelty and trouble making. Under cover of the need for a more national spirit the Congress Party in India decided early in the summer to form a rival trade union federation to combat the existing All-India Trade Union Congress. 'Communist control' was the excuse but the real object is certain to be to divide and weaken the organised workers.

The chief bone of contention between India and Pakistan is Kashmir, and an invasion by tribesmen is reported in Indian circles to have been promoted and helped by the Pakistan Government. Spokesmen of the two governments have much to say about the rights and wrongs of their respective claims to take over the territory. India, which at present holds it, promises a plebiscite; to which Pakistan writers retort that it will be faked. The real reason why the issue is so important that both sides are prepared to use military force has nothing to do with the wishes or welfare of the inhabitants. Strategically, from the standpoint of defending India (as well as Pakistan) from attack by other Powers through Central Asia it is a vital area. It has also great natural wealth in its vast forests and undeveloped coal deposits and other minerals, and its water-power may become the foundation of a great electrical development.

The ending of British rule in India was to be the opening of a new era. So said the supporters of Indian nationalism. Indeed it is. For long years capitalists and administrators plundered this conquered land in the haphazard way appropriate to the times and conditions.

Now the Indian workers and peasants are going to be exploited under home-born instead of alien masters. Their craft skill and muscular energies are going to serve in the modernisation and industrialisation of India and Pakistan, new Powers fighting for the markets of Asia. The workers there could learn much from the European countries and US, if only to avoid the costly mistakes made and still being made by the workers who first suffered from the capitalist industrial revolution that is now sweeping over Asia.

(December 1947)

Palestine and its Problems

A new state has come into existence in Palestine, the Jewish State of Israel, and it has come into existence against the intentions of the British Labour Government. This Government which, to paraphrase Mae West, has climbed the ladder of power wrong by wrong, took its stand on the Balfour Declaration of 1917 guaranteeing the Jews a national home in Palestine, but it resisted what was bound to be the inevitable consequence of the carrying out of that declaration, the demand for an independent Jewish State. In 1936 the Arab landowners inspired a revolt against the continued immigration of Jews into Palestine, foreseeing a threat to their interests in the existence of the highly industrial and commercial community that was growing up in their midst. Since then Britain, which had secured a mandate over Palestine in 1922, has been exercising a virtual reign of terror. A significant commentary on this is the following statement contained in the *News Chronicle* (28th April 1948): "Palestine Government has ended its censorship, and yesterday's papers published their first uncensored editions for 12 years – News Chronicle Correspondents, A.P., Reuter and B.U.P."

Within a few hours of the proclamation of the new Jewish State by its self-appointed Provisional Government, President Truman startled the world by publicly stating that America would recognise it. Commentators of Truman's action attributed it to a late attempt to capture the Jewish vote in the forthcoming presidential election. This is too thin. While in fact it may have this result there is far more behind the action than electioneering propaganda. Jews and Arabs in Palestine, like the Greeks, the Italians and the Jugo-slavs, are pawns in a much greater game which involves oil and the struggle between Russia and the Western Powers for economic domination. Why, for instance, has an allegedly democratic and anti-imperialist Labour Government supported the semi-feudal Arab landlords against the Jews, particularly when the leader of the Jewish nationalists, Ben-Gurion, has proclaimed himself a social democrat and labour leader in sympathy with the outlook of the British Labour Party?

The Labour Government's blundering methods in Palestine are the offspring of attempts to harmonise conflicting policies. For years anti-imperialism has been a plank in the Labour Party's programme and the withdrawal from India, Burma, and Egypt (except the canal zone) is held up as an example of the implementation of this policy. But the Labour Government is also committed to the safeguarding of the British capitalists' commercial and industrial interests; this dictates an opposite policy. Torn between the two they have failed to satisfactorily accomplish either, disappointing their working class supporters and exasperating their capitalist directors. To protect capitalist interests they must take measures to conserve the monopoly of the oil interests and safeguard the supply lines of oil, a great and growing quantity of which comes from the Middle East. A glance at a map will reveal what has guided the blundering and hesitant steps of the Labour Government in Palestine and the adjacent territories.

There are two oil pipe lines from Iraq to the Mediterranean; one through Syria to the Coast, and the other through Transjordan to Haifa. Thus it is necessary to placate or force the ruling groups in each of these territories to favour the production and transport of oil on behalf of Western capitalists. As the Arabs form the majority of the population in these territories the Arab landowners and rulers have been the principal objects of placation, not only by the Labour Government but also by their predecessors, and millions of pounds have been spent, both directly as an annual tribute to Transjordan and Iraq and indirectly under various forms of bribery, to influence a favourable attitude to the oil interests. The final result of terrorism and bribery has been to unite the Jews and Arabs in at least one direction – antipathy to the Labour Government. But the problem does not end with the territories already mentioned. Iran and the Anglo-Iranian Oil Company also come into the picture, in dangerous proximity to Russia.

So far we have only looked at a part of the picture. On Saturday, the 15th May, the *Daily Express* announced, with large headlines, Truman's recognition of the Jewish State. In the very same issue of that paper we read the following, under the headline 'Shares Boom on Wall Street': "New York, Friday. – Shares went up £250,000,000 today in the biggest day Wall Street has seen in years. Rises per share were as much as 35s. Experts think another boom market, due to rising profits and rearmament orders lies ahead."

Yes! The vultures are gathering again! What is America's interest in the Middle East and what does it portend? Why, for instance, was America so frantically concerned about the Italian elections, and why does it back British policy in Greece? In the main the immediate answer is the same as that which concerns Britain – and which finally decided the British Government to give up the Mandate in Palestine convinced that America would be forced to help carry the burden. The answer is Oil and Russian expansion; in other words Oil and Strategy. UNO, as usual, has been ignored where matters of fundamental importance to the leading powers are concerned.

Economic necessity has forced America to become a Mediterranean power to whom the future policy of Italy, Greece and the Middle East is a vital matter. The Commander of the US Mediterranean Fleet, Admiral Bieri, recently pointed out that the US Fleet intends to stay in the Mediterranean and "American forces will be allocated wherever there are American interests, in closest co-operation with the

British" (*Manchester Guardian*, 10th September 1947). Modern mechanisation, both for industrial and for military purposes, has converted oil into priority number one. In spite of their own large oil reserves neither America nor Russia can meet their growing needs out of their own production. American oil interests are pressing into the Middle East and the safeguarding of the oil life line is of paramount importance. Russia has already shown its interest in Iranian oil, and it is trying to get a strategic foothold in the Mediterranean. The whole area from the oil fields of Iran, covering the coast of Palestine and the Mediterranean, is as much a matter of concern to American capitalists as to British. So far the British capitalists have borne the costs of maintaining the oil life line. What the British Government has now done is simply throw the ball to America, and America is compelled to take the pass.

The Palestine episode is thus another move in the strategical line-up of the two major imperialistic powers – America and Russia. Russia originally backed the Arabs – then they changed over to support of the Jews. Truman's quick response was obviously aimed at getting in first and forestalling Russia. Russia has since also announced its willingness to recognise the Jewish State, but this need not prevent them from also backing the Arabs. It may be that Russia will find that its imperialistic interests will be better served by backing the Arabs. If it comes to that conclusion it will have no difficulty in finding a pretext for doing so, and we shall witness another somersault in Russian foreign policy. As an imperialist power the Russian Government is not cluttered up or inhibited by any ideals relating to democracy or the self-determination of small nations. Its methods are essentially the same as those of the Western Governments but lacking in the finesse and polish of the latter.

Whether the turmoil in the Middle East will be contained or will involve a wider conflagration (as American investors appear to anticipate) no one can at the moment determine with certainty, but what can be said is that it brings nearer the inevitable clash between Russia and the West. Both Jews and Arabs are in a position to block the oil supply but they would only ruin themselves by attempting to do so. Therefore the question is will either of them be able to turn East or West successfully for assistance.

Within the tormented area of the struggle Arab and Jewish workers have already given evidence of where the chains rub them by the strikes that have taken place against Jewish, Arab and alien masters. These Jewish and Arab workers form the vast mass of the population of the territories involved; they are the poverty-stricken exploitable material without which neither the Jewish nor Arab capitalists and landowners, nor outside capitalists, would be able to reap their harvest of profit from those rich areas. Industrially and commercially Jewish capitalists have been the progressive force. They have brought highly developed Western methods to a backward area, and in places have made the desert bloom. But with Western methods they have brought Western forms of wage-slavery and expanded under cover of nationalist ideals. For the Arab and Jewish worker neither Arab nor Jewish national independence will remove the mark of subservience from their brows. Their only hope of a life of comfort and security lies in joining with their brethren of other countries in a world socialist movement to overthrow capitalist domination in all its forms and establish Socialism in its place. Only a world Socialist system can remove from society the machinations of the oil and other capitalist interests that periodically turn the world into turmoil and bring greater misery to the millions of the workers.

Finally the personnel of the Provisional Government of Israel bears a striking likeness to the personnel of the British Labour Government. While this will not make for harmony between the two Governments it will provide another instance of how faithfully Labour Governments reflect capitalist interests.

(June 1948)

Pomp, Pageantry and Privilege

The coronation on June 2nd of a young woman by the name of Elizabeth Alexandra Mary of Windsor, as Queen of Great Britain and the British Commonwealth of Nations, is an event which, it is safe to say, has received more publicity and been the subject of more propaganda than any other peace-time occurrence of the last fifty years. Since the death of her father, the Queen has been publicised to such an extent that there can hardly be a literate person in the whole world who is not aware of the forthcoming event.

For the first time millions of people will, as it were, be inside the Abbey witnessing the ceremonial, the religious service, and the rest of the mumbo jumbo with which a Monarch is crowned. They will be there by virtue of Television, and wireless which will relate every detail of the ritual. Every organ of propaganda has been geared to the event; schools, Churches, newspapers have given it every attention all with the design to make us feel that we are part of the coronation and that we shall all be the better for it.

There can be no doubt that the organisation will prove itself efficient. The collection of notabilities from every corner of the world; the display of heraldic symbols; the presence of dignitaries with such titles as Gold Stick, Bluemantle, and Rouge Dragon will provide a magnificent spectacle beside which the productions of Hollywood will pale into insignificance. We may be sure that the belted Earls, the Dukes and Marquesses, the Society ladies, the Dowagers, the Duchesses and so forth will appear dressed in their full regalia, their diamonds sparkling, and their coronets adding lustre to the occasion.

But when the cheering has died away; when the inevitable dustcarts which follow coronations as well as Lord Mayor's Shows appear to clear the debris; when the 'captains and the kings' have departed, what will remain? When the sightseers' stands have been demolished; when the red carpets have been taken up; when the diadems and the crowns and the rest of the regalia have been returned for safe keeping to the Tower of London, what then?

If the historians and the publicists, the journalists and broadcasters are to be believed, Coronation day is to usher in a new period of glory and prosperity for this country. They assure us that whenever a Queen has ruled this land it has flowed with milk and honey, and its influence spread all over the earth. They cite the days of Queen Elizabeth and Queen Victoria as evidence for their claims, yet even the most superficial examination of those two periods will show that they are either ignorant fools or deliberate liars who by promising us the fictional glories of the past, hope to blind us to the grim, sordid realities of the present.

The Elizabethan era

What are these glories of the first Elizabethan age? It is true that then was laid the foundations of the British Empire and British mastery of the seas. It is true that British merchantmen sailed all over the world trading goods and bringing back to these shores unimaginable wealth. Colonies were established in America; pirates, cut-throats and swashbucklers flourished, prospered and were honoured by the Virgin Queen. Those not brave enough to fight the Spaniards indulged in trading in the human flesh of the African coast. Many fortunes were made in those days and it is interesting to note that some of the congregation at Westminster Abbey are there because their ancestors in the days of Queen Elizabeth were successful freebooters. But while all these things are true and while the rich and ruthless became ever more wealthy, the majority of the people of England had no share in that prosperity. For them there was work and poverty and starvation. For them the privilege of fighting to preserve the wealth of their Feudal Lords. (Strange how history repeats itself!) All the viciousness of the Elizabethan era is now glossed over with a tawdry coating of journalistic paint. But a writer of the period shows in a few words the hollowness of the claim that England as a whole was prosperous in the days of Queen Elizabeth: "The poor lie in the street upon pallets of straw, and well if they have that too, or else in the mire and dirt as commonly it is seen, having neither house to put in their heads, covering to keep them from cold, nor yet to hide their shame withal, penny to buy them sustenance, nor anything else, but are suffered to die in the streets like dogs or beasts, without mercy or shame showed to them at all ... Truly, brother, if I had not seen it, I would scarcely credit that like the Turkish cruelty had been used in all the world" (Philip Stubbs, *The Anatomie of Abuses*).

The truth is that in all ages and at all times in written history, prosperity has always been for the rich, never for the labourers, the "hewers of wood and drawers of water".

The Victorian era

If we have demolished, as is the case, the claims made about the days of Good Queen Bess, what of the age of Victoria? The Industrial Revolution had already taken place. Railways had been introduced and England had become the workshop of the world. No other country could compete in the manufacture of goods, and the world's markets were the preserve of British industrialists. Huge fortunes were built up and their possessors bought themselves titles forming a new aristocracy to replace the fast-dying old. At such a time then, surely the poor and oppressed were better off? Work there was in plenty for they were forced to toil sixteen to eighteen hours a day. Surely, therefore, the workers were amply rewarded for their toil? Nothing could be further from the truth.

Men, women and children slaved in the factories, their pay a miserable pittance, their homes hovels, their food cheap and adulterated. Epidemics, when they came, killed them off like flies. The child labourers became stunted and old before their time. There was no lack of priest or Bishop to condone this cruelty in the name of God. They praised the manufacturers for keeping children at work so that evil thoughts would not invade their otherwise idle hours.

Annual Conference, Conway Hall, 1950

During the reign of Queen Victoria, India became the "most precious jewel in the Imperial crown"; the Suez Canal came under British control, and yet a poet of that time could still write of Child Labour: "'How long', they say, 'how long', O cruel nation / Will you stand to move the world on a child's heart – / Stifle down with a mailed heel its palpitation, / And tread onward to your throne amid the mart?" ('The Cry of the Children', E.B. Browning)

And if a poet's word is not considered evidence we can refer to many factual reports given by Government Inspectors, reformers and others. In a book published just before Queen Victoria came to the throne, and dealing with conditions which prevailed well into the Victorian era, the author, J. Fielden (*The Curse of the Factory System*) wrote: "Cruelties of the most heart rending were practised upon the unoffending and friendless creatures who were thus consigned to the charge of master manufacturers; they ... were harassed to the brink of death by excess labour ... they were in many cases starved to the bone while flogged to their work ... The beautiful and romantic valleys of Derbyshire ... secluded from the public eye, became the dismal solitudes of torture and of many a murder. The profits of manufacturers were enormous; but this only whetted the appetite it should have satisfied" (Fielden did not know his capitalists!)

So much for the 'prosperity' of the Victorian era, that age of ruthless exploitation when the wealth and power of the ruling class was literally built on the blood and life of the workers.

The Coronation and its meaning

Not content with telling us that the Coronation will usher in this new period of glory and prosperity, we are told that it will be a dedication and a consecration. Bishops have prated on the holiness of the occasion, politicians, with their ability to seize every opportunity, have tried to fill us with patriotism, and the whole collection of lick-spittles, ink-slingers and columnists of Fleet Street have combined to convince us of the promising life which lies ahead.

What is this dedication and to whom in this day consecrated? Prayers for the safe keeping of her Majesty will be offered up to God; and all over the country, if the Archbishop's suggestion is followed, people will join the choir at Westminster in singing 'All people that on earth do dwell'. And in that sense perhaps it will be a day of dedication. But behind the facade of prayer and patriotism there are other interests involved which makes the Coronation a day of dedication to Mammon.

The late King's body was scarcely cold in its grave, when every junk manufacturer in the Kingdom rushed to produce enormous quantities of shoddy souvenirs. Not one avenue for making money has been neglected. Even the 'Gentry' tumbled over themselves to cash in on this 'day of consecration'. They have advertised their homes to let at fabulous rentals, from which even American millionaires have recoiled. Hotels and boarding houses, restaurants and nightclubs have put up their charges, and anybody with window-space to let on the route of the procession has been courted, bribed and enriched.

Nothing has been overlooked in this money-making jamboree called the coronation. The *Star* fashion expert tells us: "If you're fired with a desire to be patriotic through and through, so you can be … right down to your corsets. Berlei are showing – as the star item of their new summer collection – a strapless one-piece controlette in elastic net and nylon voile in a choice of red, white or royal blue."

This then is the 'holy' character of Coronation day, a day on which the money-makers will count their profits, and on which they will give their workers a day off on full pay. While they count their money they will join in the singing of the incantations at Westminster Abbey. And indeed they will have something to sing about for it is estimated that over twenty million pounds will accrue as a result of this 'day of consecration'. Is it not strange how holiness is so often linked with the 'things of this world'?

A people's coronation

Efforts have been made by means of propaganda to imbue this Coronation with a democratic flavour. For the first time, at least that is what we have been told, the people are to take part in this event. But again this claim is hollow. The only part that the 'people' will have is to stand in the streets and at their windows, or crouch before their TV sets cheering the procession of as great a collection of parasites as have ever been seen together before.

Not a dignitary involved but is a wealthy banker, landowner, Field Marshal or Major General. There will be Black rods, and Gold sticks, and Knights Pursuivants in profusion. Most of them directors of large Banking or Insurance Companies. Many of them huge landowners who are no more representative of the people than is the Queen herself, a by no means poverty-stricken personage. Surrounded as she is by these wealthy courtiers and nurtured in Palaces with a background of wealth and splendour she is cushioned off from the ordinary cares that beset the people who will stand and cheer her as she passes through the streets.

We have no personal quarrel with the Queen. As occupant of the Throne of Great Britain she has no power. The monarchy has become a mere facade of authority, a rubber stamp signature at the bottom of State documents. The Queen's whole life is regulated by strictly-defined rules and a standard of behaviour is expected which would make even the humblest of us protest.

Surrounded at the Abbey by Bankers, landowners, Labour leaders and a 'few representatives' of the Trade Unions her Majesty will perform her part, we have no doubt, with grace, charm and dexterity, and the Archbishop will intone at the right time and in the right places. The choirboys will contribute their 'Vivats', and the people whose coronation we are told this is, will stand outside and cheer. Thus it has always been; the people on the outside looking in, wearing clothes which cost less than one button of the gorgeous raiment that they have made and which they are allowed to see only at a distance. This is all the people will receive or can expect from this 'People's' coronation.

The ceremony to be performed on 2nd June has no meaning for us. It is of no consequence who sits on the throne, which flag or Royal Standard flies over Buckingham Palace; or whether her titles are Elizabeth II or I. We are not concerned with all the flummery and mediaeval mumbo-jumbo with which the event is to be celebrated. Nothing will have changed. The private ownership of the means of life will continue with all its consequences. The threat of war, the general insecurity will not be abated one jot or tittle by this glorified circus. Not one of the claims made for this event will be fulfilled as far as the workers are concerned. The promises and allurements of a brilliant future will be forgotten almost as soon as the procession has disappeared from sight.

In the Psalms, some of which will be read during the service there is a phrase which we commend: "Oh, put not your trust in Princes, nor in any child of man …" adding only the counsel to trust to yourselves, to your experience, to your knowledge to build a better Society in which all mankind will live in freedom, peace and security.

"Who would be free themselves must strike the blow."

(June 1953)

Jamaican Journeyman: job-seekers from the isle of sun and poverty

"This island excels the others for the goodness of the Ayr, and bounty of the soyl, it is for the most part a plain and even country, yielding in great abundance whatever is necessary for Man's Life" (*A True Description of Jamaica*, 1657).

On a January evening – very cold, as they say in the weather reports, and with a touch of mist, a train from the South coast arrived at a mainline London station and sent its passengers tumbling and spreading onto the platform, then towards the barrier in a jumble of suitcases and parcels, children and clothing. They were not the usual type of traveller. Their clothes were thin against the cold; many wore pyjamas as added protection, with towels around their necks and heads. Some sported wide-brimmed hats. A few came pathetically carrying stringed musical instruments. "You can always tell them", said the man leaning against the bookstall, "From a distance they haven't got any faces". Another batch of immigrants from the West Indies had come to London. It must, one thought, have been a pretty powerful Something to have brought them, the Caribbean sun still warm on their backs, to the bitterness of an English Winter.

It is impossible to accurately judge the number of Jamaicans who have recently arrived for, as British citizens, they are not compelled to register as aliens are. A reliable estimate puts the number of West Indians who came in 1954 at over 11,000 – at the end of the year about 1,000 were arriving every month. 1955 is expected to bring another 15,000, most of them from Jamaica. These immigrants are living mainly in the large cities – Manchester (in Moss Side, an older part of the City), Birmingham, Coventry and London, where the boroughs of Brixton and Paddington have taken a lot of them.

Whatever their qualifications, the Jamaicans are for the present content to take almost any job, so they mainly do unskilled work. Birmingham has nearly 300, and Oxford 20, working as bus conductors. The London Passenger Transport Board has employed some, but none for work in a bus crew. The Jamaicans are vulnerable to the rack-renter for they have come on to the end of a long waiting list for housing (in Birmingham, for example, it is 60,000) and they prefer to make their homes in areas where their countrymen are already living. The tendency to live together has hampered the Jamaican's absorption into the population at large; Birmingham is the only city to have tried to disperse them. Many are in overcrowded slums – some, it is said, owned by profiteering landlords who are themselves West Indians. The problem has aroused much concern; in Parliament it has provoked questions and a 'ten-minute-rule' private member's Bill. Several delegations from borough and city councils have been worrying the Colonial Office; it is even reported to have been discussed at a Cabinet meeting.

Jamaicans in Brixton

About 3,000 West Indians are living in the Borough of Lambeth, in South London. Most have taken homes in Brixton, packing themselves into Geneva Road and Somerleyton Road, where the houses are large and high and dowdy. To judge from the number of windows which at night are lit up, with the shadow of a dressing table mirror thrown onto faded, pinned curtains, a lot of the houses have been divided into flats and bed-sitting rooms. 'For Sale – Eight Lots Without Reserve' reads a notice outside one dusty looking residence. Is this, one wonders, the work of some rogue landlord?

On a wall in one of these roads someone has whitewashed the slogan 'Keep Brixton White'. The whitewash has been partly covered by brown paint and the weather has taken off some of the remainder. But the cool, menacing words are still just discernible and it is faintly sickening to read them in the lamplight. Yet from the evidence of a number of visits to Brixton, one would say that on the whole the Jamaicans are quite unobjectionable; as sober and as responsible in their behaviour and as modest in their bearing as anyone could wish. They have their mannerisms, it is true. In the local pub ('Select Dining Room Upstairs') they play darts with the regulars and to a man keep their hats on their heads. Some, like the two men who passed into the night, discussing how to keep warm, walk as to some inner, throbbing music. But only the chronically irascible would object to such things. There are certain London streets which have the reputation of being 'tough', so that, it is said, the police always patrol them in pairs. That is a fairly reliable guide to the amount of civic disturbance habitually expected from any given neighbourhood. Along Geneva and Somerleyton Roads the policemen walk singly. Truth to tell, there are catcalls to be heard in Brixton of a Saturday night, but they are from the local Teddy-boys and their flat-shoed girl friends, who as bearers of a white skin are exempt from having rude words written on walls about them.

Beautiful Jamaica

The Jamaicans come from an island in the Caribbean Sea – about 90 miles south of Cuba – which was discovered by Columbus in 1494 and called by him St Jago, after the patron saint of Spain. This name was changed to the Indian Xayamaca, which means 'Land of Wood and Water', an allusion to the lush vegetation and many springs which give the island its beautiful scenery. Xayamaca later became corrupted to the present name of Jamaica. The island is about 4,400 square miles in area and has many luxuriant forests which furnish abundant dyestuffs and spices and some rare cabinet woods. The mean average temperature is 78°F, the best period being January to March, when in England we are treading the cities' slush; Jamaica, of course, has its occasional earthquakes and hurricanes. Principal exports are bananas, sugar, rum (said to be the best in the world), raw coffee and cigars. An extensive fruit trade is carried on with Great Britain and New Zealand; deposits of bauxite (aluminium ore) are in development. Jamaica's population, at one and a half million, is about twice that of Manchester; nearly one half of those working in agriculture.

The island is a popular Winter holiday resort which attracts 120,000 vacationists each year, about 65% of them from America. Those lucky enough to arrive at the airport are greeted with a large glass of rum, presented with the compliments of the Sugar Manufacturers' Association. Kingston, on the south coast, is the capital – it is an ugly city with some dense slums. The principal Jamaican newspaper is the *Daily Gleaner*, a well respected publication. Cricket is the islanders' favourite game and when a Test match is being played at Sabina Park they cheerfully risk their necks at the tops of surrounding palm trees and houses to watch the game. Sometimes they are not so cheerful; they recently beat up the wife and child of an umpire who had adjudged a local hero to have lost his wicket when within reach of a century in a Test match.

Spaniards and sugar

Spain held Jamaica, with the blessing of a Papal dispensation, during a century and a half of cruelty and neglect, not untypical of its time. Little was done to develop or protect Jamaica and when a mob of ill-armed and undisciplined Englishmen under Penn and Venables invaded the island in 1655 they met little resistance. The last Spaniard left in 1660, from Runaway Bay; the English conquest was recognised in the Treaty of Madrid (1670).

The Spaniards had introduced sugar to the West Indies from the Canary Islands; this industry is now the bedrock of Jamaica's economy. The plantations, originally worked by slaves in the charge of the usually brutal and corrupt overseers, at first flourished but later were subject to the changes of economic fortune. The early eighteenth century was a time of low prices and depression but the slump was shaken off and by 1760 the industry had reached a high point of prosperity. Then, in the middle of the nineteenth century came the competition of Cuban sugar and European beet sugar, and a further decline from which the west Indies has never really recovered. Beet sugar production is heavily subsidised for strategic reasons and in any case its refining is now no costlier for the United Kingdom than that of cane sugar at the Commonwealth price, so there is no weapon of cheapness to help the Jamaican planters. Cuban sugar is a strong competitor – 75,000 tons were recently sold to Canada and it has an enviable protected market in the United States. West Indies sugar is today about 2% of the world's crop; under the Commonwealth Sugar agreement of 1951 – endorsed by the 1953 International Sugar Agreement – the islands are guaranteed an annual export quota of 670,000 tons, sold at a fixed price.

Before the war the United Kingdom and Canada stimulated the expansion of the West Indian sugar industry by granting preferential entry to its exports. This has caused the West Indies production to exceed its agreed world quota, at a time when the market is already over-stocked. This year Canada and the United Kingdom will be taking all the sugar they need; any Jamaican surplus (expected to be about 50,000 tons) will have to make its own way in the unprotected world market, with no hope of breaking into the United States. This is not an attractive prospect for Jamaica – the world price of sugar has been depressed by the glut and is now considerably lower than the price at which she sells three-quarters of her crop to the United Kingdom.

Other troubles

Jamaica has other troubles. Her citrus growers are threatened with extinction in face of competition from the USA, Israel and Spain. Her cigar industry has been forced to contract drastically and lay off several hundred workers; this once again due to competition from Cuba. Mr Bustamante, then Jamaica's Chief Minister, came to London in May, 1953, to ask for help for her island's ailing industries and to protest at the financial restrictions which force Jamaica to take 90% of her imports from Britain but forbid her to buy in the cheap dollar markets. A West Indian trade delegation came in May last year to ask for guarantees for their exports of citrus fruits, bananas, rum and cigars. The Colonial Office was firm that "... it would not be possible to guarantee a market for the whole of West Indian export crops..." This lofty refusal from Whitehall is partly due to the restrictions of Imperial Preference which the United Kingdom must enforce as a member of the General Agreement on Tariffs and Trade. For this reason the new government of Jamaica, led by Mr Norman Manley, QC, is opposed to the British Commonwealth's membership of GATT.

Any airline folder or shipping company brochure will show Jamaica as a glamorous tropical island with a history rich in the romance of Spanish treasure galleons, rum-soaked buccaneers and elegant plantation houses kept up by docile, whitely-grinning negroes. The other Jamaica, which the immigrants know, is an island of stark poverty, where 250,000 are unemployed, of a total working force of about 750,000. This is the colony with one of the worst standards of education in the British Empire, whose most troublous diseases are characteristic of its malnutrition and bad housing, hookworm, venereal disease, pulmonary tuberculosis and yaws (a skin complaint bred in dirty huts and carried by flies). Blindness is also a serious problem. Before the war a retired politician called Jamaica an Imperial slum and the description is as apt today; we can hardly blame the Jamaicans if, in the hope that things cannot possibly be worse elsewhere, they trust their luck in emigration.

Restrictions

It is likely that, given the choice, most of the Jamaicans would emigrate to the United States, but they are prevented by that country's strict immigration laws. Restrictions also bar their going to Canada and Australia. England is about the only country which offers freedom of entry and a good chance of a job. With employment easy to find at the present, there is little general resentment against the Jamaicans; this might change if British industry is hit by a slump. Then the Jamaicans would discover that England has as many hardships for them as there are springs in their native island. And, as they already know, it is so much colder.

(March 1955)

Television in Modern Life

Lambasting television is easy. The only difficult thing, indeed, must be for the critics to produce fresh variants on the bitter, derisive comments which seem all that can be found to describe the offerings of man's latest marvel. The same things were said about the films thirty years ago (those same films, by the way, now being hailed by the U-mob as aesthetic masterpieces); and, as with films, one fact brushes aside all the invective. In America families look at television for an average of five and a half hours a day, and in Britain for over half that time. Television, whatever they say about it, has become established as part of modern social life.

Obviously that does not justify its banality. It is quite true that most television programmes are stupid, noisy, mediocre and pointless, and they have become more so since 'commercial' television began in this country. But why single out television? Are not most radio programmes stupid, clamorous, mediocre and pointless, too? And most films, novels, papers and plays? Bad as television may be, it has only followed the illuminated trails blazed by every other form of mass entertainment.

In fact, much of the sneering and jeering at television is not really aimed at television at all, but at the working class. Mr Maurice Richardson, commenting on the Backward Child's – i.e. commercial television's – Birthday in the *Observer* a few weeks ago made merry with phrases like "slobbering cretin" and "the Ad-mass". Smart, easy stuff this; it would be equally easy, if less smart, for Mr Richardson to observe the U-mob lapping up stuff just as poor and twice as nasty as television in practically any West End theatre or cabaret.

Television is the passive entertainment par excellence. Indeed, if there is anything it emphasises about present-day society, it is this: the second-handedness of almost everything. The football spectator is often condemned as a passive watcher, getting satisfaction by proxy from the deeds of others, but he appears an active participant against the television-watcher – at least wrapping-up, going out of doors, meeting other men, arguing and letting off steam, while the viewer is as wholly non-participant as is possible to be.

That is only the least part of it, however. The awful, meretricious mimicry which a universal visual medium breeds has to be seen to be believed: unending imitations of imitations, until imitation is an end in itself. It applies to the artistes of course, but they are only the focal point of the pattern. See the amateur talent contests – Find the Singer, Opportunity Knocks, and so on. The dreadful thing is not that the competitors can't sing. They aren't trying to. They compete only in effectively copying the looks, gestures and antics of the stereotyped professionals.

It is this, the standardisation, the depreciating of originality, and the acceptance of prototypes for practically everything, that makes television set the seal on the trends of the last quarter-century's popular entertainment. The man in the armchair is the least noxious of its end-products. What matters much more is the man wearing other people's looks, copying other people's tricks, living by other people's judgements, and thinking other people's thoughts.

The differences between BBC television and 'commercial' resolve themselves into the latter's flamboyance – like comparing the *Telegraph* with the *Daily Mirror*. Thus ATV's newsreaders are engaging and breezy, the BBC's staid; the BBC children's hour is carefully 'improving', while ATV gives them gunplay and thunder. There is one other vital distinction, however. On ATV they give things away; on BBC they don't. The giveaway programmes are on every evening. The prizes (modest in comparison with the American ones) include £2 a week for a year, two jackpots which rise to £1000, and television sets ad lib.

The giveaway programme is a reiteration of one of capitalism's oldest myths: that if you can't climb the tree, there are always windfalls. The excitement of the thought is heaped on for the viewers. "How does it feel to win £1000? Viewers may be able to tell tonight, if the Treasure Trail reaches its thrilling climax", says the *TV Times* advertisement of Double Your Money. The 64,000 Dollar Question, in which the eventual prize is £3000, is positively ghoulish – the contestant in a glass box, macabre music, close-ups of the audience in dramatic lighting to squeeze out the last vicarious thrill.

What are the social effects of all this? The most obvious one is a loss of sociability: people go out less and welcome callers less. A few years ago there was a good deal of inviting-in to watch the television, but that has fallen off as television ownership has spread. Other forms of entertainment and recreation have lost accordingly. More beer-drinking is done at home and less in the pubs; cinemas, which kept their end up until last year, are now reporting a serious decline. And round this writer's way the local vicar circularised houses last Christmas, to apologize if his carol singers disturbed the viewers.

With this increased insularity, more attention has probably been paid to homes themselves, in the way of decorating, furnishing, and so on. At first glance that may seem a good thing, but in fact it means acceptance of the individualizing and atomizing of society that has been going on for the last hundred years – the division of labour carried to the point where each man hardly knows his neighbour. Indeed, going back to the television programmes, one of their most remarkable features is the almost hypnotic appeal of seeing other people revealed: in their occupations, in loss of dignity, or, most incredible of all, in the guise of the Man Who Eats Razor Blades, or the Woman Who Got Stuck in the Bath.

The ownership of a television set means far more than mere entertainment, however. It holds implications of prestige, of status shown by conspicuous consumption. Seven or eight years ago the mere fact of owning one was enough; the man who said: 'I watched a good play last night' was saying unmistakably: 'I've *got* a television'. That has passed, and nowadays it isn't worth having an outdoor aerial. Prestige today involves having a better, brighter and (above all) bigger set: one with a seventeen or twenty-inch screen, where you can get both programmes and don't have to turn out the light.

It is funny – and sad – this business of 'living standards'. One would imagine that having a good standard of living could mean only one thing: having plenty of good food, being adequately housed and clothed, having no debts to worry about, and being able to please one's self. Well, it doesn't. It connotes, in fact, not living at all, but possessing. The standard is seen as the rung one has reached on the acquisitive ladder. The lowest rung, below which there isn't a standard at all, is the radio-set. Above it, roughly in ascending order, come the nine-inch television, the washing machine, the refrigerator, holidays abroad, the mortgage-bought house, the big television set, and, indisputably top, the motor-car.

There are endless other things, of course – clothing, children's schooling, the sounds which come out of the radiogram; they have to be endless or the game might stop, and it can't. The common conception is that for people to be getting any or all of these things means more and more money is, by the grace of industrial civilization, being pumped into working class homes.

That can be tested. According to the *London and Cambridge Economic Service* wages currently are 176% above their 1938 level. Prices are given as 154% above 1938. In other words, wages in relation to prices (and that is the only way wages can be assessed) are just 8% more than what they were in 1938. In concrete terms, at today's prices a man with £7 10s a week is eleven shillings better off than he was before the war.

Where *does* the money for the television sets come from, then? Most are bought on hire-purchase or credit sale. The instalments can be anything from fifteen shillings a week upwards; in the case of a credit sale, when payment must be completed in nine months, they can be as high as three pounds a week. There are two answers. The first is earnings over and above wages – overtime and production bonuses; the second, that more wives go to work than ever before. Cauter and Downham's investigation in Derby found that: "The explanation of the ability of the lower-paid worker to buy a television set is suggested by the family size analysis. In fact, two-thirds of the owner-families where the chief wage-earner received £7 10s a week or less had more than one wage-earner in the family" (*The Communication of Ideas*, 1954).

The truth, then, is that television sets, like the other working class 'luxuries' are paid for by men working longer hours, their wives going to work, and both of them going without other things. It may be a pity that sacrifices are made in such a cause, but that is a different matter. Perhaps a final word may be said about the economic aspect of it. It is a mistake to think that all this – expensive means of amusement coming into ordinary homes – is a modern wonder. Before television or radio, literally every working class home had a piano. The price of a piano 35 years ago was anything between thirty and seventy pounds; it was, in fact, a far greater luxury.

Don't write off television as another machine-age monstrosity. Potentially, it can do a lot for man; as an instrument of communication, information and amusement. Its failings are not inherent in the cathode-ray tube, but are in reality the failings of social life displayed in three dimensions on a small screen. An American critic described television as a device by which a man may sit in one room and observe the nonsense going on in another. As was said at the beginning, that sort of lambasting is easy and it misses the point – which is that the real nonsense is going on in the room where the man is sitting.

(November 1956)

Hungary and Suez – Hope Amidst Tragedy

The Governments of Israel, Britain, France and Russia, when they resorted to war in October 1956 in pursuit of their own separate objectives, have at the same time struck a decisive blow to achieve something they never sought and are hardly aware of. Their tanks and bombers in a few days of destruction have helped to shatter the most hampering illusion of our generation, an illusion that has held back multitudes from taking the first step towards a real understanding of the problems facing the human race.

This illusion was the belief, held with equal fervour by democrats and Communists, and on both sides of the Iron Curtain, that there are 'two worlds', essentially different in aims and conduct.

On the one side the democrats and Labourites of the Western world believed that they and their rulers are guided by a superior moral code, are inherently against brutality, are committed to 'law not war', and to the United Nations, and are incapable of naked aggression to further their interests.

On the other side were the Communists and their followers, who believed with equal sincerity that Russia, by virtue of being a 'Socialist' country, is free from and superior to the sordid imperialism and colonialism of the West, and utterly incapable of opposing the aspirations of ordinary workers.

Now the foundations of both beliefs have been smashed into fragments. Sincere men and women in both camps are horrified and heartbroken to discover in one revealing flash that the men they reviled behave in exactly the same criminal way; that the Edens and the Kruschevs are blood brothers after all, worshippers of the same capitalist god of violence and war. The sickening dismay of those who trusted Eden, 'the friend of the United Nations', is only equalled by that of Communists who see Russian tanks smashing down Hungarian workers. For both groups the one thing that could not happen has happened.

This sudden and dramatic exposure of the sham on both sides of the Iron Curtain provides a splendid opportunity for Socialists, who alone can give a valid explanation to the bewildered adherents of the rival ideologies. Only the Socialist can explain that it is not a failure of men, but the unavoidable results of the workings of the social system. The division of the world into separate capitalist states, each seeking to achieve its own commercial ends amid the international rivalries, compels each government again and again to make a choice between using military force to achieve some gain and enduring some weakening and loss by not using military force; the ideals and temperaments of the men who make up the governments is of minor, indeed negligeable importance; they all have to use the same methods or get out.

The Socialist, too, and only the Socialist, can deal with the difficulty of the admirers of Russia. At the core of their admiration is the belief that Russia is 'Socialist', and only the Socialist can deny this fraud and explain the truth. State capitalism, the conduct of financial, commercial and trading operations by a government in place of a private company is not Socialism and has no relationship to Socialism. It is not the manner in which these operations are controlled, but the nature of the operations that constitutes them capitalist. The efforts of a government, Russian, British, Indian, or any other, to control sources of raw materials, protect frontiers and trade routes and capture markets for its exports – these activities are the cause of war, no matter how or under what flag they are conducted. The worker in every country in the world should take to heart the elementary truth that wars are not made by wicked foreigners, but at home, in the land he lives in: through the everyday activities, seemingly peaceful and innocent, of those who employ him and make profit out of him, and who seek to sell the products of his labour in world markets against the similar activities of other employers under other governments. This is the factor common to all the countries: the factor that drives governments into war and workers to their death in fratricidal combat with their fellows. But this factor is the capitalist organisation of society, and only Socialists know the remedy, the introduction on a world-wide basis of a different social system Socialism.

(December 1956)

THE 'SWINGING SIXTIES'

The 1960s proved to be a decade characterised by changing attitudes on a range of social issues and failed attempts at political change. It was this decade which saw the first signs that the post-war economic boom was coming to an end but it is remembered more for the wave of liberalisation that swept much of the 'Western World' on the back of a youth culture that had had its first stirrings in the 1950s.

The sixties was a time of radical change in the worlds of music, fashion and art. To an extent at least, this was mirrored in the appearance of the *Socialist Standard*. Pictures regularly began to appear on the front cover (and periodically inside) and colour – as opposed to coloured paper – on occasion too. The design of the *Standard* during this period was very neat, 'clean' and tidy and, in retrospect, the developments in its appearance probably lagged a little behind the radical changes sweeping the wider world of art and graphics, though at times issues of the *Standard* nevertheless began to look recognisably different from their predecessors in the decades before.

The focus of their content shifted a little too, to address the new issues arising in the political and social fields: sexual politics, the rise of the so-called 'New Left' of student radicals and Trotskyists and the attitudes engendered by the hippy movement. The decade began with then Prime Minister Harold Macmillan telling the working class that the post-war boom had meant that they'd 'never had it so good', a statement which, while rather more transparently true for the class he represented than the one he ruled over, nevertheless reflected the acquisition of consumer durables on hire purchase by a wider and wider section of the working class after the hungry thirties and war-time and post-war rationing. The years that followed proved to be anything but the calm reflection of social content he no doubt imagined they would be.

The rise of the Campaign for Nuclear Disarmament (famed for their marches from the Atomic Weapons Research Establishment at Aldermaston) was an early indication of this, and indicative of a partial change in political focus from bread-and-butter economic concerns to wider social and political ones. At its peak in 1960-61 CND had more active supporters than any other mass movement in Britain since the Anti-Corn Law League of the 1840s, a sign – if anything was – of what was to come as the decade developed.

Even the Church of England was affected by the changing attitudes that characterised the 1960s. As our article on 'The Bishop of Woolwich Squares the Circle' indicates, the Bishop of Woolwich's views were an early attempt to rationalise the prevailing Protestant faith in Britain with the ideas of a more humanistic and sceptical era where scientific progress and modernism held sway.

For many, the 1960s is remembered primarily for the development of popular music in something close to its modern form, as well as the entire music industry associated with it. Bands like the Beatles, Who and Rolling Stones were an expression of – and in turn helped to fuel – changing social attitudes, especially amongst the young, and represented the parallel generation of a distinct youth culture which set itself against the 'Establishment' and all it supposedly stood for. As the article of the 'Politics of Pop' demonstrates, some of these performers had rather more interesting and profound things to say than others. The so-called hippy movement which developed from the 'Summer of Love' in 1967 onwards was a radical outcrop of these anti-establishment views concentrating on issues such as free love, peace, abortion, feminism and drug-taking. The radical questioning of the values of capitalist society undertaken by the hippies led some of them towards socialist positions, though as our article on 'Hippies: An Abortion of Socialist Understanding' demonstrates, they were in a distinct minority.

Other, associated, anti-establishment ideas of the time were what impelled the so-called 'May Events' in Paris in 1968 when a student rebellion spread amongst much of the rest of the working class and led to unrest in other countries. This and the *cause célèbre* of the New Left in the 1960s – opposition to United States involvement in the Vietnam war – are analysed from the socialist viewpoint in two articles also reproduced here.

Finally, we include an article that is less representative of the spirit of radical change than some of the others in this section. 'Man: Ape in Wolf's Clothing' rebuts the arguments of the school of evolutionary biology which became popular in the late 1960s through the writings Desmond Morris and others. Their arguments still have an influence now and are an implicit denial that human beings could organise a socialist society of common ownership because of their supposedly innate competitiveness and aggressiveness.

"You've never had it so good"

Mr Macmillan has served the Tory party very well indeed. Along with shrewdness and other qualities he has shown himself to be a master showman in a team of showmen. But when he told the British workers that they've never had it so good, there must have been some of his fellow Tories who doubted its wisdom. A tag like this labels a politician and his party for a very long time and when their luck runs out – as it always does – they will never live it down. But a master showman has to take risks and so far the thing has succeeded beyond all possible expectations. He persuaded his followers that it is so, and then the Opposition, so that we now have Mr Anthony Crosland, Labour MP for Grimsby, endorsing it. He confessed this at a Labour Conference at Utrecht, and he told them that the British workers "now scarcely seem, either to themselves or to other classes, to be suffering from oppression or capitalist exploitation" (*Daily Mail*, 11th January 1960). It helped to win the support of a majority of the electors for the Tory party. It convinced the Archbishop of Canterbury, Dr Fisher, though it failed to win his approval. He calls it a 'dreadful phrase'. "Whenever I hear it," he said, "I say to myself in the words of Our Lord, 'how hardly shall they that have riches enter into the Kingdom of Heaven'" (*Daily Telegraph*, 11th January 1960). With his comfortable £7,500 a year he is worried lest the general affluence of the workers should imperil their souls.

But just how much substance is there in this propaganda, and how much of it exists only in the distorting imagination of the politicians and Press?

Half the Story
There is no lack of supposed evidence to back it up. Let us look at some of it.

The *Evening Standard* (1st January 1960) greeted the new year with an editorial telling us about the 'Age of Plenty'. The opening paragraph set the tone: "The age of scrimping is over. The age of affluence has begun. In the past ten years Britain has passed through a social revolution whose full impact is only likely to be felt in the new decade which has just begun. For the first time in history the greater part of this country's people – and not just the fortunate minority – have money to spare beyond their immediate needs."

Even a light-hearted journalist would hardly make this claim without evidence, and the evidence is there.

"One figure sums up the progress of this revolution. As the 1960s begin, everyone living in this country has an income higher by an average of £3 a week than at the beginning of the '50s."

But before passing on we must look more closely at the average increase of £3 a week. It was clearly derived from figures that turned up in the Press about that time. In the *Financial Times* (31st December 1959) under the heading 'Standard of Living' we were told that average personal income per head of the population jumped from £220 in 1950 to £375 in 1959. Sure enough the difference, £155 a year, is £3 a week so what more need be said? But what the writer omitted to point out was that in the same period, on official figures, the price level (cost of living) rose by 47%. To buy in 1959 what could be bought for £220 in 1950 would need £323. So the real increase was not £3 a week but the difference between £323 and £375, a matter of about £1 a week, and that the £1 a week would buy in 1959 only about half that a like amount would have bought in 1950.

Another figure published by the *Financial Times* showed 'expenditure' per head of the population (after deducting from average income the amount of taxation and the amount put aside as savings). This produced an increase between 1950 and 1959, of nearly £2 a week. But again, after allowing for the increase of prices this seemingly large increase gets cut down to a mere 4% – not a lot to show for 10 years of 'social revolution'.

It is particularly surprising that the *Financial Times* should give figures in this incomplete form because four years ago (6th September 1955) when that paper looked at similar figures published then, they pointed out what a miserable showing the figures gave when compared with 1938. They made the point that the real increase per head of the population (after allowing for higher prices) was the trifling rise of 4^1/2% as compared with 1938.

It happens to be useful to the case of those who see a vast increase of the standard of living to have chosen the year 1950 because average expenditure in all the post-war years up to 1952 (after allowing for higher prices) was actually below the pre-war level.

Mr George Schwartz in the *Sunday Times* (10th January 1960) had his own line of comment. He at least is very well aware of the fact that much of the current statistical evidence of higher incomes is merely a reflection of the steady rise in prices and a corresponding decrease in the purchasing power of money. On this occasion he wanted to make the point that booming production and exports are not a new phase in British capitalism. He reproduced columns of figures showing how 'peace and prosperity' were booming in the years 1903 to 1913. Again some very imposing figures, but when we look at prices in these ten years we see that they were steadily rising, a total rise of about 12%. Wages were rising more slowly so that the higher wage actually bought less.

Staggering truth

What is really astounding about Macmillan's boast is that, at least on average, it contains an element of truth, remembering however that the rich too are in the average figures. The state of most British workers really is a little better than it has ever been before. Of course there are large numbers of clerical workers (including most of the civil service, bank clerks and others) who are worse off than they were before the war, and some industrial workers, including London busmen, are also worse off. But with fewer unemployed and several million married women enjoying the dubious advantage of doing two jobs, home and away, working class purchasing power has gone up. But what a commentary on capitalism that this small advance can be hailed as a social revolution and set the church worrying about the corrupting influence of working class 'riches'!

Just about the turn of the year agricultural workers advanced to £8 a week for 46 hours toil. Hundreds of thousands of other men in industry and transport are on much the same level. The average earnings of women of 18 and over in manufacturing industry is £6 17s 0d a week – hardly a corrupting level of affluence. And there are over 2 million people who in the course of a year are poor enough to qualify for National Assistance – with wives and children the number is much larger.

Real capitalism

In spite of the talk about a social revolution capitalism has not changed. It is still a system of minority wealth and mass poverty and insecurity – and just at present it is profits, stock exchange prices and the emergence of new crops of millionaires that truly mark the phase of 'you never had it so good'. And the Church, with a rise of £50 million in the value of its investments in the past five years, hasn't done badly.

Just before Christmas, the *People* (20th December 1959) gave unintentionally a close-up of the capitalism we still have with us. Mr Gilbert Harding ran a charity fund and invited readers to subscribe. He was proud to report that 40,000 readers had sent in £15,000 (it later reached £30,000). In particular he recorded that 89 workers in Reading had voted to his fund the £630 held by their defunct Social Club. They had been employed by a biscuit firm but a week before Christmas the firm closed down, unable to meet the competition of larger firms. In all, 290 workers got the sack, "with not a penny in compensation from the firm," although many were likely to get other jobs, "for most of them the Christmas prospect looked bleak." Mr Harding was entitled to single out the charitable mindedness of the workers who gave the money to his fund, the money "they had scrimped and saved to put the social club on its feet."

But there was another item of interest. The *People* disclosed that when the chairman of the firm died "he left a quarter of a million pounds – all made out of biscuits."

How much more useful it would have been to point out that the quarter of a million was just part of the tribute levied by the capitalist class from the workers, not 'made out of biscuits' but out of them.

The socialist struggle has not ended, it has hardly begun, and it will achieve in due time a social system which really will be a social revolution. One in which, incidentally, it will not be necessary for workers to scrimp and save to help the discarded members of their class.

(February 1960)

A Message for Aldermaston Marchers

When your house is on fire you drop everything until you have put out the flames: and if your neighbours come into help, you are glad to see them, without asking questions whether they are vegetarians or teetotallers or anything else. So might the Campaign for Nuclear Disarmament argue, to justify the political diversity of their membership, united as it is only in the desire to abolish nuclear weapons.

We can all agree that these weapons are monstrous. The two Japanese cities were terrible enough: since then, the bombs have been made many times more destructive. The Home Office publication *Nuclear Weapons* estimated that a bomb a little smaller than that exploded by the Americans at Bikini in 1954 would cause total or irreparable damage for a radius of six miles and would certainly kill everybody within half a mile, by burns if not from other causes. A Chief Inspector of Fire Brigades has said that a hydrogen bomb on London could cause 100,000 fires – and might temporarily alter the course of the Thames. These forebodings are several years old. Now we have even bigger bombs, and rockets which can deliver them over thousands of miles. Yes, nuclear weapons must be abolished. How can it be done?

What if the governments yielded to the pressure of the nuclear disarmers and agreed to scrap their bombs? This would be worth no more than all the other solemn vows to disarm, or to refrain from taking up arms, or to be non-aggressive, which governments, when it suited them, have broken in the past. The fact that Germany in 1919 signed an agreement not to arm did not prevent her becoming a powerful military nation a few years later. The non-aggression pact of 1939 between Germany and Russia did not prevent the conflict of 1941-45. But let us suppose that governments, strangely, kept their promise to forego their nuclear weapons. That would only take us back to 1945, when wars were fought with blockbusters and flame throwers and Napalm bombs. There is nothing desirable about that. Or we could make a really good job of it and go back to the weapons of 1914-18. Or 1870 or 1415 or 1066.

APRIL 1960
No. 668 Vol. 56

SOCIALIST STANDARD

A FUTURE
WORTH LIVING
FOR

A ROCKET MISSILE *"Is this the kind of world we want? Or ..."*

Where Nuclear Disarmament Fails **ALDERMASTON MARCH**

A Voice from the Past **A MAN OR A TOOL**

Gold the Basis of Trade **RUSSIAN GOLD POLICY**

A Future Worth Living For **SOCIALISM**

6ᴰ   *JOURNAL OF THE SOCIALIST PARTY OF GREAT BRITAIN*

Of course, it is foolish to expect a modern government to run an army of longbowmen. It seems too obvious to say that as one country develops a weapon, so the others must find one similar or better. That is how the military aircraft and the nuclear bomb, for example, were born. Nowadays, no foreign minister has much of a say unless he has a fistful of H-bombs. In the last election campaign, Sir Winston Churchill said "... you are more likely to obtain a hearing for your views if you have some substantial stake in the balance of world power. And these stakes ... are still much measured in military terms." To win a stake in world power, the French and Chinese are working up their atom bombs – and the established nuclear powers, to keep their stake, have to make rockets and missiles with Hydrogen bomb war heads.

When the French atom bomb was exploded a few weeks back, General de Gaulle exclaimed, "Hurrah for France!" He knew that he was really saying hurrah for destruction and death, because that is what military power means. But military power is only necessary to modern states because in peace and war, they are struggling for economic advantage. This is a world where everything is produced with the intention of selling it profitably, which means that sellers compete for markets, manufacturers for plentiful raw material sources and transporters for trading routes. These are the disputes which, when everything else fails, are settled by force – by war. So France hangs on to Algeria for, among other things, the oil that is there. So Britain fought for years in Cyprus, because it is a base near the strategically important Suez Canal and the vital Middle East oilfields. So the last two world wars were started – and so a third could start if, for example, Russian economic influence in the Middle East or the Caribbean became too great a threat to British and American interests.

In these conditions, national states are bound to maintain a military machine to fight for the interests of their ruling classes and to equip that machine with the most powerful – and most deadly – weapons possible. It is futile to expect them to do otherwise. In 1917, it would have been suicidal for them to have thrown away their tanks, or in 1944 their bombers. In 1960 they are similarly reluctant to give up their nuclear bombs. There is only one way to deal effectively with this problem. Go to the roots. The capitalist system is the cause, from beginning to end, of modern war and the horrifying methods of its prosecution.

Marching from Aldermaston, sitting in the mud in Swaffham, or lying in jail, the nuclear disarmers deserve our respect for their concern with one of the horrors of modern society. But we can only regret that so much energy is wasted in such a topsy-turvy movement. If it is desirable to abolish one weapon of war, how much more so is it to get rid of them all? Or to get rid of war itself? Our house is burning because it is made of inflammable materials – and people will keep dropping matches. It is useless to tackle each fire as it breaks out. We must build ourselves a new house.

(April 1960)

The Bishop of Woolwich Squares the Circle

A great deal of attention has recently been focused on controversies within the Church of England by the publication of a book written by the Bishop of Woolwich entitled *Honest to God*. The book has prompted wide interest in issues basic to religion but, although this controverty has been extended within the Church itself, propositions involving the modification of assumptions fundamental to the religious outlook have been argued about for some time.

These arguments, forced upon the Church by social developments external to it, have been reluctant but inevitable, bitter and agonised. There is no doubt, however, that the publication of this book has brought these arguments under wider public scrutiny, has stepped up the intensity of the discussion, and has brought about a new phase in what is quite frankly a time of crisis for the Church of England. Its problem is how to reverse mounting indifference to it and its dogma. This may be a problem for the Church itself, which quite obviously will resent and strive against becoming a social anachronism, but in relation to the crucial social problems facing man today it is irrelevant and superfluous. The significance of the controversy is that it opens a fresh chapter in man's long struggle to free his existence from service to outside agencies – the gods.

Of all the churches in this country, it is the Church of England that has suffered most of the erosion of what was once a compelling enthusiasm for religious activities, especially in urban areas. At least until the turn of the century, the Church of England remained a powerful force that intervened actively in the everyday affairs of the community. Quite apart from providing spiritual balm to a nineteenth century working class depressed by acute poverty, it was the authoritative keeper of the community's moral conscience. It was the father confessor to an era in trouble, as well as a positive force in political and economic affairs. The pulpit was a platform, and congregations were large enough to make them worth talking to.

But since those days, the thunderous voice of the Church of England has softened to a whisper, largely ignored and unnoticed. The declamations from its pulpits re-echo around virtually empty caverns; its morality is flaunted; the soporifics that it once dispensed are now found elsewhere in more acceptable forms. But it is not a situation that has been created by mass active opposition, coherently articulated or positively demonstrated. The majority of the population are not even atheists, let alone aware and convinced of Marxist theories, but the attitude of a growing number of people is of massive indifference and crushing unconcern. The consequences for the Church are just the same. Although there is still a degree of social esteem accorded to baptisms, marriages and burials presided over by the Church, they have more significance as desirable conventions than as conscientious acts of faith; as customs they have become drained of their religious and spiritual meaning.

The steady withdrawal of active support for Church affairs does not apply in equal degree to every branch of religion in this country. Quite certainly, the Roman Catholic Church retains a firmer grip over its members than the Church of England. But there are good historical reasons for this, and whilst the Catholic Church makes it much more difficult for individuals to drift away, and although it still remains a powerful bastion of superstition based on fear and ignorance, it is unlikely either that in the long term it can resist tendencies fundamental to modern capitalism – scepticism and individual self-interest.

The dogma of the Church of England boils down to an expedient. It summed up the aspirations of a sixteenth-seventeenth century trading class seeking freedom for the development of its own activities outside the influence of the established landed interests whose political and economic power was based, at least in part, on the Roman Catholic Church, and which expressed themselves in its ideology.

The Roman Catholic Church secured subservience by the weapon of tyrannical superstition. Thus its god was a tyrant and a taskmaster; a god who imposed a duty of constant adulation and who threatened wrongdoers with the nightmare penalty of eternal damnation. Beyond this, since the Church itself was the physical embodiment of God on earth, the worship of God had to be the worship of the Church. The Catholic Church's claim was and is to be the only gateway to heaven and its followers were forced to submit to its authority on all aspects of moral and political behaviour. It involved its adherents in the agony of thorns, a hierarchy of sin, the bleeding heart of Jesus, the pain of eternally stoked hellfire and other frightening fundamentalist accoutrements of primeval religious fervour. And by means of its power over ignorant and bewildered men, it secured their economic subservience.

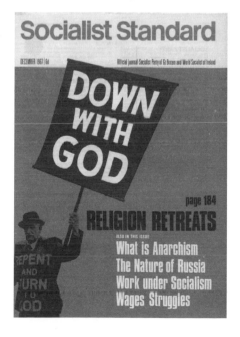

Protestantism then was the expedient ideological innovation of a dynamic social element which still felt the need for religious justification but which sought freedom from the authoritarian structures of the Roman Church. Thus with the Reformation and the establishment of the Church of England, a god was invoked who dispensed with the Church as a necessary turnstile between himself and his flock. A dogma was created that allowed entrance to heaven merely on condition of belief in the holy trinity. The expedient changing of cherished beliefs is in the long-standing tradition of the Church of England, and it is not surprising that Catholicism retains a more enduring grip over its members.

As a true child of his age, and in emulation of the image-mongering techniques of advertising, the Bishop of Woolwich believes that in order to combat the growing lack of interest in the Church and Christianity, it is necessary to change the image of its god. He holds that it is no longer acceptable to think of God as some supernatural, yet objectified, reality existing 'out there', somewhere in outer space, holding omnipotent sway over a universe of his own creation. He holds that God should no longer be thought of as an entity external to society's own existence, to whom individuals owe personal worship. For the Bishop of Woolwich, the idea of God represents all the best aspirations of man towards brotherhood, mutual tolerance and dedication to community interests. God to him is a force for common good inherited by contemporary man from the most obscure beginnings of history. Different from beer-swilling vicars singing Nelly Dean with contrived yet conscientious enthusiasm, the absurd indignity of ton-up parsons, hymns sung to skiffle and other props, the ideas of the Bishop of Woolwich form the more credible substance of today's radical theology.

The Bishop has realised that social consciousness has developed past the point of an easy acceptance of the supernatural imagery of traditional religion that sprang from social conditions in which science was in its infancy and man's technical apparatus crude. The evolving scientific culture of the space age displaces the superstitious faith of religion and reduces it to an irrelevance. It could once be truly observed and easily demonstrated that the Church was a fundamental support of capitalist society; but the order of priorities between religious faith and scientific method in a society driven towards greater technical complexity has changed all this.

Because capitalism is essentially a competitive form of society, and because this competition takes the form of struggle for commercial success both within nations and between nations, society is impelled to seek greater efficiency and productivity of labour. Thus technical change and scientific research and all the social consequences of them, including a bias towards technical education, are basic features of modern capitalist society. The fact of continued technical innovation so deeply permeates our culture that even momentous achievements are accepted with equanimity. Man lives today in an atmosphere of intense scientific enquiry which results in new discoveries daily. The means of communication are developed to a point where this new knowledge, whether it is about stars a million light years away, or the breeding habits of some obscure species of tropical fish, can be communicated immediately to all men. It is an age that emphasises the contrast between knowledge that can be proved and assumptions that require faith.

The first premise of historical materialism is that all man's thinking is social thinking; that there is no idea that man discusses, no interest that he fights for, and no ideal that he aspires to, that is not derived from social origins. When the Bishop of Woolwich denies God a supernatural existence outside human society and uses the concept to mean a social force between them, then whether he is aware of it or not, and whether he likes it or not, he has taken a faltering but definite step into the materialist camp.

In face of a developing scientific culture, the nature of religious belief undergoes gradual but definite qualitative change. Appropriately, it is during National Productivity Year that the Bishop of Woolwich articulates his death wish.

Even in the early nineteenth century, the economic structure of society was justified as being God-given, and to advocate its change was a sinful and heretical challenge to almighty predetermination. The relationship between man and God was close and personal. Earthly existence was merely a brief testing time for one's fitness to live eternally in heaven. It was a life in the service of God rather than a life of service to self. Today, even for those who are not religious, God is not thought of with the same awesome fear and only a few believe seriously that if life on earth is unsatisfactory, there remains the second chance in heaven. In the space age, the control of man's destiny is gravitating from outer space to earth itself.

Where the working class accepts allegiance to religion, to royalty or the state, or accepts a false ideology or economic subservience to the capitalist class, it denies itself the realisation of its own interests. The poverty of the modern proletariat still results from the fact that its labour operates in commodity form, is bought for wages and exploited by capitalists with a view to profit. To buy a man's labour power and set him to work is to reduce his existence to a commercial transaction and alienate his individuality.

In offering religion in more credible form to an age that is increasingly sceptical, the Bishop of Woolwich seeks to strip it of its supernatural paraphernalia and present it as an indispensable system of morals. But from the time that the Church cornered men's superstitious fear and exploited it with declamations of nature as the created province of the almighty, it has evolved to a position where it is no longer even confident in its dogma and is reduced to weak exhortations to live in good neighbourliness and brotherly love. And even these appeals are nothing more than hypocrisy since at the same time that it spuriously wishes social harmony it condones and supports a competitive economic system whose fundamental feature is the exploitation of men by men.

The evolving technical nature of capitalist society will go on revealing the Church as more and more of an outlandish anachronism and in time will heap greater and greater embarrassment upon its dogma. Yet in spite of this and of the attempts by churchmen to modify the image of the Church and alter its social role, it will retain one enduring characteristic, that of an anti-working class institution. The Church supports the present method of producing and distributing wealth – capitalism. The ideas that it disseminates, its concepts about society, and the universe it trades in, are either irrelevant or hostile to the ideas that the working class requires to achieve its economic emancipation.

Socialists seek the universal brotherhood of men, but for the Church to sloganise ideals and in practice support a system that precludes their realisation, is worse than hollow gesture, it erects a barrier to their practical achievement. What an organisation that genuinely aspires to social harmony on a world scale should do is relate to specific social situations within actual experience, and discern and illuminate and explain the reasons why men now behave in a manner contrary to their mutual interests. It should argue a valid social theory and advocate a practical course for political action that offer the sure prospect of the unity of all men based on relations of genuine social equality. Only Socialists do this.

(August 1963)

Politics of Pop

"The Commandments say 'Thou Shalt Not Kill' and half the world is in training to annihilate the other half. Nobody would get me in uniform and off to Aden to kill a lot of people I've never met and have nothing against anyway. I know people say they are against wars and yet they go on fighting them. Millions of marvellous young men are killed and in five minutes everybody seems to have forgotten all about it. War stems from power-mad politicians and patriots."

Except for the final comment, this could be a socialist speaking in Hyde Park. In fact, it is Mick Jagger of the Rolling Stones giving his views on war and militarism. On many other questions his ideas come close to the arguments which socialists use. For example, he is outspokenly anti-religious and opposed to marriage. While he does not appear to relate any of this to the class structure of society, he does at least look upon private property as a curse.

"There should be no such thing as private property. Anybody should be able to go where he likes and do what he likes."

Jagger calls himself an anarchist and, like most anarchists, his weak point is his failure to understand how capitalism works. Politicians he claims are "a dead loss" and it is they who are responsible for wars, the legal system and the rest of it.

"Politics, like the legal system, is dominated by old men. Old men who are also bugged by religion."

Socialists would reply that it is not the individuals, such as Wilson, who administer capitalism who are to blame but the system of society itself. Nor would we accept that it is the 'old men' who have landed the world in its present mess. Even Jagger must recognise that he is in the minority among young people; most youth are just as ardent supporters of private property as their fathers and grandparents. In fact, one has to look no further than some of the other groups competing on the pop scene to see just how committed they are to capitalism, religious superstitions and all.

Probably the most depressing case is the Beatles. An immensely talented and versatile group, politically they seem be about as wet as they come. One of them, George Harrison, is convinced, like Jagger, that it is the 'old men' who are the cause of the world's problems.

"I think music is the main interest of the younger people. It doesn't really matter about the older people now because they're finished anyway. There's still going to be years and years of having all these old fools who are governing us are bombing us and doin' all that because, you know, it's always them."

Confronted by this, Harrison's philosophy is to shut his eyes and pretend it isn't there. He sees an individual way out in meditation. Everything in the material world is superficial, he argues; it is only by burrowing deep inside yourself that you can find god and personal fulfilment.

"If you can contact that absolute state you can just tap that amazing source of energy and intelligence. It's there, anyway – you've just got to contact it and then it will make whatever you do easier and better. Everything in life works out better because everybody is happier with themselves."

This might be a comforting creed to someone with Harrison's wealth but unemployed workers in Birmingham or hungry peasants in Bengal are likely to be slightly less impressed by the miraculous powers of meditation. The Beatles' spiritual mentor, the so-called Maharishi Mahesh Yogi, obviously has a shrewd understanding of this and restricts his missionary efforts to the clientele of the London Hilton and such places. The Maharishi, a sort of latter-day Rasputin with mental powers that seem to be in inverse proportion to his impressive title, is at least a magnificent showman. Some of his profundities have to be heard to be believed: "I think ladies meditate comparatively more successfully because the quality of heart is more developed in the ladies than in the men, and therefore the waves of joy are more aroused, and that's why the joy is felt more. The heart is more – a mother's heart is much more much more wavy – more waves, deeper waves rise in the mother's heart than in the father's heart. An experience of bliss does need a more capable instrument of emotion."

People who fall for this sort of rot will obviously be taken in by anything and, like Rasputin, the Maharishi seems to have a low opinion of those who provide him with a comfortable living. Interviewed recently in Bremen (West Germany) he was reported to have laughingly remarked that "no matter where I am people will find in me the commodity that they want."

As well as their hatred of the 'old men', Jagger and Harrison have another trait in common – their dislike of oppression. Yet there are plenty of pop singers with other ideas – some openly racialist, others advocating dictatorship. P.J. Proby, for example, is fond of making half-witted generalisations about negroes – "They're always asking for handouts. They don't have any real dignity." Another singer with totalitarian sympathies is Scott Walker who, like Harold Wilson, has a passion for telling the working class what is wrong with them. According to Walker we have all gone flabby in the West and we ought to have this knocked out of us by a good dose of Stalinism.

"Russians have an unbelievable strength, nothing shakes them. The workers here should have the same opportunities, they should be educated on radio and television. They need a good dose of propaganda and more than anything else they need a form of dictatorship again … then we'd be all right again."

The politics of pop are worth looking at not because pop singers are anybody in particular but because most of them are from the working class and, to a certain extent, their ideas are typical of the lines which young workers think along.

One of the most widespread of their illusions is the feeling that the fundamental division in society is between young and old, rather than between the working class and the propertied class. Prejudices such as this are just as dangerous as racialism because they obscure the fact that the real conflict in society is between classes – not generations. The gulf which separates a young worker from a young capitalist is immeasurably wider than that which exists between two workers of different ages. Whatever superficial differences there might be in styles of dress or tastes in music, working men are united as a class by the fact that each one of us has to sell his labour power to the capitalists. In the same way the capitalist class stand together, whatever generation they might identify themselves with as individuals, because collectively they live off the surplus value which they wring out of the working class. It would be nice to have a few politically conscious pop singers who recognised this but, in the end, it doesn't matter that much. After all it is not a few individuals like George Harrison or Mick Jagger who are going to win the revolution but the millions of working men and women, young and old, who make up the working class.

Let's finish by giving the floor to Jimmy Saville – one of the most successful DJs in the pop business. Preaching in a church near Halifax just before Christmas he sent up a prayer to capitalism which would have warmed the heart of any Victorian mill owner or steel baron.

"For the first few years, I worked down a coal mine. Now I have hit this 'gold seam' and I say, 'Thank you, Lord, business is good'."

For the rest of us, who are still working down the mines, or in the factories and offices, how many of us feel like echoing Jimmy's pious gratitude? The only 'golden seam' we are ever likely to hit is socialism. And that won't be thanks to any gods but just to our own revolutionary initiative.

(February 1968)

How Close was France to a Socialist Revolution?

One of the most amusing reports to come out of France during the recent unrest was of one panic-stricken capitalist, convinced that his class was about to be expropriated, who loaded his car with over £1 million in cash and made a dash for the Swiss border. But his terror, ridiculous in retrospect, was matched by a corresponding euphoria in left-wing circles. Anyone accustomed to thinking along Bolshevik or anarchist lines was convinced that 'a revolutionary situation' had developed and, in Britain at any rate, there were several groups declaring that the socialist revolution had started. Already May 1968 is part of the mythology of the left and there is a generally accepted explanation of why the agitation seeped away and why the strikers drifted back to work. The French workers are supposed to have been ripe for revolution and all that was missing was "a large revolutionary organisation capable of giving direction to the demands of the working class."

This raises the whole question of what constitutes a socialist revolution. The Socialist Party of Great Britain argues that it is not enough to have thousands of demonstrators on the streets or even millions of workers occupying the factories. Above all the working class must have a clear understanding of what Socialism entails and what methods are effective in overthrowing capitalism. A grasp of socialist principles by the vast majority of the workers is a minimal condition for going forward to Socialism and no party, no matter how religiously it follows the Bolshevik tradition, can substitute for this.

If this is accepted, then we can estimate how close France came to a socialist revolution by taking a look at the demands which the workers advanced during the period of upheaval. Most prominent were the usual claims for higher wages, better working conditions, shorter hours and security of employment. (There are between two and three million workers on the minimum wage level of less than £8 a week and at least four million earning under £11 a week.) Such demands have the full support of the Socialist Party – but we must emphasise that there is nothing revolutionary about them. In fact, the wage increases that have been secured need to be put in perspective. They seem to be averaging out to a general rise of about 13% (on the basis of a 10% all-round increase and a 35% rise in the minimum wage) but this needs to be set against the fact that *nominal* wages have been rising by 6% annually over the last few years anyway. Although these increases will naturally cut into profits, the international capitalist class hastened to reassure itself that the outcome would be far from a disaster. As the Economics Editor of the *Sunday Times* put it: "The pay settlement will not be wholly adverse for France's economy. The big increase in the minimum wage will help send the poorer French firms to the wall, releasing workers for the big, profitable ones – which pay well above the minimum."

Yet the strikers did not restrict their demands simply to these issues. At numerous plants there were calls for "a radical change in the power structure" and for "participation of the workers in the running of the factory." A leader of Force Ouvrière (the social democratic trade union federation) pointed out his members were agitating for "genuine workers' participation in the policy of industry" and a senior Renault shop steward came out for nationalisation of key sectors of the economy, including all the car firms, the chemical industry and the banks. Understandably, demands such as these were greeted with rapturous delight by all those who imagine Socialism as a system of nationalisation under workers' control; but the Socialist Party rejects this view. For socialists nationalisation, whatever its trimmings, is nothing more than state capitalism. The policy of workers' control does not pose a threat to the capitalist system as long as those workers are still committed to capitalism and have not understood the socialist alternative. That this was the case in France is made clear by the fact that even the most extreme elements, such as Cohn-Bendit, went no further than the old utopian demand for equal wages. Who was urging the abolition of the wages system and an end to the market economy? For this reason, we cannot accept the claims of one young activist in St. Nazaire: "The long-term outlook is uncertain, but not hopeless. On one tier, there are the traditional union claims, which must be met immediately. On another, the government and the regime itself are in question. There is the challenge of capitalist society, of social orders based on private property."

Obviously there was a challenge to the government and the Gaullist regime but capitalism remained secure throughout.

For all that, the Socialist Party recognises that there are vital lessons to be drawn from the recent struggles of the French workers. One of the most important is the complete bankruptcy of the 'communist' parties, as demonstrated by the PCF. Another striking feature was the way in which the factories and universities were organised while the employers and authorities were temporarily eliminated. Although there was no production during the strikes, all the factory services had to be maintained. At the Renault plant at Billancourt, for example, the factory hospital was still functionning, the firemen and security officers had to keep patrolling, food had to be prepared – and so on. Even more impressive was the Sorbonne, with the students in control. A hospital service, treating those injured in the riots, was centred on the Medical Faculty and it was estimated that a daily average of 10,000 posters and hand-outs were being produced by the Fine Arts School. Yet all of this was done by unpaid, voluntary labour, by people cooperating for a common purpose. Too much should not be made of this (we are not suggesting it represented 'socialism in action') but it does at least disprove the often-heard objection to a socialist society that, if the coercive pressures of the wages system were removed, nothing but chaos would result.

Another important aspect was the role of the police and armed forces. Although vast publicity was given to the brutality of the CRS, there was less on the discontent which was building up among the ordinary police forces over their use as government thugs. Already by 18th May there were reports from the police unions of "extreme tension" in the forces. Some of the police were also adopting the tactics of the strikers themselves. An article in the *Times* mentioned that the branch dealing with intelligence on student activity had been deliberately depriving the government of information about student leaders in support of an expenses claim! This indicates that the majority of those who make up the police and armed forces are subjected to the general pressures which act on all working men and women.

As for the army, General Fourquet – the Chief of Staff – made it clear that it would obey any constitutionally elected government – even a 'communist' one. Whether Fourquet and the general meant this or not is largely immaterial for, when we are in a position to establish Socialism, the bulk of the armed forces (as with the rest of the working class) will be socialists and will understand that their interest lies not in fighting their fellow workers but in freeing mankind as a whole by stripping the capitalist class of its wealth.

If there were a working class committed to Socialism in France the correct method of achieving political power would be to fight the general election on a revolutionary programme, without any reforms to attract support from non-socialists. In fact, the first stage in a socialist revolution is for the vast majority of the working class to use their votes as class weapons. This would represent the transfer of political power to the working class. We adopt this position not because we are mesmerised by legality and not because we overlook the cynical and two-faced double-dealing which the capitalists will no doubt resort to. We say, however, that a majority of socialist delegates voted into the national assembly or parliament would use political power to coordinate the measures needed to

Socialist Standard

Official journal Socialist Party of Gt Britain and World Socialist Party of Ireland   JULY 1968 - 9d

HOW CLOSE WAS FRANCE TO A SOCIALIST REVOLUTION ?

overthrow the capitalist system. Any minority which was inclined to waver would have second thoughts about taking on such a socialist majority which was in a position to wield the state power.

But since the workers in France are still convinced that capitalism is the only viable social system, the immediate task must be for genuine socialists to concentrate their efforts on spreading socialist ideas among the working class. For this purpose an independent socialist party, which does not compromise its principles or dissipate its activity in attempts to reform capitalism, is indispensable.

(July 1968)

Why Socialists Oppose the Vietcong

Vietnam is the latest of the leftwingers' adopted fatherlands. Before Vietnam it was Algeria, before that it was Cuba, and so on back to Russia. This support for the Vietcong does not depend on what is actually going on in Vietnam, but is rather an expression of the leftwingers' dissatisfaction with certain aspects of modern society. To that extent it is irrational.

Nevertheless those who support the Vietcong imagine that they are Marxists and it is in pseudo-Marxist terms that they rationalise their support for this nationalist movement whose aim is to set up a state capitalist regime in the South similar to that in the North. The Vietcong is not a socialist movement, and by no stretch of the imagination can it be said to have anything to do with Socialism. But since those who shout for 'Victory for the Vietcong' have dragged in Marx and Socialism, we must at least refute their arguments and state why Socialists do not support the Vietcong.

Leftwingers use two basic arguments. First, that socialists should support any movement, even if it is not socialist, that weakens 'American imperialism' which they say is the main threat to social revolution throughout the world, just as Marx supported moves against Tsarist Russia. Second, and this comes from Lenin, the Vietcong and workers in the West are fighting the same enemy – imperialism – and so we should support each other.

It is true that in the middle of the nineteenth century Marx saw Tsarist Russia, the 'gendarme of Europe', as a great threat to the further social progress of mankind. He felt that if Russia overran western Europe it would crush the democratic movement and put the social revolution back for years. Therefore, he was ready to support any moves that might weaken the power of Tsarist Russia. He supported Britain, France and Turkey in the Crimean war. He stood for an independent Polish state, to be a buffer between Russia and the rest of Europe. He did all he could to expose the pro-Russia policies and intrigues of Lord Palmerston. These may seem odd activities for a socialist – and, indeed, we have criticised Marx for them. Marx argued that before Socialism is possible society must pass through the capitalist stage. But this is no automatic process; it depends on the outcome of human struggles. Russia was 'reactionary' in the proper sense of the word in that it was a threat to the development even of capitalism. Marx opposed Tsarist Russia, not because it was the strongest capitalist power, but because it was the strongest anti-capitalist power.

Looking back now we can see that Marx was over-optimistic as to the prospects of a socialist revolution in Europe. In time the capitalist states of western Europe grew stronger and the Tsarist Empire weaker, finally to be destroyed along with Austro-Hungary and Imperial Germany in the first world war. Before that even, Russia in a bid to keep its armed forces up to date had become indebted to the capitalists of France and Belgium. Well before the turn of the century we can say that conditions had changed since Marx's day. Capitalism was firmly established as the new world order. Russia was no longer a threat. The task of socialists was even clearer: to oppose all wars and nationalist movements and to work to build up a world-wide workers' movement with Socialism as its aim. This has always been the policy of the Socialist Party of Great Britain.

Today capitalism quite clearly dominates the world, in Russia and China as well as in the West. To talk of "American imperialism" as the main threat is to play the game of state capitalist Russia and China. Every up-and-coming capitalist power finds the world already carved up by the established powers. If it is to expand its influence it must clash with these powers, as Germany, Japan, Italy and Russia have found and as China is now finding. All of them, in their time, have beaten the "anti-imperialist" drum, that is, have opposed the domination of the world by Britain and France and later America. Mussolini talked of Italy as a "proletarian nation" in a class war against the "bourgeois nations". Nazi Germany stirred up Arab and Latin American nationalism. Japan advanced the slogan of "Asia for the Asians". Russia, too, and now China, like Germany before, vociferously denounce Anglo-French-American imperialism.

Naturally socialists, wittingly or unwittingly, do not allow themselves to be used as tools of some capitalist state, as most of those who shout for the Vietcong are (some know full well what they are doing). Socialists are opposed to world capitalism and to governments everywhere.

Lenin could not believe it when he learnt that the German Social Democrats had voted for the war credits in 1914. Later he worked out a theory to try to explain it, his theory of imperialism. Basically, he argued that as profits were greater in the undeveloped parts of the world capitalists were eager to invest there; this brought the capitalist states into continual conflict over the division of the world. Part of the "super-profits" of this imperialist exploitation were used to pay higher wages and provide social reforms for sections of the workers at home. They were thus led away from revolutionary socialism towards opportunism.

This theory is mistaken on nearly all counts. It has not been proved that the rate of profit was higher in the colonial territories. There is a much simpler explanation for capitalist expansion into the undeveloped world in the forty or so years before the first world war: the need to secure sources of raw material for the expanding industries at home, and then to secure strategic points to protect these sources and the trade routes to and from them. As for Lenin's explanation of reformism it is the purest nonsense. To suggest that workers share in the proceeds of colonial exploitation is to reject the Marxian theory of wages which says that wages are the price of labour-power.

But this argument was an essential part of Lenin's theory. For on it he based his strategy of support for anti-imperialist nationalist movements. If they succeeded, he believed, they would deprive the imperialist state concerned of its super-profits and so also of its ability to buy off its workers. Deprived of their share the workers' standard of living would drop and they would once again become revolutionary, affording a chance for a Bolshevik-type vanguard to seize power.

This is typical of Lenin's thinking, to rely on some factor outside of the development of the working class itself to create the conditions for social revolution. It fits in well with his contempt for the abilities of workers and his view that they should be manipulated by a self-appointed vanguard. Needless to say this short-cut to Socialism is just as much a dead-end as all the others.

Of course defeat in Vietnam, and the whole of South East Asia, would have serious consequences for American capitalism. That is why they are fighting. It would deprive them of access to many raw materials, but more important it would shift the balance of power around the pacific in favour of Chinese state capitalism.

It is not true that the Vietcong and workers are fighting the same enemy. The Vietcong are fighting American capitalism. The interests of workers are opposed not only to American capitalism but to capitalism everywhere including Russia and China. Victory for the Vietcong, as we have already explained, would shift the world balance of power from America to other capitalist powers. This is not something that is in the interests of workers, or something that they should support. There is no issue at stake in Vietnam worth a single worker's life.

The Socialist Party, then, is opposed to the Vietnam war, as to all wars. We do not take sides. Nor are we hypocrites like those who cynically use all normal people's abhorrence of the burning of women and children (as if the Vietcong did not use flame-throwers) to get them to support one side in this war. Such people do not really want an end to the killing; they want it to go on till the side they support has won. Let them at least be honest and stop trying to fool people with their phoney anti-war sentiments.

(October 1968)

Man: ape in wolf's clothing?

Perhaps the most famous of scientific frauds was the fake Piltdown Skull of 1910, a 'missing link' fabricated by a person unknown. That anonymous joker put together an ape's jaw with a human skull. Desmond Morris has grafted the most ignorant fairy tales about human society onto a body of basically sound ideas about human biological evolution. *The Naked Ape* is a barefaced hoax.

As a gimmick, Morris pretends to describe the human animal just as it would be pictured by a zoologist if it were a newly-discovered species. 'Naked ape' is a clinical term (like 'black-footed squirrel') which is supposed to denote men's most noticeable characteristics: their lack of fur. But evidently, Morris has become a rich man because to millions of his readers, nudity is a novelty. It should be obvious that the most important thing about human animals is not that they are *naked*, but that they are *clothed*. In other words, they produce what they consume; they turn the artificial into the necessary, and (like Morris) sometimes confuse it with the natural.

His book is a hymn of praise to modern capitalism. All the current practices, preoccupations. superstitions, myths and manners are, according to Morris, highly admirable. Furthermore, they are *natural* because they stem from man's past as a wolflike, monogamous, predatory killer. Frequently this approach becomes so manifestly silly that we are tempted to suspect the author of perpetrating a spoof, a sarcastic attack on the ludicrous legends of human nature: "One of the essential features of the hunt is that it is a tremendous gamble and so it is not surprising that gambling, in the many stylised forms it takes today, should have such a strong appeal."

We can safely wager that not one of the fish-eyed zombies who stand for hours in front of a fruit machine has yet thought of defending his addiction with the excuse that it stems from the bloodthirsty excitement of his prehistoric past. Derision is the only intelligent response to this sort of foolishness, yet Morris seems to be serious. Anyone with a smattering of education knows that societies have changed historically, and that customs vary geographically. But according to Morris, only capitalist man is truly human: "The earlier anthropologists rushed off to all kinds of unlikely corners of the world in order to unravel the basic truth about our nature, scattering to remote cultural backwaters so atypical and unsuccessful that they are nearly extinct. They then returned with startling facts about the bizarre mating customs, strange kinship systems, or weird ritual procedures of these tribes, and used this material as though it were of central importance to the behaviour of our species as a whole. The work done by these investigators was, of course, extremely interesting and most valuable in showing what can happen when a group of naked apes become sidetracked into a cultural blind alley. It revealed just how far from the normal our behaviour patterns can stray without a complete social collapse. What it did not tell us was anything about the typical behaviour of typical naked apes. This can only be done by examining the common behaviour patterns that are shared by all the ordinary, successful members of the major cultures – the mainstream specimens who together represent the vast majority. Biologically this is the only sound approach."

In other words, don't talk to me about filthy savages. Of course, biology has nothing to do with it. There is no evidence that different cultures are due to different biological endowments, and plenty of conclusive evidence against this. People from "all kinds of unlikely corners of the world" have been educated to be perfectly competent under advanced capitalism. Sometimes, even, the more backward the better: as in many parts of Africa, where people from stateless societies (such as the Ibo) have caught on to capitalist values much quicker than people from near-feudal societies at a more advanced stage of social evolution. For that matter, it is common knowledge that the peoples in the most advanced societies today (the Anglo-Saxons, Japanese, Russians, etc.) were for thousands of years scattered in "remote cultural backwaters" while highly successful empires sprouted in what are now wretched deserts. Morris would be very contemptuous about the "bizarre mating customs, strange kinship systems, or weird ritual procedures" of his European ancestors of 2000 years ago.

Tightly blinkered

Not that he is a racist. His point is that "the characteristics that the earlier anthropologists studied in these tribes may well be the very features that have interfered with the progress of the groups concerned." But to say this is to gloss over the weak point in his argument. If the development of civilisation has been social and not biological, then why stop the clock at one point in time and say that this particular stage of society corresponds to an inborn pattern? Is it not clear, instead, that man is capable of a very wide range of cultural behaviour, and that the modern set of conventions in marriage and politics is just one of many, all equally compatible with any of man's inborn characteristics?

Not to Morris. He constantly refers to *his* society as 'mainstream', 'healthy', 'go-ahead', 'natural', and 'typical'. His reasons for this judgement are mainly two: that capitalism has the biggest population, and that "the naked ape is essentially an exploratory species." Morris is thus a typical example of an individual tightly blinkered by the capitalist system, inside which he has been brought up. It never occurs to him that his own value judgement in placing a massive population and an exploratory drive above all other considerations is itself a result of social conditioning. It would seem to him extremely 'bizarre', 'strange', 'weird', and 'typical' to judge a society by (for instance) whether its population is happy, or whether its exploratory drives are harnessed to the satisfaction of human needs. He cannot avoid recognising the danger of capitalist war: "We are, to put it mildly, in a mess, and there is a strong chance that we shall have exterminated ourselves by the end of the century."

And, as one whose mind is open to every myth and delusion in popular circulation, Morris believes that there is a danger of world "overpopulation", so it might seem surprising that he should consider a large population the primary badge of success. But he has an answer for this: "It looks very much as though, during the next century or so, we are going to have to change our sexual ways at last. But if we do, it will not be because they failed, but because they succeeded too well."

Therefore, although the twentieth century predator is a marvellous piece of work (Morris claims his approach isn't a moral one, but his strong approval shines through every page), the writer can have it both ways. We are a tremendous success because of our animal nature; our colossal failure is due to our animal nature. He has further room for manoeuvre in man's twofold origin: that of a vegetarian primate which descended from the trees and became a hunter. Anything which cannot be 'explained' by man's predatory nature can of course be quietly slotted into his primate nature. Morris's strategy is to *assume* that all modern man's behaviour is caused by his 'nature', then to look into the current theories of man's evolutionary origins for the most plausible tie-ups with his present-day activities. Naturally they can easily be found, and this approach then becomes circular, 'proving' itself. Since Morris is quite good on biology, his obvious expertise in this field seems to give his elfin portrayal of society some authority. It is a widespread superstition that an expert in one field carries some weight in all fields, and Dr Morris has exploited this to the full. Latter-day Original Sin merchant Robert Ardrey was overjoyed to find some apparently 'scientific' support for his utterly discredited 'Man the Killer' fantasies, and commented on *The Naked Ape*: "This spectacular book by a master scientist is what every naked ape has been waiting for."

Dislike of facts

Actually Morris is more than just a specialist who imagines the universe is part of his speciality. He, along with Ardrey and Lorenz, is part of a very definite 'backlash' against social science. The problem is that modern sociology and social anthropology, even though sponsored by the capitalist state, have proved up to the hilt what socialists have long insisted: that man's most sacred institutions are not the product of his nature, but of his changing social environment. There is a very powerful and widespread dislike of this well-substantiated (and rather elementary) fact, which manifests itself in a strong appetite for the output of anyone who can undertake to 'prove' the opposite. Anthony Storr wrote in the *Sunday Times* recently: "'One quite certain principle of sociology is that very little, if any, human behaviour is inherited'. This extraordinary statement must arise from the idea that man is perfectible by altering his social institutions: a delusion to which only very old-fashioned Communists can now subscribe. We know very little about the fundamental patterns of human behaviour, but we know enough to be sure that man is not infinitely adaptable, and that we neglect biological factors at our peril."

This passage bristles with interesting details: Storr's coy recognition of the apologetic political function his views serve, the meaningless but ominous-sounding 'neglect biological factors at our peril', the casual admission that 'very little' is known about the subject of his heated denunciation, the unjustified use of the alarm-word 'extraordinary', and amid this wordy dust-storm, the one definite statement: that man is not 'infinitely adaptable', which no-one ever suggested.

Actions learned

At the risk of labouring the obvious, let us point out that all of man's behaviour results from a combination of environmental and genetic factors; that man is the most adaptable of all animals and all his deliberate actions are *learned*; that historically and geographically societies have varied very greatly in their systems of marriage, leadership (if any), property, religion (if any), and status, and that these diversities are not due to genetic differences; that to call any of these systems innate is exactly as ridiculous as to say that the grammar of the English language is innate.

The very fact that the whole human species has spent a very brief period of time (a few centuries) in Morris's "mainstream", while it spent the vast majority of its career (many tens of thousands of years) much closer to his "remote cultural backwaters", should dispel any notion that capitalism's conventions are inborn. But on one point we agree with Morris. Capitalism is the most advanced system the world has ever seen. For our part, however, this not a moral judgement. On the contrary, capitalism appeared upon the scene drenched in blood from head to foot; it sent its hideous scourges, Jesus and VD, into all "remote cultural backwaters", as the advance guard of murder, pillage, and profit. Under capitalism, genocide has become commonplace; misery the very air we breathe.

But when we say that capitalism is the most advanced social system, we mean that its *potential* for satisfying human needs is greater than that of any previous order. Capitalism is still a tremendously dynamic society, a society of unparalleled achievement, but of unparalleled waste and destruction also. Only Socialism can put the 'exploratory urge' of capitalism to the service of human happiness.

The Naked Ape does contain some well-established facts, and some reasonable speculations (though even the zoological data cannot be entirely relied upon. Some of Morris's sweeping generalisations about sex in non-human primates are falsified by Leonard Williams's observations of woolly monkeys). Furthermore, even in 1969, many workers still have a religious, sentimental view of man, refusing to believe that everything about human beings can be explained scientifically. The book may therefore do a good job here, in stripping away mystery and confusion.

Monkey myths

Violence, Monkeys and Men by Claire and W.M.S. Russel explains itself at the outset: "First, we have tried to show that violence is not the result of an innate propensity to aggression irrespective of conditions, but a response to stress in societies. Second, we suggest that violence is part of a complex of responses evolved to achieve drastic reduction of a population that is in danger of outgrowing its resources."

Here we have the familiar Malthusian view of human violence, linked up with observations of the behaviour of overcrowded captive monkeys. The main error is the confusion of overpopulation with overcrowding. In the world today there is plenty of overcrowding but no overpopulation: the general trend is the depopulation of some areas, together with the cramming of large masses of people into gigantic cities. There is plenty of room in the world.

Overcrowding does place terrible strains on workers, leading to outbursts of violence, but these must be seen in association with all the other oppressive features of life inside capitalism.

Interesting is the summary of research into monkey violence. In 1932 Zuckerman published *The Social Life of Monkeys and Apes*, based on observations of baboons in Regent's Park: "The notion of violent aggressiveness as an inherent quality of monkeys (or at least of baboons) was impressed upon a generation of scientists. By the fifties, when the crime returns from the affluent societies began to hit the headlines, the apparent results of Zuckerman's work may well have influenced a wider public, and helped to bring about the resurgence of the unconditional view of aggression. Alike in monkeys and man, it seemed, the improvement of living conditions is no guarantee against violence; aggressiveness is human nature, monkey nature, a fact of nature in the most fundamental sense."

Only in recent years have researchers begun to study apes and monkeys in the wild, though they have done so with their heads full of prevailing capitalist myths about 'human nature' and hence 'monkey nature'. These scientists have been astonished at the peaceable behaviour of wild monkeys, and at first tried to write it off as exceptional or 'unusual', but they have finally had to face the unpalatable fact that healthy monkeys and apes in the wild hardly ever fight.

The author's conclusion is that "all monkeys are peaceful in some conditions, and violently aggressive in others. Violence is a property of mammalian societies exposed to stress." They apply this to human beings, and refute the theory (held by Morris) that man's nature has been predominantly moulded by a wolflike hunting experience. For by far the greater part of the evolution of man's ancestors, after they came down from the trees, it would be truer to term them 'scavengers' rather than 'hunters'. In any case, adaptation to a hunting life would not necessarily make any creatures more aggressive within their own society,

Man and Monkey by Leonard Williams is a strange book: an idiosyncratic account of the author's relations with woolly monkeys, combined with a theory of history and society which is a mish-mash of undigested bits of Hegel, Freud, Nietzsche, Lorenz and, yes, Marx. Here we see again the naked ape syndrome, of mixing up half-baked, gossipy opinions with hard facts, in the hope that the latter will add some conviction to the former. A couple of samples: "We are all agreed that the fate of humanity depends on whether the strength of morality can cope with the instinctive drives of man." "History shows that aggressive races possessed more initiative and energy than their passive neighbours." Williams generally does reach opposite conclusions to those of Morris: he finds modern life profoundly *unnatural*.

One very clear conclusion from both *Violence, Monkeys and Man* and *Man and Monkey* is the horribly cruel treatment of our cousins the apes and monkeys, both in zoos and in the pet trade, in the interests of profit.

(September 1969)

Hippies: an abortion of socialist understanding

Everybody seems to think I'm lazy.
I don't mind – think they're crazy.
Running everywhere at such a speed.
Till they find there's no need ...

Ever since the explosion of 'Flower Power' in Summer '67, the world's working class has been aware of the Hippy movement, or as it is now more frequently called, 'The Underground'. Attitudes to the hippies have varied from amused fascination to angry revulsion. Many people have grown more hostile to them over the past two years, as their emphasis on such harmless-sounding words as 'Love' and 'Beautiful People' has declined, and their tendency to smoke pot has become more widely publicised.

In Britain the occupation of 144 Piccadilly confirmed the hippies' bad reputation – though the occupiers were not typical of the Underground by any means. Television news announcers put on their frowns for this item, were careful to identify the occupation with soccer hooliganism (both were 'violence to property'), and equally careful to avoid dragging in irrelevant details like the fact of empty houses alongside homeless people.

A wave of horror swept the country at the realisation that there were people who not only wore long hair (and obviously smelt foul, as anyone could see by looking at their TV screens), but actually believed they had a right to live without working. In one television programme, David Frost, Hughie Green and Robert Maxwell – those highly productive labourers who toil so usefully to justify their existence – led an attack on the hippies for their conscientious objection to work. When Richard

Neville (editor of the Underground magazine *Oz*) suggested that the idea of work as a duty hadn't a very ancient historical pedigree, that work in the modern world was "really a form of slavery," and that with today's productive techniques there could easily be more than enough wealth for everyone, he was devastated by Frost's crisply intelligent retorts: "Very highflown I'm sure" and "I really am an old fuddy-duddy you know."

Hippy characteristics

The hippy phenomenon is a movement, a set of attitudes, a subculture or a nuisance, according to your point of view. It consists of several hundred thousand people, drawn mostly from the working class, in the advanced regions of Capitalism. It is vaguely defined, fuzzy-edged – no one can draw up a hippy manifesto; no one can specify who is a hippy and who isn't. It differs from country to country: in America, for example, there are relatively fewer semi-hippies or weekend hippies than in Britain, for the simple reason that long hair is a much greater obstacle to getting a job in the States than in Europe. All the same, we can list some of the features which distinguish hippies from what they call 'straight' society.

First, there is age – or rather, youth. Hippies are predominantly under-thirties. Second, they have an unorthodox pattern of drugs consumption – mostly pot, with occasional recourse to acid ('pot' is now common parlance for cannabis [marihuana], and acid for lysergic acid [LSD]) and minor use of amphetamines and other pills. Or as 'straight' society (gaily swilling down immense quantities of alcohol, nicotine, barbiturates, aspirin, etc.) usually puts it: 'Hippies take drugs'. Whatever may be the medical properties of the hippies' chosen stimulants, they do have the important social property that their use is, for the time being, prohibited by the State.

Third, hippies possess a typical style of appearance: long hair, casual-to-scruffy clothes, beads, etc. And fourth, like all minority groups they have their own language: 'mind-blowing' (stimulating to the point of powerful hallucination); 'hang-up' (unfortunate disturbance of tranquillity); 'fuzz' (policemen), and so forth. It is a measure of the commercial cashing-in on hippies that virtually all of their jargon is very widely-known through its dissemination in pop music. Most of it was borrowed from other sources, not coined, by the hippies.

Fifth, hippies are preoccupied with certain forms of art, for example beat music accompanied by displays of coloured, flashing lights. Sixth, they aim at an inversion of the values of 'straight' society. They embrace spontaneity rather than self-control; childlikeness rather than sophistication; love rather than power; 'dropping out' rather than careerism; 'doing your own thing' rather than imposed uniformity; admiration for the destitute rather than for 'affluence'; disorder rather than method – and of course, Indians rather than cowboys.

Seventh, hippies often show a greater-than-average susceptibility to superstition. They are generally against established 'organised religion', but fall for all sorts of religious and mystical clap-trap which have an exotic flavour; astrology, transcendental meditation, palmistry, sunspots, or Krishna-consciousness.

Lastly, many hippies advocate a revolutionary change in society, though both the manner of achieving this, and the nature of their proposed new system (sometimes described as 'tribal' or 'communitarian') are extremely vague. An example of this vagueness was the slogan advanced in one Underground paper: 'Alternative Society Now!' – its urgent tone somewhat cancelled out by the woolliness of its descriptive content, which could scarcely be less informative. At least many hippies are clear that the major social evils of today are all bound up together, and can be removed only by a total social change. Both of the important politically-oriented offshoots of the hippy movement, the Diggers and the Yippies, make specifically Socialist proposals, such as the abolition of wages and of money. In our opinion, both these groups are doomed to futility because of their methods, but they do constitute an advance on the previously fashionable assortments of youthful radicals. This groping towards Socialist understanding is particularly impressive when set against the temporary direction of trendy Leftism in the US: flirting with black racism, romantic idolising of Guevara and similar state-capitalist prophets, or the demagoguery and vanguardism of the Students for a Democratic Society (SDS).

Causes of hippies

The Socialist argument that the majority of workers must arrive at a clear understanding of Socialism before they can get it, that a Revolution in ideas must precede the Revolution in politics and economics, is often sneered at by those who say that the mass of the population (except, for some reason, the extraordinary people who make this statement) are brainwashed robots, puppets manipulated by TV and the press.

But Capitalism is not a conspiracy. It cannot be controlled by any set of individuals, not even the Capitalist class. Current ideas provide a support for capitalism (though the 'mass media' are only a part of their reinforcement), yet Capitalism is dynamic, constantly advancing and frequently unpredictable in detail. The very ideas which defend capitalism have to be adjusted or replaced, to fit new conditions. Workers must be trained, not only to do their jobs, but also to be versatile, because their jobs are changing all the time, and also to make radical criticisms of the way capitalism is run, because otherwise inefficient and unprofitable blunders would result. As the *Communist Manifesto* put it: "The bourgeoisie cannot exist without constantly revolutionising the instruments of production ... All fixed, fast-frozen relations, with their trains of ancient and venerable prejudices and opinions, are swept away, all new-formed ones become antiquated before they can ossify. All that is solid melts into air, all that is holy is profaned ..."

Today, traditional ideas about work, leisure and 'the purpose of life' are under attack, and in retreat. Capitalism has killed God stone dead, and is stamping on the twitching corpse. Capitalism extends the juicy carrot of the 'Leisure Society' – a golden age of short working-hours and automated abundance, which is ever imminent yet never arrives. Capitalism holds aloft an image of glamour, high-powered pleasure, rest and freedom – whilst the worker's mind and body are reduced ever more thoroughly to instruments of accumulation. From the belief that work is a grim duty, consumption its reward, capitalism is shifting emphasis to the view that consumption is a duty, work something to be made rewarding.

It is in this context of irresistible change that confused vortices of rebellion like hippyism must be seen. The hippy movement has been centred in California – the most technically advanced region of the world, the window on the future. That is not an accident: it is just what Socialists and historical materialists have predicted. The embryo of Socialist ideas is constantly gestating in the womb of advanced capitalism: the foetus is aborted repeatedly, but the fertility of working class consciousness cannot be lost, and the insemination of Socialist organisation must grow more copious. The hippy movement is one of those abortions.

Hippies are a product of the youth cult, the commercialisation of young people and the 'generation gap'. But this gap is not only a construct of the publicity men: the new generation does live and think differently from its elders. Many of the things our fathers and mothers were *grateful* for (and that is a measure of the servile depths to which the working class has sunk), we *take for granted*. Young people in the advanced countries have never been brought to heel by a major slump, nor by a war at home. Their standard of consumption has generally risen steadily throughout their lives, and they confidently expect it to go on doing so indefinitely. Given this outlook, mere technical progress and

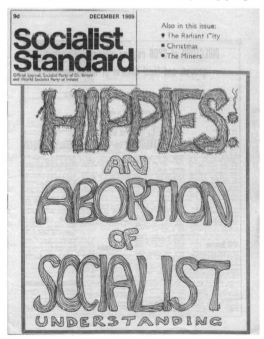

fatter wage packets lose their capacity to impress. Young workers are more likely to ask "What's it all *for*, this endless treadmill? When do we start to live?"

The rapid dissemination of hippyism throughout the advanced world is a consequence of the similarity of conditions in these counties, plus the globe-shrinking communications network: any fad, fashion, doctrine or cult, once it has popped up in one nation is almost instantly mirrored in all. This buttresses our case that the notion of a Socialist revolution in a single country is ludicrous.

The hippies' deliberate irrationality, and their earlier Love worship, are a protest against 'straight' reasonableness and logic. (In fact the very term 'straight', like the archaic 'square' reveals this). Capitalism manifests very thorough rationality in the service of intense irrationality – scientific means to insane ends. Those who don't understand capitalism's structure often find its 'logic' oppressive, and retreat into gooey, mindless sentimentality. This is a very common modern theme, exemplified in things like Godard's early films, such as *Alphaville*.

Mysticism is favoured by a reaction against modern institutional Christianity, seen as a cover for the 'straight' virtues of ambition and conformity, and mysticism links up with drug-induced hallucinations which provide escape from an aimless and insecure reality. It is romantically pretty, a source of poetry an attempt to give back to life a lost 'depth', and in its imported forms it has the flavour of more primitive societies in which alternatives to the score-card mentality of 'straight' achievement compulsion can be found.

The hippy movement is now virtually finished. Certain aspects – the dress, the jargon, the music – are steadily incorporated into a much broader and less rebellious area of commercial youth culture. 'The Underground', always a term with a more political slant, becomes infiltrated by Leftist reformists and insurrectionaries. It is to be hoped they will learn something from the Underground, for they have little to teach it.[1] A feeling of community, and a common set of values, will persist among those who smoke pot (and therefore dislike policemen), but this becomes vaguer as the habit spreads. The really important question is of future movements, perhaps partly hippy-derived, perhaps bigger, perhaps more explicitly antagonistic to the economic system.

---

1. One of these Bolshevik reactionaries, D. Widgery, recently remonstrated with the Underground, via the columns of *IT* (10th October): "*IT* would still be publishing its twee pop-star interviews two months after workers' soviets were declared on Merseyside and Clydeside." Widgery's delusional system is so fantastic that he imagines an administrative apparatus which was a symptom of Russian backwardness half a century ago has some relevance to the working class problems in the 1970s! Notice how his two chosen regions are centres for manual workers, that proportionally declining section (soon to be a minority) of the working class – a section which the Bolsheviks invest with unlimited Romantic potential. Compared to the fairytale world of the Bolsheviks, Tolkien's fables are scientific sociology, twee pop-star interviews the last word in revolutionary politics!

Criticism of hippies

A few young workers, whose anti-Capitalist tendencies were initially stirred by the Underground have progressed in their understanding to the point of embracing revolutionary Socialism, and joining the Socialist Party of Great Britain. But much more could have been accomplished if there had existed a bigger Socialist movement with the resources to put its case more loudly. As it is, a potentially fruitful upsurge of critical and anti-authoritarian ideas has in the main been diverted into reformism, anarchism and mysticism.

The hippies' emphasis on a style instead of a programme, whilst in many ways endearing, and possessing an obvious advantage for propaganda, is a grave obstacle to their progress in understanding. Distinctions of dress, hairstyle and musical taste are, after all, fairly trivial – and many hippies come dangerously close to regarding them as fetishes. Flickering lights, a psychedelic design, a whiff of incense, a Clapton guitar phrase – such things can be combined into a powerfully unified appeal to all the senses, yet Capitalist society has no difficulty in prostituting this as it prostitutes all art and all enjoyment. Whereupon the market, having squeezed the Underground dry, moves on to the next short-lived modish fad. As Wilde put it, the trouble with being very modern is that you become old-fashioned very quickly.

With the first, naive realisation that a new society is necessary, three elementary errors are committed in turn. First, it is supposed that the adoption of attitudes appropriate to the desired society will bring it closer – hence the 'Love' phase. This is quickly seen to be largely unsuccessful, since the conditions of the present system generate completely opposed attitudes. To the extent that it is successful it merely helps to reconcile people to the existing state of affairs. The next stage is to go beyond mere attitudes, to try and act as though the new society were already here. This is like trying to get out of a prison by ignoring the bars, and equally futile. After this, attempts are at last made to overhaul the system, but only piecemeal, by changing bits at a time. However the nature of the bits is mainly determined by the nature of the whole, not vice versa – as student militants are among the most recent to discover. Thus, what started out as something really radical, and in its implications revolutionary, has been shepherded back into the fold of orthodox reformist politics. Only clarity of thought, and courage in the face of the jeers about 'sectarianism' which are always hurled at revolutionaries, can break out of this vicious circle.

Now the Underground veers between two courses of action: assaults on Capitalism and attempted withdrawal from it: respectively symbolised by the occupation of 144 Piccadilly, and the move to Saint Patrick's Isle. But Capitalism will not fall before sporadic demonstrations and happenings, however defiant or amusing these may be. Neither will it let anyone drop out.

It may be argued in defence of the Underground that this is the age of exploration rather than of Principles, and that there is much value in looseness, informality, and even incoherence. But exploration is worthwhile only if it leads to discovery, looseness if it leads to firmness, informality if it leads to definable formal organisation, and incoherence if out of it emerges a new coherence. The Underground is incapable of making these advances because, though often expert at dramatising its criticism of 'straight' society, it seems quite incapable of criticising itself.

Hippies then, are only the symptoms of a sick society: Socialists the cure. Yet to those workers infuriated by the hippy way of life, we say: Don't look for scapegoats. A few 'spongers' are nothing compared to the vast wastage of Capitalism: the arms/space race, built-in shoddiness, the unnecessary monetary system, the 'sponging' of the owners of industry. To blame hippies (students, immigrants, unofficial strikers) for your troubles is to lose sight of the actual cause – which is precisely what your masters the capitalists want. Anyway, the view that people ought to work to 'earn' their subsistence is out-of-date in a world which could easily provide more than enough for everybody, with a tiny fraction of the work done today. Everything should be free; all work should be voluntary – that is Socialism.

To hippies themselves, we say: Pulling faces at Capitalism is not enough. Even talking about 'tribal' alternatives is not enough. An uncompromising stand on Socialist Principles is required before we can start to bring about the new moneyless world society.

(December 1969)

THE TURBULENT
SEVENTIES

The 1970s saw the undisputed return of economic crisis as a prominent feature of the British political scene after the years of post-war boom. This economic crisis was characterised by 'stagflation': while unemployment rose to over a million and then beyond for the first time since the Second World War, inflation also took off in spectacular fashion, the annual rate of price increases reaching 26.9% during 1976. Add to this two miners' strikes, widespread power cuts, a three-day week under Ted Heath's Tory Government, Labour Chancellor Denis Healey being bailed out by the International Monetary Fund, the infamous 'Winter of Discontent', and finally the election of the right-wing Thatcher administration in 1979, this was a decade that was anything but dull. This is not to mention the renewed 'troubles' in Northern Ireland, a spate of hijackings, the continued rise of the feminist movement, the growth of both the far left and far right, together with seemingly endless debates about the UK's relationship with what was then called the 'Common Market'.

For most of the decade the *Socialist Standard* remained rather more staid than the political events and processes it was analysing. Over the majority of this period it was even more of a text-based journal than it had been in the 1960s, with large, clear print, bold headlines and the occasional cartoon. The one apparent concession to extravagance was the glossy paper that characterised its appearance.

The heightened political activity of the 1970s saw a commensurate increase in the space devoted in the pages of the *Standard* to political enquirers and opponents. On occasion, the correspondence columns would run to several pages as those casting around for political answers to the problems of the time encountered the Party's unique analysis of events. The number of theoretical articles remained a noticeable feature of the *Standard* too, especially regarding economics, where the Party had much to say in response to both the events of the time and the arguments of the political left.

The selection of articles chosen here give a mere flavour of the analysis offered by the Socialist Party during this period, beginning with an examination of the return of the 'Irish problem' for the British government. The development of the 'civil rights movement' in Northern Ireland, supported by Catholics and the political left from the late 1960s onwards, paralleled a rise in sectarian violence between Protestants and Catholics which led to the introduction in 1969 of British troops as a 'peace-keeping' force, the Protestants vociferously seeking to defend a perceived privilege in political and economic status. The associated resurgence of terrorist activity by paramilitary organisations like the IRA is examined in 'Shadow of a Gunman – the Irish Republican Army'.

The next article, 'Up In Arms' is concerned with another political phenomenon which had earlier roots – the women's liberation movement that had developed during the 1960s alongside libertarian demands for social and sexual freedoms. As our article demonstrates, while some of the aims of the feminist movement (as it would be called today) were entirely understandable – indeed laudable – the movement as a whole was crippled in the main by its rejection of class as the primary social category in capitalist society.

Along with an article stating the positive case for socialism (the type of which became more prevalent during this period) the next group of articles deal with some of the economic problems that made the 1970s infamous. 'The End of Full Employment' details the rise in unemployment which was to make one of the key elements in the so-called 'post-war consensus' of British politics untenable, namely that governments can and should intervene in the economy to prevent the return of economic depression. 'Anti-Affluence: the Debt-ridden Society' is an analysis of the rise – and consequences – of the use of credit in society, not merely in order to pay for consumer goods during booms but as a means of economic survival during slumps. Meanwhile, inflation and the massive price rises that beset the economy under both Labour and Conservative governments alike during the 1970s is the main subject covered by 'The Crisis: Capitalism's Stranglehold on the Labour Government'.

On 1st January 1973 the UK officially joined the European Economic Community, but dissent from the left-wing of the Labour Party led then Prime Minister Harold Wilson to hold a referendum on continued membership in 1975, the first referendum ever held in Britain. 'The Common Market: In or Out – Does It Matter?' was the *Socialist Standard*'s rounded analysis of the background to the referendum and the main issues involved.

Lastly, the article 'Democracy and the Silicon Chip' is included here because of its discussion of the rapid growth of computerisation during this period and – perhaps more importantly – of how micro-electronic processors could practically assist the organisation and democratic administration of a socialist society.

Shadow of a Gunman: the Irish Republican Army

Sinn Fein was formed in 1905 and its numerous political utterances between then and the establishment of Partition leave no doubt that it represented the interests of the rising capitalist class in the South of Ireland in their struggle to achieve political autonomy in order to legislate political conditions suitable to the growth of a fledgling capitalism.

The Sinn Fein Policy Statement of 1917 summarised the utterances and actions of the organisation over the previous twelve years and made nonsense of the noble-sounding sentiments expressed by Pearse on the steps of the GPO in Dublin in 1916. The capitalist class of every country when they are striving for power pay lip-service to noble sentiments in order to rally the working class in support of their struggle and the honeyed phrases of the Declaration of the Irish Republic, with its generalisations about the Irish Nation being the property of the Irish people, were a far cry from the practical economic aspirations of the native capitalists, expressed in Sinn Fein's Policy Statement: "No possibility would be left as far as Sinn Fein were concerned for a syndicate of unscrupulous English capitalists to crush out the *Home Manufacturer and the Home Trader*" (our italics).

Despite the play with words, "English capitalists" as opposed to "Home Manufacturer", there can be no doubt about Sinn Fein's meaning: they stood for protection of the native capitalists from the competition of "foreign" capitalists. Indeed the Policy statement spells it out: "Protection means rendering the native manufacturer equal to meet foreign competition. If a manufacturer cannot produce as cheaply as an English or other foreigner only because his foreign competitor has larger resources at his disposal, then it is the first duty of the Irish Nation to accord protection to that Irish manufacturer."

This is what it was all about then! This was the bitter reality of the poet's songs, the patriot's dreams, the worker's sacrifices; this was the prize for heroism, sacrifice, murder and counter-murder, bitterness and division. The promised pot of gold at the end of the patriotic rainbow was for the Irish "manufacturer" and the "home trader"; for the worker the only gold was on his new badge of slavery, the national flag that was to adorn his poverty, fly over his slum and replace the Union Jack as a symbol of his political ignorance.

And it could not have been otherwise. Despite the heady romantics of Pearse and the phrase-mongering of James Connolly the political and economic conditions that then prevailed excluded completely the possibility of an alternative to capitalism. The purpose of the struggle was, and could only have been the political stewardship of that system; the flag that symbolised the claim of the native capitalists bore as little relevance to the problems of the working class then, as it does today.

National struggles, especially when they are waged by the very weak against the very strong, are always seen in a romantic light. They are the material for songs and romantic novels and the new masters that emerge from such struggles are not averse to the fictions and heroics which later purport to be history – 'history' which becomes an important ingredient in the fog of ignorance essential in the exploitation of the 'nation's' working class.

Our purpose here is not to deny the bravery and self-sacrificing of those who contributed these qualities in the so-called fight for freedom. Such qualities were not the preserve of one side in the struggle – they are to be found in the unfortunate combatants of any war; often, sadly, they are to be found in inverse ratio to the amount of reasoned political thought on the part of their contributors.

Our object is to show that whatever the ideas, or lack of ideas, of the membership of the Sinn Fein movement and its militant arm, the IRA, the only thing they could have achieved – and its achievement was consciously desired by the political leadership of the movement – was the maintenance of the same old failed system of capitalism out of which all working class problems arise. This was true of the IRA yesterday; it is equally true today.

If we leave aside the romantics and 'principles' and get down to the facts of working class life, now or in the twenties, it will be seen that the problems that affected the working class in Ireland under English rule were similar to the problems of the working class throughout the world of capitalism. The facts of working class life were (and since the Six Day War, namely the memory of those are!) poverty, insecurity, unemployment, homelessness, slums, as well as the violent contention, war and violence which form an inevitable sackcloth to such conditions and the economic circumstances in which they arise. These miseries did not originate in 'foreign' rule any more than they can be assuaged or eradicated by 'home' rule. The French, English, German or Russian worker under his 'own' government, lived with these problems in the same way as the Irish worker or the Indian worker, living under a 'foreign' government.

In a word, the problems of the working class in Ireland were, and remain, the problems of the working class of the world and originate in the class stratification of capitalist society. Given capitalism, these problems were inevitable; they could not then, no more than they can now, be 'planned' out of the system. They did not arise out of the 'evil' intentions, nor the blundering or stupidity of governments, 'home' or 'foreign', no more than they could be planned, prayed or fought away by brave, sincere or wise men. They were the facts of capitalism and would continue to exist for as long as the working class, the only class with an economic interest in bringing about a real change, accepted that system.

In Ireland at the turn of the century the leaders of Sinn Fein were, as we have seen, concerned with the sectional interests of the rising Irish capitalist class. They did not take issue with the fact that the system of capitalism promoted by the dominant British capitalist class resulted in poverty and misery for the working class and small farmers in Ireland – and England. Their concern was not at the fact of exploitation but rather at the identity of the exploiters – at the fact that "English manufacturers (were) squeezing out their less-powerful Irish rivals."

Sinn Fein's was not a cry from the heart at the plight of the people of Ireland but a protest from the pocket of the new bandit against the fact that the older, more resourceful bandit was not giving him a 'fair' opportunity to carry out his plunder.

But the fledgling native capitalists were not themselves capable of changing the political conditions that thwarted their exploitative function. They needed the battalions of the working class behind them to give point to their argument but to rally the working class they had to appeal to working class interests by falsely identifying the plight of the working class with the rule of the foreign capitalists.

In 1905 Sinn Fein's demands were limited to the idea of Ireland having such measure of political control as would allow for the restriction of foreign, mainly British competition in order that Irish capitalism could develop behind tariff walls and a quota system of imports. This was to be within the framework of an Ireland "hereditary to the (British) Crown ... with King, Lords and Commons for Ireland." Such evident self-seeking on the part of native capitalism was not especially conducive to this task of rallying the workers and this, along with the declining value of the system of Empire Preference, turned the Party's propaganda increasingly towards the idea of complete separatism that it had engendered in its militant wing.

Predictably, propaganda by deed took over and the Irish Republican Army evolved into an effective weapon waging war on the forces of British capitalism in Ireland.

The IRA was composed mainly of young workers and farmers largely unaware of the economic pressures that had given rise to the struggle. They were 'fighting for Ireland'! Ireland was an abstraction, a vision, a 'principle'; Ireland was the opposite of what they knew and lived with, but then they did not know that all that was hateful in the Ireland they knew was the product of centuries of class rule culminated now in the harsher vulgarities of capitalism and all that was possible for the Ireland of their vision was a continuation of the same old miseries. The law would remain to enshrine the right of one class to exploit another even if the immediate enforcers of that Law wore different uniforms. Only a flag would be changed.

When the needs of the native capitalists had been served in the treaty of 1921 the capitalist class were satisfied. For them it was a matter of regret that some sections of the IRA did not see in the establishment of conditions compatible with the economic needs of capitalism the fulfilment of their vision and if that vision – largely compounded of romanticism, heroics and a sense of comradeship – impelled such sections of the IRA to the continuance of the struggle, then it was to be put down with all the viciousness at the command of the new forces of 'law and order'.

The IRA had fulfilled its purpose; it had served the class interests of Irish capitalism and by its very nature, apart from its lofty and ill-defined notions of 'freedom', it could not have done otherwise. After the Civil War and the desertion of its leadership to the more mundane and profitable offices of capitalism such fragments as continued to exist deteriorated into a political gang that canalised the genuine discontent and revolutionary fervour of some sections of the working class, North and South, into the dream of a tomorrow that was but the pale reflection of the sad ghosts of yesterday.

During the decades that have passed the principal and tragic preoccupation of the IRA has been the useless sacrifice of the lives of young Irish workers on the altar of romanticism. Many of its members have been killed by the forces of 'law and order' it helped to create in the South. Still more have died in futile adventurism in the North and thousands of young workers have spent the best years of their lives in jails in both parts of Ireland.

Inevitably years of stagnation and infiltration by informers and police spies have brought their toll of viciousness, intimidation and death within the organisation. The counter-espionage activities of police agents have at different times caused havoc and leaks in the form of young men's bodies often been plugged with lead after arbitrary conviction by drum-head court martial. In the early Forties, after a senseless bombing campaign in England, the 'major leak' scare ran rife in the movement; after numerous bullets and some tar-and-feathers had failed to stop the stream of information to the authorities the IRA discovered that the movement's own chief-of-staff was an informer!

Possibly the only positive role played by the IRA since the Civil War was that ascribed to it by the Unionist Party – and that mainly falsely. No Unionist politician ever faced an election without discovering an IRA plot. At different times throughout the last four decades the IRA was largely a figment of the imagination of the Stormont Government – in the mid-forties the organisation could not have mustered a platoon of volunteers in the City of Belfast – but it was a useful device for stampeding those workers who were tempted to stray from the paths of Unionism. It was an almost farcical reciprocity: the Unionist Party created the conditions in which the IRA continued its tenuous existence; the IRA helped to maintain a political climate in Northern Ireland conducive to the continuance of Unionist rule.

What has it all been for ... the tragic deaths, the beatings, the imprisonments? 'For Ireland', answers the mocking voice of yesterday.

But there are two Irelands: there is the Ireland of the capitalist class which is doing quite nicely for itself and has no need for, nor interest in, the IRA; and there is the Ireland of the working class. What do they, the working class, owe the IRA? North and South for nearly six decades now members of the working class have contributed their blood in the cause of 'Mother Ireland' – and yet their problems remain. If it is accepted that these problems have their roots in capitalism and will disappear only when the alternative to capitalism, Socialism, becomes the system of social organisation then it must be recognised that the IRA have played their part in thwarting the essential unity of the working class, rendering division within the working class more deep and waylaying the working class into the blind alley of nationalism.

The organisation has declined in strength since 1922 but since then its real menace has mainly been to its own members. But the situation following on the rioting in Northern Ireland has given the IRA a new lease of life and it is true to say that from the point of view of the working class it now constitutes a dangerous ingredient in the Irish situation.

In the years following the collapse of the IRA's last military activities in the late fifties a growing section within the movement began to promote the ideas of constitutional political action along the now-fashionable 'left-wing' lines. Inevitably the latter-day ideas of one of Republicanism's patron Saints, James Connolly, began to take greater prominence in the thinking of the leadership and, just as inevitably, the nationalistic state-capitalist implications of these ideas has led the movement in the direction of the 'Communist' Party.

The events in Northern Ireland since 1968 caused a split in the ranks of the IRA but while the immediate problems posed by the troubles in the North may have triggered off this split it was the growing influence of Leninist ideas within the movement, and the effect these had on dividing the IRA's reaction to events in the North, that formed the core of the division.

The breakaway element, or 'Provisionals', as they have come to be known, were led by those who resented the growing influence of 'Communist' ideas in the organisation. Not only did such people feel that politics was an irrelevancy within the context of the Republican ideal of a thirty-two county Irish republic but the new political bias in the movement clashed with their Catholicism. When the Catholics of the North were under attack such elements saw the defence of their fellow-Catholics as an immediate priority and when this course was resisted by the official leadership the long-brewing dissension and division came into the open.

The result is that there are now two IRA's in Ireland and to confuse matters still more the 'official' group, that has moved away from the uncomplicated formula of a Republic, and now pursue a contradiction-in-terms which they refer to as a 'Socialist Workers' Republic', are known as the 'Traditional IRA' while the breakaway group still espouse the traditional cause – even if they are, at least in the troubled areas of Belfast, a mere anti-Protestant counterpart of the Ulster Volunteer Force.

The 'Provisionals', in an attempt to maintain their claim to the title IRA are beginning to refer to the other group as the National Liberation Front – a title which demonstrates not only the real differences that led up to the split but also places the 'traditionals', in the view of their erstwhile ex-comrades, in the position of stooges for the 'Communist' Party.

Members of the working class, whether in the IRA or lending support to that organisation should realise that Nationalism is the tool of capitalism. The working class have no country – they have the choice of enduring the miseries of capitalism within the confines of national frontiers or enjoying freedom in a Socialist World.

(January 1971)

Up in Arms

If the success of a movement is to be judged by the amount of popular misconception about it, then the Women's Liberation Movement have almost won. Discontented women have traditionally been a target for lewd contempt from gentlemen, and any dissatisfaction with their social conditions is often treated as a projection of sexual frustrations. Thus any woman who has ambitions above being a shorthand typist at work, a housewife at home, or a sexual vehicle in bed, is liable to be dismissed as a shrivelled spinster, or a hairy lesbian, or at any rate someone in need of a good, cleansing orgasm.

It was this sort of contempt which gave such licence for the maltreatment of the Suffragettes, who could be kicked and punched and mauled by the police and subjected, by the gentlemen of London, to such indignation as would under other circumstances have earned a court appearance for indecent assault. When the last Miss World contest was disrupted by a few Women's Lib members Bob Hope, who is not a famous anthropologist or psychiatrist or sociologist, but who was earning a few bucks as compere to the flesh parade, could attribute the incident to the only possible cause that the demonstrators were junkies. Of course, Hope was in trouble; his gag writers had not supplied him with material for such an eventuality.

So how frightening are Women's Lib? Trembling, the *Socialist Standard* went along to one of their meetings – apart part from one very old man the only unaccompanied male in the room. We looked around but found none of the obvious lesbians we had been promised. There were very few unmarried girls there and one of them was in any case a schoolgirl. What there were at the meeting were plenty of trendy young wives and mothers – articulate, angry and, since they think they are suppressed, underprivileged and exploited (as indeed they are, but more of that later) rather obsessive.

It was an amateurish affair – conspicuously so, with the projector not working and when it did the picture went far enough off the screen to make it difficult to follow. The speakers were stuck on their inferior status as wage slaves and what was billed as an open forum soon dissolved into several shy discussion groups. The girls served tea and biscuits. The one professional touch was a table flogging contraception – pamphlets, models, devices, posters – which was what the meeting was supposed to be about.

This amateurishness contrasted with the movement's professional techniques in other activities. They have, for example, shown how to get quick, plentiful publicity; their protests are thoughtfully aimed (the Miss World rumpus, and the project to rewrite fairy stories, were little short of strokes of genius) and the posters and handbills advertising their national demonstration last month were good professional jobs.

Whatever criticism we may have of them, Women's Lib represents an impetus to the glacial movement of ideas. It is impossible not to agree with some of their attitudes. We must all feel sick at the commercial exploitation of sexual appeal and it says a lot about capitalist society and women's position in it that this exploitation is so often a women's sexuality and not a man's. Who can say that they were wrong about Miss World? One of the demonstrators there later wrote in their magazine *Shrew* of what she had said, amid the uproar, to three of the beauty queens: "I managed to say we weren't against them we were for them, but against Mecca and their exploitation. 'Come on, Miss Venezuela, we're on' and the trio disappeared down the corridor."

The relevance of Women's Lib is that, although their ideas are by no means original, one of the prejudices which must disappear as property society is ended is the one which says that some human beings are by virtue of their sex doomed to a lower, less privileged social position. In spite of all the changes since the New Women were pilloried as mannish ogres, that prejudice is still in existence in one form or another. At present most women are as ready to accept their lower standing as most men are to impose it upon them. Perhaps, if they begin to question their position, they will become that much readier for the idea that privilege based upon property rights is even more noxious – and more fundamental.

Women's Lib can produce a forest of statistics to support their case that women are deprived and suppressed. In October 1969 the average earnings of women in full time employment were 47% those of men – and the gap is widening. Women get the worst, most boring and repetitive jobs. If they have children they are doomed to spend years with their heads in the nappy pail while their husbands are out in the big, exciting world of wage slavery. Ask them why they are so worked up about getting onto the same level of employee exploitation as their husbands and they point out that their economic standing conditions their social position.

But here they do not adequately meet the point. The present arrangement exists not because of any prejudice against women; rather it is the other way round. The priorities of capitalism have made the prejudices which, once they exist, are themselves a priority; little girls are given dolls and frilly clothes to condition them to accept the prejudices and the whole thing soon becomes a profitable field in its own right. When they grow up, the little girls are excluded from some jobs not because of their sex but because from the employers' point of view it is a better prospect to employ men. Recently, for example, British European Airways stated that it is not their policy to take on women pilots, no matter how qualified or experienced they are. A Tory MP complained about this discrimination but got the point of it: "… a girl may get married and pregnant – or the other way round – and the airline would lose an investment of £10,000."

Although most of the jobs which are closed, or restricted, for women are not that costly, the MP was making a fair statement of the sound, solid, sensible reasons which capitalism has for its discrimination in employment, whether against women or mental defectives or cripples – or even against wholesome men who have simply tended to change their employer more than average. We – men and women – are here up against the fact that workers are not employed as a favour to them or as an act of natural justice. They are employed with the idea of producing surplus value for their masters. There is a distinct risk that a woman who has had an expensive training will fail to produce the surplus value and will produce babies instead.

Women's Lib's answer is to make the training and the employment profitable; they campaign for free abortion and contraception on demand, and for free 24 hour nurseries so that a woman who has a baby will not be out of work for too long. Like all other reformers, they accept the cause of a problem while rejecting its effects. And what does this mean for their dignity? What does it mean, that a woman should have an abortion to keep a well paid job?

Again, why do Women's Lib go for problems which are experienced only by working class women and say that these are women's problems rather than working class ones? No female member of the capitalist class has to worry about the effect of childbirth on her earning capacity. She can have as many children as she likes and, since she can afford a 24 hour nursery all to herself, she can also carry on an interesting, rewarding occupation. Such women do not have to wait for the Pill for their sexual freedom; expensive medical attention took care of that along with everything else. Women's Lib are tackling problems which will end only when the working class end, when class society is finished.

In the meantime, they do their cause no service by obscuring the facts about their place in capitalism. It is not surprising that this leads them into mysticism of the most confusing kind. One old American Suffragist, Alice Paul, recently said: "It's hard to find a woman who's not for peace. The most fundamental way to work for peace is to work for power for women" (*Life* magazine).

Perhaps she has never heard of Golda Meir. Or perhaps never read Women's Lib declarations that they support the "… national liberation struggles in Palestine or Vietnam", partly because "… all women are sisters and wherever they're fighting we're behind them" and partly because of "… an analogy between our own oppression as women and that of peoples oppressed as nations."

It does not need a very practised political eye to discern here the signs of some busy boring from within. It shows through even the mysticism. Women's Lib say they stand for the "transformation of society" although confessing to be "… essentially heterogeneous, incorporating … a wide range of opinions and plans for action." It seems that some monotonously familiar opinions and plans are at work within the movement and it is not difficult to guess what these elements mean when they talk about transforming society.

The aims of the Women's Liberation Movement – a free association between men and women, pure of the contaminations of capitalist society – can be attained only when capitalism is no more. Conditioned as we are to capitalism's degradations, it is difficult to imagine what the freedom of socialism will be like. How it will feel, for a woman and a man to associate only because they like and respect each other. How it will be when sexual activity is not a matter of conquest and possession, not a suppressive neurosis too easily exploited to sell cars, hair sprays, washing machines, suitcases, toothpaste, politicians – but a pleasure. To reach that we need all of us to be conscious of our role in society and the reasons for it. From there we will not be far from the will to change our roles by changing society.

(April 1971)

The End of 'Full Employment'?

Unemployment has been increasing continuously for five years. It was increasing under the Wilson Labour government and the rate of increase has accelerated under the Tories. At first it was noticed that the monthly figures were higher than they had been a year earlier; then they had reached levels which were a record for seven, eight, nine and ten years; and when unemployment passed the 900,000 mark in August, this represented the highest total for thirty years – back to the beginning of the war.

Normally unemployment is expected to rise in winter and fall in summer. This summer the fall did not take place. The September figure was 280,000 more than in January and about 560,000 above September 1966. It may well reach the million mark this winter.

Every industry has been affected – private and nationalised, old and new. No section of the workers has escaped and some of the most heavily hit have been the clerical, technical and managerial. Many who have lost their jobs have little prospect of ever getting work again at their old rates of pay.

This is not the first time since the war that unemployment has reached peak levels, but the peaks go higher. In the four years 1947, 1958, 1959 and 1962 the average for the whole year just exceeded 500,000. In 1963 and 1967-69 it was about 600,000. In 1970 640,000 and for 1971 it is likely to come out at 850,000.

Of course it will drop back again sometime as markets and production pick up but there are signs that it will run in future years at levels considerably higher than it was in the nineteen fifties and early nineteen sixties, when the annual average was usually below 400,000 and often below 300,000.

One new factor is that employers' expectations about quick recovery have been undermined by the long duration of the present recession. In earlier setbacks employers expected a quick recovery with a return of labour shortage, and were often prepared to keep surplus staff on in slack times; now it has become the practice to get rid of 'redundant' workers immediately.

Why was unemployment relatively low in the early post-war years? Why is it rising now? and what will happen in the future?

Many politicians and economists have had a ready answer. They believed that governments have almost complete control of the situation and can make unemployment as high or low as they choose. This assumed control was not claimed to be total – it would not eliminate small up and down fluctuations and it might take a few months to be effective. In 1957 Professor A.C.L. Day in his *The Economics of Money*, discussing the pre-1914 ten year cycle of boom and depression, wrote: "It may now have been mastered as a result of the insight into economic processes which has been acquired in the last generation."

Even more confidence in what the government can do was expressed in the *Sunday Times* (24th May 1970) when their contributor Malcolm Crawford wrote that American bankers "know that the government can stop a recession of any magnitude, nowadays, at about six months notice," and that the steps already taken by the American government were "enough to stop the recession." (Since then Nixon has had two or three more goes "to stop the recession," but it still persists). The economic backwoodsmen of the TUC still firmly believe in this assumed power of governments.

Naturally, therefore, those economists and politicians regarded the low level of unemployment which lasted for about fifteen years after the war as proof positive that they were right in believing that Keynesian methods had changed the nature of capitalism and that serious unemployment need never be feared again.

The explanation was too simple. From the start it had one major flaw, for the same Keynesian methods were also supposed to keep prices more or less stable and not even the most zealous believer can regard the rise of prices since 1938 to a level four and a half times what it was as price stability. And now they have to explain why the Labour government before 1970 and the Tory government since 1970 could not prevent unemployment rising to levels both say are too high.

The odd thing is that though they claimed to be Keynesians they hadn't even got Keynes on their side for he didn't believe it possible to keep unemployment down to two per cent or less, which it was in those years. When Lord Beveridge hoped that, taking the good and bad years together, they could keep unemployment to an average of three per cent, Keynes dissented on the ground that Beveridge was too optimistic. Keynes did not state how much above three per cent he thought it should be but if we assume only three and a half per cent as an average, this would mean a range of, say, two and a half per cent to four and a half per cent. This would mean unemployment ranging from about 600,000 to 1,100,000. So present unemployment is Keynes' 'Full Employment'.

It is interesting to note that in America, where Democratic Presidents have from time to time been said to be operating on Keynesian lines (and Nixon suddenly announced in January that he too had been converted) unemployment in May was at a nine year record level of 6.2%, and Nixon's Chief Economic spokesman John Connally admitted in a moment of candour that, except in war-time, it has never been below four per cent (*Financial Times*, 8th July 1971). In Britain 4% would be about a million.

An examination of the causes of low post-war unemployment in Britain was made by Professor R.C.O. Matthews, himself broadly a supporter of Keynes, and published in the *Economic Journal* (September 1968). His conclusion was that, starting with the stimulus given by making good war damage of all kinds, a major cause was a prolonged investment boom and that "the decline of unemployment as compared with 1914 is to a large extent not a Keynesian phenomenon at all."

On a comparative basis he estimated pre-1914 unemployment at 4.5% and that from 1945 to 1967 at 1.8%. He expected this situation to continue, but the doubling of unemployment since 1967 has already destroyed the basis for that optimism. On one point in particular Matthews has been proved wrong. He thought that the greater job-security of the post-war years, due to employers retaining surplus workers in slack periods, would continue, but this is no longer true as the hundreds of thousands of redundancies show.

The fact is that some British industries have been losing ground and failing to keep up with the expansion of world markets. Better equipped, more efficient rivals in Japan, Germany and elsewhere have been undercutting British (and latterly also American) companies. The two devaluations of 1949 and 1967 delayed, but did not stop, this drift.

Belief in the ability of any government to secure 'full employment' at will soon came up against a complication. The 1945 Attlee government (followed by Tory governments) discovered, as Marx or even Keynes could have told them, that when unemployment is very low the workers are in a better position to push up wages and this combines with other boom developments to cut into profit margins; which in turn discourages capitalist plans to expand industry. So the governments applied their 'incomes policies' to keep wages down. It never succeeded for long. The Heath government came in with its alternative, of encouraging employers to show tougher resistance to wage claims, and warning them that if they could not pay their way they must no longer count on the government bailing out 'lame ducks' – which also adds to unemployment.

If we disregard the possibility of another world depression like that of the nineteen thirties, present indications are that the years ahead will see more unemployment in Britain, coming nearer to the pre-1914 average of four and a half per cent. But the myth of 'full employment' will die hard. The Labour Party and trade unions will go on pursuing it, for – not being Socialist – what else have they to offer?

(November 1971)

Anti-affluence: the debt-ridden society

Writing to the newspapers in protest against the receipt of unsolicited credit cards is an honourable as well as a popular occupation. Implicit in the nuisance is a degree of social flattery: those selected to be pestered in this way are the cream of shopping customers, whose bills are paid promptly and whose credit is worthy. There has been no stream of complaints and Questions in the House from the scores of thousands who, ask as they may, will get no credit cards or hire-purchase terms. These are the sometime defaulters whose failures, and a great deal more about them, are recorded in the finance companies' registers of debtors.

Once in those files, you never come out. Capitalism drives and presses us all to buy to the limits of our means, and offers devices by which those limits may be apparently stretched. But the pressure must never be yielded-to by an inch beyond the limits. The point of marketing, after all, is not that goods shall be distributed but that they be paid for. He who, lured and compelled by deferred terms or slashed deposits or simple needs, fails to meet his money commitment is as far as possible prevented for the future from buying on those terms again. Morally condemned as well, for violating the golden capitalist rule that everything has its price.

Recording and collecting

There are about three million registered defaulters in Britain. The most common ways of getting listed are by irregularity or failure in payments to one of the companies which finance trading credit, and through a County Court judgement. It does not follow, however, that the absence of such a record means credit granted automatically. An application for hire purchase or the opening of an account always means an enquiry being made. One widespread practice is to send forms to local officials likely to know something about the applicant, asking for an estimate of what he is worth and any useful information regarding him. The car-finance companies keep detailed records in which procrastination over payments is noted for future reference, even if there is no actual failure to pay.

When a debt occurs, the usual first step is a warning letter – from the legal department if the firm is big enough, from a solicitor if it is not. Some traders employ debt recovery agencies, which work on a percentage of money collected and aim, generally, to scare or embarrass the defaulter into paying up. One technique is to send a notice on blue paper, looking remarkably like a summons, with words like 'Bailiff', 'Distrain on Your Goods', 'Appear in Court', etc., printed in capitals and underlined. In other cases, collectors call on the debtor repeatedly and make themselves objectionable. No doubt there are laws against much of what goes on, but a debtor is likely to feel he is hardly in a position to shout. Car-finance firms, for instance, are known to employ men who stand on defaulters' doorsteps jingling keys and announcing their intention to take the car away – despite the fact that this cannot be done without a court order.

Penalties

If all the threatening is ineffective, a summons follows. There are two kinds, the common one being the default summons. No-one goes to court over it: the defendant has ten days to settle his debt, dispute it, or offer to pay by instalments. If he fails to do any of those, a judgement summons (the other sort) is served; he must attend the court to answer questions about his means, and the normal outcome is an instalment order. And if the instalments are not paid, a 'warrant of execution' is issued for each as its due date passes. This is simply a distraint order – the County Court bailiffs call and arrange to take enough belongings to cover the amount owed plus the Court costs. The costs are standard fees charged at each step in the proceedings, so that the repayment of a debt in these last-resort circumstances is itself an extra expense.

Until a year ago debtors could be imprisoned instead of distrained upon, by order of the Court. The purpose of 'committal orders' was to deal with people who supposedly could pay but were reluctant to do so. However, County Court judges were in the habit of making the orders almost automatically, and an impoverished defaulter was liable to be hauled to prison by the bailiff. What good was thought to be done by it, no-one knows; though its abolition aimed at reducing the pressures on prison resources, not at sense or humanity. Imprisonment orders are still made for one common class of debts, non-payment of rates to local councils. Since rates are levied under statute law, defaulters over them are summoned not to the civil courts but to magistrates' courts which continue to make committal orders.

Hard Cash

One other course of action against a debtor is the High Court writ. This is more attractive to creditors than County Court proceedings because the outcome is swifter and more relentless. The debtor has ten days following the service of the writ to file an 'appearance'. Unless he has (and is prepared to pay for) a defence, the plaintiff may then 'take judgement'. The High Court does not deal in instalment plans, and very shortly after the judgement the debtor will be called-on by a Sheriff's officer – i.e. a licenced bailiff – with a view to distraint on his possessions. However, High Court proceedings are for larger sums. The County Courts are intended to deal with actions for debts up to £700; though claims for smaller amounts can and do go to the High Court, they are not encouraged there.

It is true, of course, that proceedings for debt can be expensive to the plaintiff. The cost of solicitors' letters, and representation in court for the hearing of a judgement summons, is not recoverable. Proceedings to get back, say, £50 can well cost that amount and so have their success nullified. Many traders acknowledge this, and either write off small debts when the threats have failed or try the percentage collecting companies. Larger firms can afford the proceedings, but the fact remains that much debt-recovery is sterile: the real object is to make default an unpleasant experience, to brand the defaulter and let it be known that this sort of thing will not be tolerated.

A dirty war

'Unpleasant' is a mild word. For those who have got into debt through adversity, over-optimism or simple inadequacy in dealing with everyday matters, the consequences are harrowing and humiliating. Threats; the bailiff (or, for rates, a policeman) on the doorstep; the possibility of an auctioneer's van come to take one's belongings away, and even of being taken to prison. One wonders what future generations will think of a society in which such miseries were commonplace. There is the thought, too, what kind of people are prepared to treat other human beings like that. For judges, the question need hardly be asked. Bailiffs generally are either men who got into it through the accident of starting in associated employment when they were young, or retired policemen and the like. Loathsome as their functions are, it ought to be remembered that they are wage-workers – only daubed with more of capitalism's dirt than most of us. Certainly they suffer a penalty in social isolation: it is not uncommon for bailiffs' wives to have been in the same line of business, leaving one with the thought that most women draw the line at living with that.

Since debt is a struggle, it produces its own strategies. A debt is personal; the desperate defaulter becomes a dodger. A wife may stave off the pressures by saying her husband has gone away and left her, though bailiffs are likely to keep an eye on the house and make neighbourhood enquiries. A High Court writ has to be put actually in the defendant's hand and proceedings can start only when this has happened, making elusiveness desirable (process-servers usually are young smart-alecs ready to find fun in the chase). Likewise, when distraint is proposed a husband may claim that all the household belongings are his wife's or someone else's and therefore not seizable for his debt. This can be challenged by a creditor – the action is called 'interpleader' – but the difficulty of proof make the cases rare and seldom successful.

States of mind

Whatever the reasons for which people get in debt, it is likely to become a spiral from which extrication is hard: continually half-robbing Peter to half-pay Paul, with the result that both remain hot-breathing creditors. One of the attractions of the 'second mortgage' is that it offers the exchange of a lot of small debts for a single large one, an apparent fresh start which also can take a haunted person from the realm of County Courts to that of the High Court. But if an even keel is reached, the record of money troubles remains as a permanent disability. It is permissible for a small fee to have past judgements erased from the court registers, but they are never deleted from the credit companies' records. Extenuating circumstances are not allowed: a defaulter is marked for the rest of his life.

It is possible for defaulters to be victimised through their records. Two or three years ago someone circularised several thousand householders offering highly favourable mail-order terms. They were all in fact selected from registers of defaulters, their readiness to jump at the prospect of being allowed to buy on a credit system obscuring more rational doubts such as how the advertiser was financing his generous activities. Orders with deposits rolled in, for the money to be pocketed by an adventurer whose chief asset was a little comprehension of the states of mind that debt produces.

Must it continue?

Looking at all this: what a way to live! Yet it is part of how a very large number of people do live. Statistics about it tend to appear unbelievable because people will admit to other problems but not this one – disgrace in money matters is the deepest kind of disgrace in a money-dominated society. Nor is it anything new. The eighteenth century *London Spy* describes women in the debtors' prisons through default to tallymen. Spike May's account of pre-1920 village life, *Reuben's Corner*, refers to the village postman "walking many miles round the scattered community pushing bills and debt-summonses into letterboxes" (a different picture from the romantic one of rosy-cheeked rural bliss).

Most people under capitalism exist in quiet desperation, hair-breadths away from this sort of calamity. To talk of the proliferation of debt as a consequence of irresponsibility, of failing to cut coats according to the cloth, is beside the point. For the great majority, there chronically isn't enough cloth to keep out the cold. The respectable with credit cards and no histories of default are in debt just the same, paying monthly for what they cannot otherwise afford. Debt is a demonstration of the inescapable poverty problem of the working class. The slogan of the latest credit card is that it 'takes the waiting out of wanting'; but the only way wanting and waiting will be ended is by the abolition of capitalism.

(December 1972)

What Socialism Means

The object of socialism is to unite humanity and to solve social problems by building a society which can satisfy the universal need for co-operation and material security.

Socialism involves a creative outlook concerned with the quality of life. In association with others, the individual will develop himself as a social being. With enlightenment and knowledge, man will replace the ignorance, false illusions and prejudice from which he suffers in our own day. Socialism is the form of society most compatible with the needs of man. Its necessity springs from the enduring problems, the economic contradictions and social conflicts of present-day society. Socialist society must be based upon the common ownership and democratic control by the whole community of the means of life.

Life will be based on human relationships of equality and co-operation. Through these relationships, man will produce useful things, construct amenities and establish desirable institutions. Socialism will resolve the conflicts which at present divide man from man. Regardless of ethnic or cultural differences, the whole world community will share a common interest.

Under capitalism the whole apparatus of production are either privately owned, as in America, or state controlled by a privileged minority, as in Russia. The economies of some countries combine both private and state control. Both forms are alien to the interests of the majority, since the priorities of trade and commerce, exploitation and profit-making, dominate life. Under both forms, production for sale on the market is organised primarily for the benefit of a privileged minority.

The building of Socialism requires a social reorganization where the earth's resources and the apparatus of production are held in common by the whole community. Instead of serving sectional interests, they are made freely accessible to society as a whole. Production will be organised at world level with co-ordination of its differing parts down to local levels.

In Socialism there will be no market, trade or barter. In the absence of a system of exchange, money will have no function to perform. Individuals will participate freely in production and take what they need from what is produced. The fact that Socialism will be based on common ownership does not mean that an individual will have no call on personal effects. It means essentially that no minority will have control over or possession of natural resources or means of production. Individuals will stand in relation to each other not as economic categories, not as employers and employees or buyers and sellers, but simply as human beings producing and consuming the necessary things of life.

Socialist society will minimise waste and set free an immense amount of human labour. Armies and armament industries with their squandering of men and materials will be swept away. These will disappear together with all the wasteful appendages of trade and commerce.

Work
Work is a human need not only because it produces the material things of life, but because it is through work that man expresses his social nature.

In present society, human labour-power is the source of profit. Economic antagonism causes strikes and lock-outs. The uncertainties of trade result in dislocation and unemployment. The present chaos generates frustration and violence. Work becomes repugnant when carried on in this context of competition and exploitation. Life is a personal struggle.

In Socialism there will be a common interest in the planning and smooth operation of production. Work will be a part of human co-operation in dealing with practical problems. Work will be one aspect of the varied yet integrated life of the community.

With the change in the object of society, that is human welfare instead of profit, man will freely develop agriculture and housing, produce useful things and maintain services. As well as material production, man will freely develop desirable institutions such as libraries, education facilities, centres of art and crafts and centres of research in science and technology.

It will be a problem of social planning, statistics and research to ascertain the requirements of the community. Although these techniques are used for different ends, there is already wide experience of them. With experience of Socialist production, these planning techniques will gain in accuracy.

Once produced, goods will be transported to centres of distribution where all will have the same right of access to what is available according to individual need. It will be a simple matter of collecting what is required. As well as tradition and geography, it will be a matter of organization and practicality as to which things will require a complex world division of labour for their production and which things will be produced regionally.

Social values

The insecurities of our present acquisitive society drive men into ruthlessly selfish attitudes and actions which frustrate the human need for co-operation. With success in this competitive race goes a hollow pride; with failure there goes guilt and stigma. Against this background the failure is general because where the individual is isolated, co-operation breaks down.

Socialism will establish a community of interests. The development of the individual will enhance the lives of other men. Equality will manifest attitudes of co-operation. The individual will enjoy the security of being integrated with society at large.

Institutions

The establishment of Socialism does not call for the complete destruction and reconstruction of society. Techniques of production and some of the machinery of administration which can be transformed already exist. The task is to allow their free use and development by and for the community. With the change in the object of society from profit to human welfare will come a change in the function of social institutions. The schools and universities will no longer be concerned with the training of wage and salary workers for the needs of trade and commerce. Education will be a social amenity for life, providing teachers and a storehouse of all accumulated knowledge and skill. Education will not be rigidly separated from other aspects of life. The provision of education facilities will call for some permanent specialists, but knowledge and skill will to a much greater extent be passed on by those actively engaged in their practical application. Education will be tied more closely to the whole process of living.

There will be a body concerned with safety, the co-ordination of services in the event of an emergency, traffic regulation and the like. Here again, whilst some specialists may be required, it will be desirable for members of the community to participate as part of the normal pattern of their lives.

Institutions such as the armed forces, customs, banking, insurance, etc, will become redundant. Socialism will continue those institutions necessary to its own organization. For example, the Food and Agricultural Organization could be expanded to submit plans and execute decisions concerning world food production.

World unity

Socialism will end national barriers. The human family will have freedom of movement over the entire earth. Socialism would facilitate universal human contact but at the same time would take care to preserve diversity. Variety in language, music, handicrafts, art forms and diet etc will add to all human experience.

Democratic control

Socialism will be democratic. World policies will be subject to the control of the world community. The most complete information relevant to all issues under discussion will be made fully available. Elected delegates will carry local viewpoints to a world congress where the broad decisions on all aspects of social policy will be made. From that point, the social machinery would be implemented to carry out these decisions, subject to democratic control through both local and world bodies. Decisions affecting only local interests would be made democratically by the local community.

Whilst the general direction of social policy will be decided by the whole community, many decisions will be technical ones arising out of the problem of this policy. These decisions can be left, subject to regular democratic checks, to men and women with specialized knowledge and experience; but given the whole context of Socialism, they could only be consistent with its general aim – human welfare.

The elimination of vested interests will mean that men will have no ulterior motives influencing their decisions.

The challenge of Socialism

The greatest challenge facing humanity is the need to increase the production of wealth on an enormous scale, but this cannot be done within present capitalist society. Men and resources serve profit. On all sides it can be seen that commerce, trade and vested interests are preventing man from expanding production on a scale necessary to serve the community's needs. Socialism will provide a social framework that will enable man to get on with the job. The initial task of producing enough goods for the whole human family will be a huge one. We do not underestimate the problems of organization and production involved, but to eliminate world poverty must be one of the first tasks of Socialist society.

It is the glaring contradiction of our times that wealth is socially produced but possessed by a minority. Whereas in science, technology and in the development of the means of production man has brilliantly asserted his genius, in his relationships man suffers an abiding failure. It is this failure which is expressed in war, nationalism, racism, world hunger and poverty, unemployment, industrial chaos and social disunity. In all history, man has never suffered such universal frustration whilst having so close at hand the means of building a better world.

(July 1973)

The Common Market: in or out – does it matter?

What it's about

Europe 1945 – a shattered continent after the second war within thirty years. Industries laid waste. Millions dead. American aid pouring in trying to create a bulwark against the Russian menace. What was the future for European capitalism, as it drifted into the latter half of the twentieth century? To continue as a bunch of warring states; as competitors in the process of making, buying and selling? Or could they not become one big family? The conception of the EEC – European Economic Community – Common Market was born and the Treaty of Rome, 1957 signed by France, Germany, Italy and the Benelux countries contained the following clause: "To permit goods to travel freely without Customs Duties or quota restriction throughout the area of the six and *thus to permit manufacturers to invest on the scale that modern technology makes possible and necessary*" (our italics).

This is what it's about.

Capitalism – a system based upon class ownership of the means of wealth production and distribution – must invest in order to survive. It needs a developing technology, it needs a growing market, and the European bunch, faced with competition from America, Russia, etc., saw their Community as the answer. It was a bold step and despite constant setbacks the foundations were laid and building commenced.

Great Britain, despite the pro-European utterances of Winston Churchill, did not join. She was lumbered with the Commonwealth and any deal with Europe had to relate to New Zealand lamb, Australian butter, Jamaican sugar, etc. Harold MacMillan, Chancellor of the Exchequer in the Tory Government, even prior to the Rome Treaty had no doubts "... or we might ourselves join the Union; but this would involve abandoning the preferential system in the Commonwealth, and obviously if we had the choice of alternatives, we could not hesitate; we would choose the Commonwealth" (Llandudno, 12th October 1956).

So the British capitalists wanting the best of both worlds – the Commonwealth and a tariff agreement, formed with Switzerland, Portugal, Austria, Sweden, Denmark and Norway the European Free Trade Area (EFTA). This association was to negotiate trade terms with the Common Market. But why swim with the small fish when you can see larger fish in another pool, getting larger and threatening your existence? The Commonwealth and EFTA notwithstanding, Britain applied for membership of the EEC in 1963. The application was rejected largely due to the attitude of the French Government who wanted total commitment to a European policy – not an applicant with one foot in the Commonwealth and a certain reliance on America. "On Monday the General [de Gaulle] made it clear that he did not want Britain in, and that his reasons were political." (*Observer*, 19th January 1963). America incidentally, looked upon all these European proposals with suspicion.

But the British capitalists' appetite had been whetted. The plums in Europe seemed larger and juicier, so again application was made under the Heath Government in 1971. Suitable terms were negotiated and Great Britain became a member on 1st January 1973.

Neither the politicians nor the capitalists were united on this move. Some said the terms were not good enough; some said whatever the terms we should not be in. The Labour Party in particular were split on the issue. In their Election Manifesto of February 1974. they said our continued membership would depend upon more suitable terms being agreed. After months of discussion and brinkmanship, Mr Wilson was able to report to Parliament on 18th March, 1975. "The Government have decided to recommend to the British people that they should vote in favour of staying in the Community on the terms which I have described." Many commentators questioned whether the now acceptable terms were fundamentally different from those originally agreed but this need not concern us. And so we are being allowed to vote in the Referendum – IN or OUT. But more on this later.

Much of the discussion on the Common Market centres around the economic aspect but the EEC also entails a political angle. If such an economic set-up is to function, then the political machinery must be geared accordingly. You can't have all these separate Governments taking decisions from a Nationalist viewpoint, ignoring the greater good. So individual sovereignty will have its wings clipped. The British Parliament will not be the sole master in its own house. The European Parliament will take decisions that often seem to cut across the interests of National States.

It was also agreed by the Community, that by 1980 there would be Monetary Union with a common currency and the harmonisation of National Budgets. According to Herr Scheel "... this is the most ambitious project ever tackled by the Community."

In all the EEC was an exciting and demanding future for Capitalism. If only it wasn't such an awkward system to control and manage.

How is the Community making out?

Eighteen years on is but a passing moment in the development of European capitalism. Many of the tariff duties have been disbanded. A greater volume of trade has taken place. A workers' Charter has been formulated even to the extent of agreement on "worker participation on Industrial Boards." The politicians fall out from time to time; the Brussels administration grows and grows. Fine words are spoken about the future. And then, despite a number of advances, that awkward capitalist system starts throwing its weight about and spanners in the works. Butter; beef; wine; fish; fruit. All you might say part of the sinews of life. But not in the world of capitalism. These are commodities produced for sale with a view to profit. And capitalism in its normal anarchistic fashion has produced too much for the market

You will remember the Butter Mountain. 152,000 surplus tons at the end of 1970. A definite policy was adopted to curtail production, involving the slaughter of thousands of cows. But this didn't get rid of the butter. It was costing a bomb to store. The old age pensioners with the price reduced coupons mopped up some of it. Some official thought of a brilliant idea to feed it back to the cows. Eventually they did a deal to sell it in bulk to Russia – a deal that cost the Community millions of pounds. And butter in Paris still costs 69p per lb.

French farmers, like all farmers, are constantly demanding higher prices for their produce. To prove the point, thousands of tons of fruit have been dumped on French roads over the past few years. And then we had the fascinating pictures of French fishermen likewise tipping their catches on the roads. English egg producers, claiming to be working at a loss, demonstrate against the importation of French eggs. Dried milk, an embarrassing surplus, is being rendered unfit for human consumption and processed into animal feed. And you all know about the beef. How it is much more profitable to put it into store and get the intervention price, whilst rump steak is £1.40 per lb. And now there is the Wine Lake. The Italians have so much that they want to sell it. But the French won't have it at any price – they've put up a barrier against Italian wine. They have too much of their own for comfort. We could go on and on.

Another point about the Common Market with its great resources was the demand for labour. In fact, when Britain entered the Community, lists of jobs in Europe were pinned up in the Labour Exchanges and great play was made of how labour would be more mobile. It's a nice thought that any of the 800,000 unemployed in this country could shove off over to the continent and get a job. Their journey might not be fruitful; the Common Market members over the Channel have an unemployed army of four million. Little is said of the many thousands of migrant workers in Europe who having played their part in the development of capitalism are now out on a limb.

During the oil crisis of 1973 it might be assumed that 'the partners' would show a united front against the Arab oil producers. But national aspirations won out. All countries were falling over each other to do a deal with the Arabs.

Inflation; currency crises; restriction on production; unemployment etc., etc. These are the stock in trade of capitalism. The Common Market will never solve these problems. The EEC ship will constantly smash itself against the rocks of its own system – a problem-producing system.

The Referendum – in or out

For the first time in British History – a referendum. A device often used in other countries; Norway voted in such a manner to keep out. This vote, largely favoured by the anti-marketeers in the Labour Party, will resolve the decision for the Government. Mr Wilson, when recommending the terms said "This is one of the most important parliamentary occasions in our history." Not so. The British people are only being asked to endorse the continuation of capitalism, in or out, and they do this at every General Election. As yet, they continue to give this endorsement.

To remain in or get out has produced a weird assortment of protagonists. IN – Mr Wilson and some members of his cabinet ally themselves with Mr Heath, Maudling, the Liberal Party, the Confederation of British Industry, the Farmers' Union and generally speaking 'big business'. OUT – this includes an even weirder assortment. The Communist Party, Enoch Powell, Benn, Foot, Shore, the National Front and the TUC. A selection of the Ins and Outs is illuminating.

In: "If we came out we would end as a country with nowhere to go" (Lord Pritchard, President, Institute of Directors, *Times*, 18th March 1975).

Out: "I am really warning people in the West Midlands that the capacity of British Ministers to help industry to re-equip is going to be gravely affected by membership, and that is one of the reasons why I hope the British people will vote to withdraw" (Wedgwood Benn, speaking at Birmingham, *Guardian*, 22nd March 1975).

In: "British withdrawal from the EEC would probably cause Lucas Industries to reduce its workforce by between 8,000 and 10,000 jobs" (Bernard Scott, the Company's Executive Chairman, *Guardian*, 13th March 1975).

Out: "He told the French Chamber of Commerce in London that the TUC believed Britain should not be in a Market of which competition was the guiding principle" (Len Murray, Gen. Sec. TUC, *Evening Standard*, 7th March 1975 – perhaps Mr Murray can enlighten us as to what is the 'guiding principle' under which British capitalism works at the moment?

In: "I would not be involved in the Government if it has to take Britain out of the Common Market" (Shirley Williams, Secretary for Prices and Consumer Protection, *Guardian*, 13th March 1975).

Out: "Pop Concerts, talks to Women's Institute tea parties and trade union meetings and a a galaxy of prominent speakers including playwright John Osborne, author Kingsley Amis and scientist Kit Pedlar will be used in the fight to pull Britain out of Europe" (Get Britain Out Referendum Campaign, *Evening Standard*, 20th March 1975 – pardon us if we are not altogether overwhelmed by the galaxy of prominent speakers.)

In: "Mobilise for a Socialist Europe" (Labour Committee for Europe, advert in *Guardian*, 17th February 1975 – hardly we feel the reason why the CBI wants to keep in).

And so we could go on and on – one boring reason after another. How you will vote is your concern. We tell them to stuff their referendum. The real issue that the workers should tackle is Common Market or Common Ownership.

Where we stand

We and our sympathisers will vote. We shall register on our papers our commitment for Socialism. The question you are being asked to answer – In or Out – is of no concern to members of the working class. Whatever the outcome of the vote, Capitalism will continue. And continue it will until you and a majority like you take the revolutionary step of deciding to abolish capitalism in all its forms and to bring into being a new society.

The Socialist Party of Great Britain has only one object – Socialism, which briefly means the common ownership of the means of wealth production and distribution, democratically administered for the common good. The earth, with its untold riches would be harnessed and utilised for the benefit of all mankind. This means that human needs take priority and production centres around these. From each according to ability, to each according to need would be the guiding principle. Simply put, it means that all those sinews of life previously mentioned, and the thousand and one other things that mankind needs, would be produced to meet human satisfaction.

Socialism cannot operate in one country or in one continent. It is a worldwide concept to deal with worldwide problems. It cannot be established by any leader or so-called intellectual Left Wing group. Its very democratic nature demands that people will have to understand both the capitalist and the new society so that they play a full and responsible role in its administration. Its establishment will result from political action based upon understanding: a class-conscious act to take control of the reins of Government; then strip the capitalists of their power, their wealth, and found a new way of life.

Whilst we claim that Socialism alone can solve the basic economic problems that confront mankind, it is not a society just concerned with 'belly problems'. Its new economic basis will give rise to a new set of social relationships. Man, no longer a wage slave or an appendage to a productive machine, will be able to utilise all his potential, to blossom as a full human being.

The Socialist Party of Great Britain offers itself as your instrument for the establishment of Socialism. We offer an understanding of capitalism and some concrete ideas on how Socialism will work. But we are not leaders. You join our Party on the basis of your Socialist knowledge. We would welcome you and what you have to contribute to the only question worthy of consideration – Common Ownership or Capitalism?

Away with all the trappings of capitalism – tariffs, customs duties, monetary union, competition, buying, selling, etc. Vote for nothing but Common Ownership.

(May 1975)

The Crisis – Capitalism's Stranglehold on the Labour Government

There is of course nothing new in governments breaking pledges and turning policy somersaults, but latterly the occasions have become more frequent and more farcical. At every election since the second world war the Labour and Tory parties have undertaken to deal with inflation: to so little effect that prices have risen continuously for thirty years, with the rate of increase getting faster and faster.

It is not at all surprising that this should have happened because the governments have been running a policy of inflation in the belief that this was a way to prevent unemployment from increasing. A vain hope, because at each of the half-dozen recessions since 1950 unemployment has risen to a new higher peak – over a million in 1972 and now forecasts of a possible one and a half millions by early 1976. Instead of stopping inflation, it has been government policy first to promote it and then to try to suppress its symptoms by means of a 'Prices and Incomes Policy'.

It started in 1947 under Attlee's government and has been re-enacted half a dozen times. A long succession of failures as far as stopping inflation is concerned, but it would be churlish not to acknowledge its one happy achievement – the enrichment in the use of our vocabulary. We have had wage restraints, wage freezes, wage thaws, plateaus, pauses, ceilings, guiding lights, norms, standstills, early warnings, guide-lines, slow-downs, explosions, wage-stops, thresholds, curbs, social contracts, and a lot more.

The latest from Mr Wilson "the £6 limit on wage increases," which he admits means a lower standard of living, has a novel refinement. For years the centrepiece of the Labour programme was the 'national minimum'. The law was to be used to force 'bad employers' to become 'good employers' by making them put wages up. Now Mr Wilson threatens to use the law to prosecute employers who put wages up too much. They are, he says, 'rogue employers'. The recipients, of course, could be workers whose wages are only a small fraction of Wilson's own income.

Do they understand capitalism?

Is it really possible for government ministers not to understand how capitalism operates? And to be unaware of the inevitable consequences of their own policies? Indeed it is possible. During the nineteenth century, although capitalism regularly went through the recurring cycle of expansion, boom, crisis and depression outlined by Marx as the economic law of the system, governments, capitalists and many economists were forever expecting booms to be permanent and being amazed as each crisis blew up. There are plenty of similar examples in our own times.

Any serious student of capitalism knows that the capitalist is in business to make a profit and therefore will not invest more to expand production at those times when there is no prospect of selling the product profitably. Yet in the last recession, in 1971-72, Heath and Barber complained bitterly that though for months on end they pleaded and threatened and offered inducements for increased investment, 'nobody would listen'. Healey, Chancellor of the Exchequer in the present government, confesses to having been equally ignorant of the facts of economic life. "One thing I have learnt from my experience in the past seven months [as Chancellor]: there is no chance of investment if business expects a general and prolonged recession, however generous the tax incentives" (Report of speech, *The Times*, 5th October 1974).

Later in the same month he was again airing his ignorance, this time as guest speaker at the Lord Mayor's banquet for bankers and merchants of the City of London: "I simply cannot understand how it can make economic sense ... to keep a million active men and women idle when the nation needs the goods they could produce (*Times*, 18th October 1974).

Since when has capitalism been interested in meeting people's needs? And, in a depression, who needs additional production of unsaleable cars, motorcycles, supertankers, steel and so on?

In one respect nineteenth century British governments were better informed than governments since 1945. They knew how to prevent inflation and decided that it was in the interest of capitalism to prevent it. There was no inflation for the hundred years before 1914. Prices rose and fell by moderate amounts in booms and depressions, but the level was lower in 1914 than in 1814. Now the price level is more than seven times the 1938 level and rising fast, by far the biggest cause being the depreciation of the currency consequent on government policy.

There were always some uninfluential groups advocating inflation to cure the ills of capitalism. One was dealt with in the *Socialist Standard* in August 1906. Using the Marxist analysis the writer of the article showed that it would cure nothing and would simply raise prices: "the workers, as is usual, being the first to suffer." Another example is mentioned in *The Life and Times of Ernest Bevin*, by Alan Bullock (page 17). Bevin, trade union leader and later a minister in the Attlee government, was present in 1908 at a conference to discuss remedies for unemployment. One proposal was "the issue of paper pounds". A Liberal politician who was there thought that it was "very sensible" but politically impracticable.

After 1945 it was quite different. Influenced by Keynes (or by crude distortions of Keynes) the Labour and Tory Parties and the TUC adopted the doctrine that the government could 'manage' the economy in a way that would prevent crises and depressions occurring again. By "maintaining demand" they believed they could always prevent unemployment. Maintaining demand meant in practice printing more money and putting up prices. Keynes, whether he intended it or not, had made inflation respectable.

Marx and others on inflation

A number of economists in the past have understood that if an inconvertible paper currency is issued in excess amounts it will correspondingly put up prices. Marx's special contribution was to anchor it to his theory of value. In given circumstances a certain amount of currency will be required. If the currency consisted solely of gold coin it would represent a certain total weight of gold and therefore a certain total mass of value. If the gold is replaced by inconvertible paper money (not convertible into a fixed weight of gold) and is then issued in amounts exceeding the gold it represents, it will simply put up prices. This is the present situation. Currency in Britain in 1938 was under £500 millions. It is now over £6,000 millions. It went up £835 millions in the year to July 1975.

Those who reject this explanation of inflation can apply a test. Let them show when such excess issue took place without raising prices; or when such excess issue was halted and prices did not fall.

In December 1919, after a very fast rise in prices, a ceiling was placed on the note issue and within a year prices were falling fast and wages with them. Lord Rothschild (*Times*, 30th June 1975) recalls that German inflation was halted in 1923 by applying the recommendations of a Committee (two members of which were the banker Brand and the economist Keynes) which included the Reichsbank being "forbidden to print more notes".

Some modern 'monetarists' have confused the issue by trying to relate price movements to the total of currency plus some or all of bank deposits. Why should the act of lending by depositors to banks affect the price level? Historically there is no justification for the theory. The enormous growth of bank deposits in the last decades of the nineteenth century was accompanied by a *fall* of the price level, not a rise.

Harold Wilson used to be quite confident about how he would prevent inflation. In 1957 some of his articles in the *Guardian* were published as a pamphlet, *Remedies for Inflation*. In Section III 'What Labour Would Do' he wrote: "Ever since the Coalition Government's White Paper (Employment Policy, 1944) all major parties have been committed, on Keynesian lines, to using the Budget as a means of avoiding undue inflation or deflation. In inflationary times, therefore, all are agreed in theory on the need for public saving through a large Budget surplus, though we have felt that a number of Conservative Budgets have sacrificed financial stability to a desire for fiscal popularity."

In practice Wilson's government in 1974-5, instead of running a Budget surplus, has shown the biggest deficit in British peace-time history. Wilson says that the Government's latest measures have been forced on it by the threatened drastic fall of the pound under pressure from foreign holders of sterling, just like Labour Premier Ramsay MacDonald in 1931.

There is no sign that the bulk of the Labour ministers

5p   Vol. 68 No. 816   AUGUST 1972

Socialist Standard

Official Journal of The Socialist Party of Great Britain and The World Socialist Party of Ireland

In this issue:
IRISH CAPITALISM
ARISTOCRATS
LAING
FESTIVAL OF LIGHT
PARIS COMMUNE
EATING

The Floating Pound

THE GOVERNMENT'S decision to float the pound is yet another confirmation of the Marxian theory of inflation. Floating the pound means that the government is not using its gold and foreign currency reserves to maintain a fixed exchange rate between the pound and the dollar £1—($2.60 till 23 June). As a result the exchange rate of the £ (which is but its price on the foreign exchange market) can, depending on demand, float up or down — but in practice under present circumstances definitely down. The "Times" estimates that when, after a few months, a fixed exchange rate is restored it will be around £1—$2.40 (or its equivalent), an effective devaluation of between five and ten per cent.

Devaluation, according to the Marxian analysis, is an official recognition that due to the over-issue of a paper currency the amount of gold represented by a pound-note has been reduced. Acting on false Keynesian doctrines, successive British governments, Labour and Conservative, have denied that, given a certain level of production and trade, only a definite supply of inconvertible paper money (i.e. paper money not convertible into gold on demand) should be issued if prices were to be kept reasonably stable. And that, if more money than this amount was issued, the inevitable result would be a depreciation of the currency or, what is the same thing from another aspect, inflation (rising prices). Instead they have followed the advice of Keynes to "let the money supply look after itself" and via the Bank of England have provided government expenditure and to subsidise private capitalist industry. In the last quarter of 1971, for instance, Britain's money supply was expanded at an annual rate of 25 per cent! (The *Times*, 9 March, 1972). Only recently have a few academics come to realise what Marx, and indeed many of the bourgeois economists of his day, knew: that the inevitable result of overspending an inconvertible paper currency is depreciation and inflation.

For a trading State like Britain this can cause difficulties. For inflation (at least if it proceeds at a faster rate than in other exporting countries) raises the price of exports and makes them uncompetitive

on the world market. At the same time imports increase because of the lower prices of foreign goods. The result is a balance of trade deficit, leading to a balance of payments crisis. Also, and this is partly

Continued on page 124

and the TUC have given up their delusion that unemployment can be prevented or reduced by a further round of 'reflation' (their name for inflation). But at the moment Wilson, after years of promoting inflation because he thought it would prevent unemployment, is now declaring that inflation causes unemployment.

Some of his critics in the Labour Party and trade unions (including apparently Mr Scanlon, leaders of the engineers), think they have Marx's backing for their view that the way to deal with crises is to raise wages further. They are quite wrong. Of course Marx favoured the attitude of workers getting as high wages as they can at any time, but he did not hold that crises could be averted by raising wages. He dealt with the higher wages argument in *Capital* (Vol II, p. 475) and showed how absurd it is. Depressions end when the capitalists see prospects of profit improving. Putting wages up further would reduce profit margins not increase them.

No cure for capitalism
Because Socialists view the thirty-year Labour-Tory experiment with Keynesian fallacies as a complete fiasco for the working class it must not be concluded that we are enamoured with the prospect of returning to capitalism without inflation. With or without inflation capitalism will go on producing unemployment, crises and depressions. With Labour government, or any other government, 'managed' or left to market forces, with or without more nationalisation, capitalism has nothing to offer to the working class. The only course for the workers is to replace capitalism with Socialism.

(August 1975)

Democracy and the Silicon Chip

Karl Marx once said that the hand mill gives you feudalism and the steam mill gives you capitalism. Had he lived for another hundred years, he might have added with a wry smile that the computer gives you Socialism. The ways in which human society can be organised, is organised and ought to be organised depend on the techniques and resources which can be used in its running. The idea of a society where no one goes hungry and all co-operate to control the conditions of their existence is no more than a pipe dream unless there is the wherewithal to translate idea into reality.

It is the case of the SPGB that the wherewithal is there. The potential for providing for everyone's needs has been created by capitalism. Thanks to the development of machinery and automation, wealth can be produced in quantities which would have been unthinkable in earlier phases of human society. However, one of our greatest difficulties in getting anyone to accept our view is to convince them on just this point. For its truth is masked in capitalism. The potential for plenty is there, but it cannot be made actual. A profit system can only work with a labour force compelled to sell its energies. If an abundance of the necessaries of life were freely available, the system would grind to a halt. (Who would work at the kinds of jobs on offer in our society if they did not have to?)

We do not ask anyone to take our word for it that the problem of producing enough wealth has been solved. Rather, we refer them whenever possible to the facts unearthed by non-Socialists who are particularly concerned with such issues. (See, for example, in our pamphlet *Questions of the Day*, the chapter on the myth of overpopulation, and our Canadian companion party's pamphlet *A World of Abundance*). In this way we hope to show that hackneyed prejudices about human greed are irrelevant and that, far from being a pipe-dream, a society based on common ownership is a practical necessity.

But this is only one aspect of our case. Our aim is not just common ownership; it is democracy. For us, democracy is not an optional extra or simply a means to an end. It is part of our end, as anyone can discover by reading our Object on the inside back cover of this journal. We define Socialism as "... common ownership and democratic control of the means and instruments for producing and distributing wealth ..."

What do we mean by democracy? Amongst other things, a world in which people are not bossed around by a government or told what to do by their 'superiors'. More positively, a world where everyone takes an equal and responsible part in making decisions which affect society, without the strife which is inevitable in a class-divided society. That is one reason why we say there will be no socialist society until a majority desire it. As long as most people are content to be told what to do by elected representatives there will be no democracy in the sense defined. (Not that an electoral system is completely worthless. More of that later).

At first sight, this suggestion of literally everyone taking part in social decisions may seem as unrealistic as the earlier one of common ownership. Surely, it might be said, these matters have to be left to the experts, and surely modern populations are far too large for active participation by everyone?

Objections like these are meat and drink to political theorists and political philosophers. They think the point so obvious that they state them far more often than actually arguing for them. Yet they are not obvious. In view of the demonstrated failure of legions of experts and government advisers to solve any of the major problems of civilisation, the less said about expertise the better. On the other hand, numbers may seem a genuine problem. How can millions of people all have a say in running society?

The answer, once again is that this would be a mere 'good idea' unless the means were available to make it a reality. And the means are available. Here, too, it is a matter of pointing to existing resources and developments within capitalism. It would be futile for us to offer a blueprint, of course. The exact form the future democratic society takes will depend on the historical circumstances prevailing when it is established. But there are aspects of the technology already available which show how large numbers of people could be drawn into the decision process.

Communication is the lifeblood of capitalism. This is reflected in the facts that by 1975 over 95% of households in Britain had television sets, 53% had telephones, and world traffic in telecommunications has continued to grow at a rate of 12-15% per year (much higher than the rest of world trade). If no vested interests were involved, and if there were a desire for it, imagine how much useful information could be disseminated and how far the ordinary citizen could participate in decisions, just by replacing one old American film every week with an information-and-decision programme. People listen to proposals for some project (say, the building of a new playground or power station), discuss the issues by phone-in, and then ring in to some central point with their vote for or against.

But this is only the tip of the iceberg. Developments are now taking place which will put phones and TVs in the museum along with the stone-age axe. The device which will be responsible is the microelectronic silicon circuit. It is about one centimetre square and is made, incredibly, of grains of sand. In effect, this "silicon chip" is a tiny computer, enormously efficient and dirt-cheap to produce, which has been responsible for bringing together computer and telecommunications technology in one all-embracing 'information technology'.

The first fruits of the marriage will be available next year when the Viewdata system goes into public service. This will make available to its select customers 100,000 pages of information, any part of which can be called up on a screen literally at the touch of a button. Not only that, but the system will be fully 'interactive' – which means that as well as it giving you information, you can give it information, which it will then store. Even the feeblest imagination should be able to grasp the implication for democracy. Such technology gives the opportunity for the population to keep themselves better informed and to take a more active role in decisions than at any time since the small city-states of ancient Greece.

But back to reality. Viewdata is being developed in capitalism, which means it is first and foremost a commercial venture. It will be used not for the sake of participatory democracy but to store information for its customers – advertising agencies, financial institutions, mail order firms and the like. Moreover, systems of this kind have already begun to cause headaches in America, producing the telephone equivalent of junk mail and the hard sell. The micro-computer works its way methodically through a list of victims, automatically ringing them up to relay its recorded message to buy someone's goods. You may not want to buy them, but it's no use putting the receiver down because the computer will automatically continue to ring you back until you have heard it out.

And that is the least of it. This potential boon to mankind is not just proving to be a nuisance: it threatens to produce a crisis. Microelectronic technology is so flexible it will be throwing people out of skilled jobs such as making precision watches and cash registers. In the UK telephone equipment industry alone the number of jobs is expected to fall by 30% between 1976 and 1979. How far the capitalist system can cope with these far-reaching consequences is a problem for those who continue to support it.

Not to labour the point, here as elsewhere capitalism is double-edged. The system has itself called forth instruments which could, in a different framework, be of untold benefit. But under capitalism their use is perverted and only means further trouble. Once again, therefore, the implication is clear that we must change the framework.

The development of information technology is double-edged in a further way. At the turn of the century most political organisations depended largely on outdoor meetings for getting their message across. With the widespread introduction of radio and television this ceased to be true for the larger and richer parties. But the gap which thus opened up has begun to close again. The SPGB has managed to snatch the odd few minutes of broadcasting, and no doubt if capitalism lasts long enough we shall also, like our companion party in America, come to have our own programmes. For the technology developed by capitalism for its own needs eventually becomes available for those who wish to replace capitalism. The computer will make the dissemination of Socialist propaganda an easier and more efficient affair.

That it is something for the future. For the present all we can do is make the best use of our limited resources in what is at least a relatively open political climate. In Britain we can publish a journal and make tapes of our meetings without the threat of immediate persecution. In a one-party state like Russia we could not. We do not exaggerate the extent of this freedom: it costs a lot of money to exercise it fully, and we know that such political freedoms as we have now can be withdrawn. But equally we do not underestimate its importance. (Only a person who had never imagined living under a totalitarian regime would do that). A climate of tolerance is useful to Socialists. It is also fragile, and constantly endangered by our opponents of left and right. Their policies of confrontation and smashing this, that and the other serve only to make it easier to place further curbs on political activity. We received tangible proof of this recently, when one of our London branches lost the use of its meeting room in a pub as a result of threats between other organisations which use the room. The SPGB will have no part in such tactics, and the only force we shall continue to use is the force of rational argument.

A number of points have been made in this article to show that our aim of a democratic society is a practical possibility. There is also another kind of evidence – that of example. The structure of the SPGB is democratic, foreshadowing the future society we advocate. We have no leaders or ruling groups. Though we cannot afford a computer or even to become a customer of Viewdata, our affairs are run according to the decisions of the entire membership through instructed delegates at Annual Conference, and all our officials are elected annually, again by the entire membership. Any organisation can claim to be in favour of democracy. We ask to be judged not on what we claim but on what we do. Having nothing to fear from the presence of nonmembers (welcoming them, in fact), we have never held a closed meeting in our entire history. That is completely in keeping with our conviction that the revolution to establish the Socialist democracy will not be ours; it will be a revolution itself decided upon by a majority of humanity.

(September 1978)

'TURN TO THE RIGHT' IN THE EIGHTIES

With the change from Labour to Conservative in 1979 the infamous era of Thatcherism began. Eight Labour governments had shown that whoever runs capitalism must exploit and oppress the working class – that is its inherent nature. Thatcher's regime represented more of a change of style rather than content though. As one of the articles in this section put it, the main difference between Thatcher and Kinnock (Labour leader at the time) was that "she admits to being a swine who will do whatever the system requires of her; he lies about it".

The Tory attack on trade unions in the 1980s featured prominently in the *Socialist Standard*. Protestors attending a 1980 TUC day of action were reminded that most union leaders and Labour MPs had supported the previous Labour government's 'social contract' to keep wages down. Nineteen-eighty four was not only the year of Orwell's dystopia, but also saw the longest and bitterest coal strike since 1926. Despite widespread and heroic support, it all ended in failure and frustration. Mines were closed and many thousands of miners sacked because producing coal was 'uneconomic'. Nationalisation had not been the answer – the National Coal Board was just as exploitative and anti-worker as were the old mineowners.

Another aspect of the 1980s was the increasing evidence of a sick society. Faced with the impoverishing reality of capitalism, many of its victims responded with anti-social behaviour or a retreat into drugs. Multinational drug companies were – and still are – a growing industry, marketing tranquillisers and anti-depressants of various kinds. The decade had begun in Britain with a wave of civil disturbances (as chronicled in 'Running Riot – Britain's Urban Violence'), with young people from inner cities venting their frustration and anger at unemployment and poverty. They were taught that violence was wrong and immoral by being beaten with truncheons and sprayed with gas.

The environment was also a much-discussed theme. Around the world, workers were having their health threatened and protests concerning the dumping of radioactive waste were ignored. The Sellafield incident and the Chernobyl disaster were dealt with in the *Socialist Standard* in 1986. The wider question of the relationship between socialism and ecology was also raised, with the Greens being seen as wanting to impose on capitalism things that were incompatible with its nature. The Green Party in Britain enjoyed a short-lived breakthrough at the 1989 European elections, committed to a gradualist, reformist strategy, seeking support for a programme of environmental reforms that would leave capitalism basically unchanged, as outlined in 'Where Are the Greens Going?'

War – international and civil – continued to take its toll of human life and well-being. There was a revival of CND but, this time, to protest only against a particular type of missile. There was the Falklands War in 1982, to which the Socialist Party responded that "despite the wave of jingoistic hysteria in the press and its endorsement by Labour and Tory politicians alike, no working class interests in Britain, Argentina or the Falklands can be served by war."

Three articles reproduced here deal with various aspects of left-wing politics at the time, including the Trotskyist far left that had some success in infiltrating the Labour Party and the 'yuppies' who were arguably to have more success still. The *Standard* repeatedly noted that the left was far more coherent when it expounded on the things it despised rather than the things it proposed, and the article 'Why the Left Needs A Thatcher' is a particularly notable expression of this analysis.

Throughout the period the *Socialist Standard* marked itself out as a well-designed and structured journal with some quite striking front covers, increased use of regular columns and some special themed issues. For instance, to commemorate the centenary of Marx's death in March 1983 the *Standard* carried a 24-page supplement on 'Marx the Revolutionary'. This included articles on historical materialism, Marx the journalist, Marx and Darwin, and Engels's review of *Capital*. A special issue in February 1984 also marked the 150th anniversary of the birth of William Morris, and included his vision of the future society, his attitude to reforms and parliamentary action, and his views on work.

Running Riot: Britain's urban violence

Bristol, Brixton, Southall, Toxteth, Moss Side, Wood Green, Woolwich, Brixton again ... A wave of civil disturbances has erupted in England. As livelihoods go up in flames and mindless destruction explodes on the streets, there is a stampede on to the political stage from both wings by politicians and assorted spokesmen. They hold forth loudly to the audience – the 'general public' – about what must be done. They shake their fists and point angrily at each other. They make ominous warnings and each tries to win the support of the audience with promises to carry out the right policy. Political commentators arise and plaintive vicars descend to offer their planned remedies in the din.

A stern attitude has been struck by the government: "the law must be upheld, people must be protected" said Margaret Thatcher in her recent broadcast. Such a kind concern for people's welfare doesn't exactly square with her policy of closing down emergency casualty departments in hospitals and spending millions of pounds on murderous armoury, but then consistency is not one of her strong points. The Home Secretary, William Whitelaw, is planning measures to suppress the street violence. He advocates the use of water cannon, CS gas and increased power for the police to enable them to arrest anyone found in the area of a disturbance. He suggests that parents of those on the rampage should be punished for not controlling their children. There have also been cries from Conservative quarters to bring back the birch and to introduce the Army to 'pacify' civil disorders. The idea behind these sorts of proposals seems to be that if some people become so frustrated with the dehumanising lifestyle which capitalism imposes on the majority that they rebel violently, then you have to teach them that violence is wrong and immoral. And the way you must teach them that violence is wrong and immoral is by beating them with truncheons and spraying them with gas.

On the other hand, supporters of the Labour Party argue that the real causes of the disorders are the reactionary economic policies of this Conservative government. Inner city decay, urban deprivation and high unemployment are all identified as precipitating the riots and the Tory administration is held responsible for having bred the causes. It is true that the economic policy of this government has done much to exacerbate living conditions for many in the working class, but this government has not caused the problems of unemployment and inner city decay and its removal and replacement by a Labour administration will not solve the difficulties of life in the profit system. Not so long ago there were less than half a million unemployed in Britain. Now there are almost three million living on the dole. There are approximately thirty million workers registered as unemployed across the continent of Europe, in countries operating a great variety of economic and political administrations of capitalism from totalitarian state control to 'liberal democracies' with comparatively low degrees of state intervention in the economy. The evidence is clear enough that the trend of high unemployment, during periods of glutted production for the market, is one which moves on largely unaffected by the different economic schemes used in running production for profit. Similarly, the urban deprivation of places like Brixton, Toxteth and Moss Side was not something which grew out of the paving stones after May 1979 when the Tories won the General Election. Squalid housing and unemployment are problems which have been developing for decades and which successive Labour governments have been unable to alleviate. The recent spate of civil violence is the tip of an iceberg of discontent and frustration and it is a delusion to imagine that the problems which face us – the working class – can be eradicated by Labour plans to provide more employment (more exploitation) and more second-rate housing.

Supporters of left-wing organisations like the Socialist Workers Party have been greatly enthused by brick-throwing at policemen, which is somehow regarded as the kind of anti-establishment action of which revolutions are made, or at least from which they can be begun. The attempts to manipulate this collective aggression and stoke up more disturbance are made by ambitious crusaders who believe that if they could be elevated to positions of power on the shoulders of the angry masses, then they could charitably set to work on implementing revolutionary policies for the good of those who know no better than to oppose capitalism with damage and injury. As people who declare their support for the working class, those left-wingers have an offensively patronising view of the capacity of workers to reach socialist consciousness.

A similar enthusiasm for the rioting has been shown by the various extreme right-wing organisations like the National Front who, like the Left, regard the fury of the riot as fertile ground from which to recruit violent rebels. The nature of the political philosophy of parties like the SWP and the NF, and the degree to which the role of the rank and file membership is simply to put forward the changing slogans of the leaderships, means that enrolment to membership can be based on having your frustrations attributed to simple scapegoats which are easy to recognise like 'Thatcher' or 'The Blacks'.

The first riot in Southall was different from the others. The violence began there when several coachloads of racialists were ferried into the area, ostensibly to attend

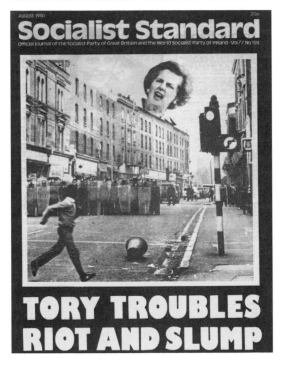

a pub concert. Shops owned by Asians were damaged and the proprietors assaulted. The violence was committed amid barked racialist slogans and provocative Sieg Heils. Local Asian residents managed to organise themselves against their aggressors while the police had taken almost their entire force away to another district, allegedly on a tip-off. In all of the other riots in London, Liverpool and Manchester, black and white workers were in the broil together. They were not race riots but poverty riots. Poverty, that is, both of wealth and ideas. The riot in Southall did not rage because local black and white residents found it impossible to exist peaceably side by side. It was fomented by violent thugs imported for that purpose. And to those who insist that there will always be an underlying tension when different cultures exist in the same district, let them travel to somewhere like cosmopolitan Kensington in London and witness how privileged 'Englishmen' have no resentment living in the same community as wealthy Arabs and Nigerians and Iranians. They have no poverty to blame on anyone, and must feel quite safe so long as we blame ours on each other.

Priests and vicars have not been slow to get off their knees to give vacuums of sympathy to victims of violence and sinister warnings to the sinners. The practicality of their advice in the aftermath of the violence is well summed up in the words of the Archbishop of Liverpool, the Most Reverend Derek Worlock, who after the destruction in Toxteth proclaimed "Out of the ashes of these last days must come new life and new hope." But then if you believe that the ultimate control of the affairs of mankind lies with a force beyond the skies, what else can you offer those suffering from socially produced hardship, but hope?

In certain degrees of poverty, especially at a time of economic crisis when there is no hope on the horizon, pent up frustration will be likely to burst into violence among those who have not considered the cause of their problems and sought to remove it. The dashed hopes and bitterness of most of those in the recent upsurges were not so much to do with the conditions of employment as the condition of unemployment. Hundreds of thousands of young members of the wealth producing class have left school in recent years to go directly on to the dole queue. The feeling of rejection and uselessness which this creates contributes to their resentment of their environment. In Toxteth, to take one example, with thousands of young people leaving school, significantly just about the time the riots broke out, the local career office was offering only twelve jobs. In the city of Liverpool, according to the latest unemployment figures, 81,000 people were chasing 1,019 job vacancies. Other factors like aggressive policing and routine stop-and-search tactics will have obviously aggravated the tensions.

The fact that the bursting frustration and desperation expresses itself in the ferocity of the riot is understandable. Capitalism is a social system which is shot through with everyday forms of 'respectable' and institutionalised violence from the teacher's cane and the policeman's truncheon to the government's tanks and bombs. From the most lighthearted comic book to the late-night documentary on the brutalities of Northern Ireland or Afghanistan we are confronted with images of violence as a method of trying to cause social change. The deeds of those participating in the riots were thoughtlessly destructive. Cars, shops and homes of fellow members of the working class were irrationally ruined. It was a foolish misdirection of anger.

Where do we go from here? It is possible for capitalism to attempt to quell the areas of extreme deprivation by pumping money into housing, industry and welfare for the poverty to become just endurable. The riots which broke in southern America in the late 1960s had their immediate causes treated with giant expenditure on welfare relief payments to the poorest families and training programmes for ghetto youngsters. The profit-system will not be burnt away, neither will it be dislodged or smashed with bricks. A few riots, even large scale rebellions, can easily enough be quashed by the authorities, and usually the rioters will be in a worse condition after the insurgence than before it. But, to borrow from Friedrich Engels, there is no power in Britain which could for a day resist the British working class organised as a body.

(August 1981)

Doing the Bulldog Thing

Some said it was war, to others it was more like comic opera. Most people's knowledge of the Falkland Islands was limited to what they had read in their stamp album but they were sure that it was a place worth defending against a vile foreign dictatorship. The Argentinians were rather better known, since their football team was once called 'animals' by the then England team manager Alf Ramsey, who was not averse to including one or two cloggers in his own side.

The British fleet which was despatched to deal a mighty blow at the invaders of the Falklands sailed out of Portsmouth trying not to look as if it was redundant. It was led by two aircraft carriers, one of which will be sold to the Australian Navy and the other scrapped. Five hundred of the sailors preparing for battle had had notices of redundancy and so had 180 of the workers in the Portsmouth dockyards where the ships were made ready. Among the crew was Prince Andrew ("a serving officer like anyone else") who truly is redundant but gets paid handsomely for it and who seemed liable to fly an expensive helicopter into battle. It was in a rather desperate patriotism that thousands of workers waved the fleet away: "We have to do the bulldog thing" urged the wife of one of the sailors, perhaps reasoning that a dead dog is better off than a live unemployed sailor.

There was too some bellicose relief. Capitalist powers devote an enormous amount of resources to training their people in how to kill other workers in a war. Servicemen are liable to become frustrated, if all their expensive training and equipment is allowed to atrophy for want of the nourishment of a nice, destructive war. So the *Guardian* could report: "The men, with their planes and missiles are, after years of war games, spoiling for the real thing". There was also some relief at the sudden emergence of this external 'enemy', who are always useful in helping persuade workers to accept sacrifices. And sacrifices, as the dole queues get longer and prices rise and rise, are what British capitalism wants from its workers right now.

The government's acute discomfiture at the "humiliating affront to this country" (the departing Lord Carrington's description) was in large part due to the fact that they had based a lot of their electoral appeal on the promise to be strong on 'defence'. Was the Iron Lady to be foxed by a bunch of gibbering foreigners who spend all their time turning out cans of poisoned corned beef? Would the Tories ever live it down? There was much praise and sympathy for the hugely suave, hugely wealthy, Lord Carrington. Even American Secretary of State Alexander Haig had a good word to say for him, forgetting that only recently he called him a "duplicitous bastard". Carrington didn't need sympathy; he retired in good order to his acres in Buckinghamshire, a green and pleasant county of which he owns a substantial amount.

There was nothing comic about the Labour Party's nauseous frenzy to exploit the situation. It was almost as if a general election had already been called. In the Commons on 30th March, Denis Healey accused the government of being "caught with its trousers down in the South Atlantic" – a phrase for the connoisseurs of Healeyisms. Callaghan, pretending to be helpful, recounted how much better the interests of British capitalism had been looked after when he was responsible. In 1977, he claimed, there was a similar crisis but the Labour government resolved it secretly, with a combination of military threat and diplomatic pressure. No MP took Callaghan's trousers down by asking why the leader of a party which once claimed to stand for international working class interests should be fishing in the murky waters of capitalist diplomacy. In fact, Carrington had been following the same policy – on this issue, as on others there is no difference between Tories and Labour – but his bad luck was that the Argentinian rulers were under pressure to call his bluff and the whole thing was played out in public.

Of course the real star of the Labour benches was Michael Foot. Belying his reputation as a doddering, ineffectual bungler, the Labour leader lashed the government for their "betrayal of those who looked to it for protection" (he was not talking about workers struggling to live on social security). "We should not," he raged, "see foul, brutal aggression successful in our world." (He was not attacking the record of past Labour governments on Korea, Malaysia, Biafra, Vietnam …) Foot's speech was applauded by the MPs as a flag-waving, drum-banging demand for the war in which, of course, he would not personally be in the front line. It was, we remember, only a few months ago that he won an affectionate ovation at a Labour Party gathering by describing himself as "an inveterate peacemonger".

Many Tory MPs were delighted with Foot's performance. One sure way of winning their respect is to make a speech calling for workers to be sent off to war. One of the more effusive – or perhaps he had merely lunched well – gurgled, "For once, you truly spoke for Britain". There was no report that Foot so much as blushed at this insulting compliment (a few days later he was calling himself "an international democratic socialist"), nor that he was perturbed by Labour MP George Foulkes' warning that "inevitably thousands of British troops will be killed." The Labour Party has never flinched from the prospect of workers dying in the conflicts to protect their masters' interests, especially if an inveterate votes-monger like Foot may be able to translate their deaths into an election win.

The Conservatives, also worried about their political standing, simply tried to shelter in a measure of fantasy. Thatcher declared: "The Falkland Islands and their dependencies remain British territory … It is the government's objective to see that the Islands are freed from occupation and returned to British administration at the earliest possible moment."

But in the reality of world capitalism 1982, places like the Falklands are not defensible by any available British force for any length of time. British foreign policy has been based on that reality for some time now. In historical fact the 'British administration' of the Islands was itself an 'occupation'. The British settlement of the Falklands was contested by France, Spain and Argentina, from the latter half of the 18th century. The Spanish were there until 1806, when the Argentinians threw them out and in 1833 a British force arrived and, politely but firmly, ejected the Argentians. The Prime Minister of the day made it plain that the British ruling class would not allow "… any other state to exercise a right as derived from Spain, which Britain had denied to Spain herself." This has never been accepted by any Argentinian government and, at the very least, they have registered an annual protest. Children there are taught about the perfidy of the British over the Falklands, rather as British children have been taught about the Germans, French, Japanese, Argentinians …

In 1851 a Royal Charter – the official sanction to the exploitation of the resources and the people – was granted to the Falkland Islands Company and since then the Islands' economy has been dominated by that company. The FIC owns nearly half the land, a third of the sheep (wool is the Islands' only product of any significance) and employs over one sixth of the population. It controls the bank, the dock and the supermarket. In 1972, after a brief spell of ownership by an offshoot of Slater Walker, the FIC was taken over by Charrington Industrial Holdings, which has big interests in fuel distribution and was probably attracted by the FIC stake in the islands' transport and warehousing and the possible presence of oil. Argentinian investors almost pulled off a stealthy take-over in 1977 but this was thwarted, partly by the Foreign Office. Charrington seemed shaken by the experience, and declared that they would never sell out to a foreign concern. Soon afterwards they were themselves taken over by Coalite, a company based in Derbyshire. Through all these machinations the workers of the Falklands plodded on, in the bare, windswept landscape, raising sheep and turning out the surplus value for whichever bunch of capitalists was appropriating the wealth they had produced.

Those workers are in the main descendants of the Scottish, English and Welsh who went to the Falklands after 1851. Most families are tenants of the FIC and live in tied cottages which they must leave when they are too old to be exploitable any longer. Until recently the majority of members of the Legislative Council were nominated by the British government. If the Falklanders prefer this kind of feudal paternalism it can only be because they think – with good reason – that life under Argentinian military rule has even less to offer them. A final irony is that, if any of them tries to take refuge in Britain they will have no automatic right of entry. The Foreign Office has promised them special concessions but, although they hold British passports, they are legally excluded because they are defined as non-patrials under the 1971 Immigration Act.

Behind the feigned concern for the fate of the Falklanders is the fact that for a long time it has been British policy, under Labour and Conservative governments, to phase the Islands over to Argentine rule. As James Callaghan pointed out in the Commons on 7th April, in a brief respite from his jingoism, there had already been negotiations about the British hold over the Falklands, which might have led to some sort of leaseback arrangement with Argentina. In 1971 a commercial agreement gave Argentina a near monopoly in fuel supply and air travel and the first big runway at Port Stanley was Argentinian built. The Director General of the Falkland Islands Office in London had this to say, about the British attitude to their efforts to resist this trend: "We have consistently not been getting sufficient support from the Foreign Office these last twelve years."

Naturally a lot of publicity was given by the British media to the transparent cynicism behind the invasion. Argentina is another country in the grip of a severe recession. At the end of March a trade union demonstration against the effects of unemployment and rising prices brought some of the worst civil disorder since the military took over in 1976. But the move against the Falklands brought a miraculous change; patriotic frenzy swamped the reality of the workers' parlous condition and of the murderous repression by which the Argentinian rulers defend their position. As the news came through there was another demonstration but this time the Argentinian workers were chanting support for Galtieri and his annexation of Los Islas Malvinas.

The hysteria and deception on both sides ensure that it will take a long time to purge the Falklands crisis of historical myth. It will be written up as an affair of honour; the Argentinians will describe it as a blow against foreign imperialism and the British as a defence of human rights. But the wars of capitalism have never protected human rights; in truth they have damaged those rights, at times destroyed them. Diplomacy – one of the practised arts of the capitalist system – cannot be an affair of honour; it must function by double-cross, concealment, treachery and lies.

So British and Argentinian servicemen went across the ocean to do battle with each other in their masters' cause. It was another doleful example of ignorant workers being easily duped by the empty jingoism of desperate politicians. Animals do it better; at least they don't take themselves willingly to the slaughterhouse.

(May 1982)

The Miners' Strike – Why?

Why did 120,000 miners join what has become the longest, bitterest and most controversial strike in the British coal industry since 1926? Clearly, it is no answer to say that they are motivated by subversive political aims or that they have all been hoodwinked by nasty Arthur Scargill and the NUM leaders. We can read this kind of facile substitute for an explanation in the propaganda press.

Economics under capitalism are concerned first and foremost with price and profit. Production is regarded as 'uneconomic' when investment of capital shows little or no prospect of leading to profit for the investor. Being "uneconomic" is not at all the same as being 'useless'. For example, dairy farming is currently 'uneconomic' within the EEC countries because more milk is produced than can be sold profitably. However, milk is desperately needed by the 40,000 children who, according to UNICEF, die of starvation or malnutrition-caused diseases every single day. So, when the economic experts say that miners are producing too much coal, this excess relates to profit rather than need. Similarly, when they say that investment in certain mines is 'uneconomic' this does not mean there is not plenty of coal in them, but that capital investment in mining such coal would be unprofitable.

Politicians like Thatcher have never forgiven the NUM for the success of their last strike. Responding to the feelings of many capitalists, her government wants to weaken the power of the miners. A leaked Cabinet Minute of 1979 explained that: "A nuclear programme would have the advantage of removing a substantial proportion of electricity from disruption by miners and transport workers."

Economists are not paid to think about the devastation of the old mining communities which pit closures cause: destroying long-established ways of life does not appear on their balance sheets. Economists are not paid to register the harsh facts that more than half of the men attempting suicide are unemployed and that the rate of successful suicides in Britain has shot up during the present recession. Nor are they paid to bother themselves about the old workers who will die this winter because they are too poor to switch on a heater. Electricity output has been reduced because there is much less market demand for it by domestic consumers, while the non-recognition of real human demand leads to the totally unnecessary social disease of hypothermia. But none of these factors is of economic significance under capitalism: let communities be converted into industrial wastelands, let thousands of useful and energetic miners be forced into idleness, let thousands be cold for lack of coal-based heating.

Myths about the State

There was once a time when miners, in the company of many other workers, were easily persuaded that the solution to the problems of the profit system was nationalisation of industry. If only the mines were owned and controlled by the government rather than by private capitalists, it was asserted, the miners would have little to worry about. Forty years ago Will Lawther, the President of the Mineworkers' Federation of Great Britain (the predecessor to the NUM), asked readers to imagine what could be achieved through nationalisation: "It would win the complete confidence of the miners and their families. Generations of suspicion and hatred would be wiped out, and an entirely new attitude developed towards the coal industry ... Only through public ownership can you really plan the effective use of Britain's coal resources, plan production on the basis of modernisation or mechanisation, and bring about complete unity between your export and domestic coalfields ..." (Foreword to *Britain's Coal* by Margot Heinemann, 1944).

Lawther goes on to predict that nationalisation would "enormously improve output and make use even of old coalfields that are looked upon as being worked out" and that "only the nationalisation of the mines can win the confidence of the miners." One can forgive miners for having been taken in by these hopes for capitalism at the time, even if – it must be added – the Socialist Party of Great Britain was then pointing out to those who would listen that nationalisation offered no solution to the workers. But now, after decades of experience of state capitalism in action, it is politically inane for workers to imagine that nationalised industries are in any way immune from the economic laws of capitalism. The NCB, as the state employer, is just as exploitative and antagonistic to the workers' interests as were the old mine owners.

The second myth which needs to be dispelled is that the state – the government, the law, the judges, the police commanders – is neutral. The state must be the political defender of the ruling class. When thousands of miners are stopped from picketing, when hundreds of miners are beaten by the police and when the funds of the South Wales NUM are stolen by the courts, it is clear that the state exists to reinforce the needs of capital. It would make no difference if the Labour Party was running the state instead of the Tories. That is why, when the Labour Party was in office between 1964 and 1970, they closed down 48 pits and made over 50,000 miners unemployed in the South Wales region alone.

In the first three months of the strike one miner was arrested every twenty minutes – 3,282 arrests in all. Over 80% of these arrests were for 'breach of the peace' or 'obstruction'. Obviously the government has instructed the police to use tough tactics in dealing with the strikers. The well-known television picture of a police officer beating a defenceless striker with a truncheon is but one of numerous examples of police brutality in a battle initiated by the state. But as ordinary workers, paid to do an unpleasant job, it is not the police workers on the picket lines who are to be blamed: the real culprits are the legally respectable and physically secure boot-boys who pull the strings of the state.

The NCB has increased its importation of cheap Polish coal which is one of the factors weakening the effects of the British miners' strike. The NUM now has an official picket outside the Polish Embassy, calling on the Polish bosses to suspend imports in order to strengthen the effects of the British strike. But when Polish miners attempted to set up an independent union of their own the President of the NUM (writing in his personal capacity) argued that such action constituted 'sabotage' and that the Polish miners should be loyal to their state bosses. The capitalists, who not for the first time are benefiting from the tactic of Divide and Rule, must be laughing all the way to the bank as they import cheap coal from their 'Communist' enemies. Reproduced below is the full text of a resolution published by the underground Solidarity union in the Warsaw region, first published in their illegal journal, CDN. It shows that the writers and supporters of this Polish resolution are thinking along internationalist lines:

"For four months the British miners have been on strike against a programme of mass closures of mines for economic reasons. The miners are threatened with unemployment. The government has rejected compromise solutions and has resorted to severe police methods against the strikers. Thousands of miners have been arrested; hundreds have been hospitalised and one has been killed.

"The government of the Polish People's Republic, despite hypocritical condemnations of the activities of the British police in the columns of the regime press and by the regime's pseudo-trade unionists, is profiting from the export of coal to Britain. It sells dirt cheap coal which has been mined in scandalously neglected working conditions and with reckless condemnation of the labour force and the coalfield. The slave labour of the Polish miner serves to break the resistance of the British miner.

"British miners! The true sentiments of Polish trade unionists towards the authorities of the Polish People's Republic and their practices was shown in the recent electoral farce which was boycotted by the workers. In the prevailing conditions of terror, the Polish workers' movement is at present not in a position to undertake protest actions. But you may be certain that as you have supported and are supporting our struggle, so we are in solidarity with you. We strongly oppose every case where force is used against workers struggling for their rights and interests" (Published in *CDN*, Mazowsze region, 26th June, 1984).

How painful it would be for the workers who produced the above resolution to know that the President, and several other key leaders, of the NUM believe that Solidarity should not exist.

What the miners' struggle has shown

As the miners' strike has not been organised by socialists, it is not surprising that tactics have been employed with which we disagree. It is possible that the division within the NUM could have been avoided; full, democratic decision-making within the workers' movement is always the surest guarantee of strength.

But the miners' struggle has shown the importance of solidarity between workers of one county and another and one country and another. The sense of common purpose and dedication which thousands of miners have shown during the strike contrasts sharply with many previous struggles in trade union history, where workers have been conned into co-operating in their rulers' interests. Let any miserable little cynic who says that workers are incapable of self-organised co-operation take a look at the tremendous achievements in communal self-help which strikers have set up.

Secondly, the strike has shown the Labour Party and its Leftist followers to be quite unable to point the miners in the direction of socialism. According to the theory, Leftists are supposed to wait for major struggles like this one in order to move in and tell the workers about the alternative to capitalism. In fact, the SWP, CP, WRP, RCP and numerous other inflatable vanguards have not produced a single leaflet between them urging the miners to transform their demands into the political aim of abolishing the wages system. As for the Labour Party, Neil Kinnock and his fellow mis-leaders have had little to offer but empty rhetoric. After all, every time the Labourites stand up in the House of Commons to tell the Tories how wicked they are, the Tories have been able to quote chapter and verse showing that previous Labour governments have run the mines in just the same way – to meet the demands of the profit system.

In any strike between robbers and robbed (with the exception of political strikes, such as when the dockers opposed immigration or the Labourites ran their phoney day of action) the Socialist Party is unequivocally on the side of the robbed. In the class war no worker and no political party can be neutral. But in expressing solidarity with workers in struggle, we point out that our sympathy and their temporary gains will be meaningless unless victory involves winning the war and not just one battle. To win the class war workers must organise as a class for the conquest of the earth and all its resources. No lesser victory is worth settling for.

(September 1984)

Leftist Wonderland: Militant in Liverpool

For those of you who are confused about what's been going on at Liverpool City Council, here are the facts:

Militant is a newspaper. The people who sell it are members of the Labour Party, although they don't support it, and supporters of Militant (the tendency, not the newspaper) although they are not members of it. The Labour Party leaders are neither members nor supporters of Militant (the tendency), and neither do they sell *Militant* (the newspaper), although you can never be sure since *Militant* newspaper sellers are notoriously shy about coming out.

The Labour Party leaders want to expel Militant supporters from the party since they think that they are wrecking Neil Kinnock's chances of moving into Downing Street after the next general election. They claim that Militant (the tendency) is in breach of the Labour Party's constitution since they operate as a party within the Labour Party, with different aims and objectives. But Labour's leaders are worried that to expel Militant might upset other Labour supporters and also, presumably, damage Neil Kinnock's election chances. So instead of expelling supporters of Militant, they have suspended the whole of the Labour Party in Liverpool – home of the Tendency's most vociferous spokesperson, Derek Hatton, who they especially want to get rid of. (There are rumours that at least some supporters of Militant are no longer so keen on supporting Hatton, but maybe we shouldn't make this any more complicated than it already is.)

Militant in Liverpool are very upset that the Labour Party is treating them in this way and assert that they, unlike the Labour leadership, are the real guardians of Labour Party conference decisions since they are resisting "Tory cuts" and fighting to "save the jobs and services for the people of Liverpool," and want to institute Clause Four of the Labour Party's constitution (the one stating that the Labour Party is committed to nationalisation). The Labour Party conference is supposed to be the main policy-making body of the party, but the leadership ignores conference decisions when they don't like them. So, just to recap, Militant, which *doesn't* agree with the Labour Party, is upholding its constitution and decisions made at conference, while the leadership, who do support the Labour Party, are ambivalent about nationalisation and Kinnock has said that he will ignore conference decisions if he doesn't agree with them. But it is Militant that looks set to be thrown out of the Labour Party for a breach of the constitution, while Kinnock is increasingly regarded as the party's saviour.

The Militant leaders of Liverpool City Council, as already mentioned, claim that they are fighting to preserve jobs and services. As part of their strategy to do this they sent out redundancy notices to 31,000 local authority workers and looked set to close down council-run facilities like daycare centres for the elderly and handicapped, children's homes, libraries, sports centres and swimming pools. Their concern for the workers of Liverpool was such that they asked them to work for nothing after they received their redundancy notices. The workers however could not understand how this was helping them (not surprising, Militant would say, since to them workers are too stupid to recognise their real interests and so need leaders like Militant to protect their interests for them). Teachers in Liverpool took the City Council to court and managed to get an injunction against the redundancy notices. But it wasn't just the teachers who were too stupid to understand that Militant were looking after their interests; just about every trade union with members working for the local authority have also shown signs of 'stupidity' by expressing their hostility to the leadership.

Militant also claims to be working for racial harmony in Liverpool and to that end they appointed a community relations officer. That appointment has resulted in almost every community group representing black people in Liverpool refusing to have anything to do with either the council or the community relations officer and trade unions have advised their members not to co-operate with him. So much for racial harmony and community relations.

Finally, Militant claims to be 'socialist'. Apart from the doubt cast on this idea by their membership of the anti-socialist Labour Party, their support for state-capitalism, their undemocratic organisation, their patronising attitude to their fellow workers, besides all that, this 'socialist' tendency has just accepted £30 million from those well-known supporters of socialism, the Gnomes of Zurich, to bail them out.

So, to sum up: Militant are members of the Labour Party although they don't agree with the Labour Party. Labour's leaders want them out because they are in breach of the party's constitution even though the leadership itself does not honour decisions made at the party's conference. Derek Hatton and his fellow Militants on Liverpool City Council claim to be acting on behalf, and in the interests, of the working class of Liverpool and demonstrate this by threatening workers with the sack or asking them to work for nothing. They claim to be 'socialist' but are quite happy to take money from a bunch of capitalist financiers who are no doubt rubbing their hands with glee at the prospect of making a financial killing from all the interest they are going to receive on this loan.

Still confused? So you should be!

(January 1986)

All Yuppies Now?

Are you young – upwardly mobile – professional? Are you the sort of person who buys downtown slums and fits them out with designer furniture and hand-painted blinds? Do you drive the sort of car which people who work in car factories can never afford to drive, listen to Suzanne Vega albums on compact discs, and check the share index in both the *FT* and *The Independent* to make sure that your highly ethical investments are looking as healthy as you do after you've been for your six-monthly BUPA check-up? If the answer is yes – sorry, yah – to those questions it is probable that you are a member of The Class of '87 – the yuppies.

Under capitalism there are two classes: the capitalists who rob and the workers who are robbed. But of course, as all trendy-minded readers will know, capitalism is not what it used to be. The working class – those cloth-capped fossils who dig coal and drive trains and have dirt under their fingernails and say things like 'Gawd blimey, mister' and 'You can't beat 'er Majesty' and 'arold Wilson' – has apparently vanished. The corpse has been buried by a team of sociologists-cum-undertakers who write for *Marxism Today* who have conducted a thorough search of the wine bars of Covent Garden and can find no trace of any horny-handed sons of toil. Even the holy trinity of the new left – Eric Hobsbawm, Ralph Miliband and Jeremy Seabrook – have announced in the columns of that robust proletarian journal, the *Guardian*, that the proletariat (they who work in factories and vote Labour) are missing, feared dead – or, worse still, 'up North'.

Both the left and the right wings of capitalism (not to mention the centre, which constitutes the Liberals and the SDP and David Owen who singularly represents the real centre) are sure that capitalism as described by Marx and the Socialist Party is old hat. Now we all live under Thatcherism. No longer are there masters and wage slaves; these are disgusting remnants of the past, entertained only in the deranged minds of people like the present writer who, in revolutionary obstinacy, insists that everyone he ever meets is either one of the bosses or one of the bossed. But if you accept the new line – as propagated by Thatcher and swallowed by her enemies in their own haste to sound indignant about it – we now live in the age of popular capitalism. And under popular capitalism you are all in one of three classes (unless, of course, you are the Queen or one of the other aristocratic parasites, in which case you are where you always were: rich, idle and useless). But the rest of us are either in class A – people who've made it – or class B – people who are making it (yuppies) – or class C – people who can't make it because they are too stupid or won't make it because they like living in squalor.

Now the object of this so-called Thatcherism is to 'make it'. Needless to say, 'making it' bears no relation to *making* anything. If you go around producing goods and services you'll never get on in the City. 'Making it' means making money. You get other people to produce goods and services and you exploit them. If you are a yuppie you are not yet in the exploiting class. (In fact – don't tell the yuppies, now – you never will be). But you act like you are heading in that direction. You do the dirty work for the capitalists. The so-called yuppie class are simply the errand boys and girls for the capitalists. They are paid extra for taking on themselves the problems of the exploiting class.

According to the Thatcher propaganda, we are all becoming capitalists now. This is a load of old twaddle. Firstly, only 19% of the British population owned any shares in the week before the BP share sell-off. So even if you define all shareholders as capitalists (which is a daft definition), that means that over 80% of British people are outside this new capitalist class. But it is not the case that workers who buy a few shares are capitalists. The test of whether you are a capitalist is easy: give up selling yourself for a wage or salary and see how long you can live on your share dividends – if you're on the last can of baked beans within a fortnight you have proved that whatever you are you are not a capitalist. The capitalist class are those people who can live without having to work: they invest in the labour of others.

Secondly, if Thatcher's policies meant that we did all become capitalists there would be no wage slaves left to produce our profits for us. If we all became the Queen, who would we have to wave at, who would there be to bring us our dinner on a silver tray? It is a necessity of class society that superiority for some can only logically exist at the expense of inferiority for most. Thirdly, there has in fact been a record number of bankruptcies under the present Conservative government. The capitalist recession is not creating vast numbers of new capitalists, as the government liars state, but squeezing out large numbers of cockroach capitalists who land with a bump into the growing ranks of the wage and salary earning class. The notion that the workers are enjoying greater prosperity than ever and that poverty is an obsolete conception is not only a myth but an unforgivable insult. Go to the Docklands area of East London – the showpiece of resplendent yuppiedom – and you will find thousands of workers without jobs or much money who are being driven out of their area because the gamblers of the City have decided to redevelop it for their own purpose.

It is not only the Tories who preach the virtues of the new yuppie vision. Nor is it confined to the Alliance, whose dream of the new Jerusalem is everyone sending their kids to progressive 'independent' (exclusive, private, fee-paying) schools and driving Volvos with push-button windows. The silly old Labour Party has decided to fall in love with the yuppies too. Bryan Gould, the genius who masterminded the Labour Party's spectacular defeat earlier this year (next time they're hiring a computer linked up to an opinion poll teleprinter to organise it for them), has decided that Labour needs to speak to a wider constituency. What this means is that Labour needs to work harder at convincing Tories that their shares are safe in Labour's hand. Gould wants Labour to go for the yuppie vote. After all, Ben Elton has made a packet posing as a socialist appealing to just such an audience. As ever, the Labour Party's tactical astuteness bears a strong relationship to a wino negotiating his way to the bus shelter. Just when the Labourites decided that there's nothing wrong with what Thatcher says about workers getting in on the Stock Exchange, what does the old Stock Exchange do? It crashes. The opportunism of the Labour Party is boundless, as they merrily proceed to urge workers to buy council houses and invest in private medical insurance and shares – as long as they're ethical. (*Marxism Today* – the theoretical organ of the Lefty Yuppie Party – is now advertising a company which will advise pseudo-Marxists with a conscience which shares they should buy if they don't want to exploit people.)

The yuppie left has become one of the more grotesque eyesores of 1980s politics. In the good old days lefties would waste our time discussing whether Russia was a deformed workers' state or a degenerate workers' state or a workers' state with minor deformities; they would quote (and often misquote) bits from Marx and insist that we Socialist Party members had failed to study our Trotsky. No longer is such rhetoric prevalent (except in Chesterfield, of course, where the whole population is currently undergoing a Collected Works of Trotsky reading course). These days the yuppie left are into 'feeling Green'. If you don't know what it is to feel Green and put yourselves in the position of a baby seal you have no right to call yourself a socialist. Coffee-picking in Nicaragua is all the rage now (even Jimmy Carter's at it) and singing South African liberation songs at book stalls displaying pamphlets about the need for armed struggle in the Third World written by Paul Foot who lives in Hampstead. If you are a male you must become what the yuppie left calls a new man, which means that you are extremely patronising to women (who are all your sisters) and must endure the rest of your life on a permanent guilt trip for the crime of being a potential rapist. It is little wonder that most wage slaves prefer the down-to-earth callousness of Norman Tebbit and his fellow gangsters to the phony, self-righteous, condescending, half-baked outlook of the trendy yuppies who constitute the left-wing of capitalist politics.

The Socialist Party is not out to win over the yuppies. We do not appeal to the 'middle class' any more than we appeal to the Wizard of Oz or the residents of Albert Square, Walford. We do not seek to trim our message to suit the prejudices of fictitious classes of people. We direct what we have to say at the working class – all workers, be they paid in wages or salaries, whether they wear overalls or carry filofaxes. Socialists do not make the leftist error of imagining that the true workers are these who live in council flats and stand on the terraces at football matches. Nor do we believe that so-called yuppies, most of whom are simply entertaining the self-delusion of privilege, are anything but workers. We have no grudge against workers who are making an extra crust out of capitalism. But they would be fools to be bought off by crusts and crumbs. The yuppies of the right who imagine that they are part of Thatcher's new elite will find out the hard way which class they are in and yuppies of the left who feel guilty for being 'privileged' people like teachers and social workers should stop boring the rest of us with their needless guilt.

(December 1987)

Why the Left Needs a Thatcher

So, Thatcher is dead, the victim of a rotten egg that she told the workers it was safe to eat. The offending chicken has been ritually slaughtered by the Guildford Association of Conservative Ladies. The funeral cortege passes slowly through the streets of London, which have been cleared of beggars the night before. Behind the coffin march vast rows of stockbrokers and workers with red-rimmed glasses and portable telephones; they have gone from deepest Surrey and deepest Sussex, from Hants and Herts and Bucks and Beds. In Dorset the firm selling black armbands (made by cheap labour in Hong Kong, of course) is expecting a boom. The cops and soldiers, saddened by the loss of an Empress, pacified by the overtime bonus paid out for funeral duties, march tearfully. Behind them shuffle the silly old proles who will weep at anything: they wept when Charles and Di got married and when the Queen Mother swallowed a trout bone (who would have believed she'd outlive Thatcher) and when The Firm got Dirty Den in *Eastenders*. They cried with joy when they received the letter telling them that Maggie was going to let them buy their council slum, and with fear when a letter came informing them that the whole estate had been bought by a property company on the Isle of Dogs. The media whores march along, forgiving the old girl for her excesses; after all, she was a character to write about. And who is this tailing on to the procession? They are weeping more than anyone. They feel deserted, they have lost a cause, Satan has descended to Hell and the children of righteousness have no-one to blame for their misfortunes. With Thatcher goes into the grave Thatcherism: a decade of leftist illusion being carried away to be chewed up by the worms. What will they do without her?

Doing what the system demands

The British Left needs Margaret Thatcher. Bankrupt of ideas or vision, all that is left for them to do is detest hers. The Left rarely talks of capitalism – except, as at the Labour conference last year, when Kinnock said that his government would have to run it better than the Tories. The aim of the left-wing has always been to establish state capitalism, the profit system planned centrally by a miracle-performing state. Eight Labour governments have demonstrated that the miracle cannot be performed. Whoever runs it, the capitalist system must exploit and oppress the working class; that is its inherent nature. So, the debate on the Left is about how to run capitalism. And to do the job as ruthlessly and callously as the system demands has come to be called Thatcherism.

Most of the Thatcher policies are hated by the Left for good reasons. Thatcher is a militant class warrior. Not even the *Daily Express* would ever have called Wilson or Callaghan that. Laws have been passed in the past ten years which have hurt workers and blunted our instruments of self-defence. The unions have taken a battering; services like the NHS, which Labour had boasted was the cream of the reformist gains, have been attacked and then attacked again. It is understandable that many workers see in Thatcher the personification of all that is wrong in society. The question they must ask themselves is, Would society have been a much better place to live in had Thatcher never come into office? The answer, based on the hard evidence of history, is that Thatcher has not been governing capitalism, but that it has governed her. Just as it governed the Labour government before she came to power. That is why the last Labour Chancellor of the Exchequer, Denis Healey, introduced the policy of monetarism as a means of cutting the state budget in a bid to deal with inflation. It was under the last Labour government that expenditure limits within the NHS were first introduced. It was the last Labour government which took on the low-paid workers of NUPE and NALGO in the winter of 1978 – when Callaghan told the unions that they would have to take cuts in real wages. Back in the mid-Seventies there were 'Fight The Cuts' rallies being organised across the country. Whose cuts were being fought but those of the last Labour government? It was under the last Labour government that unemployment doubled to the then 'wholly unacceptable' level of one and a half million.

And those Thatcher policies which Labour did not implement before 1979, they are now ready to accept as their own. Before 1979 Labour was opposed to British membership of the Common Market. Now they agree with Thatcher that Britain should stay in. Labour was opposed to selling off council houses. It is now Labour policy to sell them. Labour was opposed to selling off nationalised services, such as Telecom. It is now official Labour policy not to take back such services from private hands, lest the votes of the shareholders be lost. Labour made noises of opposition to the monstrous Tory laws aimed to limit union powers. Kinnock is now on record as opposing any substantial alteration to those laws in the event of a future Labour government. So, where does the Labour Party actually disagree with the wicked Thatcher who is supposed to stand for everything that they are against? Membership of NATO? Both parties agree that Britain should stay in. Troops in Ireland? Both parties want to keep them there. The nuclear bomb? With passionate unilateralists like Neil Kinnock, the men at the Pentagon need have no fears that both British parties of capitalism will be with them on the day. The chief differences between Thatcher and Kinnock are these: she admits to being a swine who will do whatever the system requires of her, he lies about it; she is in power, he is not.

What lesser evil?

Some of the Left are of the view that capitalism has been fundamentally changed by the Thatcher years. It is no longer the same system. It is now a new phenomenon called Thatcherism. It is, to be frank, very difficult to know what such people are talking about. The Communist Party's latest policy document *New Times*, claims that we are now living in a period of 'post-Fordism' in which the old working class has disappeared and been replaced by a new Thatcherite breed. The CP's response to these 'new times' is to seek some sort of broad, popular front reform movement, comprising every brand of political timewaster from the SNP to the SDP, with a view to offering the voters a better lifestyle under the system than Thatcher has offered them. The entire theory is flawed by two basic mistakes.

Firstly, the working class never was just that group of people who wore cloth caps and worked on the line at Ford. 'Post-Fordism' is a mourning at the funeral of a class which has not disappeared at all, but is now exploited in new areas of the economy. There are vastly more workers in the service industries now than in manufacturing, and over the last ten years the move away from making to selling has been a characteristic of the European and US economies. But the workers in these countries are still wage (or salary) slaves, legally robbed by their employers. You don't have to be a miner to be in the class struggle.

Secondly, the assumption that the way to fight a system is to concentrate all of your forces into defeating its leader of the moment is as foolish politically as it would be militarily for the Warsaw Pact to imagine that it could win the next world war by knocking off the current head of NATO. The Communist Party theorists

argue that the crucial battle is at election time when a non-Tory alliance must win
the day and slay the Thatcherite dragon. But what if a new dragon in the form of
an Owen or a Kinnock or a Hattersley is elected instead? Surely, it is the job
description and not the person appointed to do the job which is the real issue. The
point of the battle should be to put an end to the dirty job of running capitalism.
But, disloyal to the working-class interest in its death throes as much as it was at
the outset, the CP is of the view that it is better to have capitalism run by 'the lesser
evil'. And who are they, who spent most of their political history telling us that
Stalin was 'the lesser evil', to advise the workers on such matters? The foolish
tactical plans of Professor Eric Hobsbawm for a broad anti-Thatcher alliance are
to the cause of socialism what Groucho was to Marxism.

Back in 1979 the Socialist Party took the same principled position that we take
now. We are opposed to capitalism and all who seek to run it. We do not want
reformed capitalism or the profit system better managed. We are not looking for
'nice' leaders or any kind of leaders for the workers to follow. The wages system is
against the interest of the workers and only workers' self-emancipation will solve
the problems that we face. We were told not to waste our time upon such
revolutionary ambitions. Many on the Left urged us to join the Labour Party and
achieve what little could be achieved. After all, that was the party of the workers,
so we were told. The present writer was even urged by Neil Kinnock no less (when
the latter was Shadow Minister of Education and the former was a persistent
questioner at a meeting) to join the Labour Party and help swell the ranks of 'real
socialists'. We were told that with just a little harder push Tony Benn would take
the leadership and set the world ablaze. Those who joined the Labour Party in
1979 have not had much for their subscription money. The Tories have won three
elections, with millions of trade unionists voting for them, despite the fact that the
union leaders count them in as affiliated members of the Labour Party. Foot was
elected as Labour leader (to loud cheers from the Left) and proved to be an utter
failure; then Kinnock was elected as the Left's choice against Hattersley. Now
Kinnock is detested by the Labour Left – before he has even had a chance to betray
them in power.

Utter lack of principles

Most political commentators, and most of the more candid Labour leaders, do not
think that the Labour Party will win the next general election. Indeed, a split in the
Labour Party is on the cards. Where Labour is in power locally it has shown that
it can be just as ruthless at cutting essential services as the Tories. In short, after
ten years of degrading and unprincipled compromise of the few principles that
they once had, the Left stands without much hope, without much support and
with a few cranky theories of further opportunism about joining with Dr Owen,
the Greens and the Nats to form a reformist alliance. The so-called hard left

retreats annually to Chesterfield to lick its wounds, praise the achievements of Gorbachev and listen with devotion to the guru, Benn. The other hangers-on to the Labour Party (who have urged workers to vote for them in every election) have turned into parodies of themselves. The Workers' Revolutionary Party is now busy singing the praises of the Russian dictators and the SWP has degenerated further than ever, existing now as a group engaged in a few single-issue reform campaigns, such as opposition to the poll tax and – the sign of real senility – support for the Khomeni regime in its territorial conflict with Iraq. The Left which warned the Socialist Party that we would be left behind while they stormed the fortress has been left seriously wounded, largely by its own utter lack of principles.

That is why the Left needs a Thatcher. It needs that hideous voice and that look of contempt that leaves you in no doubt that you are being politically abused by the woman even when she is simply telling you the time. The hope of the Left is that hatred of Thatcher will cover up the fact that the opposition has nothing to offer in her place. The Socialist Party does have a clear alternative to the mean-minded narrowness of what Thatcher stands for. And when Thatcher is cold in her grave and another despicable faker is mouthing her lies, the call to the workers to transcend this system of misery will be as fresh and as urgent as ever.

(May 1989)

Where Are the Greens Going?

Even if turns out to be a mere flash in the pan, the result of the Euro-elections in Britain were rather remarkable. The Green Party polled some 2.3 million votes (one in seven of those who bothered to vote), overtaking the SLD (or whatever the Liberals are now called) and even pushing Labour into third place in six constituencies. This is the first time that a party to the 'left', in conventional terms, of the Labour Party has been able to make such a breakthrough, even if it can be doubted whether most of its voters saw themselves as voting for a radical alternative to Labour.

That the Greens have a far more radical programme than Labour is not open to any doubt. While Labour now openly stands for trying to run the profit system better than the Tories, the Green Party has as its long-term aim the establishment of what it calls a 'Sustainable Society'. This it defines in its basic policy document *Manifesto for a Sustainable Society* as one in which "all constituents of the environment and all activities under human control" are maintained in balance through not "using resources faster than they can be replaced, nor creating effects or products which cannot be assimilated indefinitely by the environment." Such a society could only function, the Green Party says, "within an interlocking system of small communities each as self-sufficient as possible in the necessities of life and in its own management," in which these "small, relatively self-sufficient, self-governing communities can coexist harmoniously within the framework of a greater nation and the World as a whole."

In a recent debate with the Socialist Party, the Green Party candidate for the London West Euro-constituency put it this way: " The Green Party ... offers the concept of non-polluting, sustainable, human-scale communities. No one looking for more than they need. No one striving for more than they need. No one striving for more and more to dress up their lives. Why should they? A real community knows what it needs. It looks after its own and it cares for the people around it. The success of its neighbours is part of its own success. The success of its own broad reason is part of the success of each smaller part. And knowing how every community intermeshes within the world, each community will want success for each other, throughout the world. We see a Europe of Regions where each region is built as sustainable human scale communities, each more or less self-sufficient, each taking no more than it needs. Trade is almost unknown. The economy is run on sustainable lines. We see a Europe of regions where we have broken the power of the multinationals and set the agenda for all the Continent. We see a Europe of Regions that will be joined by the rest of the world" (Jeremy Hywel-Davies, 5th May 1999).

So, what is being proposed is the abolition both of the world market, with the competition for resources and sales it engenders, and of existing centralised states, and their replacement by a worldwide network of smaller human communities providing for their own needs. This is a proposition so radically different from the profit-oriented national market economy Labour espouses that one Labour MEP, Carol Tongue, was moved to remark that it was "reminiscent of the visions of some early nineteenth century French socialists" (*New Ground* No. 16, Winter 1987/8), not that the Labour Party knows anything about socialism.

Although it would only be in the context of a socialist world that a worldwide network of decentralised, self-reliant communities could be established (not that this is necessarily the form socialism will take, though it is a form that has been favoured by some socialists, William Morris for instance), socialism is not in fact the right word since the Green Party and nearly all Green thinkers and writers see buying and selling as continuing within the smaller self-reliant communities they advocate (Murray Bookchin is one notable exception). Nevertheless, for a party committed to such a radically different conception of how society should be run to make a political breakthrough can only raise the level of political debate. Questions such as how can we free production from the tyranny of the world market, what are our needs, are smaller-scale human communities self-sufficient in basic needs desirable and possible, by what can we replace centralised states – these are the sort of questions that we would prefer to see people discussing rather than such irrelevant trivialities as should Britain join the EMS or would Kinnock make a good Prime Minister.

There is, however, the key question of how to get from here to there. The Green Party is committed to a gradualist, reformist strategy: seeking support on the basis of a programme of environmentalist reforms for the election of a Green Party government that would take steps to reduce Britain's dependence on the world market (by imposing import controls, discouraging exports).

Such a strategy won't work as the experience of the Labour Party has shown. The case of the Labour Party is relevant here in that they too originally set out to impose on capitalism something – in their case, social measures in favour of the working class – that was contrary to its nature as a profit-driven system. The Greens are also setting out to impose on capitalism something that is incompatible with its nature and, if their electoral support were to grow sufficiently to allow them to form the government, they would sooner or later come up against this restraint and learn that they could not proceed except at the expense of provoking an economic crisis, as inevitably happens when governments try to make the profit system work other than as a profit system, which would undermine their electoral support. Green government would then be faced with the choice of compromising with the system or abdicating. If the experience of Labour is anything to go by, they (or most of them) will compromise, justifying this on the grounds that a Green government of capitalism will at least be better than a Tory one.

A gap between the aims of Green Party activists and their voters is already evident. Very few of their voters in the Euro-elections will have voted for their long-term aim of abolishing the world market and centralised states; most won't even have voted for their programme of environmentalist reforms but simply used the occasion to express a justified concern about food contamination and pollution generally.

The Greens are facing the same choice of strategy as did the first socialists in Britain at the end of the nineteenth century: to build up support on the basis of the maximum programme of fundamental social change and remain small till people have become convinced of the need for the change in question or to build up support on the basis of reforms within the system and grow faster but at the price of abandoning the maximum programme or relegating it to a vague remote, non-operational long-term objective.

This dilemma is recognised by some Greens and, interestingly, the same language is being used to categorise the two competing (mutually exclusive, in fact) strategies as came into use in the socialist movement. In their recent book *The Coming of the Greens* Jonathan Porritt and David Winner distinguished between environmentalists (or 'light greens') and radical greens (or 'dark greens'). Environmentalism, they say, "is essentially a reformist movement, based on the premise that industrialism can be perfected, or at least improved, to the point where it no longer endangers the environment." They add that "probably about 95 percent of the uses of the word 'green' fit into this category," as, we would add, do 95% of Green Party voters. As to the others: "By virtue of being so far removed from power, there has always been an irrepressible streak of utopianism within the Green Party. A good thing too, some would say, in a visionless age. But this utopianism has a tendency to degenerate into 'impossibilism', manifested in a series of green-prints for the future which seem oblivious of where we are starting from in the present."

If, or more probably as, the Greens continue their present strategy of building up support for environmentalist reforms within the system rather than for their longer-term aims, then the original members can be expected to be pushed aside by aspiring Centrist politicians, from within their own ranks as well as deserters from the moribund Liberals, and derided as 'fundamentalists', 'utopians' and 'impossibilists'. Then the vision of a radically different world to today's will be thrown overboard and we'll be back to discussing whether Britain should join the EMS ... Alternatively, Greens who want a radical transformation of the world can stick to their principles but come to realise, as Socialists have done, that a sustainable society can only be achieved within the context of a world in which all the Earth's resources, natural and industrial, have become the common heritage, under democratic control at local, regional and world level, of all humanity.

(August 1989)

THE MODERN ERA

We may be too close to the end of the twentieth century to be able to provide a proper historical perspective. Nevertheless, a number of important themes may be picked out. The collapse of 'Communism' in Eastern Europe at the end of the eighties surprised many by its speed and spread. It had nothing to do with communism or socialism, but instead represented the end of dictatorial state-run capitalism and its replacement by a mix of private and state capitalism with some limited capitalist democracy. Nevertheless, it was widely hailed as a demonstration of the failure of Marxism and, conversely, proof of the superiority of capitalism.

World capitalism, however, continued on its bloody and barbarous way. The Gulf War of 1991 was a clear example of the way in which war – no matter how dressed up in nationalist or moral rhetoric – is basically fought for economic reasons. Oil and access to the means to distribute it were certainly at the root of the causes of this war. And as events at the start of the 21st century have shown, these factors have not gone away or diminished in importance.

Racist and fascist ideas continued to fester within the despair, alienation and rootlessness of class society. The press maintained their fascination with crime and criminals, and the murder of Jamie Bulger in 1993 provided yet another opportunity for them to rail at the supposed inherent evil of human beings. The articles that have been reproduced here from the *Socialist Standard* pointed out that 'evil' and fascism have social causes, rather than being a matter of the inborn nature of some humans.

Capitalism's economic troubles meant a continuing rise in unemployment in the early nineties and increased stress for those 'lucky' enough to have a job. In one of capitalism's absurd contradictions, building workers were laid off as the housing shortage grew, as chronicled in 'Building A Future'. The profit motive indeed turned useful people into beggars.

In the UK, the new Labour government elected in 1997 made little pretence of aiming to change society, just of running capitalism in a 'modernised' way. It did introduce parliaments/assemblies for Scotland and Wales, as part of plans for devolution and regionalisation but socialists oppose nationalist ideas, whatever their flavour, and as the article reproduced here indicates, voted neither 'yes' nor 'no' in the referendum.

As the decade and century ended, the Socialist Party looked back on a period when hopes for a better and safer world had been cruelly dashed, when both left- and right-wing approaches to running capitalism had failed to change or tame the nature of the beast. Poverty, starvation and misery remained the lot of so many, while a handful of billionaires and corporations dominated the rest of the world's population with their power and wealth.

The attacks on 11th September 2001 showed that a world based on division and inequality can always throw up new pretexts for conflict. Yet economic factors remained the underlying case and, just as in earlier disputes, the *Socialist Standard* maintained that wars over oil and trade routes did not justify the shedding of any working-class blood. Socialists oppose both 'sides' in such conflagrations and support only working-class unity to establish a socialist world – now as in 1904.

Socialism Has Not Failed

'Crumbling Communism', 'Failure of Socialism', 'End of Marxism' – these are the terms to which the media have echoed as the events in Eastern Europe have unfolded. Something certainly has crumbled in Eastern Europe but it has not been socialism, communism or Marxism. For this to have happened these would have had to have existed in the first place, but they did not. What did exist there – and what has crumbled – is Leninism and totalitarian state capitalism.

The Russian Empire

After the last war Russia extended its frontiers westwards by annexing parts of all its pre-war neighbours. At the same time it established a huge sphere of influence in Eastern Europe stretching from the borders of Sweden in the North to those of Greece in the South and embracing Finland, Poland, the eastern part of Germany, Czechoslovakia, Hungary, Rumania, Yugoslavia, Albania and Bulgaria.

In all these countries except Finland, identical regimes were installed to the one which had evolved in Russia after the Bolshevik coup of November 1917: a bureaucratic state capitalism where a privileged class, consisting of those occupying the top posts in the Party, the government, the armed forces and industry and known as the nomenklatura, ruled on the basis of dictatorially controlling the state machine where most industry was state-owned, a situation which gave them an effective class monopoly over the means of production.

Finland was the exception in that, after directly annexing a large chunk of what had previously been Finnish territory, the Russian ruling class refrained from installing bureaucratic state capitalism in what was left. Instead, in return for Finland giving up the possibility of pursuing a foreign policy that conflicted with Russian interests, a parliamentary regime and a private enterprise economy similar to that in Western Europe was allowed to develop.

Finlandisation

The satellite regimes installed by the Russian army after 1948 were maintained in power essentially by the threat – and in East Germany in 1953, Hungary in 1956 and Czechoslovakia in 1968 by the reality – of Russian intervention. At no time did the ruling class in these countries enjoy any degree of popular support; in fact what has been happening there could have occurred at any time since 1948 but for this threat. The reason it has happened in 1989 and not before is that, faced with internal economic and political difficulties, the Russian ruling class under Gorbachev has had to dramatically revise its policy towards its empire in Eastern Europe, and decide that it will no longer use its troops to prop up the puppet regimes there. Instead, it has informed the ruling class in these countries that they are now on their own and that they had better make the best deal they can with their subjects.

This is not to say that Russia is prepared to let these countries escape from its sphere of influence, but only that it is now prepared to allow the "Finnish solution" to be applied to them too; in other words, considerable internal autonomy going so far as a parliamentary regime and private enterprise capitalism in return for giving up the right to pursue an independent foreign policy by accepting Russian hegemony over the area.

Welcome advance

This is a startling development whose speed shows just how fast things can change and how the change to socialism could become a prospect sooner than many think. Who would have believed a year ago that by 1990 Poland, Hungary, East Germany and Czechoslovakia would have a limited, but real, degree of political democracy and would abandon state capitalism for private capitalism (or, rather, for the same sort of mixed private and state capitalism that exists in the West)?

We welcome the fall in these countries of the dictatorial regimes which have dragged the names of socialism and Marx through the mud by wrongly associating them with one-party rule, a police state regime, food shortages and regimentation and indoctrination from the cradle to the grave. The coming of a degree of political democracy there is an advance as it extends the area in which socialist ideas can be spread by open means of meetings, publications and contesting elections and in which the working class can organise independently of the state to pursue its class interests.

Collapse of state capitalism

The fall of the bureaucratic state capitalist regimes in Eastern Europe and the demise of the ruling nomenklaturas there has relevance for another aspect of the socialist case. The events in East Germany and Czechoslovakia in particular confirm our long-held view that it is impossible for a tiny minority to hang on to power in the face of a hostile, informed and determined majority. Here hard-line regimes, once it became clear that they could no longer rely on the intervention of the Russian army, collapsed in the face of mass popular pressure – fuelled by a determination, born of years of oppression, to kick out those responsible. In theory the East German and Czechoslovak ruling classes, who had shown themselves to be ruthless enough in the past, could have chosen to use physical force to try to maintain themselves in power – there is some evidence that a section in East Germany did consider sending in the troops to shoot down protestors   but in practical terms this was never really likely.

The rulers knew, through the reports of their secret police if not the evidence of their own eyes and ears, that up to 90% of the population was against them and that if they had ordered their armed forces to shoot all hell would have broken loose; the situation would have escaped from their control with a good chance of it all ending with them hanging from a lamp-post. So they decided to choose the lesser evil, as we can expect the capitalist class to do when faced with a determined, organised socialist majority, and negotiate a peaceful surrender of their power and privileges.

Private capitalism no progress

The ruling nomenklaturas in Eastern Europe are on the way out. In agreeing to give up "the leading role of the Party" and submit themselves to elections which they are bound to lose, as well as to the privatisation of large sectors of industry, they are giving up the means through which they exercised their monopoly control over the means of production. They are becoming mere politicians in charge of a capitalist state without the privileged control over production and the privileged consumption they previously enjoyed as members of a collectively-owning state-capitalist ruling class. Some of them may survive as politicians – given the tacit deal about doing nothing to harm Russian foreign policy interests there will still be a place for some pro-Russian politicians; others may be able to use the private fortunes they have accumulated to convert themselves into private capitalists, the group who are hoping to take over as the dominant section of the privileged owning class in these countries.

But a change-over to private capitalism would be no advance. There would still be a minority in society enjoying big houses, privileged life-styles and Swiss bank accounts, only these would be private capitalists instead of state bureaucrats. We therefore urge workers in Eastern Europe, if they are to avoid a mere change of exploiters, to go on and oppose the emerging private capitalist class with the same admirable determination with which they have opposed and defeated the old state-capitalist ruling class.

Socialism can only be democratic

As Socialists who have always held, like Marx, that socialism and democracy are inseparable and who denounced Lenin's distortion of Marxism right from 1917, we vehemently deny that it is socialism that has failed in Eastern Europe. What has failed there is totalitarian state capitalism falsely masquerading as socialism.

Socialism, as a worldwide society based on common ownership and democratic control of productive resources and the abolition of the wages system and the market with goods and services being produced and distributed to meet needs, has yet to be tried and more than ever remains the only way forward for humanity.

(January 1990)

Economic Causes of the Gulf War

The Prussian militarist Clausewitz declared that war was "nothing but the continuation of politics by other means" . He would have been nearer the truth if he had said that war was the continuation of *economics* by other means. Since the onset of capitalism five hundred years ago wars have been caused by conflicts of economic interest over sources of raw materials, trade routes, markets, investment outlets and strategic points and places to secure and protect these. The threatening war in the Middle East is no exception to this rule, and in fact strikingly confirms the socialist analysis of the cause of war.

Although it is rather obvious that what is at stake is oil, both sides try to play this down. Bush and Thatcher say that Saddam Hussein is a dictator whose expansionist ambitions must be checked in the interests of world peace. Saddam Hussein says that he has struck a blow for Arab Nationalism by eliminating a state tailor-made by Western imperialism to suit its interests. Saddam Hussein is a dictator and he has taken over a state created by Western imperialism, but it is not for these reasons that the West is preparing to go to war. The Western powers tolerate dictators when it suits their interests. In fact they tolerated, financed and armed Saddam Hussein himself when they needed someone to prevent Iran under Khomeini coming to dominate the Gulf area and threaten their oil supplies. And they tolerated the Indonesian invasion and annexation of East Timor in 1975 as they had that of Goa by India in 1961 without shrieking that world peace and order were threatened. The difference was that, while in East Timor and Goa only carrots grew, Kuwait is situated right in the middle of the world's largest and lowest-cost oilfields.

Oil and Empire

British imperialism made Kuwait, which remained nominally part of the Ottoman Empire, a "protectorate" in 1899. This was done not for its oil resources, which nobody even suspected existed, but for its strategic position.

At the time Imperial Germany, already squaring up to Britain in the inter-imperialist rivalry which eventually broke out as the First World War, was planning to build a railway that would extend from Europe through Turkey and Mesopotamia down to the Persian Gulf. This was the Berlin to Baghdad railway of history book fame and, if completed, would have represented an alternative and rival to the British-controlled Suez Canal as a trade route to and from the Indian Ocean and the Far East. Kuwait, a small port and pearl-fishing centre at the northern end of the Gulf ruled by a sheik called Al-Sabah, was the likely terminus for the German project. So it was "protected" by British imperialism, to thwart German imperialism.

Oil, however, was soon discovered near Kuwait, first in Persia and then in Mesopotamia. Britain acquired complete control of the Persian oilfields but those of Mesopotamia had to be shared with Germany. As Turkey had entered the First World War on the side of German imperialism, the British and French imperialists made plans to carve up the Ottoman Empire amongst themselves in the event of victory. A secret agreement in 1916 gave what is now Syria, Lebanon and the northern part of Iraq to France, and Palestine and what is now Jordan and the southern part of Iraq to Britain.

Almost as soon as the agreement had been signed, someone in the Foreign Office realised that a ghastly mistake had been made: northern Mesopotamia contained the oilfields of Mosul and Kirkuk. The French were persuaded on some pretext to agree to a rectification, and after the war the spoils were divided along the lines of today's Middle Eastern states. Iraq is just as much an artificial creation of Western imperialism as Kuwait, though its ruling class ought to be grateful that perfide Albion outwitted French imperialism, otherwise its northern oilfields would be in Syria.

Britain creates Kuwait

Kuwait remained a British protectorate when Iraq became an independent state in 1932, but the new Iraqi rulers were not happy about being deprived of a secure outlet to the Persian Gulf. A glance at a map of Iraq will show that it only has two possible outlets to the sea. The first is via the Shatt al-Arab river, but this is shared with Iran. The second is via an inlet to the west, access to which is controlled by two islands belonging to Kuwait.

At one time – in the fifties when Iraq under a pro-Western king and government seemed firmly anchored in the Western camp through its membership of CENTO, the Middle Eastern equivalent of NATO – British officials considered making some concessions to Iraq on this issue, but this was blocked by the Al-Sabah dynasty. The Emir of Kuwait, which since 1946 had become an oil-producing area with huge reserves, proved to be the better judge of his interests. On 14th July 1958 the king of Iraq and his pro-western prime minister were overthrown and killed in a military coup led by pro-Nasser army officers. The British Foreign Minister, Selwyn Lloyd, rushed to Washington to discuss the crisis. On 19 July he sent a secret telegram, recently released under the thirty-year rule, to Macmillan, the Prime Minister, in which he reported:

"I am sure that you are considering anxiously the problem of Kuwait. One of the most reassuring features of my talks here has been the complete United States solidarity with us over the Gulf. They are assuming that we will take firm action to maintain our position in Kuwait. They themselves are disposed to act with similar resolution in relation to the Aramco oilfields in the area of Dhahran, although the logistics are not worked out. They assume that we will also hold Bahrain and Qatar, come what may. They agree that at all costs these oilfields must be kept in Western hands. The immediate problem is whether it is good tactics to occupy Kuwait against the wishes of the ruling family."

Selwyn Lloyd went on to discuss the options, including turning Kuwait from a protectorate into a colony, i.e., annexing it as Iraq has just done, but rejected this in favour of another option:

"On balance, I feel it very much to our advantage to have a kind of Kuwaiti Switzerland where the British do not exercise physical control" (*Independent*, 13th September).

This was the solution eventually adopted and in 1961 Kuwait was granted "independence" in the sense of no longer being subject to direct "physical control" by Britain. Iraq immediately moved its troops up to the border – and British troops had to be rushed in to prop up the artificial Middle Eastern "Switzerland" that their government had just set up.

Kuwait survived and its rulers prospered. Thanks to revenues from oil, the ruling Al-Sabah dynasty became one of the richest families in the world, overtaken only by fellow oil *nouveaux riches* the Saudi royals and the Sultan of Brunei, and far surpassing other dynastic billionaires like the Queen of England and Juliana of the Netherlands.

The Shatt al-Arab War

Iraq meanwhile also developed its oil resources and revenues, which were mainly used to build up its armed forces so strengthening the grip of the military on the state. Iraqi politics came to consist of coups and plots and counter-plots amongst the leaders of the armed forces. Out of these Saddam Hussein emerged as top dog in 1979.

The current Iraqi regime, though in fact a military dictatorship pursuing the national interests of Iraqi capitalism, has as its ideology the Pan-Arab Nationalism of the Baath party. Iraq, however, is by no means purely an Arab country since up to a quarter of its population speak Kurdish rather than Arabic, and the attempt to impose Baathism in the 1970s led to a revival of the armed revolt of Kurdish nationalists in the North of the country, where the oilfields of Mosul and Kirkuk are situated – which explains why Iraq has been prepared to use all means, including, more recently, poison gas, to retain the area.

This revolt was encouraged as a means of weakening Iraq by the Shah of Iran, whose country had a long-standing dispute with Iraq over the control of the Shatt al-Arab river. The dispute went back to the time of the first commercial exploitation of Iranian oil before the First World War and concerned Iran's demand for access and protection for its bordering oil wells and installations.

The Shatt al-Arab is the name of the river formed by the confluence of the Euphrates and the Tigris. From the Iranian town of Khorramshahr to the sea it forms the frontier between Iraq and Iran. Safe, free navigation in this waterway is absolutely vital to Iraq as its main port, Basra, can only be reached via the Shatt al-Arab. Without this, Iraq becomes virtually a land-locked country, dependent on other countries for the transit of its imports and the export of its main product, oil. Its vulnerability in this respect was well illustrated by the ease and speed with which the pipelines via Turkey and Saudi Arabia were closed to enforce UN sanctions (and by the fact that a third pipeline via Syria had long been closed by the Syrian government for political reasons).

The Shah's strategy worked and in 1975 a treaty was signed between Iraq and Iran under which Iraq ceded control of the eastern side of the Shatt al-Arab to Iran in return for Iran withdrawing its support for the Kurdish nationalists. When, however, the Shah was overthrown in 1979 and Iran began to slip into chaos, the tables were turned. The Iraqi ruling class decided to use the occasion to attack Iran and regain control of the whole of the Shatt al-Arab and perhaps more. So began, in 1980, one of the longest and bloodiest wars of modern history. The war lasted eight years and led to the death of about one million people – all for control of a strategic commercial waterway.

The Western powers were happy to let the war go on, using Iraq to block any

SEPTEMBER 1998 ● Vol. 94 No. 1129 ● Price £1.00

The *Socialist* Standard

Journal of The Socialist Party
Companion Party of The World Socialist Movement

● Irrelevant Euro
● Feudal relics
● War crimes

The futility of treaties

Page 4

Iranian take-over of the Gulf region. When, however, Iran began to attack shipping in the Gulf in 1987, the West was forced to send its own taskforce of warships and warplanes to the area to protect the free flow of its oil supplies.

Why Iraq invaded Kuwait

The war ended in 1988 in a stalemate, with Iraq in control of some Iranian territory but with the port of Basra blocked. This put pressure on Iraq to turn to its other possible outlet to the sea: that blocked by Kuwaiti control of the islands of Warba and Bubiyan.

The Iraq-Iran war strikingly confirmed a point made in 1938 by the Iraqi Foreign Minister in discussions with his British counterpart:

"Iraq would like to rent a piece of land from Kuwait for establishing a deep harbour and connecting it to the Basra railway line, since Iraq could not guarantee navigational safety on the Shatt al-Arab in the case of an Iraq-Iran dispute. (Quoted in press release on 'The Political Background to the Current Events' issued by the Iraqi Press Office, London, on 12th September, pages 16-17).

The present Iraqi Foreign Minister, Tariq Aziz, has made it quite clear that Iraq's motives for taking over Kuwait were economic, commercial and strategic. In a letter on *The Kuwait Question* sent to all foreign ministers on 4 September he denounced Britain for having created and sustained since 1899 an "artificial entity called Kuwait" which cut off Iraq from "its natural access to the waters of the Arab Gulf", and went on to say that all Iraqi governments since the establishment of the state of Iraq in 1924 had insisted that Iraq must have Kuwait "to guarantee its commercial and economic interests and provide it with the requirements necessary for the defence of its national security."

King Hussein of Jordan brought out the same point, in a message broadcast on the American TV network CNN on 22nd September, when he said that Iraq had been seeking "an agreement with Kuwait that would secure it an independent access to the sea which it considers of vital national interest."

The phrase 'vital national interest', invoked by both sides in the threatening war, is the key as in the mealy-mouthed language of diplomacy this refers to issues over which states are prepared to go to war in the last resort.

Iraq emerged from its war with Iran with a huge financial debt and a desperate need for money to pay for reconstruction. With oil revenues as virtually its only source of income, Iraq favoured using the OPEC cartel to push up the price of oil by restricting its supply. Since this was in the interests of a number of other OPEC members, including Iran, some move in this direction was agreed. However, two countries in particular – Kuwait and the United Arab Emirates – failed to apply this. They consistently exceeded their quotas, so preventing the price of oil from rising.

The reason why the emirs and sheiks and sultans of the Gulf pursued this policy was not shortsightedness or cussedness. It was because it had become in their economic interest to do so. The Al-Sabah family had not wasted all its riches on horse-racing, gambling and gold-fitted bathrooms. Most of it had been re-invested in capitalist industry and finance in the West, so much so in fact that a large part of Kuwait's income came from these investments. In other words, the Kuwaiti and other Gulf rulers had become Western capitalists themselves and not just oil rentiers – with the same interest in not having too high a price for oil.

Iraq regarded this refusal to take steps to raise the price of oil as a plot to prevent it recovering from the war. Combined with their long-standing claim to Kuwait as a means of obtaining a vitally-needed secure trade route to the sea, this decided the Iraqi ruling class to take military action. On the night of 1st/2nd August Kuwait was invaded and later annexed. As an additional bonus, the Kuwaiti oilfields when added to the Iraqi ones make Iraq potentially almost as big a producer sitting on as big reserves as Saudi Arabia.

Why the West is going to war

Bush, and Thatcher who happened to be in America on a lecture tour, reacted quickly, issuing an ultimatum to Iraq not to move further down the coast and take over the Saudi oilfields and dispatching a battle fleet to the Gulf for the second time in three years.

Iraq probably had no intention of invading Saudi Arabia, but America had every interest in finding an excuse to send troops to protect the Saudi oilfields. Since 1950 these had been an American preserve: under an agreement with the King of Saudi Arabia European oil companies were excluded and US ones, grouped together as ARAMCO, given a monopoly.

In preparing for war by dispatching troops to the Gulf, Bush is applying the policy enunciated by Carter in his 23rd January 1980 State of the Union message: "Let our position be absolutely clear: An attempt by any outside force to gain control of the Persian Gulf region will be regarded as an assault on the vital interests of the United States. It will be repelled by use of any means necessary, including military force."

The Gulf, he explained, was of "great strategic importance" because "it contains more than two-thirds of the world's exportable oil" and because the Strait of Hormuz at its mouth is "a waterway through which much of the free world's oil must flow". At the time the immediate threat was seen as coming from Russia which had just invaded Afghanistan, but the Carter Doctrine applied equally to threats to American oil supplies from other states like Iran and now Iraq.

In Britain the *Sunday Times* (12th August), which has called for war since day one of the crisis, has been equally frank: "The reason why we will shortly have to go to war with Iraq is not to free Kuwait, though that is to be desired, or to defend Saudi Arabia, though that is important. It is because President Saddam is a menace to vital Western interests in the Gulf, above all the free flow of oil at market prices, which is essential to the West's prosperity."

If war breaks out in the Middle East, the issues at stake will be purely economic and commercial: access to the sea and a high price of oil, on the one side, and control of oilfields and a low price of oil, on the other. Neither of which are issues justifying the shedding of a single drop of working class blood.

(November 1990)

What the Fascists Need

It is too easy to hate fascists. The sight of chanting skinheads, half Stormtrooper of the Year 1932, half late-adolescent tantrum, fills us with memories of a genocidal past and fears that the jackboots are being polished up again. Ridiculous screwballs stand in East End markets with swastika tattoos, boots for brains and snarling detestation for the world in which they are impotent merchants of mean-spirited outrage.

What are we to say to them – or think of them? 'Drive the Racists of the Streets!' says the wallposter from the people who brought us 'The Socialist Motherland'. But who would be left on the streets except for rival sects of Leninist paper sellers arguing over whose central committee will make the most effective job of dictating over the proletariat? There are hundreds of thousands of racists on the streets. There are one or two in most of our houses. Are we supposed to give them all a good doing? And what good is a sore head to a racist – racism thrives on battered minds.

It is all too simple to paint caricatures of the monstrous jackbooted swine. Television pictures show us them in Germany, spewing hate before them, like primitive fertiliser spreaders. Not just murderous thoughts, but now they burn and kill and rejoice at the suffering of their enemies. Just like British workers did when bombs fell on Iraqi cities and who knows how many burned to death or were crushed in an underground medical centre. And when the conscripts met their death as the *Belgrano* sailed away from the Falklands exclusion zone, were not we told by the Mad Priestess that we should rejoice at the victory? Rejoice as men drown and babies are buried under rubble and bombs unknown to the non-professional terrorists explode with priestly sanction. Where does war stop and monstrous atrocity start?

The fascist moron follows his leader. The comical sight of fancy-dress Nazis doing their Mosley impressions to a few dozen Bash Street Kids from Povertyville is almost worth a smile. Of course, nobody will be smiling when the petty-führer's words have been heard and another black family gets a petrol bomb or kicking on the way home. But there is an amateurish hooliganism about such viciousness: not an army but a venomous gang of no-hopers.

The military moron follows his leader and is paid well for it. The barking, and often barking mad, führer is given medals and 'our boys' are allowed to play with more than home-made bangers. The pseudo-militarism of the neo-Nazi boneheads, drilling in Hackney Marshes for the day when Enoch gives the word to get the Asians, is all rather ridiculous. Not so the official military training camps where violence is taught as a respectable art.

Fascists breed on false divisions. They seek to turn us against each other, as if life is not hard enough having to share the misery as one unhappy family. But what is new about the propaganda of Divide and Rule? It is the basis of all nationalism. "He's one of *our* lot; he was born under *their* flag. *He* is *our* enemy." Fascists might be the ultimate flag-fetishists, grasping on to their little Union Jack rag on the end of its pointy stick as if it is their lifeline to lunacy, but they did not invent them. The flags, and all the other emblems of nationalist idiocy, were here long before boys with muscles and not many brain cells decided to call street violence a political philosophy. Let's rock against racism, by all means, but let's do a bit of rocking against nationalism while we're at it. How often is it the case that the right-on lefties who want to smash all racists find no difficulty in supporting the narrow bigotry of trendy nationalism?

So, why fascists? What horrible moment in history set in motion such movements of undiluted venom? The dung-like soil in which fascists are bred is fear. Because behind those hard-as-rock, we're gonna-get-you looks of enmity to the world, what we are seeing are a load of frightened people who are confused, threatened and deeply alienated from their social selves. The fascist is the human who aspires to be anti-human. The social nature which allows us to co-operate allows them to seek refuge in artificially constructed groups based on skin colour, flag colours, football team colours – colour-blind fascists often have a hard time with their pseudo-identities. The unique ability to use language is adapted by the fascists into a snarling, animalistic rage of incoherence. Rational discourse is swapped willingly for brute feeling. That is what the fascist wants life to be. Everything else seems to have failed.

It is a miserable, frustrating and disempowering alienation which is the lot of many under the profit-system – and so many more than those who are foolish enough to go down the fascist path – which is at the root of the fascist mentality. Alienation from a society where life as a conscious being seems unimportant and negligible leads some – perhaps many – to seek comfort in the false security of national, racial and vanguardist loyalty. As the squeeze gets tighter, with a deepening world recession and the collapse of the elementary security offered by the welfare net, is it any surprise that new size twelves are slipping into new jackboots in the futile search for an honourable place within capitalist history?

The psychology of despair is one of the main symptoms of a society which converts the vivacity of the individual into purchasable chunks of labour power to be bought as cheaply as possible – and often left on the shelf to rot. The fascist mentality is part of the rot. And just as you don't blame the woodworm for the damp and dingy wall in which it thrives, it is futile to blame the rotten fascist for the stupidity of his position.

Fascism is a celebration of irrationality. The National Front should be called the Irrational Front. The confused wage slave is capitalism's very best friend. And confused, irrational, unscientific thinking will not be cured by socialists learning to fight better than the fascists. When it comes to brutality we are willing to come last. What the fascist needs is to be hit in those cerebral parts least used and most in need of life support. What the fascist needs, in fact, is to be educated by those who see him not as a despicable fascist, but as a bloody stupid worker.

(February 1993)

After Bulger

We live in unfriendly times. As neighbourhoods have made way for wretched anonymous tower blocks, so neighbourliness has become outdated. It is not that people have chosen to become careless and uncooperative; as social animals we are never happier than when we are able to behave in mutuality, empathy and compassion towards our fellow human beings. But the way that life has come to be organised conspires against our will to be human. "There is no such thing as society", said Thatcher, and her words were met with howls of protest by those who did not want her words to be true, and by blushes of embarrassment by those who knew just how true her words were becoming. For the truth is that community is now little more than a quaint ideal, a sociologist's buzzword. The depressing reality is that more than ever we live in a society which does not resemble anything very social.

This sense of crushing alienation, which was once a mere term of jargon employed by those who had read Marx (who wrote about how workers are alienated not only from the product of their labour, but from their very selves as creative beings who are transformed into robotic profit-producers) is now inescapable. The city streets are settings for fear and loneliness. Housing is designed according to the cheap measurements of profits for rapacious landlords whose concern for comfort, dignity or social fellowship in the place where we live simply does not exist. The transport system is unsafe and its weary users shuffle ritualistically to and from wage slavery in various conditions of unease, stress and anger. Services are running down – the basic needs of workers are too expensive to bother with, so let us dwell amongst the refuse of late twentieth century squalor. This is our environment. For most of us saving our environment is not about trees and forests and fish ponds; they are out of reach and survival within the urban wasteland is about dodging the dog mess and hoping that it will be someone else's house that they break into.

An alienated world of non-community turns others into strangers and strangers into enemies. People turn in on themselves and draw lines like stone fortress walls around their lives, their emotions. And within the darkness of these enclosed lives horrible, unthinkable abuses occur. People like to speak about "the freedom of the individual", as if being atomised, isolated and excluded from social cooperation were somehow a form of liberation. It is not; it feels horrible inside those fragile, impoverishing, life-limited walls of the alienated human's existence. And this is where awful nightmares come to life. Yesterday's unthinkable becomes today's headline and, perhaps, tomorrow's routine.

Why did two ten-year old boys kill a two-year old boy? No simplistic answers are on offer here. If you want to blame someone or something there is no shortage of scapegoat hunters on the market. The boys had access to sick videos. One of these, in the home of one of their fathers, appears to depict a crime much like the one they committed. Who made this video? That 'artist' of our age was not in the courtroom as the boys sobbed. Perhaps he is working right now on a new work of cinematic art which reproduces the killing in question. And if there is a market for it ... an audience with cash to pay for thrills from screen violence ... plenty of profit in that, so what can be wrong? And who are the government to condemn such an entrepreneur? How can a government which sells arms to dictatorships and torture equipment to the highest bidder state any but the most hypocritical objections to films which celebrate gratuitous slaughter? Were there no two-year old babies in Baghdad when British and American bomber planes went on their killing spree in defence of the profits and power of the unelected dictator of Kuwait? Let those who kill children, and celebrate it within their daily lie sheets, claim no moral highground now that the murders are beyond the law.

The boys played video games for hours. These games now outstrip the music record industry in sales. When once (in 'the bad old sixties', of course) kids sang that all you need is love and dopey parables about two little boys with their two little toys, now for hours on end they stare at video violence turned into a game. Press this button and Kill, Kill, Kill ... and then put in another pound and your licence to kill begins all over again. Killing without consequence. Just as the victim of a shooting in a bad American film limps away and returns in the next scene ready to run the New York marathon, so the message of these 'games' are that violence never really hurts. How about a game where you insert your pound and the machine boots you in the balls?

As life has become more of a miserable struggle to survive in the face of debt and the dole and a dreary environment, so entertainment has come to be about releasing anger. The racist louts who killed a teenage lad at a bus stop because they imagined that his skin pigmentation made him a threat were probably briefly entertained by their bullying victory. The kids in Manchester who captured and tortured a young girl might have had a brief high, and the list could go on. The truth is that the list is a very, very long one.

This capitalist system under which we all live – even if we many deny that they do, and most do not even know that they do – has committed against us the greatest of crimes. It has denied us our freedom to be innocent. Contrary to the medieval remains which lurk within Christian minds of professional pessimists like the Bishop of Liverpool, babies are not born evil. The whole notion of evil belongs in the museum of antiquated follies. Would Hitler have been a Nazi dictator if he was your brother?

We are born neither good nor bad. To imagine otherwise is as sensible as to imagine that we are born with a preference for Pepsi rather than Coke, a genetic inclination to rape rather than pass the parcel. We are born to be within the world as it is. And the world as it is right now is not a happy place in which to be born.

Millions and millions of children are born into conditions of such material constraint that it is amazing they grow up fit for anything. Some do not emerge fit for anything. The wounds suffered as a result of authoritarian parenting, of sexual and violent abuse (both misuses of power) and of squalid and ignorant upbringings are injuries which were once unthinkable – or at least, unthought about. Perhaps, if capitalism had been removed long ago, these effects would have been of a lesser magnitude and we could go in greater innocence towards creating our futures.

As this century comes to an end the hard, unpalatable fact (perhaps even for many socialists) is that the psychological pain caused by the artificial way of organising life under capitalism has led to a loss of innocence for most of us. Put plainly, we have all been much more hurt by this system than it is easy to admit. And that is why there will be more horror stories to fill the gutter press. More and worse, until we get rid of this system.

The reformists, who were always wrong, now stand mute before what is to them an inexplicable breakdown in civilised culture. After all, had they not set up a welfare state, with its ever-ready social workers and free schools for the poor? But the kids can't stand the schools and see no point in going when all they must learn is to become unemployed – sorry, 'Job Seekers'. The churches talk about the collapse of the family, with their eyes carefully averted from the disaster zone of the family which heads their religion. But when Norman Tebbit said to fathers that they must get on their bike and look for work (and families don't fit on bikes, you know) and the smug bankers threw tens of thousands out of their repossessed homes into the insecurity of hostels, then what real chance did the children of those families have?

Now Tory ministers cry for moral education in the schools. But what reasonably sensible school student would for one minute accept moral instruction from that rabble of corrupt and callous rogues? And what moral depravity would characterise the child who received an A+ in the exam set by exploiters to test the sturdiness of the-soon-to-be-replaced exploited?

All that is left for capitalism is blame. Guilt is the final cudgel in their diminished ideological armoury. As the 1990s come more and more to resemble the 1930s, no lessons are learned by our masters' mouthpieces who set the tone of the media. The best that they could do was whip up hysteria. Releasing the names of the two 'guilty' boys and delighting in the waste of their lives places the British tabloid press several rungs further down the moral ladder than these little boys have ever had a chance to descend. These were the headlines of the tabloid press on Thursday 25th November, the day after the two boys' conviction for murder:

Daily Mail: EVIL, BRUTAL AND CUNNING.

Daily Mirror: FREAKS OF NATURE – The faces of normal boys but they had hearts of unparalleled evil.

Daily Star: HOW DO YOU FEEL NOW YOU LITTLE BASTARDS?

All of the above appeared with pictures of the little boys – pictures that would ensure the victimisation of them and their families for many years to come. The articles within these rags stooped to any claim in their eagerness to cast blame on these children. The editors and the journalists and the sort of vile readers who throw rotten eggs at prison vans were comforted by this orgy of attributing guilt to the feeble and infantile targets of popular wrath. What they did not report were the four suicides this year within the juvenile detention centre in west London where life for the guilty ended in the defeat of all hope. And while they screeched and yelled about the "unparalleled evil" of two confused and antisocial boys they did not report how killers of exactly the same age are employed by such armies as the Tamil Tigers in Sri Lanka or the government side in the civil war in Sierra Leone. ("Since the civil war began in 1991 children as young as eight years old have been used by government forces in Sierra Leone to execute suspected rebels, sometimes cutting their heads off with machetes", readers were informed by the *Independent* on 2nd December last year). But why worry anyone's narrow minds with such distant, legalised atrocities to which our rulers have uttered not a word of meaningful condemnation? How much easier it is to concentrate little minds on the guilty faces of little children (the freaks, the bastards, the murderers) and rest content that the origin is in the unequalled blackness of their hearts.

Sometimes, through the fog of confusion which is how life is viewed by many people, and despite the brutalised indifference which seems to be the price of keeping afloat within the relentless competition to afford any kind of a life, certain events make us especially sad. These events are very largely selected for us by unaccountable media chiefs whose employees orchestrate public grief on such occasions. That does not diminish the authenticity of our sadness. After all, we are human beings. We are social animals. And sometimes, after a Warrington bomb or an Ethiopian famine disaster, a collective nerve is touched. And then what?

Socialists do not indulge in piety. That can be left to those who prefer to respond on their knees with their eyes shut. We leave moral self-righteousness as their monopoly as well. No sugary sentiments of love for little children will be heard from us. It is only under a system where the material stimulus to love and care is lacking that 'loving thy neighbour' is promoted as some great virtue. No proposals here for teaching children what is right and wrong; not under a system which would have willingly taken those sane children only five years further into their lives and taught them to kill strangers as paid members of the British army.

Occasional sadness is a sign that we have not been wholly brutalised. Just as the fact that the overwhelming majority of children do not adjust willingly to the competitive, vicious and violent norms of the capitalist ethos is proof that this system has not and will not desensitise us all. To punish the dehumanised for what an inhumane world has taught them to become is as wise as to lock a dog in a kennel and then beat it for barking. The fact is that the kennel door is unlocked. It does not have to be like this.

(January 1994)

Building a Future

I am one of the many tens of thousands of construction workers who are currently unemployed. Disunited, we must be patient and wait. Surviving on the State-prescribed pittance as pliant trapeze artistes on the unravelling 'safety net' which so enchants reformers. Turning useful people into beggars is a historical, and inevitable, principle of the capitalist system. Perhaps this time, we have got to be extremely patient before capitalist investors decide that the opportunity of making profits from our labour power is a distinct possibility. Until then we must needlessly hang on, suffer quietly, await our masters' call.

Twenty-eight years ago, when I started working as a hod-carrier on the buildings, the economic circumstances were quite different from today. The demand for labour was high, consequently wages and degrees of freedom had been rising. Capitalism was in the boom phase of its cycle, and the construction industry anticipating even larger profits was in the process of restructuring itself. The design of buildings was slowly beginning to change, as were materials. Every aspect of what is a labour-intensive industry had to be cost effective.

Cash-in-the-hand wages were starting to become the norm for bricklayers and hoddies in London. No sick pay, holiday money or wet time for us, after all we were screwing the State, weren't we? Being a nomadic trade – I have had well over a hundred jobs – where being a realist is forced on you, the majority took full advantage of the economic situation. It was quite usual for men to jack because there was no crack on the job, tea-breaks were too short, or, because you couldn't get a sub when you wanted it. The sub was very important, its availability was one indicator of an employer's liquidity. It was a simple case of once bitten twice shy. Nearly everyone who has worked for sub-contractors for some time gets bumped, at the first sign the realists abandoned ship before it sank.

The Monday Club was in full swing at this time. If 50% of the workforce turned up on a Monday the subbie was in raptures all day about how loyal his 'boys' were. Building trades unions at this time were generally recognised as the niche of opportunists, liars, and the bribeable. Consequently, negotiations over wages took the form of "we want another shilling an hour". If it wasn't forthcoming, then the tools were immediately thrown into the bag and the ladder descended. A new start was just a phone call away.

It was fully understood that what we built during a working week was worth more than what we were paid, it was wholly transparent. The remainder being shared by the layers of pimps that thrived through our labours, this too was understood and despised. Creating profits, through the unremitting appropriation of surplus value from its workers, is the sole function of the construction industry. Building homes, etc is purely incidental to the process.

No boom lasts forever. The speculative jamboree of overproduction ended abruptly and inevitably. A few capitalists went bust. The shrewd, and well-connected ones are still there, conniving their way out of their latest short-lived binge. The long boom was over, and those few freedoms have never returned. The barbed-wire around the sites was in the process of being re-erected, and a new reality was beginning, one that over the coming years would increasingly subjugate the realists.

New income tax laws had been imposed, and were strengthening. Tax was being deducted at source which meant a 30% reduction in wages for those without exemption certificates. We were now self-employed – small businessmen no less. A great many workers, inspired by media reports of large sums of money to be earned, had travelled to London. These were among the first to taste the dole. Realists understand that they are disposable. Skint, most of the smaller and more liberal subbies were back on the scaffold with their 'boys'. The illusion that they had been more than just intermediary workers in the production of profits was still obstinately imprinted on their thwarted minds.

A small elite of subbies were now in a position to more effectively exploit for their masters those who were still in work. Afternoon tea-breaks disappeared and have never returned. Apprenticeships, which had been declining rapidly amongst firms since the rise of the subbie in the early sixties, were now just a source for contrite prattle by reformers. The derisively-paid, and deftly-worked improvers became their replacement. The week in hand was introduced, and the sub became extinct.

Competition between workers became more ferocious than ever. It was common practice when starting a new job to be put to work with the fastest bricklayer on the job; if you didn't keep up, you were down the road before breakfast. Few workers now questioned this, and some gained pleasure from it. Guilt, if you thought you hadn't done enough, and fear of what might happen, became as inseparable from your being as the trowel was from your hand.

A brutal system can create brutes, and the surviving subbies seemed to be in agreement on the type of foreman that they needed to run their jobs. Only the thug would do, no knowledge of bricklaying was necessary. A bully with a watch and few scruples replaced the tradesman. The old boys said that they'd seen it all before, no-one really believed them.

Semi-literacy, and a knowledge of various state institutions, form the background for many bricklayers and labourers. Alcohol, and latterly drugs, are an integral part of the everyday working life for most. When the sack can arrive at any moment, to anyone, regardless of ability, just "to keep 'em on their toes"; where working conditions can vary from working in shin-high mud, to ramshackle scaffolds; where names and faces over the years become a blur, simply because of their frequency. And forming friendships is fraught with problems, then escapism becomes a necessity. And callousness a shield.

It's an upside-down world under capitalism. Those who are most useful suffer the lowest social esteem. But, laze in a masterfully-built mansion, and devise ways of turning human sweat into profit and you are to be admired, knighted even. After all, how would we cope without them, once the plans had been drawn and the footing dug and concreted, the walls built and then plastered, the joist and trusses nailed into place, and the roof battened and slated. Surely, we would be lost without a parasite to then sell the building?

A common dream, voiced amongst many workers that I came into contact with through the years was to build one's own home. A few achieved it. Some of those have now lost it. The possibility for all to achieve this dream can become a reality. By uniting, together we can begin the work of tearing down the barbed-wire that surrounds our lives, and bring nearer the day when we can establish socialism, and with it our freedom.

(July 1994)

The Referendum: where we stand

A Parliament for Scotland? An Assembly for Wales? Unable to agree among themselves and afraid to go ahead without popular support – last time they put this to a referendum their proposals were thrown out – our rulers have decided to ask us our opinion on the matter.

We should be flattered, but don't be fooled. These proposals are part of a smokescreen to disguise the fact that the Labour Party cannot deliver, and no longer wants to deliver, social reforms aimed at shifting wealth and power from the privileged few to working people.

Labour has always accepted the profit system. They used to believe they could humanise it by social reform legislation. Not any longer. Bitter experience has taught them that where reforms and profits come into conflict, it is reforms that have to give way. The last Labour government under Callaghan ended up applying this and Blair had promised to do the same even before he became Prime Minister.

The Labour Party fully accepts now that priority has to be given to profits and no longer promises more spending on social reforms. But, to distinguish itself from the Tories, Labour still wants to retain a reforming image. But how? By finding reforms which don't come into conflict with profits. Constitutional reforms fill the bill perfectly. They don't interfere with profit-making. They don't cost more money. And they give rise to an illusion of change.

It is in this light that the Labour government's proposals for a Scottish Parliament and a Welsh Assembly should be seen, along with their proposals for turning the House of Lords into a huge non-elected quango and for elected mayors and other such gimmicks. But it's all completely irrelevant as far as ordinary people are concerned.

Constitutional reform is of no benefit or relevance to us. It leaves our lives and the problems the profit system causes completely unchanged. Exploitation through the wages system continues. Unemployment continues. A crumbling health service, a chaotic transport system, a polluted environment, failing schools, rising crime and drug addiction and the general breakdown of society all continue. As far as solving these problems is concerned, constitutional reform is just a useless irrelevancy.

Deficient Democrats

Naturally, Labour wraps its irrelevant, constitutional reforms up in democratic rhetoric. Elected assemblies in Edinburgh and Cardiff, we are told, would be an extension of democracy, bringing power nearer to the people, so how can Socialists not be in favour of this?

Yes, Socialists are in favour of democracy, and socialism will be a fully democratic society, but full democracy is not possible under capitalism. Supporters of capitalism who talk about 'democracy' always mean only political democracy since economic democracy – where people would democratically run the places where they work – is out of the question under capitalism, based as it is on these workplaces being owned and controlled by and for the benefit of a privileged minority.

You can have the most democratic constitution imaginable but this won't make any difference to the fact that profits have to come before meeting needs under capitalism. The people's will to have their needs met properly is frustrated all the time by the operation of the economic laws of the capitalist system which no political structure, however democratic, can control.

It is not imperfections in the political decision-making process that's the problem but the profit system and its economic laws. And the answer is not democratic reform of capitalism's political structure but the replacement of capitalism by socialism.

As a society based on common instead of class ownership of the means of production, socialism will fulfil the first condition for a genuine democracy. Because it will be a classless society without a privileged wealthy class everyone can have a genuinely equal say in the way things are run. Some will not be more equal than others, as they are under capitalism, because they own more wealth. Socialism will be a society where the laws of profit no longer operate since common ownership and democratic control will allow people to produce to meet their needs instead of for the profit of a few as today.

The argument about elected Scottish and Welsh assemblies bringing power nearer to the people might have something in it if, even within the limited context of mere political democracy, the proposed assemblies were going to have some real powers. But they are not.

All their money is to come from the central government, and the only 'power' they will have will be to rearrange slightly how the limited amount of funds they will be given is to be spent. In other words, they will have no more power than existing borough and county councils.

They will be part of the administrative arm of central government and their members will be no more than elected civil servants spending central government money. All that would happen would be the introduction of another layer of elected bureaucrats. Another trough for the professional politicians to get their snouts into perhaps, but of no significance to ordinary people.

If our rulers want to reform the machinery of capitalist government in this way, that's up to them. But spare us the pretence that it's some great extension of democracy.

Nasty Nationalists

Also urging a 'yes' vote are the Nationalists of the SNP and Plaid Cymru. They see the sham parliament with token powers that is on offer as a step towards their goal of an independent parliament with full powers to impose taxes and make laws.

This argument for voting 'yes' cuts no ice with Socialists either. We are not nationalists – in fact we are implacably opposed to nationalism in whatever form it rears its ugly head – and we see the establishment of an independent Scotland or Wales as yet another irrelevant, constitutional reform. One of the last things the world needs at the moment is more states, with their own armed forces and divisive nationalist ideologies.

Nationalism is based on the illusion that all people who live in a particular geographical area have a common interest, against people in other areas. Hence the supposed need for a separate state and a separate government to defend this separate interest.

This flies in the face of the facts. All over the world, in all geographical areas, the population is divided into two basic classes, those who own the productive resources and those who don't and have to work for those who do, and whose interests are antagonistic.

The non-owning class have a common interest, not with the owning class who live in the same area, but with people like themselves wherever they live. The interests of workers who live in Scotland and Wales are not opposed to the interests of those who live in England – or France or Germany or Russia or Japan or anywhere else in the world.

Nationalists like the SNP and Plaid Cymru who preach the opposite are spreading a divisive poison amongst people who Socialists say should unite to establish a frontierless world community, based on the world's resources becoming the common heritage of all humanity, as the only framework within which the social problems which workers wherever they live face today.

This is why Socialists and Nationalists are implacably opposed to each other. We are working in opposite directions. Us to unite workers. Them to divide them. So, insofar as the proposed assemblies in Scotland and Wales are a sop to nationalism – as to a certain extent they are – that would be more a reason for voting 'no' than for voting 'yes'.

Useless Unionists

So, what about voting 'no'? It's tempting. After all, Socialists don't want constitutional reform (we want socialism) and a 'no' vote would be a repudiation of the divisive doctrines of the narrow-minded Scots and Welsh Nats. But in the end the point at issue – a mere constitutional reform which will leave profit-making, exploitation, unemployment and all the other social problems quite untouched – is so irrelevant that it is not worth taking sides.

In addition, those leading the campaign for a 'no' vote – various businesspeople and the Tory rump – are conservatives in both senses of the term. They want to leave things as they are. They don't want to change anything. We don't see any point in diverting our energies to changing the constitution but we certainly want things to change. We want people to change the economic and social basis of society and establish socialism in place of capitalism. So we've nothing in common with them.

They fear that the proposed change will be the first step on a slippery slope leading to the break-up of the United Kingdom. Maybe, though this is not the opinion of Labour and the Liberals who are also Unionists.

The leading 'no' campaigners, too, are nationalists. Not of course Scottish or Welsh Nationalists, but British Nationalists, since that is what the Unionists are, spreading the poison that it is all the people in the British Isles who have a common interest against people everywhere else. But Socialists are just as much opposed to British Nationalism as we are to Scottish or Welsh or any other nationalism.

Just because we are not prepared to back the efforts of Scottish and Welsh Nationalists to break away from the United Kingdom – and vigorously oppose their efforts to split the trade union movement – does not mean that we are Unionists. We don't support the Union. We just put up with it while we get on with our work of convincing people to reject world capitalism in favour of world socialism.

Vote for Socialism

So we shan't be voting 'yes' or 'no'. We shall, however, be voting. We'll be going to the polling station and, since they are not giving us this option on the voting paper, we'll be writing the word 'SOCIALISM' or 'SOSIALAETH' across it.

If you want socialism, we urge you to do the same, as a way of registering your support for world socialism and your rejection both of separatist Welsh and Scottish nationalism and of unionist British nationalism.

(September 1997)

A Century Passes

They were the worst of times. They were the even worse of times. The century which offered the promise of providing abundant wealth for all has been characterised by the jackboot, the mushroom cloud and the sizzling stink of McDonald's culture.

At the beginning of the twentieth century there were high hopes and big ideas. It was to be the Age of Science. Industrialisation had made it possible to produce plenty for all. It was to be the century of Democracy. Votes for all meant that the people's voice would count from now on. So, what happened?

Capitalism happened. It began as the capitalist century and it ends in the same rut. Capitalism is not an ethos or a state of mind. It is a system. It is based upon minority class ownership of the means whereby we live and production for profit. Its economic laws are inviolable; there is no democratic mandate strong enough to force capitalism to operate against its inherent, systemic nature. A ceaseless conflict between the accumulation of profit and the satisfaction of needs, and an attendant struggle between those who possess the means of wealth production and those who produce goods and services, is innate to capitalism. The problems which result from this conflict and struggle are not accidental or the results of bad government: they are endemic to the system. It is no more possible to eradicate from capitalism the conflict between profit and need than it would be to make cancer of the body compatible with good health.

There have been two main approaches to capitalism in the twentieth century: the liberal Left and the conservative Right. The former have expressed a sentimental opposition to the effects of capitalism. This reaction against the beast is not insincere or without ethical force. It is based upon a humane distaste for what capitalism is doing to society. The Left has spent much of this century expressing this distaste, often with compelling eloquence and force. It has busied itself with endless schemes to remove this and then that effect of capitalism. The Left has never been a single movement for change, but a diverse collection of fragmented campaigns, each hoping that the moral virtue of their position can break down the iron bars of the capitalist prison. Some of the bars have indeed been bent, and others, once bent for a while, have been straightened and strengthened. The Left has only ever concerned itself with remedying effects. Even when it has adopted apparent alternatives – Russia, nationalisation, welfare states, Cuba – these have only ever been state-run versions of capitalism. The tragedy of the twentieth-century Left has been its self-righteous belief in the moral power of its chosen sentiments alongside a deeply conservative resistance to fundamental alternatives to the system which it has derided as utopian and unrealisable.

The conservative Right has accepted the brutal rationality of the capitalist system and has spent the century seeking to justify as inevitable everything that is cruel and socially divisive. In terms of capitalism, they have been right. In opposing every measure for the long-term improvement of life under capitalism they have recognised a truth which is that you cannot impose rules of moral decency upon a system which can only thrive well by being exploitative, oppressive and callous. At its worst, and historically most unforgivable, the Right has embraced the sickest and most disfiguring of the twentieth-century's ideas: racism, national chauvinism, dictator-worship and pride in war. Bevan was right, of course: Tories are lower than vermin. But the Tories were right as well: Bevan's moral outrage was one long piss in the wind of history.

If one attempted to draw up an inventory of capitalism's casualties in the twentieth century it would be longer than the collected works of any encyclopaedia. How many people have had their lives destroyed in its pointless wars? How many more have had bodies ruined by injury in war? Or in industrial accidents where human safety has been sacrificed for profit? How many have been thrown into its prisons simply for violating the laws of property and class rule? How many were gassed to death for being the wrong 'race'? How many were thrown from their jobs and forced to stand idle? How many were denied an education that would allow them to develop their full potential? How many died waiting for health care? How many starved to death in a world of plenty? How many gave up hope and killed themselves? How many are there left who feel battered and only partly alive after years of struggling with money?

The inventory can be expanded and the depressing statistics, some of them unknowable because the victims are countless, tell the story of a wasted century. Yes, of course there were great moments and we will remember them – but they have occurred despite the system and not because of it.

At the end of the twentieth century the mood contrasts sharply with the hopes of the beginning. The reformers, once so confident, have become meek and modest. In 1900 they campaigned to end unemployment once and for all. Now they campaign to stop extra means-testing of the disabled unemployed. They started out intending to ban bombs (though never all of them); they've ended the century seeking to ban bomb testing, though not the weapons themselves. There has been an undignified and squalid accommodation by the Left to the logic and even the rhetoric of capitalism. At the same time, the Right has learned a few tricks of presentation about appearing to be caring and humane. The two historic wings of capitalist ideology have merged into a single, mushy fudge of dull consensus.

It is this bland acquiescence to an endless future of capitalism   'the end of History', if you don't mind – which characterises the politics of the conventional political vision for the next century. You want to know what the future looks like? Well, look in your rear-view mirror and you'll get a pretty good picture. Yes, it will be capitalism with modems and moving pavements and viagra and tikka flavoured Big Macs, but there is no vision of anything new or challenging or exciting.

Close to parliament, and now overtowering it, is a vast Wheel. People can buy seats on the Wheel and whizz round and round until their money runs out and they must pay again. What an appropriate emblem for the twentieth century. You pay. You go round in circles. You get back to where you started. You pay again. It is historically fitting that the Wheel stands over parliament, reminding it and us of history's demented rhythm in this passing century. We paid. We went round in circles. We got back to where we started. We paid again. Anyone for a twenty-first century spin? Anyone feeling slightly sick of the sensation?

(December 1999)

The Middle East Connection

"The first war of the 21st century" was how Bush has described the events sparked off by the suicide – and murderous – attacks on the World Trade Center in New York and the Pentagon in Washington on 11th September. A chilling reminder that, under capitalism, things are going to be no different this century than they were in the last. But Bush's claim was not entirely accurate, since the attack on America that Tuesday was the continuation of a conflict that has been going on for half-a-century, irrupting from time to time in open warfare: the struggle for the control of the oil resources of the Middle East.

America didn't share in the carve-up of the Ottoman Empire after the First World War but managed to get a foothold in the Middle East with the establishment of the state of Israel in 1949 as a colonial outpost, a puppet state peopled and run mainly by European immigrants to serve as their proxy gendarme in the region. Rivalry between the Western powers continued – and still continues – throughout the period but fifty years ago they were joined by a new rival: a section of the local capitalist class. In 1951 the Mossadeq government in Iran nationalised the oil industry and was overthrown in a Western engineered coup. Then there was the Anglo-French-Israeli attack on Egypt in 1956 for nationalising the Suez canal, at the time the main trade route for bringing Middle East oil to western Europe. Then the Yom Kippur war of 1973 at a time the post-war boom was coming to an end and which helped accelerate this. Then the Gulf War, ten years ago, to take back the Kuwaiti oilfields which Iraq had grabbed from the West, a war which has continued ever since at a lower level of intensity with regular bombings of Iraq by US and British warplanes.

The conflict in Chechnya too had an oil dimension, since a planned pipeline to get Caspian Sea oil out westwards made control of Chechnya of strategic importance to Russia. In fact, the collapse of the Russian state capitalist empire re-opened the Caspian oilfields to Western penetration and control, bringing Afghanistan into the equation as a possible alternative route via Turkmenistan for a pipeline to get Caspian oil out without having to pass through Iran.

The West's rivals for the control of the Middle East oilfields and the trade routes to get the oil out, as well as of the strategic areas and points to protect these, have been sections of the local capitalist class in the region. The ideology they used, to begin with, to get a mass following was an anti-imperialist nationalism which had a leftwing tinge and even employed a 'socialist' terminology. This was the ideology of Mossadeq in Iran, Nasser in Egypt, of the Baathist regimes in Syria and Iraq and of the PLO in the 1970s.

It is still a significant political force but, since the 1980s, has more and more been challenged by Islamic fundamentalism as the ideology of those who want local capitalist, rather than Western imperialist, control of the oil resources of the Middle East. A key factor in this change was the triumph of the 'Islamic revolution' in Iran in 1979. But not to be neglected is the influence of the long-established fundamentalist regime in Saudi Arabia which, while not anti-Western, used a part of its oil rents to wean Arab militants away from leftwing nationalism. This had been encouraged by America as part of its struggle with Russia for world hegemony. It is now a notorious fact that Osama Bin Laden – a billionaire member of the extended Saudi royal family – was armed by America and sent into Afghanistan to fight against this country falling under Russian control.

That those who attacked America on 11th September should have been Islamic fundamentalists was therefore no surprise. This has become the ideology of many of those in the predominantly Muslim countries of the Middle East who want to wrest control of the oil resources of the region from the West for the benefit of local capitalists.

The West's reaction has been revealing. A grand coalition is being organised to combat 'terrorism'. But not terrorism in general. The Western powers are not concerned about the Tamil Tigers or ETA or the IRA or the various South American guerrilla groups. They are out to get Islamic fundamentalist terrorism because this is the rising ideology of their rivals for control of the Middle East oilfields. This, not terrorism in general, is the threat to the supply of this key resource. Russia has no problem in joining this coalition since its oil supplies too have been challenged by the same movement, as in Chechnya.

The one accurate thing Bush, Colin Powell and the US media have said about the attacks on the WTC and the Pentagon was that it was an 'act of war'. It was. The latest act in the 50-year struggle for the control of Middle East oil. This of course is not how they see it, or rather, how they present it. For them it is an attack on 'civilisation' and 'freedom-loving people everywhere' and (Blair's favourite) 'democracy'. It is appalling, virtually unbelievable, that any human being would hijack an airliner full of people and deliberately fly it into a tower block where thousands more worked. It is also true that the establishment of Islamic States everywhere would undo the Enlightenment and plunge the world back a thousand years (and has done so in Afghanistan). But this is not the issue.

The Islamic fundamentalists who flew those planes would indeed completely suppress freedom of thought and speech and replace rule by elected politicians by the rule of ignorant and obscurantist priests, but those who trained and sent them weren't attacking America because it was 'democratic'. They would still have attacked America even if it had been a fascist dictatorship or a Christian theocracy.

Socialists of course appreciate the existence of secular, political democratic forms, limited as we know they are, and wouldn't want to see these replaced by an Islamic State. But 'democracy' as an ideology is something different. It is based on the idea that everybody living under a democratic state (as a state allowing the election of certain state officials) shares a common interest. This is a lie that socialists challenge.

Under capitalism, whatever the political form, society is divided into two classes with conflicting interests: those who own and control the means of production and the rest of us who have to work for them. This is not changed if the excluded majority are allowed to vote for those who run the political side of capitalism – and who define the 'common interest', inevitably since they are governing on behalf of the capitalist class, as in fact the interest of that class.

What Blair and the others call 'democracy' is by no means democracy in the full sense of the term, which can only exist in the classless context of a society based on the common ownership and democratic control of the means of production. Their democracy is the inevitably limited and narrowly political democracy that is the most that can exist under capitalism. But, in any event, it is not even this stunted, political democracy that is at stake. It is oil.

So, the line-up in the next – military – episode in the continuing struggle for control of the oil resources of the Middle East is, on the one side, a section of the local capitalist class using Islam to rally mass support and, on the other, the Western capitalist powers using 'democracy' as their ideology to win mass support for war. But 'Islamic State' versus 'Democracy' is only the ideological smokescreen disguising the real issue at stake: control of oil resources and trade routes. It is not an issue worth the shedding of a single drop of working-class blood.

As Socialists we declare our opposition to both sides in this war and call on the working class of the world to unite to bring capitalism to a rapid end so that no more lives are sacrificed to further the economic interests of rival sections of the world capitalist class.

(October 2001)

A Hundred Years

This year is the centenary year of the Socialist Party of Great Britain, our organisation having been founded in June 1904. But we have mixed feelings on the matter.

In one sense to still be in existence represents a failure since it means that socialism – our objective – has not been achieved. Had it been, there would no longer be any need for a socialist party, which would have long since been disbanded. Our aim in 1904 was to see ourselves go out of existence as soon as possible. To work ourselves out of a job. That we do still exist is therefore undeniably a sign that we have not succeeded.

But this lack of success is not so much ours, or at least not essentially ours, as we never imagined that the growth of the majority socialist understanding required to establish socialism depended on the campaigning efforts of socialists alone. It is the lack of success of the class of wage and salary workers in general. It's up to them, not us, to establish socialism. But, distracted by Labourite reformism on the one hand and Leninist state capitalism on the other, workers failed in the course of the past hundred years to see the need to abolish the fundamentals of capitalism – the class monopoly of the means of production and the profit motive – if the social problems they face are to be solved. And that's why we are still here.

It is also true that we have never won any election, but then, for us, elections are only a means not an end. We have never been interested in winning elections as such, in getting socialist bums on to the benches of the House of Commons at any price. Socialists will enter parliament when enough workers outside it want to send delegates there, mandated to formally wind up capitalism. But this situation has not yet arisen.

In any event, even in politics, 'power' is not the only standard by which to judge success. Politics is also about ideas and their survival and effect. Here we can claim some modest success. We have not only survived as an organisation, for instance producing this journal every month since the first issue in September 1904, no mean achievement when you look at the fate of our one-time rivals over the years, the SDF, the ILP and the Communist Party. We have also kept alive the idea of socialism in its original sense.

At the time the Socialist Party was formed there was widespread agreement as to what socialism was – a system of society based on the common ownership and democratic control of the means of production – even though there were widely divergent views as to how to get there. Here it is those who argued, against us, that the way to socialism was to get into parliament on a programme of reforms to capitalism and then to gradually re-form capitalism into socialism, who have failed. Not just to achieve socialism, or to make any progress towards it, but even to keep alive the idea of socialism as the alternative society to capitalism. The same goes for the partisans of the regime that used to exist in Russia. They, too, came to abandon the original idea of socialism, redefining it to mean the state management of the wages system, or state capitalism.

Since socialism – common ownership instead of class monopoly; production for use instead of production for profit – remains the only practicable alternative to capitalism, and the only solution to the problems thrown up by capitalism, we continue to advocate it. But, it is fair to say, we don't want to have to still exist for another hundred years.

(January 2004)

NAME INDEX

GENERAL INDEX

LIST OF AVAILABLE
SOCIALIST PAMPHLETS AND BOOKS

Ecology and Socialism	£1.00
From Capitalism to Socialism how we live and how we could live	£1.00
Socialism – As a Practical Alternative	£1.00
Some Aspects of Marxian Economics	£1.50
How The Gods Were Made by John Keracher	£1.50
Marxism and Darwinism by Anton Pannekoek	£1.50
How We Live and How We Might Live by William Morris with a modern assessment	£1.50
The Right To Be Lazy and other articles by Paul Lafargue	£2.00
Marxism Revisited	£2.00
Socialist Principles Explained	£2.00
The Market System Must Go! Why Reformism Doesn't Work	£2.75
A Socialist Life by Heather Ball	£3.75
Are we prisoners of our genes?	£4.75
All of the above	£19.00

For six or more of any publication, reduce total price by a third.
All pamphlets are available from Head Office at cover prices

Prices include post and packaging
Please make all cheques and postal orders payable to:
The Socialist Party of Great Britain
52 Clapham High Street, London SW4 7UN

ECOLOGY AND SOCIALISM

One of the major problems of capitalism is pollution – as capitalists cause long term damage to the environment for short term gain. This pamphlet outlines the Socialist case for a better, cleaner world run for people, not for profit.

£1.00 including postage and packing

FROM CAPITALISM TO SOCIALISM
... how we live and how we could live

Contrasts the present state of life with what a future Socialist world would bring, and then suggests what kind of political action can be taken to bring Socialism about.

£1.00 including postage and packing

SOCIALISM – AS A PRACTICAL ALTERNATIVE

Sets forth the practical proposition that Socialism entails and develops further arguments into ways in which a sane society based on social equality and cooperation could operate.

£1.00 including postage and packing

SOME ASPECTS OF MARXIAN ECONOMICS

A series of articles culled from the Socialist Standard explaining the real nature of modern economic problems and the failure of 'conventional economics' to solve them.

£1.50 including postage and packing

HOW THE GODS WERE MADE
by John Keracher

A classic reprint of a text defending the materialist conception of history. In doing so it explains the Socialist opposition to religion. The text comes with an introduction by the North East Branch of the Socialist Party.

£1.50 including postage and packing

MARXISM AND DARWINISM
by Anton Pannekoek

A classic reprint of a text that puts in context our origins as an animal species and also our social nature as a key part in the development of society. The text comes with an introduction by the North East Branch of the Socialist Party.

£1.50 including postage and packing

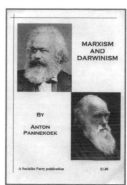

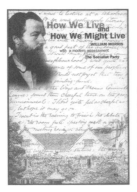

ECOLOGY AND SOCIALISM
by William Morris
with a modern assessment

A clear exposition of what Morris saw as being wrong with society in his time and how a moneyless, tradeless society based on common ownership and democratic control would have to be the basis of any healthy arrangement of human affairs. Includes a 14-page modern assessment by the Socialist Party.

£1.50 including postage and packing

THE RIGHT TO BE LAZY
and other articles
by Paul Lafargue

A reprint of Marx's son-in-law's classic text. Makes the clear point that any imaginary right to work under capitalism is just a wage slave's 'right' to be exploited. Includes a collection of other important articles written by Lafargue not easily available in print and an introduction by the Socialist Party.

£2.00 including postage and packing

MARXISM REVISITED

A lively document of a series of five talks given by members of the Socialist Party as part of a weekend seminar in 1998. Titles are as follows: 1: Who the hell was Karl Marx? 2: Was Marx a Leninist? 3: The fetishism of commodities. 4: Has the modern market superseded Marxist economics? 5: Is the Socialist Party Marxist?

£2.00 including postage and packing

SOCIALIST PRINCIPLES EXPLAINED

This pamphlet is a basic introduction to our case, and ideal for people who have just come across Socialist ideas or who are thinking of joining. It explains in simple language our object and each of the eight principles.

£2.00 including postage and packing

THE MARKET SYSTEM MUST GO!
Why reformism doesn't work

Explains why the Socialist Party advocates the revolutionary transformation of existing society rather than piecemeal reform, like the Labour Party or Conservatives. It is a detailed backup to our more introductory pamphlets putting the case for genuine revolutionary change.

£2.75 including postage and packing

A SOCIALIST LIFE
by Heather Ball

A collection of short stories by *Socialist Standard* writer Heather Ball. Many readers liked her distinctive writing style, finding it full of charm, warmth, humanity and humour. Sadly, Heather died before she could complete her writing project. This collection, published by the Socialist Party, presents the case for Socialism on the basis of individual, everyday experience.

£3.75 including postage and packing

ARE WE PRISONERS OF OUR GENES?

The argument that our behaviour is determined by our physical inheritance may pose as science, but in reality it is a socially determined prejudice used as part of a crude political ideology. Faced with such objections to socialism, the first thing that needs to be done is to clarify what is going to be meant by the term 'human nature'.

£4.75 including postage and packing

LIST OF AVAILABLE CDs

Middle East War For Oil

1. Israel, the Intifada and the Peace Process	£5.50
2. The 1991 Gulf War – Crisis and Aftermath	£5.50
3. The Socialist Party and War	£5.50
Set of three:	£12.00

The Strategic Choice before Socialists: Lessons from 100 Years Ago

William Morris and the Hammersmith Socialist Society	£5.50
Robert Tressell and the Social Democratic Federation	£5.50
Set of two	£8.00

We also have a wide range of meetings and talks on tape – the full list is available from Head Office

Prices include post and packaging

Please make all cheques and postal orders payable to:

The Socialist Party of Great Britain

52 Clapham High Street, London SW4 7UN

GIVEN UP ON GETTING THE FACTS?

TURN OVER A NEW LEAF!
SUBSCRIBE TO OUR JOURNAL
THE SOCIALIST STANDARD

One year	£12
One year (low/unwaged)	£7
Voluntary supporter	£20
Europe	£15
Rest of the world	£22

Please make all cheques and postal orders payable to:

The Socialist Party of Great Britain

52 Clapham High Street, London SW4 7UN

WORLD SOCIALIST MOVEMENT

The Socialist Party
52 Clapham High Street, London SW4 7UN, UK
email spgb@worldsocialism.org

Socialist Party of Canada/ Parti Socialiste du Canada
PO Box 4280, Victoria BC V8X 3XB, Canada

World Socialist Party (New Zealand)
PO Box 1929, Auckland NI, New Zealand
email wspnz@worldsocialism.com

World Socialist Party of the United States
PO Box 440247, Boston MA 02144, USA
email: wspboston@mindspring.com

World Socialist Movement website
www.worldsocialism.org

OVERSEAS CONTACTS

Belgium
email martyn.dunmore@pandora.be

Denmark
Graham C Taylor, Spobjergvej 24, DK-8220 Brabrand
email grahamt@sol.dk

Gambia
World of Free Access
email wfa70@hotmail.com

Germany
Norbert email weltsozialismus@gmx.net

Norway
Robert Stafford, Lingelemveien 62A, 3225 Sanefjord, Norway
email hallblithe@yahoo.com

Uganda
Socialist Club, PO Box 217, Kabale

The Socialist Party of Great Britain

Object

The establishment of a system of society based upon the common ownership and democratic control of the means and instruments for producing and distributing wealth by and in the interest of the whole community.

Declaration of Principles

The Socialist Party of Great Britain holds:

1. That society as at present constituted is based upon the ownership of the means of living (i.e. land, factories, railways etc.) by the capitalist or master-class, and the consequent enslavement of the working class, by whose labour alone wealth is produced.

2. That in society, therefore, there is an antagonism of interests, manifesting itself as a class struggle, between those who possess but do not produce and those who produce but do not possess.

3. That this antagonism can be abolished only by the emancipation of the working class from the domination of the master class, by the conversion into the common property of society of the means of production and distribution, and their democratic control by the whole people.

4. That as in the order of social evolution the working class is the last class to achieve its freedom, the emancipation of the working class will involve the emancipation of all mankind without distinction of race or sex.

5. That this emancipation must be the work of the working class itself.

6. That as the machinery of government, including the armed forces of the nation, exists only to conserve the monopoly by the capitalist class of the wealth taken from the workers, the working class must organise consciously and politically for the conquest of the powers of government, national and local, in order that this machinery, including these forces, may be converted from an instrument of oppression into the agent of emancipation and the overthrow of privilege, aristocratic and plutocratic.

7. That as all political parties are but the expression of class interests, and as the interest of the working class is diametrically opposed to the interests of all sections of the master class, the party seeking working class emancipation must be hostile to every other party.

8. THE SOCIALIST PARTY of Great Britain, therefore, enters the field of political action, determined to wage war against all other political parties, whether alleged labour or avowedly capitalist, and calls upon the members of the working class of this country to muster under its banner to the end that a speedy termination may be wrought to the system which deprives them of the fruits of their labour, and that poverty may give place to comfort, privilege to equality, and slavery to freedom.

(This declaration is the basis of our organisation and, because it is also an important historical document dating from the formation of the Party in 1904, its original language has been retained.)

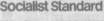
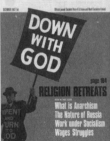

Power and Policy in China

Second and Enlarged Edition

Parris H. Chang

The Pennsylvania State University Press
University Park and London

Library of Congress Cataloging in Publication Data

Chang, Parris H   1936–
    Power and policy in China. 2nd enlarged edition

    Includes bibliography and index.
    1. China—Politics and government—1949–
I. Title.
DS777.55.C375   320.9'51'05   78–50773
0–271–00543–2 (cloth)
0–271–00544–0 (paper)

To my Mother
and
To the memory of my Father

Preface

Since the first edition of this book went to press in April 1975, many important events have taken place in China. These include the death of Chou En-lai in January 1976, the disgrace of Teng Hsiao-p'ing in April 1976 following a riot in Peking, the death of Chairman Mao in September 1976, a coup one month later which ousted from power four top radical leaders (the "Gang of Four") and elevated Hua Kuo-feng to the party chairmanship, and Teng's unprecedented political rehabilitation in July 1977. The Eleventh CCP Congress met in August 1977 to ratify a new leadership lineup and approve a new set of policies. Indeed, since October 1976, the post-Mao leadership has lost no time in stepping up efforts to modernize China's agriculture, industry, national defense, and science and technology. Going hand in hand with the drive for development of the national economy has been an intensive campaign to ferret out the Gang's followers and supporters at all levels and to eliminate the ideological and political influence of the radicals.

In this new edition, I analyze these events and examine the political conflicts and leadership and policy changes of the past three years in some detail. In addition, Appendixes A and B have been updated. This book presents a picture of concentric circles of Chinese leaders involved in conflict and a consensus-building process and takes issue with the "Mao in command" notion. The validity of this "pluralistic" model that I suggested in the 1975 edition has been highlighted by the political conflicts of the past few years and it remains a highly useful and relevant approach to analyzing the post-Mao politics.

I wish to acknowledge my indebtedness to a number of people who made this publication possible. I am grateful to Chris Kentera and John Pickering of The Pennsylvania State University Press for providing the incentive to work on the new edition. The last stage of research and writing was completed in Honolulu in December 1977, and special thanks go to Jack Lyle, Godwin Chu, and other members of East-West Communication Institute at the East-West Center for their generous hospitality, intellectual stimulation, and other assistance. I have benefited greatly from Godwin Chu's insights on Chinese politics. The expert typing of the manuscript by Ann Gillis, Alison Miura, and Karen Katayama of the Institute is highly appreciated. As always, I owe a great deal to Ting Wang in Hongkong, who generously supplied to me valuable research materials over the years.

Parris Chang

Honolulu
January 1978

Acknowledgments

The research and publication of this book would have been impossible without help from many quarters. My debts are far too numerous to acknowledge completely, but there are a number of people and institutions whose support and assistance cannot go unmentioned.

I owe a special personal and intellectual debt to Professor Doak Barnett, who has for many years lent his encouragement and support to my studies of Chinese politics. He was my academic adviser at Columbia University, gave me a basic education on contemporary China, and stimulated and supervised the writing of my doctoral dissertation from which several chapters of this book derive. At Columbia University, I also had the good fortune to study with Professors Zbigniew Brzezinski, O. Edmund Clubb, Roger Hilsman, and James Morley, who have greatly contributed to my intellectual development.

I am grateful to several colleagues in the field who took time to read the manuscript at its various stages and offered valuable comments. In our numerous conversations in Hongkong and at the Center for Chinese Studies at the University of Michigan, Allen Whiting provided me with many illuminating insights into the dynamics of the Chinese leadership. His encouragement, understanding, and willingness to assist a beginner are greatly appreciated. I also thank Gordon Bennett, Thomas Bernstein, Seweryn Bialer, Alexander Eckstein, C.T. Hu, John Fincher, Michael Pillsbury, Robert Scalapino, Richard Solomon, Frederick Teiwes, James Townsend, and the late John M.H. Lindbeck, who read all or parts of the manuscript and whose suggestions resulted in many improvements in this book. I wish especially to thank John Fincher, who read the entire manuscript several times and gave me invaluable advice on the scope of the study, and Robert Scalapino, whose penetrating criticism led me to reshape and refine interpretations and analysis I have obstinately maintained.

I owe special thanks to Ting Wang of the Contemporary China Research Institute of Hongkong, who generously shared with me his immense knowledge of China and his lifetime collection of research materials, and to many cadres on the mainland (whom I shall not name) I talked to during my tour of China in 1972, who provided me with first-hand information on some personnel and policy issues and significantly enhanced my understanding of Chinese politics.

I wish to express deep appreciation to Vernon Aspaturian, Robert S. Friedman, and Thomas Magner, colleagues at The Pennsylvania State University, for unfailing encouragement and support.

Several institutions have generously supported and assisted the preparation of this book, and it is a pleasure to express my gratitude. Research grants provided by the Contemporary China Studies Committee of the East Asian Institute at Columbia University from 1967 to 1969 enabled me to do field research in Hongkong in 1967–1968 and complete the first draft of the study. In the final stages of research I received timely research grants from the Liberal Arts Office for Research and Graduate Studies of The Pennsylvania State University.

Various libraries and research institutions and their staffs generously provided research facilities and rendered other helpful services. I wish to thank particularly Richard Sorich of the China Documentation Center at Columbia University, Weiying Wan of the Asia Library at the University of Michigan, Yee-fei Lau of the Universities Service Center of Hongkong, and staff members at the Institute of International Relations in Taipei and the Union Research Institute of Hongkong for valuable assistance. I am grateful also to the editor of the *China Quarterly* for permission to incorporate here portions of my article published in the journal earlier.

The skills and talents of a number of people have greatly expedited the completion of this book. I wish to thank Carole Schwager, who carefully edited the manuscript and coordinated the book production; Susan Mandarino, Karen Sweeney, and June Cutler, who devoted countless hours to typing several drafts of the manuscript; and Kathleen Shelton and Marsha Church, who helped compile the index.

Finally, I am most grateful to my wife, Shirley, and to our daughters, Yvette and Elaine, who have shared and endured the travails of my academic life, and whose patience and understanding are a source of constant encouragement which sustained me in my long and arduous years of authorship.

As always, I take sole responsibility for any errors and imperfections in the subsequent pages.

Parris H. Chang

University Park
April 1975

Contents

Abbreviations

APC	Agricultural Producers' Cooperative
CC	Central Committee
CCP	Chinese Communist Party
CPGC	Central People's Government Council
CPPCC	Chinese People's Political Consultation Conference
CPSU	Communist Party of the Soviet Union
CRG	Cultural Revolution Group
GAC	Government Administrative Council
GPCR	Great Proletarian Cultural Revolution
KMT	Kuomintang (The Nationalist Party)
MAC	Military Affairs Commission (Committee)
MD	Military District
MR	Military Region
NCNA	New China News Agency
NPC	National People's Congress
PLA	People's Liberation Army
PRC	People's Republic of China
RC	Revolutionary Committee

Introduction

Until the advent of China's Great Proletarian Cultural Revolution (GPCR) in 1966, leaders of the Chinese Communist Party (CCP) had carefully concealed their differences from the public and had largely succeeded in nurturing an image that Communist China was a monolithic society governed by a unified, cohesive leadership—an image which was accepted by quite a few outside observers. The violent leadership conflicts and the attendant political upheavals in China during the GPCR shattered that myth of monolithic solidarity. Since 1967, the Chinese Communists themselves have rewritten their own history and propagated a theory that in the CCP there was a "struggle between the two lines" extending back over many decades—between the proletarian revolutionary line represented by Mao Tse-tung and the bourgeois revisionist line represented by Liu Shao-ch'i and other "capitalist power-holders." According to the theory, these "capitalist power-holders" had attempted to restore capitalism in China and had overtly or covertly sabotaged, obstructed, and opposed Mao's revolutionary line.

Is the reinterpretation more credible than the old myth? By examining China's policy-making process and policy disputes at the decision-making level before the GPCR I hope to ascertain where the truth lies. Five major policy issues are analyzed in this book: the Twelve-Year Agricultural Program, administrative decentralization, the commune movement, the Socialist Education Campaign, and the ideological rectification campaign. In analyzing the formulation and implementation of these policy issues, this study is designed to shed light upon the following questions: In the period covered by this study, were China's policy-making processes tightly controlled by a few top leaders who, in essential agreement, made all major decisions, which were then carried out by a highly centralized bureaucracy? Or were there much more complicated political processes at work in China in those years, in a system that was in reality less cohesive and monolithic than it appeared? Were there significant differences among the CCP leaders on various policy issues? What role did Mao Tse-tung play in the policy-making process, before and after the Great Leap Forward? What were the roles of

Liu Shao-ch'i, Chou En-lai, and other leaders at the center? Were the leaders at the center divided into factions? Did leaders at the regional and provincial level play a role in the policy-making processes? To what extent were local cadres a factor influencing policy-making—at least in the implementation stage? Were policy shifts simply a matter of a few leaders who largely agreed on their objectives and shifted policies in response to changing conditions? Or were policy shifts related more to conflict among leaders and to a changing balance of power in party councils? In structural terms, where were the loci of decisions? Did the loci of decision-making change over time?

Although the answers to these and other questions will be set forth in the subsequent chapters, the major conclusion of the book can be summarized at the outset:

1. Policy-making in China involved a complicated conflict and consensus-building process with many actors and many problems which—although distinctive in many respects—had some similarities to political processes elsewhere.

2. Although Mao played an extremely important role in the system—different from the less important role he played after the early 1960s—he was frequently blocked and frustrated by other leaders, and he was not always "in command," as some scholars have maintained.

3. When Mao maneuvered on various occasions to push his policies, he sought "outside" support to overcome his opponents at the center; consequently, the arena of political conflict was expanded, and more actors were drawn into participation in the resolution of conflict.

4. Despite Mao's enormous power, policy was significantly influenced by debates and conflict among the leaders; the major shifts in policy followed an oscillating pattern between the conservative and radical orientation, as a result of shifting coalitions and balance of power in the decision-making councils.

5. Leaders and cadres at the provincial and lower levels did have an effect on policy during the implementation phase in a variety of ways, although they may not have directly participated in its formulation.

Placed in the context of political science literature, my study of the policy-making process in China falls into the tradition of so-called descriptive or behavioral decision theory, which is concerned only with how policy-makers *actually* behave, whether the outcome is admirable or not,[1] and I have adopted an elite approach, viewing policy-making in China as an elite occupation. Political scientists have questioned the validity of this approach partly because an elite is not easily identified in a political system or subsystem, and partly because those who assert the existence of elite power structures cannot empirically prove that the elite exert power over a variety of policy issues.[2] In the case of Communist China, there is no question that a ruling elite does exist; this ruling group until the Cultural Revolution, consisted of most of the 193 full and alternate members of the Central Committee (CC) of the CCP,[3] and its total number was approximately 800.[4] These 800 persons satisfactorily meet the theoretical requirement for an elite model as suggested by Dahl: "a controlling group less than majority in size, that is not a pure artifact of democratic rules . . . a minority of individuals whose preferences regularly prevail in cases of differences in preference on key political issues."[5]

Inasmuch as an elite did exist in China, it makes sense to focus on how this elite allocated value in society. In such an analysis of the behavior of policy-makers, we are concerned with policy-makers' expectations, the values they sought to maximize, their role demands, motivational and strategic factors, the socioeconomic constraints upon them, and their interaction with one another, on the one hand, and with the bureaucracy and the society as a whole, on the other. Thus while concentrating primarily on policy-makers, this study is intended to avoid some of the pitfalls of the "totalitarian model" which concentrates on "the dictator, his whims, the political intrigues among those around him."[6]

For purpose of analysis, the policy-making process in Communist China is divided into five stages: problem-identification, initiation, consensus-building, authorization, and implementation.[7] *Problem-identification* refers to gathering of information and definition of problems. *Initiation* or recommendation embodies the generation and proposal of solutions to cope with the identified problems. *Consensus-building* involves efforts to obtain support for the proposed solutions as well as efforts to neutralize or overcome opposition. *Authorization* or prescription refers to the formal enactment of solutions by those who have the effective and legitimate authority. *Implementation* or application involves the execution of the authorized measures in specific situations.

Terms such as "power," "influence," "policy," and "decision," which appear very frequently in this book, are defined briefly here. Many definitions have been given to the concept "power" in the social science literature. "Power" is defined in terms of the capacity to affect or modify the behavior of another group or individual, or it is defined as the production of certain intended effects, or as the process of affecting the behavior, attitudes, or outcomes of others, or "power" is sometimes synonymous with the causation of a change in another's behavior or attitude.[8] In this book "power" or "influence" refers to affecting, controlling, modifying, altering, or causing some activity, behavior, attitude, or outcome in an individual or a group. The analysis of power or influence in policy-making is, in a sense, a search for an explanation of why decisions turn out the way they do.[9] When we say that Mao Tse-tung had power over a given decision, we are explaining the decision in terms of Mao. Thus "power" and "influence" are used interchangeably here, although other writers may differentiate. According to

Lasswell and Kaplan, for instance, power is a special case of the exercise of influence, and power is different from influence in general because of its implied threat of sanction.[10]

Although "policy-making" and "decision-making" are used interchangeably here, "policy" and "decision," intimately related concepts, are used differently. "Policy" refers to goals, the means chosen to carry out these goals, and the actual distribution of values which is designated by the term "decision." In other words, policy includes decisions as one form of stipulation or determination of value distribution.[11]

In addition, Chinese Communists hold a peculiar concept of "decision," which renders analysis more difficult. According to the party's general secretary prior to the Cultural Revolution, Teng Hsiao-p'ing:

> Many important directives of the Central Committee were first sent out in *draft form* to local organizations, which were asked to suggest revisions after they had discussed them and *put them tentatively into operation; they were issued in official form only after being revised in the light of the opinions received*—a process which takes several months, sometimes even more than a year, to complete. The Central Committee also permits local organizations to modify its directives according to local conditions if they really find it impossible to carry out the directives as they are.[12] (Emphasis added)

It appears that Chinese Communists did not regard a "decision" as hard and irrevocable but as an idea that would evolve continually in the course of application (implementation). In this regard, it is more productive to treat policy-making as an ongoing process, using the authoritative decision itself as a focal point of analysis, as Richard Snyder suggests.[13]

Five major policy issues constitute a good sample for examining China's policy-making process. The case study approach is used because it is not sufficient to analyze the structure of policy-making by examining only China's state and party constitutions, legal statutes, and other authoritative policy statements. This alone cannot insure an understanding of how China's political system has actually functioned. A good many of the rules and procedures of government which are followed in practice may have been the result of precedents. Such rules and procedures may be understood and observed even though they are not formalized; they may function alongside of, or in place of, formal rules. Therefore as a guide for understanding the policy-making process in China, case studies of how policies are made may prove more reliable than simple analysis of formal rules and official statements made by Peking.

Several considerations influenced the selection of the five cases. Each received substantial press coverage, and the available information about them makes it possible to undertake detailed analysis. Each was an issue of conten-

tion among the leadership and underwent a great many changes; they therefore are a good basis for the analysis of underlying influences on the Chinese
policy-making process. Although the book does not deal with the GPCR in
great detail, except its initial stage (1955–66), its focus on the issues of contention and political conflict in the CCP leadership and on some of the dynamics in the system should clarify the GPCR and Chinese politics since the
second half of the 1960s.

The main sources used in this book are materials published in the People's
Republic of China, particularly the speeches of the party leaders, official
statements, documents and regulations issued by the CCP and the government, and newspapers, periodicals, and books. These are supplemented by
secret Chinese Communist documents and unpublished speeches by Mao that
have become available outside of China, Red Guard posters and newspapers,
refugee interviews, and studies made by scholars on China. The use of Chinese
sources, particularly secret documents and Red Guard publications, raises
some methodological problems.

Questions arise as to the validity of relying on the public Chinese Communist communications as the major sources for studying a topic such as
policy-making processes in Communist China. It is argued, and with much
truth, that Chinese official statements and mass media are full of propaganda
material and often do not report "facts"; moreover, they are frequently
couched in generalities, and they obscure reality by using Marxist jargon
and clichés. Furthermore, important aspects of the policy-making process are
often deliberately cloaked in secrecy by Chinese leaders; meetings that are
held secretly and decisions made may be announced later or not at all. This
practice conceals much that an observer needs to know to follow a line of
action through from start to finish. All these facts point to the handicaps and
limitations one has to reckon with in using Chinese Communist materials.

On the other hand, however, it would be wrong to regard all information
in the Chinese mass media as mere propaganda. No ruling group can rule by
coercion alone; to govern a big country like China and to try to persuade the
vast Chinese population to support its policies, the CCP has constant need to
communicate its directives to the masses, and this is done mainly through the
mass media. More than 28 million party members (last official figure, reported
in 1973) and hundreds of thousands of party activists upon whom the CCP
relies in carrying out its policies cannot be guided effectively on the basis of
secret channels of communication alone. For these reasons, not only official
statements but the mass media as well provide important sources of information for studying various Chinese policies and the goals of the regime.[14] Even
materials used in propaganda often reveal the motivation of the leadership
and the problems encountered.

Besides materials published for public consumption, there are a number of
secret Chinese official documents that have now become available in the

West. These documents reveal much valuable information which either clarifies issues or confirms speculations made by outside observers. Surprisingly enough, the language used in the secret channels of communication does not appear to be different from the language used in open channels, and the issues raised in these secret documents are also discussed in the press (either simultaneously or subsequently), though in somewhat vaguer terms.

The most important secret documents available are twenty-nine issues of the secret military journal *Kung-tso T'ung-hsun (Bulletin of Activities)*, covering the period of 1 January to 26 August 1961.[15] The bulletin was published by the PLA General Political Department and distributed to the Communist military officers at the regimental level or higher; the top-secret issues of the bulletin were distributed only to divisional officers. These bulletins contain extremely frank speeches by top military leaders, resolutions and reports of the Military Affairs Commission of the party's CC as well as from other sections of the army, and much valuable information on China's economic and social conditions. These copies of the journal are said to have been smuggled out of China after Khanbas overran a Chinese regimental post in Tibet in the late summer of 1961; they were subsequently acquired by the U.S. State Department which, in turn, made them available to academic libraries.

Less widely known but equally important are the so-called Lienchiang Documents. In March 1964, Nationalist Chinese commandos raided Lienchiang Hsien in Fukien province and captured documents totaling more than 200,000 words. Among these documents were resolutions of the Tenth CC Plenum of the CCP, directives of the CCP Fukien Provincial Committee and of the CCP Lienchiang Hsien Committee, reports of rural communes and brigades, as well as statistical charts and circulars on the Socialist Education Campaign and on various problems in the communes. The Nationalist Chinese authorities reprinted the Lienchiang Documents for restricted distribution. An English translation of these documents, entitled *Rural People's Communes in Lienchiang*, was published by Hoover Institution in 1969.

In addition, several other secret Chinese Communist documents secured and made available by the Chinese Nationalists have been used in this study. The authenticity of these documents is supported by the fact that at the time they were drawn up, public Chinese Communist sources were making statements that reflected the contents of these documents;[16] furthermore, Chinese Communist actions strongly indicated conformity to the programs outlined in these documents.

Red Guard publications, which mushroomed in China during 1966–67 because of the Cultural Revolution, have become an important new source for students of Chinese Communist affairs. These publications carry, among other things, many articles attacking and denouncing opponents, real and imagined, of Mao Tse-tung and the Cultural Revolution, and they reveal information relevant to the period of this study. Therefore I have selectively used some of these Red Guard sources, particularly in parts of Chapters 4 and 5. The authoritativeness and accuracy of the Red Guard materials do pose problems for the users, because many articles printed in the Red Guard publications are politically motivated and frequently are obviously biased and distorted.

In using the Red Guard materials, I have always tried to doublecheck other Chinese Communist or Western sources of the 1950s and the 1960s to determine whether a particular item is corroborated or reliable. After reading most of the available Red Guard publications, I have tentatively come to the following conclusions: their value judgments on the individual purge victims (e.g., assertions on their motivations for doing or saying certain things) are generally distorted and must be viewed with skepticism; information pertaining to facts ("who did what and when?") appears to be fairly reliable. For instance, information about several unpublicized party conferences in the early 1960s and the contents of some of Liu Shao-ch'i's unpublished speeches or interviews revealed by the Red Guard publications subsequently were confirmed by the official *People's Daily*.[17]

One major methodological problem of using the Red Guard materials is to ascertain the authoritativeness of the Red Guard sources. Where did the Red Guards get the information for their articles? Were they in a position to know what happened in the CCP leadership in the 1950s and early 1960s? Available evidence indicates that some Red Guard groups were closely associated with, if not directly controlled by, the CC Cultural Revolution Group (CRG) headed by Ch'en Po-ta and Chiang Ch'ing (Madame Mao).[18] It is quite possible that articles attacking major party figures which appeared in the publications of these organizations (many of which were reprinted in other Red Guard newspapers in other cities) were based on information supplied by the CRG. Without direct access to the sources at the highest level and the classified party archives, it would have been impossible for the Red Guards to quote directly from the private correspondence and unpublished speeches of people like Liu Shao-ch'i and to report a number of top-level party meetings and decisions made there.

Undoubtedly, articles in Red Guard publications and, since 1967, in the *People's Daily* as well have reinterpreted many past facts to suit current political need, yet they have also revealed facts hitherto unpublicized and shed new light on issues of contention in the CCP leadership and on modes of operation of the political system. With care and caution, and reading between lines, it is still possible to make significant use of the Red Guard materials.

Chapters 1 to 6 of this study are devoted to events and issues centered around the five selected policy issues. Chapter 1 discusses the background and the initial intraparty disputes on the Twelve-Year Agricultural Program during

1955–57. Chapter 2 focuses on problems of administrative decentralization. Chapter 3 deals with the implementation of the Twelve-Year Agricultural Program after the fall of 1957 and the chain of events leading to the establishment of the communes in the summer and fall of 1958. Chapter 4 analyzes the adverse effects of excessive decentralization and the communization program and inner-party disputes over the Great Leap Forward. Chapter 5 deals with the fate of the Twelve-Year Agricultural Program, the reversal of administrative decentralization, the reorganization of the commune system, and the retreat from the Great Leap Forward. Chapter 6 analyzes the Socialist Education Campaign and the rectification of cultural circles as well as a series of events that set the stage of the GPCR. Finally, Chapter 7 summarizes the findings of these case studies and offers some generalizations regarding the policy-making process in China. The names and positions of approximately one hundred Chinese officials mentioned in the book are listed in Appendix A.

1

The Dispute Over the Twelve-Year Agricultural Program

Two Different Strategies of Socialist Construction

In China's economy, the role and the importance of agriculture cannot be overstated; the agricultural sector has provided not only food for the entire population but also 90 percent of the raw materials for consumer goods industries and 75 percent of the exports with which China paid for its industrial imports. Poor agricultural harvests not only affect food supply but also have an almost immediate and direct impact on industrial products and export capabilities.

Thus the lag in agricultural output has been a serious problem for China's leaders. Farm production through the years has grown only slowly, possibly just enough to keep pace with population growth. Harvests have fluctuated, depending on weather conditions. Increased rate of industrial growth clearly demands increased agricultural output.

Two distinct approaches or strategies of economic development have been contending against each other since the early 1950s. One strategy for increasing agricultural output, which will be labeled "radical" for want of a better term, stresses structural changes in the economy and assigns a greater role to political mobilization and subjective human factors such as attitudinal change and class consciousness. It advocated, for example, collectivization of agriculture to replace the system of private farming. Early agricultural collectivization, in this view, would not only facilitate a more rational and efficient organization of labor and use of land but would also make it easier for the state to collect agricultural surpluses and speed up capital accumulation. Moreover, this approach favors greater utilization of organization and political mobilization in agriculture (and in the economy as a whole) and was planned to rely on institutions of economic control as prime instruments for resource mobilization and allocation essential to economic growth.

A different strategy, which will be labeled "conservative" or "pragmatic," places a greater emphasis on providing material incentives to the peasants and supplying chemical fertilizers and modern agricultural machinery to the countryside. Citing the example of Soviet collectivization, proponents of the conservative approach opposed a premature change in the system of agricultural production and argued for the postponement of collectivization until China's industry was ready to support the creation of large-scale, mechanized collective farms. Their argument was that a lack of qualified cadres makes it unwise for the government to exert too much control over production lest it have an adverse effect on peasant zeal to produce. Rather, material incentives such as providing more consumer goods, higher farm prices, distribution of more income to the peasants, and more free markets would be the best ways to induce the peasants to produce more. Finally, though such measures would inevitably use more of the scarce resources available for the industrial (particularly heavy) sector, it was suggested that a more balanced—even though somewhat slower—economic growth would remain the wisest course.

The Zigzag Course of Collectivization

On 31 July 1955 Mao Tse-tung, chairman of the CCP, delivered a speech to a meeting of the secretaries of provincial, municipal, and autonomous-region party committees calling for an acceleration of agricultural collectivization.[1] This was Mao's first important policy statement since his major article "On People's Democratic Dictatorship" presented in July 1949, three months before the establishment of the People's Republic of China in Peking.

The speed of agricultural socialization had been a matter of dispute within the party since 1953. Attempts were made in the spring of 1953, the fall of 1954, and the spring of 1955 to increase the tempo of collectivization. As a result of serious opposition within the party, both at the center and in the provinces, and resistance from the peasants, these efforts had to be modified or slowed down.[2]

Many Chinese leaders were well aware of the lessons of the Soviet collectivization in the 1920s.[3] Vice-Premier Teng Tzu-hui, concurrently director of both the State Council (Cabinet) Seventh Staff Office and the Rural Work Department of the CC in the CCP, articulated in July 1954 the views of those who advocated a cautious approach: "As the USSR possessed the various necessary conditions [for collectivization] at the time, it was right for her to act thus. We, however, have not the necessary conditions ... moreover, the Chinese peasants' conception of private ownership is relatively deep, while our rural task is heavy and we have not enough cadres."[4]

In March 1955 the State Council issued a "Directive on Spring Farming and Production," which ordered the cadres to slow down agricultural collectivization and reorganize and consolidate the existing Agricultural Producers' Cooperatives (APC's).[5] In line with this "go-slow" approach, Vice-Premier Li Fu-ch'un's "Report on the First Five-Year Plan" to the National People's Congress on 5 July 1955 specified that by 1957 only one-third of the peasant households would join the elementary APC's.[6] Thus, up to the summer of

1955, the principle of "gradualism" had prevailed. Then suddenly at the end of July Mao intervened and attempted to reverse the moderate policy that was being implemented.

To understand Mao's justifications for speeding up collectivization, it is useful to keep in mind China's overall economic situation in the mid-1950s. First, farm production from 1949 to 1955 had increased only slowly, possibly just enough to keep pace with population growth. Agriculture, however, occupied a decisive position in the nation's economy; the agricultural sector had provided not only food for the entire population but also 90 percent of the raw materials for consumer goods industries and 75 percent of the exports which China exchanged for capital and industrial goods abroad.[7] The poor agricultural harvest in 1954 had not only affected food supply but also had an immediate adverse impact on industrial production and export capabilities and hence on the accumulation of capital in 1955.

Moreover, the level of living in China was low and the voluntary rate of saving was correspondingly low, yet capital accumulation would have to come almost exclusively from domestic savings. Therefore some form of compulsion would be required to achieve the desirable rate of saving. Since China's population was overwhelmingly agricultural, the bulk of savings would have to be sought in the agricultural sector so that some form of agricultural organization would have to be introduced to control the volume of consumption and generate maximum agricultural surplus.

It was within this economic context that Mao argued for the acceleration of agricultural collectivization. His basic arguments, as advanced in his speech of July 1955, are summarized in the following points:

1. China's rapid industrialization would have to rely on a sustained big push in agricultural production; this could be accomplished only through collectivization.

2. Collectivization would bridge the gap between the ever-increasing demand for marketable grain and industrial raw materials, on the one hand, and the generally low yield of stable crops, on the other.

3. Collectivization would facilitate a more rational and efficient organization of labor and use of land.

4. Collectivization would enable the state to exercise a greater degree of control over the Chinese population, would allow the government to effectuate a desired high rate of capital accumulation, and would ensure the state's supply of any available surplus.

Also very much in Mao's mind was the alleged "class struggle" in the countryside (Section IX).[8] The land reform had created a class of well-to-do peasants, and some enriched themselves by money-lending and speculative activities; on the other hand, the majority of poor peasants, lacking technical know-how and sufficient means of production, were still subjected to poverty.

If tendencies toward polarization of the peasantry were not checked, Mao warned, they would negate any positive results of the land reform, and the countryside would have to undergo another violent struggle such as the one in the land reform campaign.

Finally, Mao argued that the peasant masses were strongly for the collectivization. He maintained that the poor and the lower middle peasants (who represented 60 to 70 percent of the rural population), because of economic difficulties, were "disposed to choose the socialist road and energetically respond to our Party's call for cooperation" (Section II). It was Mao's firm belief that the peasants' zeal for the new system would induce them to work harder and that collectivization would generate a "high tide of agricultural production."

Some of Mao's colleagues, while agreeing with the need for increased agricultural production and the goal of eventual agricultural socialization, differed with Mao on the methods and timing of achieving these objectives. They were very skeptical about the ability of the cadres at this stage to institute and manage the APC's and especially about Mao's claim concerning the peasants' eagerness to join the APC's. They argued that the present pace of development of the APC's had gone beyond "the level of the cadre's experience" and "practical possibilities" or "understanding of the masses" (Section VI). They also cited the experience of the Soviet Union to criticize "impatience and rashness" in carrying out collectivization in China at that time.

Up to the summer of 1955, some of Mao's colleagues had been able to argue successfully for a more gradual policy and avoidance of a too radical approach which might deprive the peasants of their incentive and enthusiasm to produce. The evidence that other top CCP leaders had slowed down the collectivization drive was revealed in Section III of Mao's speech in July 1955:

> With the adoption of a policy of what was called "drastic compression" in Chekiang province—not by decision of the Chekiang Provincial Party Committee—out of 53,000 APC's in the province 15,000 comprising 400,000 peasant households were dissolved at one fell swoop in 1955. This caused great dissatisfaction among the masses and the cadres, and it was altogether the wrong thing to do. A "drastic compression" policy of this kind was decided on in a state of terrified confusion. It was not right, too, to take such a major step without the consent of the *Party Center*. As early as April 1955, the *Party Center* gave the warning: "Do not commit the 1953 mistake of mass dissolution of APC's again, otherwise self-criticism would again be called for." But certain comrades preferred not to listen. (Emphasis added)

Subsequently, throughout China 200,000 APC's were said to have been disbanded.

Mao's words revealed the existence of a group of officials powerful enough to obstruct the will of the "party center."[9] Who were they? Mao, in this speech, used the term "some comrades" or "certain comrades" twenty times, and "they" fifteen times to refer to those who disagreed with or obstructed rapid collectivization, but he did not identify them. They were not confined to provincial-level officials who actually implemented the policy of "drastic compression," since the decision to dissolve APC's was not made at the provincial level, as Mao clearly indicated. Some powerful top-level leaders of the CCP must have been involved because they were in a position to defy the April 1955 warning of the party center and to dissolve APC's on a large scale.

The denunciations of the purged party leaders during the Cultural Revolution have shed new light on the dispute over collectivization in the spring of 1955. Liu Shao-ch'i and Teng Hsiao-p'ing are alleged to have been the prime movers in the slowdown of collectivization:

> In 1955, following Chairman Mao's great call, there was an upsurge in agricultural cooperation throughout the country. But taking the opportunity of Chairman Mao's absence from Peking, China's Khrushchev [i.e., Liu Shao-ch'i] once again plotted criminal activities against "rashness." In May of that year, he and another top Party person in authority taking the capitalist road [i.e., probably Teng Hsiao-p'ing] concocted the reactionary policy of "holding up," "contraction," and "readjustment," and he personally ratified a plan for drastically cutting down the number of cooperatives. In a little over two months, 200,000 cooperatives were disbanded in the country.[10]

Liu had long been considered a believer of the theory of "mechanization before cooperation," and he had told a Conference on Propaganda Work in 1951, "Only with the nationalization of industry can large quantities of machinery be supplied to the peasants, and only then will it be possible to nationalize the land and collectivize agriculture."

According to Liu's own account, he did not take the initiative, although he did approve the proposal to dissolve the APC's. The initiative was said to have come from Vice-Premier Teng Tzu-hui, who was then in charge of the regime's overall rural policy: "In 1955 Comrade Teng Tzu-hui proposed the retrenchment and dissolution of 200,000 cooperatives. The Central Work Conference, over which I presided, made no refutation of this proposal, and virtually approved his plan. Later Teng Tzu-hui retrenched and dissolved 200,000 cooperatives at a Central Committee Rural Work Conference."[11]

Liu's story appears to be closer to the truth. It is plain from both accounts that the proposal to disband APC's did not originate with Liu, and probably not with Teng Hsiao-p'ing; it was initially sponsored by someone else (by Teng Tzu-hui, according to Liu). When the proposal was presented to the Central Work Conference for decision, however, neither Liu nor Teng Hsiao-p'ing opposed it. Whether Liu supported the proposal cannot be determined on the basis of available evidence. It is quite probable, however, that Liu did not fight against the dissolution of these APC's; since he was the presiding official of the conference, Liu's failure to oppose the proposal might have facilitated its approval.

Teng Tzu-hui had on the record strongly advocated a policy of gradualist collectivization and material incentives for peasants.[12] Although he was never a member of the Politburo, he was in charge of the regime's rural policy; thus if, as is alleged, he did make the proposal to cut back APC's, this view would have carried great weight in the interparty circle. Li Hsien-nien, a Vice-Premier and concurrently Minister of Finance, was among those repeatedly opposed to rapid collectivization, as his self-criticism later implied.[13] Vice-Premier Ch'en Yun, a Politburo member who was in charge of China's overall economic policy, and appeared to have consistently advocated a gradualist strategy toward economic development,[14] may have also supported Teng Tzu-hui. There is also evidence that in the provinces there was a widespread feeling against rapid collectivization.[15] In short, there seemed to be a consensus (although probably not unanimity), involving an important segment of the leadership, which opposed rapid collectivization at that time. The decision of the May 1955 Central Work Conference to cut back APC's probably reflected this consensus.

Lui Shao-ch'i's confession, quoted earlier, revealed several pieces of information on China's decision-making process. Most significant is the fact that when Mao was absent, Lui was in charge. The Central Work Conference —a forum not stipulated in the party constitutions of 1945 and 1956—was actually an enlarged meeting of the Politburo or its Standing Committee attended by both Politburo members and selected non-Politburo party officials; the Work Conference could make decisions on key issues as binding as those of the Politburo or the CC.[16] And the Rural Work Conference, such as the one convened by Teng Tzu-hui, seemed to be concerned with operational and technical matters.

Mao's Call for Help from Provincial Leaders

Confronted with opposition within the party center, Mao apparently chose to bypass the regular decision-making bodies and appeal directly to provincial-level leaders. By this maneuver, Mao appeared to enlarge the arena of policy debate to include the provincial-level secretaries so that he might try to obtain their support to overcome his opponents in the center. At the end of July 1955, just after he had returned from an extensive tour of the provinces where he must have sought support from the provincial secretaries,[17] Mao convened a conference in Peking of the secretaries of provincial-level party committees (a forum stipulated in neither the 1945 nor the 1956 party constitution).

Mao severely attacked the conservative tendencies in the party in his speech to the provincial leaders; he castigated those party officials who championed a "go-slow" policy of collectivization as "tottering along like a woman with bound feet, always complaining that others are going too fast." He called for the organization of 1.3 million lower APC's by October 1956 (a 100 percent increase in fourteen months), and for the conversion of some of these into higher (advanced) APC's.[18] Mao then envisioned that all peasant households would join lower APC's by 1960. In his speech Mao also asked provincial secretaries to "go back and look into the question [of collectivization], work out a program suited to the actual situation, and report to the CC within two months." Mao promised to "hold a discussion and make a final decision" within two months.

With this instruction, Mao staked the tremendous prestige of his position and the great strength of his leadership on the issue of collectivization. Pressure was exerted and attitude on this issue became a yardstick for measuring each official, both high and low, for his loyalty to Mao. The impact of Mao's speech was swift and impressive: cadres in the provinces immediately drew up plans to intensify collectivization and new APC's were established everywhere. For instance, in Kiangsu the number of APC's increased from 35,773 in July to 121,494 in early October, and the Provincial Party Committee revised its plan to suit the new situation.[19] In Shantung more than 78,000 new APC's had been set up by the end of September 1955, surpassing the number laid down in the plan drawn up by Shantung's Provincial Party Committee. In Kwangtung, at the Provincial Party Congress, T'ao Chu spoke on Kwantung's "First Five-Year Plan Centered on Agriculture" and promised to increase the number of APC's from 16,000 to 70,000 within six months.[20]

The Speed-Up of Collectivization

By the time the Enlarged Sixth Plenum of the Seventh CC was convened on 4 October 1955, the leap in agricultural collectivization was already a *fait accompli* in many provinces. This apparent success tended to vindicate Mao's position, implying that he had been correct and decisive. On the other hand, the success also seemed to show that Mao's colleagues in the center were guilty of "rightist" deviation—they had been too conservative to properly assess the socialist consciousness of the masses and did not sufficiently believe in the ability of the party "to lead the peasants along the road to socialism." With his own position strengthened and that of his opponents weakened by the actual development, Mao now proceeded to push through his collectivization program and convened the Plenum to formally endorse and legitimize the campaign that had already been launched—as well as to criticize rightist tendencies.

When the Plenum opened on 4 October Ch'en Po-ta delivered a speech, "Explanations of the Draft Decision on the Question of Agricultural Co-operativization."[21] In the course of his speech, Ch'en revealed for the first time that he was "doing some work in the Central Committee Rural Work Department"; later he was identified as one of the Deputy Directors of that department. Until he was purged in 1970 Ch'en Po-ta had been Mao's brain-truster for over thirty years, frequently feeding ideas to Mao and giving sub-stance to Mao's visions.[22] Very likely it was Ch'en who had advised and worked closely with Mao in 1955 on the drive to accelerate the pace of col-lectivization. Therefore Mao picked Ch'en to offer official explanations for the new line, bypassing Teng Tzu-hui (director of the Rural Work Depart-ment), who was opposed to it. On 11 October the Plenum formally adopted the decision which, among other things, called for the basic completion of lower APC's by the spring of 1958.[23] This new target represented a two-year advance over the schedule set by Mao's July speech.

The meeting, however, was by no means one-sided; in Mao's own words, which were never made public in China, the conference saw "a big debate."[24] It may have been the provincial party secretaries who carried the day for Mao. Although few of these provincial secretaries were then members of the CC, and those who were not could not vote, they did attend this enlarged CC plenary session and it seems plausible that they spoke out strongly for Mao.[25] If that was the case, when the provincial leaders (who were closer to the problem of implementing rural policies than the leaders in Peking) said Yes, it may have made it difficult for the central leaders who opposed Mao's views to say otherwise. As we shall see later, on numerous subsequent occasions Mao appeared to take actions designed to mobilize support from provinces to overrule opposition in the center.

Mao thus scored an impressive victory in the fall of 1955 and his July speech was then made public for the first time. His personal intervention to impose his views appeared to settle for the time being the debate within the party on the question of collectivization which had evolved over the preceding three years; as Vice-Premier Ch'en Yi admitted at the time, this enabled certain comrades (probably himself included) "to turn from their mistaken paths to the correct road of Marxism-Leninism."[26]

A few other high party officials who opposed the collectivization drive made self-criticisms. For instance, Li Hsien-nien recanted the error of "em-piricism"; probably speaking for other colleagues as well as himself, Li stated that "in the past we were not in doubt about the general line and the center's policy on agriculture. . . . But empiricism frequently characterized our view of the tempo of agricultural collectivization."[27] Li added: "Some of our comrades heed only the negative reactions and not the positive reactions [of peasants]. They underrate the consciousness of peasantry and underrate the leadership of the Party. In these circumstances they cannot but commit serious errors."

Vice Premier Po I-po also endorsed the new policy in a *People's Daily* (17 November 1955) article entitled "Agricultural Cooperation Should be Closely Linked Up with Technical Reform of Agriculture," although between the lines he appeared to show continuing doubts and argue more strongly for technical reform than socialist transformation. In addition to agricultural cooperation (i.e., socialist transformation of agriculture), Po considered mechanization, electrification, and chemicalization of culture, or the technical reform of agriculture, another important aspect of the socialist transformation movement. He maintained that technical reform of agriculture should correspond to the needs of socialist transformation of agriculture and give an impetus to socialist transformation of agriculture, and that only the use of modern techniques could raise the productivity of agriculture continuously. He emphatically stated, "Only after the productivity of agricultural production has been highly developed can the superiority of cooperation be further demonstrated and fully developed."

Curiously enough, Teng Tzu-hui was silent. Although he was singled out for criticism by Mao during the Plenum for having committed "empirical rightist errors," he may still have clung to his own position.[28] Shortly after the Plenum, Liao Lu-yen and Ch'en Cheng-jen were appointed deputy directors of the State Council Seventh Staff Office. As pointed out earlier, Ch'en Po-ta, a theoretician and Mao's brain-truster, had been appointed one of the deputy directors of the CC Rural Work Department before the October CC Plenum. These two institutions were the highest state and party agencies in charge of the regime's rural policy and both were headed by Teng Tzu-hui. Although Teng was not purged then, Mao appointed those who favored his programs to dilute Teng's power and authority. Teng apparently remained at cross-purposes with Mao, and he was to suffer politically for his conviction: when the First Plenum of the Eighth CC was convened in September 1956, Teng was the only vice-premier who was not elected to the Politburo.

The Initiation of the Twelve-Year Agricultural Program

A Brief Sketch of the Draft Program

It was in the context of the inner-party disputes over the tempo of collectivization and Mao's victory leading to the speed-up of collectivization that the draft "Forty-Article 1956–1967 National Program for Agricultural Development" was launched on 25 January 1956, at a Supreme State Conference meeting.[29] The draft program called for continuation of the fairly radical line pushed by Mao since the previous summer. Capitalizing on the accelerated momentum of socialist transformation in the autumn and winter of 1955–56, Article 1 stipulated that "all provinces ... should, in the main, complete agricultural cooperativization in its elementary form and set themselves the goal of getting about 85 percent of all peasant households into APC's in 1956." This was a further upward revision of the timetable set in the October 1955 CC Plenum, accelerating the schedule by two years. According to Article 2, higher-stage APC's were to be formed by 1957 in "areas where APC's are on a better foundation," and by 1958 the "main work" of organizing them was to be completed throughout the country.

Many other ambitious goals were included. By 1967 per *mou* (1 mou = 1/15 hectare or 1/6 acre) grain and cotton yields were to be increased more than 100 percent in three major regions of the country (Article 6); grain output was to increase from the 1955 figure of over 150 catties (1 catty = 1/2 kilogram or 1.1 pounds) to 400 catties in areas north of the Yellow River, from 208 to 500 catties in the areas south of the Yellow and north of the Huai River, and from 400 to 800 catties in the areas south of the Huai,[30] while the average annual yield of ginned cotton was to be increased from the 1955 figure of 35 catties to 60, 80, or 100 catties depending on local conditions. Within three to five years, 6 million two-wheeled double-bladed plows and other farm tools would be put into service as the first step toward mechanization (Article 12). The major diseases and the four prevalent pests were to be wiped out within twelve years (Articles 26 and 27). Illiteracy was to be eliminated within five to seven years (Article 19), and local road systems and broadcasting networks were to cover the country by 1967 (Articles 30 and 31).

Of these tasks, with the exception of a few that were to be undertaken by the state or with the assistance of the state such as the production of the two-wheeled double-bladed plows, the majority would have to be carried out by the peasants themselves. Liao Lu-yen, in a report explaining the draft program, said that it "principally calls for its realization by means of reliance on the peasants themselves, using the manpower, material and financial resources of the 500 million peasants."[31] The draft program was said to have been designed to raise the peasants' "material and cultural living levels," but this goal could be achieved only after the draft program was fulfilled. The draft program promised the peasants not material rewards now but a rosy future attained through hard work.

The heart of the program was to increase agricultural production by expanding cultivated areas through reclamation and irrigation and by improving the unit area yield through irrigation, application of fertilizers, close planting, deep plowing, soil improvement, conservation, pest control, and any other means possible. Thus an approach emphasizing the mass mobilization of labor, which was to become a hallmark of the Great Leap Forward two years later, originated in 1956. As Chou En-lai told the Second Plenary Session of the Second CPPCC National Committee on 30 January 1956, the draft program was only the "minimum program" for agricultural development; he said that the massive strength of the peasantry could be relied upon not only to complete but to overfulfill the draft program ahead of schedule.[32] China had 120 million peasant households. Article 23 stipulated that a man from each household would work 250 workdays and a woman 120 workdays each year, a total of 370 workdays a year for each household, making a total of 44 billion workdays for the whole country. The amount of labor that the peasant used directly in field work was said to be roughly two-thirds of all workdays. Thus, based on Chou's calculation, the peasants would still have 14.8 billion workdays each year to be used for various measures for increasing production and other work. Total and massive labor mobilization was to be the key to realizing the goals stipulated in the draft program.

The Initiation

The process through which the draft program was formulated and the manner with which it was presented to the public deserve close attention. The original suggestion of the draft program was said to have come from Mao himself;[33] in November 1955 Mao exchanged views on the development of agriculture with the secretaries of fourteen provincial party committees and together they "agreed" on the so-called Seventeen Articles. These Seventeen Articles, apparently without approval by legitimate decision-making bodies, were transmitted to the rural areas, where they produced a "colossal mobilization force." Their contents, however, are not known to the outside world. In January 1956, after more discussions with provincial party officials, Mao expanded the Seventeen Articles into Forty Articles and produced the first version of the draft program. In mid-January 1956, members of the CC, provincial party secretaries, and other community officials in the government, all of whom were then attending a meeting convened by the party's CC, were briefed by Liao Lu-yen on the contents of the draft program.[34]

In line with the regime's united front strategy at that time, Mao made efforts to involve other groups in the political process. The CC of the CCP invited 1375 prominent non-party members in Peking, including scientists, industrialists, businessmen, educators, and representatives of the "democratic" parties and groups, to attend a series of meetings to give advice and suggestions. Some valuable ideas were said to have been offered, and revisions were made accordingly. The second draft of the draft program was then adopted by the Politburo on 23 January 1956.[35]

Two days later, on 25 January, with great éclat, the draft "1956–1967 National Program for Agricultural Development" was presented to the Supreme State Conference for discussion. According to the press release concerning it, the meeting was attended by more than 300 people, including not only important Communist officials in the government but also non-Communist officials and many prominent "democratic" personages.[36] This was the first time that Mao used this symbolically important body of the Chinese government to launch a very important policy.[37] And Mao then continued to use the Supreme State Conference as a platform from which to make important policy pronouncements. The presence of non-Communist officials and representatives of "democratic" parties gave the appearance of national support for the draft program and the party.

The program, labeled a draft, was not meant to be final for at least a few months. As stated in its introduction, the draft program was to be distributed to local party committees at all levels and to all departments concerned for comments and suggestions. Opinions would also be solicited from the public by 1 April. On the basis of these opinions, the Seventh CC Plenum, which was scheduled to meet on that date, would draw up a final plan. Meanwhile, local party and government organs at all levels, as well as all departments concerned, were instructed to review their plans of work and, on the basis of the draft program, draw up new plans for their community or agency. Thus the draft program was not simply a draft, but it was in a sense to become operative even before final approval by the CC.

Publicity and Propaganda

Persuasion as well as coercion is stressed by the Chinese leadership. A mass propaganda campaign, which usually precedes and accompanies the implementation of a policy, has been an invariable ingredient of the policy-making process in China. Following the announcement of the draft program, an intensive publicity campaign was launched to publicize it and to arouse the enthusiasm of the masses as well as that of the cadres. Premier Chou En-lai made a report (cited above) to the Second Plenary Session of the CPPCC, presenting an optimistic picture of China's countryside after the goals of the draft program were attained. National newspapers published editorials and feature articles to eulogize the draft program and urge the masses to work harder to attain the goals prescribed.[38] Response from the provinces was swift and impressive. Party officials in Kiangsi, Shansi, Hopei, and Kansu immediately called meetings to study the draft program and to revise their working plans accordingly.[39] In other provinces, the press enthusiastically propagandized the draft program, and officials vowed to achieve its objectives even sooner than the projected date.[40]

Implementation

With great fanfare, various provinces began to map out plans in accordance with the spirit of the draft program. For instance, in Shensi secretaries of the special district and *hsien* party committees attended an enlarged plenary session of the Provincial Party Committee in February 1956, in which the "Plan for the Thorough Implementation in Shensi of the Draft 1956–1967 National Program for the Agricultural Development" was adopted.[41] In Kwangtung, T'ao Chu (governor and secretary of the Provincial Party Committee) presented an ambitious draft "Seven Year Plan for Agricultural Development" to Kwangtung's CPPCC, pledging to fulfill all the targets set in the draft national program by 1962, five years ahead of schedule.[42] In addition to provinces, *hsien*, cities, and even mass organizations published their programs based on the draft national program and launched campaigns to execute them. For instance, Shenyang city (Mukden) in Liaoning province drew up a "Twelve-Year Agricultural Plan" for the city.[43] The Forestry Departments of the provincial governments of Szechuan and Shensi each formulated a "Ten-Year Forestry Plan,"[44] and the All-China Federation of Democratic Women had its version of a Twelve-Year Plan.

Meanwhile, unprecedentedly large numbers of peasants were mobilized to reclaim wastelands, to repair and build irrigation and water conservancy works, and to engage in many other construction projects. A Tientsin newspaper reported that the peasants were so occupied by these assignments they had no time for subsidiary occupations.[45] The cadres, engaging in what many critics later called "reckless advance," were under great pressure from their provincial superiors to undertake many tasks at once and to achieve the goals of the draft program ahead of schedule. The draft program also gave the local cadres an added impetus in the movement for agricultural collectivization, and the target date for the completion of the socialist transformation was frequently advanced.

For instance, the plan in Shensi province cited earlier stipulated that 90 percent of all peasant households were to join the APC's (including the higher level APC's) before the spring tilling of 1956, and that more than 90 percent of all peasant households were to join the higher APC's before the spring tilling in 1957. This was one year ahead of the schedule outlined in Articles 1 and 2 of the draft national program. Kwangtung, a latecomer to land reform, also set the same target. Thus at the end of December 1955, 75 million peasant households, or 63 percent of the nation's total, had joined APC's; three months later the number of peasant households joining APC's had increased to 88.9 percent or 206,680,000, and 54.9 percent of the nation's peasant households were already in the higher APC's.[46]

The cadres, spurred on by their superiors to attain the target, evidently acted rashly in herding the peasants into APC's. They often ignored the principles of "voluntarism and mutual benefit" as prescribed by the central authorities, forcing the peasants to join APC's and surrender their properties without due compensation. In some localities peasants were forced to invest their money in the APC's against their will, and in many cases their deposits in banks or remittances from other areas were frozen by overzealous cadres.[47]

The peasants, especially those who were better off, were dissatisfied and resentful. Although peasant resistance was rarely well organized, many instances were reported. The peasants slaughtered livestock and draft animals instead of surrendering them to the APC's; this situation was serious enough, even before the initiation of the draft program, that the State Council in December 1955 issued a directive ordering cadres to protect draft animals.[48] As soon as the draft animals became the property of the APC's, their mortality rate rose rapidly. According to a survey conducted in Kiangsu province, some 60,000 head died during the winter of 1956 and the spring of 1957; in Shantung, 30 percent of the draft animals were declared to be weak or incapacitated.[49] There were also frequent reports of peasants' absence from work, indifference to common property, disregard of orders, and even acts of sabotage.[50] The news that cadres were forcing peasants to invest their money in the APC's created a panic, with peasants in many localities withdrawing their savings from banks, concealing their money, and refraining from buying even needed articles, which resulted in "an abnormal situation in the rural market."[51]

Cadres' lack of experience in managing the APC's and the resulting mismanagement further exacerbated the difficulties of the APC's. Whereas the cadres might be very skillful in political manipulation and in conducting political activities, these functions were significantly different from those of organizing and operating economic production, especially agricultural production. To formulate plans of production for an APC of several hundred households, to allocate labor and farm tools adequately among different production teams working on different crops, to compute wage points for the peasants performing different types of labor—all their new functions must have been a very complicated and difficult job to say the least. In a speech in May 1956, Teng Tzu-hui frankly admitted that mismanagement and faulty planning had greatly contributed to the defects of the APC's.[52] The rapid growth of the APC's led to a universal shortage of competent cadres to do the job of planning, managing, and accounting adequately. Many units, even after their first year of operation, could not establish regular accounting systems. Thus it was almost impossible to distribute income correctly, and irregularities dampened the enthusiasm of the members.

Many APC's, again according to Teng Tzu-hui, had no overall production plans. Food crops and cotton were overemphasized (because they were targets in the draft program) at the expense of other economic crops; agriculture was overstressed, and subsidiary occupations were neglected. According to a

survey of Liaoning province during the first quarter of 1956, sideline production registered a 40–50 percent decline compared with the corresponding
period in 1955.[53] Sideline production generally represented 30–40 percent of
the peasants' total income, and the falling output in economic crops and
sideline occupations greatly affected the peasants' cash income and increased
the difficulties in their daily life. On 2 May 1956 the editorial in *Ta-kung Pao*
stated that the decline of subsidiary production was one of the main causes of
the occurrence of "certain stagnant conditions" in China's rural economy.
According to Teng Tzu-hui, the decline of subsidiary production adversely
affected not only the economic balance of society and the supply of raw
materials for certain industries but also the supply of export materials.[54]

The Shelving of the Program

The First Sign

By April 1956 it must have become apparent to the Chinese leaders that the
national economy was encountering some serious problems. The Seventh CC
Plenum, which was originally scheduled to meet 1 April to approve the draft
program, failed to meet (although the Politburo did);[55] the draft program was
therefore not approved by the CC, as had been planned.

Probably as a result of the late March to early April Politburo meeting, on
4 April the CC of the party and the State Council of the government issued
an important joint directive to stop the tendencies of "reckless advance" in
socialist construction.[56] It reprimanded enterprises, departments of the party,
and government organs at all levels for trying to do everything at once—
attempting to fulfill the draft program "with a single stroke in two or three
years." On the other hand, the joint directive also blamed the APC cadres for
extravagance, waste, and abuse of manpower. Many APC's were said to have
constructed various projects unnecessary to production, purchased farm
implements and transport facilities in excess of actual need, and even built
clubhouses and offices and bought large quantities of cultural entertainment
equipment and nonproductive supplies.[57]

Tendencies of "reckless advance" had resulted in excessive investment,
general economic overexpansion, overemphasis on production and quantity,
creating bottlenecks and causing financial difficulties. The full extent of the
economic crisis caused by the "reckless advance" was revealed one year later
at the NPC in June 1957, when Minister of Finance Li Hsien-nien estimated
total overspending at more than 2 billion *yuan*. Chou En-lai also announced

a 20 percent cutback in 1957 capital construction investment.[58] A fascinating example was the overproduction of the two-wheel double-bladed plow. In the first half of 1956 alone, 1,400,000 were produced and although 800,000 were sold, many by compulsory means, only half of these were actually used because they were either too heavy for the draft animals or not suitable for the soil in most areas. One authoritative source admitted that the overproduction of these plows caused a shortage in the supply of steel and affected priority construction projects.[59]

It was under these circumstances that the Politburo met in an enlarged session from late March to early April. Both the problems afflicting national economy and the difficulties in the countryside resulted largely from the rapid collectivization drive and poor management of the APC's, as well as from the attempts to achieve the goals of the draft program ahead of time, all of which served to vindicate the position of those party officials who advocated gradualism. The issuance of the 4 April joint directive appeared to indicate that their counsel had prevailed once again in the party's highest decision-making body.

Following the Politburo meeting, another conference of the provincial secretaries was convened. At this conference, top provincial officials may have been briefed on the shift of the regime's rural policy as well as on the question of de-Stalinization in the Soviet Union.[60]

Khrushchev's sudden denunciation of Stalin at the Twentieth Congress of the Communist Party of the Soviet Union (CPSU) appeared to have created unexpected political vibrations in China, which may have hurt Mao's political standing as well as his policies, including the draft program. In light of the de-Stalinization in the Soviet Union, the Chinese leaders apparently decided to review their leadership, particularly Mao; as a result, the political atmosphere changed, and some major domestic policies, such as the draft program, changed accordingly.

It will be recalled that Khrushchev, in a secret speech to the Twentieth Congress of the CPSU in February 1956, suddenly unveiled and attacked Stalin's crimes and megalomania. That serious dismay was created in Peking by Khrushchev's action was suggested by the fact that from February to the end of March the Chinese media were silent on the question of de-Stalinization, even though the question was already being bitterly debated throughout the Communist world and had already resulted in defections from some Communist parties. The first public Chinese reaction was the publication in the *People's Daily* (30 March) of a translation of "Why is the Cult of the Individual Alien to Marxism-Leninism?," a *Pravda* editorial of 18 March which severely criticized Stalin. On 5 April, after almost two months of soul-searching, the Chinese leadership published in the *People's Daily* an editorial entitled "On the Historical Experience of the Dictatorship of the Proletariat," which was said to have been written "on the basis of a discussion at an enlarged meeting of the Politburo."

Stalin previously had been portrayed in China as almost a demigod, and the CCP had adopted many Stalinist measures. Moreover, like Stalin, Mao had pursued a policy of rapid collectivization. Had someone in the party begun to question Mao's style of leadership and his cult of personality as a result of Khrushchev's attack on the dead *Vozhd*? For Mao, there was an urgent need to avoid the charge that he was following Stalin's footsteps.[61] Thus the editorial, while conceding Stalin's "serious mistakes," affirmed Stalin's positive role as an "outstanding Marxist-Leninist fighter" who had defended Lenin's line of industrialization and collectivization against the enemies of Leninism. The editorial contended that Stalin's errors were committed late in his life— when he indulged in the cult of the individual, violated the party system of democratic centralism and collective leadership, and fell victim to subjectivism by divorcing himself from reality and the masses.

Perhaps in anticipation of a possible challenge to Mao's leading role, the editorial emphasized the important position of leaders in history: "It is utterly wrong to deny the role of the individual, the role of forerunners and leaders." A leader begins to make serious mistakes only when he "places himself over and above the Party and the masses." However, it was implied, there seemed to be no danger of this in China now. The editorial pointed to a 1943 Party Central Committee resolution on methods of leadership which stressed the mass line. The implication was that the CCP, under Mao, had consistently observed this "Marxist-Leninist" method of leadership.

The fact that a few months later, during the Eighth Party Congress, the new Party Constitution dropped the term "thought of Mao Tse-tung" from its preamble,[62] an action allegedly first proposed by Marshal P'eng Teh-huai and then supported by Liu Shao-ch'i,[63] seemed to suggest that Khrushchev's attack on Stalin had emboldened some CCP leaders to criticize or at least question Mao's personal leadership. Even if Mao's colleagues did not wish to embarrass him in public, Mao himself may have felt compelled to observe the system of collective leadership and change somewhat his strong personal style of leadership. In a new political atmosphere when collective leadership was emphasized, other top party officials who opposed Mao's rapid collectivization policy but were forced to go along in the fall of 1955 may have reasserted themselves and argued against rash approval of the draft program. Perhaps Mao felt that in the interest of collective leadership he would have to accede to the opposition and allow the draft program to be shelved.

It is interesting to note that "collective leadership" was now applied even to the publication of the 5 April editorial, a policy statement which was based on the "discussions of an enlarged meeting of the Politburo." The editorial carried no name of any active Chinese leader, not even Mao; by contrast, only two months earlier Mao had been conspicuously identified with formulating and proposing the draft program.

It should be pointed out here that in the spring of 1956 Mao had adopted a new posture, manifested in a secret speech, "Ten Great Relationships," which he delivered to an enlarged Politburo session on 25 April.[64] Foreshadowing his celebrated speech "On Correct Handling of Contradictions Among the People" in February 1957, the speech in April 1956 called the party's attention to the ways of correctly handling ten basic relationships or contradictions confronting the Chinese polity, including the following:

1. The relationships between industry and agriculture and between heavy and light industries.
2. Those between coastal industries and inland industries.
3. Those between economic construction and national defense.
4. Relationships among the state, the co-ops and the individual.
5. Contradictions between the central and local authorities.
6. Those between the Han people and the national minorities.
7. Those between the Party and non-Party people.
8. Those between revolution and counter-revolution.
9. Contradictions between right and wrong, inside and outside the Party.
10. Problems in international relations.

What is truly remarkable about this speech is that, in addition to showing a sober recognition of the wide range of economic and political problems in China, Mao embraced a number of solutions which made him look like a "liberal," both in politics and in economics. For example, he spoke in favor of giving material incentives to the peasants, which had long been advocated by other top leaders who were in charge of economy and which Mao had criticized earlier (and was to criticize again in 1958). Did Mao adopt the new posture due to a genuine change of heart or was he responding to political pressures resulting from China's economic difficulties and the de-Stalinization campaign? This cannot be answered with certainty. In any case, the shift seemed to be good politics from Mao's point of view. By drifting to the right, Mao, a shrewd politician, may have hoped to occupy the consensus position that had emerged in the new political context of the spring of 1956 and to preempt the issues from his critics.

The Conservatives in Ascendancy

Thus in the spring of 1956 the political momentum generated by Mao's collectivization drive of the previous summer gradually slowed down, and the official enactment of Mao's draft program as a major policy was blocked or at least delayed for the time being.[65] The political current in Peking began blowing to the right, and the 4 April Central Committee-State Council joint directive and Mao's speech were straws in this new wind. A further indication of the new trend was provided by an editorial of the *People's Daily* on 20 June

1956, "Oppose Both Conservatism and Hastiness."

Ostensibly opposing both conservatism and hastiness, the editorial in fact aimed at the tendencies of "reckless advance" which were said to have occurred "after combating conservatism [since the second half of 1955]." "That hastiness is a serious question," stated the editorial, "is due to the fact that it exists not only among the cadres of the lower levels and that in many cases the hastiness manifested at the lower levels is the result of pressure applied by the higher levels." Further, "As soon as the forty-article draft Agricultural Program was announced, all organizations vied with each other to set unrealistically high targets lest they should be accused of rightist conservatism and all departments looked forward to immediate success in their work," implying that those defects were related to Mao's draft program.

Finally, the editorial admonished cadres to adopt an attitude of "seeking truth in facts" and to apply as a criterion to combat rightist conservatism and hastiness the so-called criterion of objective practical possibility (what falls behind it is rightist conservatism and what exceeds it is hastiness). It is not inconceivable that these sentences were written with Mao in mind, since he had criticized rightist conservative thinking and had said these words: "The problem today is that many people think impossible what is in fact possible if they exert themselves.[66]

According to a recent revelation of Wu Leng-hsi, former director of the New China News Agency, the editorial was first drafted by Teng T'o, the editor-in-chief of the *People's Daily*, then revised by Lu Ting-yi and Hu Ch'iao-mu, two top officials responsible for propaganda, and finally approved by Liu Shao-ch'i.[67] Mao, unenthusiastic about the editorial when Liu went to him for his last clearance, wrote "I do not want to read it" on the draft of the editorial, although it was subsequently published. The publication of this editorial may have left Mao smarting for, according to an unpublished text of Mao's speech delivered to the Nanning Conference in Kwangsi (a meeting convened by Mao and attended by some Politburo members and regional party secretaries) in early 1958, he reopened the case of that June 1956 editorial, calling it a "mistake" and criticizing it for having undermined the spontaneous initiative of the masses and cadres and resulting in losses to the national economy.[68] Wu further asserted that Mao's criticism was really directed against Liu Shao-ch'i, who allegedly was the initiator of the movement against "reckless advances."

In the course of the Cultural Revolution, everything Liu (and other purged victims) did and said in the past was reinterpreted to discredit him; therefore any specific charge against him (or others) must be treated with caution. With regard to the movement against "reckless advance" in 1956, it may not be entirely true that Liu and the aforementioned officials, all of them disgraced in the Cultural Revolution, were prime movers;[69] the main pressure could have come from any of several directions.

One source of this pressure seemed to be Premier Chou En-lai who, since the beginning of 1956, had urged the party to relax its control over the intellectuals who possessed valuable technical and intellectual resources needed for China's socialist construction but who were politically tainted in Communist eyes because of their Western or non-Communist education. In an important speech, "On the Question of Intellectuals," addressed to a special conference of the party on 14 January 1956, he called for the party to make a better use of China's underemployed intellectuals, to give them more scope and initiative, to provide them better working conditions, and to maximize their support for the task of socialist construction.[70]

Another source of pressure was a group of top party-government officials in charge of the economic administration, especially Ch'en Yun.[71] The criticism and attempts to check excesses created in the process of socialist transformation of the economy generated what Mao later called a "miniature typhoon." Even Mao himself probably unintentionally encouraged the political shift to the right. This had something to do with his "Ten Great Relationships" speech on 25 April and another speech to the Supreme State Conference on 2 May in which he signaled his support of liberalization toward intellectuals and advanced the celebrated slogan "Let a hundred flowers blossom and a hundred schools of thought contend."[72]

Taken at their face value, these two speeches by Mao showed that he was quite capable of flexibility and pragmatism and was willing to shift his stand to abide by the consensus of leadership when he confronted political difficulties. Even if he himself was merely engaged in a political maneuver and did not really subscribe to a set of policies advocated by other top leaders, his pronouncements tended to strengthen the hands of those leaders who wanted to slow down the hectic economic policies Mao initiated since the previous summer and make legitimate the more pragmatic themes they were to sound starting in May 1956.

Thus emboldened, they began to openly criticize the rashness with which the APC's were organized and the draft program was implemented. They spoke at length of their sympathy for "the peasants' burden" and began to push for more consumer goods, relaxation of control, and other measures to alleviate tensions and deficiencies generated by the socialist transformation of agriculture, industry, and commerce in Chinese society. It is true that these themes had already appeared in Mao's speech on 25 April, but other party leaders seemed willing to go farther than Mao, and other party officials apparently capitalized on the fact that Mao had endorsed those ideas to justify their advocacy and to expand the limits of economic liberalization, perhaps much to Mao's chagrin.

In early May 1956, a speech addressed to the National Conference of Model Workers by Teng Tzu-hui, which was mentioned earlier, deplored the problems caused by the rapid forced collectivization. Speaking to the same conference, Chia T'o-fu, Director of the State Council Fourth Staff Office (which was then in charge of light industry) and Minister of Light Industry, came out strongly for developing light and particularly consumer goods industries.[73] Since in both the conception and execution of the First Five-Year Plan (1953–57) heavy industry was to receive and had thus far actually received priority while light industry had played only a limited secondary role, Chia's new theme was not insignificant. He reiterated his arguments in June when he spoke to the NPC, and he was backed up by an editorial of the *People's Daily*.[74]

New themes also emerged from the economic reports of Li Fu-ch'un, Ch'en Yun, Li Hsien-nien, and Teng Tzu-hui delivered to the third session of the First NPC in June 1956. These included placing more emphasis on light industry, improving the living conditions of the people, and the necessity for giving more incentives to the workers, peasants, and even the bourgeois capitalists.[75] Ch'en Yun stressed the importance of securing the bourgeois capitalists' cooperation and the desirability of using their production techniques and management expertise. Teng Tzu-hui regarded the proper distribution of APC income as the most pressing problem and urged "less deduction, more distribution" as the basis for solving the relationship between the state, the APC, and the members. Teng also candidly admitted that "not a few mistakes and defects" had occurred in the course of the collectivization movement. He severely reprimanded the local cadres' waste of manpower and resources, the overburdening of the peasants, unrealistic target-setting, use of coercion, mismanagement of APC's, and so on. Nevertheless, he maintained that the chief responsibility lay with "the departments concerned at upper levels," which "were hasty and bit off more than they could chew." The most severe and thorough criticisms were made by Chou En-lai in the Eighth Party Congress, which will be discussed later.

A shift toward "soft" policies was also manifested through concrete actions. It was announced that a fixed rate of interest, 5 percent, was to be paid for seven years to the capitalists whose enterprises were placed under joint state operation.[76] The NPC's Standing Committee also passed a resolution to increase the portion of land to be retained by APC members.[77] The controls exercised over former landlord elements and the rich peasants also were relaxed, and some cadres were criticized for discriminating against the former landlord and rich peasant families.[78] The Model Regulation for an advanced Agricultural Producers' Cooperative, adopted on 30 June 1956, permitted former landlords and rich peasants to join as regular members.[79]

The Eighth National Congress of the CCP, September 1956

The Eighth Party Congress was an event of great significance for the CCP. It was the first national party convention since the party successfully seized power in mainland China in 1949; in fact, it was the first such meeting since the Seventh Party Congress was convened in the spring of 1945, several months before the defeat of the Japanese in World War II. Compared with the Second Session of the Eighth Party Congress in 1958, the 1956 meeting was characterized by realism and moderation. In its proceedings, delegates were informed not only of the achievements but also of the difficulties of the regime's programs. The conservatives, who had apparently achieved ascendancy since the spring, seemed to prevail in the Congress, and many statements articulating their views were fully aired. For instance, Ch'en Yun defended the placement of many "bourgeois" capitalists in managerial positions of the joint enterprises and justified this step by stressing the need to use their know-how and managerial expertise; that is, former owners would still be useful after the change to public ownership. Ch'en also urged that the sphere of free economy be expanded and more subsidiary occupations be managed by individual APC members, so that peasants' incentive would be increased and production would rise.[80] Teng Tzu-hui's prescriptions paralleled those of Ch'en Yun, and he advocated more distribution and less accumulation in the income of the APC's.

Two other top economic officials, Li Hsien-nien and Po I-po, supported a policy of increasing material incentives by raising the procurement prices of farm products and improving people's living conditions. Po I-po said: "Experience shows that when the relationship between accumulation and consumption was properly dealt with, a harmony was evident in the economic life of the state and a favorable effect resulted in the development of industry and other branches of the economy and in the improvement of people's living conditions." He added, "Whenever we tried to undertake more industrial construction or other construction and made too big state budgets and planned too big capital investment, haste always made waste, and man-made strain was caused to the national economy."

Premier Chou En-lai's "Report on the Proposal for the Second Five-year Plan," which was adopted by the Party Congress, affirmed a moderate line for the national economy. In this report, Chou made some very factual remarks in which he frankly admitted problems and difficulties upsetting China's national economy. He candidly stated:

> Many of the shortcomings and mistakes in our work are inseparable from subjectivism and bureaucracy among the leadership. Some leading comrades sit on high, do not approach the masses, are ignorant of the actual conditions, and are subjective in dealing with questions and making arrangements for work. ... Moreover, bureaucracy at high levels fosters commandism at lower levels.

Referring critically to the draft agricultural program, Chou said that there was a tendency in some departments and localities to do everything at once and do it everywhere, taking no account of actual conditions, and recklessly running ahead. This kind of mistake, he added, affected the state's priority construction projects and gave rise to difficulties in finance and waste of manpower and material resources. He pointedly stated, "such a tendency recurred in the beginning of 1956, following the publication of the draft *National Program for Agricultural Development.*"

Although Premier Chou and others openly criticized mistakes only in the implementation of the draft program, their criticisms were actually directed against the program itself. Criticisms of the faulty implementation would eventually have discredited the program politically. Such implications were not lost on the participants in the Party Congress, particularly Mao himself. The reason other top party leaders refrained from directly criticizing the program was that such a criticism would amount to a personal attack on Mao, the initiator of the program and, by extention, the myth of the infallability of the party leadership—this they would want to avoid. Even the criticism of the administrative errors was not made lightly; it was only in the context of Mao's political eclipse that other party leaders reasserted themselves to air their views.[81]

Under these circumstances, it is not surprising that the draft National Program for Agricultural Development was not adopted. Instead, a moderate document issued jointly by the CC and the State Council on 12 September 1956, on the eve of the Party Congress,[82] may have been intended as a substitute. The draft program, a major party policy document only a few months earlier, was conspicuous by its absence at the deliberations and the proceedings of the Party Congress. Teng Tzu-hui, the major spokesman for the regime's rural policy, did not refer to it in his speech on agricultural production. Liu Shao-ch'i, in his Political Report, mentioned it only once in passing.[83] Chou En-lai in his report (cited above) referred to the draft program in a critical manner. The proposals for the Second Five-Year Plan adopted by the Party Congress failed to mention the draft program, which two years later was hailed by Liu Shao-ch'i in his Political Report to the second session of the Eighth Party Congress as having set "great goals for rural work" and having given a "correct orientation for the development of the entire work of socialist construction." Thus eight months after its emergence in January 1956, the draft program had fallen into oblivion.

Mao's political eclipse was furthered by a new arrangement in the leadership hierarchy in September 1956. In line with the new political trend placing great emphasis on collective leadership, the First CC Plenum, which met on 28 September, in addition to electing Mao Tse-tung chairman of the Party CC and Politburo also elevated four other top party leaders, Liu Shao-ch'i, Chou En-lai, Chu Teh, and Ch'en Yun to vice-chairmen of these two powerful bodies. These five men and the party's General-Secretary Teng Hsiao-p'ing formed the Standing Committee of the Politburo, the leadership nucleus of the CCP. The four vice-chairmen were already top party leaders, but their elevation to vice-chairmanship, newly created posts in 1956, served to indicate their rising political influence vis-à-vis the chairman. In the summer of 1966, when Mao had his final say, these four vice-chairmen were dropped and Lin Piao was selected by Mao as the sole vice-chairman. The CCP leadership has, over time, displayed the apparently contradictory dual characteristics of one-man rule and collective leadership. The manifestation of one characteristic over the other is an obvious function of changes in the balance of power of the top leaders.

In light of political and social and economic developments since the summer of 1955, Liu Shao-ch'i's characterization of the rightist and leftist deviations from the party's general line was fairly informative and significant. Liu had the following to say in the Political Report which he presented to the Eighth Party Congress:

> In the last few years the tendency of deviating from the Party's general line to the right has manifested itself mainly in being satisfied merely with what has been achieved in the bourgeois-democratic revolution, in wanting to call a halt to the revolution, in not admitting the need for our revolution to pass on into socialism, in being unwilling to adopt a suitable policy to restrict capitalism in both town and countryside, in not believing that the Party could lead the peasantry along the road to socialism, and in not believing that the Party could lead the people of the whole country to build socialism in China. . . .
> The tendency of deviating from the Party's general line to the "left" has manifested itself mainly in demanding that socialism be achieved overnight, in demanding that some method of expropriation be used in our country to eliminate the national bourgeoisie as a class, or some method be used to squeeze out and bankrupt capitalist industry, and commerce, in not admitting that we should adopt measures for advancing, step by step, to socialism, and in not believing that we could attain the goal of socialist revolution by peaceful means. Our Party resolutely repudiated as well as criticized those two deviations.

Liu's reconstruction of leftist and rightist deviations was more than an exercise in rhetoric; it rather accurately pictured the debate between two different strategies of economic development or "schools of thought" and hinted at disputes among CCP leaders over the strategy and tactics of socialist construction in China.

Whereas it is fairly easy to discern these two distinct approaches to socialist construction, the identification of individual CCP leaders with the two points of view is difficult. At the risk of oversimplification, those who had the actual responsibility for running the national economy—Premier Chou En-lai, Vice-Premiers Ch'en Yun, Teng Tzu-hui, Li Fu-ch'un, Po I-po, and Li Hsien-nien—may be considered members of the conservative group, while Mao and those who specialized in the party administration—Liu Shao-ch'i, Teng Hsiao-p'ing, and P'eng Chen—constitute the radical group. It should be emphatically stated that with the two exceptions of Mao, who consistently pushed for revolutionary change, and Teng Tzu-hui, who persisted in his own conservative viewpoints, most other leaders had often changed their positions under different circumstances and were willing to accept the policy decided by the party at any moment. And Chou En-lai was a reputed "tide-watcher," well-known for his ability to sense and move with the political tide. Leaders like Liu Shao-ch'i, Teng Hsiao-p'ing, and P'eng Chen were thought to be "hardliners" in the 1950s because they tended to take a radical stance, but they shifted and adopted the conservative approach in the 1960s in the wake of the disastrous Great Leap. On occasions even Mao was flexible and acquiesced in measures repugnant to his known preference, although after 1958 he became closely tied to the Great Leap programs and came to personify the radical approach.

The dispute between the two approaches was not the conflict of leadership factions or cliques, and those leaders who pursued the same approach did not appear to belong to the same faction. Within the CCP leadership, factions based on personal ties or historical associations (e.g., the field army ties) have in fact existed,[84] and as the leadership unity was shattered and the top leaders were locked in bitter struggle in the 1960s, the old ties were reactivated and factional cleavages became a salient element in Chinese politics. In the 1950s, however, factional conflict had little effect on the dispute over strategy of economic development, perhaps with the exception of the P'eng Teh-huai affair in 1959 (see Chapter 4 for details). The conflict over economic policies in the 1950s was conflict between "opinion groups."[85] The opinion groups consisted of leaders who shared the same view on a given issue, but the "membership" was never constant as individuals shifted their stance. Moreover, there were different opinion groups on different issues, and those who held the same view on one issue did not necessarily stand together on other issues.

Major changes in policy in the 1950s and early 1960s can be attributed to shifting coalitions of opinion groups at the center. Furthermore, when the views of the "radical" group prevailed, there would be a "big push" that unfolded radical measures. But when the views of the "conservative" group prevailed, there followed a period of retreat and consolidation which employed a different power mix in policy implementation.

Thus the shifts in policy followed an oscillating or alternating pattern, a kind of a dialectical pattern, between conservative and radical policies. Peking's pendulum had swung to the left during the fall of 1955 and throughout the winter of 1955–56 when collectivization was stepped-up and the draft twelve-year agricultural program was launched. The momentum of this leftward swing was slowed down in the spring of 1956 as the political forces in the party regrouped; thereafter, the pendulum began to swing to the right as the views of the "conservative group" prevailed. As a result, Mao's grandiose draft program failed to secure final approval while the regime devoted its efforts to making adjustments and solving "contradictions."

The 12 September 1956 party-state joint directive on the APC's, mentioned earlier, was a sober document embodying the same comparatively sober and factual line of thought found in the speeches of Chou En-lai and other top economic officials during the Party Congress. It frankly discussed a number of problems afflicting collectivization and the rural economy, particularly the importance of individual "sideline" production, realistic target-setting and plans, avoidance of "commandist" behavior toward peasants, more distribution of income for payment and less for accumulation, the institution of a free market, and the appropriate size (not too large) for APC's. Despite these prescriptions (some of them significant concessions to the peasants), they did not seem to measure up to the difficulties in the rural economy and therefore could do no more than palliate the deficiencies of the collectivization system.

It is obvious, if only from Mao's own admission, that criticism of and opposition to the collectivization within the party continued throughout the winter of 1956–57, constituting in Mao's phrase a "miniature typhoon."[86] The harvests in 1956 were disappointing, and food shortages were reported in many areas. In Kwangsi, for instance, many peasants died of starvation; the situation was serious enough that the province's first party secretary, Ch'en Mang-yuan (a candidate member of the CC), two provincial party secretaries, and several other lesser officials were dismissed.[87] Peasant discontent was widespread; as noted earlier, they slaughtered draft animals and damaged public properties, and in some places large-scale withdrawals from APC's forced their dissolution.[88]

Mao's speech on "The Correct Handling of Contradictions Among the People" in February 1957 suggested a new approach to China's economic problems primarily through political action and ideological education. He sought solutions to "contradictions" in Chinese society through attitudinal changes of the intellectuals and their active support in socialist construction, and the education of the party cadres in a new working style. The efforts to rectify party cadres and to win over intellectuals in the spring of 1957, however, unexpectedly resulted in the intellectuals' direct challenge to the foundations of the Communist rule and bitter attacks against the abuses of Communist officialdom.[89] In early June the rectification campaign of the party was transformed into an "anti-rightist" movement; thereby the party launched a counterattack against "bourgeois rightists." Nevertheless, the image of the party leadership had already been severely tarnished.

In the meantime the events of the summer of 1957 had done nothing to improve the economic and particularly the agricultural situation. The palliative measures prescribed in the joint directive of September 1956 were insufficient and hence ineffective. It is true that the weather of 1956 and 1957 was unfavorable. Typhoon Wanda, said to be the worst in fifty years, swept through many provinces in early August 1956, doing heavy damage to crops and properties, and both flood and drought were reported in large areas of China in 1957. Many poor peasants and rural cadres, however, candidly blamed the system of collectivization, the unified grain purchase policy, and other "man-made" factors for the failure in harvests. They said that collectivization had been pushed too far and too fast, that the state's grain policy had squeezed too much out of the peasantry, that the APC's were inferior to *tan kan* (private farming), and that the peasants' living conditions were worse after they joined the APC's.[90]

The Chinese campaign showed organizational skill and control techniques far superior to those of Stalin's collectivization drive in the 1920s and the 1930s, resulting in a smoother transition and little bloodshed.[91] The peasants' resistance was largely ineffective and rarely organized. It does not follow, however, that China's collectivization was a resounding success. Despite their brilliant achievement in effecting structural change in the countryside and in bringing the peasants under tight control, the Chinese Communists did not bring about the desired increase in farm output—a very important, if not the most important, goal of collectivization. There were many reasons for this failure, some technical and others political.

The view of the "pragmatic coalition" in the party, as articulated by Teng Tzu-hui, was that the policies of collectivization and of unified grain purchase had generated many "contradictions," conflicts between APC members and the cadres, between APC's and the state, between the poor peasants and the middle peasants, and so on.[92] Teng argued that to increase agricultural production, these "contradictions" must first be "correctly" handled. His prescription was, in essence, that the party must make more concessions to the peasants and give them more material incentives to promote production.

This line of argument, which may have received the support of many of the cadres specializing in agricultural affairs, seemed to have prevailed in the party up to the eve of the Third CC Plenum. A National Rural Work Conference, held in early September 1957, reviewed the party's policy toward APC's and agricultural production.[93] Presumably, conclusions reached there were then approved by a Politburo meeting, and three directives were issued in the name of the CC on 14 September 1957, one week before the Third Plenum was convened. The directive, entitled "On the Improvement of Production Administration in APC's," instructed cadres to dissolve large APC's and restrict the size of each to one hundred households (equivalent to a natural village) and each production team to twenty households, a move apparently contrary to the wish of Mao Tse-tung, who had advocated a larger organization.[94] The directive unequivocally stated:

> As a result of practice in the past years, it has been proven that big co-operatives and big teams are generally not suited to the present conditions of production. . . . Therefore, except for a few big co-operatives which are really run with success, all the existing co-operative farms which are too big . . . should be appropriately reduced in size. . . . Once the size of the co-operative farm has been fixed, an announcement should be made that there will be no change for the next ten years.

This meant that the size of the APC's was to be further reduced, for the joint directive of September 1956 had stipulated that the size of APC's should be about 100, 200, and 300 households in mountainous, hilly, and plains regions, respectively.

The same directive, in a sense, also "decollectivized" the system of collective management to a degree by transferring the authority of production from APC's down to both production teams and subsidiary occupation groups, which in turn were to delegate authority to individual households. In other words, the collective element in the management of the APC's was to be restricted: production teams and subsidiary occupation groups were to decide their own production plans within the framework of a "unified management," the "three-guarantee" system was to be widely introduced, and an individual (household) production responsibility system was to be stressed to increase incentives.[95] Unnecessary collective labor was to be avoided to conserve manpower. Another directive stipulated that concessions were to be made to the middle and rich peasants in policies concerning the means of production and distribution of collective income, and APC members were to be permitted to raise and keep a certain number of livestock.

If these measures had been fully implemented, the cooperative system as it then existed in China's countryside would have been drastically modified; collectivist elements would have been substantially reduced and the active role of individual peasant households increased.[96] Before these profound changes could take full effect, however, the "radical" segments of the party leadership again dominated the decision-making councils and mapped out a different developmental strategy that charted a new course of action. Thus the cycle was repeated: an intensive, highly organized nation-wide campaign, followed by a period of retreat and consolidation, which in turn was replaced by another intensive campaign.

The Revival of the Program

The Regroupment of Political Forces

The "hundred flowers" episode and the subsequent "anti-rightist" campaign in the summer of 1957 had enormous political and economic repercussions. Shocked by the negative responses of the "bourgeois" intellectuals, Mao and other leaders began to reassess various policy assumptions of the past. As a result, they formulated a different developmental strategy in which the role of intellectuals (such as scientists, engineers, technicians, managerial and planning staff), who were now politically tainted, was to be deemphasized in the course of socialist construction. With regard to dissensions on economic policies, events during the summer of 1957 put the supporters of a radical line, including Mao himself, in a very strong position. On the other hand, the same events made it difficult for anyone in the party to criticize the radical policy in any way without incurring the charge of rightism; the position of the "conservatives" was correspondingly weakened.

Initially, Mao's rectification and the "hundred flowers" relaxation were supported by the liberal elements in the party, who argued for the relaxation of control, and particularly by officials responsible for economic affairs, who were then pushing for a more moderate line, but it was obviously opposed by some other political groups. For instance, some officials in the cultural propaganda apparatus of the army openly voiced their dissent.[97] Party officials in various fields, either unable to genuinely grasp Mao's dialectic and theory of "contradictions" or determined to protect their own prerogatives, criticized the rectification campaign as a rightist deviation.[98] Mao's scheme of rectification, which used an extra-party force, the intellectuals and "democratic" parties, to criticize the party cadres, was understandably unwelcome by the party's organization men. There is some indirect evidence that top "organization men" Liu Shao-ch'i and P'eng Chen were against Mao's rectification policy.[99]

The shocking events of the late spring and early summer during the "hundred flowers" period finally led to a political realignment. Mao, who apparently had initially overruled the opposition of the "organization men" to launch the rectification campaign, now apparently came to a quick change of mind and joined hands with them to pursue the "anti-rightist" campaign.[100] Apparently the balance of power among the party leaders changed and soon thereafter, in the fall of 1957, there was a shift of the regime's economic policy.

Clashes Between "Radicals" and "Conservatives" at the Third Plenum

On 10 October 1957 the *People's Daily* published a brief communique announcing that the Third CC Plenum had been held between 20 September and 9 October 1957. According to the communique, the Plenum was an enlarged meeting, in which the secretaries of the provincial and autonomous regions and special district party committees participated. Three Politburo reports were delivered, by Teng Hsiao-p'ing on the rectification campaign, by Chou En-lai on wages and welfare, and by Ch'en Yun on changes in the system of economic administration and the problem of raising agricultural output. The Plenum "basically" passed the 1956–1967 National Program for Agricultural Development (revised draft), regulations for improving the system of industrial management (draft), regulations for improving the system of commercial management (draft), regulations for improving the system of financial management and of division of authority over financial management between center and regions (draft), and regulations on the question of employee wages and welfare (draft).

Dissension on policy among the party leaders was suggested by the unusual length of the proceedings and the party's subsequent failure to make public the two important Politburo reports presented by Ch'en Yun and Chou En-lai. Generally a CC Plenum is preceded by a Politburo meeting, which is held to prepare for it, and the reports of the Politburo, such as the three that were presented to the Third CC Plenum, are first approved by the Politburo and then by the CC. If this practice was observed in the September 1957 meeting, why was Teng's report published while the other two were not?

It is probable that Mao did not attend the Politburo meeting which presumably approved the three Politburo reports.[101] *Possibly he disagreed with some of the decisions made in that Politburo meeting.* As argued earlier, the supporters of a "pragmatic" economic policy had prevailed since the second half of 1956 and their influence apparently resulted in the three CC directives which were issued on the eve of the Third CC Plenum, probably upon the conclusion of the Politburo meeting. The fact that Ch'en Yun, an outspoken advocate of the "pragmatic" line, delivered the Politburo report on the economy indicated that the same approach underlying these three directives was adopted initially and that the "pragmatic coalition" still had an upper hand in the early part of the meeting.[102]

But suddenly, at the end of the CC Plenum, the draft twelve-year National Program for Agricultural Development, symbolic of a radical mobilization approach in agriculture and the economy as a whole, was unexpectedly resurrected. It was unusual that the revised draft program was introduced by Teng Hsiao-p'ing's report, which dealt primarily with the rectification campaign.[103] Furthermore, a speech (not report) on agricultural production made by Teng Tzu-hui to the Plenum, a portion of which was later made public,[104] reiterated the main points contained in the three aforementioned CC directives and failed to endorse the revised draft program, which was surprising in view of the fact that it became one of the major items on the agenda of the Plenum.

All of the evidence suggests that the draft program was reintroduced to the Plenum late in the meeting,[105] probably as a result of Mao's initiative. Mao seems to have suddenly turned the tables, as he had in 1955 on the issue of collectivization, when he was assured of new support, and challenged the opponents among his colleagues by presenting his own policy. Another parallel with the 1955 dispute over collectivization is indicated by the fact that before the Third Plenum Mao also traveled extensively in the provinces, where he may have picked up support from the provincial secretaries, many of whom had been brought into the CC since the 1956 Eighth Party Congress.[106]

The proceedings of the Third CC Plenum were said to have been punctuated with "enthusiastic discussions." The unusual length of the meeting indicated that the CC engaged in hot and serious arguments. Exactly what procedures were subsequently used to resolve policy differences among the party leaders can only be a matter of conjecture. On the basis of available evidence, formal votes seem to be a rarity in such meetings.

It has been postulated that a last minute switch from "conservative" to "radical" policies at the Third Plenum may have been triggered by the Soviet launching of Sputnik on 4 October 1957.[107] This scientific achievement might have convinced Mao—judging from his later remark in Moscow that "the East wind is prevailing over the West wind"—that the balance of forces in the world had shifted and now favored the socialist camp. Mao, Schurmann suggests, may have invoked the changed international situation to argue against the "conservative" policies and to justify pushing the revised draft program through the Plenum.

In any case, Mao's victory in the Third Plenum was not total, inasmuch as the revised draft program was only "basically" passed, implying reservations by some of the party leaders. It was stated that further revisions, based on suggestions to be solicited from the peasants, would be made; the draft would then be submitted to the party's National Congress for approval and finally be enacted as formal legislation by the state organs.[108]

Significant revisions were later made in the original draft program, presumably to placate the "conservatives." For instance, whereas the 1956 draft called for the APC's solving their need for fertilizer by their own efforts, it was now promised that the government would invest more in manufacturing chemical fertilizer (5 to 7 million tons and 15 million tons were set as the production targets to be achieved in 1962 and 1967, respectively). Several targets and requirements set in the 1957 draft were more modest than those of the 1956 draft: cotton yield per *mou* was reduced from 60 to 40 catties for some areas, the expansion of rice acreage was cut from 310 to 250 million *mou*, plans for the two-wheeled double-share plows were dropped, and the number of annual workdays required of women was reduced from 120 to 80. Another important addition in the 1957 version was a subparagraph in Article 29 recommending that "Except in a few nationality areas, birth control and planned parenthood should be publicized and encouraged in order to avoid too heavy a burden on living expenses and in order to give the children a better education and good opportunities for employment."[109]

Despite these changes, the revised draft program was still a very ambitious and unrealistic program. Its revival represented a radical departure from the more moderate economic line which the regime had pursued since the second half of 1956.

On 13 October 1957 Mao convened the Supreme State Conference to discuss the revised draft program. The conference was attended by some sixty people, including "democratic" personages as well as party leaders (as stated earlier, the meeting in January 1956, when the draft program was first made public, was attended by more than three hundred people and enjoyed great publicity). On 14 October the revised draft was submitted to a joint session of the Standing Committee of the NPC and the Standing Committee of the CPPCC for discussion; this joint session also "basically" approved the draft program. These deliberations by the Supreme State Conference and the other two institutions had not been called for, as far as is known on the basis of the public record, in the Third Plenum communique. In all probability Mao still felt it was important to use available instruments to enlist support for his program. T'an Chen-lin, a member of the CC Secretariat, made a report on the revised draft to the joint session of the NPC and the CPPCC Standing Committees. This was T'an's "debut," so to speak, as a spokesman for "radical" agricultural policy; later he would appear with increasing frequency throughout China to propagate the "radical" line on agriculture.

Honan as a Microcosm of National Politics

The provincial politics of Honan from 1955 to 1957, like national politics in the same period, went through a full cycle: big push (usually in the form of an intense, highly organized campaign), relaxation of control (adjustments and consolidation), and then another push. The province of Honan, despite its peculiarities, presented in a sense a microcosm of the leadership disputes over the strategy of socialist construction as well as the turmoil and problems which had characterized the entire country in the collectivization drive of 1955–57. An intensive study of provincial political processes in Honan may shed light on the interactions between the national capital and provincial capitals and further our understanding of China's overall political processes.

Honan, like most other provinces, responded to Chairman Mao's call in July 1955 for accelerating collectivization, creating a "socialist" upsurge in its countryside in the winter of 1955–56. Soon after the draft twelve-year agricultural program was announced by Peking at the end of January 1956, Honan also adopted a twelve-year program which provided an added impetus to the collectivization drive. In 1956 there were 26,221 APC's in the province, each having an average membership of 358 households; among them were 808 large APC's, each of which embraced over 1000 households.[110] The cadres of Honan, spurred on by the desire to meet the targets set by the party leaders, evidently had acted rashly in organizing the new APC's, and in the process they had met strong resistance from the peasants. There was large-scale slaughter of draft animals in the countryside aimed at avoiding their surrender to the management of the APC's.[111] The summer weather of 1956 was unfavorable in Honan as in many other areas of China, and there was a severe food shortage in Honan.[112] The peasants who had been induced to join the APC's by promises of increased income were discontented when benefits did not materialize.

During the winter of 1956 and the spring of 1957, widespread dissatisfaction in the villages and desertions from the APC's were reported in many areas of Honan; a party publication characterized this as an "anti-social adverse-current"; in Lingju Hsien, for instance, there was a large-scale dissolution of the APC's and much turmoil allegedly arising from sabotage by the landlords, rich peasants, counterrevolutionaries, and bad elements.[113] The circumstances were so serious that Honan's Provincial Party Committee deemed it necessary to file several reports to the CC in Peking.[114] In Yungcheng, Hsiayi, and Minchu'an Hsien, it was also reported that the landlords and rich peasants had allied with the prosperous middle peasants to oppose collectivization. They assaulted the cadres, distributed the draft animals, foodstuffs, and farm tools among themselves, and dissolved the APC's.

Honan's Provincial Party Committee, then led by Wu Chih-p'u, governor and second secretary of the party and a CC member, regarded the situation as a sharp class struggle between the landlords and peasants. The provincial committee launched a counterattack against "class enemies" and backed the local cadres in strong actions to "turn the anti-socialist tide and safeguard socialism."

In the spring of 1957 P'an Fu-sheng, first party secretary of Honan and a CC alternate, on sick leave in Peking since the summer of 1954, returned to his job in Honan. After the winter of 1956, the CC had decided to launch a "rectification" campaign to eliminate "commandism" among the cadres and keep the party in touch with the masses. Mao's speech "On the Question of Correctly Resolving Contradictions Among the People" in February 1957 set a new tone. In line with the new policy, P'an termed all the disturbances "contradictions among the people," not between antagonistic classes, and indicated that they should be settled accordingly.

During this period, P'an and his two close confidants in the Honan Provincial Party Committee, Yang Chueh (a secretary) and Wang T'ing-tung (deputy secretary-general) emphasized that the major contradiction in the rural areas was the grain question, expressed primarily in the relation between the leaders and the led. Apparently paraphrasing Mao's 1956 speech on "Ten Sets of Relationship," they set out ten major contradictions (problems) found in Honan: the shortage of grain and fodder; natural calamities which hampered production; water disputes between communities; shortage of draft animals; contradictions between the free market and the state unified purchase system; contradictions between promotions to higher schools and getting employment for their graduates; the relation between city and countryside and between supply and demand; the minority problem (Muslim members of the APC's demanded to be allowed to withdraw); contradictions between the Party and the non-Party people, especially the "democratic" personages and the intellectuals; contradictions between centralization and decentralization, between vertical and horizontal leadership.

P'an believed that most of these contradictions manifested themselves in the relations between the leaders and the led, and he blamed the "commandist" behavior of the officials for the difficulties. He subsequently repudiated the previous views and decisions of the Provincial Party Committee on the incidents in the APC's, attacked the leadership of Wu. Chih-p'u, and even took punitive action against some forty cadres who had committed "commandist" actions in those incidents.

P'an apparently had misgivings about agricultural collectivization, believing that it contributed to Honan's shortages of grain and animal power and decline in agricultural production. On one occasion P'an was alleged to have vilified the cooperative system in these words: "The peasants were not equal to beasts of burden in the past, but are the same as beasts of burden today. Yellow oxen are tied up in the house and human beings are harnessed in the field. Girls and women pull plows and harrows, with their wombs hanging down. Collectivization is transformed into exploitation of human strength."

P'an also criticized collectivization in Honan as being the result of "reckless advance"; he said that the APC's were oversized, private plots retained by peasants were too small, the peasants' lot was too hard, and production enthusiasm was low. As the First Secretary of the province, P'an was squeezed between pressures from below to feed the population and the orders from above to fulfill various state targets. His interests and responsibilities were to maintain order and develop production in a way that would satisfy both his superiors and his constituents. In the wake of difficulties resulting from collectivization, he sent his confidants Yang Chuch and Wang T'ing-tung to several counties to conduct investigations and study the ways by which the morale of the peasants could be raised and production could be developed.

In May 1957 P'an instructed the Rural Work Department of the Honan Provincial Party Committee to formulate measures to provide incentives to peasants. A simple document drafted by the Rural Work Department was found unsatisfactory by P'an; according to P'an's critics, it was then redrafted by Wang T'ing-tung in accord with P'an's wish and was later announced as "The Propaganda Outline for the Encouragement of the Development of Agricultural Production." In many aspects the outline diverged from the guidelines set by Peking: it permitted APC's to reduce their size and the peasants to withdraw, encouraged the reclamation of land by individuals, enlarged the size of private plots and raised the amount of grain reserved for APC members, encouraged the development of family subsidiary occupations, and opened the free markets.

The outline sharply divided the Provincial Party Committee's Standing Committee; some members put forth opposite suggestions, but P'an only made changes in wording and went ahead with efforts to implement it. Although it also met opposition from some officials on local levels, P'an, as first party secretary, held a strategic position for eliciting support and overcoming opposition. From the end of June to mid-July, for instance, P'an and his supporters in the Provincial Party Committee simply ignored and bypassed the Provincial Party Committee as a decision-making body and proceeded to implement the new policy. P'an convened a conference of the secretaries of the Special District, *Hsien*, and City Party Committees and called two separate meetings of the directors of the staff office of the Hsien Party Committees. At these meetings he examined and reviewed the results of the implementation of the "propaganda outline" in each locality.

These conferences appeared to be effective mechanisms through which party officials could follow up and supervise the execution of policy on the local level. For instance, Lingju Hsien's party secretary, who allowed only 47 out of 743 households that applied to leave the APC's, was reprimanded and instructed to take a more liberal attitude. The Hsinhsiang Hsien Party Committee, which was lukewarm toward the new policy and had deliberately omitted in the "propaganda outline" an article permitting the peasants' withdrawal from the APC's, was ordered to correct the omission.

P'an also challenged the theory that large cooperatives were superior to the smaller ones: "Big cooperatives are nothing better. In a big cooperative there are more contradictions among the people." He cited the example of Liuling Cooperative in which members had to walk some 10 *li* and queue up before they could talk with the director.

P'an and his supporters criticized the provincial committee for its past policy of setting up big APC's and insisted on reducing the size of APC's as far as possible. It was revealed later that the number of APC's in Honan doubled in a few months—increasing from 26,221 to 54,000 from the spring to the summer of 1957, each averaging 180 households, with the smallest containing less than 30.[115] Some hard-line local cadres voiced strong opposition to the breaking up of large APC's, so that 495 large APC's (out of 808) were retained.

P'an also took a more liberal attitude toward peasants' withdrawal from their APC's. He openly stated that peasants' withdrawal from APC's did not mean they would not follow the socialist road. Seven measures on withdrawal from APC's drafted by the Rural Work Department of the Honan Party Committee in accord with P'an's instructions were vetoed by the Standing Committee of the CCP Provincial Committee. P'an, however, did not give up his attempt; he and his supporters relied on the conferences of the directors of general offices of the *hsien* committees to push lower cadres to split up large APC's.[116]

To survive and thrive in a highly centralized political system like that in China, provincial leaders must constantly keep a watchful eye on Peking to detect any shifts in the power combinations of the top leadership or in policies,[117] and they must be flexible and adequately opportunistic to bend to the political wind. In the early summer of 1957, P'an Fu-sheng was not quick enough to detect changes in the party's line, and his insensitivity seems to have hurt him politically. The orientation of the "rectification" campaign gradually changed, and by mid-June it had become a part of the "anti-rightist" struggle. The editorial "What is This For?" (*People's Daily*, 8 June 1957) was a clear call for a halt to criticisms of the party, and during the next few days a series of *People's Daily* editorials pressed the counterattack against the "rightists," signaling a reversal of policy at the highest level.

P'an apparently did not read these signals clearly. The press in Peking was violently denouncing the rightists, but P'an was slow to act. After the "anti-rightist campaign" was finally launched in the capital of Honan, P'an reportedly still urged the party members to return the stormy assault of the rightists with criticism as gentle as "a breeze or mild rain," and he restrained the party members from using mass meetings or violent methods in struggling against the rightists.[118] When the Jungyang Hsien Party Committee initiated its own anti-rightist campaign and issued instructions to the cadres in the *hsiang* and the APC's "to mobilize the masses to uncover and combat the bourgeois rightists on 9 July 1957,[119] P'an, without consulting his colleagues in the Standing Committee of the Provincial Party Committee, sent out a directive to party committees on all levels in Honan forbidding the launching of the campaign in the organs below the *hsien* level.[120] P'an continued to call contradictions between the rightists and the party "nonantagonistic," and he claimed that the struggle between the two roads in the rural areas had been fundamentally settled. He ordered the Jungyang Hsien Party Committee to revoke its instructions and reproached it for having "created artificial tension in the countryside and fostered commandist tendencies."

The evidence does not really suggest that P'an wanted to develop capitalism in Honan and that he colluded with the "rightists" outside the party to attack the CCP, which he was later accused of doing. Rather P'an appeared to be more concerned with increasing economic production and mitigating the disruptive effects of the anti-rightist movement in Honan.

The tactics used by provincial officials to cope with demands from above indicate that through their control of the flow of information, provincial officials often enjoyed a great degree of autonomy and were in a good position to evade central supervision. For instance, when P'an Fu-sheng was summoned to Tsingtao in late July 1957 to attend a conference of provincial party secretaries, he detected obvious changes of tone in Mao's speech. Being an astute politician, P'an deleted from his previously prepared report those data critical of collectivization and added other materials showing the positive aspect of the rural economy in order to please Mao. On his return from Tsingtao in early August, P'an allegedly twisted Mao's instructions to justify his policy in Honan; he revised the outlines of his report, inserted several remarks made by Mao at Tsingtao, distributed the outlines, and, in the words of his critics, "wanted to give the fifth session of the Provincial Committee an impression that the Party center had endorsed the outlines of his report."[121]

P'an's "double-dealing" tactics might have succeeded had not his chief rival in the province, Wu Chih-p'u, who had just attended a Central Grain Conference, apparently also become aware of changes in the attitude of some top central leaders, particularly Mao, which encouraged him to challenge P'an back home. Thus in the fifth enlarged session of the Honan Provincial Party Committee, P'an's policies and leadership were fiercely attacked by an anti-P'an coalition led by Wu Chih-p'u. He was accused of denying the existence of class struggle in the rural areas, opposing collectivization and the state's grain purchase policy, pursuing capitalist policies, protecting and allying himself with the rightists, conducting factional activities, and many other anti-party words and deeds. P'an was forced to revoke the propaganda outline and stop its execution; he was also compelled to review his leadership and engage in self-criticism.[122]

It is plain that political forces in Honan, as well as in the nation, had undergone a realignment, with the radical elements now holding an upper hand. Attempting to fortify his position, which had already been undermined, P'an undertook an inspection tour of the countryside and produced a report to show that he was quite aware of class struggle and that he had been tough on "capitalist" tendencies in the rural areas.[123] When Mao visited Honan soon after, P'an was able, in the words of his critics, to "show off" his survey report and "deceive the Party center and cover up his own errors."[124]

The victory of the "radical" force in the national scene, following the clashes between the "radicals" and the "conservatives" in the Third CC Plenum, had an important bearing on the fight between P'an and Wu in Honan. When the second session of the First CCP Honan Provincial Congress was held between 12 November and 2 December 1957, T'an Chen-lin, a secretary of the CC and now the spokesman for Mao's radical line, was present to speak on the "current situation at home and abroad, the rectification campaign and the leadership over the production high tide in the countryside."[125]

P'an Fu-sheng was in hot water; this can be seen from criticism leveled against him by the Provincial Congress:

> For a short while prior to the 5th Plenum of the Provincial Committee (when P'an was in command), the Provincial Committee erred in denying the struggle between the two roads in the countryside and put restraint on cadres and the masses at a time when unlawful landlords, rich peasants and well-to-do middle peasants imbued with capitalist ideas cooperated with the bourgeois rightists in cities in their attack on the socialist system. In handling the relations between the State, APC's and the peasants, the Provincial Committee also erred in speaking for the well-to-do middle peasants and took certain economic measures that suited the capitalist spontaneity.[126]

Although it was not until the Second Session of the Eighth CCP National Congress in May 1958 that P'an Fu-sheng was openly denounced by name, and not until the Ninth Enlarged Plenum of the Honan Provincial Party Committee in June 1958 that P'an was formally replaced by Wu Chih-p'u as first secretary of Honan,[127] yet there are some indications that P'an was already out of Honan's political picture by the fall of 1957.[128] Obviously, the "conservative" forces in Honan (and in the nation as well) had lost, and the radicals in Honan led by Wu Chih-p'u had won. As a result, politics in Honan was radicalized and, before long, the repercussions of events there were widely felt on the national scene—a subject we shall return to in Chapter 3.

2

Administrative Decentralization

The Background

China's Communist rulers, like their predecessors throughout Chinese history, have been plagued by the problem of a proper division of power between central and regional or provincial authorities. On the one hand, China is so large and heterogeneous that it has been proven politically unfeasible, administratively inefficient, and economically counterproductive for the central authorities to monopolize all decision-making powers and administer the entire country directly; these are strong arguments in favor of decentralization and of delegating to local authorities discretionary power. On the other hand, the Chinese leaders have been wary of the regionalism and warlordism of China's history and of powerful regional Communist leaders' tendency toward creating "independent kingdoms"; they have therefore been equally reluctant to delegate unrestricted authority to local political organizations. Over more than twenty years of Chinese Communist rule, conflicting political, economic, and ideological pressures have worked for either centralization or decentralization; consequently, the central-local power relationship has vacillated between the two poles.

From the time of Communist takeover in 1949 until 1952, the regime instituted a highly decentralized administrative system. It divided the nation into six so-called Great Administrative Areas covering North China, Northeast China (Manchuria), Northwest China, Southwest China, East China, Central-South China. Except for Manchuria and North China where "peoples' governments" were established, a Military and Administrative Committee was set up in each of these areas as the highest local organ of state power. These regional authorities, headed by top Communist leaders, had substantial power and exercised a significant degree of autonomy; they directed and supervised the work of the provincial-level units within their jurisdiction on behalf of the national government.[1]

Gradually, as the political power of the new regime was consolidated, leaders in Peking began to tighten control over the regional authorities. In November 1952 these regional bodies were abolished and in their places six less powerful Administrative Committees were established.[2] Two years later, these six Administrative Committees as well as the six CCP Regional Bureaus which functioned in the same areas were abolished. Most of the top party or government officials in the provinces were recalled to Peking during 1952–54 to work in the central party or government apparatus. (These leaders included Kao Kang, Li Fu-ch'un, Po I-po, Nieh Jung-chen, Jao Shu-shih, Ch'en Yi, Lin Piao, Teng Tzu-hui, Hsi Chung-hsun, Teng Hsiao-p'ing, Liu Po-cheng, Yeh Chien-ying and K'ang Sheng.)

Other factors also contributed to the rapid centralization of power in Peking. In the economic sphere China's First Five-Year Plan (1953–57), which essentially emulated the Stalinist model of economic development, necessitated centralized planning and execution of major economic programs. Thus the Central People's Government Council (CPGC), in announcing the abolition of the regional administrative machinery in 1954, made the following statement:

> The planned economic construction of the country demands further strengthening of the concentrated and unified leadership of central government. In order to enable the central government to lead the provinces directly, reduce the organizational levels, improve work efficiency, overcome bureaucratism ... and to strengthen the leadership of provinces, the administrative machinery at the levels of the Great Administrative Areas shall be abolished.[3]

Another factor was political. "Independent kingdoms" allegedly created by some regional leaders, notably Kao Kang and Jao Shu-shih, also precipitated the central leadership to do away with the regional bodies and centralize power in Peking. Kao and Jao were based in Manchuria and East China, respectively, during the early 1950s, and in 1953 they headed the State Planning Commission and the Party's Organization Department, respectively. They were said to have attempted to maintain exclusive control over these areas and departments and used them as their bases to "oppose the Central Committee and usurp its authority."[4] The nature of the Kao-Jao incident was apparently a struggle between the regionally-based leaders and the centrally based leaders, particularly Mao's top associates, such as Liu Shao-ch'i and Chou En-lai.[5] Kao and Jao formed an "anti-party alliance" and recruited supporters among the provincial officials. Their factional activities were detected by Mao's top associates in 1953 or even earlier, and a national conference on financial and economic work in the summer of 1953 and a national conference on organizational work in September of the same year had already tried to deal with their challenge.[6] In February 1954 the Fourth Plenum of the Seventh Central Committee, which was presided over by Liu Shao-ch'i in Mao's absence, made the decision to purge Kao and Jao; this decision was then formally approved in a resolution in the National Conference of the Party in March 1955. The Kao-Jao incident tended to strengthen those centrally based leaders who had a vested interest in curtailing local autonomy and thus fostered the tendency toward a higher degree of centralization of control in Peking.

Since then the provinces have come under the direct control and supervision of the central leadership without an intermediate regional layer of government. After the summer of 1960, six bureaus of the party's CC were reestablished to coordinate and supervise the provincial party committees, but no parallel governmental organs at the regional level were set up. The 1954 constitution prescribes a highly centralized unitary system; it vests certain powers in the provinces but the central authorities may revoke them. The provincial government is constitutionally less a self-governing political entity than the administrative arm of the central government, or in the words of the constitution, the local administrative organ of state. The same kind of tight central control also extends to a few outlying border regions, populated by a large number of non-Han minority nationalities, even though the constitution designates these areas "autonomous areas" and their governments "organs of self-government." Under such systems individual departments under the provincial governments (People's Councils) function in many respects like branches of various central ministries.[7]

The Problems of Excessive Centralization

Late in the First Five-Year Plan (1953–57) a centralized administrative system had evolved, because concentration of administrative authority was deemed necessary for unified planning and direction of many economic programs. However, the excessive growth of central bureaucratic power had generated some unanticipated problems, and the Chinese leaders began to call for a readjustment of the administrative powers and functions such as those between the central and local authorities. Liu Shao-ch'i had the following to say on this subject in his Political Report to the Eighth Party Congress in September 1956:

> ... during the past few years, some departments under the central authority have taken too many jobs and imposed too many or too rigid restrictions on local departments and ignored special circumstances and conditions in the localities. Even when they should have consulted with the local authorities, they did not do so. Some departments issued too many formalistic documents and forms, imposing too much of a burden on the local authorities. This not only did not facilitate the work of the local authorities, but dissipated the energies of the central authority and fostered the growth of bureaucracy. ... It is absolutely necessary for

the central authorities to devolve some of their administrative powers and functions to the local authorities.[8]

What had happened was that in the course of the expansion of economy and the socialization of industry and commerce, various industrial and economic ministries in the central government had come to control a large number of factories, mines, and enterprises. The concentration of authority in Peking over enterprises scattered through the country unavoidably gave rise to bureaucratic delays in making decisions and settling daily questions; for instance, permission had to be obtained from the ministries if enterprises were to acquire fixed property worth more than 200 *yuan* (approximately U.S. $100).

Since all lines of command led to Peking, the provincial authorities, limited in the allocation of resources and in management of finance and personnel, were unable to use their own initiative to examine and act upon any assessment of the potentialities of the given area from a viewpoint which transcended interindustrial boundary lines. This particularly impeded the development of provinces that were not favored by central economic planners; thus the majority of large new industrial projects built during the First Five-Year Plan were centered in Hupei (Wuhan), Inner Mongolia (Paotou), Szechuan (Chungking), Kansu (Lanchow), Shansi (Taiyuan), and Honan (Loyang).

The high degree of centralization placed enormous power in the hands of the ministries in Peking and also gave rise to a tendency toward ministerial autarky. This was partly the result of the chronic uncertainties of supplies, which led to the reluctance of any minister to rely on other ministries, so that each set up his own "ministerial" supply base. But another part of the explanation for ministerial autarky lay in the unworkability of the coordinating procedures in the face of the growing complexity of the economy. The burdens of planning and coordination had grown with the growth of the economy itself.[9]

In the words of one Western economist, the high degree of centralization of economic power had caused the system to break down.[10] As a result, there was a gradual devolution of authority to various ministerial "independent kingdoms" and in some cases even to enterprises or local government. This was indicated by Liu Shao-ch'i, who called for proper coordination of the initiatives displayed by the central economic department with those of local economic organizations:

> Some central departments did not pay enough attention to the development and overall arrangement of local authorities ... some local authorities went blindly ahead building and expanding certain industries, regardless of whether there was enough equipment in the country to spare for them, and without reference to the resources and other economic conditions in the localities concerned.[11]

A top-level Chinese economic planning official also revealed that "some areas" decided on major items of capital construction without the approval of the state or of higher levels, diverted raw material from key construction projects of the state, and in some cases even detained materials that were in transit.[12] He added that careless plan formulation, followed by repeated revisions, had resulted in priorities being neglected, as well as in waste of both capital and raw materials and in unbalanced plan fulfillment.

The Initiatives for a Change

In April 1956 Mao spoke of "contradictions" between the center and provinces in an important speech, "Ten Great Relationships," presented to an enlarged Politburo session. Referring to the excessive control of the provinces by the center, Mao stated:

> Now there are dozens of hands interfering with local administration, making things difficult for the region. Although neither the Center nor the State Council knows anything about it, the departments issue orders to the offices of the provincial and municipal governments. All of these orders are said to have initiated from the Center, thus putting great pressure on the regions. Forms and reports are like floods. This situation must change and we must find a way to deal with it.
>
> We must promote a consultative style of work with the regions. Nothing can be initiated by the Center of the Party without having consulted the regions concerned. We hope the departments of the Center will take note of this. Everything must go through the process of consultation before an order is issued, if the matter concerns the regions.[13]

Mao then set forth a principle of "combining centralization of powers with decentralization" to guide the distribution of powers between the center and the provinces, hoping to achieve both "uniformity and individuality." He claimed that the relationship between the central and local authorities was still suffering through lack of experience and suggested that the matter be further discussed, but the speech made it unmistakably clear that he favored the expansion of local power.

What had motivated Mao to champion the expansion of local power, particularly in light of the Kao-Jao affair, is intriguing. Whereas Liu Shao-ch'i and Chou En-lai may have regarded the Kao-Jao alliance as a challenge to their power, Mao did not view it as a direct threat to his own position. There is little doubt that Mao was genuinely concerned with the problems and difficulties caused by excessive centralization. The shortcomings of China's First Five-Year Plan, which was based on the Stalinist model, and the problems arising from centralization of power in the central apparatus were candidly admitted by the CCP leaders themselves and undoubtedly served as an important impetus for change.

Mao's dialectical view of the world was another important factor. Franz Schurmann reasons that because Mao believed in a dialectical process he was convinced that centralism and democracy (decentralization), discipline and freedom, or uniformity and individuality could be combined in a "unity of opposites."[14] In this dialectical view, decentralization was intended to unleash creativity and initiative from below, and democracy could be better served by giving greater scope of freedom to the regions. Here also lies a distinct Maoist strategy of economic development which explicitly rejected the Stalinist model underlying China's First Five-Year Plan and provided an alternative model in which the provinces would be given a bigger role and more initiatives in propelling China's economy forward.

Mao's dialectical view and strategy of economic development along with the shortcomings that existed in the regime's administrative system, however, may not offer sufficient explanation for the subsequent reform and the particular means of that reform. Like many other important changes in economic and political fields in China and elsewhere, the efforts to decentralize power were partly motivated by a genuine need for reform of the economy and administrative efficiency and partly devised (and opposed) by individuals or groups of political actors who had varying interests at stake.

Seen in this perspective, Mao's inclination to sponsor decentralization appears to have been motivated by political considerations: he sought to weaken the power of several top economic officials of the party identified with the central government apparatus who were opposed to his policies and to shift control of the national economy to the provincial authorities who, as evidenced by the dispute over the speed of collectivization the previous summer and fall, were generally responsive to his command. His political tactic was to balance different political groups, to play the provincial forces off against the centrally based leaders.

Mao's identification of the relationship between the central and local authorities as an important issue legitimized open discussion of the problem and obviously boosted those who favored decentralization. Speaking to the NPC in June 1965, apparently in answer to criticism, Premier Chou En-lai promised a "more concrete definition of the division of power between central and local authorities."[15] From May to August the State Council called a series of national meetings to study the question of improving the state administrative system. According to Chou, a draft resolution for improving the state administrative system was introduced into these meetings, and the State Council extensively solicited views from different circles on that plan.[16]

The pronouncements made during the proceedings of the Eighth Party Congress indicate that the CCP leaders had by that time reached a consensus that excessive centralization, which had resulted from emulating the Soviet model, must be changed to allow local authorities a larger role. This was indicated by Chou En-lai's report:

> In the Second Five-Year Plan period, an increasing number of construction projects in the country will be undertaken by the local authorities or completed through the concerted efforts of the central and local authorities. Therefore, to afford local authorities free scope for their initiative is an essential condition for the accomplishment of our socialist construction ... we must and can, in keeping with the principles of unified leadership, level-to-level administration, devising what is appropriate in each locality and in each case, define more clearly the respective sphere of jurisdiction of the central and local authorities, and improve the state administrative system, so that local initiative can have a free scope.[17]

Chou also introduced seven general principles to be followed in the coming reform of the state administrative system, incorporated into the "Proposals for the Second Five-Year Plan" and formally adopted by the Party Congress.

Changes in the administrative system—involving an enlargement of the power of provincial authorities—were proposed in response to the pressures exerted by provincial forces. Inasmuch as the decentralization would have increased provincial control over industry, finances, and economic planning, it no doubt had substantial political appeal to the provincial leaders; therefore they themselves may have pushed for it. The growing political weight of the provincial forces—as suggested by the election of twenty-six provincial officials to the CC in the Eighth Party Congress in September 1956—would have enabled them to exert greater political pressure than before to obtain concessions from the central leadership.

The final decisions in the process of reform were slow to come. Although the CCP leaders agreed in principle that the local authorities must be granted greater powers, they appeared to disagree over the exact way by which decentralization should be instituted. In 1956 and particularly in 1957 different views found expression in various economic journals.[18] In these discussions, each official stressed the merits of his own approach, but their disagreements also had obvious political overtones.

The crux of the debate, in fact, was not merely to find a workable balance between centralized control and decentralized authority but to determine whether the central or local authorities would exercise ultimate power over many matters. Provincial officials naturally pressed for far greater decentralization and for the authority of provincial leaders to control and operate the enterprises in their regions. Economic officials who were entrenched in the state administrative apparatus favored the retention of the ministerial control system; they wanted only a modest decentralization of authority to the provinces and continued reliance on the ministries to give coherence and direction to the economy.

Clearly articulating the views of the central economic officials was an article published in September 1957 by Hsueh Mu-ch'iao, director of the State Statistical Bureau and a vice-chairman of the State Planning Commission. Proposing changes in the economic planning system, Hsueh advocated "big planning combined with small freedoms," a principle which he attributed directly to Ch'en Yun.[19] According to this principle, the central economic coordinating agencies (such as the State Planning Commission and the State Economic Commission) would impose direct control over only a small number of vital economic activities. For the other economic activities not covered by direct central control, either the central economic agencies would only set targets, thereby granting ministries, provincial authorities, and enterprises a greater degree of operational autonomy, or it would allow enterprises a free hand to set targets and formulate production plans according to market situations, and let commercial ministries exercise regulatory control according to supply and demand.

What Hsueh called for was a system of unified leadership at the top and separate management by lower-level authorities, in which various ministries, provincial authorities, and enterprises would all be allowed greater discretionary powers, which was a significant modification of the principles put forth by Chou En-lai at the Eighth Party Congress by which the provincial-level authorities alone would benefit from the proposed decentralization. For the enterprises administered by the central government, the State Council (or the economic coordinating agencies), the ministries concerned, and enterprises should each have their special responsibilities, but the local party-state authorities on the spot would have the right to "supervise" these enterprises. For the enterprises administered by the local authorities, the central government would only provide policy guidance and set broad targets, which the local authorities would be allowed to adjust.

The changes in the economic administration proposed by Hsueh called for simultaneously giving greater decision-making powers to the ministries, provincial governments, and enterprises and substantially reducing the powers of the supreme economic coordinating bodies such as the State Planning Commission and the State Economic Commission in Peking. The ministries, which would then inherit the powers of these top economic coordinating bodies, might benefit most from the new arrangement.[20] The scope of decentralization to the provincial authorities, as proposed by Hsueh's article, was limited. This may have reflected the practical consideration that not all economic agencies in the provinces were staffed with competent cadres capable of planning and directing major economic programs. For example, Yunnan,

Kweichow, and Ninghsia—all among backward parts of China—were at first excepted from taking over certain industries from central ministries on the grounds that their administration was not yet competent to do so. On the other hand, power was apparently at stake; centrally based officials were not inclined to surrender the control of the national economy to the provincial officials.

The approach outlined in Hsueh's article may well have characterized Ch'en Yun's report on the proposed changes in the system of economic administration which was presented to the Third CC Plenum in September 1957. If this was indeed the case—which I am inclined to believe—then the fact that the promulgated regulations embodied principles significantly different from those Hsueh put forth in his article suggests that Ch'en's report was not well received by the Plenum. This body, which devoted much time to examining the reform of the system of economic administration,[21] may have been divided, but a scheme of decentralization different from that proposed by Ch'en was "basically approved" (implying reservations by some CC members). Since Ch'en Yun's report was not accepted, or, at least, his proposal was not adopted completely, his report was not made public either at that time or later.

Much of what happened in the proceedings of the Third CC Plenum remains unknown. There is, however, evidence that there were serious dissensions in the Plenum and that the approval of the revised twelve-year agricultural program and the measures of decentralization, which represented a shift toward the left, came as a result of changes in the balance of power in the CC (as noted in Clashes Between "Radicals" and "Conservatives" at the Third Plenum, ch. 1). The changes were brought about by a coalition of provincial leaders (who demanded a greater decentralization of power to the provincial authorities), Mao and the "radical" group (who were pushing for a radical economic line), and party administrators[22] (who wanted a tighter party control of the government activities and saw a greater decentralization of power to the provincial authorities, in which the party maintained a dominant role, as increasing the party control of the economy and curtailing the power of the central state organs). From the fall of 1957, the party's decision-making councils tended to be dominated by forces identified with the central government apparatus, with only an occasional voice of dissent being heard.

Decentralization Measures

On 15 November 1957 the State Council, acting on the decision of the last CC Plenum, promulgated reforms in the system of industrial, commercial, and financial administration.[23] In the field of industry, the most important change was twofold: the power of provincial authorities was increased by transferring to their control many enterprises previously managed by the ministries of the central government; and the operational authority of the enterprises was increased by reducing the number of their mandatory targets.

Control of industrial enterprises in China was divided between the industrial ministries of the central government and the corresponding organs of local authorities. Before 1957–58, the industrial ministries of the central government (Ministry of Light Industry, Ministry of Textiles, various ministries of Machine Building, and so on) exercised direct control over a great number of factories and mines all over the country. Until 1959 these industrial ministries in Peking were directed and coordinated by the State Council's Third, Fourth, and Sixth Staff Offices, which dealt with, respectively, heavy industry, light industry, and transport and communications; in 1959 they came under the control of the State Council's Staff Office of Industry and Communications under Vice-Premier Po I-po.[24] In the CC of the party, a Department for Industry and Communications Work directed and supervised the work of the state agencies.

By the decree of November 1957, enterprises in consumer goods industries (most of which were then controlled by the Ministry of Light Industry), nonstrategic heavy industry, and "all other factories suitable for decentralization" were to be "transferred downward" to the local (primarily provincial) authorities. Most plants of importance were to be retained under direct control of the central ministries. These included producer goods industries, large and important mining concerns, oil refineries, electricity networks, the national defense industries, and a few other key industries (e.g., paper manufacturing).

The provincial authorities now would not only assume operational responsibilities for a broad range of industries coming under their control, and receive 20 percent of these enterprises' profits, but would also achieve greater influence over centrally controlled enterprises. For the enterprises still retained under the control of central ministries, a system of "central-local dual leadership— with the central authority as the main—is to be followed, and the leadership and supervision by local authorities is to be strengthened."[25] In other words, although the vertical links of the ministries were to be paramount for these centrally controlled enterprises, the horizontal ties to and leadership by authorities on the spot were to be greater than before.

In the provinces and the lower level administrative units, the control and influence of the party committee over the government agencies was very substantial. To transfer control of an enterprise from a ministry to a local authority was to transfer immediate control of the enterprise to the party committee of that local authority. Thus the decentralization of 1957–58 had the effect of greatly increasing the economic power of provincial and other local party committees. Donnithorne and Schurmann, as well as others, have pointed out that horizontal control—control in a particular geographical area—soon became identified with control by local Party committees, particularly in the levels below the province.[26]

In the field of commerce, as in industry, considerable authority devolved from Peking to the provinces and to the local authorities. The Decree on the Reform of the Commercial Management System, promulgated in November 1957, placed a broad range of previously centrally controlled commercial agencies and enterprises under local control. For instance, processing plants belonging to commercial ministries of the central government were, with a few exceptions, to be transferred to the control of the commercial departments of local authorities. Wholesale depots, large refrigeration plants, and granaries were placed under dual central and provincial control, although the central government was to continue to be the senior partner.

The State Council now set fewer and less complex annual targets for commercial work. Profits of enterprises, like those of industries, were, by the 1957 decree, to be divided between central and provincial authorities in the ratio of 80–20; only the profits of grain sales and foreign trade were to go to the central government. Provincial authorities were given the right to set some prices in their areas of jurisdiction.

The specialized corporations which marketed various commodities were to be merged with national ministries or local departments engaged in commercial activities. These changes resulted in a great loss of power for the Ministry of Commerce, which previously had controlled many of the national and local corporations. Now the local corporations were absorbed by local departments, over which the Ministry of Commerce could exercise small influence. In fact, the ministry headed by Ch'en Yun underwent a major reorganization in 1958.[27]

Financial reforms were in line with the general decentralization of economic administration that was introduced at this period, although no major organizational changes were called for. "The major improvement," according to the 1957 directive, was "to clearly and definitely define the scope of revenue and disbursements of local finance, to appropriately enlarge local authority in financial management, and ... to increase the flexible power of local authorities."

Before the 1957 reform, provincial-level authorities in all provinces except Peking, Shanghai, Tientsin, and Liaoning had no significant local sources of revenue and had to obtain grants from the central government to meet their "normal annual expenditure.[28] Their power in financial management was also tightly restricted, authorization from the Ministry of Finance was needed for local expenditure, and numerous items in local budgets were controlled by the central government. The reform now drastically changed the picture; the central government would no longer control each item of local revenue and expenditure, and local authorities would be assigned definite sources of revenue that they would then be expected to use to meet all their normal expenditures.

Three sources of revenue were allocated to the local authorities: fixed local revenue, the local share of profits of state and joint state-private enterprises under the central and provincial government, and the adjustable share of certain revenues.[29] Fixed local revenues were those revenues from the state and joint state-private enterprises already under local control before the 1957 decentralization, several minor taxes, and "other local revenue." The adjustable share of certain revenues to which the local authorities were entitled included commodity circulation tax, merchandise tax, industrial and commercial tax, and agriculture tax. This arrangement was designed to give the provincial authorities greater financial power and improve their financial position vis-à-vis the central authorities as it increased the scope of their initiative. In addition, provincial authorities were authorized to reallocate revenues and expenditures as needed as long as the approved figures for overall balances were not overstepped to the central government's detriment.[30]

Provincial authorities could now levy special taxes and use their own initiative in raising funds by methods they themselves chose, such as issuing bonds, although these methods were subject to approval by the higher authorities.[31] Moreover, central ministries were no longer to transmit detailed financial plans and quotas to provincial-level departments, a provision which, if strictly observed, would curtail the powers of the ministries severely.[32]

During 1958–60, local authorities at all levels appeared to have substantially enhanced their financial independence as a result of the rise in extrabudgetary funds available to them.[33] These funds were items of revenue at the disposal of local authorities (or enterprises) which were not entered in the budgets and which might be used without approval of higher authorities. They were derived mainly from a part of the profits retained by enterprises, major repair reserve funds, supplemental wage funds, and local surtaxes.[34] It was estimated that at the beginning of 1958 extrabudgetary income in general amounted to the equivalent of some 20 to 30 percent of the budgetary revenues of local authorities of all levels; for *hsien* and municipalities, the estimate was 40 to 50 percent, rising in a few cases to as much as 70 percent.[35]

Capital investment reportedly constituted the largest single item of expenditure for extrabudgetary funds. In certain departments in Taiyuan Municipality in 1959, for example, 46 percent of total expenditure from extrabudgetary funds was used for capital investment purposes.[36] Two Chinese writers pointed out that many of the local construction projects undertaken at the time of the Great Leap were financed in this way.[37] Since these funds were invested in new projects largely without prior central approval and in competition with the state's key construction projects for materials, equipment, skills, and manpower, their unsupervised use tended to render economic planning impossible and in many ways contributed substantially to the chaos of the Great Leap Forward.

Going a step further than previous decentralization measures and reflecting the much more radical atmosphere of 1958 was the reform of the planning system which was decreed by a joint party-state directive in September 1958.[38]

The major innovations of the reform were stated in an article in the State Planning Commission's journal *Planned Economy* in September 1958 as follows:[39] (1) the establishment of a new planning system—the "double-track" system—in which local equilibrium was to play a leading role and the ministries and local authorities were to cooperate; (2) decentralized control; (3) strengthened cooperation and coordination; and (4) planning by the central authorities was to cover only the "balance transfer" of major commodities and not the total production in the country.

The previous system of planning, the "single-track" system, had operated primarily on a vertical production-branch basis, with the central ministries holding the dominant position vis-à-vis the provincial authorities in the formulation of the national economic plan. Under this system, the most important "plans of balance" with respect to major commodity branches were compiled by central ministries in charge of the individual commodity branches, and provincial plans were made an adjunct of the plans of the ministries. It was, in essence, a scheme of centralized planning primarily for the benefit of the centrally controlled enterprises, and thus it tended to neglect the interests of the locally controlled enterprises.[40]

The double-track system was designed to effect the "organic integration of balancing by production branches and balancing by local authorities" with the leading role assigned to the local authorities. Thus plans for balancing the supplies and uses of major commodities were to be regionally based, and even the plans of centrally controlled enterprises were to be integrated in the regional plans. Like other measures of decentralization, the new system of planning was based on the principle of dual leadership by both the central ministries and local authorities; however, the horizontal leadership of the territorial party committees was to have priority over the vertical leadership of production branches;[41] thus in determining plans of enterprises in their areas the local authorities would occupy a position superior to the ministries.

The double-track system required the local authorities to compile and coordinate the plans of their subadministrative units (*hsien* and special district) and of the enterprises in their locale. The plan was to be constructed from the bottom up, primarily on the basis of horizontal territorial balances. After the provincial plans had been balanced by the economic cooperation regions, they were to form part of the unified national plan. These successive horizontal balances were to comprise the primary plans; the vertical production-branch plans compiled by the ministries were to take second place. The final national plan would be based on these two types of plan.

According to the directive on planning, only nine "important" items of planning were to remain under central control: the output targets of the most important industrial and agricultural commodities (e.g., steel and grain); total national capital investment, major capital projects, and new productive capacity for important commodities; the balancing and transfer of important raw materials, equipment, and consumer goods; the total state revenues and expenditures, provincial revenue remittances and subsidies, credit equilibrium, and distribution of capital grants; total wages, total number of employees, allocation of manpower at the national level; volume of railway freight and freight turnover; and so on. Other targets, including total value of industrial output, irrigated acreage, total circulation of commodities, and local transport, would no longer be fixed by the central government. They would be decided by the local authorities and the ministries between themselves in planning conferences. Even the centrally controlled targets might be adjusted by local authorities as long as state plans were fulfilled.

Subject to the overall fulfillment of state plans, the provincial authorities were now allowed considerable freedom in rearranging and adjusting output targets, using investment funds, and adjusting both the overall scale of investment and investments in individual projects. In financial matters as well as in plans for labor, commerce, local transport, and education, a similar latitude was to be allowed to the provinces.[42] If state plans were fulfilled for the main raw materials, equipment, and consumer goods, the provincial authorities might distribute these, using their own discretion; this allocation of power to provincial authorities was later extended to cover central government enterprises within their territories.[43]

Before the 1958 reform, the planning system was on a vertical production-branch basis; as noted earlier, the central ministries held the leading position, and they tended to develop an attitude of self-sufficiency. This tendency was reversed after the 1958 reform, but a tendency toward provincial autarky was generated. Under the new system the planning unit was a geographical area—usually a provincial-level unit—and every unit aspired to become as self-sufficient as possible and thus tended to ignore the needs of other units. The resulting disruption of the regular flow of supplies between areas or provinces was extremely serious in 1958–59.[44]

The 1957–58 decentralization of powers from the central government to the provinces was paralleled by a modest decentralization from the provincial level to the special districts (and municipalities) and below them to the *hsien*. The degree of this decentralization probably varied from province to province, for an editorial in *Ts'ai Cheng* (9 June 1959), the organ of the Ministry of Finance, complained that some provincial-level authorities were giving too much financial responsibility to special districts and *hsien*. As a result of decentralization of control over enterprises, *hsien*, like the provinces, divided certain revenues with higher level authorities[45] and thus derived a high portion of their revenue from profits and taxes of industrial and commercial enterprises; for example, 70 to 80 percent of the revenue of one *hsien* in Honan was reported to come from such sources. The financial position of the *hsien* authorities was further improved by the rise in extrabudgetary funds since 1958, which offered more initiatives to the *hsien* in economic activities.

For control over many agricultural functions and other economic activities the province was, of course, too large a unit, thus the leadership of the *hsien* and municipalities was increased in activities such as those relating to demonstration farms, water conservancy campaigns, and other small-scale industrial programs. During 1958–59, the leadership of the *hsien* over local industries was encouraged and given wide publicity by the regime;[46] in fact, the development of local industries was termed one major strategy that would make possible a great leap forward in industrial development.[47] At a lower level, the communes, which were established in China's rural areas after the summer of 1958, were urged to become self-sufficient units, and they exercised considerable power at the local level.

The amount of power exercised by the subprovincial authorities probably varied considerably between provinces, and there were intraprovincial variations in size and in management and distribution systems of communes. A great latitude was given to these subordinate authorities in 1958, particularly in the field of agriculture.

The decentralization that was implemented in 1958 was quite different from, and more drastic than, what was reflected in the three regulations issued in November 1957. As originally envisaged, the decentralization transferred considerable power to the provincial authorities, but the central authorities continued to retain a very high degree of control over economy. Furthermore, the decentralization measures were to be carried out "step by step," and changes in the administrative system would be tried in 1958 and then thoroughly carried through during the Second Five-Year Plan.[48] However, as the radicals' grip on the party's policy-making machinery became tighter in the winter of 1957–58, and the position of the conservatives became weaker, gradualism and caution were discarded. Hence at the Nanning and Chengtu conferences in the first quarter of 1958, both called by Mao and attended by selected Politburo members and provincial party secretaries, new decisions resulted in decentralization proceeding more quickly and covering a larger scope of activities.[49] For instance, whereas the decree of 1957 stated that for the time being only a few textile enterprises were to be decentralized, by June 1958 all factories in the textile industry were reported to have been transferred down to the local authorities. The same decree also stipulated that most plants of importance in the producer goods industries were to be retained under direct control of the central ministries, but decentralization in heavy industry in 1958 was also reported to have covered a wider range of enterprises than indicated by the original directive. Thus some 80 percent of the enterprises and institutions controlled in 1957 by the economic industries of the central government had been handed over to the provincial-level authorities by the end of June 1958, and the share of the locally controlled enterprises rose from 54 percent of the industrial value produced in 1957 to 73 percent in 1958.

The Consequences of Decentralization

The foregoing decentralization measures greatly expanded the powers of the provincial authorities. The declared purposes of the 1957–58 reform in industrial administrative systems were to "suitably enlarge" the authority of provincial-level units over the management of industry, and to "suitably enlarge" enterprise personnel's managerial authority. The reform was different from Hsueh Mu-ch'iao's proposal, which advocated, as noted before, a limited decentralization to provinces and enterprises but retained strong ministerial powers.

If these provisions had been strictly implemented, enterprise managers would have enlarged their powers, counterbalancing the new power of provincial authorities—who then might not have accumulated the immense powers that they did.[50] However, as a result of the anti-rightist movement in 1957–58, enterprise managers, most of whom were regarded as "bourgeois rightists," were subjected to heavy political attack, and the powers that they might otherwise have exercised devolved into the hands of enterprise party committees, under the control of the provincial party apparatus, in a spirit that was called "politics takes command."

Thus provincial authorities—particularly those in control of the party apparatus—not only assumed control over the enterprises assigned to them but also extended their powers, through the system of central-local dual leadership, over the enterprises in their areas which were still under central jurisdiction. They acquired greater power over allocation of resources and target-setting as well as greater control over personnel, including those working in centrally controlled enterprises. In addition, the assignment of definite sources of revenue to provincial authorities and the new measures allowing profit-sharing significantly improved the financial position of the provincial authorities. However, it is impossible to generalize on a nation-wide basis; the extent of provincial autonomy varied greatly. Which enterprises were to fall within provincial jurisdiction and the degree of provincial authority over those still under central ministries varied; provinces varied in resources and in efficiency; and some provinces benefited from the decentralization measures more than others. The relative positions of central ministries and provincial authorities depended on the ministries and provinces concerned, on the enterprises involved, the matters at issue, and the personalities involved.[51]

The chief victims of the decentralization—in terms of loss of influence—were the various industrial and commercial ministries which lost many of their powers; clearly the central government apparatus as a whole was considerably weakened in its role in economic affairs. Early in 1958, the State Council carried out a sweeping reorganization by merging and abolishing many of its ministries and directly affiliated agencies, in an intensive drive called "structural simplification." Many cadres in the State Council were transferred down to work in the provincial and lower level organs or to take part in physical labor in 1957–58. The number of ministries and other agencies was reduced from forty-one and twenty-four in 1957 to thirty-one and fifteen in 1958–59.[52]

The 1957–58 decentralization fostered tendencies toward provincial self-sufficiency and localism: as the province became the most important unit of economic planning in the national economy, each province attempted to construct an independent industrial complex within its borders.[53] This development, coupled with the unsupervised use of extrabudgetary funds in capital construction, resulted in keen competition for materials and equipment, which, in turn, led to a virtual breakdown in the allocation system and in transport. Hence the uncertainties of supply made it more necessary than ever for each province to try to become self-sufficient, disregarding the needs of other provinces.

Given these decentralization measures, some degree of localism or departmentalism was probably inevitable; this was the cost to be paid for "bringing local initiative into full play."[54] In fact, the problems of localism or departmentalism were not unanticipated, and the Chinese Communists initially seemed confident that these problems could be overcome by "strengthening the Party's leadership"[55] and by the coordination and supervision of several interprovincial agencies known as the "economic cooperation regions." In 1957–58, after the provincial authorities were given greater control over the economy, the party purged many provincial leaders who were accused of deviations of localism, ensuring that the provinces would not use their enlarged power to challenge the center.

The control of the party, unlike that of the central government, was not decentralized. Many official statements stressed the unified leadership of the party over industry and other economic activities.[56] The central party leadership, however, failed to foresee that the provincial party secretaries, who were supposed to be agents for maintaining the party's centralized control over the provinces, would become identified with the administration of their provinces; they often displayed "departmentalist" tendencies, defended the particular policies and interests of their own areas, and found themselves impelled to advance their provinces' interests in negotiation with the central government or other provinces.[57]

Another important measure—the creation of the regional coordinating bodies designed to supervise the provinces—was not effective, either. Late in 1957 the Chinese leaders had divided the country into seven large "economic cooperation regions," each embracing several provincial-level administrative areas. Each region was intended to be an administrative mechanism between center and province.[58] Each "economic cooperation region," according to a joint party-state directive issued in September 1958, was to plan and coordinate economic activities of the provinces under its jurisdiction as well as develop an integrated complex of industry, enterprises, and institutions dealing with industry, agriculture, commerce, and education within its borders.[59] By this directive, economic coordination and increased self-sufficiency were to be achieved at the regional level, not within provinces.

However, the economic cooperation regions, during the brief period of their existence, apparently did not possess and could not develop a meaningful administrative structure to handle the task originally assigned to them.[60] The scheme of economic cooperation regions seems to have been discarded by the party in early 1959, for nothing more was heard of them after this. Thus no effective regional economic coordinating agencies appear to have functioned during 1958–59, when decentralization and the Great Leap Forward attained their fullest support. Insofar as the range of political authority was a determining factor in economic decisions, economic coordination and cooperation as well as considerable economic self-sufficiency tended to develop at the provincial level.

The far-reaching decentralization carried out after the fall of 1957 seems to have contributed in many ways to the economic crisis in China from 1959 to 1962. The decentralization drive coincided with the Great Leap Forward movement. Mao believed the Chinese economy could not be operated as a single entity from Peking, and provinces must be assigned a bigger role in propelling the economy forward. In fact, decentralization was regarded as one of the strategic developments that would make the Great Leap Forward possible.

The forceful implementation of the Maoist strategy of economic development after 1957 gave the provincial authorities a greater control over the economy; they then undertook many initiatives in economic construction, including some that were irrational and ill-conceived. Since economic planning (i.e., control) had been decentralized and no effective regional coordinating bodies existed, undesirable tendencies displayed by the provincial authorities, such as the construction of independent industrial complexes within the provinces and the unsupervised use of the extrabudgetary funds in capital construction, were not checked for a long while. The cumulative effect of these developments was an excessive economic overexpansion and "overinvestment" or waste of resources.[61] As a result, the development of China's economy was retarded and the image of the CCP leadership was severely tarnished.

3

Communization in China's Countryside

The Prelude

As noted in Chapter 1, the Third CC Plenum revised the twelve-year agricultural program. Despite some modifications, the program as a whole was very ambitious and unrealistic. It now appears that the passage of this program signaled the party's switch to a radical line in economic development strategy. The new line, however, was not immediately translated into a new and full-scale economic drive. Although a large-scale irrigation and water conservancy campaign was launched soon after the Plenum, it differed little initially from the regular routine campaign conducted annually at the end of an agricultural season. The Chinese leadership itself appeared to be somewhat uncertain as to what ought to be done. Their uncertainty could be detected in the first *People's Daily* editorial on the revised draft program, which did not appear until 27 October 1957, eighteen days after the Third CC Plenum was closed. The editorial was ambiguous; it restated various targets of the draft and dutifully endorsed the revised draft program, but it failed to call for specific action.

Some cadres which seemed to have misgivings about the revised draft program resisted the idea of another "reckless advance." This was suggested by several articles written by members of provincial cadres stressing the need to overcome "conservatism" when implementing the draft program.[1] Furthermore, cadres in the APC's, *hsiang*, and even *hsien* were found, to the dismay of the central leadership, to have become too closely identified with the interests of their local communities and the peasants.[2] Unless something drastic was done, so the Chinese leadership reasoned, the party could not expect its new policy to be effectively implemented.

Uncertainty regarding Soviet aid in China's Second Five-Year Plan also may have been a factor in the delay in implementing new policies; at that time the Chinese Communists appeared to be unsure of the nature and extent of the economic assistance they would obtain from Moscow. It is now generally believed that Mao did not secure a new Soviet credit or other economic assistance when he made his second trip to Moscow in November 1957.[3] This could have removed some elements of uncertainty Chinese leaders felt concerning the new economic strategy and reinforced Mao's own belief that new measures to achieve a breakthrough in agriculture were more necessary than ever if China was to continue to step up her exports to finance her industrial imports and to repay her debts to the Soviets.

In any case Mao, soon after his return from Moscow in the second half of November, left Peking and traveled extensively in the provinces. In the course of his tours, he attended provincial party congresses in Shantung and perhaps other provinces.[4] He also held several regional meetings with provincial officials in which he may have actively promoted his new economic line and sought support.[5]

Struggle in the Provincial Party Hierarchy

The party's policy of political liberalization in the first half of 1957 (i.e., the "hundred flowers") and its sudden reversal in the summer of the same year (the "anti-rightist" movement) had produced much confusion among party members, who were already, it seems, divided over the question of the "correct" agricultural policy. The provincial party congresses held soon thereafter, in the winter of 1957–58, provided forums in which the leadership could put forth an official interpretation of recent events, defend the consistency of the party's handling of the rectification campaign and the ensuing anti-rightist campaign, and attempt to unify party members' thinking.

A report on Shanghai's Municipal Party Congress, held in December 1957, is very revealing. At this congress "some" party members were reported even to have challenged Mao's views on "contradictions among the people":

> The session accorded adequate discussion to the current domestic situation and the principal contradictions during the period of transition; it leveled criticism at the erroneous ideas cherished by some Party members. These members, since the victory in the anti-rightist struggle, had questioned the correctness of the direction of correctly handling the contradictions among the people. They described as "rightist" some of the Party's basic policies: the policy on intellectuals, the united front policy of "long-term coexistence and mutual supervision," and the policy of "letting all flowers bloom together and diverse schools of thought contend."[6]

Whereas some criticized rightist deviations in politics, others had misgivings about the leftist tendency in economic policy. In his report to the municipal party congress K'o Ch'ing-shih, the secretary of the CCP Shanghai Bureau and the first secretary of the Shanghai Municipal Party Committee, said:

> Some of our comrades have thought that our work in Shanghai has

"advanced recklessly" in all branches. . . . They have maintained a view diametrically opposed to that of the Party. They regard the revolutionary attitude of achieving "more, faster, better and more economic results" as "recklessness" and "love for pre-eminence and ostentatious achievement. . . ."

So we must criticize such rightist conservatism, because it has already caused us some damage. Since the second half of last year, 1956, there has been little mention of the policy of "more, faster, better, and more economic results," plans based on the National Agriculture Program have not been carried out with the same vigor and enthusiasm, and the revolutionary zeal for work of many people has subsided. This is really abnormal.[7]

Paraphrasing Mao's preface to the *Socialist Upsurge in China's Countryside*, K'o said that the problem now was the interference of rightist conservatism from many directions and that many things thought impossible would become possible if only adequate efforts were exerted, and he introduced a slogan: "Join the group that promotes progress, don't join the group that promotes retrogression."

K'o may well have been one of the first regional party secretaries to join "the group that promotes progress" and give enthusiastic support to Mao's policy, for a few months later he advanced to the Politburo ahead of six other Politburo alternates. K'o's report was prominently featured in the *People's Daily*, and an editorial note stated that the issues and questions raised in the report had nation-wide significance.[8]

Indeed, the problems discussed in K'o's report were not unique to Shanghai; provincial first party secretaries in some other important provinces were preoccupied with the same problems and sang the same tune in their party congresses.[9] In these congresses, those who questioned Mao's rectification policy, and particularly those who questioned the radical new economic policy, were bitterly attacked. In the winter months of 1957–58, the more moderate elements in the party were silenced, although perhaps not convinced, and the political climate in the nation became radicalized.

The Socialist Education Movement

Even before the Third Plenum, the countryside was caught up in an intensive "socialist education movement." From the Eighth Party Congress, the press emphasized the need to rectify cadres' commandism and bureaucratism, and the "correct handling of contradiction among the people" was a main theme of propaganda in the spring and summer of 1957. One of the three directives of 14 September 1957 contained instructions for APC cadres to rectify their work styles to placate the peasants and avoid commandism. The Third CC

Plenum changed this policy. Teng Hsiao-p'ing's "Report on the Rectification Campaign" did call for the rectification of the cadres, but the emphasis shifted to education for socialism, that is, intensification of the ideological indoctrination of the rural population and cadres.[10]

Under the previous policy stressing material incentives and concessions to the peasants, the influence of the well-to-do middle peasants and rich peasants had increased in the countryside, or in the jargon of the Chinese Communists, the struggle between the two roads—socialism versus capitalism—in the countryside had become very sharp. The purpose of socialist education, according to Teng Hsiao-p'ing, was to win over the peasants to the socialist road and to criticize the bourgeois ideology of the prosperous middle peasants. Socialist education was to overcome their influence, as well as expose and counterattack the alleged sabotage carried out by the landlords, rich peasants, and "bad elements."

Before the socialist education movement could be launched, the party decided that local cadres must first undergo ideological remolding. Many local cadres were found to be tainted with rightist ideology and, worse, were too closely identified with the interests of the peasants. For instance, there had been widespread criticism by cadres in Shantung and Kwangtung of the unified grain purchase policy; they said "it resulted in the peasants' shortage of food," "it squeezed too much out of the peasants," "the amount of food rationed for the peasants is too little, not enough to eat," "the government drove the people to rebellion"; many cadres allegedly adopted an attitude of "rather resisting the government than offending the peasants."[11] These cadres also complained that collectivization was proceeding too swiftly; they said "the APC was not really superior," "the advanced APC was worse than the elementary one, the elementary APC was worse than the mutual team, and the mutual aid team was no better than independent farming."

According to a survey in Tu Hsien in Shantung, of 882 cadres surveyed, 10–15 percent were opposed to the unified grain purchase policy, 10 percent considered the amount of grain rationed to the peasants to be insufficient, and 30 percent exaggerated the damage done by natural calamities, reported more people than they really had in the APC's, or concealed the amount of grain actually produced, thus permitting the APC's to deliver less to the state and distribute more among their own members.[12]

The extent to which persuasion is emphasized as a means of enforcing the party's policies has been an outstanding characteristic of China's political system. This point was clearly illustrated by a series of so-called three-level and four-level cadres' conferences held in various provinces during October 1957.[13] In these conferences of local officials, expression of dissenting views was encouraged. It was not that the Chinese Communists supported principles of unrestricted free discussion but rather that they believed it would be better to have "negative" opinions openly expressed. Once expressed they could then be discredited and refuted by means of "positive" arguments, and the people holding wrong ideas could then be educated and rectified.

Reports of these "free debates" reveal the defects, shortcomings, and "contradictions" thought to exist by those who actually implemented the party's policies. It is questionable whether the cadres who criticized the policies of collectivization and unified grain purchase were genuinely convinced by the official lines of argument used to justify these policies. Nevertheless, the Chinese Communists were willing to take the trouble to conduct "debates" and by this means to try to remold the doubting cadres' thoughts, a policy whose origin lies in the Chinese leaders' almost mystic faith in ideological remolding and attitudinal change as well as their adherence to the "mass-line" technique of leadership.

After these cadre conferences, meetings were held in the APC's to educate peasants in socialism; the "landlord" and "capitalist" elements were attacked, and the peasants were subjected to intensive indoctrination. The following report from Honan is typical of what happened in many provinces:

> In pursuance of the directive of the Party's Central Committee regarding the rectification campaign, a general debate was conducted in the cities and countryside [of Honan] as to the two roads—socialism or capitalism, repulsing the onslaught of the bourgeois rightists, landlords, rich peasants, and counter-revolutionaries, and overcoming the spontaneous tendency towards capitalism among the well-to-do middle peasants. The people were thus enabled to distinguish right from wrong on major issues, draw a clear line between the enemy and themselves, and see more clearly the necessity of pulling down the white flag of bourgeois ideas and hoisting in its stead the red flag of proletarian ideology. ... [14]

The Hsia-fang Movement

Coupled with the socialist education movement was the *hsia-fang* movement, the "transfer down" of cadres from higher to lower levels of authority. The *hsia-fang* movement proceeded gradually, beginning after the Eighth Party Congress in September 1956; the anti-rightist campaign and the decision of the Third CC Plenum gave a special impetus to the movement. For instance, at the end of October 1957 the Liaoning Provincial Party Committee convened a conference of municipal and special district party secretaries which decided, in accordance with "the spirit of the Third CC Plenum," to transfer down 200,000 cadres by April 1958. The Kirin Provincial Party Committee also held an enlarged plenary meeting which transmitted the "spirit of the Third CC Plenum" and approved plans to simplify organizational structures and to transfer down 100,000 cadres by April 1958.[15]

The motivations of *hsia-fang* were varied and complicated: the party wanted to cut down overlapping organizations in the state machinery and reduce superfluous staff to improve administrative efficiency, it wanted to reduce administrative expenses, and it wanted to keep cadres in contact with the masses. In addition, the party intended to reform the "rightist" technicians and intellectuals through labor; in the aftermath of the anti-rightist campaign, the rightists were bitterly attacked and sent down to the front line of production. Most of all, the party wanted to strengthen its leadership of the lower levels.

Since many local cadres were thought to have identified too closely with local interests, and to be unresponsive to the commands of the party, the *hsia-fang* movement in some areas may have been aimed primarily at replacing local cadres with "outsiders," thereby checking any trends toward "localization." A series of reports on *hsia-fang*, released by various provinces, stressed the aim and the achievement of strengthening the leadership in lower and basic party and governmental organizations. For instance, in Honan province 5000 cadres were sent down from the *ch'u* (district) level to take over the leadership posts of *hsiang* (administrative villages), and at least three ch'u-level cadres were assigned to each *hsiang*.[16] In addition, 61 special district-level cadres were sent down from the provincial and special district party committees to the *hsien* (county) level to strengthen the party leadership at that level. Most of them became *hsien* party secretaries, and in 52 *hsien*, or 61 percent of the total, the post of *hsien* first party secretary was assumed by cadres newly transferred down. In Kwangtung, among the 180,000 *hsia-fang* cadres, 30,000 were sent down to basic units to strengthen "the leadership over agricultural production."

The developments sketched above—the anti-rightist campaign, the socialist educational campaign, the attacks on the party's moderate elements in the provincial party congresses, and the *hsia-fang* movement—silenced critics of the party's new radical policy and increasingly radicalized the atmosphere in the country. The radical atmosphere was accentuated by a so-called two-anti (anti-waste and anti-conservatism) campaign launched in the first quarter of 1958. A party directive on this campaign equated conservatism with waste; it instructed cadres to immediately do away with "obsolete" norms and systems that would hamper production and challenged cadres to "think and act" bravely to invent new ways and new models to promote a great leap in every sphere of work.

These campaigns gradually laid the political and ideological ground for the Great Leap Forward in the winter months of 1957–58. At this stage, however, measures that would be used to bring about the Great Leap had probably not yet been formulated in detail, although the concept of some sort of a big push—especially a breakthrough in agriculture—had already become evident soon after the Third CC Plenum. In many respects it was the moves toward implementation of the twelve-year agricultural program which set in motion a series of developments that led to communization and the subsequent disastrous reversals resulting from the Great Leap Forward.

The Initial Stage of Communization

The Twelve-Year Agricultural Program as a Catalyst of the Communes

The core of the twelve-year agricultural program was, as noted earlier, to step up agricultural production. The program set output targets of 400, 500, and 800 catties of grain per *mou* for three regions in the nation, and 40, 60, 80, and 100 catties of cotton per *mou* for four regions. It also set production targets for other areas of work. To accomplish these goals, the peasants were expected to improve and construct irrigation and water conservancy facilities, gather manure and accumulate fertilizer, adopt "advanced" farming methods such as deep plowing and close planting, carry out soil improvement, and undertake ten other measures designed to increase agricultural production. The key to success was total mobilization of labor for these purposes.

The APC's provided the Chinese Communists with a handy mechanism for the control and mobilization of labor. Moreover, the cadres could use this mechanism to support various construction projects through allocation of APC resources, in the form of public accumulation funds,[17] and by organizing labor to work on these projects and to launch other campaigns.

When the draft program was introduced in 1956, most of the APC's were in the process of being established, the cadres were preoccupied with organizing and consolidating the APC's, and attempts at mass mobilization could be undertaken only on a limited scale, although even this limited mobilization resulted in charges of "reckless advances" on many fronts in the first half of 1956. When the revised draft program was adopted in 1957, collectivization was complete, 97 percent of the peasant households were in the APC's, and the party had consolidated its control in the rural areas. There was therefore considerable truth in the claims made by Chinese Communist officials that the system of collectivization was one of the best ways of implementing the National Agricultural Program.[18]

In December 1957 the Communist regime called several national conferences to discuss methods of implementing the program. The aged Chu Teh, then vice-chairman of the PRC and a member of the Politburo Standing Committee of the CCP, who had rarely involved himself in agricultural matters, came to the fore and argued vigorously for the twelve-year agricultural program in these conferences. Several main ideas emerged from these meetings: the need to emphasize overall planning (to combat "departmentalism") in work, the need for the party committees at various levels to take full command and tighten control, the need to rely on local material and financial resources, and the need to mobilize the peasants on a large scale.[19]

The first measure that embodied these lines of action was the water conservancy campaign, in the winter of 1957–58. By the end of 1957 more than 60 million peasants reportedly had been mobilized to construct irrigation and flood control works. There had been a debate among the cadres as to whether small- or large-scale projects would be emphasized, and this debate carried broad economic and political implications. There were some who argued that the large-scale projects would be more economical in terms of investment, manpower, and resources, and that water conservancy work required technical knowledge; therefore, such people argued, the enthusiasm of the masses could not supplant the necessary technology.[20]

Large-scale projects, however, could be implemented only with investments from the state, and the Chinese leadership was not willing to divert to the agricultural sector resources heretofore channeled into industry. Thus small-scale projects were to be emphasized, enabling "the state to spend little money and to rely on the masses."[21] The rationale, according to T'an Chen-lin, was that small-scale projects best fitted the principle of achieving "more, faster, better, and more economical results."[22] Since they could be built in a shorter period of time with the local resources—especially the manpower—of the APC's, they were "more and faster"; since they could be expected to produce quick economic returns, from the viewpoint of production, they were "more economical, hence better." The small-scale projects did not demand much technological knowledge, therefore "politics" could take command, and the party cadres could mobilize the peasant masses to work in a water conservancy campaign of unprecedented magnitude.

The peasants were also mobilized to work in many crash programs which, like the irrigation and water and soil conservancy campaigns, were designed to bring about a great leap in agriculture. There were energetic programs for fertilizer-accumulation, expansion of double and multicrop acreage, soil improvement, deep plowing, close planting, pest control, land reclamation, the improvement and manufacturing of farm tools and machinery, and so on.

Campaigns to build and expand local industries went hand in hand with campaigns to increase agricultural production. For instance, construction projects such as dams and flood control works needed cement, pumps, equipment, water mills, and other irrigation instruments; land reclamation and other farm work required more plows, farm implements, and agricultural machinery. The local authorities, maximizing the use of labor and mobilizing all available domestic resources in the spirit of thrift and economy, built and operated tens of thousands of small factories in areas such as iron and steel (including backyard furnaces), machine shops, power generation, coal extraction, and fertilizer production as well as in the more traditional textile and food processing industries.[23]

Small and medium-sized industries were emphasized because they would "spend little money, do many things and bring about quick economic returns."[24] The rationale was based on a strategy of economic dualism, officially termed "walking on two legs" in Chinese Communist pronouncements. The bulk of the modern sector's final product would be exported or reinvested and used for its own continued expansion and growth; very little would be diverted into the agricultural sector.[25]

On the other hand, the growth of the rural sector was to rely "on the masses," that is, on local resources. Labor-intensive small-scale industries would be developed by using simple, locally manufactured equipment, local labor, and local raw materials. A typical example was the construction of more than 600 dams in Antung Hsien of Liaoning by using straw and sand to substitute for rolled steel and cement, a "feat" that was given wide publicity. The development of local industry would absorb rural surplus labor[26] and lower the cost of transporting raw material to urban industrial centers; in addition, the products of local industries could be used to satisfy rural demands for consumer goods, tools, agricultural machinery, and other requisites of farm production. The proliferation of local industries was facilitated by the decentralization of economic decision-making in many fields after 1957. The transfer of authority over a number of industrial and commercial enterprises to the provincial and *hsien* governments (where the party was in an increasingly dominant position) placed economic planning functions under greater local party control. This enabled "politics to take command" and the initiative of the masses to be given full play, while the professionals and technicians were further restricted in their activities.

Thus China had in effect adopted a new formula for economic development. During the First Five-Year Plan, China applied the Stalinist development strategy with some modifications, so that industry, especially heavy industry, was emphasized at the expense of agriculture. But since the Chinese economy depended so heavily on agriculture, the neglect of investment in the agricultural sector slowed the growth of industry. After the dispute within the party as to whether more resources should be channeled into agriculture in order to effect a more balanced growth in the economy, a strategy evolved, after much debate and improvisation, which would permit and foster the simultaneous development of agriculture and industry.

The Amalgamation of the APC's

As various crash campaigns simultaneously unfolded, many problems emerged. Labor shortages became apparent; the APC's were too small and their administrative structure inadequate to meet the situations created by the water conservancy campaign and later by the Great Leap Forward. Local cadres began to experiment with different solutions in a spirit of the new slogan: "One must dare to think and act."

Women were mobilized to take part in physical labor in the fields, mess halls, nurseries, and other institutions for collective living which began to be organized to save time and free women from household chores; new work organizations were tried as peasants were organized into specialized "squads" or "brigades" to carry out the same tasks (such as rice-planting or ground-preparing) in one field or village after another.[27] One measure that had a most important effect was the enlargement of the size and expansion of the functions of the APC's. The amalgamation of APC's, which started in March 1958, was a major step toward the subsequent communization, although the establishment of communes per se may have not been envisaged at this early date by provincial and lower officials.

The size of the APC's had been a matter of controversy within the party for years. Mao was known to have advocated a larger organization; his favorable editorial comments in an article "On the Superiority of the Large Co-ops" often were quoted by cadres to justify the enlargement of the size of APC's. In September 1957, however, as noted earlier, a CC directive instructed cadres to break up large APC's and restricted their size to 100 households.

The APC was originally conceived as an economic organization primarily engaged in agricultural production. In the course of development, however, it steadily expanded its scope of activities and, in many cases, began to compete with the government of the *hsiang* in exercising certain functions.[28]

In the summer of 1957, cadres in Fukien made an attempt to have the APC's absorb banking and commercial functions from the Credit Co-ops and the Supply and Marketing Co-ops by merging these three kinds of co-op into one single unit [*San she ho yi*].[29] The Credit Co-ops were basic units linked to the People's Bank at the *hsiang* level, and the Supply and Marketing Co-ops were the lowest unit under the All China Federation of the Supply and Marketing Co-ops. The rationale for the merger was to effect better coordination among them; with the two other institutions under the direct control of the APC's, "departmentalism" would be eradicated and harmony would prevail in all their work.

The proponents of the merger reported that many contradictions existed among these three independent units at the basic level. The Credit Co-ops often urged peasants to deposit money when the APC's were encouraging peasants to invest their money in the APC's; the Credit Co-ops, because of their special financial responsibilities, often did not respond to applications for agricultural loans when the peasants were in need. Moreover, the Supply and Marketing Co-ops maintained too rigid a standard in their purchase of local products, the merchandise they carried often did not cater to the needs of peasants, and their location and office hours were sometimes inconvenient for the peasants.

To resolve these "contradictions," the Party Committee of Ch'ing Chiang Special District in Fukien dispatched an ad hoc work group to Nanan Hsien to test the amalgamation. The results of this experiment were reported in the *People's Daily*. An editor's note accompanying the report suggests that the central authorities were not at that time particularly enthusiastic; the note termed the amalgamation a new "working method" but pointed out several problems that would arise, including changes in the command systems of each. The paper also solicited opinions from those engaged in rural work; several articles expressing conflicting views were subsequently published in the *People's Daily*. The idea of amalgamation along these lines apparently evoked little interest in Peking at the end of summer 1957, for thereafter nothing more was said about it (although, as will be noted below, the experiment continued).

However, by the spring of 1958, as a result of the massive water conservancy campaign of the previous winter and other efforts at implementing the revised draft program, the motivation for reducing the size of APC's and checking the expansion of the functions of the APC's had significantly changed. The development of numerous crash campaigns in agriculture and local industry demanded increasing supplies of manpower and resources, which most of the APC's were unable to provide. It was argued that "localism" on the part of the APC's was not conducive to overall rational planning of the water conservancy programs, that many irrigation projects constructed separately by the APC's were small and inferior in quality, and that in many cases the frequent disputes among the APC's and among *hsiang* concerning land and water adversely affected the progress of their work.

Under these circumstances, neighboring APC's, *hsiang*, and even *hsien* learned to pool resources, take concerted actions, and institute unified planning and management to build dams, reservoirs, and other construction projects. Cadres in several localities began to ask for the expansion of the APC's; for instance, at Szekutun Hsiang of Shanchen Hsien in Honan, fourteen APC's were merged into four larger APC's in March 1958, although this move was not publicized at that time.[30] Expansion of the size of the APC's was designed to solve the problems discussed above and to strengthen the party's control in rural areas by cutting across the local ties of APC cadres who allegedly had too close an identification with the interests of their own groups or communities.

In early March 1958, an *NCNA* dispatch from Fukien reported that one year of experimentation in the amalgamation of the three kinds of co-op [*San she ho yi*] in Lientang Hsiang of Nanan Hsien produced impressive results, and the Fukien Provincial Party Committee summed up the experiences and decided to popularize them throughout the province. This *NCNA* dispatch was carried by *Ta-kung Pao* (13 March 1958) but, surprisingly, not in the

People's Daily, which suggested that the central authorities still had some reservations. During the month of March, *Ta-kung Pao* continued to publicize the news of *San she ho yi* in other provinces, but the *People's Daily* was conspicuously silent.

On 2 April the *People's Daily* ended its silence on the subject of merging various co-ops and endorsed the idea by headlining the amalgamation of the APC's, the Credit Co-ops, and the Handicraft Co-ops in Shansi Province. The turning point may have come at a meeting of regional officials in Chengtu sometime in March, when Mao made a "suggestion" to provincial officials to combine small APC's into larger units.[31] No formal decision on merging the APC's was taken in this conference, but Mao's "suggestion" probably added impetus to the trend. Some provincial officials, perceiving Mao's favorable attitude, proceeded to enlarge the APC's even before formal steps were taken in this direction.[32]

In early April 1958, for instance, cadres in Fukien merged three *hsiang* into one large *hsiang* and twenty-three APC's into one very large APC; on 12 April the *People's Daily* approved such a move for the first time, in headlines on the first page. In late April more than 3000 APC's in Lu Hsien, Szechuan, were merged into some 700 large ones, with the average membership of each increasing from 60 to 250 households. Meanwhile, Honan's Hsinyang Special District Party Committee set up, on a trial basis, a large APC of 6000 to 7000 households in both Suip'ing Hsien and P'ingyu Hsien. The enlarged Weihsiang (Sputnik) APC of Suip'ing, which soon was claimed to be China's first commune, was formed out of twenty small APC's in four *hsiang* on 20 April 1958; when this was merged with seven more APC's in late June, the commune embraced a total of 9369 households.[33] In May and June small APC's of the two *hsien* were gradually amalgamated into larger units. Similar actions were taken in Liaoning in May.

The amalgamation of the APC's laid the groundwork for later moves toward communization. The Chinese Communists, in fact, claimed that the communization movement started in the spring of 1958, although many elements of the commune system had existed before that time.[34] On the other hand, however, it is not certain whether the Chinese planned communization at this early date. It now appears more likely that many policy actions were taken on an ad hoc basis and were based on improvisation and reactions to unanticipated problems, that the full implications and consequences of these actions were not clearly foreseen or totally grasped at the time, and that communization progressed piecemeal rather than being planned in advance.

The Enactment of the Great Leap Forward

In an enthusiastic, radicalized atmosphere, the Second Session of the Eighth Party Congress met in May 1958 and approved the party's new "General Line for the Socialist Construction," thereby officially launching the Great Leap Forward. The Leap had actually started a few months earlier; in fact, the NPC session of February had called for a "Great Leap Forward," demanding a huge increase in the production targets of many main branches of industry. These targets then were scrapped and raised repeatedly.

Before the opening of the Party Congress, Mao traveled extensively in the provinces for several months to promote his radical line. He came into personal contact with, and may have won support from, various provincial secretaries, seven of whom were subsequently promoted to the CC at the May session.[35] In the Fifth CC Plenum immediately following the party congress, K'o Ch'ing-shih and Li Ching-ch'üan, first party secretaries of Shanghai and Szechuan, respectively, and T'an Chen-lin, a secretary of the CC Secretariat specializing in agricultural affairs, were elevated to the Politburo, advancing over six alternate Politburo members.[36] Lin Piao, a member of the Politburo, was elected a member of the Standing Committee of the Politburo and vice-chairman of the CC of the party.[37] Two of the top economic officials, Li Fu-ch'un and Li Hsien-nien, who were also members of the Politburo, were added to the Secretariat, presumably coopted by Mao to help implement his new economic policies.

Although proponents of the Great Leap policies were firmly in control of the party, a significant number of party officials in the center and in the provinces, vaguely identified by the press as tide-watchers [kuan-ts'ao p'ai], account-settlers [suan-ch'ang p'ai], and retreat-promoters [Ch'u-t'ui p'ai], had questioned and sometimes directly opposed the wisdom of the party's embarking on the radical course. The opposition to the party's policies was considered significant enough that Liu Shao-ch'i took a clear note of it and devoted an extraordinary amount of attention to the critics of the Great Leap policies in his keynote speech to the May session of the Party Congress.[38]

According to Liu, "some comrades" had opposed the line of rapid collectivization in 1955 and had charged that the leap forward of 1956 was a reckless advance"; they had misgivings about the principle of "more, faster, better, and more economically" as expressed in the twelve-year agricultural program; and in 1957 they had dampened the initiative of the masses, thus hampering progress, particularly on the agricultural front. The introduction of the revised draft program in the Third Plenum, Mao's militant call to overtake Britain in production, and the mass initiative evoked by the rectification and anti-rightist campaigns led to an all-round leap forward, and many of those comrades who had expressed misgivings had "learned a lesson." But, Liu added: "Some of them have not yet learned anything. They say 'We will settle accounts with you after the autumn harvest.'" Liu challenged the critics to await the autumn harvest for the results of the new policy by saying: "Well, let them wait to settle accounts, they will lose out in the end."

There was further evidence of inner-party opposition in mid-May 1958, when ten provincial first party secretaries wrote a series of articles in the *People's Daily* attacking the conservatism of "some cadres" who allegedly refused to believe in the possibility of a rapid economic progress and opposed an all-round leap forward.[39] These provincial secretaries adopted a posture of all-out support for the Great Leap and tried to persuade others to make intense efforts to bring it about. If the conservative cadres were not convinced, they were at least intimidated and silenced by purges carried out in early 1958.

In the provinces, many "rightist" officials were expelled from the party or dismissed from their leadership positions in this period. These provincial purges, most of them reviewed by the Party Congress in May, covered twelve provinces. The purge victims included four alternate CC members, one provincial first secretary, eighteen members of standing committees of provincial committees, five provincial secretaries, ten members of provincial committee secretariats, four governors, and ten vice-governors, as well as approximately twenty-five other officials holding important party or government positions at the provincial level.[40] In almost every purge differences over rural policy were involved, and in seven of the twelve provinces it was apparently the most important policy issue. In eight provinces charges of localism were also leveled against the purge victims.

In the center there was no open purge, yet the influence of those who had argued for a cautious approach seemed to be considerably undermined. Vice-Premier Teng Tzu-hui, concurrently director of the CC Rural Work Department and of the State Council Agriculture and Forestry Staff Office, and hitherto the regime's top spokesman for agricultural affairs, was pushed into the background; although he was not formally deprived of his positions, at least some of his responsibilities were taken over by T'an Chen-lin, who now outranked him in the party hierarchy.

The influence of Ch'en Yun, and possibly the influence of Chou En-lai as well, was weakened in 1958.[41] Both had been critics of the "reckless advances" of 1956—and thus indirectly were critics of Mao's collectivization drive and the draft twelve-year agricultural program. Their reports to the Third CC Plenum in the fall of 1957 were not published, and they may have advocated a material incentive approach which clashed with Mao's approach. They may even have opposed the decentralization measures pushed through in the Third Plenum, whose implementation considerably weakened the central government apparatus and transferred much of the power to direct the national economy to the party cadres at local levels. For opportunistic or other reasons, three top economic officials, Li Fu-ch'un, Li Hsien-nien, and Po I-p'o, who formerly articulated conservative viewpoints, now changed their tactics and took the lead in promoting the Great Leap policies.

Against the background of the radical trend in the policy-making councils, the second revised draft of the twelve-year agricultural program was formally approved by the Party Congress in May 1958, and it was scheduled to be officially enacted by the NPC in 1959. In the mood of the Great Leap Forward, new targets were adopted and many earlier targets were raised upward.

The 1958 version of the draft program was never published, despite the fanfare it received in the summer of 1958. The revisions made at the time are known only through T'an Chen-lin's explanatory report.[42] According to T'an, targets for the production of oil-bearing crops were added to the existing production targets; the yields on products such as ground nuts, rapeseed, and soya beans were to be doubled or tripled by 1967; the target of 40 catties of cotton per *mou* for some areas was raised to 60 catties, thus restoring the original goal set in the 1956 draft. A separate article was now devoted to close planting. This "advanced" experience, after being tested in some localities with what one report called "spectacular" results, was to be emulated throughout the nation. T'an admitted, however, that "close planting" "has often run up against resistance from conservative and backward ideas." Therefore the enactment of a separate article in this connection was to "give greater impetus to the popularization of close planting."

The principle of mass mobilization and maximization of the use of local resources was also formally written into the program. According to T'an, in the section on water conservancy, "three emphases" (emphasis on small-scale projects, on water storage, and on APC resources) were inserted to give that policy greater prominence. The article on mechanization and electrification is said to have been redrafted. There is no way of knowing how the article was rewritten, however, since the text was never made public. One source suggests that the changes came as a result of Mao's intervention.[43] At the Chengtu Conference of March 1958 a policy document entitled "Opinions on the Problem of Agricultural Mechanization" was formulated on Mao's initiative, and it was later approved by the Politburo. The document is said to have called for the mechanization of agriculture through the massive manufacture of small machinery by local industries and through reliance on local economic strength. In a similar vein, T'an Chen-lin stated in May 1958:

> The new version of mechanization reflects the great mass movement to improve farm implements now being used in the Country. It takes into account the possibility that semi-mechanization and mechanization of agriculture may be realized through the expansion of small-scale local industries, and it makes the point that the budding technical revolution in agriculture is a stepping stone to semi-mechanization and mechanization.[44]

An important amendment was also made to the provision regarding education. Agricultural middle schools were to be established on a large scale in the countryside by using local APC resources, and "work-study" education programs were to be actively promoted. The Chinese Communist regime had undertaken a reexamination of its educational system in late 1957 and early 1958, and one of the main conclusions reached by the authorities was that the government, central and local, could not afford the tremendous expenditures required to achieve the regime's educational goals.[45] The regime therefore decided that the only realistic course to follow in pursuing its goals was to assign the major part of the task of establishing and running schools in the countryside to the APC's. Accordingly, a rapid establishment of great numbers of *Min pan hsueh-hsiao*, or "schools run by the people," took place in late winter 1957 and early spring 1958. A dispatch of the *NCNA* on 10 June 1958 said 61,000 such schools had been set up between February and May 1958.

Honan as a Pacesetter

The newly revised draft program made no mention of the communes, the new type of rural organization which was to emerge in China's countryside shortly thereafter; it is not clear whether the Party Congress in May discussed the establishment of this new form of rural organization. However, various elements of the commune system, including new institutions for collective living (such as the public mess halls, nurseries, and sewing teams), new methods of organizing labor (such as labor armies and specialized labor brigades), and trends toward the amalgamation of APC's into larger units, had already developed in the countryside before the spring of 1958. A central party directive on merging the APC's issued in May gave a further impetus to cadres to enlarge the APC's.[46]

The province of Honan was the pacesetter in the amalgamation of APC's; later it also played a significant and leading role in bringing about China's communization. Honan's prominent role in these events can be attributed to two factors.

The geographic factor is very important. Honan is crisscrossed by several major river systems, the Yellow, the Huai, the Wei, and their tributaries; rainfall in the province reaches a maximum in July, with virtually all the precipitation occurring from May through September, and floods have been frequent.[47] In fact, both in 1956 and in 1957, Honan suffered severe floods, causing serious damage to crops and properties. Drastic steps would therefore be necessary to control the floods and reduce their damage in the future. Thus Honan was in the forefront of the water conservancy campaign in the fall and winter of 1957–58,[48] and in October and December of 1957 two national conferences concerning the campaign were held in that province.

Between fall 1957 and spring 1958, 8 billion cubic meters of earth and stone had been moved in water conservancy projects (whereas only 360 million cubic meters were moved in the previous eight years), and the area of irrigated land had been extended from 4.3 to 17 million *mou* or 86.6 percent of arable land of Honan. At the peak of the campaign, as many as 10 million peasants were organized to work on various irrigation and flood control projects in that province. Peking publicly praised Honan as "the province that has made the most rapid progress in the current mass water conservancy program."[49] Thus Honan succeeded through concerted organization and use of its large population (over 44 million in 1958) combined with its relatively high incidence of natural calamities.[50] The unusual degree of organization that was introduced into the countryside to undertake the tasks of the Great Leap also laid the groundwork for the later merger of APC's. A revealing example was provided by a 9 May directive of the Honan provincial authorities:

> Collaboration shall be worked out between *hsiang* and *hsien*, among APC's and brigades and teams, between mountainous regions and the plains, and between cities and villages. . . . All APC's shall make due arrangements for living requirements of their members during May and June. . . . Headquarters for directing the summer harvest and cultivation shall be established in all administrative districts, *hsien* and *hsiang* to unify the forces available and to bring about concerted action.[51]

In response to this directive it was reported on 20 May that "organizations have been set up in all parts of the province to direct the summer harvesting and sowing work. . . . Creches, babycare groups, sewing groups, temporary mess halls, and centers for old people have been set up to enable more peasants to be free from domestic chores."[52] It was clear that by wheat harvest time in late May the countryside of Honan had been turned into what Hofheinz called "a veritable honeycomb of local organizations."

In addition, the factional struggle in the politics of Honan, discussed in Chapter 1, was another major factor making Honan the cradle of the communes. The conservative First Party Secretary P'an Fu-sheng, who had been on sick leave since 1954 and returned to Honan in the spring of 1957, attacked the leadership of Wu Chih-p'u, the second party secretary and governor, who had ruthlessly established collectivization in Honan. P'an and his followers later broke up many large APC's, reversed extreme measures implemented by Wu, and instituted some "capitalist" measures to give peasants incentives for agricultural production.

The provincial leadership of Honan was thus divided into two major groups, one led by P'an, who favored a moderate rural policy emphasizing material incentives for the peasants and opposing a rash approach toward collectivization, and the other led by Wu, who advocated the opposite. Besides policy differences, the conflicts between these two top provincial officials in Honan were probably exacerbated by their personal feud. Whereas P'an was the superior of Wu in Honan (P'an came to the Honan Provincial Party Committee in 1953 and replaced Wu as the senior secretary there), Wu became a full CC member after September 1956, outranking P'an, who was only an alternate CC member. The accusations that P'an violated the principle of "democratic centralism" by relying on his two confidants (who had served under P'an before their transfer to Honan in 1953), disregarding the regular party decision-making organs, at least suggested that factionalism was an element in the politics of Honan.

As pointed out at the end of Chapter 1, the ascendancy of the "radicals" in the CC after the Third CC Plenum in September 1957 enhanced the position of Wu Chih-p'u and his followers in Honan and enabled Wu to gain an upper hand in his struggle with P'an. Thereafter, Wu Chih-p'u was virtually in control of Honan's policy-making and P'an was absent from Honan for "health" reasons, although his disgrace was not publicly revealed until the Party Congress in May 1958.[53]

Changing the guard in Honan probably generated pressure on cadres in that province to enlarge APC's. The motivations for doing so were mixed and complicated. Some cadres were composed of real activists, mindful of the favorable attitude of the provincial authorities. Members of other cadres were sensitive to the new atmosphere in the provincial capital and aware of Wu's attitude, perhaps wanting to play it safe and please the new boss. Officials at all levels in Honan, who might have had misgivings about the establishment of large APC's consisting of several thousand households, might well have been afraid of being linked with the "rightist-leaning" conservatism of purged P'an Fu-sheng and might have thus felt compelled to go along with their colleagues or even subordinates who dared to "think and act."

A "suggestion" to merge the APC's made by Mao at the Chengtu Conference in March 1958 probably reinforced Wu's own inclinations and was immediately acted upon. In Wu's own account, Honan had already started a large-scale amalgamation of small APC's in April, and in the following two months it assumed the proportion of a mass movement. When small APC's (each of which generally coincided with a natural village) were merged into larger units, and when work organizations were changed in response to new tasks assumed by peasants in the spring and summer of 1958, changes in the existing APC administrative framework were unavoidable.[54] The new type of rural organization—in the form of the commune—was soon introduced by the Chinese Communists.

The Establishment of the Communes

The Crystallization of a New Concept

In the summer of 1958, the Chinese Communists had created *Jen-min Kung-she*, or People's Commune, a new economic, social, and political unit in China's countryside. The reasons they chose the name People's Commune to designate the newborn organization are not totally clear. The word commune was used by the Chinese Communists before—when they staged an uprising in the city of Canton in December 1927 they set up the Canton Commune, which lasted for three days. However, the more likely source of inspiration is the Paris Commune of 1871, which was specifically compared to the People's Commune by Chinese officials in 1958.[55] It is well known that the experience of the Paris Commune fascinated the Chinese Communists,[56] and they may therefore have adopted the term to honor their romanticized image of the Paris Commune.

If the word commune was indeed borrowed from the Paris Commune, the concept of the People's Commune bore no resemblance to the source. In fact, the concept was articulated gradually over a period of several months. When Mao spoke to the Chengtu Conference in March 1958, there were several striking passages in his speech which suggest that he may have already had various features of the new system in mind at this early date. There is, for example, Mao's call on those present to study and think boldly about such issues as "the law of value," the private ownership of property, the role and future of the family, and the future "Communist distribution relationship of to each according to his need," all of which were issues prominently featured in the discussion of the commune system in the summer and fall of 1958.[57]

In late spring and early summer the concept of commune was refined further by Ch'en Po-ta, Mao's brain-truster. The first hints of the crystallized concept of the future organization appeared in the third issue of *Hung Ch'i* on 1 July 1958. Using the example of a small APC (Hsukuan No. 1 in Hupeh), Ch'en Po-ta urged other APC's to emulate this APC's methods of building and managing small industries by "transforming a co-op into a basic-level organization of agricultural and industrial cooperation, namely forming a People's Commune which combines agriculture and industry."

A more elaborate conception of the commune appeared in another article by Ch'en in the following issue of *Hung Ch'i* (16 July 1958). Entitled "Under the Banner of Chairman Mao Tse-tung," Ch'en quoted Mao:

> Our direction is to combine, step by step and in an orderly manner, workers (industry), peasants (agriculture), businessmen (exchange), students (culture and education), and soldiers (military) into a large commune, which is to constitute our nation's basic social unit. In this kind of commune, industry, agriculture and exchange are the people's material life; culture and education are the people's spiritual life which reflect their material life. The total arming of the people is to protect this material and spiritual life.

And Ch'en added his own statement: "Mao Tse-tung's thoughts on this kind of commune are the conclusion he has derived from the experiences of real life."

For the first time, a succinct statement of a new type of sociopolitical organization was forcefully put forth. These lines, written by Ch'en Po-ta, *Hung Ch'i's* chief editor, who was also reputed to be Mao's personal secretary and ghost writer, and printed in the party's most authoritative theoretical journal, could not be taken lightly. They probably reflected the fact that Mao's ideas about the commune system had crystallized to a large extent by that time.

Mao's decision (it was apparently his decision, not that of the party) to establish communes, meanwhile, was being passed down to provincial officials in mid-July 1958 by T'an Chen-lin, who attended the regional conference in Chengchow.[58] This was confirmed later by a correspondent for *Hung Ch'i:*

> The original purpose of the cadres in Hsinyang Special District (Honan) in amalgamating the APC's was merely to create a larger unit in order to facilitate construction. When they attended the meeting in Chengchow, comrade T'an Chen-lin told them the ideas of comrade Mao Tse-tung and the CC on integrating industry, agriculture, commerce, education, and militia into a large commune. Since then, they have begun to call [enlarged APC's] "communes."[59]

It thus seems probable that *Weihsing* (Sputnik) commune was formally established in July, probably after this meeting, and not in April as is often assumed.[60]

Provincial officials also indicated that they had not thought in terms of establishing a new rural organization in the form of communes before Mao instructed them to do so. Referring to what had occurred in the spring and early summer of 1958 in the countryside—the merger of APC's, changes in the methods of organizing labor, new institutions for collective living, and the expansion of local industries—Wu Chih-p'u wrote in *Hung Ch'i* (no. 8, 1958):

> This was, in essence, already the start of the movement for People's Communes. But people were not yet aware of the real nature of this development. *Only after comrade Mao Tse-tung gave his directive in July, 1958 regarding the People's Communes did they begin to see things clearly,* realizing the meaning of this new form of organization that has appeared in the vast rural and urban areas, and *feel more confident and determined to take this path.* (Emphasis added)

Party officials of other provinces made similar statements giving credit to Mao for pointing out the new direction of agricultural development—that is, communization.[61] Before totally committing himself Mao decided to take a good look at the countryside, and in the first half of August 1958 he visited the rural areas of Hopei, Honan, and Shantung.

On 6 August 1958, Mao, during a tour of Honan, inspected the Ch'iliying

Commune and its facilities; the commune was said to have been established "according to Chairman Mao's instruction." The press carried a vivid and detailed report of Mao's activities, and recorded this interesting conversation:

> Chairman Mao smiled and said to Wu Chih-p'u: "Secretary Wu, it looks very hopeful! I wish all of Honan were as good as this." Wu Chih-p'u said: "If there is one commune like this, then there will be many other communes like this." Chairman Mao said: "Right. If there is a commune like this, then there can be many more."[62]

Mao appeared to be impressed and pleased by what he had seen. On 9 August he visited a Shantung village; in the course of a briefing, when he heard that Peiyuan Hsiang was ready to set up a large collective farm, he said: "It is better to set up the People's Commune. It has the advantage of integrating agriculture, industry, trade, education and militia, and is easier to lead."[63] This seemingly casual remark was headlined in the *People's Daily* and became a "go-ahead" signal for many cadres, who began to prepare for communization even though this new form of organization had not yet been formally authorized by the party's legitimate decision-making organs.

The Formal Authorization

On 17 August 1958 the Politburo of the CCP held an enlarged session at Peitaiho, a summer resort not far from Peking, to consider, among other things, the question of communization. On 29 August the Politburo formally passed a resolution to institute communes in the rural areas—a historic decision which subsequently plunged China's national economy into a process that resulted in serious dislocations. What motivated the Chinese Communists to embark on the communization program? Why did a collegium of rational leaders authorize a social and economic change of such vast magnitude with little advance planning or preparation?

Ideologically, the communes symbolized a spurt ahead toward the ultimate goal of a Communist society. Since the spring of 1958, the prevailing atmosphere within Chinese society had tended to encourage the idea that Communism was just around the corner, and at least some Chinese Communists apparently regarded the commune system as a quick steppingstone into their utopia. The influence of ideology on the decision to institute communes is indicated by the 1958 Peitaiho Resolution, which termed the communes "the best form of organization for the attainment of socialism and gradual transition to Communism."

There were undoubtedly more practical considerations underlying the commune decision; the commune system was seen by its proponents as a solution to various problems that existed in the APC's. One of these problems was so-called localism or departmentalism, which many APC's had displayed: the APC's were concerned only with their interests, to the exclusion of the interests of other APC's and even of the state. For instance, a state farm near Peking with an abundant water supply refused to let a neighboring APC share its water, and the APC retaliated by digging a deep well near the state farm, thus drying the water supply of the state farm.[64] An experimental team from Peking University planted some valuable fruit trees on the land of an APC, but the APC workers ploughed them up to make way for food crops. And there were many other disputes among the APC's over the land and water resources.

The unprecedented massive water conservancy campaign of 1957–58 and the Great Leap Forward drive had imposed many new tasks on the APC's; the APC's, generally small in size and meager in manpower and resources, found themselves unable to meet the requirement of new circumstances. For example, forty-eight APC's in Hsiachia Hsien of Honan, in response to the call of the water conservancy campaign, had independently constructed some eighty small projects along both banks of the Tanshui; but due to lack of manpower and inability to mobilize enough resources, these projects, poor in quality, were subsequently destroyed by floods.[65] Elsewhere some APC's had iron ore but no coal, while others had coal but no iron ore, and their work was hampered.

Each of these was a minor irritation of a local nature, but hundreds of thousands of APC's throughout China had the same problems, creating serious trouble for the central leadership, which was committed to bringing about a great leap in industrial and agricultural production. Thus the commune decision may be seen as an attempt to meet immediate needs: communes which merged small APC's into larger units aimed at solving conflicts of interest among the APC's and at providing a more efficient mechanism to organize labor and mobilize local resources on a large scale and for overall planning and management.

Furthermore, the commune system was an essential component of Mao's Great Leap strategy, the strategy of "walking on two legs." The surplus garnished from the modern section of the economy would be reinvested and used for the continued expansion of that sector, whereas the rural sector was to rely on itself and the local resources for growth. Labor-intensive small-scale industries would be developed as well as operated by the communes using simple, locally manufactured equipment, local labor, and local raw materials. Thus the commune system may be seen as an economic control lever for resource mobilization and allocation as well as an instrument for rural industrialization which would make the Great Leap Forward possible.

To a certain extent, military considerations affected the decision to set up communes because some Communist leaders, particularly Mao himself, seemed to believe that the communes would enhance China's defense capability in a "people's war." Following the enlarged session of the Military Affairs Commission of the party in June 1958, which criticized those who favored foreign military theory and discarded the party's own revolutionary traditions and experiences, there was a renewed emphasis in the PLA on people's war and the party's military traditions.[66] The revival of the militia in the summer of 1958 and, to a lesser degree, the militarization of the peasantry coincided with this development. Apparently Mao saw the communes as the ideal framework within which the militia could be organized.[67] Thus the communization became connected, even if only indirectly, with questions of military strategy and national defense.[68]

These were probably some of the considerations underlying the decision of the Chinese leadership, and particularly Mao himself, to embark on the course of communization. Mao and some of his supporters in the provinces appear to have forced the hand of the Politburo. Before the Politburo met in Peitaiho on 17 August, communization had already been in full swing in some parts of China, particularly Honan, Liaoning, and Hopei; this fact and Mao's endorsement of the new system, which was widely publicized in the press, as noted earlier, tended to present a *fait accompli* to the Politburo, which had no alternative but to give formal sanction.

Chinese official statements made it clear that the Peitaiho Politburo Resolution on Communes was based on Mao's proposal. We do not know whether Mao's Politburo colleagues, particularly those who had persistently advocated a moderate policy in the past, genuinely favored such a course of action; however, none of them spoke directly against the decision to set up communes at that time.[69] The structure and functions of communes were among the topics that came under prolonged discussion in the Peitaiho Conference, which lasted two weeks, from 17 to 30 August,[70] but it appears that very little advance planning had been made to communize the countryside on a nation-wide basis.

Beginning in 1959 P'eng Teh-huai and other Chinese Communists criticized the commune movement, saying it had been launched too hastily, and indeed the suddenness of the 1958 commune decision stood in striking contrast to the debate, experimentation, and preparation that preceded the collectivization campaign of the mid-1950s. Possibly Mao had become more assertive in 1958 following his disappointment with the overcautiousness or conservatism of his colleagues. Or after the collectivization drive of 1955–56, in which Mao achieved what generally had been considered impossible by most of his Politburo colleagues in the summer of 1955, Mao may have become "dizzy with success" and hence tended to underestimate the difficulties involved in the communization campaign. It is also possible that other CCP leaders, including those who attacked the commune system later, did not regard the commune decision as irrational or disastrous in 1958 and did not anticipate that the commune system would so severely affect agricultural production in the following years.[71]

P'eng Teh-huai provided a clue to the thinking of the CCP leadership in the summer of 1958. Many top officials, including P'eng, fell victim to the party's own propaganda as they were misled by the rosy—and grossly exaggerated—reports of bumper harvest in China at the time of the 1958 Peitaiho Conference and mistakenly believed that the grain problem had been solved.[72] This ill-founded optimism, in P'eng's opinion, was largely responsible for the premature introduction of the free supply system, symbolized by the slogan "eating rice without pay" [ch'ih-fan pu-yao-ch'ien], which developed much extravagance and waste and raised false expectations. Thus the optimism about the food supply—which was not borne out by reality later—had, to some extent, affected the thinking of the Chinese leaders when they approved the commune resolution at the 1958 Peitaiho Conference.

The Peitaiho Resolution on Communes, published in the *People's Daily* on 10 September, almost two weeks after its approval, was a curiously vague document. It formally designated the new rural organization the "people's commune" [jen-min kung-she], although it had been called by many different names in different localities. It also outlined some broad principles for organizing and administering the communes, but these guidelines were too general and imprecise to be useful for local cadres in an innovation of such vast magnitude. This would further suggest that the Chinese Communists, even those who had earlier had a vague concept about this new form of rural organization, had not carefully planned the commune movement in advance. In fact, several months after the Peitaiho meeting, the central authorities were still unable to provide detailed operational instructions to cadres about the form, structure, and functions of communes.[73] Consequently, local cadres were compelled to improvise and make their own decisions; disorder and confusion arose from divergent practices in different communes and different localities regarding the size, structure, and system of ownership and distribution.

One week before the Peitaiho Resolution was published, the *People's Daily* of 4 September published the charter of the Weishing (Sputnik) Commune in Honan Province and an accompanying editorial designed to provide some guidance to cadres on how to set up a commune. The experience of establishing the commune system in Honan had received by far the largest share of publicity in the national papers between mid-August and mid-September 1958.[74] Examples of organizing and running the communes in Honan were publicized as models to be emulated by other provinces. It appears that cadres in Honan had provided Mao and other proponents of the commune system with a rough blueprint of an operative commune.

Thus policy regarding the commune system was not formulated by the top leadership alone; rather it was the product of interactions between the top leaders and local cadres. Policy could not be formulated by single decisions, however fully considered. A vast number of lesser decisions accompanied the basic ones, and the way in which each basic policy was carried out also affected its substance. The decision to launch the communes was made at the center; however, local cadres had already, on their own initiative, taken actions moving in this direction (i.e., changes in labor organization, collective life, and the amalgamation of APC's). Provincial cadres and particularly those in Honan had consequently provided some ideas relevant to the concept and management of a "commune," which inevitably affected the decision made by the top leaders on communization.

Establishing the Communes

During the enlarged Peitaiho Politburo session which met from 17 to 30 August 1958, and particularly in the period immediately following the meeting, the press, radio, tatzepao [wall posters], and all other mass media were mobilized to launch a propaganda campaign on communization. The mass media served not only as an instrument of persuasion to stimulate enthusiasm and mobilize the support of the masses for the commune system, but also as an important channel of official communication through which the party could quickly disseminate orders, instructions, and other official directives to local cadres to publicize those practices and examples designed to be emulated and popularized.

While the propaganda campaign was launched in the mass media, the party's channels of internal communication—meetings, official correspondence, and so on—were also employed to communicate specific instructions regarding communization from central to provincial and then to local authorities. Provincial first secretaries were present at the enlarged Peitaiho Politburo Conference; in the proceedings there they were informed of the party's new policies and of the thinking and intentions of the top leaders. Even before the official Politburo resolution to establish the communes was made public, some of the more "activist" first secretaries had already acted.

The Hopei Provincial Party Committee issued a directive to cadres in that province to organize communes on 29 August, the same day that the Politburo resolution on the communes was approved.[75] Three days after the Politburo conference opened, the Fukien Provincial Party Committee called a telephone conference of secretaries of special district, municipal, and hsien party committees in the late evening of 20 August. Kuo Liang, secretary-general of the Fukien Provincial Party Committee, "transmitted" the instructions of the Central Committee and of the provincial first party secretary, Yeh Fei (who was still in Peking), to organize the communes on a large scale.[76]

In most provinces, however, instructions filtered down to lower authorities only after the Politburo Conference had been concluded. Hupeh and Shansi Provincial Party Committees held meetings on 4 September to direct the work of and make arrangements for communization in their provinces. The Kwantung Provincial Party Committee's Rural Work Department sponsored a meeting of the directors of the Rural Work Departments of Special District Party Committees from 30 August to 1 September; this was designed to study "practical problems involved in organizing the communes and to make arrangements for setting up the communes on a trial basis."[77] Meanwhile, written directives were also issued by the Szechuan and Chekiang Provincial Party Committees, and these provided more detailed and specific guidance for implementing communization than did the Peitaiho resolution.[78]

Communization in Chekiang

The processes by which communes were established in Chekiang can be reconstructed from published materials.[79] Hangchow, the provincial capital of Chekiang, was an urban center surrounded by suburban districts where a high percentage of the population were peasants engaged in agricultural production. After Honan's communes and Mao's favorable remarks on organizing communes were publicized in the *People's Daily*, the Rural Work Department of the Hangchow Party Committee began to prepare for communization in its rural areas.[79] It sent cadres to Honan and other places that had already established communes to learn their experiences; at the same time, it began to organize "*shih-tien*" [experimental] communes in six *hsiang*.

Lungch'ing, Suanglin, Tangnan, Liangt'u, Choupu, and Chien Chiao were chosen as experimental sites not because they were typical *hsiang* but rather because they were not. These *hsiang* had strong and talented leadership; their cadres were able to plan the establishment of communes in addition to managing production; the level of consciousness of the masses was reported to be high; and the size of these *hsiang* was relatively small, ranging from 2500 to 3500 households; moreover, each of these *hsiang* contained a market town.

On 29 August 1958 (the day the enlarged Politburo meeting at Peitaiho passed the resolution to set up communes in the rural areas), Communization Work Teams dispatched by the Hangchow Party Committee arrived at these *hsiang* and started to work. A propaganda campaign, its content and methods already mapped out by the Propaganda Department of the Chekiang Provincial Party Committee, was launched to "liberate human thought," to elevate the class consciousness of the masses, and to establish the superiority of the commune system, which was said to be the steppingstone to an ideal Communist society.

All available resources and means, including local newspapers, wall posters, tabloids, loudspeakers, propaganda teams, theatrical groups, movie teams, and mass meetings, were mobilized to saturate the masses with intensive propaganda. Mass meetings were held in each APC to "debate" typical questions: Can we do better in the (agricultural) production? How can we do it? Do we want to set up a commune? What are its advantages? Can we sucessfully manage it?

In these "debates," according to *Chekiang Jih-pao*, different shades of opinions were expressed and the peasants gained a good education, elevated their understanding, and voluntarily called for the establishment of communes. Subsequently, tens of thousands of "petitions" to set up communes and "applications" to join them were prepared by the peasants and presented to their *hsiang* party committees.

By 9 September each of these six *hsiang* had organized one commune, and the work of experimentation had come to an end. From 16 to 19 September the Hangchow Municipal Party Committee called a four-level cadre conference attended by more than 1100 cadres from the municipality, *Ch'u*, *hsiang*, and APC's.

The conference was devoted to studying party documents, such as the Politburo Resolution on Communes, directives of the CC and the Chekiang Provincial Party Committee, and the relevant editorials of the *People's Daily*. In the course of studying documents, APC cadres' tendencies of "departmentalism" and "individualism" (manifested in misgivings toward forming communes with less well-off APC's) were criticized, and cadres undertook criticism and self-criticism. As a result, the cadres' Communist consciousness was said to have been raised, and it was claimed that they became convinced of the necessity and superiority of the commune system.

The experiences of organizing the six initial communes then were summed up in writing by the Municipal Party Committee and distributed to the cadres for study in meetings. Through this device, the officials in the Hangchow Municipal Party Committee tried to show lower cadres how to implement the party's policy of communization and directed the attention of cadres to specific problems encountered during the "*shih-tien*" phase.

For instance, the efforts of cadres to set up a commune in Liangt'u *hsiang* met with a cool reception from the peasants as the cadres there failed to stress the economic benefits that would immediately follow the establishment of the commune. On the other hand, the experiences of Suanglin *hsiang* were singled out for praise and emulation because party cadres there allegedly relied on the mass line method and fully mobilized the masses to take part in the "debates"; these cadres appear to have kindled a certain degree of enthusiasm among the peasants through promises of great economic progress and benefits.

The conference also discussed and plotted detailed programs for communization and production for various localities, made concrete arrangements for their execution, and assigned cadres to the communes which were to be set up thereafter. As soon as the conference was concluded, cadres went back to their posts and started to organize communes on a large scale.

Despite local variations, the methods and procedures for organizing the communes appeared to be fairly uniform throughout China.[80] In the beginning, a few communes were to be set up on a trial basis; these were called *shih-tien* [spot experiments]. In these experiments, techniques of operation and organizational forms for the communes were tested, modified, refined, and "perfected." Experience gained in this process was then "summed-up" and popularized so that cadres in other places would benefit from these "advanced" experiences and apply them to organizing the communes in their own localities.[81] Much valuable experience could be gained from this leadership technique. By setting up experimental communes, the party could concentrate qualified talent on a few spots to work out, through trial and error, techniques of "social engineering" suitable for use on a vast scale. The operational methods thus devised and "perfected" could then be followed by less imaginative or competent cadres in other areas. This approach not only demonstrated operational know-how to cadres in a mass drive but also helped persuade the laggards. Liu Shao-ch'i had perceived the susceptibility of the masses to persuasion as early as 1939, when he prescribed the following:

> In our work we should break through at one point to give an example to the masses and let them see and understand things by themselves. Only by giving demonstrative examples to the masses can we encourage them, particularly the intermediate and backward elements, by affording them the opportunities and facilities to understand the problems, thereby instilling in them confidence and courage to act under our Party's slogans and to culminate in an upsurge of mass enthusiasm.[82]

It must be pointed out, however, that the "*shih-tien*" technique has very little in common with the concept of scientific experiment as generally understood in the West. "Spot experiments" were undertaken by the Chinese to disarm opposition and win acceptance for party policy, to polish, to perfect, and most of all to demonstrate certain organizational methods. There was no attempt to find out whether the measure under experimentation could really work in all localities. As pointed out earlier, when the Hangchow Municipal Committee picked six *hsiang* in the suburbs of the city in which to organize communal *shih-tien*, the "samples" it chose were not typical or ordinary *hsiang* but rather were chosen because they were atypical.

The formal government machinery seems to have played a secondary role in the course of organizing the communes, since it was rarely mentioned in the press. Rather, it was the party that took charge of the operation. As in many previous mass campaigns, the party organization, from the province down, would first set up an ad hoc "Communization Campaign Office" and assign special personnel (usually party secretaries) to take responsibility for planning and directing the campaign in a given area.[83] The communization campaign office would then dispatch work teams to engage in *shih-tien*. Usually, the *hsien*-level party organization would function as the "command post" to direct the campaign;[84] occasionally, however, provincial working groups also participated at the *hsien* or even *hsiang* level, especially in setting up a few initial model communes.[85] After the *shih-tien* stage was completed, conferences of three-level or four-level cadres (*San-chi* or *ssu-chi kan-pu hui-yi*), that is, cadres from the *hsien*, *ch'u*, and *hsiang*, sometimes with cadres from the APC party organizations, were called to make systematic preparations for large-scale implementation of the commune movement.

In these meetings, cadres were required to study, through lectures and small discussion groups, such relevant documents released by the higher authorities as the Peitaiho Politburo Resolution, directives from the CC and the Provincial Party Committee, and certain editorials of the *People's Daily* and *Hung Ch'i*. The lessons gained from *shih-tien* and the "advanced" experiences of other localities or other provinces were also introduced and discussed.[86] Many provinces actually sent cadres to Suip'ing Hsien in Honan, the cradle of the commune system, to make a field study;[87] this is a further indication of the impact of Honan's communes on the other parts of China.

Concrete plans and measures for communization in each locality later were decided upon and worked out in detail. In the planning sessions, cadres were reindoctrinated with the party's premises and goals, their misgivings about or opposition to the commune system were overcome or silenced, and efforts were made to kindle their enthusiasm. Such meetings performed other important functions. They formed a link in the party's chain of command through which the authority of the top leaders could flow down and reach cadres at the basic level. They also served as training sessions in which cadres were informed of detailed provisions of the party's policy on communization and were taught organizational techniques and operational methods.[88]

Before each commune was set up, a propaganda campaign tailored to the local situations was initiated. The *hsien*-level party organization usually was in charge of the propaganda work within its territorial jurisdiction; it mobilized and organized all available resources and mechanisms to distribute intensive propaganda among the masses.[89] The Peitaiho Politburo Resolution, several editorials in the *People's Daily*, and propaganda directives issued by provincial party authorities repeatedly enjoined cadres from using coercion to force peasants into the communes; instead, peasants were to be convinced and won over through education, persuasion, and the mass line method.[90]

In this propaganda campaign the masses were subjected to intensive indoctrination in Communist ideology to elevate their class consciousness; in addition, more instrumental themes—for example, the shortcomings of the

APC's and advantages of communes—were stressed in all the propaganda activities; in particular, many extravagant promises of rapid economic progress were made to the peasants.

The mass meeting was another mechanism used for persuasion. In many *hsiang* and APC's party cadres organized meetings to "debate" typical questions: Shall we establish a People's Commune? What are its superior qualities? Can we successfully manage a commune?[91] These meetings and "debates" were carefully planned and conducted by local party cadres; dissenting views were allowed and encouraged, or even planted, and then were roundly refuted and condemned, and the arguments in favor of the commune were forcefully put forward.

"Fair play" was not the aim of the "debates"; dissenting views could not be allowed to "confuse the masses" or to appear as attractive as the "positive views." The purpose of juxtaposing two different views was "to make the red flag redder and to make the masses recognize what is a 'white flag.'"[92] In the course of "debates," the commune system was characterized first as *ta* (i.e., large in manpower and resources) and second as *kung* (public, or more socialistic, as a system of ownership); on the other hand, the APC was characterized as *hsiao* (small in capital), *shao* (having less manpower), and *pen* (characterized by *pen-wei chu-i*, i.e., departmentalism).

Even the relatively "backward" Chinese peasant could easily infer which type of organization was "preferable," and the peasants were thus "persuaded" to join the communes. Through such manipulations the Chinese Communists secured the population's consent, although the process was clearly less than fully "voluntary." Although the peasant masses may not have been heartily convinced by this kind of manipulation, yet the Chinese Communists' emphasis on persuasion, rather than merely on compulsion, was certainly a very striking feature of the process.

Furthermore, these mass meetings served a useful purpose: they provided a forum through which the party reached the peasants, most of whom were at least partially illiterate, and the party was able to propagate its policies effectively. The debates and the clear-cut dichotomy characterizing the communes as good and the APC's as bad helped peasants understand the content of the party's policies. Finally, these meetings gave the peasants a sense of participation, which probably facilitated the party's efforts in mobilizing their support.[93]

The emphasis on propaganda, education, and persuasion in mass campaigns showed that the Chinese leadership took the mass line principle seriously. This leadership doctrine preaches that the party's policy and methods of work must be based on popular support and that "commandism" must be avoided. Mao once stated this guiding principle in the following terms:

In all practical work of our Party, correct leadership can only be developed on the principle of "from the masses, to the masses." This means summing up [i.e., coordinating and systematizing after careful study] the views of the masses [i.e., views scattered and un-systematic], then taking the resulting ideas back to the masses, explaining and popularizing them until the masses embrace the ideas as their own, stand up for them and translate them into action by way of testing their correctness. Then it is necessary once more to sum up the views of the masses, and once again take the resulting ideas back to the masses so that the masses give them their whole-hearted support.[94]

The propaganda activities, the mass meetings, and the "debates" of August–September 1958 were intended to "convince" or "persuade" peasants that communization served their interests best and thus should be accepted gladly. An image of a voluntary, spontaneous movement was propagated as the masses filed "petitions" and "applications" to join communes.[95] The party propagandists claimed loudly that the communes were the result of the "spontaneous demands" of the masses.[96] On the other hand, however, since the mass line doctrine rejected "tailism" as an incorrect leadership method, the cadres were instructed not to blindly follow "wrong" demands of the masses. If the masses could not clearly see their true interests in the commune system, it was because their class consciousness had not yet been adequately elevated or because they were victims of evil propaganda and counterrevolutionary ideologies. Therefore the party was expected to do what must be done, and the party organization at all levels had to "stand in the forefront of the movement to lead the masses."

4

Intraparty Dissension over the Great Leap Forward

The Phase of Disillusion

The establishment of the communes in rural China was certainly an epoch-making event; within a brief span of several months in the fall of 1958, the Chinese Communist leaders, with minimum resistance, imposed on the vast rural population a radically new form of organization. To be more exact, one month after the passage of the Peitaiho Resolution, more than 90 percent of China's 127 million peasant households were organized into 23,397 communes.[1] At the time, however, many of these communes existed in name only; the party instructed cadres to put up the "skeleton" of communes and wait until after the autumn harvest to reorganize APC's into communes.[2]

Communization involved a structural integration of the *hsiang* or township government (administrative village) and the collectives (mainly APC's but also other co-ops) as well as a significant territorial expansion of the basic units of local administration. In addition, changes in the system of ownership and income distribution in the rural areas accompanied the reorganization. It was only after the harvest in September that cadres in many areas began to seriously face the realities of organizing communes.

Dizzy with Success

In implementing the party's programs of communization, overzealous local cadres often stepped beyond the limits set by central authorities, which resulted in many excesses. The Chinese leadership later blamed the difficulties of the national economy largely on the mistakes committed by local cadres' implementation of central policies. There was undoubtedly some basis of truth in this charge. The excesses manifested in the cadres' implementation of communization (as in the land reform movement in the early 1950s and the collectivization drive in 1955–56) were probably inevitable; a mass movement such as this, which derives its power from mass enthusiasm and initiatives, creates its own momentum. In addition, the bias of the Chinese Communists toward leftism, as reflected in the slogan "better leftist than rightist" [*ning-tso wu-yu*], resulted in a tendency, clearly recognized by top Chinese leaders, for lower cadres to advance recklessly.[3]

But it would be wrong and unfair to place the entire responsibility for the disastrous effects of communization on cadres, groups that were merely carrying out the party's policies—many of which, in fact, were unrealistic, overambitious, ill-planned, and unsound. The top CCP leadership, more than anyone else, must take the blame.

In the fall of 1958 an atmosphere of "blind optimism" seems to have pervaded Chinese society; there was much talk in the Chinese press about the prospects for an immediate transition to communism, and some party leaders, including Mao himself, appeared to be persuaded that the pace of communization could be very fast without causing serious difficulty. The CC tried on several occasions to provide guidelines and to caution local cadres to move slowly, but instructions from the top were often ambiguous and imprecise and at times self-contradictory.

For instance, the Peitaiho Resolution of 29 August had stipulated that 2000 households would be the normal size of a commune, but it also permitted some places to set up communes of 6000 or 7000 households in accordance with local needs. One provision of the resolution instructed provincial and *hsien* cadres not to encourage the formation of communes of more than 10,000 households, but at the same time it told them not to oppose communes of such vast size. The national and provincial press, attempting to stimulate peasant enthusiasm for the commune system, had meanwhile publicized the "superiority" of bigger organization. In a millennial atmosphere, local cadres either ignored the CC guidelines or took advantage of the flexibility in the Peitaiho Resolution, and they proceeded almost uniformly to set up big communes.

In ten provinces alone, there were 1628 communes having a membership of 5000 to 10,000 households, 516 communes having a membership of 10,000 to 20,000 households, and 51 communes having more than 20,000 households.[4] Party officials at the *hsien* level tended to think that "the bigger the communes the better" and ordered the formation of large units, sometimes comprising 100,000 households, which of course proved unwieldy.[5] The Peitaiho Resolution also instructed cadres to form *hsien* federations of communes; in many localities, the whole *hsien* was organized, on paper at least, into a single commune containing as many as 500,000 people.[6] The Chinese leadership must have gotten carried away, so to speak, for they made almost no effort to discourage the formation of large communes, which could not be efficiently run because of a lack of sufficient qualified cadres.

The average number of households per commune for the whole of China at the end of September 1958 was estimated to be 4600, varying from 1400 in Kweichow to 9800 in Kwangtung; in the country districts within the municipalities of Peking and Shanghai, the number of households per commune exceeded 11,000. A general pattern was discernible in the size of the communes: the largest (on the average) communes were found in China's most modernized areas, which had the best transport facilities; conversely, the smallest (on the average) number of households per commune occurred in relatively underdeveloped and sparsely populated provinces.[7]

The Peitaiho Resolution held that one *hsiang* should equal one commune; if this privision had been strictly followed, then the total number of communes would have been about 80,000 instead of 26,400, since there were approximately 80,000 *hsiang* in China before communization. It turned out that a commune usually absorbed several or even a dozen *hsiang*. Most cadres in the absorbed *hsiang* found that their positions were eliminated, and they were either sent down to the first line of production or they were demoted to work in posts less important or powerful than those they had previously held. Although cadres in the APC's continued to serve as cadres in the new production brigades after communization, they were now subject to tighter control by the communes and found their power correspondingly diminished. Dissatisfaction among this group of basic cadres was widespread; they complained that whereas the communes had become bigger, their positions had become smaller [*she ta kuan hsiao*].[8]

Besides *ta* (bigger in size), the commune system was also characterized by the Chinese Communists as *kung* (more "socialistic" in ownership and distribution system). Before communization, the major elements of production, such as land, farm implements, and draft animals, were owned by the APC's, and the peasants could still retain a small plot of land. After communization, all the properties of the APC's were converted into the collective ownership of the communes, and peasants' private plots, house sites, and other means of production which had been retained by peasants were also handed over to the communes.[9] *Hung Ch'i* on 1 September 1958 approvingly stated that in many communes the "last vestiges of private ownership" were removed, and "in certain aspects, things had gone beyond the stage of collective ownership."

Understandably, peasants were discontented, and incidents of sabotage occurred in several provinces.[10] Overzealous local cadres also confiscated the private property of peasants—including bicycles, watches, and radios—and aroused great anxiety among the peasants. The editorial in *Hung Ch'i* on 16 September, designed to refute "rumors" spread by "class enemies" that all private property would become public, instructed the cadres in unequivocal terms that certain categories of private property, like small strips of land by the side of houses, and a small number of fruit trees as well as small livestock, and personal property such as home furnishings, clothing, bedding, and items such as bicycles, watches, and radios should not be touched.

In spite of this injunction, many local cadres proceeded to confiscate not only peasants' private plots but also their personal property.[11] Domestic sideline occupations, too, were widely suppressed on the pretext that peasants would have little time for anything other than collective work. The closure of rural markets also had an adverse impact: there were severe shortages of pigs, poultry, vegetables, and fruit as well as such items as straw sandals, coir brooms and raincoats, bamboo hats and baskets.[12] Since the APC's had to turn over all collectively owned properties to the communes as "shares," some cadres took the lead in distributing APC properties and reserve funds among their members before their APC's were merged into the communes.[13] In other cases, cadres and peasants of the wealthier APC's demanded that all APC's contribute equal "shares" to the communes. The tendency toward "departmentalism" shown by these cadres and peasants led the CC to issue repeated warnings that "education in the Communist spirit should be given to the cadres and masses." The party exhorted them to "accept the difference (in shares) with an easy conscience," not to "settle every small item of accounts or to square everything, and not to haggle over minor matters."[14]

In the fall and winter of 1958 there was a widespread practice called "one equalization and two transfers" [yi-p'ing erh-t'iao]. In many places cadres which may have taken too literally the propaganda promoting the rapid transition to Communism equalized the income of each peasant and transferred properties of wealthier production brigades (equivalent to former APC's) to other brigades, sending the labor force of one brigade to work for other brigades without compensation. Although the morale and incentive of peasants in the wealthier brigades were seriously affected, this practice was not corrected until the spring of 1959.[15]

The system of distribution in communes, which had important implications for peasants' incentives, evoked a great deal of discussion within the party during the autumn and winter of 1958. In the Peitaiho proceedings, according to Vice-Premier Li Hsien-nien, "some comrades" (presumably more radical elements) proposed a system of "eating rice without pay" (a free grain supply system).[16] Initially, the party appeared to have rejected that proposal; the editorial in the People's Daily of 4 September indicated that free supply of grain would have to be postponed to the distant future. The Peitaiho Resolution, which was made public on 10 September, cautioned cadres not to hurry the change from the original system of distribution (payment according to hours and workdays) to "avoid any unfavorable effect on production."

In spite of this injunction, the supply system was introduced during September in a number of provinces.[17] Some cadres in the provinces were anxious to exceed even that swift pace set by the party leadership in the advance to Communism. On the other hand, one suspects that the impetus may have been given by the radical elements in the party, including Mao himself. Mao, in a tour of Anhwei, was quoted on 16 September: "Since one commune can put into practice the principle of eating rice without pay, others that possess the equal conditions can do the same. Since rice can be eaten without pay, clothing can be had without pay in future."[18] This was no formal directive, but for cadres in the provinces, anything Mao said would probably have the same or even greater effect.[19]

The rationale for adopting the supply system was complicated. In practical terms, the existing system of distribution tended to favor families with a strong labor force or with better skill; most of these probably belonged to middle and upper-middle peasants. It also created inequalities between peasants. The supply system would favor peasant households with a small labor force, most of whom could probably be classified as poor or lower-middle peasants—those who were dependent on the assistance of the party and were regarded as the party's allies in the communization campaign. Ideologically, the supply system, embodying the Communist principle "to each according to his need," was an advance beyond the socialist principle of "to each according to his work," and thus appealed to enthusiasts who wanted to effect the fast transition to Communism. In addition, there was a romantic yearning for the return to Yenan experiences, when the Chinese Communist supply system provided free food and goods to their cadres and troops in base areas.[20]

All of these reasons were articulated by Chang Ch'un-ch'iao in an article in Chieh-fang (Liberation), the semimonthly theoretical organ of the Shanghai Party Committee.[21] The article also advocated total restoration of the Yenan supply system and complete abolition of the current wage system, which Chang termed "unequal" and "bourgeois." Wu Leng-hsi, former director of the New China News Agency, claimed that the basic ideas of Chang's article had been expressed by Mao at the Peitaiho Politburo Conference.[22] Wu also said that Mao ordered the reproduction of Chang's article in the People's Daily and personally wrote an accompanying "Editor's Note" basically affirming the theses of that article.[23] (It is significant that in 1975, unhappy with wage differences in China, Mao renewed his earlier call for changes in the remuneration and distribution system and that Chang, in strong support of Mao, published a signed article in the April 1975 issue of Hung Ch'i to attack the bourgeois rights.)

In October and November, the problem of wages and supply was roundly debated, and different shades of opinion were expressed in both the People's Daily and Hung Ch'i.[24] Although the People's Daily did not come out editorially in favor of any particular solution, allegedly a result of inner-party dispute,[25] there were many enthusiastic reports on the free supply of grain in the provinces, and a "half supply, half wage system" was almost universally adopted throughout China.[26] In some provinces, such as Honan, the list of free supply items even included clothing, medical care, maternity benefits, education, wedding and funeral expenses, and recreation, in addition to food.[27] In this particular province, the percentage of the total commune income allocated for distribution (both supply and wages) was also very low; whereas the central authorities reportedly stipulated that 60 percent of the commune incomes were to be distributed,[28] in many communes in Honan the distributed income constituted only 30 percent of the total commune income.[29]

In late fall 1958 problems and difficulties began to emerge, caused in part by certain irrational programs of the Great Leap Forward and communization and in part by the excesses of cadres at provincial and lower levels. Many communes were simply too big, and the cadres were incapable of coordinating the multiple enterprises within them. In Shantung, most communes existed without production plans, and the press urged each commune to map out a unified production plan.[30] The peasant masses, spurred on by the cadres, had worked excessively hard since the winter of 1957; after this year of sustained intensive mobilization, they—and even the cadres—began to suffer from physical exhaustion.[31] The excessive "Communist style" (*Kung-ch'an Feng*, a pejorative term), as manifested in the cadres' overemphasis on the accumulation and investment (in relation to distribution) of the supply portion of the distribution, and in the cadres' requisition of peasants' private property, denied many peasants material incentives to work and produce.

The Wuhan Plenum—A Tactical or Genuine Retreat

In mid-October 1958 such major economic officials of the regime as Li Hsien-nien and T'an Chen-lin conferred with officials from the northern and northeast provinces at an important conference; they discussed many problems that had emerged in the communes.[32] In November many Politburo members went out to the provinces to determine what had gone wrong. Between 2 and 10 November Mao called a meeting in Chengchow which was attended by some of Mao's Politburo colleagues and a few regional party leaders.[33] Later (21–27 November) Mao called a meeting in Wuchang, whose participants included the first secretaries of the provincial party committees.[34] Formal meetings and informal consultations continued, and finally the enlarged Sixth CC Plenum was held in Wuhan from 28 November to 10 December 1958.

The Plenum was the party's first systematic attempt to come to grips with organization, management, administration, and distribution problems that had arisen as a result of the establishment of communes. In the preceding few months, the central authorities, aside from giving some broad guidelines, had failed to issue detailed, concrete instructions on these questions; the cadres in the provinces, relying on the "wisdom of the masses," had largely taken things into their own hands, and much confusion had arisen from divergent practices in different places. For example, before the Wuhan Plenum, there were two, or three, four, or even five administrative layers under different communes in different places in Liaoning Province, and these administrative layers were called by different names.[35] In Wuhan, the Chinese leadership stipulated a three-level administration for communes throughout China.

The Resolution on Communes adopted by the Wuhan CC Plenum on 10 December 1958 showed that the Chinese leadership had become more sober and realistic. An examination of the issues dealt with in the resolution also reveals the unmistakable interaction of ideological and practical considerations in the party's councils. It appears that the influence of the radical elements in the party had peaked in the fall of 1958 and began to decline with the Wuhan Plenum.

Section IV of the Resolution reaffirmed the rights of commune members to retain individual means of livelihood, small farm tools, and domestic animals and stated that commune members were again permitted to engage in small domestic sideline occupations, on condition that these would not harm collective production. To increase peasants' material incentives, the resolution cautioned that the scope of free supply should not be too wide;[36] it clearly stated that the system of wages paid according to work done must take "first place for a certain period" and "an important place over a long period" and warned that any negation of the socialist principle "to each according to his work" at this stage would "dampen the working enthusiasm of the people" (Section III). The Chinese leaders obviously were aware that Communism was not just around the corner,[37] and the Resolution addressed some "good-hearted" but "overeager" comrades, who had thought the process of building a socialist country in "fifteen, twenty or more years" was too slow, saying that "every Marxist must soberly realize that the transition to Communism is a fairly long and complicated process of development" (Section II).

In the months preceding the Resolution many cadres had apparently been harsh and "commandist" in pushing peasants into communes. On many occasions central authorities told local cadres to use persuasion; nevertheless, their exhortations for local cadres "to stand in the forefront of the communization movement," to get peasants "organized along military lines," and to enforce strict discipline in agricultural production may have encouraged cadres to place greater reliance on means more effective than persuasion—coercion. The Wuhan Resolution now admonished cadres to manifest a "comradely" style of work, with no rudeness or "commandism"; it also instructed them not to become "dizzy with success" and not to exaggerate (Sections VI and VII).

Finally, the resolution called on party committees at all levels to "make full use of the five months from December this year to next April" to check up on and consolidate the people's communes in their own areas. In the second half of November 1958, Shantung, Anhwei, Honan, and other provinces had already organized 10,000-man inspection corps to go into the rural areas to study problems in the communes; they discovered that the way income was distributed (too little was allocated for distribution and too much was distributed on the basis of free supply), the long hours of work, and cadres' "commandist" behavior had aroused widespread peasant discontent.[38] These findings presumably led the party leadership to prescribe the corrective measure contained in the Wuhan Resolution.

The most astonishing news of the Wuhan Plenum, however, was Mao Tse-tung's decision not to be a candidate for a second term as chairman of the PRC in the 1959 election, which had party approval. In the spring of 1959 the NPC elected Liu Shao-ch'i to succeed Mao.

There was speculation at that time outside of China that Mao was being pushed aside or demoted because of the failure of the commune movement. There is no solid evidence for believing this to be the case;[39] indeed, although Mao relinquished his government post, he continued to hold the chairmanship of the party—the real locus of the power in the regime. One major reason for Mao to give up the chairmanship of the government, a primarily procedural and ceremonial position, was probably Mao's desire to concentrate his attention upon "questions of the direction, policy, and line of the Party and state," as indicated in Peking's official statement.

Moreover, in stepping down Mao probably was trying to avoid the kind of successional struggle that occurred in the Soviet Union after Stalin's death in 1953. In a speech in October 1966, Mao himself alluded to this:

> For considerations for the security of the country and in view of Stalin's experience, two lines [of leadership] were arranged—I was on the second line and other comrades on the first. . . . I was on the second line, I didn't take charge of the daily routine. Many things were done by others in the hope that this might increase their prestige, so that when I go to see God the country won't receive such a shock [as it may otherwise]. . . . [T]o divide the Standing Committee [of the Politburo] into the first and second lines and to let them take charge of the Secretariat was my idea.[40]

The division of the Politburo Standing Committee into "two lines" of leadership—the first at the "operational" level and the second at the policy level—in the 1950s (probably during the Eighth Party Congress in 1956) was, according to Mao, his way of training the "revolutionary successors." The elevation of Liu Shao-ch'i to the chairmanship of the PRC can thus be seen as a step to ensure that Liu would succeed Mao when he died and would settle the succession issue when Mao was still alive.

Mao's decision to step down as head of State in favor of Liu, however, certainly cannot be considered politically innocent and entirely free of other political motivations. Being sensitive to the successional struggle in the Soviet Union after Stalin, Mao may have been attempting to avoid any denunciation of his own leadership by some Chinese leaders after his death by installing one top CCP leader who had his utmost confidence and who could be relied upon to continue the course of Chinese revolution which he had chartered. Up to 1958–59, Liu was certainly this man.[41] It is also possible that in the winter months of 1958–59 Mao anticipated opposition to his leadership as a result of his Great Leap and communization programs, therefore he stepped down as head of state in favor of Liu in the hope that he would deflate his opposition and strengthen his support from Liu.[42]

In any case, the election of Liu Shao-ch'i in the NPC session in April 1959 did surprise many people. Some observers outside China had predicted that Marshal Chu Teh, then vice-chairman of the Republic, would succeed Mao, and reports reaching Western diplomatic sources in Peking had indicated that Chu Teh was an active "candidate" for the post.[43] The elevation of Liu Shao-ch'i to chairmanship of the PRC, even though it was merely a ceremonial post, gave him tremendous prestige and signaled to the party ranks that he was second in command and Mao's designated successor.

Anna Louise Strong, a veteran American Communist residing in China at that time, visualized the communization campaign as a battle—a sudden push ahead, a retreat for consolidation, and then another advance. She described the communization campaign of the summer and fall of 1958:

> Any swift advance, in battle or social organization, produces rough edges. The foremost troops outrun the main force and take posts where the new front cannot yet be stabilized.... But the drive has natural limits and a pause comes for regrouping. The general staff must be ready to fix the new front line forward which the main forces may quickly advance and which they can firmly hold. Some of the foreposts can be fortified, the rest drawn back for safety and the rear brought up. A new front is consolidated for some later advance.[44]

The autumn upsurge had pushed 99 percent of the peasants into communes —the "foremost troop" had outrun the "main force" and taken the posts which the main force could not hold. Thus the Wuhan Plenum was an occasion for consolidation. There is considerable basis of truth in Strong's observation. Late in 1958 the Chinese leaders had uncovered some problems through preliminary investigations, inspections, and various formal and informal meetings, and they then prescribed a period of five months in which to take corrective measures. However, there were no clear indications at that time that the Chinese leaders intended to backtrack from what they had done, nor did they appear to have foreseen or anticipated at the Wuhan Plenum the kind of social and economic crises into which China would soon be plunged.

In fact, at the Wuhan meeting the party continued to urge communes "to go in for industry in a big way" and optimistically put forward excessively ambitious targets for economic development in 1959. Steel output was to be increased from an estimated 11 million tons in 1958 to 18 million tons in 1959; grain output was to be increased from an estimated 375 million tons in 1958 to about 525 million tons in 1959. As it turned out, the party's "new front" was not consolidated and the party, instead of advancing, was compelled to retreat even further in 1959 and later.

Further Retreats

In the course of their checkups, the Chinese Communists began to uncover many serious problems in the communes. For example, in his "Investigation Report of the Humeng Communes," published in the *People's Daily* on 25 February 1959, T'ao Chu (first secretary of the Kwangtung Provincial Party Committee) denounced as undesirable one widespread practice among brigades and teams, who concealed their harvested crops from higher authorities and divided the concealed grain among their own members. He attributed this manifestation of "departmentalism" to the failure of the communes to take into account the differences between brigades and between teams when income was distributed. The communes were reportedly unable to provide unified production plans for their numerous brigades, work was assigned day by day, and the militarization of work methods resulted in inefficiency and waste of labor power. According to T'ao there was much discontentment with the mess halls and the new system of distribution under which malingerers and weak peasants now got the same food and benefits as hard and strong workers.

From the end of February to early March 1959, many Politburo members and provincial secretaries met quietly at Chengchow in an enlarged Politburo session—the Second Chengchow Conference—to review the state of communes and compare notes on their checkups.[45] They realized that something more than what was prescribed in the Wuhan Plenum had to be done to effectively cope with the defects they had discovered. After the conference, the party issued secret directions which instructed communes, among other things, to enforce a system of "three-level ownership, three-level accounting," with the brigade as the basic accounting unit.[46]

In the original commune system the commune owned all the means of production in its component parts (production brigades and production teams) and operated as the sole accounting unit to distribute income for all the commune members. Before the Chengchow revision, although the production brigade formed a business accounting unit, its gains and losses were pooled into those of the commune as a whole, and the brigade was not permitted to allocate its own resources; this fact had an adverse effect on the incentives of the brigades, particularly the prosperous ones. The transfer of the right of ownership back to the brigades (most of which were formerly advanced APC's, equivalent to a natural village in scope) and the move to make the brigade the basic accounting unit set the proponents of the original commune system back a long way; the transition to ownership "by the whole people" and to Communism was to be retarded further. In spite of the unfavorable ideological implications, however, the regime was compelled to attend to accounting and administrative problems at the commune level, and, particularly, to the discontent and slackened efforts on the part of the peasants in the brigades and teams who were now receiving insufficient incentives. The party also reprimanded overeager cadres for committing "one equalization and two transfers" and ordered them to return properties requisitioned improperly from brigades and teams and compensate the peasants for their losses.

By the second half of February greater emphasis was placed on establishing a system of "production responsibility."[47] Some authorities on production management were transferred from the communes down to the brigades and from the brigades down to the production teams. The brigades and the teams were required to fulfill their contracts and meet the quotas assigned to them, but they were allowed to manage their own production work. These were sensible administrative arrangements designed to restore morale and work incentives; however, ideologically they represented backsliding, showing that the "bigness" and "socialist" nature of the original commune system did not work. Target-setting had become more modest and realistic; both the *People's Daily* and *Hung Ch'i* recommended to commune cadres that targets be fixed in contracts at 15–20 percent below the highest level attainable to give production brigades extra incentives to work for bonuses.[48]

"The Whole Country as a Chessboard"—The First Attempt at Recentralization in the Spring of 1959

The 1957–58 decentralization, giving local authorities control of industrial construction and production, and the encouragement of local industries had given rise to some serious problems. The increased autonomy of the provincial authorities over the management of the economy correspondingly weakened the ability of the central authorities to plan, coordinate, and allocate resources. There was a strong tendency for provincial authorities and even communes to become self-sufficient, and this tendency toward autarky was fostered by a breakdown in the allocation system and bottlenecks in transport. Communes, in their efforts to "go in for industry in a big way," retained many superfluous materials.[49] Provincial authorities, attempting to build up comprehensive industrial complexes within their own provinces, had set up and expanded various industries, almost regardless of cost. As a result, many key raw materials were in short supply, the state's priority projects were adversely affected, and the situation was out of control.[50]

These developments greatly alarmed the central leadership, which now denounced the "departmentalism" of the provincial authorities. The party called for a return to centralized leadership in the development of industry and stressed the need for overall planning and better coordination in a *People's Daily* editorial, "The Whole Country as a Chessboard" (24 February 1959), which emphasized the need to distribute investment funds and construction projects around the country in an orderly way and to determine production targets and allocate raw materials according to a "single national plan." Probably in reply to criticism of inconsistency directed against the new line, the editorial asserted that centralized leadership as implied in the concept of "the whole country as a chessboard" did not contravene the policy of administrative decentralization and would not hamper local initiatives and flexibility. The editorial added: "Dispersionism and departmentalism violate democratic centralism and are contradictory to the spirit of the whole country as a chessboard."

In discussing problems of capital construction in an article in *Hung Ch'i* (1 March 1959), Ch'en Yun also had much to say about "the whole country as a chessboard." Ch'en emphatically stated that only when a national industrial complex had been built would it be possible to build regional industrial complexes and that only after regional industrial complexes had been set up would it be possible to establish industrial complexes in the provinces. Ch'en criticized provincial authorities for prematurely attempting to build complete, independent industrial complexes within their borders.[51] He termed these efforts "impractical," "harmful to the overall arrangement," "diluting the collective strength," and "retarding the speed of socialist construction," and he admonished provincial authorities to show their Communist spirit and to overcome departmental tendencies.

Ch'en Yun, who previously had misgivings about excessive decentralization, probably felt his earlier skepticism vindicated by the prevailing conditions. In the *Hung Ch'i* article, he virtually argued for recentralization. For instance, he proposed that a system of priorities should be instituted and the principle of a "chessboard" strictly observed. Construction projects were to be ranked in order of importance to the country according to "the purview of the central government"; materials, major equipment, and the labor force were to be uniformly controlled and allocated by concerned central government departments and provincial authorities to insure "first, the accomplishment of national plans and then, if there is a surplus, to carry out regional or local projects."

A similar proposal was expounded by Chou En-lai in his "Report on Government Work," which was delivered to the NPC in mid-April 1959. To guarantee proper fulfillment of planned targets, Chou stated, it was necessary to draw up "10-day, monthly, or quarterly time-tables" for the most important products or projects, and it was also necessary for leading organs of the central and provincial authorities to send inspectors to check on progress and quality.[52]

Some curiously contradictory overtones could be detected in Chou's speech. On the one hand, the speech contained many frank and realistic statements; it argued in favor of unified planning and coordination at the national level, further checkups and consolidation of communes, implementation of the corrective pressures decided upon in the preceding few months, adaptation of plans (targets) to objective realities, and the need to keep manpower engaged in agricultural rather than industrial tasks (agriculture should employ no less than 80 percent of the manpower). On the other hand, Chou also talked at length about the correctness of the 1958 "general line" and continued to call for another "great leap" in 1959 to achieve the fantastic targets set the previous December (525 million tons for food grain and 18 million tons for iron and steel).

The ambivalence of Chou's speech probably reflected the political and economic context of that moment. The Seventh CC Plenum had been held in early April in Shanghai, shortly before the NPC meeting. Some CC members who had had doubts about the overambitious targets for 1959 set at the Sixth CC Plenum the previous December proposed revising them downward. The CC was divided and the proposal was not approved.[53] Red Guard sources later reported that P'eng Teh-huai and Mao clashed in the proceedings; P'eng reportedly voiced opposition to Mao's "assuming command in person" and "discarding the Standing Committee of the Politburo," and, in return, Mao was said to have criticized P'eng.[54]

Apparently many top Chinese leaders were victimized by their own dramatic propaganda, as they daily assailed the public with inflated statistics. P'eng Teh-huai's account provides some clues to the confusion and bewilderment of the Chinese leadership during the last quarter of 1958 and early 1959:

> At that time, from reports sent in from various quarters, it would seem that communism was around the corner. This caused not a few comrades to become dizzy. In the wake of the wave of high grain and cotton output and the doubling of iron and steel production, extravagance and waste developed. The job of autumn harvesting was handled crudely and without consideration of cost, and we considered ourselves rich while actually we were still poor. More serious, in a rather long period of time, it was not easy to get a true picture of the situation. Even up to the Wuchang conference and the conference of secretaries of provincial and municipal Party committees in January this year [1959], we had still not been able to find out the realities of the overall situation.[55]

Other leaders felt the same way. Thus Teng Hsiao-p'ing instructed the State Planning Commission and the State Economic Commission to identify major problems and propose solutions and bring them to the following Central Work

Conference for discussion. He also ordered the New China News Agency to collect various data and information to make the top provincial leadership aware of the objective realities.[56]

Before long, however, the Chinese leadership, including Mao, grasped the seriousness of the problems confronting them and decided to make amends and slow the pace of the Great Leap. This was suggested in Mao's secret "Letter of Instruction" sent to the party committees at all levels down to the communes and production teams on 29 April 1959 through an inner-party communication medium, *Tang-nei t'ung-hsin* [*Correspondence within the Party*].[57] In the letter Mao admonished the cadres to be more modest and realistic in setting grain production quotas, to refrain from issuing impractical orders on matters such as close planting, and to speak the truth and not give false reports. He was well aware that low-level cadres were under immense pressures to falsify information because the high-level authorities bragged, applied pressure, and indulged in empty promises, and he specifically rebuked these erroneous leadership styles. The letter was significant in at least two ways. It shows that Mao had again switched to a conservative position, placing himself at the head of a more conservative consensus within the party. Moreover, by criticizing the work methods and manner of implementation, Mao intended to shift the blame for economic difficulties from the policy and the policy-maker to the cadres who improperly executed the policy.

The provincial secretaries' reaction to the low key sung by Mao was apparently mixed; some officials were dismayed or puzzled. Li Ching-ch'üan (the first party secretary of Szechuan who was promoted to the Politburo in May 1958 because of his enthusiastic support of the Great Leap programs), for instance, reportedly characterized the letter as "blowing a cold wind" and "making people waver at a crucial moment." In a meeting called to convey Mao's instructions to his own subordinates, Li allegedly warned lower officials not to "take a one-sided view of the letter and let peasants do what they like." To soften the negative impact of the letter, Li was said to have told secretaries of Special District and Municipal Party Committees to understand the letter "from the positive aspect" and allegedly refused to lower the high grain targets and change the rules for close planting (between 300,000 and 400,000 rice stalks per *mou*) set earlier by the Szechuan Provincial Party Committee.[58]

In any case, beginning with the Wuhan Conference, the party swung slowly but inexorably to the right. During the spring and early summer of 1959, the press criticized those tendencies that were closely identified with the Great Leap: too much reliance on mass enthusiasm and not enough careful and realistic planning and experiment; overestimating the capacity of the human will and subjective spontaneity while underestimating the importance of objective factors; overemphasizing speed and quantity at the expense of rising costs and lowered quality; exhibiting bureaucratism and commandism which were harmful to the cause of the party; and so on.[59]

As in 1956, the more radical elements of the party had overplayed their hand, and, in turn, the "conservatives" had much to criticize about "reckless advances." But one major difference between the debates in the summer of 1959 and those in the second half of 1956 is the fact that the disputes within the party in 1959 were not contained; rather they cracked open the party leadership.

The Showdown at Lushan

In early July 1959 an enlarged Politburo conference was convened at Lushan, a summer resort in the province of Kiangsi.[60] Attending the conference were important officials of the party, government, and the PLA, in addition to regular members and alternates of the Politburo. The tasks facing China's top leaders at Lushan required a comprehensive review of the Great Leap programs and the formulation of measures to cope with problems that had beset the national economy.

Most, if not all the participants were by this time well aware of the short-comings of the Great Leap and were probably convinced that some revision of existing policy was inevitable. To the surprise and anger of Mao, however, many of his Great Leap policies came under direct frontal attack by a so-called anti-party group led by P'eng Teh-huai. This was the most serious opposition within the party that Mao had encountered since establishing himself as the undisputed leader of the CCP in 1942.

Before discussing the Lushan proceedings, P'eng's attack on the Great Leap policies must be placed in proper perspective. The background of the Army-party friction in the 1950s is a good starting point.

The PLA and the Party [61]

Party control over the army has been a strong tradition and accepted leadership doctrine for the CCP leadership. Since its inception in 1928, this system of party control has remained essentially unchanged in general outline, although parts of it have at times received more or less emphasis than others. However, the modernization of the PLA, the increasing emphasis on technology and modern warfare by those party officials in charge of military affairs, the rise of a young professional officer caste after the Korean War, and the adoption of the Soviet military experiences generated some unanticipated consequences. Under the vastly changed circumstances of the mid-1950s, the relevance of the pre-1949 revolutionary model, of the old procedures and practices regulating the army's internal and external social behavior, and of the Maoist military doctrines were increasingly questioned by many PLA men. In short, within the PLA there was a sense of impatience with the system of political control.

On numerous occasions the party displayed overt dissatisfaction over various "deviations" in the PLA; for instance, on 1 July 1958 the organ of the PLA charged:

> . . . purely military views, warlordism, and doctrinairism have revived among a part of the personnel. They assert that that collective leadership of Party committees is not adapted to the requirements of modernization and regularization. One-sidedly stressing the suddenness and complexity of modern warfare, they assert that the system of Party committees will impede the better judgement and concentration of command. They even openly advocate liquidation of the system of Party committee leadership. Further, they liquidated and restricted the activities of Party committees in leadership and political work.[62]

Several weeks later, the same paper also blasted those who advocated "technology first" and questioned the competence of political officers in military affairs:

> There are those who concentrate excessively on modernization, and advocate the weakening of party leadership, and try to weaken political work. . . . They pay lip-service to political leadership, but they believe that modernization is not related to and is in a different class from politics. . . . [63]

Beginning in 1956, the party leadership attempted to rectify undesirable tendencies in the PLA through a rapid succession of campaigns. Political education was intensified for both officers and men; party committees in the PLA were rebuilt and strengthened; PLA officers' privileges were curtailed, and an "officer to the ranks" movement was launched. In spite of—or perhaps because of—these endeavors to strengthen political control and restore "revolutionary" traditions, the PLA's relationship with the party apparently deteriorated.

It is necessary to note that what the PLA objected to was not party control or party leadership per se, for, after all, the top leadership of the PLA consisted of party leaders; rather, what the PLA objected to was a series of specific measures which the party tried to enforce in the PLA. However, the PLA, as a distinct political group, also had its special interests. Many of the party leaders in charge of the PLA may have found that the logic of the special function of the PLA (e.g., national defense) and the special interests of their "constituents"—let alone personal ambition and other considerations—compelled them to resist or obstruct policies which they viewed as inimical to the PLA and to lobby for policies more in line with the interests of the army.

Consider the issue of PLA participation in the regime's various socialist construction campaigns.[64] The party claimed that "the PLA is the army of the people, it must regularly maintain close relations with the masses, and nourish itself with what is acquired from the struggle waged by the masses," and the party ordered the PLA to actively participate in and support socialist construction.[65] In January 1956, when the party's draft twelve-year agricultural program was launched, the PLA's Political Department drew up a twenty-article "Program for Participation and Support by Army Units in the Agricultural Cooperative Movement and Agricultural Production" by which the PLA would support the draft program with "practical action."[66] From 1956 to 1959, PLA units reportedly contributed "freely" 4 million, 20 million, 59 million, and 44 million workdays, respectively, to agricultural tasks such as sowing, harvesting, land reclamation, and irrigation work.[67]

By 1956, "a number of people [in the PLA] [took] the view that for the army to help the people in production and take part in certain social activities in leisure hours [would] hinder training."[68] The increasingly nonmilitary demands made on the PLA during the period of the Great Leap also increased misgivings and opposition within the PLA. As Hsiao Hua revealed:

> There is a definite conflict between participation in national construction and training in their respective demands for time.... Needless to say, as the Army is an armed combat organization, it must carry out its task as a "work force" in such a way that its task as a "combat force" is not affected.... It is obviously wrong to think that, as no war is going on at present, the Army should exert itself mainly in the direction of production construction, or to set too high requirements concerning the Army's participating in construction and labor production. Anything that may weaken war preparations and training tasks is impermissible.[69]

It was this kind of divergence between military priorities and other (political, economical, and ideological) priorities that was at least partly responsible for the growth of friction between the party and the PLA leadership. During 1956 and 1959, the cumulative effect of the numerous nonmilitary demands made on the PLA either brought latent opposition into the open or created new opposition. On the eve of Army Day (31 July 1958), Marshal Chu Teh, apparently speaking on behalf of the party, severely indicted some elements in the PLA in an article entitled "People's Army, People's War," in the *People's Daily*:

> There are people who advocate an exclusively military viewpoint, who have a one-sided regard for military affairs and look down upon politics,

have a one-sided high regard for vocation and technique and look down upon ideology, have a one-sided high regard for the role of individuals and neglect the collective strength of the Party and the masses. They only deal with tactics and technique, but not strategy; they only want the army but neglect the function of masses of the people; they only pay attention to national defence, but not to the significance of economic construction to national defence.

The appointment of senior provincial party secretaries to serve in the capacity of first political commissars in the military regions or military districts to strengthen party control—a trend that became discernible particularly at the height of the Great Leap—was an indication of the party's doubts about the PLA and its leadership. Marshal Lin Piao, who had been inactive for some time, was elevated to the Politburo Standing Committee and made a vice-chairman of the party in May 1958; this was generally attributed to Lin's improved health. However, Lin's promotion also may have been an early sign of Mao's displeasure with the performance of Minister of Defense P'eng Teh-huai, who was in overall charge of the regime's military affairs, and of contemplation or preparation on Mao's part for changes in the top leadership of the PLA.

In fact, immediately after this session of the Party Congress, the MAC held an enlarged meeting, from 27 May to 22 July, to undertake a comprehensive critical review of the current PLA line of military construction with the aim to "destroy slavish ideology" and "bury dogmatism." In a speech to the group-leader forum of the conference on 28 June, Mao severely criticized the PLA efforts at emulating the Soviet experiences and rebuked General Hsiao K'o, then vice-minister of defense and director of the Military Training Department, for having warlord mentality imbued with "bourgeois ideology, dogmatism, and feudal ideology."[70] Although Mao did not single out P'eng Teh-huai for criticism, there seems to be little doubt that the meeting and Mao's speech were directed against P'eng inasmuch as he was then in charge of the regime's overall military affairs and should be responsible for the shortcomings in the PLA work.

Evidence contained in the secret PLA *Bulletin of Activities* makes it clear that army-party relations worsened partly because of the differing priorities of the PLA and the party leadership, and partly because some politico-military policies which the party emphasized were opposed by leaders of the army. For instance, P'eng and some other PLA leaders were obliquely or directly accused of advocating an "erroneous military line," opposing army participation in production, favoring "unreasonable military systems and formalities," neglecting party branches at the company level, and preferring foreign military theory to Mao's own doctrines.[71]

It is argued, however, that in themselves these reasons were insufficient for P'eng to challenge Mao at Lushan in 1959; another important factor that motivated P'eng's "anti-party" activities, for which he was ultimately dismissed, is believed to have been a "fundamental disagreement over policy towards the Soviet Union with special military implications."[72] According to Gittings, an expert on Chinese military affairs, P'eng fought for military collaboration with the Soviet Union and may even have been willing to sacrifice some measure of control over China's military affairs to secure continued military assistance, possibly including nuclear weapons or technology.[73] The Chinese leadership, however, chose a different course of action, one which subsequently led to the rupture of military arrangements between China and the Soviets, reportedly on 20 June 1959,[74] less than two weeks before the Lushan Conference.

If P'eng's attack on the Great Leap policies and the commune system were motivated primarily by his dissatisfaction over China's policy toward the Soviet Union and the military relations between the two nations, as Gittings argues, P'eng did not show it at Lushan, judging by the evidence available. Information released to date suggests that he chose to act as a member of the Politburo speaking exclusively on economic matters, rather than as a dissatisfied minister of defense pleading a case on military grounds. P'eng and other PLA leaders had legitimate reasons to be concerned with the regime's economic policies. The food of the PLA had to be supplied by the peasantry, soldiers were recruited largely from the countryside, and the livelihood of the peasants had a direct impact on the troops' morale. Besides, the PLA had to help maintain peace and order, and if the peasants should revolt, it would doubtless have the ultimate responsibility for suppressing them. There is little doubt that P'eng and his colleagues were dissatisfied with the economic policies of the Great Leap and communes; his dissatisfaction was clearly reflected in a poem he composed in the fall of 1958:

> Grain scattered on the ground, potato leaves withered;
> Strong young people have left to smelt iron, only children and old
>   women reaped the crops;
> How can they pass the coming year?
> Allow me to appeal for the people.

The Challenge of P'eng Teh-huai

Considerable information, considered credible, has now come to light concerning the party's meeting at Lushan in 1959. It indicates that when the enlarged Lushan Politburo Conference started, the participants were divided into small discussion groups according to regions, and P'eng Teh-huai was assigned to the northwest group.[75] A movement to critically review the shortcomings of the so-called Policy of the Three Red Banners had been fostered by an anti-leftist campaign preceding the conference, as noted earlier, and the ground rules calling for "big democracy" at the Lushan Conference seem to have created a somewhat uninhibited atmosphere.[76] Many party leaders may thus have been encouraged to speak out more boldly than they had before. It was probably under these circumstances that Marshal P'eng Teh-huai, who reportedly attacked the Great Leap and the communes in unequivocal terms in the discussions with the northwest group during 3–10 July, set out his criticisms of current policies in a lengthy "Letter of Opinion" which he presented to Mao and distributed to the members of the Lushan Politburo Conference on 14 July.[77]

While praising the achievements made as a result of the general line and paying lip service to Mao's brilliant leadership, P'eng's attack was a strong one even though it was couched in careful terms. P'eng blamed the party leadership for being misled by an "air of exaggeration" to overestimate grain production at the time of the Peitaiho Conference in the previous year and to conclude that food problems were settled. He criticized the party leadership and, by implication, Chairman Mao, for prematurely diverting the peasants' efforts to adjust to the needs of industrial production. The party's understanding of the development of iron and steel production was characterized, in P'eng's words, by "serious one-sidedness." P'eng also criticized the party for its alleged lack of careful and realistic planning and for its failure to specify concrete and practical measures in many areas. P'eng chided "not a few comrades" who, misled by the achievements of the Great Leap and the ostensible enthusiasm of the mass movement, had developed pronounced leftist tendencies and wanted to "jump into Communism in one step."

Leftist tendencies, in P'eng's opinion, were manifested in the premature negation of the principle of "exchange at equal values," in the premature raising of the slogan "eating rice without pay," in the blind propagation of certain techniques without proper advance testing, and in the substitution of the principle "politics in command" for certain economic laws and scientific rules. He held that "petty-bourgeois fanaticism" was responsible for these leftist deviations. P'eng is alleged to have said that "if the Chinese workers and peasants were not as good as they are, a Hungarian incident would have occurred in China and it would have been necessary to invite Soviet troops in."[78]

He was not the only top leader who criticized the "Three Red Banners." Chang Wen-t'ien, a candidate member of the Politburo and the senior vice-minister of foreign affairs, is also reported to have made several speeches attacking the Great Leap.[79] Some evidence suggests that P'eng and Chang may have acted in coordination. On 24 April 1959 P'eng led a "military good will" mission to the capitals of the Warsaw Pact powers, and on the same day Chang left for Warsaw to attend a meeting of the foreign ministers of the Warsaw Pact powers in an observer's capacity. Before and during the Lushan Conference, both P'eng and Chang reportedly had many contacts, and, according to P'eng's confession,

... both comrade Chang Wen-t'ien and I harbored the right-leaning thought and also had discussed things in advance. Furthermore, because both of us harbored prejudice and malcontent against comrade Mao Tse-tung, this urged us to attack the Party together. Although no concrete plan had been mapped out for such an attack, yet it was quite obvious that we two shared the same feelings and worked in coordination.[80]

According to P'eng's own account and other sources, Huang K'o-cheng, a member of the CC Secretariat and chief of staff of the PLA, Chou Hsiao-chou, a candidate member of the CC and first secretary of the Hunan CCP Committee, and a number of other high-ranking party officials (to be identified later) also spoke against the Great Leap and the communes. Besides criticizing the Great Leap and commune policies, Chou Hsiao-chou was alleged to have given P'eng detailed information on the defects of these policies and supplied P'eng with the "ammunition" to attack the party's "Three Banners."[81]

P'eng Teh-huai and his "anti-party clique" may not have intended to overthrow Mao's leadership in the party, as charged. What they in fact attempted was the modification of the party's Great Leap policies. Yet if their endeavors had been successful, Mao's prestige and authority, which were now so closely associated with those policies, would undoubtedly have been tarnished severely.

Having received P'eng's "Letter of Opinion" on 17 July, Mao reportedly spoke for some forty minutes at the Lushan Conference on 23 July.[82] He is said to have declared that he welcomed criticism but that he hoped his audience would "withstand" criticism and not be misled or discouraged. He refuted the charges that the party was divorced from the masses and that the institution of communization, public mess halls, and other mass movements constituted "petty-bourgeois fanaticism"; he claimed that 70 percent of the 500 million rural population actively or tacitly supported the party's programs.[83] Mao asserted that the major shortcomings of the Great Leap were manifested only in "the shortages of vegetables, hairpins and soap, and a tense market situation for a certain period." He admitted that "petty-bourgeois fanaticism" had stirred up the "wind of Communism" for a few months, and for this he held cadres at the *hsien* and commune levels responsible; but he stated that this mistake had been rectified and had in fact had a "favorable" educational effect.

At one point Mao virtually made a self-criticism. He said that he was personally responsible for what went wrong during 1958–59 because he did not understand economic planning and took too much into his own hands. At the same time, however, he implicitly blamed this on the failure of Premier Chou En-lai to assume his responsibilities, and he criticized Vice-Premier Li Fu-ch'un and the State Planning Commission, which Li headed, for not having done the necessary planning work.

Mao confessed that he had originated the idea for a mass movement to smelt iron and steel, which subsequently involved 90 million people in a battle on the "steel" front. In a rather sad and emotional way, he lamented that he had no male offspring, "one son having been killed [in the Korean War] and the other being mad." Quoting a curse uttered by Confucius,[84] Mao attributed his family tragedy to divine punishment for initiating policies that had caused much human suffering.

Some of Mao's attackers may have been silenced or restrained by Mao's speech. In P'eng Teh-huai's own account, he and Chang Wen-t'ien felt "tense" after listening to Mao's talk, and Chang remarked that "things could not be discussed further."[85] P'eng, however, was determined to press his case further, to "clear up some vague ideas."[86]

Whether P'eng had organized the dissidents in advance to launch coordinated attacks in the proceedings of the Englarged Politburo Conference at Lushan is debatable, but it is an intriguing question. The party subsequently condemned the activities of the "anti-party clique" headed by P'eng as "purposive, prepared, planned and organized," and P'eng did not totally deny these accusations.[87] That P'eng's views were not without sympathetic hearers in the CC was barely noted by a passage of the resolution which observed that his activities "could and did mislead a number of people." Some observers now believe that P'eng launched his attack at Lushan with the foreknowledge and support of Russians, having been in personal contact with Khrushchev himself.[88] P'eng and his "anti-party clique" do appear to have done some lobbying behind the scenes before and/or during the Lushan Conference, and many high-ranking PLA officers were reported to have endorsed P'eng's "Letter of Opinion."[89] In addition, a number of Politburo members and lesser personalities apparently supported P'eng initially but did not hold out to the end.

Lin Po-chu, member of the Politburo and a patriarch figure of the party, may have supported P'eng from beginning to end.[90] Information made available since the initiation of the Cultural Revolution claims that Marshal Chu Teh, a member of the Politburo Standing Committee and a vice-chairman of the CC, also sided with P'eng Teh-huai and voiced criticisms of the Great Leap.[91] Mao's sarcastic references to the "Military Club" [*Chunshih chu-lo-pu*][92] and his alleged remarks that he would organize guerrilla bands "if the PLA chooses to follow P'eng Teh-huai"[93] suggest that a large number of PLA leaders were behind P'eng.

Was Mao overwhelmed by his critics at the enlarged Politburo Conference —as Khrushchev was by his opponents in June 1957?[94] Mao may have felt that his leadership position was endangered by the opposition of some of his powerful associates. As the debates between his attackers and defenders continued indecisively to the end of July, Mao reportedly sent for other CC members who were not then present at Lushan and whose support he badly needed[95]—a maneuver which General Huang K'o-cheng is reported to have labeled "calling for reinforcements."[96]

On 2 August Mao turned the enlarged Politburo Conference into a formal CC Plenum, a forum he may not have planned at the outset. Apparently confident of the support that would come from his "reinforcements," Mao's tone changed markedly; he now accused his critics of being "right opportunists" and described their criticism of his policies as the "frantic attack of right opportunists on the Party."[97] Although P'eng Teh-huai and his "anti-party" group were subsequently defeated, the defeat came only after what a *Red Flag* editorial labeled a "test of strength."[98]

From the context of events before the Lushan meeting and developments thereafter, the position taken by various CCP leaders (other than those who have already been identified) during the Mao-P'eng confrontation seems to be of interest, but precise information on this subject is not available. Lin Piao is reported by the Red Guard sources to have vigorously defended Mao's policies, and there is no reason to believe otherwise. Despite the charges to the contrary since the GPCR, Liu Shao-ch'i did throw his support behind Mao.[99] Premier Chou En-lai apparently went along with Mao too. Ch'en Yun, a vice-chairman of the party and a member of the Politburo Standing Committee, had frequently championed a conservative economic line and was a critic of Mao's Great Leap programs, yet he failed to back P'eng at Lushan. In fact, Ch'en was not even present at the Lushan proceedings; according to one Red Guard report, he was on sick leave in Manchuria when the Lushan meeting was in session and he expressed surprise and regret when informed of P'eng's activities.[100] Other top economic officials, including Li Fu-ch'un, Li Hsien-nien, and Po I-po, who had expressed misgivings on Mao's economic measures in 1956, "have now stood firm," in Mao's own words, and did not join forces with the P'eng group;[101] as noted before, they had shifted ground in 1958 to support Mao's Great Leap programs.

In view of the fact that P'eng received support from only one of the seven members of the Politburo Standing Committee (Marshal Chu Teh) and was opposed by four other members (excluding Ch'en Yun and Teng Hsiao-p'ing, who were not present), that he received support primarily from the military officials, and that he failed to recruit to his side more civilian party officials, and particularly those in charge of the economy, his opposition to Mao seemed to lack a broad political appeal. Even though a large number of the PLA leaders backed him, P'eng's challenge to the party leadership, when short of threat or use of naked force (of which P'eng was presumably capable, since both he and his collaborator, General Huang K'o-cheng, had the authority to deploy troops), and when the arena of conflict was the CC where Mao and his supporters had greater control, could result only in defeat.

During the last part of the Lushan Plenum, after being subjected to criticisms and denunciations, P'eng made a formal self-examination.[102] In addition to confessing errors in his attack on the Great Leap and Mao, P'eng also admitted a number of mistakes he had made in the 1930s and 1940s, all of which involved disputes and conflicts with Mao. P'eng is alleged to have said he had adopted a "quarrelsome attitude" toward Mao and for a long time had had "an extremely wrong personal prejudice" against Mao. He also gave a brief account of his relations with Chang Wen-t'ien and Huang K'o-cheng.

On 9 September 1959 P'eng sent a letter to Mao in which he alluded to his past mistakes, regretted his failure to follow Mao's guidance in the past, regarded Mao's "well-intentioned and sincere criticism as a blow" to him, and asked for permission to leave Peking to visit communes so that he might steel and remold himself ideologically "in the collective life of the working people."[103]

P'eng, Chang Wen-t'ien, Huang K'o-cheng, and Chou Hsiao-chou were later officially named members of the "anti-party" clique and were dismissed from their executive posts in the government and the party, but they retained their membership in the party's Politburo and CC.[104] Meanwhile, Lin Piao, Lo Jui-ch'ing, and Chang P'ing-hua replaced P'eng, Huang, and Chou as minister of defense, PLA chief of staff, and first secretary of CCP Hunan Committee, respectively. The surprisingly lenient treatment meted out to P'eng and the other members of the so-called anti-Party clique for their severe offense—challenging the party's leadership—may well have been due to the fact that they commanded substantial support.

With regard to policies concerning the communes, the Lushan Plenum reaffirmed changes in the structure of the communes that had been previously made in the Second Chengchow Conference in March:

> At the present stage a three-level type of ownership of the means of production should be instituted.... Ownership at the production brigade level constitutes the basic one. Ownership at the commune level constitutes another part.... A small part of the ownership should also rest in the production team.[105]

Thus the production brigade would recover the land, animals, and implements that had been taken over by the communes since the fall of 1958, and they again would be the basic accounting unit, whereas the powers at the commune level were drastically curtailed. The Plenum also admitted the exaggeration in the 1958 agricultural production figures released earlier and scaled down the claimed output of grain and cotton from 375 and 3.5 million tons to 250 and 2.1 millions, respectively; it also lowered the 1959 target figures about 10 percent.

The Aftermath of Lushan

Following the Plenum, an extraordinary nationwide campaign was launched against rightist tendencies and "rightist opportunists"; it was accompanied by passionate reaffirmation of the Great Leap policies and exaggerated adulation of Mao's leadership.[106] In many provinces, meetings of provincial and lower-level cadres were held to wage struggles against "rightist thinking, rightist sentiments and rightist activities"; "rightist opportunists" and those imbued with "rightist thinking" were exposed and subjected to serious criticism.[107]

As a result, many party officials, fearing guilt by association with the "rightist opportunists," were reluctant to implement a number of the more practical policies introduced in late 1958 and early 1959. Trends toward realism and pragmatism that had clearly emerged since the spring of 1959 were suddenly halted. In some respects, the momentum of the campaign actually made the Party swing again to the left.

For instance, the system of "production responsibility"—farm output quotas based on individual households [*pao ch'an tao hu*]—which had been acclaimed in the spring, was now denounced by the party as "reactionary"; it was held responsible for having degraded the "big and public" features of the commune system and having converted it into a "small and private" system.[108] Whereas in April and May 1959 Mao (in his Letter of Instruction) and the propaganda organs had placed great emphasis on modest target-setting and on "leaving a margin," three months later the party condemned this sober attitude as "conservatism."[109] This radical "backlash" also resulted in a nation-wide drive to restore commune mess halls and in a frenzied but abortive attempt to set up urban communes.

It subsequently became clear that many party officials were victimized by the "anti-rightist opportunist" campaign.[110] A number of officials disgraced —dismissed or demoted from their original posts—were PLA leaders who either had close working relationships with P'eng Teh-huai or were otherwise implicated in the P'eng affair.[111] The first category included at least T'an Cheng, director of the PLA General Political Department and a secretary of the Central Secretariat, Hung Hsueh-chih, director of the PLA General Rear Services Department, and Hsiao K'o, director of the PLA Military Training Department.[112] The second category included at least Teng Tai-yuan, commander of the Army Railway Corps and minister of railways, Teng Hua, commander of the Shengyang Military Region, and a few civilian officials such as Hsi Chung-hsun, vice-premier and secretary-general of the State Council, and Chang Chung-liang, first secretary of the Kansu Provincial Party Committee.[113] Since all of these PLA leaders were also members of the CC, they may have been the members of the "military club" that Mao referred to in the 1959 Lushan Conference.

Most of the other officials adversely affected by this campaign did not appear to have close relationships with P'eng Teh-huai; they probably held "rightist" views similar to P'eng's, however; that is, they criticized Great Leap and commune policies.[114] Two vice-premiers, Ch'en Yun and Teng Tzu-hui, also slipped into relative obscurity during this period, but available evidence is insufficient to establish their connections with P'eng Teh-huai's "anti-party" activities. Teng Tzu-hui, like Ch'en Yun, had consistently advocated conservative economic policies in the mid-1950s, and he is believed to have been a critic of Mao's Great Leap and commune programs, but his eclipse seemed to precede the Lushan showdown. Sources that became available during the Cultural Revolution indicated that most of the victimized officials in the "anti-rightist campaign" of 1959 were provincial and lower-level cadres.[115]

Whereas the Communist regime ended its first decade of rule on 1 October 1959 with many splendid achievements to its credit as well as serious problems to solve, the regime's second decade was beset with enormous difficulties from the outset.

Severe drought struck many provinces in 1960. In addition, a typhoon and floods, said to be the worst in fifty years, hit twenty provinces, causing very serious damage.[116] Approximately 900 million *mou* of farmland in the country were reported hit by floods, drought, wind, insects, or waterlogging; of this total, some 300 million *mou* of land were severely hit, with some areas suffering complete crop failures.[117] The calamities in 1960 were particularly disastrous since "they came on the heels of the heavy natural calamities which swept over 600 million *mou* of farm land in 1959."[118]

Overambitious Great Leap and commune programs, coupled with cadres' excesses and aggravated by severe natural calamities, resulted in acute food shortages, serious economic disarray, widespread popular discontent, and a serious loss of moral among party and military cadres. In many places calamities precipitated peasant revolt. In Honan, the cradle of the commune system and showcase of many radical Great Leap policies in 1958, for instance, there was widespread starvation and "armed banditry"; desperate peasants who had access to arms (because they were militia members) organized themselves into strong armed bands in Hsinyang, Kaifeng, and other special districts, causing social disorder, and the Chinese authorities had to launch an all-out military and political effort to "suppress the counter-revolutionaries and pacify the countryside," inflicting numerous casualties.[119]

5

Retreat from the Great Leap Forward and the Reorganization of the Commune System

The Fate of the Twelve-Year Agricultural Program

The 1956–1967 National Program for Agricultural Development, which had rarely been mentioned since the fall of 1958, came back into the news in the spring of 1960. The party reiterated the need to "fulfill" the goals of the program, even though at the height of the exhilaration (and exaggeration) of the Great Leap, many of these same goals had been reported to have been surpassed. In April 1960 the NPC formally enacted the Twelve-Year Agricultural Program.[1]

T'an Chen-lin, appointed a vice-premier of the State Council in 1959, made a report on the program.[2] T'an claimed that in 1959 504 *hsien*, 28 percent of the total 1786 *hsien* where grain is grown (or in terms of acreage, 286,700,000 *mou*, 24 percent out of a total 1,200,000,000 *mou*), had achieved or surpassed the program's targets for per *mou* grain yields (400, 500, or 800 catties); 204 *hsien*, 20 percent of 1027 cotton-growing *hsien* (or in terms of acreage, 36,484,000 *mou*, 42 percent of a total of 85,000,000 *mou*), produced over 60, 80, or 100 catties of ginned cotton. In 1959 there were more hogs, it was claimed, than the target figure for 1962. The average annual income of each member of the rural population in 1959 was claimed to have reached about 85 *yuan*, which was close to the average income level (80 *yuan* per person) of the prosperous middle peasants before agricultural cooperation, and it was reported that income reached the target set for 1962 ahead of time.

The "four pests" (rats, sparrows, flies, and mosquitoes) had allegedly been eliminated; and some diseases like smallpox and bubonic plague had already been virtually wiped out or effectively controlled. T'an further claimed that the irrigated areas in China had increased by 550 million *mou*, and that 610 million *mou* were now able to withstand drought for 30, 40, or 70 days, as called for by the program. Soil improvement had covered 450 million *mou*, or 60 percent of the total 700 million *mou* of lowlands subject to waterlogging. The area sown to better seeds reached 1.8 billion *mou*, or 80 percent of the total sown area.

Despite these extravagant claims, the 1959 and 1960 harvests were poor;[3] food shortages were severe, and Peking was forced to import grain from

Western countries to feed its population. Floods and droughts disproved the claim of "achievements" made in the irrigation and water conservancy campaign of 1957–58. Even by T'an's own admission, the efforts to increase grain and cotton—the core of the program—had achieved only a limited success; less than one-fourth of the *hsien* had met the targets for average annual per *mou* output of grain and cotton, and most of these areas had a high-yield record before.[4]

In his speech to the NPC meeting, T'an appealed to the nation to exert greater effort to fulfill the program two or three years ahead of schedule. The party's organ endorsed the call in an enthusiastic editorial;[5] immediately thereafter, cadres in the local areas were directed to mobilize the peasants to work for another great leap in agricultural production. The renewed emphasis on the program in the spring of 1960 by the CCP leadership, particularly the party's attempt to achieve the goals of the program ahead of schedule, was ill-timed, for the prevailing conditions of China's agriculture should have induced the policy-makers to prescribe more realistic measures, as they actually did subsequently, rather than attempt another leap.

The CCP leadership failed to take timely actions to salvage the agricultural crisis in the spring of 1960 for several reasons. In the wake of the Lushan affair, the leadership was apparently impelled to defend and reaffirm the correctness and validity of Mao's policies in order to uphold and restore Mao's prestige and authority, which had been tarnished at the Lushan meeting. The renewed campaign to push the twelve-year agricultural program, in addition to the urban communes, should be viewed in this political context.

It is possible that Nikita Khrushchev's attack on Mao's policies also caused the CCP leadership to react very emotionally and a bit irrationally. Khrushchev's open derision of the peoples' communes in his conversation with United States Senator Hubert Humphrey in December 1958 and his disparaging remarks about the commune system (which could only be taken as direct criticism of the communes in China) in a public speech in Poland in July 1959—both events publicized by the American press—apparently infuriated Mao.[6] A proud and stubborn man, Mao may have become more defiant in the face of Soviet criticism and more doggedly determined to prove the correctness of his policies, regardless of the consequences.[7]

A remark attributed to Liao Lu-yen, minister of agriculture in 1961, provided a clue to the thinking of the CCP leaders and highlighted their defiant mood in 1960: "That things have now come to such a pass is largely attributable to the years before and after 1960 when fired by the passion of the moment and irritated by Khrushchev's rebuke, desperate steps were taken to tackle things in a big way, regardless of consequence."[8] In the fall of 1962, Mao made an admission: "There was a period of time in 1960 when this problem [rectification of errors in agriculture and industry] was given insufficient attention."[9] Mao attributed this to the "advent of revisionism which pressured us, and our attention was shifted to opposing Khrushchev."

If the foregoing analysis has any validity, then it can be said that the actions of the Chinese leaders in the spring of 1960 were influenced at least partly by emotions aroused by Khrushchev's criticism of Chinese policies. This kind of human element is not always easy to discern and document, but it must be present in any policy-making process, since policy-makers are of course subject to emotion and human failings. Policy decisions therefore seldom result from rational deliberation alone, often reflecting the human ingredients.

The Twelve-Year Agricultural Program that was enacted by the NPC in April 1960 was identical with the revised version of October 1957 (which is less ambitious than the 1956 and 1958 versions), except the sparrow, which had been found to be the natural enemy of insect pests harmful to fruit trees, was replaced by bedbugs in the list of "four pests," as proposed by T'an Chen-lin. Even though the APC's had been supplanted by the communes, articles on and references to that institution remained intact, and the existence of the communes was not noted in the program. This may have been a case of legislative sloppiness by the NPC, but it also highlights the role of the NPC in China's policy-making process: the NPC was a rubber stamp; it simply put a seal of approval on the bill as presented by the party leadership without even making technical amendments. Interestingly enough, T'an Chen-lin, throughout his speech to the NPC, failed to make any references to the second revised draft of the program which had been approved by the second session of the Eighth Party Congress in May 1958. The 1958 version, reflecting the radicalized atmosphere of that time, contained higher targets and a number of new goals.

The 1956–1967 National Program for Agricultural Development fell into oblivion after April 1960, and little has been said about it.[10] The top policy-makers in the party, including the original proponents of the program, may have lost interest in it, for in fact it had proven to be a failure.

The approaches toward increasing agricultural production—massive mobilization of labor, intensive application of labor, greater emphasis on structural change and ideological motivation—which had been symbolized by the program and advocated by the radicals of the party, including Mao, proved counterproductive in many respects. The stress on ideological motivations and attitudinal change underlying Mao's almost mystic faith in the malleability of human nature was a poor substitute for incentives and resulted in serious peasant discontent. The structural changes in agriculture brought about by the establishment of first the APC's and then the communes, and the utilization of these control mechanisms to effect maximum resource mobilization in the rural areas, had achieved only a limited success and in fact by 1959 had reached the point of diminishing returns.

Many Chinese Communists by now were well aware that sustained agricultural growth would require major technological reforms in agricultural production. The Twelve-Year Agricultural Program was a step in that direction, but the measures it stipulated were insufficient and inadequate because they emphasized labor-intensive techniques and underestimated the need for capital investment.

In conjunction with technical improvements in agriculture, an intensive campaign had been conducted during 1958 and 1959 to implement the "eight-point charter for agriculture," which had been introduced by Mao in 1958 after he "applied the advanced principles of agricultural sciences and summarized the rich experience of the peasant masses in the practice of production."[11] The excessive and indiscriminate application of techniques such as close planting and deep plowing, in disregard of divergent soil and climate conditions, not only wasted large amounts of labor but contributed substantially to crop failures in many localities.

In light of the relatively labor-intensive farming techniques practiced in China even before collectivization, increasing agricultural production required greater capital investment in agriculture. Throughout the 1950s, however, Peking had been unwilling to divert significant amounts of investment resources, heretofore channeled into industry, and particularly heavy industry, to agriculture, and state investment in agriculture had been relatively small.

In 1958, the radical group in the party had formulated a new approach to agricultural investment: local resources and labor were mobilized on an unprecedented large scale to work on labor-intensive investment projects such as irrigation, flood control, and land reclamation and to raise unit yields in agriculture through close planting, deep plowing, and the like, as well as to promote the expansion of small-scale local industry. The party planned to use the output of these local industries to satisfy rural demands for manufactured consumer goods, tools, agricultural machinery, and other requisites of farm production, while most of the modern sector's product would still be saved and used for its own continued growth. This was one of the main ideas behind the slogan "walking on two legs"—a strategy of dualism designed to bring about the simultaneous development of agriculture and industry.[12] Instead, however, this strategy helped to produce the profound economic chaos in China between 1960 and 1962.

The "Agriculture-First" Strategy

Confronted with acute food shortages and serious economic dislocation, and shocked by the sudden withdrawal of Soviet technicians from China, the party was compelled to scrap the Great Leap, modify the commune system, and improvise measures to cope with the serious crisis from the second part of 1960 on. The regime's past policies, which had been riding the tide of the "anti-rightist" campaign, momentarily swung to the left after the Lushan Conference. Gradually, however, the prevailing crisis situations swung the pendulum back to the right as the "anti-rightist" campaign ground to a halt and "conservative" elements steadily regained a predominant voice in the councils of the party.

In the summer of 1960 a Central Work Conference was convened at Peitaiho, to be attended by all provincial first party secretaries. The proceedings of the conference were not given publicity in the media, but subsequent events indicate that the conference must have decided to change drastically the priorities of economic policy—above all by mobilizing available resources to support agriculture. Fragmentary evidence suggests that it was at this conference that the party discussed or decided upon the reestablishment of six CC regional bureaus (which had been abolished in 1954)[13]—a decision which was announced by the party at its Ninth CC Plenum in January 1961.

After the work conference, the shift toward an "agriculture-first" policy became clearly discernible. In an article in *Hung Ch'i* in September 1960 Liao Lu-yen, minister of agriculture, stressed that agriculture must be the foundation of the national economy and that the basic policy of the party must be to take agriculture as the "foundation" and industry as the "leading factor."[14] It is true that the agriculture-first policy had been discussed by various CCP officials since the fall of 1959 and that Mao was credited with initiating the policy in 1959,[15] yet the policy had not been seriously implemented up to the summer of 1960. In the last four or five months of 1960, "all the people to agriculture and food grains" became a nation-wide slogan in China, and concrete steps finally were undertaken to implement the new line.

The policy of making the production brigades the major units of ownership, accounting, and production in the communes was reiterated and reemphasized in the public media. For instance, on 16 September 1960 an editorial in the Canton *Nan-fang Jih-pao* (*Southern Daily*) instructed cadres to thoroughly implement the new policies and encouraged the production brigades and commune members to undertake "multiple enterprises" and subsidiary occupations in addition to growing food grains; the proceeds of such diversified undertakings were to be kept by the brigades for their members. Apparently in answer to charges that these measures represented a backsliding from the original system of ownership at the communal level, the same editorial disclosed that "On the basis of the experiences gained in the People's Communes over the past two years, our Party has recently set the period of transition from the system of ownership by the production brigade to the system of ownership by the People's communes at five years." In other words, the retreat was to be only temporary; when the situation improved, the party would advance once more.

It appears that many of the pragmatic and rational measures introduced since the spring of 1959, including the agriculture-first policy, had not been effectively implemented, and in some cases had not been implemented at all. The campaign against the "rightist opportunists" launched after the Lushan Plenum and the efforts to reassert the validity of Mao's policies were one of the major factors, as previously indicated. In mid-May 1960 T'ao Chu stated the following:

> Recently, the bud of rashness has again appeared in some places. There is a desire to speed up the transition of the system of ownership by the brigades to the system of ownership by the communes. Communes have improperly used the material resources and labor power at the lower levels to strengthen the commune-owned economy. Some other people go to the other extreme; they think that failure to observe totally the principle of exchange at equal value and distribution according to work means equalitarianism.[16]

In many localities the party's distribution policy (to each according to his labor, and payment based mostly on wages), which was clearly stipulated after the Wuhan Plenum in December 1958, was not implemented. In Kwangtung, "idealist" and extremist cadres claimed that "the more the payment in supplies and the less the payment in wages the better." The cadres added meat, fish, and fruit to the five basic items originally stipulated for free supply.[17] In the distribution of free rations, these cadres gave the same treatment to men and women, old and young, and people capable and incapable of heavy physical labor. According to Nan-fang Jih-pao (2 September 1960), "more and more goods are supplied while less and less is paid in wages, and some brigades cannot afford to pay wages for a long time.... [This] dampens the people's enthusiasm for production to a considerable degree." In the suburbs of Peking, cadres wanted to distribute less and retain more, because "the availability of more funds on hand can help develop the economies of the communes at a faster pace."[18]

Many cadres resisted the party's policies because their own interests were involved. Since the transfer of rights of property ownership and production authority from the communes to the brigades would inevitably reduce the power of cadres at the commune level, some cadres refused to carry out the changes, justifying their action on the grounds that the changes would "affect the unified leadership of the communes and hamper the fulfillment of production plans."[19]

Huang Huo-ch'ing, first party secretary of Liaoning, blamed the "departmentalism" of cadres in Liaoning, one of China's most important industrial provinces, for the failure to implement effectively the party's "support-agriculture" policy:

Not all the comrades grasped the great significance of industrial aid to agriculture as a measure to speed up agro-technical reform. Some functionaries of certain factories and mines showed rightist conservatism and departmentalism; they maintained that fulfillment of their production tasks came into conflict with the aid to agriculture. Some regarded the communes as "poverty-stricken relatives" and held that industrial aid to agriculture was "one-way help" and "additional burden."[20]

In an editorial of 17 July 1960 the *People's Daily* emphatically instructed industrial enterprises to forgo other considerations and promote the idea that agriculture should be the foundation of all things, giving top priority to supporting agricultural production.[21] And in November 1960 the party dispatched a secret "Twelve-Article Urgent Directive on Rural Work" to cadres at all levels, instructing them to carry out the provisions of the directive thoroughly and faithfully.[22]

The directive reduced the scope of power at the commune level and enlarged the authority of the brigades to make them economically and administratively viable units (articles 1 and 3). It demanded that cadres stop trying to equalize peasants' income by transferring workers without regard for the quality of work that resulted, a policy known as "one equalization and two transfers" [*yi-p'ing erh-t'iao*].[23] It returned to peasants private plots, which had been confiscated in 1958, and permitted peasants to undertake family sideline occupations (article 5) and sell their products in the rural trade fairs (article 10). The directive also stipulated that more collective income should be allocated for distribution and less for accumulation and that more than 70 percent of payment to the peasants must be in wages.

The restoration of private plots and the opening of free markets were the only provisions that had not been announced before the directive. The fact that the party deemed it necessary to reiterate the other provisions and disseminate new instructions in the form of an "urgent directive" was a further indication that policies had not been earnestly implemented by lower cadres up to that time.

China's New Economic Policy

In January 1961 the CC, which had not met formally since August 1959, held its ninth plenary session in Peking. This was a very critical moment—the food supply crisis was at its worst, and shortly before, in the summer of 1960, the Soviet government had torn up many agreements concluded with Peking and had withdrawn from China Russian experts and technicians along with the blueprints of unfinished industrial plants and factories.

The CC reaffirmed the agriculture-first policy pursued since the summer of 1960:

> The whole nation in 1961 must concentrate on strengthening the agricultural front, thoroughly carry out the policy of taking agriculture as the foundation of the national economy and of the whole Party and the entire people going in for agriculture and grain production in a big way, step up and support agricultural production by all trades and professions.[24]

Although the communique of the plenum did not specifically mention the twelve-article urgent directive, the plenum presumably discussed and approved it. The new agricultural policy was combined with an industrial policy based on "readjustment, consolidation, filling out and raising standards." In concrete terms, the new line meant that economic activities had to be readjusted, capital investment had to be cut back, consumer goods industries and industries that could produce goods of value to agriculture were to be favored, and quality rather than quantity was to be emphasized. The communique also formally announced two other important party decisions: to establish six regional CC bureaus and to intensify the rectification campaign, which was already in progress.

Recentralization and Rectification

The regional bureaus were established, in the words of the communique, to "strengthen leadership" of the party center over party committees in the provinces. In the course of decentralization and the Great Leap, provincial authorities, and particularly provincial party committees, had acquired greater power (at the expense of central government ministries) in the management of economy. Provincial party secretaries, supposedly agents of the central party control, tended to become identified with local and particularistic interests and to become preoccupied with problems of their provincial administration, so that many displayed "dispersionist" and "departmental" tendencies.

In the spring of 1959, as noted previously, heavy emphasis had been placed on the principle of "the whole country as a chess board," and some measures were put forward to recentralize and tighten control over the provincial authorities. The establishment of the new regional party bureaus was a further step toward recentralization—it would provide the central leadership with an additional organizational instrument to supervise the provinces more closely.[25] These regional bodies, judging from their institutional setup, were expected to perform major economic functions on a regional basis, in addition to their regular political functions.[26]

In 1961 the regional bureaus were assigned the priority task of supervising the ongoing rectification campaign. In the words of the communique of the Ninth CC Plenum, the rectification campaign was to be carried out throughout the country "stage by stage" and "area by area," to help cadres "raise their ideological and political level, improve their method and style of work and purify the organizations" by cleaning out the extremely few bad elements who had "sneaked into party and government organizations."

The party publicly admitted that counterrevolutionary incidents had taken place and that the party's functionaries had committed various unlawful acts. The primary targets of the 1961 rectification campaign, however, were obviously the "leftist" elements who were described by the communique as "good-willed and well-intentioned" but without a "sufficiently high level of ideological consciousness." They were accused of lacking sufficient understanding of the distinction between socialism and Communism and between the socialist ownership by the collective and the socialist ownership by the people as a whole, of the three-level ownership in the People's Commune with the brigades as the foundation, of the principles of exchange of equal value and to each according to his work. In short, the campaign was directed against "leftist tendencies."

Some of the more radical provincial-level proponents of the Great Leap were disciplined in the course of the rectification campaign. Wu Chih-p'u, Honan's first party secretary who had played a leading role in the communization movement in 1958 and ruthlessly implemented many Great Leap programs (which had helped cause widespread famine and peasant revolt) in 1958–60, was demoted to second party secretary in 1961 and was later transferred from his post in Honan.[27] Chang Chung-liang, first party secretary of Kansu, was purged in 1961, partly as a result of serious famine and starvation that had occurred in that province in 1959–60.[28] The 1960–61 purge or demotion of province-level first secretaries in Chinghai (Kao Feng), Shantung (Su Tung), and Anhwei (Tseng Hsi-sheng) also may have been related to "leftist" mistakes they committed during the Great Leap period. These three first secretaries had played a leading role in the 1958 purges of "conservative" officials in their provinces, and when these officials won reinstatement their prosecutors' positions were undermined.

Changes in the Original Commune System

After Mao relinquished the chairmanship of the Republic in April 1959, and particularly after the Lushan confrontation in which Mao's prestige and self-esteem were badly scarred, he appeared to gradually withdraw from active participation in the policy-making councils. Either because Mao was unwilling to preside over the liquidation of his utopian programs or because of opposition pressure within the leadership or preoccupation with the widening Sino-Soviet rift—or, more probably, a combination of all these factors—the reclamation of the disasters of the Great Leap and commune programs was largely carried out by Mao's colleagues. They were known to have sought Mao's final approval of major policy decisions,[29] yet Mao no longer introduced them, as he often had in the past (this may be less true in regard to key foreign policy issues, such as Sino-Soviet relations). The importance of the function of policy initiation should not be overlooked; those who initiate are in a better position to define problems, present alternatives, and structure choices. Since Mao no longer initiated policy, he lost a large measure of control over the decision-making process.

For instance, when Mao convened a Central Work Conference at Canton in March 1961 to consider, among other things, the reorganization of communes, the chairman discovered to his chagrin that, without his prior knowledge, Teng Hsiao-p'ing, the party's general-secretary, had already made certain key decisions on the plan concerning the reorganization, which was drafted under Teng's supervision.[30] Presented with the fait accompli, an irritated Mao asked sarcastically: "Which Emperor has decided these?"[31] Even though Mao expressed displeasure and scolded Teng for making decisions in advance of the meeting, he was apparently compelled by the prevailing instability of the rural economy to sanction or at least acquiesce to the plan. The meeting subsequently approved the "Draft Regulations on the Rural People's Communes."[32] It seems that when Mao no longer initiated policies and withdrew from active participation in policy-making process, those who controlled the CC Secretariat increased their power since they were in a position to exercise control over the agenda of the party conferences and over the preparation of policy proposals for deliberation at the conferences.

The new sixty-article draft redefined the nature of the communes as well as their ownership and distribution systems, watering down the original (1958) concept considerably. It clearly stipulated the various functions and division of labor among the three layers of the commune, a move intended to check abuses by officials at the commune level; it also decentralized most powers previously vested in the commune level, passing these powers down to the brigade and team levels—which in a sense was a concession to "localism."

In addition to reducing the size of the communes and brigades and prescribing that 5 percent of the farmland in a given commune be set aside for private plots, the sixty-article "Regulations" elaborated on the measures provided for in the twelve-article "Urgent Directive" and presented them in a more detailed and formalized manner. Party committees at all levels were instructed to discuss the new document and to insure its thorough understanding and faithful implementation by cadres.

Reaction to the sixty articles was apparently mixed, with most cadres and soldiers in the PLA reportedly warmly supporting the party's new policy. However, the party felt compelled to reply to "some cadres and soldiers" who articulated misgivings such as the following: Do communes still have "ten superiorities"? Is there still any difference between the people's communes and the advanced co-operatives when big communes are being divided into small ones and earnings are made proportional to labor, and when self-retained land continues to exist?[33] Where did the "five styles" come from? Why is it that the wind of "Communist style" has been blowing all over the nation?[34] And some cadres questioned whether the promotion of private plots, family sideline occupations, and free markets "would affect collective production and develop capitalism."[35]

Party propagandists were at pains to defend the party leadership from the obvious charge of having turned backward and being inconsistent. They maintained that the "Three Red Banners" (the general line for socialist construction, the Great Leap, and the communes) were still correct, and that the measures prescribed in both the twelve articles and the sixty articles had been consistently advocated by the CC and Chairman Mao, and they blamed the difficulties of the national economy on overzealous cadres who had stirred up the "communist wind" (i.e., excessively stressed egalitarian tendencies) as well as on cadres' mistakes in the execution of party policies. However, this line of argument was hardly convincing; in fact, not a few cadres reportedly attributed responsibility for the "five styles" to the central authorities, and some even said that without the commune there would be no "five styles."[36]

The CCP leadership clearly began to display a greater sense of realism. Expertise, rational planning, efficiency, and pragmatism were again emphasized.[37] The critics of the Great Leap policies who had been sidelined in 1957–58 and again in 1959–60 during the anti-rightist-opportunists campaign were gradually rehabilitated—a tacit admission that these critics had been at least partially correct.[38]

In 1961, a number of Politburo members went out to rural areas to undertake what were called "squatting investigations" [*tun-tien tiao-ch'a*]. For instance, Liu Shao-ch'i spent forty-four days in three communes in three different *hsien* in Hunan from 2 April to 15 May 1961.[39] Also in April and May, both Teng Hsiao-p'ing and P'eng Chen spent one half month in the rural areas of Hopei carrying out intensive investigation.[40] Ch'en Yun was in the suburbs of Shanghai for three weeks from June to July.[41] Even P'eng Teh-huai and Chang Wen-t'ien reportedly went out to rural areas to undertake "investigation and study."[42]

The obvious change in the top leaders' working style probably resulted from their realization that they had not received accurate information about China's political and economic conditions, which they needed to form correct workable decisions. Hence the Central Work Conference in March 1961 instructed leading cadres at all levels to conduct personal "investigation and study" to help them understand the situation on a firsthand basis.[43] The study of "On Investigation Work," an article written by Mao in 1930, was now required reading for cadres.[44]

In conducting these "squatting investigations" top leaders stayed in a given locality long enough to closely survey the grassroot conditions. Thus they obtained information that might otherwise have been concealed by lower-level officials or might have failed to reach the top levels of the party through official channels of communication. This subject is discussed further in Chapter 7.

A Realignment of Political Forces

The political climate in China had changed considerably since the second half of 1960. The CCP leadership manifested anxiety and a sense of urgency, in contrast with an earlier attitude of resolution and defiance in the face of internal difficulties and Khrushchev's criticism. Officials who had been most closely linked with the Great Leap and commune policies at the provincial level, and probably at lower levels, were disciplined, and critics of these policies who had been demoted or dismissed reasserted themselves and succeeded in "reversing the verdict" [fan an], that is, they won reinstatement.

Moderate policy views were now well received in the party. Several of the top economic officials of the regime, including Ch'en Yun and Teng Tzu-hui, who were known for their conservative views and criticisms of the Great Leap and commune policies and who had been politically inactive during 1958–60, must have felt vindicated by the prevailing conditions. From 1961 on men like Ch'en Yun and Teng Tzu-hui reemerged on the political scene and actively participated in the policy-making processes.[45] Members of the Politburo who previously had been inclined toward the "radical" group and supported Mao's economic measures, including Liu Shao-ch'i, Teng Hsiao-p'ing, and P'eng Chen, also changed their stance. Whether the lessons they learned from the failure of the Great Leap had honestly changed their minds or whether they were merely being opportunistic cannot be determined. In any case, political forces in the party underwent a gradual, almost imperceptible realignment from the second half of 1960, with the advocates of the moderate policy in charge of the party's policy-making councils.

The conversion of Liu Shao-ch'i into an ardent advocate of moderate policies in the early 1960s was both interesting and politically significant. Before the Cultural Revolution in the second half of the 1960s, Liu had generally been regarded by Western observers as a hardliner.[46] In the two speeches Liu made in 1957 and 1958, he showed himself to be a staunch supporter of the Great Leap and closely identified himself with Mao.[47] Liu succeeded Mao as chairman of the republic in April 1959, apparently because he had Mao's confidence, for although he had differed with Mao on the questions of collectivization in 1955 and the "hundred flowers" in 1957, when the party decision was made, Liu went along with Mao.

The Great Leap and commune programs generated harmful consequences by the time the Lushan Conference was called into session in July 1959, and Liu had begun to doubt their value. The Lushan meeting was originally intended to be a working conference to deal with defects in the economy and modify some of the radical policies that were being pursued, but Peng Teh-huai's attack on Mao upset the original plan.[48] Although Liu threw his support to Mao in Mao's confrontation with P'eng Teh-huai,[49] he was apparently preoccupied with the economic dislocations caused by the Greater Leap. The accusation that Liu hoisted the "ensign of combating the Left deviation" at the Lushan proceedings and schemed to "tamper with the already prepared summary of the meeting and turn it into an anti-Left document"[50] suggests that Liu was concerned with curbing excesses of the Great Leap.

Mao's withdrawal from active participation in the leadership in 1960 put Liu squarely in the forefront. The responsibility for overcoming the economic disaster now rested on the shoulders of Liu, who now was working closely with Ch'en Yun, Teng Hsiao-p'ing, P'eng Chen, and Po I-po. During his seven-week squatting investigation in Hunan Liu probably got a clearer picture of the state of the economy; in May 1961, in fact, he warned a Central Work Conference that the true situation in the nation was worse than had hitherto been realized by the leadership.[51] From that time on, Liu apparently became more outspoken in his criticism of the defects of the Great Leap and the commune programs and supported a series of measures that were long advocated by the "conservative" group in the 1950s. Although Liu's criticisms were largely directed against the cadres and their implementation of Mao's programs, Mao probably saw these criticisms as aimed at himself. The disagreement between Mao and Liu grew steadily; although there was no open and complete break between the two until 1966, in retrospect, it is clear that Liu's "rightist deviations" of 1961–62, which were criticized by Mao in the summer of 1962, undermined Mao's trust in Liu.

P'eng Chen also had generally been regarded as a "hardliner"; in 1957 he, like Liu Shao-ch'i, was said to have taken a tough position toward the party's liberalization policy.[52] Nevertheless, there is evidence to suggest that P'eng had become critical of Mao's leadership by 1961, if not earlier. It was the *Peking Wan Pao* [*Peking Evening News*] and *Ch'ien Hsien* [*Front Line Monthly*], both controlled by P'eng Chen's Peking party apparatus, which in 1961–62 published the satirical political essays entitled "Evening Chats at Yenshan" and "Three Family Village," which subtly attacked the Great Leap.[53] It is difficult to believe that this was done without P'eng's approval—or at least knowledge.

In 1961 P'eng reportedly established an "Office of Policy Research" under the Peking Municipal Party Committee and staffed it with his own "brain-trusters."[54] This office is said to have conducted a series of intensive investigations into the commune system, industry, finance and trade, and other fields. *Peking Jih-pao* also claimed that P'eng Chen organized his aides to undertake a critical examination of orders and directives issued by Mao personally and by the central authorities during 1958–60, allegedly for the purpose of uncovering errors and mistakes committed by Mao.[55] The authenticity of these reports is difficult to judge, but the evidence does suggest differences evolved between P'eng Chen and Mao.

The realignment of party leaders as well as Mao's loss of his magic grip on some of his followers had crucial implications for policy-making. In the second half of 1961, the party further reorganized the commune system, introducing revisions more extensive than those presented earlier in the sixty articles.[56] The size of the communes, brigades, and teams was reduced, and the teams (generally twenty to thirty households in size), which had already been granted greater powers in managing production, were made the basic "ownership" as well as "accounting" units of the communes.[57] Thus the widely propagandized "big and public" features of the 1958 commune system could no longer be found in the drastically reorganized communes.

In December 1961 the party formulated another major policy document—the seventy-article "Regulations on Industry, Mines and Enterprises"—to try to cope with serious disarray and pressing problems in industry.[58] This document was drafted under the close supervision of Vice-Premier Po I-po, assisted by Sung Jen-chiung (then the first secretary of the CCP Northeast Bureau and during 1956–60 minister of the Third and Second Machine-Building Ministries), and was approved by a Politburo meeting chaired by Liu Shao-ch'i.[59] As noted earlier, since the Ninth Plenum in January 1961 the party had emphasized an agriculture-first strategy and had reshuffled its priorities of economic development; the seventy-article "Regulations" now outlined concrete and systematic measures to implement these broad policy lines.[60]

The provisions of this document clearly indicate that many policies associated with the Great Leap were reversed. Except in a few specially regulated cases, all capital construction programs were to be terminated (articles 3 and 4) and all industrial enterprises set up in haste and in defiance of economic rationality (i.e., those suffering financial loss) were to be closed down (article 9). Industrial production was to be reoriented toward serving the market—that is, satisfying consumer demands (article 2). Workers' material incentives were to be more carefully studied, the piece-wage system was to be restored, and better working conditions and other welfare benefits were to be provided (articles 25, 26, 27, 67, 68, and 69). Rationality, rather than mass movement, became the dominant theme of industrial management; factory managers (*ch'ang chang*) were once again given production authority, and the importance of engineers and technicians in production processes was reemphasized (articles

30 and 52). Quality was favored over quantity, and a system of strict quality control was established (articles 34, 35, and 36).

The Reversal of Verdicts

In January 1962 an enlarged Central Work Conference was held in Peking, attended by 7000 people, most of them provincial and lower-level officials. The immediate objective of the conference was to prepare a comprehensive review and a "summing-up" of the regime's policies of the previous three years.[61] This occasion was similar to the Lushan Conference in 1959, for again the Great Leap and commune programs received heavy criticism.

The consensus that emerged from the January 1962 enlarged Central Work Conference apparently was that the party, without abandoning the slogans of the Great Leap, would have to scrap its ambitious programs and pursue a rational and pragmatic course of economic development. Liu Shao-ch'i apparently set the tone of the conference when he said that the catastrophic failures of the Great Leap were "three parts natural calamities and seven parts human failings" [*san-fen t'ien-chai, ch'i-fen jen-ho*] and admonished party officials to learn the necessary lessons from these painful experiences.[62] Among the top leaders only Chou En-lai and Lin Piao came to Mao's defense.[63]

The rehabilitation of the critics of the Great Leap and the victims of the 1959 "anti-rightist-opportunist" campaign, which had expanded gradually after late 1960, apparently was an important item on the agenda of the conference. Subsequently Red Guard sources reported that the official line adopted by the party was, in Liu Shao-ch'i's words, that "those who shared P'eng Teh-huai's views, provided that they had not colluded with foreign countries, would be permitted to reopen their cases."[64] The matter, however, did not rest there; those who had done the purging or had benefited from the purging seemed to have resisted the move, and the top leaders were compelled to speak out again.[65]

The following statement by Liu Shao-ch'i, republished in 1962, deserves to be quoted at length; it unmistakably reflects a negative attitude toward the "anti-rightist-opportunists" campaign and the attendant purges:

> When opportunist ideas and differences of principles arise in the Party, we must, of course, wage struggles to overcome those ideas and errors of principle. This definitely does not mean that when there are no differences of principle and no opportunist ideas in the Party, we should deliberately magnify into differences of principle divergences of opinion among comrades on questions of a purely practical nature.
>   Comrade Mao Tse-tung has said: "... *the Party must on the one hand wage a serious struggle against erroneous thinking, and must on the other hand give the comrades who have committed errors ample opportunity to wake up to*

their errors. This being the case, excessive struggle is obviously not appropriate."
The *"Left"* opportunists were clearly *wrong in their attitude toward inner-Party struggle.* According to these almost hysterical people, any peace in the Party was intolerable—even peace based on complete unanimity on matters of principle and on the Party line. Even in the absence of any differences of principle in the Party, they deliberately hunted out targets, dubbed some comrades opportunists and set them up as "straw men" to shoot at in inner-Party struggle. They thought that such erroneous struggle and such shooting at "straw men" were the magic formula for developing the Party and achieving victory in the revolutionary fight of the proletariat.[66] (Emphasis added)

Although this statement (based on a statement which first appeared many years earlier) restated ideas Liu had preached since 1939, the new messages contained in the revised text (the italicized sentences) are important, especially in the new political context of 1962 when Liu was attacking the "left" opportunists. We need not accept at face value charges recently leveled against Liu that the republication in 1962 of his 1939 treatise, *How to be a Good Communist*, represented an open challenge to Mao. Nor can one assume that the charges made by Maoist propagandists that Liu was behind the "anti-party" group at the 1959 Lushan meeting and later actively sought P'eng Teh-huai's reinstatement are necessarily correct.[67] Rather it is more likely that Liu's promotion of a policy of rehabilitation was motivated by his genuine concern over the harmful effects generated by the excessive purges and struggles that had taken place in the party. Undoubtedly, at a time of serious national crisis, the party needed to unite its members and mobilize all of its talent to cope with the various problems it faced. Acting as a "unifier" in the party, Liu could and must have enhanced his image and prestige among many party members.

In 1961–62 P'eng Teh-huai was dramatized as the contemporary "Hai Jui" in a historical play, *The Dismissal of Hai Jui*, which was performed throughout China and was well received by China's attentive public. Wu Han, a vice-mayor of Peking and a well-known playwright and historian, pictured Hai Jui as a righteous Ming Dynasty minister who returned land to peasants and brought oppressive and corrupted officials to justice only to be cashiered for his efforts through court intrigue. In the play, the demand was made that the unfair dismissal be reversed so that this "righteous official" could again serve the people.[68] The contemporary meaning of the drama was apparently not lost on Mao; in fact, he said that "The crux of the 'Dismissal of Hai Jui' is the question of dismissal from office; the Emperor Chia Ch'ing dismissed Hai Jui from office. In 1959 we dismissed P'eng Teh-huai from office and P'eng Teh-huai is 'Hai Jui,' too."[69]

Undoubtedly Mao was irritated, to say the least, by the demands being made to reinstate critics of Great Leap policies; and he may have been particularly embittered by open sympathy being shown to Marshal P'eng Teh-huai by the intellectuals. During 1961–62, T'eng T'o, a party secretary of the Peking Municipal Committee, Wu Han, and Liao Mo-sha, director of the United Front Work Department of the Peking Party Committee, together or separately wrote many essays "in the guise of recounting historical anecdotes, impartial knowledge, telling stories and cracking jokes" that surreptitiously mocked Mao, criticized his policies, pointed to his errors, and subtly praised his critics.[70] In domestic policy, for example, they satirized at the "follies" of the Great Leap, characterizing it as "boasting," "indulging in fantasy," and "substituting illusion for reality." In foreign policy, they indirectly ridiculed Mao's famous slogan "The East Wind Prevails over the West Wind" as "great empty talk."

The economic crisis in 1960–62 had come to vindicate P'eng Teh-huai's earlier criticisms and had made him a martyr in the eyes of some Chinese. Mao had been proven wrong, and his prestige appears to have been tarnished, judging from the writings of Wu Han, Teng T'o, and other intellectuals in the party.[71] Perhaps emboldened by the evidence of sympathy for the cause he fought for, in June 1962 P'eng produced an 80,000-word "petition" to appeal for a "reversal of verdict" in his case.[72] Mao may have been further distressed by P'eng's action, which suggested that P'eng had not learned his lesson after the Lushan incident and had not repented.

The Role of Ch'en Yun[73]

In the party's further swing to the right in 1962, Ch'en Yun appears to have been a major moving force behind many policies of economic rationalization. Supporters of Mao now claim that Liu Shao-ch'i admits that he "trusted Ch'en Yun too much and listened to his views too one-sidedly." Under Liu's aegis, Ch'en was appointed head of a "Five-Man CC Finance and Economy Group" established in 1962 to take charge of the regime's overall economic and financial policies.

From 21 to 23 February 1962, Liu Shao-ch'i reportedly convened an enlarged session of the Politburo Standing Committee in the west chamber of Chungnanhai, Peking (often referred to by the Red Guard press as the "West Chamber Conference") to follow up various suggestions made at the January CC Work Conference. The West Chamber Conference, which was also attended by the regime's top economic officials, reportedly heard Ch'en Yun present a report on "Current Financial and Economic Conditions and Certain Measures." Excerpts reported in Red Guard publications indicated that Ch'en Yun's indictment of the Great Leap was merciless but that his diagnosis of the state of the national economy was essentially realistic; he prescribed drastic measures to salvage the situation.

Teng Tzu-hui also is said to have discussed and recommended Anhwei's "responsibility farm system," under which each peasant household was to assume responsibility for agricultural production on the farmland contracted to it. The conference, according to Liu Shao-ch'i's account, "did not oppose this proposal." A "certain comrade," as Liu Shao-ch'i recalled, even went so far as to propose the permanent distribution of farmland to each peasant household and advocated the policy of "*san ho yi shao*" [three reconciliations and one reduction], that is, making peace with the imperialists, reactionaries, and revisionists and reducing aid to the world revolutionary movements.

In 1967 Ch'en Yun was identified as the "villain" who had advocated the distribution of collective lands to peasants. He was quoted as having said in the summer of 1962, when the Nationalists were threatening to invade the mainland, that the peasants could be relied upon in the coming battle with the Nationalists if they had a stake in their own land.

The Politburo, it is said, later endorsed Ch'en Yun's report to the West Chamber Conference and asked him to speak again to "leading cadres" of the CC departments and the State Council. Ch'en Yun's speech was subsequently disseminated to officials at the provincial level for "discussion"—a practice often used by Chinese leaders to inform lower officials of the thinking at the top.

In May 1962 a report prepared by Ch'en Yun's five-man CC financial and economic group was approved by Liu Shao-ch'i, who was presiding over the Politburo in the absence of Mao. Although details of this report are not available, it probably proposed a drastic reorientation of economic priorities and further extension of rational measures to boost economic production. Faced with a *fait accompli*, Mao was reportedly furious; in Liu Shao-ch'i's words, "the Chairman was not in the least in accord with our evalution of the situation and our way of doing things."

Confronted by an acute food shortage, widespread social discontent, and serious economic disruptions, the majority of the party leaders appeared to be willing to take drastic measures to boost the peasants' incentives for production and to disregard temporarily the political and ideological implications of such measures. Thus a system called *san tzu i pao* [three freedoms and one guarantee], which subsequently was denounced repeatedly during the cultural revolution,[74] is said to have been instituted in 1962. This system allowed peasants to farm private plots as well as reclaim wasteland for their own use, to operate family sideline occupations, and to sell their produce in the free markets; in addition, each household was responsible for certain output quotas on the public land assigned to it.

In some cases, collective lands were divided among peasants on a long-term basis in the 1962 period, and some peasants were even permitted to leave communes to engage in private farming. Teng Hsiao-p'ing allegedly quipped: "So long as it raised output, *tan kan* (literally, going it alone, i.e., private farming) is permissible; white or black, so long as the cats can catch mice, they are good cats."[75] These concessions, a desperate attempt to salvage the Great Leap, considerably weakened the collectivist elements of agricultural production.

Retreats in the Model Province—Honan

Honan was a pacesetter in the communization movement in 1958; under the leadership of the leftist first secretary, Wu Chih-p'u, the province received much nation-wide publicity for carrying out radical Great Leap measures. In 1960–61, severe natural calamities and human failings [*t'ien tsai jen huo*] resulted in enormous economic dislocations in this province. Many areas of the province suffered complete crop failure; hunger was widespread, and large numbers of peasants fled Honan. Armed peasant revolts occurred in several special districts, and the Chinese authorities had to use troops to suppress these "counterrevolutionary" activities, inflicting numerous casualties.[76] In 1960 or early 1961, First Secretary Wu Chih-p'u was demoted to second secretary and later shifted to a position outside of Honan. Liu Chien-hsun, the first secretary of Kwangsi Chuan Autonomous Region, was transferred to Honan to head the Honan Provincial Party Committee in 1961.

Two months after the 7000-cadre enlarged Central Work Conference met (January 1962), T'ao Chu, first secretary of the Central South Regional Bureau, came to Honan to deal with the critical situation there. At Chengchow, the provincial capital of Honan, T'ao Chu presided over a work conference (also called the Chung-chou Guest House Conference) which was attended by secretaries of provincial, special district, and municipal party committees of Honan, to formulate measures for agricultural recovery.[77] In response to the critical conditions prevailing in Honan's rural economy, the conference prescribed several "capitalist" measures which downgraded collective management in agricultural production and placed greater emphasis on peasants' material incentives.

Some dissenting voices were raised during the conference by apparently leftist party officials. T'ao Chu ridiculed these officials as "leftist remnants" and rebuked cadres in Honan for being "inept and reckless." In reply to a suggestion that some measures were "capitalistic," T'ao Chu retorted: "You are afraid of capitalism but not malnutrition." "You are afraid of this or that, but not of people's starvation." "Capitalism is much better than 'starvationism' and 'malnutrition-ism.'" Defending a measure to lend collective land to peasants, T'ao Chu declared: "Give the peasants a piece of land, some seeds, let peasants escape with life." The conference produced two documents, "The

CCP Honan Provincial Working Conference Summary" and "The Six-Year (1962–67) Plan for Agricultural Recovery and Development of Honan Province," which T'ao Chu subsequently presented to the CC; reportedly they were approved by Liu Shao-ch'i.

Based on these two documents, the Honan People's Provincial Council issued a "Notice on the Measures for Encouraging Agricultural Production," which stipulated strong measures to boost peasants' incentives. For instance, the production teams were instructed to allocate 7 percent of the collective land as private plots of peasants; these private plots would be farmed by individual households on a long-term basis, and the proceeds were to be kept by peasants and exempted from the state's system of unified purchase. Draft animals and livestock belonging to the collective were divided among individual peasants for use and care, and the peasants were to get one, two, or three "legs" for each new-born animal as a reward.

In areas that were difficult to work, peasants might be allotted additional pieces of good land on loan from the production teams. When this measure aroused strong opposition from many cadres as well as large numbers of poor and lower-middle peasants, Liu Chien-hsun, who had replaced Wu Chih-p'u as Honan's first party secretary in 1961, had a reply: "If we may eat food imported from capitalist countries, why cannot we loan land?"[78] In Feng Ch'iu Hsien, 210,000 mou, or 23 percent of the collective land, were loaned to peasants for private farming, and in some grave disaster areas as much as 80 percent of the collective land was farmed by peasants individually.[79] In Honan at that time, the peasants had a new adage: The private plot is a son of one's own begetting [ching-sheng tzu], the loaned land is an adopted son [yang-stu], and the collective land is an orphan [ku-erh].

In July 1962 the Honan provincial authorities handed down another document, "The Summary of the Provincial Party Standing Committee Conference," which provided for a system of "guaranteed production quotas by households."[80] Individual households now were to underwrite the output of a piece of collective land assigned to them; they would receive rewards if they overfulfilled the quotas but would receive fines if they failed to meet the quotas. This measure undoubtedly was designed in large part to enforce a system of production responsibility and provide production incentives for the peasants; however, the measure obviously undermined collective agricultural undertakings which the Chinese authorities had been stressing since agricultural collectivization in the mid-1950s.

Mao Stages a Comeback

In the face of severe economic and social crisis in 1960–62, Mao either reluctantly acquiesced or was compelled to accept a Chinese version of the New Economic Policy mapped out by his colleagues, and temporarily, at least, he lost a large measure of control over the decision-making process. He apparently felt that under Liu Shao-ch'i's stewardship things had gone too far, so as soon as the economy showed signs of recovery in the second half of 1962, Mao reasserted himself, demanding repeal or restriction of various "revisionist" measures that had been taken to repair the disasters of the three preceding years.

When a Central Work Conference was held at Peitaiho in August 1962, top leaders holding different views clashed. According to later reports on this conference in Red Guard and other sources, Mao vehemently denounced the policy allowing peasants' private farming [tan kan] and the system of production responsibility [pao ch'an tao hu], which he felt threatened to undermine China's collective agriculture. He criticized Ch'en Yun by name for initiating tan kan and blamed Li Hsien-nien's commercial policy for having "undermined the collective economy and facilitated private farming."[81] Furthermore, Teng Tzu-hui, Mao's long-time critic who was said to have actively promoted the system of production responsibility in 1962, was ousted from the directorship of the party's CC Rural Work Department and the State Council's Agricultural and Forestry Staff Office.

At this conference Mao complained that the State Planning Commission (headed by Li Fu-ch'un), the State Economic Commission (headed by Po I-po), and the Finance and Trade Staff Office of the State Council (headed by Li Hsien-nien) had become "independent kingdoms."[82] Finally, Mao severely criticized Liu Shao-ch'i for having followed a "rightist" policy line.[83]

Apparently, for the first time since 1960, Mao actively intervened once again in the policy-making processes; according to Liu Shao-ch'i, after the Peitaiho meeting Mao took the initiative in drafting a decision for the "further strengthening of the collective economy" and a decision on commerce.[84] Another source reported that Ch'en Po-ta, Mao's confidant, clashed with Li Hsien-nien and others over the draft of a "Decision Concerning Commercial Work" at the Tenth CC Plenum, held from 23 to 27 September 1962.[85]

During the Peitaiho Conference in the summer of 1962, and at the following Tenth CC Plenum, Mao made it clear that he was opposed to the current policy of rehabilitation; he talked at great length on the importance of class and class struggle and warned his colleagues against the danger of the development of "revisionism" in China.[86] Not a few party officials obviously regarded Mao's analysis of objective conditions as inaccurate and his ideological prescription irrelevant to the concrete problems faced by the nation.[87] They were keenly aware that many measures termed "revisionist" or "capitalist" were indispensable for stimulating peasants' production through increased incentives, and they felt that such measures had, in fact, contributed substantially to the post-1961 economic recovery. Precisely because Mao was unable to refute arguments such as these, he shifted the dispute to the ideological level, and thus he attempted to turn the issue into one of political life and death for the proponents of "revisionist" or "capitalist" economic measures. In a socialist political system like China to advocate capitalism is a cardinal sin; ostensibly, the Cultural Revolution was launched to overthrow those "power-holders in the Party taking the capitalist road."

In any event, it appears that Mao did not succeed in getting all he wanted. It is true that after the Tenth Plenum the party reemphasized class struggle and increased its ideological control by violently attacking "revisionist" trends in all fields.[88] It is also true that Mao pushed the party to launch a Socialist Education Campaign in the countryside after the Tenth Plenum, and the party prohibited the practice of dividing land among individual households, cut back excessive private cultivation, again stressed collective undertakings, and tightened control over the rural trade fairs and peasants' speculative activities.[89] Most of the existing economic measures which had contributed significantly to China's post-1961 economic recovery, however, were not seriously affected by these measures or Mao's active intervention.[90] Possibly Mao's efforts to reverse current policies were blocked by a majority in the CC who were opposed to letting Mao "rock the boat" again.

The "Decision Concerning Further Consolidation of the Collective Economy of the People's Communes and the Development of Agricultural Production," which was approved by the Tenth CC Plenum, continued to uphold the principle of "agriculture first" in economic development and set the order of the priority in the economic plan as agriculture, light industry, and heavy industry.[91] It also called for a more reasonable unified grain purchase policy and higher farm prices to "mobilize the peasants' enthusiasm for the collective undertaking," and it affirmed the right of peasants to maintain private plots and to operate family sideline occupations.

The Plenum also approved a revised sixty-article document, the "Draft Regulations on the Rural People's Communes," which formalized the revisions in the original commune system that had been made de facto since late 1961.[92] The regulations now formally stipulated that production teams constituted the basic units of accounting in the communes; that is, the teams could carry out independent accounting, assume responsibility for their own gains and losses, and manage their own income and distributon—practices that had been in effect since the second half of 1961. Furthermore, the regulations emphatically stated that the size, ownership, distribution, and management systems of the reorganized communes would not be changed for at least thirty years.[93] In fact, the relatively moderate commune policies pursued before the Tenth Plenum seemed to remain essentially unchanged from 1963 to 1966, despite the widespread unfolding of an intensive "socialist education campaign" in the Chinese countryside.[94]

Although the three-level commune administrative structure continued to exist throughout the mid-1960s, many elements of the 1958 commune system were abandoned. In fact, by 1962 the commune system had been "decommunized" to a considerable degree. The production team (twenty to thirty households in size and generally equivalent to a lower APC) has since then owned the major means of production, constituted the basic accounting unit of the commune, and exercised independent production authority—a reversion in many respects to the system of lower APC's as it existed in 1955.

Before the Tenth CC Plenum in September 1962, central authorities had steadily recentralized control in the sphere of economy. As noted earlier, the creation of the six CC bureaus in 1960–61 was an important step in that direction; each of these regional bureaus was expected to supervise closely a group of provinces in the nation's six large regions. During the proceedings of the CC Working Conference at Peitaiho in August 1962 and at the Tenth CC Plenum in Peking the following month, the issue of economic planning was among the major problems discussed by the Chinese leaders.[95] Steps were being taken to strengthen the control of planning and coordination functions by the top economic agencies of the central government, although this control had been reduced in 1958–59. In November 1962 the State Planning Commission received seven notable new vice-chairmen, in addition to its original thirteen vice-chairmen. These new vice-chairmen were Po I-po, T'an Chen-lin, Li Hsien-nien, and Teng Tzu-hui, all of whom were vice-premiers of the State Council, as well as Ch'en Po-ta, chief editor of *Hung Ch'i*, and two lower ranking economic officials, Sung Shao-wen and Yang Ying-chieh, who had been dismissed from this position in 1959 for criticizing the Great Leap. In 1962, the Third Five-Year Plan was said to have been scheduled for 1963–67; therefore these appointments were probably made to strengthen the work of the State Planning Commission. The inclusion of both "radicals" (T'an and Ch'en) and "conservatives" suggested that both groups were watching closely the future direction of the nation's economy.

There were also some signs that the central authorities had further tightened their control over the financial sector. An article in *Hung Ch'i* in 1962 advocated that the banking system perform and strengthen its supervisory functions over the economy through careful extension of credits and strict loan-repayment enforcement. "All credit activities, settling of accounts, and disbursement of cash throughout the country must be concentrated in the national bank."[96] This was supported by other writers discussing financial work: "In matters of financial control, the major power must be concentrated in the central government and the power of local authorities and of economic units must be reduced."[97] The recentralization of financial power from provinces to the central government was paralleled by a similar recentralization within the provinces, to curtail the financial autonomy of lower local authorities. "Authority in the management of national finance must be concentrated in the three levels of central government, great administrative regions [sic], and the provinces; the authority of financial management of special districts, *hsien* and below must be reduced."[98]

The Chinese leadership was by now aware that China is too big for central authorities to administer directly from Peking. This realization, and the painful experiences resulting from excessive provincial decentralization during the Great Leap, probably accounted for the move in 1960–61 to establish CC regional bureaus to help supervise the provinces. There is some indication that these regional bodies (in theory, they are "dispatched organs" of the party's CC and are therefore different from the "military and administrative committees" and the "administrative committees" of the early 1950s, which formed a layer of local government in the overall government hierarchy) had fulfilled some of the functions of economic coordination among provinces, functions which the regime in 1958 apparently expected would be performed by the "economic cooperation regions." For instance, the CC regional bureaus were reported to have sponsored "material exchange conferences" to promote intraregional cooperation and to smooth out allocation problems within their regions.[99] In practical terms, these measures were designed to effect a more efficient use of local resources, to transfer unused supplies and equipment from one intraregional enterprise to another, and to achieve savings in transportation by stopping unnecessary interregional cross-hauling. Politically, the promotion of this policy was probably intended to check the tendency toward provincial autarky by curtailing the autonomy of provincial authorities in economic matters.

To perform the tasks of coordinating and supervising political, economic, and other activities in the provinces, the regional bureaus would need some degree of authority and administrative machinery of their own, and it appears that each of them was delegated considerable power and developed a significant set of administrative organs.

The efforts at recentralization during the 1960s, however, did not result in a return to 1957, that is, the pre-decentralization era in the distribution of power over management of the economy and the structure of economic control.[100] Centralization and decentralization now accommodated one another, in a system similar to one that Hsueh Mu-ch'iao had recommended in 1957. On the one hand, the central government apparatus regained considerable power lost in the decentralization of the late 1950s, but the earlier "ministerial system" was not restored in any full sense. On the other hand, the enterprises in the hands of managers and technicians were granted a certain degree of autonomy over the management and operation of economic production, as evidenced by several provisions in the seventy-article "Regulations on Industry, Mines and Enterprises" of 1961.

Despite various measures to curtail provincial power in the 1960s, provincial authorities retained considerable control (de jure or de facto) over many economic activities. After the decentralization of 1957–58, which had given great powers to the provinces, it was probably difficult for the provinces to relinquish these powers. Provincial-level units that had especially large resources—Szechuan, Kwangtung, Liaoning, Shanghai, and Peking—or provinces that were headed by officials of relatively high party stature— Shanghai, Szechuan, Inner Mongolia, and Peking—probably enjoyed greater power and independence in their relations with the center than other provinces with less resources or less powerful provincial officials.

The central-provincial power relationship, in fact, had undergone subtle but significant qualitative changes since 1957–58. Unlike the period preceding the Great Leap when the central leadership alone made decisions and imposed them on the provinces, since the early 1960s the central leadership regularly involved the provincial leaders in the decision-making process at the highest level. This widened political participation took place within the institutional frame-work of the central work conference, which was convened at regular intervals from 1960 to 1966 and which was connected with decisions on important policy issues.[101]

The decentralization of power to the provincial authorities in the late 1950s greatly enhanced the importance of provinces as bases of political power. Moreover, the role of local leaders in China's overall political structure continued to grow as national leaders found it politically expedient and necessary to involve local party leaders in top-level decision-making. As the top CCP leadership became divided in the 1960s, different factions attempted to enlist the support of the provincial leaders to tip the balance in a policy debate, and their political power accordingly increased. To put it in another way, as a result of the dissension in the CCP leadership in the 1960s, the arena of political conflict has been expanded and those situated below the upper echelons of the leadership hierarchy, such as the provincial leaders, became directly involved in the resolution of conflicts among top leaders; thus the scope of participation in power conflicts widened and a new elite became established.

Ironically, the party's regional bureaus, created in 1960 to serve as the central leadership's loyal "watchdogs" over the provinces, have subsequently turned out to be the centers of regional autonomy. Initially, the six bureaus were headed by three loyal provincial leaders and three other party officials dispatched from the center. In time, however, all of them became identified with their own regions and developed their own "independent kingdoms" with substantial autonomous bases of support in the regions and came to resist the command of the central authority. Such regional autonomy manifested itself most clearly at the height of the Great Proletarian Cultural Revolution (1966– 67), and the central leadership could only oust these obdurate regional leaders from their regional strongholds by pushing the PLA into the picture. Since the GPCR, the PLA-dominated provincial power bases appear to be even more intractable and difficult to manipulate.

6

Setting the Stage
for the Cultural Revolution

The tumultuous events in China since the summer of 1966 created a political drama of the highest order. In a crusade called the Great Proletarian Cultural Revolution (GPCR), Chairman Mao invoked the support of China's fanatical revolutionary youth to ferret out "those in the party who take the capitalist road." The GPCR then generated political and social turmoil on a scale not approached in China since 1949. Not only have many party and government institutions been seriously disrupted, and not only have veteran officials, from the CC down to the local levels, been decimated, but the facade of a coherent, unified leadership has been shattered, and the image of the regime has been tarnished almost beyond repair in the eyes of the Chinese population.[1]

The GPCR began when Mao decided it was necessary to oust some of his "comrades-in-arms." As pointed out earlier, Mao's control over the party was weakened substantially when his grandiose Great Leap and commune programs failed, sending him to the political background as other CCP leaders came to the fore to save China from profound economic crisis. A set of pragmatic policies sponsored by Liu Shao-ch'i and others extricated China from the crisis by the fall of 1962, but Mao was alarmed by Liu's leadership, which, in his view, was leading China to the path of revisionism and "restoration of capitalism." Despite Mao's persistent efforts to reimpose his policies and assert his leadership, he found himself unable to make the party responsive to his will, for other leaders who controlled the party organizations had used sabotage, obstruction, and passive resistance to frustrate his goals. Mao became convinced that if he were to control the direction of the Chinese Revolution and carry out his own revolutionary vision, he would have to remove from positions of authority those leaders "who are taking the capitalist road."

The Socialist Education Campaign (SEC)

While a series of liberal policies adopted by the CCP leadership from 1960 to 1962 significantly contributed to China's post-Leap economic recovery, they also generated problems and consequences that Mao regarded as undesirable.

First and foremost was the peasants' "spontaneous tendency toward capitalism." The "three freedoms and one guarantee" system so weakened the regime's economic control over the peasants that they tended to forgo the collective undertakings of the communes to "rely on the private plots to get money and on speculation to get rich." Free markets had the effect of encouraging peasants to engage in peddling and in speculative activities instead of farming—which the Chinese Communists considered a dangerous tendency of the peasants to leave "the socialist road for the capitalist road." So long as the agricultural output increased and peasants' livelihood improved, many rural cadres condoned or even cooperated with those efforts.

A general relaxation of social and political control during 1960–62 encouraged a revival of "feudal" practices such as religious festivals, arranged marriages, and witchcraft. In the ranks of the party, and particularly among the rural cadres (most of whom were not members of the party), doubt, cynicism, and demoralization were widespread after the failures of the Great Leap. Members of many rural cadres, believing their burden of leadership too rigorous and incommensurate with their rewards, wanted to quit. A further problem was the widespread corruption among rural cadres, as was the growth of "commandism" and "bureaucratism" in cadres' working style.[2] It was in this broad social, economic, and political context that the SEC was initially launched in response to Mao's admonition to the Tenth Plenum: "never forget the class struggle."[3]

By February 1963, four months after the Tenth CC Plenum, the SEC was well under way in many provinces. Although officials claimed that great progress had already been made in restricting peasants' "capitalist" tendencies and in improving the morale, work habits, and political consciousness of both cadres and masses, defects in carrying out the SEC were conceded by those cadres who supervised it. Up to that time, the SEC was relatively lifeless—it clearly lacked the kind of tension, intensity, and momentum seen in many of the mass movements of the 1950s. The low key of the SEC may be attributed to two major factors: numerous cadres, both high and low, had suffered physical and mental exhaustion and become weary of mass campaigns after the experiences of the Great Leap; moreover, since agricultural output had barely recovered from the "three lean years," many party leaders and rural cadres were apprehensive that a violent SEC would once again disrupt economic production, like many of the mass campaigns of the 1950s had, and they therefore placed greater emphasis on increasing production than on waging class struggle.

This was unsatisfactory to Mao, who held that the class struggle should be the primary focus of the SEC.[4] He asserted that in Chinese society there still existed classes, class struggle, and struggle between socialism and capitalism, and he pointed out various class struggle phenomena in society. On the basis of his perception of reality in China, Mao intended the SEC to be a revolutionary movement of cosmic scale:

This struggle is one for the re-education of men; for the reorganization of revolutionary class force to wage sharp and effective struggles against the forces of capitalism and feudalism which are launching an audacious attack upon us; it is a great movement to suppress their counter-revolutionary activities and to remold the majority of these elements into new men: it is also a campaign for the joint participation of cadres and the masses in productive labor and scientific experiments, with a view to bringing our Party a step further in becoming a more glorious, greater and more correct Party, and making our cadres well-versed in politics and in business operations, both red and expert, well integrated with and supported by the masses, instead of being divorced from the masses and considering themselves officials and overlords. After the completion of this education movement, there will emerge in the whole country a climate of brightness and prosperity.[5]

To put the SEC back on the correct course, Mao intervened. In a Central Work Conference in February 1963, Mao described the "success" Hunan and Hopei provinces attained when class struggle was given prominence in the SEC, and he urged other localities to emulate that experience. Those cadres who had failed to emphasize class struggle or had paid insufficient attention to the class struggle phenomena were criticized. Many cadres were rebuked for having adopted "an attitude of indifference" toward various class struggle phenomena, thereby "letting the phenomena continue and develop."

Not much detail of the February party meeting is known; the available information indicates that Mao imposed on the party a new approach to the SEC—an approach that was underlined by Mao's slogan: "Once class struggle is grasped, miracles are possible." After the meeting, various provinces began to experiment with the new approach in selected areas. Shortly thereafter, reports from provinces began to pour into the CC claiming that many cadres had mastered socialist education work and that the work of SEC had been carried out with good results.

This would tend to prove the "correctness" of Mao's approach to the SEC and bolster his position. Subsequently, Mao put forth the "First Ten Points," which were adopted by another Central Work Conference in May 1963. He defined the characteristics of the contemporary historical stage, the nature of contradictions, and salient political issues in Chinese society, and he provided the directions and guidelines for resolving these contradictions and implementing the SEC. This document was the first major policy directive concerning the SEC and was clearly intended by Mao to guide the campaign along the course he desired.

The party professed that the document was based on reports of rural conditions filed by provincial and lower officials. Certain operational methods that were regarded as "successful" in some provinces, including Hunan, Hopei, Honan, and Chekiang, were standardized and written into the document as "advanced" experiences to be emulated by other provinces. As in the mass movement before, the top leadership did not provide concrete operational guidelines in advance; rather it relied on the "creativity" and initiative of individual provinces to work out methods suitable to their localities. In this way, the provincial and lower authorities had a considerable degree of freedom in implementing central directives. Furthermore, some provincial authorities actually affected, if only indirectly, the nationwide implementation of the central directives, as their "advanced experiences" were singled out by the central authorities as models to be emulated by other localities. The local autonomy in policy implementation and the kind of interaction between central and local authorities were among the striking characteristics of the regime's policy-making process, as noted earlier.

The implementation of the SEC is indicative of the change in Mao's role. Unlike the period of 1960–62, when Mao withdrew, to a large extent, from party deliberation of domestic policies, from the time of the Peitaiho Conference in the summer of 1962 Mao frequently interjected himself into the policy-making process. In a sense, Mao was a different political actor after the Peitaiho Conference—he had unmistakably displayed the will and tenacity to fight for his programs. This new image of Mao apparently gave him considerable political influence.

Whereas Mao was now actively involved in the deliberation of the party councils, he did not closely supervise the day-to-day party administration. According to Mao's own account in October 1966, the Politburo Standing Committee was divided into a first line and a second line, and he himself was in the second line, presumably meaning that he was to concern himself only with the most important decisions and with defining policy goals. The power of controlling and overseeing the daily tasks of governing China fell largely into the hands of Liu Shao-ch'i, Teng Hsiao-P'ing, and other members of the party Secretariat. Consequently, these party officials were able to sabotage, obstruct, or change Mao's policy if they happened to disagree with it. This is exactly what happened to the SEC.

About four months after the First Ten Points were promulgated, another directive on the SEC, "Some Concrete Policy Formulations of the Central Committee of the Chinese Communist Party in the Rural Socialist Education Movement" (also known as the "Second Ten Points"), was put forth by the party.[6] In the course of the GPCR, official Chinese sources revealed that the author of this document was Teng Hsiao-p'ing.[7] Purporting to supplement the contents of the SEC and to solve "a number of problems concerning concrete policies" emerging from the implementation of the First Ten Points in the preceding months, the Second Ten Points substantially modified the spirit and softened the impact of the SEC as set forth in its predecessor.

For example, Article II, Section 6 stressed that the development of the SEC "should be closely coordinated and connected with the production work."

The intense concentration on the SEC prompted some cadres to ignore production work; the new directive now demanded that "at no stage of the movement should production be affected" and that "measures taken during the course of the movement should be helpful to production." To prevent excessive, indiscriminate class struggle from adversely affecting production, the drafters of the new directive set limits by spelling out detailed, concrete guidelines on all aspects of the struggle. Thus cadres were warned to carefully distinguish between the class enemies and the "hoodwinked" backward masses, between the spontaneous capitalist tendency and the speculation and profiteering, on the one hand, and proper family sideline occupations (including private plots), proper activities of marketing and trading of commune members, on the other (Article III). A set of measures, such as private plots, sideline occupations, and "free markets," which had been provided in the 1962 sixty-article "Regulations on the Rural People's Communes," was once again emphasized; it was also stated that whether the sixty articles have been well implemented should be a yardstick in judging the result of the Socialist Education Movement (Article II, Section 5).

Furthermore, despite lip service paid the class struggle, the new directive apparently sought to moderate the disruptive effect of the SEC on production and to prevent alienation of the majority of the peasants who were more resourceful and enterprising farmers. The majority of upper-middle peasants were held to be "laborers and our friends," capable of taking the socialist road, although even they were likely to display "capitalist" tendencies. Measures of struggle employed against enemies were forbidden against the upper-middle peasants who showed "capitalist" tendencies; rather, Article V recommended patient criticism and education to win them over. In the case of children of rich peasant-landlords, the majority were said to have never directly participated in exploitation and were explicitly included in the 95 percent of the masses who were to be "consolidated" during the SEC (Article X). With respect to cadres who had made mistakes, most of their problems were said to be "nonantagonistic" in nature; even those cadres who had ties with class enemies were regarded as being qualitatively different from the class enemies themselves and to be dealt with by education and reform (Article VI). This optimistic assessment of contradictions and the overall lenient treatment of the masses and cadres prescribed by the new directive seem to negate the premise of intensified class struggle in Chinese society, which this directive was supposed to correct.

Not surprisingly, therefore, the Maoists criticized the Second Ten Points for using the method of "removing the burning brands from the boiling cauldron" to negate "the essential content of the struggle between the two classes and between the two roads and completely discard the line, principles and policies" of the SEC as set forth by Mao.[8] The accusation obviously is distorted and exaggerated; yet in light of what actually took place, the distortion and exaggeration in this and other charges are not totally unfounded.

Whatever discrepancies existed between the two directives, however, did not seem to be apparent to Mao. The authors of the second directive professed only to "supplement" the first and to set out clear-cut criteria for implementing concrete policies—the first directive was not contradicted directly or explicitly. Phrases and slogans were copied from the first directive to repeat very nearly the same thing on matters such as class struggle and the need to mobilize the masses. Even when the authors redefined issues and set new limits, they used terms very similar to those used by Mao. This adroit subterfuge, coupled with Mao's withdrawal from the supervision of daily policy implementation, blinded Mao for a time to the fact that the true intent of his own policy was being ignored.

Thus only in June 1964, nine months after the Second Ten Points were formulated, did Mao again step forward to intervene. In a Central Work Conference, which was a meeting of the Politburo Standing Committee attended also by the first secretaries of the party's regional bureaus, Mao formulated the following six criteria[9] for measuring the success or failure of the SEC:

1. We must see whether the poor and lower-middle peasants have been truly aroused.
2. Has the problem of the Four Uncleans among the cadres been resolved?
3. Have the cadres participated in physical labor?
4. Has a good leadership nucleus been established?
5. When landlords, rich peasants, counter-revolutionaries and bad elements who engage in destructive activities are discovered, is this contradiction merely turned over to the higher levels, or are the masses mobilized to strictly supervise, criticize, and even appropriately struggle against these elements, and moreover retain them for reform on the spot?
6. We must see whether production is increasing or decreasing.[10]

All except the last are political criteria and thus contrast sharply with the primarily economic yardstick, the sixty-article Regulations on the Rural People's Communes, as stipulated in the Second Ten Points. The introduction of new criteria at least suggested that Mao was displeased by the way with which the SEC had been pursued and that he was repudiating, even if only indirectly, those who were responsible. Apparently it was also at this meeting that "Organizational Rules of Poor and Lower-Middle Peasant Associations" were adopted.[11]

The work of organizing a "revolutionary class army" had been urged since May 1963 in the First Ten Points. Since then, efforts had been made in various parts of the country to recruit and organize poor and lower-middle peasants. The directive of the Second Ten Points was somewhat ambivalent; although it promoted the establishment of peasants' organizations in terms very similar to its predecessor, it also elaborated methods and procedures to be followed and criticized cadres who set up such organizations overnight by administrative order. By suggesting caution and by pointing out unresolved problems with regard to organizing rural class ranks (Article IV, Sections 1 and 5), the authors of the Second Ten Points may have intended to slow down such activities. In any case, the Organizational Rules adopted in July 1964 finally gave concrete form to, and formally defined the functions of the peasant organizations and settled problems that had previously been left open.

Two of the tasks of the peasant associations were to "carry on resolute struggle with the forces of capitalism and feudalism" and "to assist and supervise the various level organizations and cadres in the rural people's communes to do a good job of managing the collective economy."[12] This may mean that local party organizations failed in carrying out these tasks, for otherwise it would be unnecessary to undergo such "organizational tinkering." If the peasant associations were designed to serve as separate "watchdog" bodies in the rural areas, why were they to be subjected to the leadership and control of local party organizations, as stipulated in the "Organizational Rules"? The ambiguity of the role of the peasant associations perhaps reflected the continual dissension in the CCP leadership over the SEC.

Mao's efforts in June 1964 and on earlier occasions showed that he was determined to carry out his vision of the SEC. But his repeated intervention and assertion of his authority indicate that he was encountering resistance, and the SEC was not following the course he had charted. Other party leaders did not oppose Mao directly and they never challenged his authority to set basic policy decisions, even when they disagreed. Although Mao could and did make basic policy decisions, his overall ability to control events was diluted because other party leaders who controlled the operation of the party and supervised policy implementation were in a strategic position to revise and modify his guidelines and thwart his true intent, as they clearly did when Mao championed the SEC. He called for the campaign at the Tenth CC Plenum, but it was led "astray" soon after it was launched; from February to May 1963 Mao tried to put it back on the "correct" path, first by issuing the First Ten Points. A few months later, this "correct" orientation was sidetracked by the introduction of the Second Ten Points, and Mao felt compelled to intervene once again in June 1964. This cycle was to be repeated when Liu Shao-ch'i later took over the management of the SEC.

In the fall of 1964, the SEC entered a new phase as Liu came to the forefront to direct the campaign. There is no way to know whether he was responding to Mao's intervention in June or whether his extensive "investigation and study" tour in Hunan in August 1964 convinced him that cadres were not carrying out the SEC adequately; other considerations, or a combination of all these factors, may have motivated him to personally take charge of the implementation of the SEC. Wang Kuang-mei, Liu's wife, was also actively and prominently involved.[13] Liu's stewardship of the SEC and Wang Kuang-mei's involvement were subject to scathing attack by Maoists during the GPCR. The "crimes" Liu is alleged to have committed can be summarized as follows: on the basis of Wang's "T'aoyuan Experience," in September 1964 Liu produced the "Revised Second Ten Points" which were "left" in form but "right" in essence and in opposition to the line set by Mao; in addition, he "wrote off" the struggle between socialism and capitalism and took excessive punitive action against basic-level cadres to "protect the handful of capitalist power-holders in the party."[14]

These and other charges leveled after Liu's disgrace were obviously intended to blacken his reputation and to meet new political exigencies; they purposely distorted and obscured what Liu actually did in the second half of 1964. Maoist reinterpretation of past events notwithstanding, the fact still remains that Liu did play a guiding role in the SEC during the second half of 1964 and that his management was found wanting and repudiated by Mao as early as January 1965.

Mao was irritated by Liu's "mispresentation" of the purpose of the SEC. Following his eighteen-day tour of Hunan in August 1964, Liu delivered a speech to the high-ranking officials of the CC departments and of the Peking Party Committee in which he stated that the SEC should be oriented toward solving "the contradiction between the Four Cleans and the Four Uncleans" in politics, ideology, organization, and economy; in Liu's view, problems in Chinese society were derived from "the overlapping of contradictions within the party and contradictions outside of the party, or the overlapping of [antagonistic] contradictions between the enemy and us and the [nonantagonistic] contradictions among the people."[15] By juxtaposing the "antagonistic" and "nonantagonistic" contradictions, Liu, according to Mao, downgraded the importance of the "antagonistic" contradictions in society and thus surreptitiously shifted the focus of the SEC away from struggle between the "two lines." For this, he was subsequently accused of pursuing an erroneous policy line which was "right" in essence but "left" in form.

The "leftist" manifestations of Liu's line were to be found in the excessive purge of basic-level cadres. On the basis of Liu's own theoretical formulation, he appeared to have placed equal, or perhaps greater emphasis on the resolution of the contradiction "among the people." He held that the contradictions among the people had found expression in an "irregular relationship" between the cadres and the masses. Therefore, for him, the complete solution of the problems of cadres, that is, their "Four Uncleans," was the "most important condition for successful consolidation of over 95 percent of the peasants."[16] The cadre problem was viewed by Liu as quite serious. In his speech of August 1964 cited above, he claimed that one-third of the rural leadership was not "in our hands" and that the party had not won but actually lost the battle in the revolutionary struggle of the past year. The Revised Second Ten Points also stated that the cadres, aside from being "unclean" economically, had failed to draw a line between allies and foes, forsaken their own principles, discriminated against poor and lower-middle peasants, fabricated their background and family history, and thus they became unclean in politics and organization. Following this new critical assessment of the cadre problem, Article VI recommended harsher treatment of cadres. In practice, throughout the late fall of 1964, a great number of basic-level cadres were publicly criticized by the "mobilized masses" and many were dismissed from office.[17] Although Liu was undoubtedly responsible for this state of affairs, it does not follow that his "striking at the many" was intended to "protect the few" at the top,[18] as the Maoists have charged.

In addition, Mao and Liu apparently disputed certain operational techniques. Liu, a typical "organization man," stressed leadership and control from above and empowered the "work teams," which largely consisted of outside personnel from higher levels, to direct the SEC. The emphasis on the role of the work teams in the SEC would tend to circumscribe the revolutionary fervor of the masses below, for although the Revised Second Ten Points spoke at length of the need to boldly mobilize the masses, it clearly meant that the mobilization was to be led and directed by the work teams from above (Article II, Sections 1 and 3). Liu did not basically object to arousing the masses; rather, as an "organization man," he was likely to see any threat to the position and prerogatives of the party organization, thus he wanted mass enthusiasm kept within bounds to guard against a situation in which mass spontaneity could get out of hand.[19]

Liu and Mao also disagreed over the effective method of information gathering. Liu wanted leading personnel of the SEC to "squat at points," that is, to remain in villages to secure information directly from the masses instead of merely calling meetings to listen to reports and reading materials prepared by others (Article II, Section 2). In his August 1964 speech, Liu disparaged the method of "investigation and research," which Mao had long advocated, by claiming that the "investigation meeting," hitherto used by cadres to collect information, "did not work in many cases" and "could not uncover problems." Mao apparently took Liu's remarks as a personal insult and later pointedly reaffirmed the effectiveness and correctness of the "investigations and research" method in a formal party document, the "Twenty-Three Points"; Liu was to apologize for his "denial of the Chairman's thought" in his self-criticism in October 1966.[20] This is just one of many policy conflicts that became personalized.

By the end of 1964, the deviations in Liu's handling of the SEC had become apparent to Mao and he began to take steps to put the SEC back on the path he desired. The first such indication was a statement in the editorial of the

People's Daily on 1 January 1965: "The principal contradiction in China today is the (antagonistic) contradiction between socialism and capitalism. ... The Socialist Education Movement ... is directed precisely at carrying further the solution of this contradiction."[21] The shift of the orientation of the SEC was unmistakably clear in a new directive, "Some Problems Currently Arising in the Course of the Rural Socialist Education Movement" (also known as the Twenty-Three Points), which was said to have been drafted under Mao's personal guidance in a Central Work Conference in January 1965. This directive listed three different interpretations of the "contradictions" in Chinese society, which the SEC was to solve:

    1. The contradictions between the Four Cleans and the Four Uncleans.

    2. The overlapping of contradictions within the party and contradictions outside of the party, or the overlapping of contradictions between the enemy and us and contradictions within the people.

    3. The contradictions between socialism and capitalism.

Article II of the Twenty-Three Points termed the first two (Liu's formulations) "un-Marxist-Leninist" and affirmed the third "Marxist-Leninist" and "decidedly in accord with the scientific theories" of Mao. Although Liu's name was not explicitly mentioned, it was beyond any doubt that the clarification was undertaken to correct his earlier "mispresentation."

Similarly, although the Twenty-Three Points did not explicitly and totally repudiate Liu's Revised Second Ten Points (in fact, both contained some of the same formulas and prescriptions), there was no doubt that Mao had actually intended to provide a new guideline for the SEC. Mao's intention was clearly reflected in a passage in the Preamble of the Twenty-Three Points which stated: "If this document should contradict previous central committee documents concerning the Socialist Education Movement this document should uniformly be taken as the standard." In several places, the Maoist document directly contradicted the provisions of the Revised Second Ten Points and the T'aoyuan Experience.[22] Thus Mao once again asserted his personal authority to establish a new overall policy line for the SEC.

The party meeting in January 1965 seemed to mark an important turning point in the intraparty conflict. Several sources claim that it was during the drafting of the Twenty-Three Points that Mao became suspicious of the loyalty of men like Liu and Teng, and that he had already decided to purge the highest echelons of the party in early 1965.[23] Thus the Twenty-Three Points sounded a novel and curious note by stating that the key point of the SEC was "to rectify those people in positions of authority within the Party who take the capitalist road"—a phrase that was to become a leitmotiv of the much larger struggle that began unfolding in 1966.

If Mao had actually had a plan to purge some of the top leaders in early 1965, his timetable was temporarily interrupted by the escalated war in Vietnam in February.[24] The expansion of United States war efforts aroused fear of a direct Sino-American military confrontation and an invasion of the Chinese mainland in the minds of many Chinese officials, probably including Mao himself. At a time like this, it would not be opportune to further divide the party by undertaking purges, and Mao apparently temporized. In fact, the press and radio in the spring and summer of 1965 drastically toned down the themes of class struggle in Chinese society and focused on the consolidation of cadres and masses. However, after the danger of a Sino-American confrontation subsided and when Mao's earlier doubts on the loyalty of top party leaders were reinforced by new evidence of resistance to his command in the fall of 1965—an event that will be discussed later—the GPCR could begin.

Reform in the Cultural and Ideological Spheres

During the socioeconomic crisis of 1960–62, the party had relaxed its stringent political control over society, and there was a thaw in the cultural and ideological spheres.[25] It was in this "permissive" period that dissenting writers and intellectuals, most of whom were members of the party, expressed basic disagreement with the party policies. Writings published by men like Teng T'o and Wu Han even satirized Mao's leadership and his Great Leap programs.

Mao began to fight back at the Tenth CC Plenum. For Mao, the heresy and criticism by the writers represented an assault by the "bourgeois" forces against socialism in China. Thus he told the Plenum: "Using novels to carry out anti-Party activities is a big invention. In order to overthrow a political regime, it is always necessary to prepare public opinion and carry out work in the ideological field in advance. This is true of the revolutionary class as well as of the counter-revolutionary class."[26] Mao argued that although the bourgeoisie had been overthrown in China, they attempted to use the old ideas, old culture, old customs, and old habits of the exploiting classes to corrupt the mind of man and conquer his heart to attain their goal: restoration of their rule. He therefore called for rectification in the areas of culture and ideological work.

Mao's outburst in the Plenum had an immediate, although short-lived, effect. T'eng To and his colleagues no longer published their "Evening Chats at Yenshan" after September 1962. Chou Yang, a deputy director of the CC Propaganda Department charged with overseeing the regime's literary and art work, hurriedly convened a "Symposium on Literary and Art Work" in mid-October to transmit the "spirit" of the Tenth Plenum. Adopting what the Maoists called "two-faced tactics," Chou made a mild self-criticism as a concession to Mao's criticism, on the one hand, but he affirmed his own leadership by claiming that "the basic situation of the literary and art circles is good" and "not too many things in opposition to the Party and Marxism have been published," on the other.[27] Shortly after, in November, Chou allegedly sponsored a "Symposium on Confucius" in Shantung, the birthplace of Confucius, to glorify this ancient sage and his teachings.

Later disclosures made during the GPCR presented the first clear picture of this tug-of-war between Mao and his followers, on the one hand, and those who controlled the regime's cultural and propaganda apparatus, on the other. Beginning in September 1962 Mao repeatedly called for total reform in the fields of culture and ideology, and his followers sought to bring this about. Yet those in the "Establishment" were at best lukewarm to Mao's demand, which they apparently viewed as an attack on the particularist concerns of their profession. Outwardly, they bowed to the Maoist demands for reform and rectification; in reality, they paid lip service to Mao's criticism while continuing to ignore his demands. Each time Mao spoke out, they would convene meetings to transmit Mao's instructions and undertake rectification, but each rectification campaign would soon peter out with exaggerated claims of the very accomplishment the campaign had not actually produced.

Closely involved in Mao's efforts to rectify the cultural and ideological spheres was his wife, Chiang Ch'ing. Late in 1962 she became actively engaged in the reform of Peking Opera and energetically promoted the "revolutionary modern drama." She demanded that art serve politics and that the Peking Opera and other theatrical forms primarily portray workers, peasants, and soldiers in socialist revolution and construction, turning from "ghosts," "emperors," "generals," "ministers," "scholars and beauties"—themes that had hitherto dominated China's theater. The Peking Party Committee and the Ministry of Culture, which controlled the best known and most prestigious Peking Opera organizations, refused to cooperate, and her endeavors in Peking were obstructed and sabotaged.[28] This was not surprising. Officials in the cultural "Establishment," some of them China's best known literary figures, resented the intrusion of Chiang Ch'ing in their affairs, since they regarded her as a layman in cultural work. Her personality did not win friends either; on occasions her sharp tongue, arrogance, assertiveness, and disregard for "protocol" irritated party leaders P'eng Chen, Lu Ting-yi, Chou Yang, and others, who perhaps then became more determined to stand in her way.[29] Thus policy differences were intertwined with personal conflicts. Frustrated in Peking, Chiang Ch'ing turned to Shanghai to seek support for her theatrical reform.

The Shanghai Party Committee was then headed by K'o Ch'ing-shih, a Maoist stalwart, who was concurrently first secretary of the party's East China Bureau, mayor of Shanghai, and a Politburo member. K'o expressed total support for Mao's art and literary reform and had already in early 1963 urged workers in the art and literary fields to emphasize the successes of the past thirteen years. K'o's proposal was given a cold reception by key officials in the party's Propaganda Department; when a meeting on "Literary and Art Work" was convened by that department in April 1963, Chou Yang was quoted as having said that "All themes in writing can reflect the spirit of our time" and that writers should "not consider the portrayal of the present as our only major task."[30] In spite of the cold shoulder of officials in the central apparatus, K'o and Chang Ch'un-ch'iao, director of the Propaganda Department of the Shanghai Party Committee, mobilized the manpower and resources under their control to provide Chiang Ch'ing with a base of operation. Shanghai became the pacesetter of "revolutionary modern drama" and in late 1963 sponsored a festival of modern drama, the first of its kind in the nation, to show off the achievements of theatrical reforms in the East China area. The activities of Chiang Ch'ing and K'o Ch'ing-shih were apparently disliked by the officials in the regime's cultural establishment and therefore failed to receive any publicity in the national media at that time.[31]

The foot-dragging of key party officials in the cultural and propaganda hierarchy stymied the reform and rectification campaign that Mao had demanded. Seeing his wishes largely ignored, Mao intervened again and again and kept pressing those in charge to carry out his will. In December 1963, when commenting on a report submitted by K'o Ch'ing-shih, Mao sharply criticized the serious problems in literary and art circles:

> In all forms of art—drama, ballads, music, the fine arts, the dance, the cinema, poetry and literature, and so on—problems abound; and the people involved are numerous; in many departments very little has been achieved so far in socialist transformation. The "dead" still dominate in many departments. Isn't it absurd that many Communists are enthusiastic in promoting feudal and capitalist art, but [show] no zeal in promoting socialist art?[32]

Mao's sharp remarks drew immediate response. On 3 January 1964 Liu Shao-ch'i and Teng Hsiao-P'ing called a symposium on literature and art in the name of the Party CC to discuss criticisms Mao had raised.[33] Chou Yang, in his report to the symposium, sidestepped Mao's criticism and described the shortcomings of the leadership in literature and art as a "failure on some occasions to exercise a tight enough grip" on work and "failure to make enough effort in cultivating and affirming the new things of socialism," but basically he affirmed the achievements in literary and art circles. Liu approved Chou's speech and declared that "The question is one of comprehension for the great majority in literary and art circles. There also are some who are double-minded and anti-Party. They must be criticized but must not be opposed as though they are rightists." With regard to the reform of drama, Liu echoed the Maoist demand on the staging of plays on contemporary themes, but he also affirmed the value of historical plays and voiced opposition to "dogmatism in art." In the following months, rectification meetings were convened by organizations in literary and art circles and they basically parroted the line set by Chou and Liu in January.

In June and July 1964, under the aegis of Mao, a "Festival of Peking Opera with Contemporary Themes" was held with fanfare in Peking, and many plays with contemporary themes were staged for a vast audience including Mao and other top party leaders. Bowing to the pressure of Mao and his followers, officials in charge of the party's cultural and ideological affairs now feigned great enthusiasm in promoting the revolutionary drama and seized initiatives from Chiang Ch'ing and her followers. Thus Lu Ting-yi made the opening address, P'eng Chen presented a keynote speech, and Chou Yang made the summation remarks at the festival.[34] The speech Chiang Ch'ing gave on 23 June to a symposium of artists and theatrical workers taking part in the festival was not reported,[35] nor the two operas produced under her personal supervision given any special attention in the media at that time. Although Establishment officials now endorsed the idea of infusing the Peking Opera with contemporary themes, they continued to uphold traditional art; official accounts of the festival made it clear that "plays on contemporary themes, traditional items, and new historical plays will coexist" in the future.[36]

At the end of June 1964, the CC Propaganda Department submitted a report to Mao intended to call a halt to the rectification campaign in the All-China Federation of Literary and Art Circles (ACFLAC) and its affiliated associations —a campaign which it had reluctantly launched six months earlier in response to Mao's criticism.[37] Mao, who was obviously enraged by the perfunctory manner in which his instructions were carried out, again made an extremely harsh indictment:

> In the last 15 years, these associations and most of their publications (it is said that a few of them are good) and by and large the people in them (that is not everybody) have not carried out the policies of the Party. They have acted as high and mighty bureaucrats, have not gone to the workers, peasants and soldiers and have not reflected the socialist revolution and construction. In recent years, they have slid down to the brink of revisionism. If serious steps were not taken to remold them, at some future date they are bound to become groups like the Hungarian Petofi club.[38]

It was probably around this time that a special organ of the CC, the "Five-Man Cultural Revolution Group," was set up to direct and oversee a sweeping "cultural revolution"; P'eng Chen was the head of this group, and Lu Ting-yi, K'ang Sheng, Wu Leng-hsi, and possibly Chou Yang were its members.[39]

On 2 July, less than a week after Mao's outburst, the CC Propaganda Department again called the officials of the ACFLAC and the Ministry of Culture to a meeting to make arrangements for carrying out a rectification campaign.[40] From the second half of 1964 on, after repeated intervention by Mao, it looked as if the rectification campaign that Mao had envisaged was finally "taking off" in earnest.

Thus many literary figures and their works were subject to attack in the press and magazines. The "crimes" for which they were assailed ranged from propagating revisionist themes such as "class harmony," "bourgeois humanism," and "ghosts are harmless," to beautifying capitalists and uglifying peasants and workers and party cadres, to eulogizing capitalism and opposing socialism.[41] Various literary journals were also criticized for publishing "poisonous weeds," for failure or lack of enthusiasm in responding to Mao's earlier call for rectification, for laying more stress on the past than on contemporary subject matter, and for refusal to publish the works of young writers.[42] During the rectification campaign of 1964–65, the careers of numerous literary figures and cultural officials were adversely affected; the notable ones included T'ien Han, Shao Ch'uan-lin, Yang Han-sheng, Mao Tun (minister of culture), and Hsia Yen, Ch'i yen-ming, and Ch'en Huang-mei (three vice-ministers of culture). In the ideological field, the most notable casualty was Yang Hsien-chen, a member of the CC and principal of the Higher Party School (1955–61), who advocated a bizarre theory of "combining two into one," allegedly in opposition to Mao's theory of "dividing one into two."

Chou Yang, the regime's "cultural czar," and his superior in the CC Propaganda Department, Lu Ting-yi, who were most responsible for the conditions in the cultural and ideological fields that caused Mao's wrath, emerged unscathed from the rectification campaign; Lu was even appointed minister of culture in January 1965 when the Ministry was reorganized. They were able to weather the storm by publicly repudiating their subordinates—a tactic which the Maoists described as "sacrificing the knights to save the commander."

In the mind of Mao, the campaign had not gone far enough, however. Several outspoken critics of his, including Teng T'o and Wu Han, had been spared. Apparently Mao neither forgot nor forgave his detractors, particularly Wu Han, who wrote the play "The Dismissal of Hai Jui," which, Mao believed, had sung the praises of P'eng Teh-huai and clamored for P'eng's rehabilitation. Hence when a Central Work Conference was held in September 1965, Mao singled out the play and its author for criticism and proposed that those in charge of the "cultural revolution" take action to publicly condemn the play and its author from the perspective of class struggle.[43]

Mao's demand at the conference went unheeded. Some party leaders were genuinely concerned with the war in Vietnam, which had grown more intense in February, and feared a possible direct Sino-American military confrontation; they may have reasoned that it would be wise to rally all segments of society behind the party and not alienate and further divide the population by waging struggle against the intellectuals at a time of national crisis. In fact, Liu Shao-ch'i and Teng Hsiao-p'ing had considered the campaign too excessive since 1964 and at a meeting of the Secretariat on 3 March 1965 had decided to end it; soon after that the great majority of newspapers and magazines quietly dropped criticisms of "bourgeois" writers and "reactionary academic authorities."[44] Personal considerations may have motivated several party leaders such as Teng Hsiao-P'ing and P'eng Chen to shield Wu Han; they maintained that he did not warrant the kind of struggle that Mao called for. Wu was a vice-mayor of Peking and P'eng Chen's protege—his disgrace certainly would reflect unfavorably on the prestige and authority of his boss. Allegedly, Wu was also a close friend and a bridge partner of Teng Hsiao-p'ing.[45]

As pointed out earlier, Mao had already entertained doubts on the loyalty of those in the first line of leadership; these doubts were now strengthened by fresh evidence of resistance to his command, so he decided to act. Since the central party apparatus and the Peking party machine were in the hands of his opponents, Mao was compelled to turn to the Shanghai Party Committee for a base to prepare and launch attacks against Wu Han and, by implication, his powerful protectors. This was recounted by Mao himself in October 1966:

> Then Peking couldn't do a thing; nor could the center. It was in September or October last year when this question was raised: If there was revisionism in the Center, what would the regions do about it? I felt that my views couldn't be accepted in Peking. Why wasn't the criticism of Wu Han started in Peking but in Shanghai? This was because there were no available men in Peking.[46]

Thus on 10 November 1965 the *Wen Hui Pao* of Shanghai published an article by a young leftist literary critic, Yao Wen-yuan. The article, innocently entitled "On the New Historical Play 'The Dismissal of Hai Jui,'" proved to be the first shot of the Great Proletarian Cultural Revolution. Although the article used the name of Yao, it was actually written at the instigation of Mao, who was in Peking, and under the close supervision of Madame Mao, who took a special trip to Shanghai.[47]

The attack on Wu Han and his play immediately alarmed P'eng Chen and his aides in Peking. After careful deliberation, P'eng decided to ignore Yao's article by not reproducing it in the media of Peking; but he was not ignoring the attack—he instructed his aide to ring the *Wen Hui Pao* to find out who was the "backer" of Yao's article.[48] For two weeks, Yao's article seemed to have generated no public impact—it was reproduced by only one newspaper, Shanghai's *Chieh-fang Jih-Pao*, on 12 November. To give greater publicity to Yao's article and to reach more readers outside Shanghai, on 24 November Mao arranged for the Hsin Hua Bookstore of Shanghai to print the article in pamphlet form, and the bookstore sent urgent cables to its sister stores throughout the country soliciting orders. On the same day, four provincial newspapers, *Chekiang Jih-Pao*, *Fukien Jih-Pao*, Nanking's *Hsin-hua Jih-Pao*, and Shantung's *Ta-chung Jih-Pao*, reprinted Yao's article, and *Anhwei Jih-pao* and *Kiangsi Jih-pao* followed suit on 25 and 26 November, respectively, but all of these papers were in the East China area. It looked as if P'eng Chen had largely succeeded in circumventing the publicity and minimizing the impact of Yao's attack on Wu Han.

Meanwhile, Mao appeared to be actively working behind the scene and was gradually receiving active support from other top leaders. A politically astute Chou En-lai, who had often joined the winning side, apparently jumped on Mao's bandwagon at this critical juncture, for on 28 November he called a meeting to press P'eng to have Yao's article reproduced in Peking's newspaper. Bowing to the pressure, P'eng permitted the organ of the Peking Party Committee, *Pei-ch'ing Jih-pao*, to print the article on 29 November.

Mao's most crucial support, however, was to come from Lin Piao, a vice-chairman of the party and the minister of defense, and a few other PLA leaders. Similiar to his maneuver during the 1950s in which he enlisted the support of provincial political forces to overcome opposition at the center, Mao turned to the PLA for support, broadened its political roles, and involved the PLA in political conflict resolution in the 1960s. He succeeded in coopting Lin Piao and used the PLA as a new base of power to fight his opponents who controlled the party machinery.

The first sign of PLA open support for Mao came on 29 November 1965, when the army organ, *Chieh-fang-chun Pao (Liberation Army Daily)* reproduced Yao's article. Furthermore, the army paper added an "Editor's Note" attacking Wu Han's play for having propagated politically erroneous themes and denouncing it as a "big poisonous weed." On the following day the *People's Daily* also reproduced Yao's article but added its own "Editor's Note," said to have been written by P'eng Chen, to counter the indictment made by the army paper. The note asserted that the issues involved in Wu Han's play were "academic" and that the evaluation of Hai Jui and the play should center on "questions of how to treat historical characters and historical plays, of using what perspectives in studying history, and of employing what artistic forms to reflect historical characters and historical events," and it urged those in the fields of history, philosophy, and literary studies to take part in a free debate on these "academic" questions.[49]

Clearly, the note was drastically different from that of the *Liberation Army Daily* and it said nothing of the political offenses of Wu Han's play. It seems likely that P'eng Chen intended to divert public attention from dangerous political implications that Mao had drawn from the play and to confine the debate to less harmful issues of historical scholarship and historiography. According to Mao himself, however, the crux of Wu Han's play, "The Dismissal of Hai Jui," was not faulty scholarship but its insinuation that the dismissal of P'eng Teh-huai at the 1959 Lushan Conference had been unjust and its portrayal of Marshal P'eng as the righteous Hai Jui.[50] Mao wanted to have Wu Han punished for political "crimes" in attacking his own leadership; he suggested this to P'eng Chen on several occasions. Only in this light can the significance of P'eng Chen's maneuver, and his audacity in resisting Mao, be fully appreciated.

For several months, beginning in December 1965, the criticism of Wu Han's play in the media largely revolved around the theoretical questions of historical scholarship in accordance with the tone set by the *People's Daily*, the prestigious authoritative organ of the party's CC. Although there were many articles criticizing Wu Han on various theoretical grounds, some defended him and attacked Yao's article.[51] Wu Han himself published a "self-criticism" in the *Peking Daily* on 27 December in which he confessed errors in the theories of "moral legacy" and of "historical materialism" but dodged the political offenses he was accused of in Yao's article.[52]

This episode concerning Wu Han once again demonstrated that Mao, despite his persistent efforts, was unable to enforce his will when party leaders who disagreed with him controlled the party machine. P'eng Chen, however, did not oppose Mao openly and directly; the tactics P'eng used were those of subterfuge, obstruction, and passive resistance. When repeatedly pressed by Mao to repudiate Wu Han openly, P'eng went along outwardly, but in fact he shifted the basic orientation of the attack and used different ploys to shield Wu Han from political criticism. P'eng's efforts at evasion and diversion culminated in the "Outline Report on the Current Academic Discussion" (also known as the "February Outline Report"), which he produced in the name of the Five-Man CC Cultural Revolution Group in early February 1966.[53] With the support of both Liu Shao-ch'i and Teng Hsiao-p'ing, the report was allegedly approved *pro forma* in a Politburo Standing Committee session chaired by Liu on 5 February; it was issued to the party organization on 12 February to serve as the guideline for the cultural revolution.[54] By this manipulation, P'eng had hoped to use the sacred aura of party authority to legitimize his policy and to ward off the attack of Mao and his supporters.

Those in the Maoist camp now were preparing for a final showdown with P'eng Chen and his allies, and the PLA under Lin Piao's stewardship become more closely involved in the conflict. On 2 February 1966 Madame Mao was entrusted by Lin Piao to convene a "Forum on the Literary and Art Work in the Armed Forces" in Shanghai.[55] At the conclusion of the eighteen-day forum, a summary report was prepared under Chiang Ch'ing's guidance; it was revised three times by Mao before its release.[56] The "Forum Summary" did not confine itself to the literary matters in the armed forces, it spelled out the Maoist position, policy, and intention on the cultural revolution in the nation. It pointed out that the literary and art circles had basically failed to carry out Mao's instructions and that the cultural front was dominated by an anti-party and anti-socialist "black line"; moreover, it called for a "great socialist revolution on the cultural front" and the complete elimination of this black line and stated that the PLA "must play an important role in the socialist cultural revolution."[57] The Maoists later claimed that the summary was "in direct opposition to the counter-revolutionary 'February Outline Report,' and launched a vigorous attack on the counter-revolutionary revisionist line."[58] Clearly, Mao had secured the full backing of Lin Piao and was involving the PLA on his side to fight P'eng Chen and his allies in the central party apparatus.

Mao's opponents, undoubtedly aware of the dire consequence if all the PLA leaders were to intervene and to side with Mao, desperately tried to ward off the involvement of the PLA in the domestic power struggle. To accomplish this aim, they sought to turn the attention of the PLA toward the external enemy—the Americans—by advocating a bigger and more active Chinese role in the Vietnamese war.

To fully understand how the Vietnamese war became intertwined with China's domestic politics, we must briefly review the dispute over foreign policy at that time. As the war in Indochina escalated after February 1965, and the Chinese leaders feared an eventual American invasion of the Chinese mainland, a heated debate arose among the CCP leadership as to what China should do under these dangerous circumstances. One "hawkish" option, as articulated by Lo Jui-ch'ing, then PLA chief of staff, was that China should adopt a "forward" or "active defense" strategy in that China would "give more effective support" to the Vietnamese Communists and intervene actively in the war to defeat the Americans. To deter the Americans from using nuclear weapons against China and to bolster China's defense, Lo favored China's reconciliation and united front with the Soviet Union.[59]

On the other hand, a "dovish" option supported by Mao and Lin Piao sought to avoid a direct military confrontation with the superior armed might of the United States by following a low-risk response. They rejected Lo's hard line because it would greatly increase the risk of war with the United States and opposed the demand for reconciliation with Moscow because they regarded the Soviet "Modern Revisionists" as an even worse enemy than the American Imperialists.[60] Instead, they advocated a "defense in depth" or "people's war" strategy. As articulated in a major treatise by Lin Piao, "Long Live the Victory of People's War," published with éclat in the *People's Daily* (3 September 1965), the strategy called for a people's war on China's soil against the invading enemies. Unlike Lo's hawkish stance asking China to intervene in the Indochina war, the Mao-Lin group wanted to fight only after China was attacked or invaded by the Americans. To justify such a low profile, Lin's essay asserted: "Revolution or people's war in any country is the business of the masses in that country and should be carried out primarily by their own efforts"; the people must not rely upon foreign assistance.

Although the "dovish" posture gained an upper hand and Lo Jui-ch'ing was purged in December 1965,[61] the "war and peace" debate continued and was entangled with domestic political considerations. For example, P'eng Chen, who previously supported the Mao-Lin option and was vehemently opposed to a united front with Moscow,[62] shifted his position in the first quarter of 1966, when he endorsed the formation of a "broadest international united front" in opposition to American imperialism in the course of negotiations with a Japanese Communist Party delegation which sought to rally the support of the Chinese, Russian, and other Asian Communists to aid Hanoi.[63] A Chinese report that P'eng Chen proposed to head a CCP delegation to attend the Twenty-Third Congress of the CPSU in Moscow in March 1966—a proposal which was turned down by Mao—also suggested that he had adopted a more conciliatory attitude toward Moscow.[64] Apparently, realizing that his handling of the ideological rectification campaign had alienated Mao and that his political survival was in danger, P'eng Chen reversed himself and joined those who favored rapprochement with the Soviets and a tougher policy against the United States in Indochina.[65]

Standing together with P'eng Chen on this issue were Liu Shao-ch'i and Teng Hsiao-p'ing.[66] Several domestic political considerations appear to have underlain their advocacy of a united front with the Soviet Union and a more active Chinese role in the Indochina conflict. First, if China should go to war with the United States, or if the crisis intensified, the PLA and its leaders would be preoccupied with the external situation, and Mao would be denied the use of the PLA in the internal power struggle. Failing that, Mao's opponents may have seen the militant policy they advocated as a means to captivate the anti-American elements in the party and the PLA so as to win their support in the eventual showdown with Mao and his supporters.

It is well known now that the controversy over China's policy toward the Vietnamese war was decided in favor of the Mao-Lin group. China did give substantial materiel to Hanoi and even dispatched highway construction and maintenance workers, but the Chinese refrained from sending combat personnel to Vietnam to fight with the Vietnamese. The assurance by Washington that the United States had no intention of escalating the conflict beyond the borders of Vietnam and did not seek the destruction of the Hanoi regime may have been used by Mao to win the approval of his "dovish" policy in the party. Ironically, as Karnow points out, "by minimizing the American threat to China, President Lyndon Johnson unwittingly provided Mao with the respite he required to trigger the Cultural Revolution."[67]

In late March 1966 Liu Shao-ch'i left Peking to visit Pakistan, Afghanistan, and Burma; he did not return to North China or East China until 20 April. Soon after Liu was away, P'eng Chen came under attack. On 28 March Mao denounced P'eng Chen and the "February Outline Report" for undermining the Cultural Revolution and protecting bad people; he confided to K'ang Sheng his intention to disband the Five-Man Cultural Revolution Group and to reorganize the CC Propaganda Department and Peking Party Committee.[68] After being informed of Mao's criticism, P'eng on 1 April set up a "three-man group" in the Peking Party Committee to repudiate Teng T'o, thus attempting to pacify Mao.[69] From 9 to 12 April K'ang Sheng and Ch'en Po-ta specified and denounced P'eng's "crimes" in a session of the CC Secretariat which was also attended by Chou En-lai.[70] The meeting resolved to revoke the February Outline Report and set up a new organization under the Politburo Standing Committee to carry out the Cultural Revolution. On 16 April Mao convened a meeting of the Politburo Standing Committee at Hangchow and P'eng Chen was summoned to account for his wrongdoings.[71] On 18 April the organ of the PLA issued an editorial, "Hold Aloft the Great Red Banner of Mao Tse-tung's Thought, Actively Take Part in Socialist Cultural Revolution"; the editorial paraphrased the Forum Summary of the PLA and declared war on the anti-party, anti-socialist "black line" in the cultural front.[72] At the end of a four-day struggle in the Hangchow Politburo Standing Committee, on 20 April (the second day after Liu Shao-ch'i returned from Burma), P'eng was for practical purposes removed from power. Whether Liu had been deliberately kept away at a crucial moment when one of his important allies was being removed can only be a matter of conjecture.[73]

The political demise of P'eng Chen was subsequently made official by a CC circular issued on 16 May after a Politburo Standing Committee meeting which had been in session in Hangchow since the second week of May. The 16 May circular revoked the February Outline Report and announced the dissolution of P'eng Chen's Five-Man CC Cultural Revolution Group and the formation of a new Cultural Revolution Group under the Politburo Standing Committee.[74] By this time, the cultural establishment which had obstructed Mao's demands for reform had crumbled. Lu Ting-yi, who made his last public appearance on 28 February, seemed to be in political disgrace soon afterward; his political fate was sealed on 8 May during a Politburo meeting when his "crimes" were exposed.[75] Chou Yang had become ill in January 1966, and he then began to relinquish his official duties. The targets of Mao and his supporters, however, were not confined to these persons. The 16 May circular had called for repudiation and dismissal of the "bourgeois representatives" who "had wormed their way" into the party, the government, the military, and various cultural organizations.

In response to Mao's "mobilization order," "revolutionary students and teachers" in Peking's educational institutions began to rise up to attack officials of the school administration. The students were further encouraged when the old Peking Party Committee was reshuffled and Li Hsueh-feng, then first secretary of the North China Bureau, became its new chief. On 25 May Nieh Yuan-tzu, a teaching assistant at the Peking University, and her six followers put up what Mao later called "the first Marxist-Leninist big-character poster in the entire country" to denounce an educational official of the Peking Party Committee and Lu P'ing, the president of the Peking University and secretary of its Party Committee.[76] Lu immediately organized his supporters in the university to demonstrate in support of the university administration and to wage a struggle against Nieh and her followers, who were denounced as counterrevolutionary traitors, bad elements, and so forth.[77] As a result of Mao's phone call to K'ang Sheng, the text of Nieh's poster was broadcast by Radio Peking throughout the nation on 1 June and published in the *People's Daily* the following day accompanied by a positive commentary.[78] Emboldened, Maoist students in Peking and other cities soon followed the example of Nieh to attack their school administration, thus ushering in a new mass movement of the GPCR. Maoists later referred to Mao's intervention in the Nieh incident as Mao's "great strategic measure" which kindled the flame of the GPCR throughout China.

Liu Shao-ch'i and Teng Hsiao-p'ing had no alternative but to fight back in self-defense. Like P'eng Chen, they could not afford to oppose the GPCR openly; what they did was to control its direction and circumvent the mass movement which threatened to disrupt the established political order. In early June, Liu hurriedly convened a Central Work Conference in Peking to formulate a guideline for the GPCR, the "Eight Articles of the Central Committee," which prescribed restrictions on the actions of the "revolutionary masses."[79] The meeting also authorized the dispatch of "work teams" by central and local party organizations to various schools and institutions on the pretext of giving leadership to the GPCR. Liu himself gave the following account:

> At a certain period before 18 July, Chairman Mao was not in Peking. I took the lead in carrying out the daily, regular business of the party Central Committee. The state of the cultural revolution in various sectors of Peking city was reported at the central conference, over which I presided, and I made mistaken decisions and gave mistaken approval there. One wrong decision I made, for example, was the decision that a work team would be dispatched at the request of the various central ministerial committees and the Chinese Young Communist League headquarters. At the time, the various central ministerial committees and the Chinese YCL headquarters quite actively requested the dispatch of work teams to various areas. Through the recommendation of the new Peking municipal committee, work teams were dispatched not only to various schools but also to various organs.[80]

On 3 June the first work team was sent to Peking University by the Peking Party Committee. Bowing to the pressure of the Maoists, the new Peking Party Committee dismissed Lu P'ing and took measures to reorganize the Peking University administration, but it authorized the work team to assume all the power of the University Party Committee, thereby retaining the control of the GPCR in the university. Just as in the various stages of the SEC, work teams were the instrument with which the "organization men" in the party attempted to control the mass movement from above. In accordance with the current central policy, and following the example of the Peking municipal authorities, various provincial authorities soon dispatched work teams to schools to provide similar leadership. Initially the work teams appear to have been welcomed by most students and to have established their "revolutionary credentials." In the name of the provincial authorities, they quickly removed the top officials in the school administration and organized students to wage a struggle against the deposed school administrators, blaming them for having suppressed and undermined the GPCR.[81]

Soon, however, leftist students discovered that the work teams, in assuming the power of university authorities, were simply a new manifestation of their former suppressors, and the repeated struggle sessions (e.g., Kangaroo courts, trials) organized by the work teams against the school administrators and alleged rightist professors and students represented a cunning attempt to confine the GPCR within schools and to shift the targets of attack away from "capitalist powerholders" in the provincial party apparatus. Therefore, at least if later Maoist reports are to be credited, opposition against the work teams gradually rose and subsequently became widespread. But the work teams hit back hard at their critics. They were able to manipulate the slogan "To oppose the work teams is to oppose the party"[82] to maximum advantage, and in most instances they won support from the majority of students.

If we are to believe later reports—most of them emanating from Maoist sources—the work teams were very harsh toward the "revolutionary masses." In many cases, the work teams struck at those who had the audacity to oppose their leadership as "counterrevolutionaries," "conspirators," and so forth, and organized their supporters to struggle and persecute the dissidents. In Peking's Tsinghua University, for example, when K'uai Ta-fu, a student leader, and his followers hung a big-character poster attacking the work team, Wang Kuang-mei (Madame Liu Shao-ch'i) and other members of the Tsinghua work team allegedly instigated the "hoodwinked masses" to struggle against K'uai and branded K'uai and more than 800 "revolutionary teachers and students" as "counterrevolutionaries" and "pseudo-leftists but actual rightists," and they enforced "white terror" (i.e., police brutality, considered characteristic of the capitalist system) that caused the death of one person and impelled many persons to commit suicide.[83]

There are indications that student opposition to the work teams was directed and manipulated behind the scenes by Mao's top aides in the CRG or at least had their blessing. When the case of K'uai was brought up at a high-level party meeting in early July, K'ang Sheng defended K'uai. Allegedly, Liu Shao-ch'i denounced K'ang for "failure to understand the situation," and K'ang pointed out that "forbidding K'uai Ta-fu to bring his complaint to the Central Committee at least is not in accord with state law and is in contravention of Party regulations." Reportedly, Ch'en Po-ta supported K'ang's viewpoint and sent two CRG members, Kuan Feng and Wang Li, to Tsinghua to pay a visit to K'uai, who was in custody.

Mao quickly learned of the Liu-Teng efforts to counterbalance and "subvert" his opening moves; there followed a massive and decisive Maoist attack. By June 1966 Lin Piao had already moved reliable troop units to the Peking area and appointed General Fu Ts'ung-pi as the new commander of the Peking garrison. On 18 July 1966, after an absence of almost eight months from the nation's capital, Mao returned to Peking to personally direct the campaign against the Liu-Teng leadership. For example, he called a Central Work Conference on 21 July to review the product of work teams and pushed through the conference a decision to recall the work teams. On 26 July the *People's Daily* publicized with great fanfare the news and picture of Mao's swim in the Yangtse ten days earlier—a ploy to dissipate doubts in the minds of many Chinese officials about Mao's state of health and to signal to cadres at all levels that he was still in active control. And on 5 August, four days after the opening of the acrimonious Eleventh CC Plenary Session, which was packed by "revolutionary teachers and students," Mao himself wrote a big-character poster to "bombard" the "bourgeois headquarters"; the poster assailed the leadership of the GPCR by Liu Shao-ch'i and Teng Hsiao-p'ing in June and July 1966 and attacked Liu's policy errors in 1962 and 1964.[84]

In the course of the Plenum, Mao and his supporters, under circumstances which still remain mysterious to outsiders,[85] managed to discredit the leadership of Liu and Teng and censured them for having produced and enforced an erroneous "bourgeois reactionary line." The Plenum also reshuffled the Politburo, elected Lin Piao as the sole vice-chairman of the party and Mao's successor, and formally approved Mao's blueprint for the GPCR—the now-celebrated "Sixteen-Point Decision," which endorsed Mao's call to purge "those power-holders within the Party who take the capitalist road."[86]

The censure of Liu and Teng and the attack on their policies in the Plenum suddenly put the provincial leaders in a highly vulnerable political position. It had been demonstrated that Mao possessed the power to redefine issues and he had ruled the policies of Liu and Teng both politically and ideologically erroneous. Thus the provincial leaders, to their dismay and horror, found themselves the executors of a policy line denounced by none other than Mao himself as having "enforced a bourgeois dictatorship and struck down the surging movement of the great cultural revolution of the proletariat."[87] Few provincial leaders had any intention of opposing Mao; indeed, all of them had been at great pains to display their loyalty to Mao by carrying out the policies laid down by Liu and Teng in the name of the central leadership, policies which they very likely believed had Mao's endorsement. Yet now, in the midst of rapidly changing events, they found themselves standing on the opposite side of Mao and directly involved in a furious political conflict. Consequently, they had good reason to fear and suspect that they would become primary targets in the purge projected in the Plenum's Sixteen-Point Decision.

The Maoist leadership did nothing to allay their misgivings. On the contrary, it added to the provincial leaders' fears and suspicions by both words and deeds. Rightly or wrongly, the provincial leaders interpreted a rapid succession of developments as an unmistakable sign that a sweeping purge by Mao was under way: Lin Piao's speeches at the Peking Red Guard rallies on 18 and 31 August; the simultaneous press campaign which enthusiastically acclaimed the "rebellion" of the Red Guards and "revolutionary rebels" and encouraged them to go to provinces to storm the "bourgeois headquarters" and "drag out" the capitalist power-holders; and the subsequent activities of the Red Guards and "rebels" in response to these orders. Under the prevailing conditions, the provincial leaders felt they could not take a chance, so they used all the resources at their disposal to devise a number of strategies for self-preservation. Their efforts in turn provoked the Maoist leadership to press harder and to attempt to oust the recalcitrant provincial officials from positions of power. As a result, the conflict escalated rapidly and continuously on both sides, up to the end of 1966, when there was no turning back.[88] Then, in 1967 and 1968, the Maoist effort to remove these officials and to destroy the party-government organization in which they were firmly entrenched resulted in almost total disruption of Chinese society and brought China to the brink of civil war.

Mao's Sources of Power and His Political Strategies

After the Tenth Plenum in September 1962 Mao on several occasions forcefully intervened in the policy-making process, yet he still had to overcome considerable resistance by other party leaders before he was able to impose on the party the policy lines he desired. In fact, these policy lines were often surreptitiously modified by other leaders in the course of implementation, increasing Mao's anger and frustration. He felt compelled to launch an all-out attack on his opponents and to recapture control of the direction of Chinese revolution. During the spring and summer of 1966, although Mao and his supporters were apparently in the minority, he succeeded in disposing of powerful opponents like P'eng Chen, Teng Hsiao-p'ing, and Liu Shao-ch'i even though they controlled the party machine and commanded a large number of followers in the CC. A few observations on Mao's sources of power and his political tactics are in order.

One important source of Mao's power was organizational: he had been the chairman of the CC of the party since 1945. As the party's head, he had the authority to make basic decisions and direct the party organizations, and this authority gained wide acceptance in the polity. One informal arrangement in the leadership operation, the division of "first line" and "second line" in the Politburo Standing Committee, may have solidified Mao's authority. This arrangement had others manning the first line—the actual management of society—while Mao was in the second line concerning himself with defining basic policy goals and making important decisions.[89] Although this arrangement was not strictly followed in the 1960s and other party leaders did in fact exercise the power of definition, they rarely challenged Mao's leadership position in the open, even when they were fighting against him.

Mao's power never depended only on the office he held. It also derived from the history of the CCP movement: Mao was the principal organizer of the party and the architect of the Chinese Communist revolution after 1935. Furthermore, the force of his personality and intellect gave him immense influence; he was characterized by charisma, total political commitment, great self-confidence, and imagination and originality in applying theories to specific conditions as well as an outstanding ability to evoke strong loyalty from followers.

Mao's ability to assert his authority was greatly enhanced by his capacity as the top ideologist of the regime: he had made numerous authoritative ideological pronouncements and constantly manipulated political symbols. He alone possessed the prerogative to assess the state of the nation and define the salient issues in society. Mao's ideological role contributed much to his political influence; his ideological pronouncements set goals, constrained choices, and set the parameters within which specific problems were tackled. This was clearly reflected in the SEC. Even when other party leaders did not genuinely share Mao's diagnosis of and prescription for China's problems, they were obliged to justify their own policies on Mao's ideological formulations and base the legitimacy of these policies on Mao's thought. Although they often resorted to a tactic that the Chinese Communists fittingly describe as "waving the red flag to oppose the Red Flag," they had to accept the Maoist premises and, in the long run, reinforce the primacy of Mao.[90]

Furthermore, the elevation of the "thought of Mao Tse-tung" to the level of a new political creed and Mao's skill in manipulating political symbols gave him tremendous leverage over his opponents. The formation of a strong personal cult of Mao gradually turned Mao into an institution, and the thought of Mao became "a new standard of legitimacy and correctness with which the actions and opinions of many top leaders were to be judged."[91] Other party leaders were thus disarmed from opposing or attacking Mao publicly, inasmuch as Mao had become the source of authority and correctness and they could not base a claim to legitimacy in opposition to Mao.

In addition to taking full advantage of his political and ideological authority, Mao also skillfully manipulated issues to get what he wanted. One of the issues he manipulated was Sino-Soviet relations. There is no question that Mao, for a variety of reasons, was bitterly hostile to the Soviets, and particularly to Khrushchev. It now appears that Mao deliberately escalated the dispute between Peking and Moscow so that he could deter his colleagues from taking the "revisionist" road and compel them to adopt the anti-revisionist programs he favored at home. For example, the celebrated July 1964 article "On Khrushchev's Phoney Communism and Its Historical Lesson for the World" launched a scathing attack on revisionist trends in the Soviet Union not merely to criticize the CPSU leadership but to hold the Soviet Union up as a "negative example" for the entire international Communist movement, and most specifically for China.[92] Khrushchev's revisionism, the article asserts, "sounds the alarm for all socialist countries, including China, and for all Communists and Workers' Parties, including the Communist Party of China." In the course of providing an ideological diagnosis of the origins, nature, and consequences of Khrushchev's revisionist policies in Russia, the article also diagnosed what had been going amiss in Chinese society:

> Classes and class struggle still remain, the activities of the overthrown reactionary classes plotting a comeback still continue, and we still have speculative activities by new and old bourgeois elements and desperate forays by embezzlers, grafters, and degenerates. There are also cases of degeneration in a few primary organizations; what is more, these degenerates do their utmost to find protectors and agents in the higher leading bodies.

From Mao's point of view, combating foreign revisionism worked to prevent revisionism at home. This strategy had enormous consequences. The bitter attack on the Soviet Union generated in Chinese society hostility toward the Soviets and had the effect of deterring those in the CCP leadership who, for whatever considerations, might push for a rapprochement with Moscow. The attack on Khrushchev's revisionism tended to discredit ideologically policies that smacked of revisionism and to deprive of legitimacy those who might justify their policies, whether in the military, economic, or other fields, on the "advanced" Soviet experiences. Most important, the attack on Khrushchev's revisionism committed the CCP politically and ideologically to what must be done about preventing revisionism in China and enabled Mao to impose on the party his anti-revisionist programs. Thus, not surprisingly, the SEC and many other measures taken by the regime from 1962 to 1966 were based on Mao's fifteen-point program (put forth in the treatise "On Khrushchev's Phoney Communism") and on his other prescriptions to prevent revisionism and to ensure successful continuation of the revolution in China.

Another issue that he manipulated was his own succession. When he called for training and bringing up China's "revolutionary successors" in July 1964, he was genuinely concerned with the future of China's revolution and wanted to cultivate worthy revolutionaries of the younger generation who would carry out his revolutionary vision. In raising the question of "revolutionary succession," Mao also appeared to be raising the issue of his own succession,[93] although he had earlier designated Liu Shao-ch'i as his heir-apparent and the issue of his succession seemed to have been settled. Before the Eleventh Plenum in the summer of 1966, Liu's status as Chairman Mao's successor had added much political weight to his already enormous power and enabled him to speak with very great authority on a wide range of issues, yet, precisely because Liu had become so powerful and because his leadership had not lived up to Mao's expectations, Mao was having second thoughts.[94] Mao's grooming of Lin Piao and the approbation of the PLA before the nation may be seen as an attempt to build up a new heir or a "counterheir." When Mao listed five requirements for the "worthy successors to the revolutionary cause of the proletariat" (in "On Khrushchev's Phoney Communism") he introduced the yardstick with which he wanted to measure the "candidate" to his mantle.

Mao's manipulation of his own succession served definite political purposes. He could pressure Liu to display unquestioned loyalty to Mao and whole-hearted support for his policies; failing that, Mao could undermine Liu politically through withdrawal of endorsement. He could also sow dissension among other top leaders by making them compete to succeed him. Furthermore, he could use his succession as "bait" to cajole and win supporters from the ambitious aspirants among the top leaders. P'eng Chen, until his downfall, widely regarded by outside observers as a contender to succeed Mao, appeared to have been "courted" by Mao. In September 1964 the press accorded him the honor of being Mao's "close comrade-in-arms" for the first time; after that his responsibilities steadily increased (e.g., he was appointed head of the Five-Man CC Cultural Revolution Group and first vice-chairman of the NPC Standing Committee).

Mao's victory in the political struggle in 1966 should also be attributed to his ability to gain the allegiance of Lin Piao and to mobilize the support of the PLA at crucial moments. Beginning in 1963, Mao had gradually built up the PLA as a "counterinstitution" to the party. As a result of his call for the nation to emulate the PLA, PLA methods of organization, operation, and ideological training were presented as models to be learned by all political, economic, and social organizations, including the party itself. Mao's call was an indirect rebuke to those who administered the party, for it meant they had not done their jobs properly, and the nationwide campaign to emulate the PLA in the mid-1960s boosted the prestige of the PLA. The establishment in the party and government organizations of a network of "political work departments," clearly modeled after the PLA's political commission system, enabled the PLA to extend its influence into the operations of the party and government, since these political departments were staffed largely by political cadres transferred from the PLA and by civilian cadres who were sent to PLA schools for training.

In the course of Mao's tug-of-war with P'eng Chen over the Wu Han case, the *Liberation Army Daily*, the organ of the PLA, voiced strong support to Mao's cause and helped sway to Mao's side those party officials who were uncommitted. In the spring of 1966, the army paper openly rivaled the *People's Daily* and clearly indicated the PLA's intervention on Mao's side, which enabled him to overcome the stubborn resistance of P'eng Chen.[95]

In the summer of 1966, PLA support was crucial to Mao's defeat of Liu and Teng. There were reports that troops loyal to Lin Piao were moved into Peking in June 1966; in fact, Fu Ts'ung-pi, a long-time aide of Yang Cheng-Wu, the newly appointed acting chief of staff, took over the command of the Peking garrison at this juncture, and the *People's Daily* editorial board was reorganized on 1 June and placed under the control of the PLA. It is not known whether troops were used to intimidate Mao's opponents during the Eleventh Plenum. Nevertheless, it seems obvious that PLA leaders played a vital role in the victory of Mao and the defeat of his opponents in the Plenum; this can be seen from the fact that three marshals of the PLA, Yeh Chien-ying, Hsu Hsiang-chien, and Nieh Jung-chen, were rewarded by their promotions to the Politburo.

Finally, Mao's long experience in political in-fighting and his political acumen served him well in his struggle with his opponents in 1965-66. When situations were unfavorable, before he could be certain of victory, Mao would temporize, wait for "suitable climate and soil," and avoid hasty actions. Behind the scenes, however, Mao carefully prepared the ground for a decisive assault—he formed the coalition and recruited political allies (Chou En-lai, Lin Piao, etc.) and organized his supporters into action. His tactics of "divide and rule" and "take one at a time" kept his targets isolated politically and prevented them from taking concrete actions. Such clever maneuvers often misled his opponents and kept them in the dark as to his true intent, thus enabling him to concentrate his strength to strike at them one by one, first Lo Jui-ch'ing in December 1965, then P'eng Chen in April 1966, and finally Liu and Teng in July and August 1966.

7

Conclusion:
A "Pluralistic" Policy-Making Process

Thus far we have examined in some detail the formulation and implementation of a number of policies. The following pages summarize the major findings of this study and make additional observations on China's political system.

Politics of Conflict

Despite Mao's continual imposition of his own policies on China's political process, disputes and dissensions in the leadership were frequent and intense, even during the period when Mao exercised a fairly tight reign. Consequently, policy was significantly affected. The policy shift tended to assume an alternating pattern between conservative and radical policies, following a change in the balance of power in the decision-making councils. In other words, when the radical view prevailed in the party, the political pendulum would swing to the left, policies to effect rapid revolutionary changes would be pushed, and the leadership would stress mobilization of the masses and the ability of human will to overcome objective limitations. When the conservative view gained an upper hand, however, the political pendulum would swing to the right, the radical policies would be moderated and "consolidation" (retreat) would become the order of the day, and material incentives for the people as well as objective conditions would receive attention.

This peculiar pattern of policy oscillation was noted by Skinner and Winckler, who identified eight cycles of "radicalization" and "deradicalization" at the national level between 1949 and 1968.[1] Each cycle, according to these authors, went through six phases: normalcy, mobilization, high tide, deterioration, retrenchment, and demobilization; and each phase witnessed changes in the goals of the regime, its prescriptions for leadership style, the actual behavior of cadres, and the compliance behavior of the population. Dynamics that caused these changes, according to Skinner and Winckler, were provided by the interactions between the leadership and the population on the one hand and among the leaders themselves on the other.

That disputes and conflicts have divided the CCP leadership is now beyond doubt. Are these conflicts the manifestations of the "struggle between the two lines" (capitalism versus socialism), as the Chinese communists have asserted since the GPCR? It seems clear from this study that CCP leaders, including those disgraced during the GPCR, shared a common belief system and agreed on many basic goals. Commitment to a common ideology and goals notwithstanding, there are enormous diversities in all the sources and components of the CCP ideology and there are many levels of understanding and diverse interpretations to which each ideological tenet is susceptible. It is far from the truth for the Maoists to claim that Liu Shao-ch'i and other fallen leaders are "capitalist power-holders" who intend to restore capitalism in China. Their disputes with Mao, as shown in the case studies here, pertained to timing, speed, methods, and tactics of socialist construction.

Were these policy disputes and conflicts merely "honest disagreement" among the CCP leaders or did they involve a struggle for power? Some policy disputes arose from differences in judgment among leaders who, due to the different nature of their work, maintained divergent perspectives. Teng Tzu-hui, the regime's top agricultural official until his political eclipse in the autumn of 1957, showed genuine concern for the burden of the peasants and consistently fought against Mao's radical rural policy through the 1950s. He paid a heavy political price for his conviction: he was removed as director of the State Council Staff Office of Agriculture and Foresty (until 1959 State Council Seventh Staff Office) in October 1962, and the CC Rural Work Department (the highest agricultural organ in the party), which he had headed, was abolished in September 1962.

Teng Tzu-hui's conservative outlook was shared to different degrees by leaders such as Ch'en Yun, who specialized in economic affairs. Inasmuch as they were in a better position to know China's economic realities, they became more sensitive to objective limitations. These economic officials in the party, in contrast with party officials working in other functional areas, tended to be more cautious and placed greater emphasis on "economic" methods rather than "political" methods to foster economic development.

Teng and other economic officials, however, were not entirely oblivious to their roles and the interest of their bureaucracies. It is a truism that bureaucracies everywhere generate and guard their own special interests. In fact, one can argue that it was in Teng's interest to promote measures that would increase the peasants' zeal for production, for he depended on the peasants to fulfill the targets on the basis of which the agencies he headed were to be judged. Similarly, other top economic officials also had vested interests in increasing agricultural production because agricultural output directly and immediately affected the performance of other sectors in the economy. The PLA leaders from time to time also displayed their "departmentalist" tendencies; for example, when the PLA was asked by the party to take part and assist in various economic construction tasks during the second half of the 1950s, many military leaders demurred because they feared these tasks would interfere with the training and normal routines of the PLA. Thus policy disputes in China manifest many of the traits characteristic of bureaucratic politics generally.

P'eng Teh-huai's attack on the Great Leap and commune policies, which resulted in his dismissal as minister of defense, has been attributed by some writers to his conflict with Mao in other policy areas, notably military policy and Sino-Soviet military relations.[2] To what degree P'eng's criticism of Mao's leadership at Lushan was motivated by P'eng to settle his old scores with Mao in their personal conflict can only be a matter of conjecture.[3] Political actors are human beings; on occasions their human hopes and fears, human greatness and human failings—impossible to document—can become the overriding motivation of their political action.

Policy conflicts frequently were intimately tied to power struggle among leaders. In the case of administrative decentralization, those party officials who were entrenched in central ministries wanted only a gradual limited transfer of power to provincial authorities because it was in their interest to have ministries retain control over economic planning and administration. On the other hand, for obvious reasons, the provincial leaders generally supported a far-reaching decentralization of power to the provinces. Although arguments were presented on the merits of the various types of decentralization measures considered, the stake was power to be gained or lost.

Similarly, events on the eve of the GPCR provided ample evidence of power plays among the rival leaders. Power considerations figured prominently in the disputes over the Socialist Education Campaign, ideological rectification campaign, and China's policy toward the Indochina war. Both the Maoists and their opponents used the conflicts to enhance their own positions and to undercut their rivals.

Multiplicity of Political Participants

Another outstanding characteristic of China's policy-making process was its relative openness—"open" in the sense that the process was not monopolized by a few top leaders who largely agreed on their objectives and made major decisions alone. Rather, the process was accessible to a significant number of party officials below the top level of the leadership hierarchy (the Politburo and its Standing Committee), many of them from the provinces, and these officials affected, in various ways and in varying degree, the formulation and implementation of the regime's policy.

Although the CC, as an institution, rarely initiated policy measures, the top leadership sought and took into account opinions of CC members, many of whom occupied key positions in both the central and provincial apparatus relied upon to implement central directives. Exactly how the "anticipated reaction" of the CC members conditioned and shaped a decision of the Politburo is hard to gauge; nonetheless, the influence was certainly present, although perhaps indirect or limited. When the top leadership was deadlocked, however, policy conflicts at the top were carried to the CC for resolution; consequently, members of the CC were drawn into participation in settling disputes and making momentous decisions which, at times, changed the political fate of powerful leaders (e.g., P'eng Teh-Huai and Liu Shao-ch'i).

There seemed to be a special kind of political actor in Communist China, one who did not occupy high official position and rarely appeared in the public limelight, yet was able to shape the course of events from behind the scene. Some of these "silent power-wielders" were the personal aides or advisers to the top party leaders. For instance, Teng Li-ch'un, Liu Shao-ch'i's political secretary, was able to get things done through phone calls he made,[4] for what he said was thought by other party officials to reflect the wishes of his boss. Ch'en Po-ta, Mao's brain-truster and political confidant, had been underrated by outside observers in the past; materials available since the Cultural Revolution reveal that he often made "suggestions" to other party officials or fed ideas to Mao which led Mao to intervene, but he was apparently resented by others for having both access to and the ear of the Chairman.[5] Chiang Ch'ing, Chang Ch'un-ch'iao, and Yao Wen-yuan had become prominent political figures since the second half of the 1960s, but before the Cultural Revolution they largely operated behind the scenes. They advised Mao on various issues and he seems to have lent a willing ear to their views, which subsequently became political stimuli in the policy-making process.[6] Hsu Li-ch'un's official position was not very high—he was one of the several deputy directors of the CC Propaganda Department after 1961—but he allegedly was P'eng Chen's political advisor and frequently assisted P'eng in drafting important party documents, including the February Outline Report of 1966. We lack detailed and complete knowledge of the "silent power-wielders" in China, but it is possible that there were Chinese counterparts of Harry Hopkins, Theodore Sorenson, Richard Goodwin, Bill Moyers, H.R. Haldeman, and the like in Peking, advising and influencing the thinking of top CCP leaders and thus decisively affecting the policy of the regime.[7]

Cadres at the provincial and lower levels also had a significant impact on the policy-making processes. These cadres controlled the flow of information and through the manipulation of information they affected the leaders' perception of realities and indirectly shaped their policy choices. A good example is the highly exaggerated reports on industrial and agricultural production and on the miraculous results of deep plowing and close planting during 1958 and

1959, all of which either misled the top leaders or reinforced their established predilections. Nevertheless, they constituted an input which ultimately affected the policy output of the regime.

Moreover, the top leadership relied on the bureaucracy to project its will. Policy defined at the top by the leaders had to be translated into concrete actions by cadres at lower levels, who had to make a host of secondary decisions which frequently affected—and even altered—the substance of original policy. The character of the policy formulated by the CCP leadership seems to have contributed substantially to the leeway lower cadres had in the implementation stage. More often than not, policy directives by the top leaders only defined broad goals and left the cadres to "*hsiang pan-fa*," that is, to use their ingenuity to get things done. Since lower cadres were compelled to find and mobilize the necessary resources, human and material, to accomplish prescribed goals, they often had to take implementation very much into their own hands Bureaucrats in China, as elsewhere, had their own motivations and particularistic interests. They would not automatically implement central directives that clashed with their interests; they had to be pushed into action. At times they evaded or tried to bend the directives to suit their needs. Frequently the action of the leadership was a response to problems created by bureaucratic evasion or inertia.

The CCP leadership seemed well aware of the difficulties in maintaining a responsible bureaucracy and had developed an elaborate set of bureaucracy-controlling techniques to enforce its ruling priorities [8] One of the techniques was the use of a "campaign approach" to policy implementation. The reliance on this technique, as Barnett points out, enables the leadership to mobilize and concentrate all efforts on achieving the defined objective at a given time, to break through the bureaucratic routines, and to combat the tendency toward bureaucratization.[9]

The use of the campaign approach in implementing policy may have solved some problems, but it created others. "Crash" campaigns inevitably resulted in undesirable side-effects and excesses. This was the case in the wake of the accelerated collectivization drive and the implementation of the twelve-year agricultural program and in many "crash" programs during the Great Leap Forward. Spurred on by higher authorities to fulfill and overfulfill various targets, and under constant political pressure and ideological exhortation to appear "progressive," local officials were often compelled to opt for targets even higher than those imposed on them and to do everything to achieve the impossible.

A mass movement which derives its power and effectiveness from the initiative and enthusiasm of lower cadres necessarily generates its own momentum, which the top leadership cannot always control. The tendency toward excesses in the course of such campaigns probably is an inescapable hazard in a totalitarian regime; the same phenomenon was also present in the

Soviet system, particularly during Stalin's collectivization campaign in the 1930s.[10]

The actions of the lower officials in the implementation stage—whether they involved evasion, distortion, poor compliance, or overcompliance—inevitably created new situations and new problems ("feedback") to which the top leaders had to react; they then had to make new decisions. In this sense, lower cadres can be said to have participated, at least indirectly or negatively, in policy initiation.

On certain occasions, however, lower cadres played a less indirect and more positive role in originating policies. The communization movement in 1958 is a good example. The available evidence indicated that the decision to establish communes was first made by Mao and then formally ratified by the Politburo in the Peitaiho Conference in August 1958. Mao, however, and perhaps his Politburo colleagues as well, were greatly influenced by local leaders and cadres in Honan, the cradle of the commune system, who provided not only ideas relevant to the concept of the new rural organization but also concrete examples of operative communes. In other words, the choices of the top leadership were, in a sense, structured by cadres in Honan. In fact, several communes in Honan were selected by the CCP leadership as models to be emulated throughout China[11] and as such they greatly affected the ways in which the commune system developed throughout China in the fall of 1958.

Thus policy in Communist China was not made by a few top leaders alone; actors possessing different political resources participated, directly or indirectly, in each stage of the policy-making process and affected, in a variety of ways, the decision-output of the regime. A political actor's resources may come from his control of a segment of the party-state apparatus, or from one or more official positions which grant decision-making authority in a formal sense; or a political actor with no important official position still may have access to the top party leaders. Political resources may also stem from the functions the political actors perform, such as cadres' implementation of leadership policies, and from the opportunities to control or manipulate the flow of information. An actor may also derive political influence from his expertise on a given issue or from the fact that he speaks for a wide public; for instance, an agricultural official will have influence on agricultural matters.

Expansion of Political Participation

According to the CCP constitution of 1956, when the CC is not in session (as was often the case) the Politburo or its Standing Committee is the highest decision-making body in the party. The principle of democratic centralism, on which the CCP is organized, is designed to keep the effective decision-making power of the party in the hands of a few people at the top of the leadership hierarchy. In fact, when the top leaders in the Politburo (those in the Politburo Standing Committee) were in essential agreement among themselves, matters rarely went beyond this inner circle, for the decision they made by themselves would carry enough political weight to gain acceptance by others.

Despite the fact that Mao wielded enormous political influence, he did not always carry the day. As shown in our case studies, many of the programs he favored were modified or blocked by other party leaders who held different views. As leadership unity broke down and top leaders were involved in policy conflict, they were compelled to go to the CC or other large political forums to settle their differences. Consequently, officials outside the inner circle increasingly took part in policy decision and conflict resolution.

To project his will, Mao often engaged in politicking to seek wider support and used various maneuvers to overcome his opposition. In July 1955, for example, Mao appealed directly to provincial leaders, over the heads of his colleagues in the Politburo, to gain support of a radical collectivization policy. This maneuver enabled Mao to secure the overwhelming support of most provincial party secretaries and to disarm opposition from his colleagues at the center. In the late 1950s, when Mao was promoting his Great Leap programs, he actively enlisted the backing of provincial leaders and used such support to overcome resistance at the center.

Such maneuvers by Mao, designed to redress the balance of power in his favor, resulted in the expansion of the arena of political conflict and mobilization of new participants into the policy-making process.[12] Furthermore, after the collapse of Mao's utopian programs in the early 1960s, and as Mao was opposed and politically eclipsed by other party leaders who controlled the party machinery, he went outside the party to seek support. As is well known now, Mao turned to the PLA, coopted it, and used PLA intervention to remove P'eng Chen, Liu Shao-ch'i, Teng Hsiao-p'ing, and others from positions of power in the regime in 1966.

From the summer of 1966 on, Mao went one step further by extending the political conflict to the "public" arena; he mobilized extra-party forces—the student Red Guards and "revolutionary rebels" drawn from workers and youth—to push his GPCR crusade. The resistance to Mao's radical goals was so widespread and prevalent in the party organization at the center and in the provinces and Mao's supporters within the party councils were in the minority, that he had no alternative but to enlarge the area of conflict and invoke the aid of the "masses" to crush his opposition within the party. The participation of the masses in the political conflict reached a climax after January 1967 when they were extolled by the Maoist leadership to launch an unprecedented all-out assault against the entire power structure and to seize power from the "capitalist power-holders." In emulation of the 1871 Paris Commune rebellion, the Red Guards and "rebels" rioted, occupied party headquarters and government buildings, ousted and in many instances handcuffed party and government officials, paralyzed the party and government authorities, and produced chaos in public social order.

Some political scientists have measured the degree of political development in a polity by the scope of political participation. The explosion of political participation in China after January 1967, which was unstructured and anomic, can hardly be seen as a sign of political development, however. Rapid increase in mobilization and participation, in the absence of effective and strong political institutions, produced not political development but what Huntington calls "political decay."[13]

The subsequent intervention by the PLA and the tight control it imposed on the Red Guards has considerably arrested the trends toward political decay. PLA intervention in politics has generated new problems, however; during and since the GPCR, PLA leaders have assumed important political functions and their political influence expanded enormously at the expense of civilian officials. Opening the floodgate to military intervention when he pushed the PLA into the political arena, Mao found himself plagued by the refusal of PLA leaders to "return to the barracks."[14]

The Policy-Making Structure

The final question is where, in structural terms, the real loci of power lay in China's system in the period covered by this study. During the second half of the 1950s, when Mao was an active participant in the policy-making process, the process was, in a sense, more personalized and less routine; Mao had used various institutional devices to initiate policies and mobilize support for them. One of these was the Supreme State Conference which he convened on fifteen occasions as chairman of the People's Republic from 1954 to 1959. Another device Mao used was the meeting of provincial party secretaries and the ad hoc party conference. Mao also frequently used the press, through interviews, articles he wrote, and news reports, to initiate policies and make known his approval or disapproval of certain measures. And still another device he used was to write comments on reports that were submitted to him by his colleagues and subordinates, which frequently induced these officials to undertake new actions. In contrast, when Mao was less active in the 1960s, forums such as the Supreme State Conference and meetings of provincial party secretaries and the ad hoc party conference were rarely convened. The policy-making process was, in a sense, routine and institutionalized; work conferences of the Politburo and the CC were used regularly to discuss and approve policies which appeared to have been initiated by individual Politburo members, and mass campaigns became less frequent as policies were implemented through established normal institutional channels.

The supreme political authority in China, before the Cultural Revolution, was clearly vested in the CCP. In the CCP, the Politburo or its Standing Committee was the most important locus of decision; all major policy measures of the regime had to be approved, at least formally, by the Politburo or its Standing Committee. When the Politburo was divided, as it was over the pace of collectivization in 1955 and over a number of economic issues in the fall of 1957, party officials outside of this innermost circle appeared to become involved in the decision phase. On these two occasions,[15] as at the Lushan Plenum in August 1959, the CC apparently was the ultimate organ for deciding the issues and settling the disputes among the top leaders.

On various occasions when the top leadership appeared to be divided, forums such as enlarged Politburo sessions, central work conferences, and enlarged CC plenums, which were attended by nonmembers as well as members of the Politburo or the CC, were apparently used to decide major policy decisions. When Mao actively intervened in the policy-making processes in the 1950s, he frequently used regional party conferences which were attended by both Politburo members and provincial leaders to discuss and apparently also decide major policy questions.

Thus the locus of decisions may be seen as the arena of political conflict, and the choice of a particular arena was itself "political," since it would determine the political actors to be involved and the procedures to be used in solving conflict. We may also conclude that when the top leadership was divided, the arena of political conflict expanded, and those who were below the topmost level in the leadership hierarchy became involved in decision-making and conflict resolution.

In analyzing the operation of the Politburo, it is possible, on the basis of our case studies, to distinguish, tentatively, between decisions which have not been made by the Politburo as an institution but only formally approved by it and those that have been subject to full-dress debate in the Politburo. Reportedly, certain important economic measures in 1962 were proposed by the Five-Man Central Financial and Economic Group established in 1962 and headed by Ch'en Yun and were formally approved by the Politburo presided over by Liu Shao-ch'i. Similarly, the seventy-article Regulations on Industry, Mines, and Enterprises were reportedly drafted under the auspices of Po I-po (who was in charge of the regime's overall industry and communications policy) and approved by a Politburo meeting chaired by Liu Shao-ch'i. Most individual Politburo and CC Secretariat members had areas of specialization and appeared to be in charge of different broad functional areas (e.g., the military, foreign affairs, propaganda). It is possible, on the basis of available evidence, to postulate that these Politburo and Secretariat members in their individual capacities made some important decisions within their own special areas of responsibility, and that these decisions were probably then approved by the Politburo with or without full-dress debates.

Thus it appears that issues and measures that finally reached the Politburo had already been screened to some extent, and the ultimate choices of the top leadership had to some extent been defined in advance. This situation may have been inevitable. Unless individual Politburo and Secretariat members had screened issues and defined problems, decision-making in the Politburo would have been hopelessly clogged.

Although various state institutions are empowered by the 1954 state constitution with important policy-making functions, their actual role in the policy-making process is much less significant than that of the party. The NPC, according to the constitution, is the highest legislative organ of the nation; in reality, however, its functions were merely dressing decisions of the CCP leadership with legality and serving as the "transmission belt" of the party leadership; it had little to do with actual initiation or authorization of the government programs. The NPC was convened regularly in the 1950s and was, presumably, informed of the developments in the nation, but the party even dispensed with this formality in the 1960s. The party did present the twelve-year agricultural program to the NPC for formal enactment in April 1960. By this time, however, all the basic decisions about the program had been made, and the approval of the NPC was only the culminating formal ratification of the policy-making processes which had preceded it. The establishment of the communes, which resulted in major changes in the local administrative structure of the state, was effected by a party directive alone, without the NPC's formal action.

The State Council, on the other hand, was more directly involved in the regime's policy-making processes. It was the party's "executive arm," responsible for the implementation of the regime's policy. Most important, the State Council, with its ministries and agencies, administered the nation's economy. During the period covered by this study, the premier and nine of the sixteen vice-premiers of the State Council were also members of the Politburo and obviously participated in the making of decisions within the party. Even when basic policy guidelines were set by the party, the State Council had to make many administrative decisions in the course of implementation.

Thus several institutions were involved throughout the policy-making process. For instance, those agencies connected with planning, decision, and execution of rural policies in the center would at least include the Ministry of Agriculture (headed by Liao Lu-yen), the State Council Seventh Staff Office (later renamed Agricultural and Forestry Staff Office, headed by Vice-Premier

Teng Tzu-hui), the CC Rural Work Department (also headed by Teng Tzu-hui), the Secretariat (in which T'an Chen-lin had the primary responsibility over rural policies), the Politburo, and the CC.

The twelve-year agricultural program and the commune program would require the support or at least cooperation of each of these six groups. Opposition by any of the first four groups would presumably be handled by removing the dissenting official or officials. In the fall of 1955, Teng Tzu-hui's power in the State Council Seventh Staff Office and in the CC Rural Work Department was already diluted by several newly appointed deputy-directors, and from 1957 on, his functions were largely taken over by T'an Chen-lin, although he was not formally removed from those two posts. Vigorous disagreements within the Politburo would be settled by the CC or by removing dissenting individual members. Ch'en Yun was rendered inactive in 1959–60 and after fall 1962 presumably because he was critical of many Great Leap measures.

Beyond these central party and government bodies, a host of organizations from the provinces down to the communes are also involved in national policy-making processes, primarily because they have to carry out the central directives. The purge of provincial and lower-level cadres in 1957–58 and in 1959–61 suggested that the performance of these officials was not equal to the expectations of the top leadership and they had to be removed to facilitate the goals of the leadership.

The regime's most important decision-making bodies in the period covered by this study were, of course, the Politburo (its regular session and working conference), the CC (the regular and enlarged sessions), and the ad hoc party conference. The ad hoc party conference, such as the Tsingtao Conference of July 1957, Hangchow Conference and Nanning Conference of January 1958, or Chengtu Conference of March 1958, is not a formal party organ, for there is no provision in the party constitution for its existence and functions. In practice, however, it did make important decisions, and the legitimacy of these decisions was never questioned in Communist China.

Once a policy decision was adopted at the top, it then filtered down through various communication channels for implementation by lower levels. One of these channels was the mass media, particularly the party's central organs, the *People's Daily* and *Hung Ch'i* (which replaced *Hsueh-hsi* in June 1958), and the provincial newspapers published by provincial party authorities. Another channel was official directives of all sorts issued by the party and the government, some of which were made public in the press. And still another important channel was the conferences, such as those meetings convened regularly by the party and by government functional departments (the rural work conferences, the conferences of the party secretaries in charge of industry, etc.), and "conveyance meetings" (*ch'uan-ta hui-yi*), which were convened by the leading official of a functional or geographical unit specifically for conveying to his subordinates instructions from above. The meetings of the NPC, the CPPCC, and the CC also performed important communication functions.

To a very striking degree, rarely seen in other political systems, the Chinese Communists used oral communication to transmit vital information. Although this mode of communication had certain advantages,[16] often it blocked the flow of information. Transmitting central directives by word of mouth, local officials could easily reinterpret or distort them to suit their needs, thus frustrating the goals of the central leadership.

Top leaders were aware of this problem and used various means to ensure the compliance of executing agencies. For example, party and government organizations regularly filed reports, which filtered up the bureaucratic hierarchy. Another mechanism was conferences in which officials not only received information or instructions from above but also presented reports [*hui pao*] informing the higher authorities of the work of their units. The higher authorities frequently sent investigation teams or the top leaders themselves undertook inspection tours to gather information. In addition, agencies such as the State Statistics Bureau and the New China News Agency and, to some extent, letters written to the party, government, and the *People's Daily* also provided information on the state of the nation.

Was the Chinese leadership insulated from reality by the nature of the system it presided over or by the character of its own information-gathering agencies? Available evidence makes it clear that there are pressures built into the Chinese political system which operate to block channels of communication. Every dictatorship has a tendency to breed sycophancy and conformity, and Communist China is no exception. When the views of the leadership on certain issues were known, lower officials tended to send back reports that confirmed its preconceptions. For example, when Mao suggested in 1958 that close planting could increase farm production, many provincial party secretaries went out of their way to "prove" the correctness of Mao's idea, and its indiscriminate application later resulted in severe crop failures. In 1958–59, when the Chinese leadership demanded a great leap in industrial and agricultural production, lower officials, responding to the pressures or the climate of expectations at the top, transmitted false information and inflated statistics to higher authorities. Since the Chinese Communists often equated caution with rightist deviations, cadres felt compelled to juggle data to conceal failure of performance or compelled to opt for targets that could not realistically be met.

The so-called squatting investigations undertaken by many top leaders since 1961 indicate that the CCP high command tried very hard to collect information on a first-hand basis. This type of investigation is somewhat different from what the Chinese leaders had done in the 1950s. They did conduct inspection tours frequently in the 1950s, but these tours appeared to be superficial; it is questionable whether the top leaders, whose entourages usually consisted of local senior party officials, would have the opportunity to hear or see things objectionable to the local leaders in their "guided" tours.[17]

This was precisely the point raised by Liu Shao-ch'i. In an interview with the "work group" of the Hunan Provincial Party Committee in April 1961, Liu allegedly criticized Mao's method of "investigation and study" and stated that investigators sent by higher authorities were often deceived by local officials who were skillful in concealing failures and falsifying data.[18] Liu was said to have prescribed a new method of investigation which called for investigators to undertake investigation in their own hometowns. The rationale, according to Liu, was that investigators, instead of relying merely on the official sources of information and the cooperation of the investigated, could count on their relatives and friends, who would be inclined to tell the truth about the local conditions and would thus be able to uncover problems and obtain needed information.[19] Whatever merits Liu's method of "squatting investigation" may have had, it would appear to be too wasteful for top officials to "squat" in the countryside to collect information and not to attend to other important tasks in Peking.

Mao's Roles

In Studying China's political system, one can hardly fail to be impressed by the enormous power Mao wielded. He was the undisputed leader in the Chinese system; on many occasions, he displayed an impressive ability to defy all institutions and intervene in any policy matter he considered of vital importance. In China's policy-making process, Mao played several important roles.

First he was an ideologist. On numerous occasions (his speeches on collectivization in the summer of 1955, on contradictions among the people in February 1957, and on class struggle in September 1962; his statement incorporated in the treatise "On Khrushchev's Phoney Communism" in July 1964) Mao provided an authoritative assessment of the state of the nation and pointed toward a purposeful goal for the next phase. In other words, Mao determined the nature of a given period, identified different social forces and contradictions in society, and defined problems in the political arena at each important turning point. Pronouncements such as these tended to condition the policy alternatives the regime subsequently mapped out; even Mao did not dictate policy measures, but his political diagnosis had the effect of establishing the parameters within which problems were tackled.

A second role Mao played in the policy-making process was political balancer and arbiter. Mao, as the leader of the party and the nation, had to mediate conflicting interests of society (which were represented to a certain degree by his colleagues who were in charge of different segments of the bureaucracy or different functional "systems") and fix priorities among their conflicting goals. Mao's speech "Ten Great Relationships," addressed to an enlarged Politburo session on 25 April 1956, is typical of Mao's efforts to reconcile contradictions in the major sectors of Chinese society—contradictions between agriculture and industry, between light and heavy industry, between national defense and economic construction, between the central and local authorities, between the collective and the individuals, between the Han people and minority nationalities, and many others.

Furthermore, Mao played the role of an innovator in the policy-making process. In many instances, it was Mao's initiative that resulted in launching a new policy or reversing an ongoing policy. For example, he promoted the collectivization drive in the summer of 1955. At that time, when other party leaders had clearly favored a "go-slow" approach toward organizing peasants into the APC's, Mao argued vehemently for stepping up the tempo of collectivization in a secret speech to a meeting of provincial party secretaries at the end of July 1955; consequently, the "go-slow" approach was discarded and an intense nation-wide campaign was launched to accelerate agricultural collectivization.

In addition to his intervention in the issue of collectivization, numerous other examples of Mao's vigorous initiative can be cited. In January 1956 he initiated the ambitious twelve-year agricultural program—reportedly he not only provided basic ideas for the program but also personally supervised its formulation and drafting. In the spring of 1956 he actively promoted a liberalization policy toward intellectuals, and in the first quarter of 1957 he pushed for a party rectification campaign, apparently against the counsels of many of the "organization men" in the party. He resurrected the twelve-year agricultural program in the CC Plenum of September-October 1957, and in doing so he again reversed a more cautious rural policy pursued by the party up to that time. In a series of conferences with provincial leaders at Hangchow, Nanning, and Chengtu in late 1957 and the first quarter of 1958, Mao actively and vigorously campaigned for his ambitious Great Leap programs. In the summer of 1958 he gave a "go-ahead" signal to launch the communes throughout China. In the fall of 1962 he pushed the party to launch the Socialist Education Campaign, and in the fall of 1965 he set in motion the Great Proletarian Cultural Revolution.

Political Constraints upon Mao

Enormous as Mao's power was, he sometimes did not have his own way. This study provides ample evidence that other party leaders frequently were able to block his policy or modify its substance. In other words, Mao was not "in command" all the time; he encountered opposition from his Politburo colleagues, and his capacity to enforce his policy fluctuated considerably.[20]

For example, the disaster of the Great Leap politically eclipsed Mao, and other party leaders seized the opportunity to initiate new programs. The question of who exercises power to initiate policy is of great political significance, for the initiator is in the position of choosing problems or issues to be placed on the agenda of the political system and determines the subjects for debate. He who defines problems and proposes alternatives carries enormous political power. In the context of the American political system, one writer has observed:

> The definition of alternatives is the supreme instrument of power; the antagonists can rarely agree on what the issues are because power is involved in the definition. He who determines what politics is about runs the country because the definition of the alternatives is the choice of conflicts, and the choice of conflicts allocates power.[21]

To a considerable degree, this observation is equally applicable to Mao's participation in China's policy-making process. In the second half of the 1950s when Mao constantly intervened in the policy-making process to exercise "leadership," his influence was paramount. After the Lushan confrontation with P'eng Teh-huai and in the wake of the disastrous failures of the Great Leap and commune programs in the early 1960s, for a variety of reasons Mao no longer played the role of an innovator who initiated policies, especially domestic policies, and he abstained, to a considerable extent, from participation in the policy-making process. Consequently, Mao's influence in the policy-making process declined substantially.

With Mao's reduced role in the initiation of policy, there was a corresponding growth in the power to initiate by other CCP leaders, particularly Liu Shao-chi'i, Chou En-lai, Teng Hsiao-p'ing, Ch'en Yun, Lin Piao, P'eng Chen, and Po I-po. The CCP was experiencing a different kind of leadership in the early 1960s as political power appeared to become more diffuse and individual Politburo members appeared to exercise greater influence over policy on their special functional "systems." Although Mao was undoubtedly kept informed of major domestic developments and his approval was sought for important decisions, yet as he was now in the "second line" and "did not take charge of the daily routine," he increasingly found himself unable to impose his will on the party.

It seems clear from the events in 1965–66 that Mao found himself "stone-walled" by other party leaders like Liu Shao-ch'i, Teng Hsiao-p'ing, and P'eng Chen, who tightly controlled the party machinery, and felt compelled to launch the GPCR to purge these "capitalist power-holders," thus removing constraints upon himself and regaining control of the party.

Scholars frequently compare Mao with Stalin and consider Mao China's Stalin. It is doubtful whether Mao ever held the kind of absolute power that the Soviet dictator wielded after 1935. True, Mao clearly dominated China's policy-making process in the second half of the 1950s; but even then he had to resort to extensive politicking to win support outside the Politburo. In the 1960s, however, Mao appeared to have lost much of his "power to persuade," thus he had to use extraordinary measures to destroy his opponents politically. Although he succeeded in creating a wreckage—personal and institutional—during the GPCR, his destructive acts reflect more of the failure of his leadership and the loss of his ability to persuade than his power to command compliance.

To fully understand the constraints Mao faced, it is necessary to analyze the roles and power of other top leaders in the CCP and some of the "operational codes" the CCP leadership observed. First, most Politburo members, and particularly those in the Politburo Standing Committee (or those in the Secretariat before the 1956 Party Congress) were leaders of great stature; they fought alongside Mao against the Japanese and the Chinese Nationalists, and each of them made significant contributions to the success of the Communist revolution in China. In other words, these leaders achieved positions of power by their own merits and did not owe their positions to Mao. Unlike the relationship between Joseph Stalin and other Politburo members of the Soviet Communist Party after the 1930s, which can be characterized as the master and lackeys, the relationship between Mao and most of his Politburo associates was one of coequals, with Mao as the first among equals.[22]

Over the years, Mao's growing cult of personality and his acquisition of the "routinized charisma"[23] of the party after the Communist victory in 1949 gave him enormous prestige and influence among the rank and file and tended to enhance Mao's position vis-à-vis his Politburo colleagues and undermine the one-time relationship of relative equality. For political expediency, Mao's colleagues often inflated Mao's cult and publicly affirmed his undisputed leadership position. Nevertheless, Mao's power was never absolute; other CCP leaders did share with Mao control of important political resources in the system, the most important one being control of the party organization and the authority vested in it, and they represented in varying degrees counterweights to Mao's power. Even in the 1950s when Mao was actively and closely involved in policy formulation and execution, he by no means monopolized all the policy-making power. On occasion, such as after Khruschchev's de-Stalinzation speech in 1956, other party leaders invoked the principle of collective leadership to constrain Mao.[24]

Moreover, decision-making is not a one-man show; because of inherent limits on the time, energy, and intelligence of a single individual, Mao simply could not decide all vital issues in a wholly planned society like China. Therefore, if for no other reason than this, Mao had to, and did, in fact, divide the labor and share the power with other top leaders. Thus Liu Shao-ch'i, the party's senior vice-chairman, was in charge of party affairs in the 1950s, and after succeeding Mao as head of state in the spring of 1959, he wielded more power than before. Liu was virtually the acting chairman of the party in Mao's absence from the national capital, which was quite frequent in the 1960s. Liu presided over the Politburo meetings and exercised the important and powerful functions of balancing, coordinating, and integrating conflicting interests of various sectors of the system.

Other members of the Politburo Standing Committee, with the exception of the very elderly Chu Teh, also took charge of a major functional area.[25] For instance, Premier Chou En-lai had the overall responsibility for government administration and the conduct of foreign relations (probably with the exception of intra-Communist bloc affairs); Ch'en Yun was responsible for overall economic policies until his political eclipse in 1959; Lin Piao was in charge of military affairs after he was elected to the Politburo Standing Committee in May 1958; and Teng Hsiao-p'ing supervised the party apparatus and probably also managed intra-Communist bloc affairs. Aside from these seven top leaders in the Politburo Standing Committee, other members of the Politburo and the secretaries of the CC Secretariat who were not Politburo members also had their special areas of responsibility;[26] they tended to become closely identified with particular sectors of the political system and strove to protect the special interests of their "departments."

It can be argued that in a nation as huge and diversified as China, some measure of division of labor and collective decision-making is certainly necessary, as in all political systems. Moreover, China does not have real collective leadership when Mao stands above all others and repeatedly throws his weight decisively into the political arena. Nevertheless, other party leaders were able to severely checkmate Mao by vetoing and blocking policies Mao favored. The alleged division into "first line" and "second line" in the Politburo Standing Committee, which allowed other top party leaders to exercise operational or administrative power while Mao, in the "seond line" exercised "legislative power" (making basic decisions), did not prevent those in the "first line" from making basic decisions either. For one thing, there cannot be clear-cut distinction between operational and "legislative" power in China, and those who execute policy can and frequently do remake policy. At times Mao either elected or was forced to abstain from deliberations of the party councils; consequently, other party leaders made their own decisions and the thin line between the operations and "legislative" functions became totally blurred.

As pointed out, Mao sometimes was much less involved in actual implementation of policy in the 1960s, and the control of the party apparatus devolved into the hands of Liu Shao-ch'i, Teng Hsiao-p'ing, and others. These leaders built up water-tight "independent kingdoms" to spurn the interference of Mao and his supporters. Mao himself actually complained in October 1966 that Teng Hsiao-p'ing had "stonewalled" for six years, and had not informed him of the work in the CC Secretariat. What Teng and others did, especially after January 1965, was more than bureaucratic foot-dragging; they used their positions of strength and mobilized resources available to them to fight for their political survival.

Moreover, these leaders, sensing Mao's intention to remove them after January 1965, allied with one another and took concerted actions for mutual defense. These leaders included Liu, Teng Hsiao-P'ing, P'eng Chen, Lu Ting-yi, Yang Shang-k'un, and possibly Lo Jui-ch'ing, all of them entrenched in control of the party apparatus (the last five being members of the CC Secretariat, the party's highest administrative body). In opposition to the Liuist faction was the Mao-Lin faction, which included Mao, Lin Piao, Chou En-lai, Ch'en Po-ta, and K'ang Sheng, who plotted and made preparations separately or together for the final showdown. Factional cleavages and struggle, which apparently had little part in the policy conflicts over economic issues during the 1950s and were not the salient element in Chinese politics prior to the 1960s, suddenly assumed a pivotal importance in the political scene in the 1960s as the two groups were locked in bitter conflict.

Under such circumstances, former personal and working ties gained new significance. A large number of CC members who had worked under Liu Shao-ch'i and P'eng Chen in north China during the 1930s, many of whom (including P'eng Chen) were imprisoned by the KMT authorities and allegedly signed an anti-Communist manifesto to regain freedom, rallied to the side of Liu and P'eng.[27] Their political survival would depend on the fate of Liu and P'eng, for they knew too well from past experience that purges of a top leader would also victimize his former associates. This apprehension was further reinforced by the Maoist propagandists who, through a reinterpretation of history, insinuated that those who had written self-incriminating statements were cowards and traitors and deserved to be purged. Such twists and turns of events reactivated the historical ties, exacerbated the factional conflict, and hardened the opposition to Mao, all of which would in time force Mao and his supporters to go outside normal party channels in order to launch the GPCR.

Political constraints upon Mao have come not only from his opponents but often from his allies and supporters. To secure the backing of Lin Piao and his followers in the Fourth Field Army group, for example, Mao reluctantly made concessions to Lin even in matters which he considered of crucial importance. Thus Lin became the authoritative spokesman and interpreter of Mao's policy and thought after 1965, greatly expanded his base of power, particularly during the GPCR, by placing his own followers in key positions, and was made the sole vice-chairman of the party and Mao's successor during the Eleventh CC Plenum in August 1966. All of these matters had undoubtedly received Mao's consent, something which he would in time regret; but, in retrospect, the consent appears to have been a *quid pro quo*, a political payoff, which he had to give to obtain Lin's all-out support.

The case with Premier Chou En-lai seems somewhat similar. Although Chou had been regarded by most Western observers as the symbol of moderate political forces in China, he was a political "swinger," ready to take any stance and swing to the side that served his own interest, as the case studies in this book show. In the course of the seesaw conflict between the Liuists and the Maoists in the mid-1960s, Chou lent his support to Mao and may have advised and planned with Mao from late 1964 to depose P'eng Chen and Liu. Chou's support during this crucial period and whatever contribution he made to the ultimate defeat of Liu Shao-ch'i in the summer of 1966 were undoubtedly appreciated by Mao. Nonetheless, Mao was known to harbor serious reservations about Chou. In a letter to Lin Piao on 15 September 1966, for example, Mao criticized Chou for being eclectic and "not consistently honest" and expressed doubts on Chou's integrity (loyalty) in "his late years."[28] However, what refrained Mao from turning the spearhead of struggle against Chou at that time, according to the letter, was that Chou "had done a great deal of beneficial work for a long time, and few in the Party can match his ability"; hence Mao thought it politically expedient to have Chou join "the proletarian headquarters for the time being and let him handle a few problems."

Regardless of his real feelings toward the radical goals of the GPCR, Chou went along with the Maoists at least on record, chanting the radical line and heaping praises on Chiang Ch'ing, and permitted his State Council subordinates to be attacked by the Red Guards, or even engaged in self-criticism. By such acts, Chou managed to establish his identification with Mao's "proletarian headquarters" and enhance his revolutionary credentials. Furthermore, political turmoil and economic disruptions caused by the GPCR, particularly after the winter of 1966, made Chou highly indispensable to Mao. His eloquence, political skill, and administrative talent enabled him to mediate among rival political groups, moderate excesses of the Red Guards, and maintain a modicum of order in China's national economy and foreign relations in the face of massive upheaval. Such were the circumstances under which Chou, perhaps against the wishes of Mao, was allowed to gradually assume the overall management of the GPCR from the Cultural Revolution Group (CRG), a body which was set up in May 1966 to propel Mao's crusade.

The shift might not have been significant had Chou and the CRG leaders seen eye to eye on the goals of the GPCR and on methods of carrying out the goals, but obviously they did not. On the one hand, the CRG leaders such as

Ch'en Po-ta and Chiang Ch'ing were political radicals; they wanted to change the status quo completely, they extolled violence, incited the revolutionary rebels to launch an all-out attack on the Establishment, and sought to destroy the existing power structure in China through a revolution from below to be carried out by the masses, in the image of the Paris Commune. On the other hand, however, Chou En-lai was politically moderate or conservative during the GPCR, inasmuch as he was devoted more to restricting the scope of political conflict, curbing violence and other excesses, and, most important, preserving the very political system which the CRG radicals vowed to overturn. Of course, Chou was pragmatic enough to accept reforms when they seemed inevitable, but he would effect as little change as possible to the power structure; he was a "reformist" at most, and not a revolutionary like many of the CRG leaders. At times he professed the same radical goals, but he was not really committed to them; his cooptation of the radical line, however, did facilitate his takeover of the management of the GPCR as well as the moderation of its radical goals.

Mao and the CRG leaders were fully aware of Chou's "double-dealing" but could do very little to change the situation. For one thing, Mao highly valued Chou's ability and regarded Chou as indispensable to him. For another, Chou's management of the GPCR appears to be supported by powers in the party and the military hierarchy. Perhaps most important, Mao may have perceived the threat of Lin Piao, who had expanded his influence too much during the GPCR, and Mao considered Chou a would-be ally against Lin Piao. There is some evidence that Chou was an element of Mao's anti-Lin Piao coalition, which carried out a step-by-step struggle with the Lin Piao group after the Lushan CC Plenum in August-September 1970.

Siding with Mao in every round of intra-party struggle since the 1950s, Chou En-lai displayed his consistent loyalty to the Chairman. Whatever reservations Mao may have, he was not in a position to deny Chou a place in the top leadership hierarchy. This fact, coupled with the absence of leaders who could match Chou's seniority and merits, after the elimination of Chou's peers Liu Shao-ch'i and Lin Piao, allowed Chou to emerge from the Tenth Party Congress in August 1973 as a leader with power second only to Mao.

The political rehabilitation of Teng Hsiao-P'ing, denounced by the Maoists as the Number Two top "capitalist power-holder" during the GPCR, is still another illustration that Mao had not ruled by fiat but was engaged in political "give and take." After Lin Piao's downfall and Mao's attempt to remove or neutralize the opposition of Lin's followers entrenched in the party and PLA leadership hierarchy, Mao had to rally the support of all political forces and make deals with them. Possibly Teng's rehabilitation, revealed in his first public appearance in April 1973, was one such deal exacted from Mao by Teng's allies and associates of the former Second Field Army. Since then, Teng has gained surprising political prominence, including elevation to the Politburo around January 1974. Given his extensive military background during the period of struggle, and his ties with PLA leaders, Teng is one of the very few top CCP leaders who has empathy toward the PLA leaders and at the same time is respected and trusted by them; hence he is believed to have been instrumental in the orderly carrying out of the major reshuffle of the PLA regional leaders in December 1973.

In addition, certain rules of the party apparently had the effect of limiting Mao's power. One such rule, for example, is to ban the use of terror against dissenting cadres in the party, particularly members of the CC. This rule, which was formalized in the early 1940s by the Chinese Communists to avoid the repetition of Stalin's methods in the CCP, has been observed with consistency. In handling the disgraced cadres, particularly those who held high positions in the leadership hierarchy, Mao either reduced their power, as the case of Ch'en Yun and Teng Tzu-hui, or relieved them of it, as the case of P'eng Teh-huai, P'eng Chen, Liu Shao-ch'i, Teng Hsiao-P'ing, and a host of "capitalist power-holders" in 1966–68, but he did not threaten them with death. Some of Mao's critics in the 1950s, such as Ch'en Yun and Teng Tzu-hui, and more recently Teng Hsiao-P'ing, came back to reassert their political influence after a period of political eclipse; similarly, a large number of lesser party officials, some in the center but mostly in the provinces, who were disgraced because of their criticism of the Greap Leap or their opposition to the GPCR in the 1960s succeeded in winning "reversals of verdict" and secured rehabilitation—not posthumously.

Whatever political merits this particular mode of management of opposition may have, over the years it may have tended to reduce Mao's ability to elicit compliance and impose his will. Inasmuch as the punishment for those who dared to criticize or oppose the top leadership was simply personal disgrace and retirement, and not a matter of life or death, they were less inhibited in asserting themselves. That P'eng Teh-huai wrote an 80,000-word letter to the CC in June 1962 in which he attacked Mao's policies and demanded reversal of the verdict on him should be viewed in this context. Conceivably, those who have been purged in the course of the Cultural Revolution may plot a comeback in the future. Their physical existence alone resembles something of a political alternative to those in power, and the availability of a "counter-elite" constitutes a continuing threat to the "ins" and makes it difficult for them to consolidate their control in the wake of the Cultural Revolution.

Postscript I
The Last Stand of the Maoist Revolution

The political upheaval in China dramatized by the sudden ouster of four top radical party leaders (the "Gang of Four") in October 1976, barely one month after the death of their patron, Chairman Mao Tse-tung, once again brought into sharp relief many of the burning issues and deep-seated conflicts which have gripped and divided the CCP leadership in the last decade. These conflicts also involved a struggle for leadership succession. It is within this broad context that China's political drama has been staged since the early 1970s.

Conflict over Mao's Succession

Addressing the Ninth Party Congress, convened in April 1969 to mark the "victorious close" of the Cultural Revolution, Mao Tse-tung called for "a congress of unity and a congress of victory." The unity and victory that Mao called upon the Congress delegates to forge proved elusive, however, for a new, intensive intraparty struggle flared up not long afterward, involving both Mao and his successor Lin Piao in a life-and-death battle.

Without question, Marshal Lin Piao and his followers had greatly benefited from the GPCR. Not only had Lin replaced Liu Shao-ch'i as Mao's successor and become the sole vice-chairman of the party, but he had also placed many of his followers in the Fourth Field Army in key positions and substantially expanded his base of power. For example, Lin promoted a fellow Fourth Field Army leader, Huang Yung-sheng, commander of the Canton MR, to the post of PLA chief of staff in March 1968, bypassing many equally, if not more highly qualified men, including several incumbent deputy chiefs of staff. In addition, Lin put his followers from the Fourth Field Army and his wife in control of the "Administrative Unit" of the MAC, the regime's supreme military decision-making body. Moreover, Lin replaced more than 300 senior military officials at various levels with his own men and made considerable inroads into the power base of other military factions.

When the Ninth Party Congress was convened, Lin's men packed the meeting. He was the featured speaker, delivering the political report to the Congress, and the Congress adopted a new party constitution containing an unprecedented provision which salutes Lin Piao and sanctions his succession to Mao (a provision which was allegedly inserted at Lin's behest): "Comrade Lin Piao has consistently held high the great red banner of Mao Tse-tung's thought and has most loyally and resolutely carried out and defended Comrade Mao Tse-tung's proletarian revolutionary line. Comrade Lin Piao is Comrade Mao Tse-tung's close comrade-in-arms and successor."

In the newly elected CC, approximately 46 percent, or 127 of the 279 members, were career soldiers, and in the 25-member Politburo, 13 were military representatives. In these two highest decision-making bodies of the party, Lin's supporters constituted the largest and most influential group. In the post-Congress period, the military continued to dominate the party and, under Lin's stewardship, the army managed to control nearly every aspect of life in China, defying the "unified leadership" of the party.

There seems to be no question that PLA domination of China's political system was the basic cause of the conflict between Mao and Lin Piao and that Mao came to perceive Lin's enhanced position as threatening his own power and leadership. Mao clearly had neither anticipated nor desired this situation, for it was contrary to his dictum of party control, and after the GPCR a suspicious Mao apparently viewed the situation with grave apprehension. When the party's CC met in a plenary session at Lushan from late August to early September 1970 to consider, among other things, a draft of the new state constitution, and Lin Piao spoke in favor of retaining the post of head of state, in disagreement with Mao, who wanted to abolish the post, Mao's distrust of Lin was strengthened and he apparently decided shortly thereafter to curtail Lin Piao's power and to reassert the party's control over the military.

Moreover, Mao and Lin also clashed over a major foreign policy issue. In the wake of the bloody Sino-Soviet armed conflicts along the Ussuri in March 1969 and in Sinkiang later that summer, some Chinese leaders including Mao and Premier Chou apparently perceived a genuine danger of large-scale Soviet military action against China; their anxiety may have been heightened by veiled Soviet threats of nuclear attack on China in 1969 and in 1970. The overwhelming concern for national survival impelled the Chinese leadership to adopt a new foreign policy strategy seeking to improve relations with the United States and to use the United States as a counterweight against the Soviets. The new strategy found concrete expressions in U.S. National Security Advisor Dr. Henry Kissinger's secret meeting with

Premier Chou in Peking in July 1971 and the announcement that President Richard Nixon would visit China in the following year.

The drastic turnabout in China's approach toward the United States—long regarded as China's main enemy—was apparently opposed by Lin Piao, who was an outspoken proponent of the "dual adversary strategy": opposition to both American imperialism and Soviet revisionism simultaneously. Exactly how, why, and on what grounds Lin argued against the decision in the Party Council for a Sino-American rapprochement has never been made public. The veiled criticism in Chinese sources that Lin advocated "isolationism" and capitulation to the revisionists suggests that he probably opposed "opening" to the United States as a means to defuse the danger of Soviet attack, and may have advocated some measures to seek rapprochement with the Soviets instead, or with the United States and the Soviets simultaneously.

This renewed conflict within the party reached a climax in September 1971 when Marshal Lin Piao suddenly disappeared from China's political scene. According to Peking, the treacherous Lin was killed in a plane crash in Mongolia on 13 September 1971, attempting to flee China after an abortive plot to assassinate Mao and usurp the leadership. The Lin Piao affair and the subsequent drive by the Maoist leadership to purge Lin's alleged co-conspirators and accomplices brought new traumas within China's political apparatus.

Not least of these was the fact that Mao twice cultivated and designated a "counterrevolutionary," "bourgeois careerist," and "renegade and traitor" as his revolutionary successor. The extension of purges to several scores of ranking party and military leaders after Lin's downfall further polarized and divided the Chinese leadership. Most serious of all, Lin's demise reopened the issue of the succession to Mao.

In this connection, the Tenth Party Congress of August 1973 would have been an opportune occasion to build a new leadership team and, most importantly, to make arrangements for Mao's succession. Indeed, the Congress did endorse a new leadership team, but it was an uneasy coalition of contending political forces.

Included in the twenty-five-member Politburo were party and government bureaucrats, provincial leaders, military men, radicals, and model workers and peasants. Several features of the Politburo composition merit comment. First, with the elimination of Lin Piao and his top associates, military representation on the Politburo was halved. Second, eight Politburo members were concurrently first party secretaries in the provinces. Increased representation for provincial forces—an emerging trend since the 1960s—continued to underline the growing importance of the territorial base of power in Chinese politics. Third, in terms of distribution of power, the new Politburo represented a gain for the radicals and their supporters; the radicals as a group recovered from the setback in the Ninth Congress and increased their representation.

On the nine-man Politburo Standing Committee, the regime's supreme decision-making body, the active participants in policy deliberations were Mao, Premier Chou, Wang Hung-wen, Yeh Chien-ying, Li Teh-sheng, and Chang Ch'un-ch'iao. (One should probably exclude K'ang Sheng, who was in poor health, and the aging Tung Pi-wu and Chu Teh.) Thus Wang, Li, and Chang, who were identified with the radical cause during the Cultural Revolution, clearly had sufficient strength to promote the leftist view and as such they were in a position to act as a counterweight to the moderates.

Most curious of all, the Congress failed to designate a would-be successor to Mao. Despite the fact that Premier Chou was clearly the most powerful man under Mao and greatly enhanced his status through his able conduct of China's foreign relations, notably the improvement of Sino-United States relations, and the normalization of Sino-Japanese ties, he was not duly deputized as Mao's successor. Instead, Mao made a move to groom his own successor by elevating a young labor organizer from Shanghai. The spectacular rise of Wang Hung-wen was one very startling feature of the Tenth Party Congress. Wang was not only elected second vice-chairman of the party—a ranking that placed him third in Peking's hierarchy—but he was given the rare honor of presenting the report on the revised party constitution.

Born in 1935 to a peasant family in Kirin province, Wang took part in the Korean war and worked in a factory in Shanghai from the mid-1950s; when the GPCR started in 1966, he was still an obscure, low-level security cadre in Shanghai's seventeenth cotton mill. Under the leadership of two Shanghai radical officials, Chang Ch'un-ch'iao and Yao Wen-yuan, Wang organized and led workers in Shanghai to rebel against local conservative authorities in 1966 and 1967. After the Maoists seized power in February 1967, Wang was appointed a deputy director of the Shanghai Revolutionary Committee (RC). In subsequent years, he worked closely with Chang and Yao in Shanghai and Chiang Ch'ing in Peking. Moving steadily up the career ladder, Wang was elected to the CC in 1969, was named a Shanghai party secretary in early 1971, and was transferred to the central party apparatus after the summer of 1972. In April 1973 he was also elected director of Shanghai's Federation of Trade Unions. As a vice-chairman of the party, Wang outranked his political patrons, Chang, Yao, and Chiang Ch'ing, as well as most other senior party leaders.

Wang's rapid rise to political prominence at the Tenth Party Congress took people both inside and outside China by surprise. If he did possess any unusual credentials, they had never been publicized.[1] There seems no question, however, that he enjoyed the special favor of Chairman Mao and that he was close to Mao personally. This can be seen in part from the fact that in the fall of 1973 Wang received French President Georges Pompidou and other visiting foreign dignitaries outside Mao's residence and took part in the meetings of the foreign leaders with the Chairman. Mao's grooming of Wang notwithstanding, subsequent developments, including the opposition of veteran officials (which we will detail later), were to undo his succession arrangements.

Backlash against the GPCR

In many important ways, Chinese politics and leadership conflicts in the 1970s continue to be shaped by the GPCR and its aftereffects. Initiated by Mao, the GPCR was aimed, among other things, at shaping Chinese society according to Maoist revolutionary values and removing from power those "capitalist-roaders," like former head of state Liu Shao-ch'i and former Party General Secretary Teng Hsiao-p'ing, who allegedly were pursuing a counterrevolutionary revisionist line to restore capitalism in China. The celebrated Sixteen-Point Decision, approved by the party's Central Committee (CC) on 8 August 1966, formally sanctioned Mao's call for purging all capitalist-roaders from the leadership and for creating a new power structure firmly committed to Maoist revolutionary goals.

But once started, the GPCR developed a momentum of its own, and no one, including Chairman Mao himself, proved capable of controlling its pace and direction; consequently, it generated large-scale severe political and social chaos in China. From 1966 to 1968, tens of thousands of Red Guards and "revolutionary rebels" who responded to Mao's call for rebellion against capitalist-roaders in the leadership rampaged about the country staging anti-rightist demonstrations, wresting power from incumbent local officials in what were termed "seizures of power from below," and shattering the existing party and government machinery in many provinces. A considerable number of alleged capitalist-roaders in the party were "dragged out": they were not only dismissed from their leadership posts but were also subjected to a terribly humiliating ordeal of public "self-criticism" and "struggle" meetings. Many ranking party officials were even paraded through the streets wearing dunce caps, and some were physically abused.

Was the GPCR really necessary? What did it accomplished? The legitimacy and the rationality of the GPCR has been an issue of contention in the leadership since the late 1960s. As can be expected, the protagonists of the GPCR strongly defended the correctness of the campaign and lauded its achievements. For example, Mao termed the GPCR "absolutely necessary and most timely for consolidating the dictatorship of the proletariat, preventing capitalist restoration and building socialism" and praised it as "a powerful motive force for the development of the social productive forces in our country." The late Lin Piao, who went all-out to support the GPCR, claimed the gains of the campaign as the "greatest" and its losses as the "smallest."

The radical leaders, who worked closely with Mao and Lin to plan and push the GPCR in the 1960s and were beneficiaries of the crusade, had been staunch defenders of its legitimacy and accomplishments in the 1970s. Their political *raison d'être* rested on the affirmation of its values. Thus they asserted that the GPCR had achieved the following positive results:

> The three-in-one combination of the old, the middle-aged and the young has invigorated leading bodies at all levels, and millions of successors to the cause of proletarian revolution are tempering themselves in accordance with the fine requirements set by Chairman Mao. The revolution in art and literature exemplified by the model revolutionary theatrical works has resulted in an efflorescence of creative work in socialist literature and art. The revolution in education is advancing ... in the direction pointed out by Chairman Mao, and gratifying results have been achieved in the efforts to transform schools into instruments of the dictatorship of the proletariat and bring up workers with both socialist consciousness and culture. The revolution in health work is overcoming the rural shortage of doctors and medicines, barefoot doctors are steadily maturing.... By entering May 7 cadre schools, going down to do manual labor and studying afresh, a large number of cadres have increased their awareness of the need to continue the revolution and regained their revolutionary youthfulness. More than ten million school graduates have gone to the vast countryside where they are persevering in the revolution and growing sturdily.[2]

On the other hand, numerous party officials took a negative view of the GPCR and vehemently disputed the positive results claimed by its defenders. Some are said to have openly challenged the rationality of Mao's violent method; for example, they asked: "Since Liu Shao-ch'i and his handful usurped part of the power in the dictatorship of the proletariat, it needs only an order from Chairman Mao to dismiss them from office, why should the present [violent] method be adopted?"[3] It is only natural, moreover, that those party officials who were actually toppled from power and persecuted during the GPCR should harbor resentment against the movement and what it represents. They not only have questioned its legitimacy but also have criticized it for having demoralized and divided party ranks and having produced severely adverse consequences for the nation.

The attitudes of these veteran party officials were critically described in a long report delivered to the "Central Study Class" on 14 January 1974 by Wang Hung-wen, the party's vice-chairman since August 1973, who was an active supporter and a beneficiary of the GPCR. Wang's remarks explain some of the background issues underlying China's current political upheaval and thus are quoted at length:

> The problem is that today there are some comrades in our ranks, including Party and non-Party members, who, just as seven or eight years ago, still do not comprehend the GPCR; they do not take it seriously and do not work hard for it. Some of them even confound right and wrong and confuse black and white; a few individuals even color the GPCR pitch black and depict it as a ravaging flood or a predatory beast, and some say that they shudder at the thought of the GPCR. It is stated in the Constitution approved by the Tenth Party Congress and in the resolution of the Party that the GPCR will be carried out many times in the future. But some say that the GPCR was totally unnecessary and it should not be carried out any more. In particular, the senior and middle-level cadres have divergent views. Some of them say: "The GPCR has scored a great victory nationally, but we do not see it here." What they mean is that if victory cannot be seen here and there, then, in aggregate, it cannot be seen in the whole country; why was, then, the GPCR necessary? . . . Some people do not distinguish between right and wrong; they blame the GPCR for whatever is wrong in some units, or call it the sequela of the GPCR.[4]

Wang's remarks clearly indicated that the issue of the GPCR had polarized the party ranks and that those officials who were disgraced sought to take revenge against their former persecutors. Again, to quote Wang Hung-wen:

> There is still another kind of people who are totally oblivious to the fact that the GPCR has struck down two bourgeois headquarters, thereby preventing the state from changing its color; instead, they have been engrossed with the attacks by the masses, and upon rehabilitation and back in power, they try to rectify the masses whenever an opportunity presents itself. . . . Some say: "Since we were dragged out and struggled against during the GPCR, we will have to settle the accounts [with our persecutors]. We are already very generous for not charging interest, but what is there to prevent us from taking vengeance? We must loudly warn such comrades: it is too dangerous, what do the masses owe you. . . . If you must settle accounts with the masses, they have the right to again seize the power back from you."

To the dismay of Mao and the radicals, the legitimacy of the GPCR and the policy innovations (socialist "newborn things") it introduced were further undermined by the infamous affair of Lin Piao inasmuch as Lin was the prime mover of the GPCR. Moreover, the campaign to repudiate Lin's heinous crimes that began in 1971 not only reflected unfavorably on the GPCR but also tended to discredit the radicals who were intimately associated with Lin.

The campaign to criticize Lin Piao's crimes and to ferret out his followers in the leadership ranks also gave a new impetus to the drive to rehabilitate cadres ousted during the GPCR—a development that had serious adverse implications for the values of the GPCR. The political forces pressing for the rehabilitation of veteran cadres found it politically expedient to blame Lin Piao for excessive and indiscriminate purges and for opposition to the correct treatment of erring cadres. Such a deliberate maneuver to implicitly link the opposition to cadre rehabilitation with Lin Piao's ultraleftist mistakes may have politically disarmed the radicals and others in the regime who, for political, ideological, and other reasons, strongly resisted the restoration of disgraced cadres. Apparently Mao himself also found it necessary to rally the support of anti-Lin Piao forces in the regime; thus he at least acquiesced in the rehabilitation of the GPCR victims to fill some of the key leadership positions following the removal of Lin's followers.

Indeed, a large number of disgraced veteran cadres, including even those who had committed serious political crimes in the eyes of Mao and the radicals, were "liberated." An outstanding example was Vice-Premier Teng Hsiao-p'ing, formerly the party's secretary-general and concurrently vice-premier of the State Council; in 1966 he was purged and vilified as "the second top capitalist-roader in the party" and, disgraced, disappeared from public life until April 1973.

The restoration of these former capitalist-roaders to office had serious political implications. Their political comeback squeezed out, or blocked the political advance of young cadres who were promoted during the GPCR, and weakened the power base of the radical leaders who achieved rapid political prominence as a result of their support for the GPCR. Meanwhile, the reinstatement in recent years of those who opposed the GPCR also increasingly calls into question the legitimacy of the GPCR; in fact, under the guise of denouncing Lin Piao's ultraleftist crimes, the conservatives did their utmost to discredit the GPCR and its "newborn things." Moreover, once restored to power, they moved step by step to modify and dilute innovations introduced in the GPCR and resurrected policies which Mao and his radical supporters had sought to do away with.

The Battle to Reaffirm the GPCR

It was in this shifting political context that Mao and his radical supporters had repeatedly tried from 1973 to 1976 to arrest what they saw as a process of "retrogression and restoration" and to reaffirm the values of the GPCR. The opening move of the radicals' offensive was a concerted blast in the summer of 1973 against the college admission policy which, since 1971, had placed more and more emphasis on academic standards, less on political criteria. The conduit of this attack was a letter written by Chang T'ieh-sheng, a youth in China's northeastern Liaoning province, who failed his college entrance examination. Under the manipulation of Mao Yuan-hsin (Chairman Mao's nephew), a radical party secretary in Liaoning, Chang's letter was prominently displayed in the *Liaoning Daily* on 19 July 1973 and reproduced in the front page of the *People's Daily* on 10 August.

According to Chang, who had finished junior middle school in 1966, gone to the countryside to work in a commune in 1968, and become the leader of a production team there, he had spent some eighteen hours every day at his work since his rustication. The heavy work load left him no time to review his middle-school lessons, and he was therefore unable to answer the questions in geometry, physics, and chemistry on the college entrance examination. Chang complained bitterly: "To be very frank, I am not impressed by, but rather resent, those bookworms who just fooled around and did not do any useful work in the past several years; the examination has been monopolized by those obsessed with going to college." He claimed that he would have been able to answer all the questions if he had taken two days out for preparation, but that he did not give up his productive work during the busy summer season to study. Moreover, he asserted that his political background, family, and social relations were "clear," that his ideology and world outlook had taken a "flying leap" in the past five years, and that he did not feel ashamed of himself for being unable to pass the tests required by the current admissions system.

In publishing Chang's letter, the *Liaoning Daily* also printed an editorial note raising questions about the system. The note asked:

> Should the cultural tests be chiefly aimed at understanding the appli-
> cant's ability in analyzing and solving problems, or at checking how
> well he remembers his middle-school lessons? Should the main criterion
> for enrollment be based on an applicant's constant behavior in the three
> great revolutionary movements [class struggle, production struggle,
> and scientific experiment], or on the marks of the cultural tests he
> takes? Should the intellectual youths be encouraged to actively receive
> reeducation by the poor and lower middle peasants and the working

class, and to try hard to do well and fulfill their work, or divorce themselves from the three great revolutionary movements and study behind closed doors [a cardinal sin attributed to the "revisionist" educational line of Liu Shao-ch'i]?

There is no question that the radicals made the Chang case their cause célèbre and used Chang's criticism of the entrance examination system to reassert the values of the GPCR. In fact, the radicals concocted Chang's protest and used the incident to attack Premier Chou En-lai's stewardship— or so we were told after the purge of the radicals in October 1976. Chang T'ieh-sheng, who became an "anti-establishment" hero and a national celebrity of sorts after the summer of 1973, was made the scapegoat and placed under arrest as soon as his political patrons were disgraced.

In addition to education, the radicals mounted the "anti-Lin Piao, anti-Confucius campaign" in early 1974 with the avowed objective of checking the trend toward "rightist restoration." As an editorial in the *People's Daily* on 21 February 1974 made crystal clear, the campaign (contrary to the belief of some Western scholars) was not an academic debate—it was closely connected with the ongoing leadership conflict and a battle to defend the GPCR:

> We must combine the criticism of Lin Piao's "restraining oneself and restoring the rites" with cardinal issues of right and wrong in the class struggle and the struggle between the two lines at the present moment. We must criticize the crimes of the Lin Piao anti-Party clique in negating the GPCR. . . . We must criticize the fallacies of the Lin Piao anti-Party clique viciously maligning newly emerging socialist things.

Under cover of criticizing the figurative Lin Piao and Confucius during the campaign, the radicals were in fact attacking the conservative veteran cadres in the leadership. In particular, Premier Chou was the target of assault in many articles which ostensibly were repudiating Confucius.[5] The radicals' emphatic attack on a saying of Confucius—"Revive states that are extinct, restore families whose line of succession has been broken, and call to office those who have fallen into obscurity"—was unmistakably directed against the rehabilitation of cadres disgraced during the GPCR.

In the campaign, the radicals also had commissioned articles to vindicate Ch'in Shih Huang (the first Emperor of the Ch'in Dynasty), a notorious tyrant in China's history. He was particularly extolled for unifying China under one empire and setting up a strongly centralized system in the place of "ducal states."[6] His burning of classics and burying alive of hundreds of scholars were described as progressive measures which facilitated consolidation of political control.

Inasmuch as Lin Piao allegedly equated Mao with the Ch'in tyrant and denounced Mao as the "biggest despot in Chinese history who dons Marxist-Leninist clothes but implements the laws of Ch'in Shih Huang," and the Communist persecution of intellectuals resembles what the Ch'in emperor did, one can infer that extolling the Ch'in emperor and his rule was an attempt to defend Mao and his unpopular policies. Moreover, the glorification of the system of centralized control set up by the first Ch'in ruler also provided the ideological justification for curtailing provincial autonomy and curbing the political roles of regional PLA leaders. The policy of cutting back the political roles of the PLA was in fact carried out through a wholesale transfer of virtually all top regional PLA leaders in December 1973. Through this dramatic reshuffle, the central party leadership not only managed to move regional PLA leaders from their long-held bases of power but also relieved them of top provincial party and government posts they had held concurrently, and filled these posts with civilians.

The radicals' vociferous attacks on the trends of "retrogression and restoration" did have some effect. This was most clearly reflected in the cultural and educational areas where the values of the GPCR had been strongly reasserted. The radicals' denunciation of the conservative trends in Chinese society also created political and ideological pressures which imposed constraints on the veteran officials and arrested temporarily any further political shift to the right. There was circumstantial evidence that Chairman Mao was dissatisfied with Premier Chou, whose stewardship had helped foster the resurgence of a conservative tide in China's polity, and that the thinly veiled campaign against Chou in the media in the first half of 1974 was carried out with Mao's consent, if not his active encouragement. At the same time, Chou was becoming relatively inactive, partly through his illness (he had cancer) and hospitalization. Yet there is no question that he also encountered political difficulties. Capitalizing on circumstances, the radicals sought to dump Chou from the premiership and seize control of the State Council (cabinet) in the course of the Fourth NPC meeting, scheduled for January 1975.

Teng's Political Comeback

Although the NPC was, according to the 1954 state constitution, the highest legislative organ of the nation, it failed to meet after January 1965 due to political turmoil generated by the GPCR. After the Ninth Party Congress was convened in April 1969, Chinese leaders were engaged in preparation to convene the Fourth NPC to approve a new constitution and to approve a new government leadership lineup. A draft of the new constitution was discussed and "basically approved" in a CC Plenum held at Lushan in late August 1970. However, during the proceedings, a serious dispute between Mao and Lin Piao arose as Lin spoke in favor of retaining the post of head of state (to which he aspired), while Mao insisted on abolishing the post. The intensification of the Mao-Lin struggle thereafter and the subsequent Lin Piao affair rendered it impossible for the Chinese leaders to reach agreement on important issues. Consequently, the projected NPC meeting did not take place.

When the Chinese leadership met for the Tenth Party Congress in August 1973 in the wake of the Lin Piao affair, they agreed to convene the Fourth NPC soon thereafter, and this decision is included in Premier Chou's Political Report. Again, due to political disruptions created by the anti-Lin Piao, anti-Confucius campaign and, most important, to leadership dissension on the new government leadership lineup the Chinese leaders were forced to postpone the meeting of the Fourth NPC. Then, in the fall of 1974, they were once again in earnest preparation for the NPC and scheduled it for the following January as Chairman Mao called for the whole party and the army to "forge unity" and achieve "stability."

Before the NPC met to approve the new constitution and government appointments, various political groups were actively jockeying for position. Although Premier Chou had been hospitalized, he was not idle; reportedly, he frequently consulted with Teng Hsiao-p'ing, Yeh Chien-ying, and Li Hsien-nien in his hospital room.[7] The radicals apparently saw the forthcoming NPC as an opportunity to get rid of the ailing Chou; therefore in October 1974 they dispatched Wang Hung-wen to Changsha, Hunan, to see Chairman Mao and to persuade the Chairman to dump Chou and to nominate Chang Ch'un-ch'iao as the new premier.[8]

We do not have the minutes of the Mao-Wang meeting; therefore we cannot know what transpired in the conversation. According to the story released by Peking after the purge of the radicals in October 1976, Mao rebuffed Wang and reaffirmed his confidence in Premier Chou when Wang badmouthed Chou and other veteran leaders. This may not have been the true story, however. There was circumstantial evidence in 1974–75 that initially Mao was receptive to the plan of the radicals, but that he quickly backed off when he saw the opposition of the veteran officials was too strong.

If a story circulated within China can be believed, Chou had graciously agreed to step down as premier when informed by Wang Hung-wen of Mao's "concern" for his health, but other veteran leaders in the Politburo overruled him. When an enlarged Politburo meeting was called in November or December 1974 to deliberate on the new State Council appointments, there was reportedly a shouting match between Marshal Chu Teh and other veteran leaders on the one hand and the radical leaders on the other. The overwhelming majority of those present strongly favored reappointing Chou as premier despite his failing health and were opposed to the nomination of Chang Ch'un-ch'iao, who seemed to enjoy Mao's backing. To ensure that the premiership would not fall into Chang's hands in case of Chou's death, the veteran leaders also took steps to elevate Teng Hsiao-p'ing over Chang in leadership status, placing Teng in a strong position to take over from Premier Chou.

Here a few words on Teng's return to the political scene are in order. As mentioned earlier, Teng was reinstated as a vice-premier in April 1973, after seven years of political disgrace. During 1973 and 1974, he steadily rose in political prominence. At the Tenth Party Congress, he was elected a CC member; four months later (in December 1973), however, he was admitted into the Politburo and appointed a vice-chairman of the party's MAC. Several factors accounted for Teng's rapid political comeback.

First, in the wake of the Lin Piao affair and the drive against powerful Lin supporters in the regime, the leadership had an urgent need to broaden its base of power by rallying the support of all anti-Lin forces; the rehabilitation of Teng and many other veteran officials was a necessary step to meet such a political exigency. Second, as the purge of a large number of veteran officials during the GPCR had adversely affected the running of government and management of the national economy, there was a widely felt need to reemploy the talents of many officials sidelined since the GPCR, and Teng, as a skillful administrator with much experience in both domestic and external affairs, obviously had assets which placed him in demand. In retrospect, however, a third factor appears to have been even more crucial—the failing health of Premier Chou, who was known, if only within the top leadership, to be suffering from cancer as early as 1972. Anticipating death in the near future, Chou appears to have played a major role in securing Teng's rehabilitation in 1973 and to have actively promoted Teng as his own successor thereafter.

There is no doubt that Mao himself had at least acquiesced in Teng's return to power.[9] Beyond that, Mao may even have considered Teng's return politically useful. For example, Teng's military background and his close personal ties with many ranking PLA leaders may have made him, in Mao's estimation, an ideal person to handle a host of problems arising from party-PLA relations and help reestablish firm political control over the military establishment. And Teng quickly proved his worth to Mao in this respect, for he was instrumental in arranging and carrying out an orderly changeover of regional PLA leaders in December 1973, whereby a number of key military leaders were transferred from their long-entrenched "independent kingdoms" and stripped of positions in the provincial party and government apparatus. It is possible that, in consenting to Teng's return, Mao and other radicals may initially have had a devious plan to coopt Teng

—to win him over to their side and use him to checkmate Chou and divide the conservatives. Indeed, for a while it looked almost as if Teng meant different things to different groups in the regime and was being courted by all—a very advantageous political position which enabled him to wield considerable influence.

Much to the chagrin of Mao and the radicals, however, Teng turned out to be an "unrepentant capitalist-roader" after all. In the conflict between the radicals and veteran officials during the anti-Lin Piao and Confucius campaign in 1974, for example, Teng sided with the veterans and helped crush the offensive launched by the radicals. There is no question that Teng commanded wide political support among the veteran officials. He was their answer to Chang Ch'un-ch'iao, who until the end of 1974 seemed to have been a strong contender to succeed Premier Chou and take over the control of the State Council. Much to the displeasure of Chairman Mao, during the CC Plenum and the NPC meeting in January 1975, Chou was reappointed premier, and Teng was made a vice-chairman of the party, senior vice-premier of the State Council, and PLA chief of staff. Overall, the veteran officials, including quite a few victims of the GPCR, were in control of the key posts in the State Council. It is true that Chang Ch'un-ch'iao was appointed second vice-premier and director of the PLA General Political Department; however, the radicals as a group suffered a severe setback.

Also indicative of the predominance of the conservative forces in the leadership was the fact that the new state constitution approved by the NPC formally endorsed the right of peasants to farm private plots and engage in subsidiary production, reaffirmed the principle of income distribution according to labor ("to each according to his work"), and guaranteed to citizens the right of private ownership.[10] These provisions have been long considered necessary by veteran administrators like Chou and Teng to ensure the people's incentive to work and to boost China's economic development, but they had been opposed by Mao and the radicals as ideological backsliding and as condoning and expanding the "bourgeois right."

The major personnel and policy decisions taken at the January 1975 meetings of the party and the NPC clearly ran counter to Mao's wish. However, possibly because he lacked sufficient support at that time to block or reverse them, he chose instead to dissociate himself from them by staying away from both meetings. Moreover, he soon moved to negate these decisions by inspiring a new campaign to study "the theory of proletarian dictatorship."[11] Mao was quoted as having complained in advance of the January decisions that despite Communist rule since 1949, China still retained the birthmarks of the old society in adhering to "an eight-grade wage system, distribution to each according to his work and exchange by means of money" —all systems that "are scarely different from those in the old society" and which "provide the soil and conditions for engendering the bourgeoisie and capitalism."[12] Yet, to Mao's consternation, the CC and the NPC not only failed to eliminate these vestiges of the old society, but instead took decisions that, in Mao's view, consolidated and strengthened the "bourgeois right."

Mao's response was the new campaign to restrict the bourgeois right; he called for a firm "dictatorship of the proletariat" over the bourgeoisie. Not surprisingly, the Chinese media, which were dominated by the radicals, gave enormous publicity to the campaign, with the clear objective of downgrading and discrediting those decisions approved at the January meetings. In March and April 1975, Yao Wen-yuan and Chang Ch'un-ch'iao, both prominent radical leaders, published signed articles in *Hungch'i*, the party's theoretical organ, to support Mao's political offensive. Besides fiercely attacking the bourgeois right itself, they also inveighed against "people like Lin Piao" and cadres in the party who supported the policies that safeguarded and strengthened the social base of the bourgeois right, accusing them of helping to restore capitalism in China.

Meanwhile, the veteran leaders in the party, including Chou En-lai and Teng Hsiao-p'ing, remained conspicuously silent; at least, none of them publicly expressed support for the campaign as Yao and Chang had done. More than that, according to subsequent Maoist charges, they actually opposed the campaign to restrict the bourgeois right and tried in every way to block criticism of the policy of material incentives.[13] There seems little doubt that the veteran party leaders were fearful that the premature elimination of wage differentials and excessive emphasis on egalitarianism would dampen the working incentives of the masses and jeopardize the goal of building China into a powerful and modern socialist country before the end of the century—a major objective proclaimed by Premier Chou at the NPC. Thus they evidently sought to play down Mao's call for unremitting class struggle in Chinese society and to place heavy emphasis instead on the maintenance of unity and discipline and on leadership efforts to boost the national economy.

Policy Disputes and Power Struggle

It is in this context that the seemingly baffling and bizarre charges leveled at Teng by Mao and his radical followers in 1976, accusing him retrospectively of having concocted a revisionist line of "taking the three directives as the key link" become comprehensible.[14] According to the charge, Teng put two earlier directives of Mao Tse-tung—to promote stability and unity and to develop the national economy—on a par with the February 1975 directive to study the theory of the dictatorship of the proletariat, describing the three directives as "interrelated and inseparable" from one another and "the key link for all work." Mao's angry retort to Teng's interpretation of the directives was: "What 'taking the three directives as the key link'! Stability and unity does not mean writing off class struggle; class struggle is the key link and everything else hinges on it." [15] By juxtaposing Mao's three separate directives and giving them equal importance, Teng was allegedly denying the primacy of class struggle and promoting stability and unity and China's economic program at the expense of ideology—a cardinal sin in Maoist politics.

The economic program which Teng was implementing had been approved by a plenary session of the party's CC and presented to the NPC in January 1975 by Premier Chou. The program was a two-stage plan for the development of China's national economy which, according to Chou, would build "an independent and relatively comprehensive industrial and economic system" by 1980 in the first stage, and "accomplish the comprehensive modernization of agriculture, industry, national defense and science and technology before the end of the century" in the second stage, so that China's national economy would be "advancing in the front ranks of the world." [16]

The basic goals of the economic program were probably not at issue within the leadership; what had been in dispute are the means by which they were to be realized. Indeed, 1975 was a crucial year in this respect, for plans were being mapped out for the Fifth Five-Year Plan due to commence in 1976. With Chou in steadily deteriorating health and confined to the hospital, Teng, as senior vice-premier, probably took the leading role, a good position from which to influence decisions but one also exposed to attack. Available evidence suggests that Teng strongly favored a major economic drive and pushed for it at a number of conferences he attended between May and October 1975 concerning steel, the national defense industries, military affairs, agriculture, education, and science and technology. [17] This may have given rise to later allegations that Teng used the "four modernizations" as "a big club" and incited people to fan up an "economic gale" and a "gale for vocational work." [18]

According to subsequent charges in the Chinese media, Teng's "revisionist line" was embodied in a lengthy, comprehensive policy paper—a "blueprint" for the restoration of capitalism in China. The paper in question, "On the General Program for All Work of the Party and the Nation," was allegedly prepared under Teng's guidance in the summer of 1975, completed in draft form on 7 October, and intended for publication shortly thereafter to serve as the general program for all work during the next 25 years. [19]

Judging by the passages quoted in the Chinese press, the paper did indeed place great emphasis on economic development and gave top priority to the "four modernizations." It also sought to impose greater discipline on workers by introducing stricter rules and regulations for factory and enterprise management. The paper called for rectification (leadership reorganization and/or policy change) in nine areas: industry, agriculture, communications and transportation, finance and trade, science and technology, culture, education and public health, literature and art, the army and the party. This rectification allegedly represented a systematic effort by Teng to remove cadres promoted during the Cultural Revolution and replace them with his revisionist followers who would carry out a reversal of verdicts on the GPCR.

In response to Teng's call for rectification, officials in several departments mapped out concrete plans for action in the fall of 1975. In August and September, a twenty-article plan "Concerning Certain Problems in the Speed-Up of Industrial Development" was reportedly formulated.[20] From 18 July to 26 September a newly appointed "capitalist-roader" in the Academy of Sciences prepared an "Outline Report of the Academy of Sciences" under Teng's close supervision. The report was submitted to a conference at the Academy attended by Teng at the end of September, and it was approved as a guide for the work of the Academy and of the nation's scientific-technological establishment as a whole. In the field of education, a similar report outline was said to have been under preparation by Chou Jung-hsin, Minister of Education, in early October 1975.[21]

From what has been revealed concerning the thrust of these plans and Teng's role in shaping them, it appears that Teng believed that various measures instituted during the GPCR, by placing too much emphasis on ideology and political considerations, were retarding China's economic development and therefore needed to be "rectified." One very important issue had to do with the GPCR innovations in education. These innovations had placed heavy emphasis on political indoctrination, practical training, and combining education with labor; had downgraded theoretical knowledge and research; and had required college students to be admitted on the basis of political qualifications. Teng, however, evidently viewed the GPCR changes as lowering academic standards and impeding China's efforts at modernization, and he wanted students to be admitted to advanced education primarily on the basis of their academic credentials. Teng is quoted as having complained that "the quality of education is low," that "scientific research has lagged behind," and that these deficiencies "have hampered the four modernizations." He allegedly called "not reading books" and "not having culture" the "greatest danger" and the "greatest crisis" today.[22] Other statements attributed to Teng are similar in thrust:

> Quite a few problems have developed in our schools. Some students can't even read. The Chairman says students should be putting their studies first. Chou Jung-hsin, you are the Minister of Education; there are currently a lot of problems to do with studying, why haven't you said anything about it?

> Scientific and technical schools should be well-run. You have to choose those students who are good in mathematics, physics, chemistry, and foreign language. The children of cadres should not be given privileges ... we are in a crisis.[23]

What emerges from the "facts" adduced to "prove" Teng's opposition to the policies of the GPCR and his design to effect a "capitalist restoration" is a picture of a practical-minded, blunt man strongly committed to China's economic growth. Many of the remarks attributed to Teng show him to be quite a pragmatist. For example, he allegedly said that he cared "only about a rise in the national economy, not about how it was to be done." More specifically, he considered material incentives necessary for "mobilizing the enthusiasm" of workers and peasants, advocated a return to "relying on specialists in running factories and academic institutes," and was willing to import foreign technology and machinery to speed up China's economic growth. For this he was accused of opposing Mao's precept of "putting politics in command" and of trumpeting "servility to things foreign" instead of adherence to the Maoist principle of self-reliance.[24]

In short, the radicals portrayed Teng as harboring essentially the same pragmatic outlook that prompted his frequently quoted 1961 remark: "It doesn't matter whether a cat is black or white; any cat that catches mice is a good cat"—a heresy that figured prominently in his initial downfall during the GPCR. In 1975, as in the 1960s, Teng's pragmatism was seen by the radicals as a direct challenge to Mao's insistence upon revolutionary purity and values, and once more it got him into political hot water. This time, however, Teng apparently recognized the political risk he was taking and chose to go ahead anyway. He is quoted as having remarked: "I am not afraid of being toppled a second time."[25]

The ongoing political conflict in China, however, has not been merely a struggle over principles—pragmatism versus revolutionary purity, for example—and over policy issues, important though these may be. It has also been very much a struggle for power in which Teng was prominently involved. In its latest phase, this struggle has centered on the promotion of young cadres and the rehabilitation of old ones, and as such, it has a vital bearing on the choice of China's leaders in the post-Mao era.

The promotion of young cadres was, without question, the most important plank in the "platform" of the radicals. To perpetuate the innovations of the GPCR, the radicals realized that they must have political power, and that therefore they must place their supporters in positions of authority in the leading organs at all levels. Hence they termed the promotion of young cadres "a major issue of right and wrong" and a yardstick by which to measure a person's attitude toward the "GPCR and Chairman Mao's proletarian revolutionary line." More than that, they sought to institutionalize their young followers' right of access to positions of authority by pushing through the insertion in the 1973 Party Constitution of provisions sanctifying the principle of "combining the old, the middle-aged, and the young."

On the other hand, there is no question that Teng and other veteran party officials resented the fact that their former tormentors from the GPCR— the radicals and their young followers—had been catapulted into positions of power. Teng is said to have disparaged these young cadres who "rise like a helicopter" and to have insisted that they should only "be promoted step by step."[26] Moreover, Teng took measures to undermine the radicals' political influence. In the spring of 1975, for example, he apparently seized transcripts of interviews Chiang Ch'ing had given an American scholar, Roxane Witke, in the summer of 1972 to censure her for self-aggrandizement, divulging state secrets, and violation of other party rules.[27] For two months during April, May, and June 1975, Teng led the struggle against Chiang Ch'ing, subjecting her to self-criticism and personal humiliation.[28]

Meanwhile, Teng did not spare other radical leaders, either. He led a concerted political attack on Chang Ch'un-ch'iao and Yao Wen-yuan when they initiated a criticism of "empiricism" in the spring of 1975, seeking to discredit the veteran cadres *en masse*, and provoked massive angry reactions from the veteran officials. The incident was apparently serious enough that even Mao issued a reprimand against Chang and Yao. In their eagerness to push the campaign against the bourgeois right, the radicals had somehow stirred up labor unrest in many provinces in the summer of 1975 and severely embarrassed the regime. Apparently Teng held the radicals, particularly Wang Hung-wen, responsible and censured them for their leadership blunder.

In contrast to his negative and even hostile attitude toward the radicals, Teng patronized the veteran cadres, many of them reviled and purged during the GPCR. He made no secret of his belief that the toppling of "some good party cadres" had been an error, and he called for their speedy rehabilitation and restoration to positions of responsibility.[29] In 1975 alone, probably under Teng's aegis, seven rehabilitated cadres were appointed first secretaries, and many more were appointed secretaries of provincial party committees.[30] A considerable number of personnel changes also took place in the PLA's central and provincial hierarchy during 1975, especially after July, and out of some thirty new appointments at the center, more than a score went to rehabilitated PLA cadres.[31]

The return of these veterans to high positions was part of the effort made to implement Teng's "General Program for All Work of the Party and the Nation," which called for rectification in all areas of activity and particularly for revamping the various organs of leadership. In the eyes of the radicals, these personnel changes threatened to have still wider political ramifications. The restoration of rehabilitated officials to key posts in the party and the PLA would enable Teng to consolidate his control over policy and to strengthen his own power position with a view to preempting the succession to Chou's post and, eventually, to Mao's mantle. These implications of Teng's actions were obviously not lost on Mao, and the Chairman initiated a series of counter-measures beginning in late summer 1975.

Mao's Last Stand

At the end of August 1975 a campaign of criticism centering on the classic Chinese novel *Water Margin* was begun. The press quoted Mao as having complained that Chao Kai, the founder of the rebel group in the novel, was excluded from the roster of 108 heroes after his death, and that Sung Chiang, who succeeded Chao Kai as the leader of the rebels, changed the name of the rebel headquarters from *Chü-yi T'ing* (Uprising and Solidarity Hall), which symbolized revolution, to *Chung-yi T'ang* (Loyalty and Solidarity Hall), symbolizing acceptance of existing political and social order.[32] Ostensibly, the criticism was directed at Sung Chiang for having capitulated to the landlord class and betrayed the cause of rebelling peasants in thirteenth-century China; in reality, it was directed at Sung Chiang of modern times—Premier Chou En-lai—and other capitulationists (e.g., Teng Hsiao-p'ing) who would bow to revisionism and betray Mao's revolutionary line.[33]

Here it is necessary to clarify the confusion created by Peking's efforts to rewrite history after the purge of the "Gang of Four." Peking's publicists now claim that Mao's criticism of *Water Margin* was never directed at his close comrade-in-arms Chou En-lai or at Teng, but that Yao Wen-yuan and Chiang Ch'ing twisted Mao's critique of the novel, tampered with Mao's instructions, and maliciously changed the criticism of the novel into a political campaign against Chou, Teng, and other leading party, state, and army cadres.[34] Is this credible? Obviously, Peking's leadership has to preserve Mao's image as an infallible benevolent leader, so it tries to exonerate Mao and blames the campaign against Chou and Teng on the disgraced radicals. In so doing, however, the leadership of China today has depicted Mao as a hapless, isolated political figurehead, victimized by the intrigue and manipulation of his wife and radical cronies. As a matter of fact, Mao was quite active and vigorous through April 1976 and actively took part in the anti-Teng campaign.

It should be pointed out that Mao seemed to be a victim of his own obsession. Having witnessed Khrushchev's de-Stalinization, Mao may have become obsessed with the fear that the revisionists in the CCP would attack him posthumously and eliminate his place from history. Hence in 1966 his rival Liu Shao-ch'i was reviled as "China's Khrushchev." In 1975, his obsession again manifested itself in his complaint that Chao Kai had been excluded from the roster of 108 heroes. Perhaps Mao was fearful that the fate of Chao Kai could befall him, so he was determined to make a last stand against the would-be capitulationists in the leadership.

In the fall of 1975, the attack on the "right deviationist wind" came into sharp focus. Responding to a letter from a Tsinghua University official, Liu Ping, who complained about the deterioration in academic standards, Mao called for a revolutionary mass debate at Tsinghua. The debate quickly unfolded and spread to other academic institutions in November and December, as revolutionary teachers and students put up posters denouncing the critics of educational reform and accusing them of seeking to reverse verdicts on the GPCR.

With the *People's Daily* editorial on 1 January 1976, one week before Premier Chou died, the struggle entered a new phase. The editorial contained a portion of Mao's comment on the three directives, which was to become a leitmotif and a major charge against Teng in the anti-rightist campaign, and signaled the expansion of the campaign to issues other than education.[35]

The death of Premier Chou on 8 January removed whatever constraints Mao and the radicals may have felt previously and enabled them to attack Teng directly. In addition, the need to appoint a premier to succeed Chou meant that if they did not block Teng at this stage he would become premier and would be in a position to preempt Mao's own succession subsequently. Although Teng was not removed from his party and government posts until 7 April, the process was begun some two and a half months earlier. At an enlarged meeting of the Politburo, Mao and the radicals, probably in defiance of majority opinion (this was, after all, the same Politburo that had approved Teng's reascent to power), prevented Teng's nomination and named Hua Kuo-feng acting premier.

Despite Mao's direct personal involvement in the campaign to dump Teng, Teng appears to have been backed by many veteran party officials. In Peking, a number of Politburo members, including Yeh Chien-ying, Chu Teh, Liu Po-cheng, and Li Hsien-nien, reportedly protested Mao's move against Teng; few party leaders in China's twenty-nine provincial-level units came out to express public support for Mao's campaign and some apparently boycotted it. That Teng was not without considerable political support was revealed in the charges that after Premier Chou's death, Teng's followers "went about establishing extensive contacts" and "surreptitiously plotted to write letters to the Party Central Committee" to demand Teng's appointment as premier.[36] The support was also implicit in the massive demonstrations in Peking and other Chinese cities in early April. The demonstrations that broke out in Peking and other cities, while an expression of support for the late Chou and his policies, reflected at least indirectly on Teng, whose rehabilitation and grooming for the premiership were more Chou's doing then anyone else's. This, more than any other factor, may account for the haste with which Teng was removed in the wake of the Peking T'ienanmen Square incident.

On the other hand, the demonstrations were directed unmistakably against those who were behind the campaign to criticize policies associated with Chou and Teng. For example, many posters and placards denounced Chairman Mao's wife, Chiang Ch'ing, who was known to be playing an active role in the campaign, and Yao Wen-yuan, the leading radical ideologue. Some of the demonstrators also explicitly attacked Mao himself, chanting "the era of Ch'in Shih Huang is gone," "gone for good is Ch'in Shih Huang's feudal society."[37]

The dismissal of Teng Hsiao-p'ing from all leadership posts and the elevation of Hua Kuo-feng to first vice-chairman of the party and premier of the State Council, which were effected by two Politburo resolutions on 7 April 1976 following Chairman Mao's proposal,[38] can be regarded as a compromise, a stalemate, or a victory for the radicals, depending upon one's perspective. However, as subsequent events will demonstrate, the real winner was Hua Kuo-feng, who emerged from the anti-Teng campaign and the T'ienanmen Square riot the strongest contender for Mao's mantle. While much remains obscure, what evidence exists tends to suggest that Hua rose suddenly to political prominence during February-April 1976 through a set of fortuitous circumstances.[39] In other words, he was simply lucky—at the right place at the right time.

Hua's good luck began in early February 1976 when he was unexpectedly designated acting premier by Mao after Premier Chou's death. Hua received the appointment not because of his seniority (he became a member of the Politburo only in 1973 and was only the sixth ranking vice-premier in the State Council), nor because of any exceptional talents or administrative experience he possessed; rather, he was the least objectionable to the rival political forces in the leadership and was not regarded as a threat to them.[40] The fact that Hua was designated only acting premier also strongly suggests the tentative nature of his appointment. However, the turn of events in the following two months, particularly the T'ienanmen Square incident, greatly strengthened Hua's political position. What happened was that in light of pro-Chou and Teng demonstrations in Peking Mao had no choice but to forcefully confer confidence in Hua and to grant Hua the number two position in the regime. In so doing, Mao knowingly or unknowingly made Hua his heir-apparent and completely wrecked whatever plan he had devised in 1973 for structuring his own succession.

Understandably, the radicals were dissatisfied with Hua's elevation. They now saw Hua as a political obstacle and directed attacks at him in their continuous struggle to remove from office other "capitalist-roaders" in

Peking and in the provinces.[41] To be a target of the radicals' attack turned out to be a blessing in disguise for Hua, because many veteran officials (e.g., Marshal Yeh Chien-ying) who may otherwise have had misgivings toward Hua previously now rallied behind him to contain the radicals' offensive.

In any case, the anti-rightist crusade which was launched in Mao's name gradually lost momentum months before Mao's death in September 1976. Several reasons accounted for the inability of the radicals to move the campaign. There was considerable support among China's powerholders for the modernization programs and they stonewalled the anti-rightist campaign which they saw as detrimental to China's best national interests. Moreover, as Mao's health deteriorated after June, the radicals who previously administered the campaign in his name now had great difficulty convincing the cadres that the campaign was still under his personal leadership. The uncertainty concerning Mao's role apparently further emboldened the powerholders to resist the campaign.

The huge earthquake in the T'angshan-Tientsin area at the end of July also dealt the anti-rightist campaign a crushing blow. Although the Chinese authorities have revealed little information, the casualties, material damage, and economic losses inflicted by the earthquake were obviously of immense proportions. In the wake of the disaster, attention of the people and the cadres was directed toward the relief work and economic construction—a situation which naturally enhanced the role of the administrators and gave them more political clout. On the other hand, the radicals' call to "deepen the great struggle to criticize Teng Hsiao-p'ing,"[42] at a time when almost everyone was preoccupied with the calamities, was both irrelevant and callous; it not only failed to generate support but it also aroused resentment. Even before Mao died, many Chinese already viewed Mao's failing health, a giant meteor that hit Manchuria in March, and several major earthquakes in May and in the summer as indications that Chairman Mao had lost the "Mandate of Heaven" and the end of his rule was approaching—a view which severely undermined Mao's authority and damaged the influence of the radicals who often acted in his name. In fact, the radicals felt compelled to condemn the "theory of the Mandate of Heaven," denouncing the talk of traditional Chinese cosmology as an evil trick of the Confucianists and class enemies.[43]

With Mao's death on 9 September 1976, the anti-rightist campaign quickly came to a halt. Without Mao's backing, the radicals were simply unable to push the unpopular campaign against the strong resistance of the nation's conservative political forces. Moreover, less than a month after Mao's death, the radicals were ousted from the leadership, and immediately the political equation changed drastically. With the radicals' disgrace, the last stand of the Maoist revolution also collapsed.

Postscript II
China's New Phase

On 6 October 1976, not one month after the death of Chairman Mao, his four protégés who were the radical leaders in the party were arrested and removed from power in a lightning coup in Peking. These radicals, who have since been labeled the "Gang of Four," were Wang Hung-wen, Chang Ch'un-ch'iao, Chiang Ch'ing, and Yao Wen-yuan. The coup not only marked, in the words of Hua Kuo-feng, the "victorious close" of the GPCR launched by Mao in 1966, but it also abruptly terminated the colorful careers of these radicals who had made a spectacular political breakthrough in their quest for national power during the tumultuous decade of 1966–76. Before we proceed to analyze the October coup and the events that followed we should briefly examine the radicals' sources of political power and their operations, for the radicals were not only the driving force of Chinese politics up to 1976—their actions will leave a deep imprint on China's polity for many years to come.

The Radicals Seek National Power

Until their ouster in October 1976, the radical leaders were a closely knit group, and perhaps the most powerful faction in the Chinese leadership. Their rise to political influence dated back to 1965–66: when most senior party officials appeared to have deserted or opposed Mao, they rallied behind the Chairman and worked intimately with him to plan and prepare the GPCR crusade. They had ready access to Mao and were close to the Supreme Leader personally and ideologically. They held important leadership positions, controlled the propaganda apparatus at the center, dominated the central party headquarters, and were in a strategic position to dispense patronage.

Although firmly entrenched in Peking, the radical group suffered from a lack of strong support in most provinces (with the exceptions of Shanghai, Liaoning, Anhwei, and Kansu), where conservative powerholders dominated the local power structure. To compensate for this weakness, the radical group had in the first half of 1970s restructured such mass organizations as the urban militia, trade unions, and youth leagues, placing their followers in control and using these organizations to challenge local authorities as well as expand their base of support. Indeed, in a dozen or so provinces, the radical leaders succeeded in placing their followers from the mass organizations in leading positions within the provincial party committees.[1]

In spite of their enormous political resources, opposition to them was formidable. They had earned the enmity of China's conservative political forces by attacking the power structure and challenging the vested interests of the establishment since the GPCR, and they had generated much political ill-will by breaking not a few careers in their climb to the apex of power in China. Moreover, most veteran party and PLA leaders are survivors of the Long March and Civil War and valued highly their pre-1949 revolutionary record; they resented the sudden jump to eminence of the radical upstarts whose credentials rested solely on the promotion of the GPCR after the 1960s, and they were dead set against the radical group's attempt to capture the national leadership. In her bid to assume Chairman Mao's mantle, Chiang Ch'ing was particularly handicapped by the Chinese prejudice against women in high political office. In other words, the radical group had to fight an uphill battle. Yet they had no choice but to wage a struggle while Mao was still alive, for they needed Mao's support or, at least, had to invoke his name in what they tried to accomplish. Against this background, we may understand better their relentless campaigns and political maneuvers during 1973–76.

Manipulation of Authority Symbols

Since the GPCR, Mao had become the most important source of legitimacy in the regime. Inasmuch as the radicals were personally and ideologically close to Mao and controlled the propaganda apparatus, they were in a strategic position to explicate Mao's views, use his name, or forge his instructions, and otherwise manipulate the symbols of authority in the regime according to their needs. The radicals' handling of an epithet attributed to Mao, "Going against the tide is a Marxist-Leninist principle," is a good illustration. The slogan was written into the 1973 Party Constitution and used by the radicals as an ideological weapon to mobilize their supporters to challenge the conservative powerholders. Thus Wang Hung-wen emphatically stated in his report to the Congress that "a true Communist must act without any selfish considerations and dare to go against the tide, fearing neither removal from his post, expulsion from the Party, imprisonment, divorce nor guillotine."[2] Likewise, the radicals coopted the policy of cultivating "revolutionary successors" and manipulated the principle of combining the old, the middle-aged, and the young in the leadership positions to advance their cause. To legitimize their own status and promote their followers to positions of authority, they inserted into the 1973 Party Constitution provisions which sanctified the principle of combining the old, the middle-aged, and the young.

It should be pointed out, however, that the radicals were not alone in this game and that other political leaders also exploited Mao's authority for their own purposes. That Teng Hsiao-p'ing coopted Mao's three separate directives, reformulated them, and presented them as "the key link for all work" in 1975 is one of the many outstanding examples.

"Managing News" and Conducting Propaganda Warfare

Like manipulation of authority symbols, "news management" has been part of the political game in China.[3] Because the radicals (particularly Yao Wen-yuan) controlled the regime's propaganda apparatus, the mass media became a weapon in their struggle for power. This is apparent in their use of the media after 16 September 1976: their massive and concerted efforts to propagate a behest Mao allegedly made shortly before his death—"Act according to the principles laid down"—was a cunning attempt to justify Chiang Ch'ing's succession to Mao's leadership role.[4]

Numerous other cases can also be cited to illustrate how the radicals used the media to enhance their position and undermine that of their opponents. For example, Yao told cameramen to take pictures of "all of the Politburo members" during Mao's mourning period in order to downgrade Hua Kuo-feng's leading place in the minds of China's television viewers, while much publicity was accorded to Chiang Ch'ing's flower wreath in the news and on TV.[5] With the connivance of the radicals, cameramen also took pictures focusing on Chiang Ch'ing standing in the middle of the Politburo group during the 1976 National Day celebration gathering, purporting to give the Chinese people the impression that she now occupied the center stage. In October 1975 Hungch'i was ordered by Yao Wen-yuan not to print Hua's summation speech at the "National Learn-from-Tachai Agricultural Conference." When Premier Chou En-lai died in January 1976, Yao sought to denigrate Chou's image by forbidding the television station to show a documentary film on Chou's career, and he gave instructions to the media to circumvent publicity on Chou's memorial service and withhold news stories on the people's mourning.[6]

Moreover, from 1973 to 1976, the radicals launched a series of intensive propaganda wars. Under Yao's overall direction, the Writing Group of

Peking and Tsinghua Universities (using such pen names as Liang Hsiao, Po Ch'ing, Kao Lu, and Liang Hsiao-chang), the Writing Group of Shanghai (using the pen names Lo Ssu-ting, K'ang Li, Shih Lun, Shih Feng, Chai (cho) Ch'ing, and many others), the Writing Group of the Ministry of Culture (using the pen names Chu Lan and Chiang T'ien), and the Liaoning University Writing Group (supervised by Mao Yuan-hsin) published hundreds of articles in a concerted propaganda blitz.[7] These articles focused on three broad issue areas: attack on the veteran party and PLA leaders (e.g., Chou, Teng), whom the radicals sought to topple; defense of the values and "newborn things" of the GPCR; and promotion of the Gang of Four, particularly Chiang Ch'ing (through the glorification of Empress Lu and Empress Wu Tso-t'ien) to succeed Mao.[8]

In this connection, one should note the Shanghai journal *Hsüeh-hsi Yi P'i-p'an* (*Study and Criticism*), published from September 1973 to September 1976. Ostensibly attached to Futan University, the journal was a "theoretical" organ of the Shanghai CCP Committee, supervised by Hsu Ching-hsien, a party secretary of Shanghai and staunch follower of the Gang of Four. During its three years of publication, it became a formidable propaganda weapon of the radical leaders as it trumpeted offensives against the veteran leaders and their policies (to be examined later). Moreover, the magazine helped mobilize the followers of the radicals throughout the nation and they took their cue from it to attack the local powerholders.

Cooptation

As noted previously, the radicals sought to legitimate their young followers' right of access to positions of leadership by pushing through the insertion in the 1973 Party Constitution of provisions sanctifying the principle of combining the old, the middle-aged, and the young. Indeed, a large group of young cadres had been patronized and promoted since the GPCR by the radicals.[9] Rightly or wrongly, youth and junior cadres in the bureaucracy considered the radical leaders "supporters of the youth," "protectors of the youth," and "representatives of the newly emerging forces" in the regime,[10] and supported the radicals' efforts to defend the values of the GPCR and attack the conservative veteran powerholders.

Radical leaders' cooptation of supporters was not confined to youth, however. To the extent the radicals were in a position to dispense patronage, they were also able to draw ambitious, opportunistic party and PLA officers to their side. Chiao Kuan-hua, China's former Minister of Foreign Affairs, is an outstanding example. He was considered a political moderate and a confidant of Premier Chou, but he switched to the side of the radical group after the T'ienanmen Square riot in April 1976, either out of an instinct for political self-preservation or because the radicals promised a high leadership position (e.g., vice-premiership, membership in the Politburo). In addition to Chiao, scores of veteran officers both in the center and in the provinces—those who had been opportunistic and too eager to cooperate with the radical group in return for its power in appointment and dismissal—have been ousted since October 1976.[11]

Hua Kuo-feng, Ch'en Hsi-lien, Chi Teng-kuei, Wu Teh, and Wang Tung-hsing also appeared to have worked closely with the radicals when Mao was still alive; at times even Premier Chou, Yeh Chien-ying, and Li Hsien-nien felt compelled to go along with the radicals. Using Mao's authority and ex-ploiting Chinese officials' opportunism or loyalty to the Chairman, the radicals were often in a position to impose their views.

Building a Mass Base

Although firmly entrenched in the party's central apparatus, the radical group suffered from a lack of support in most provinces (with the exceptions of Shanghai, Liaoning, Anhwei, and Kansu), which were dominated by con-servative powerholders. To compensate for this weakness, the radicals had sought to coopt supporters among the provincial officials through a combi-nation of patronage, cajolement, and political threat, and they had some successes, as noted previously. Their most notable and successful endeavor, however, was the building of grassroots support through control over mass organizations in the provinces. In the first half of the 1970s, the radical group took the lead in reorganizing trade unions, youth leagues, women's asso-ciations, and the urban militia, placing their followers in control of these organizations (or winning over leaders of these organizations to their side), and using these organizations to challenge local authorities as well as expand their base of power.

Instrumental in the efforts of the radical group to forge mass support, particularly among the workers, was Wang Hung-wen. He appeared to have been popular with, and admired by, workers, possibly because he was once a worker himself and they regarded him as sympathetic to their interests. Consequently, workers were receptive to his lobbying and solicitation and became loyal followers of the radicals.

The radical group's power to dispense patronage also helped them gain support. Indeed, through the radicals' intervention in a dozen provinces, their supporters in the mass organizations made it into the provincial leadership nucleus.[12] Although these mass organization representatives were unable to control local events, they were in a position to checkmate the conservative powerholders and deadlock the party committees in many provinces in 1974–76.

Constructing the "Second Armed Forces"

The radicals knew too well that "political power grows from the barrel of a gun" and that they needed military backing in order to contend for the supreme party leadership. Hence they did what they could at once to place their supporters in positions of leadership at all levels of PLA hierarchy and coopt PLA officials who were already in high office to their side.[13]

On the other hand, the radical leaders realized that they were unpopular among the veteran PLA leaders, the overwhelming majority of whom were extremely hostile to the GPCR and would be opposed to the radical cause in the future,[14] so they sought to build up a "second armed forces" as a counterweight against the PLA and as an instrument in their struggle for Mao's succession. Thus in the early 1970s, Chang Ch'un-ch'iao and Wang Hung-wen began to organize and arm the urban militia from among the workers in Shanghai. One very important feature of this paramilitary organization was that it was placed under the command of the Shanghai Federation of Trade Unions (which was headed by Wang), and not under local PLA authorities as in the past.

After the fall of 1973, the radicals actively promoted the Shanghai experience in "militia building" and, in spite of opposition by PLA authorities in many localities, succeeded in getting the central authorities to sponsor the Shanghai model throughout the nation. In joint directive number 162 (1973), the State Council and the MAC of the party instructed other provinces to "learn and extend Shanghai's fresh experience in reorganizing and building militia." Although PLA leaders in many provinces boycotted the directive and refused to surrender the command of the militia, in quite a few provinces the followers of the Gang of Four did secure control over urban militia units and, from 1974 to 1976, they echoed the radical group's campaigns to attack the veteran powerholders through strikes and anomic activities.

As in the case of mobilizing labor support, Wang Hung-wen played a vital role in reorganizing urban militia and placing radical followers in positions of leadership, and prior to his downfall he had intended to set up the "People's Republic of China Militia Command Headquarter" with himself as its Commander-in-Chief.[15] After Mao's death, Wang allegedly instructed his cohorts in Shanghai to distribute weapons and ammunition to the militia units in preparation for armed conflict. After the four top radicals were arrested in Peking on 6 October 1976, some militia units in Shanghai were prepared to launch an armed struggle; reportedly the dispatch of troops from Nanking under the command of Hsu Shih-yu and of marines from the East China Sea Fleet led by Su Chen-hua preempted the potential rebellion.

Campaigns against the Establishment

From 1973 to 1976, a series of campaigns were launched by Mao or in his name to repudiate Lin Piao and Confucius, to criticize the practice of "taking the back door," to study the theory of proletarian dictatorship, to criticize the Chinese classic *Water Margin*, to "beat back the right-deviationist wind," and to repudiate Teng Hsiao-p'ing, among others. Some of these campaigns, such as the one against Lin Piao and Confucius, raised a number of highly academic and theoretic questions (e.g., assessment of Ch'in Shih Huang, periodization of ancient Chinese history, interpretation of the doctrines of Confucius and Legalists)—questions which did mislead some Western scholars—but the campaign was by no means an academic debate over theory.[16]

For example, an article by Shih Lun, "On Worshipping Confucianism and Opposing Legalism," published in *Study and Criticism* (September 1973), which ostensibly criticized Lu P'u-wei (a Ch'in dynasty premier) was actually directed at Premier Chou En-lai.[17] Yao Wen-yuan had the article written and had it reproduced in *Red Flag* in October 1973. During the same campaign, the media under Yao's control published numerous articles attacking the figurative Confucius—the present-day Confucianists in the Chinese leadership. The article "Confucius and the Confucianists Are a Small Handful of Political Swindlers" by K'ang Li (*Study and Criticism*, February 1974) was a thinly veiled attack on Chou En-lai; it was reproduced by *Red Flag* in the following month with its title changed to "Confucius and Lin Piao Are Both Political Swindlers." Another article by the same author in May 1976 in the *Shanghai Journal*, "Ssu-ma Kuang in Office after One Year," presented insinuations against Hua Kuo-feng.

In other campaigns, such as the campaign against "taking the back door" and the "anti-rightist campaign," principles as well as concrete important policy issues (e.g., values of the GPCR, affirmation of "newborn things") were debated. At heart, however, was very much a struggle for power. Throughout these campaigns, the radicals invariably used the propaganda instruments at their disposal to mobilize support for themselves, to initiate attacks on trends and policies they considered undesirable, to discredit and topple veteran leaders, and to enhance their own chance for Mao's succession.

Downfall of the Radicals

The power struggle between the radicals and other leadership groups in the CCP reached a climax in the month following Mao's death in September 1976. In the first week of October an anti-radical coalition composed of diverse leadership elements rallied behind Hua Kuo-feng, then first vice-chairman of the party and premier, and on 6 October they staged a coup that deposed the radicals.

The coup used to purge the radicals represented an ominous change in the rules of the political game and set a dangerous precedent in the leadership conflict. In the wake of Mao's death, the radicals were actively conspiring to seize power and after 16 September they began to propagate in the media Mao's alleged behest "Act according to the principles laid down" to pave the way for Chiang Ch'ing's succession. The radicals appear to have held a trump card in their hands—they possessed or forged Mao's political will which anointed Chiang Ch'ing to succeed the deceased Chairman—and they were to call a Politburo meeting on 8 or 9 October to act on Mao's behest. Confronted with such an exigency, Hua Kuo-feng and Yeh Chien-ying were forced to take a preemptive action against the four radical leaders.

The coup would not have succeeded, however, if it was not actively supported by a key individual, Wang Tung-hsing, Mao's lifelong security officer and commander/commissar of the "8341" unit—an army-sized special security troop which at once guards China's elites and keeps a close watch on them. If Wang chose to side with the Gang of Four, the coup might not have been attempted in the first place, for it could have precipitated a civil war. *The People's Daily* has confirmed that Wang's 8341 unit arrested the radical leaders: "At the crucial moment when the Gang of Four was about to launch a counterrevolutionary coup . . . the 8341 unit . . . under the direct command of Chairman Hua and Vice-Chairman Yeh, firmly carried out the order of the central committee and acted promptly to deal a crushing blow to the Gang of Four."[18]

Wang's move against the radicals was most intriguing, particularly when his career and political associations are considered. To begin with, Wang had worked closely with Mao for more than four decades until Mao's death in September 1976 and is, without question, a staunch Maoist. He was closely involved in Mao's GPCR crusade in the 1960s and he rose to political prominence because of it—he became director of the CC General Office in 1966, an alternate Politburo member in 1969, and a full Politburo member in 1973. Like the radicals, Wang is a beneficiary of the GPCR and has a political stake in preserving its legitimacy. In fact, Wang appears to have been on good terms with Chiang Ch'ing, at least until early 1970s,[19] and quite a few former members of Wang's 8341 unit, such as Chih Chun and Hsieh Ching-yi, who headed Tsinghua University, were staunch supporters of the Gang of Four.

On the other hand, however, Wang must have become apprehensive with the intrigues of the Gang of Four and felt his power and access to Mao threatened by their maneuvers. Whether or not Wang Tung-hsing approved of Mao's grooming of Wang Hung-wen is unknown to us. He could have been irritated by the quick rise of the young upstart from Shanghai and particularly by Wang Hung-wen's intrusion into his "sphere of influence." It is known, for example, that the staff office under Wang Hung-wen had issued party directives bypassing the CC General Office and performed other functions previously monopolized by Wang Tung-hsing. Moreover, Wang must have seen the attempt by Chiang Ch'ing to place Mao Yuan-hsin (Chairman Mao's nephew) as the deputy director of the CC General Office and the political commissar of the 8341 unit as steps to usurp his own power.[20] It is not clear if, and to what extent, Chiang Ch'ing did succeed in making inroads into Wang's "independent kingdom." Sometime in 1975–76, however, Mao Yuan-hsin reportedly served as Chairman Mao's "liaison officer";[21] in that position he relayed reports to the Chairman, conveyed Mao's directives to others, and was apparently able to control other leaders' access to the sick old man.

Circumstances such as these would partly explain why Wang turned against the Gang of Four following Mao's death. He also may have calculated that if the Four took over control of the leadership, his own political usefulness to them would be substantially reduced, and he might face elimination since he possessed too much incriminating information about them. He was undoubtedly aware that the Four had made too many personal and political enemies among China's powerholders, and to side with the Four would not only be fighting a losing cause but would help dig his own political grave.

In addition, there were a number of major considerations which motivated Wang to rally behind Hua Kuo-feng at the critical moment in early October 1976. In personal terms, Hua seems to have been modest, unassuming, and not an abrasive person—a kind of leader Wang would find easy to work with. Politically, Hua was appointed first vice-chairman of the party in April 1976 by a Politburo resolution recommended by Mao—thus allowing Hua to claim Mao's personal imprimatur—and he was supported by other leaders including Yeh Chien-ying. Yet the decisive factor that swayed Wang to champion Hua's cause was probably the cold calculation that he could really be a "kingmaker" and an indispensable man to Hua.

Wang's role in the coup in Peking in early October 1976 is well-known by now. On 7 October 1976, the day following the arrest of the four radical leaders, the Politburo held an enlarged session, attended by provincial leaders flown into Peking for the occasion, to receive briefings by Hua, Yeh, and Wang Tung-hsing on the arrest of the Gang and to select the party's chairman.

According to a reliable source inside China, Wang extolled Hua in his speech, endorsed Hua's succession to Mao, and quoted Mao as explaining to him three reasons for appointing Hua acting premier in January 1976: "First, he [Hua] has had experience in the work at the prefectural and provincial levels and his performance as Minister of Public Security over the past several years is not bad. Second, he is loyal and honest. Third, he is not stupid."[22] Inasmuch as Wang was so close to Mao, his words probably carried great weight. Thus, on the same day, the Politburo approved Hua to be chairman of the CCP and its powerful Military Affairs Committee, making him Mao's successor.

At the very moment when Wang's security guards were arresting the Gang of Four and its hardcore elements in a well-coordinated surprise move, other preventive military actions were also taken against the supporters of the Gang. In Peking, for example, the PLA units quickly disarmed the militia in the nation's capital and forestalled any possible uprising of that paramilitary organization. Ground forces and naval units led by Hsu Shih-yu and Su Chen-hua, respectively, were dispatched to Shanghai, the radical stronghold, and overpowered some militia units which had planned to make a last-ditch armed resistance.

Ever since the arrest of the Gang, a sweeping purge of its followers in the nation has been set in motion. As of early 1978, the purge is still in progress. Among the important victims of the purge have been the following:

1. Those in the inner circle of the Gang, such as Mao Yuan-hsin, a political commissar of Shenyang MR and Mao's "liaison officer" in 1976; Chih Chun and Hsieh Ching-yi, leaders at Tsinghua University who were the radical group's brain-trusters and directed a very vociferous and powerful propaganda outlet ostensibly attached to the Tsinghua and Peking universities (Liang Hsiao); and Wang Mang-t'ien (a relative of the Chairman), a party secretary of Tientsin and concurrently a Vice-Minister of Culture, and Yu Hui-yung, Minister of Culture, among others.

2. Supporters of the Gang in Shanghai, virtually the entire Shanghai leadership prior to October 1976 (e.g., Ma T'ien-shui, Hsu Ching-hsien, and Wang Hsiu-chen, all party secretaries in Shanghai; the press attack on Ma was most virulent, calling him a shameful example of veteran cadres who sold their souls to the Gang of Four).

3. Scores of leading cadres in the party, government, and PLA who supported the cause of the radical group, including veteran officials who had been coopted and the radicals' followers who had been placed in positions or responsibility; some typical examples of officials who rose quickly because of political patronage and are now out of favor are Sung Chien, vice-premier, Wu Kuei-hsien, an alternate Politburo member and vice-premier, Yao Lien-hui, vice-chairman of the NPC standing committee.[23]

4. Followers of the Gang in such mass organizations as the militia, trade unions, and youth leagues.[24]

5. Those officials who have otherwise been implicated with the Gang, such as Chang Shu-chih, commander of Honan MD, Keng Chi-chang, secretary of Honan, Wu Ta-sheng and Yang Kwang-li, both secretaries of Kiangsu. (Most of those weeded out in Peking's current effort to reorganize the provincial government leadership teams can be included in this category and their number is increasing.)

It is true that some officials who were patronized by, or were formerly close to, the Gang have been spared and even coopted into the new leadership; Ni Chih-fu, a worker-engineer who was elected an alternate Politburo member in 1973, defected from the Gang, and was elevated to a full member of the Politburo in August 1977, is one such. But the purges already carried out may have effectively wiped out the leadership elements of the radical political forces in China. Moreover, China's current powerholders have conducted a massive campaign to weed out a large number of radical supporters in the subprovincial leadership organs and to break, once and for all, the radical group's bases of support in the polity. According to information released by Peking, over 7 million people have been recruited into the CCP since 1973, and out of the 35 million party members in 1977 more than half joined the organization since 1966. Apparently the overwhelming majority of these new recruits, and particularly those new members since 1973, have had strong radical ties and they have been the targets of the anti-leftist rectification campaign.

The Political Shift to the Right:
The Eleventh Party Congress

Since October 1976, the balance of Chinese political forces has changed drastically. On the one hand, the radicals have been ousted from power, their supporters scattered, and their bases of power shattered. On the other hand, the conservative forces have had an upsurge.

One of the clear manifestations of the conservative ascendance is the spectacular, unprecedented second political comeback of Teng Hsiao-p'ing. In July 1977, at the party's CC plenary session, Teng was formally reinstated to all the leadership positions he lost in April 1976. The decision to rehabilitate Teng was not an easy one, for it was opposed by some of China's most powerful leaders. It appears that Hua Kuo-feng, Wang Tung-hsing, Wu Teh, Ch'en

Hsi-lien, and Li Teh-sheng, all of them members of the Politburo who either had voted for Teng's ouster in April 1976 or had benefited from his downfall since, or were otherwise apprehensive of his threat to their power, tried to block Teng's political comeback. They may have argued that inasmuch as Teng's dismissal was enacted by a unanimous Politburo resolution on Chairman Mao's proposal, the reversal of the verdict on Teng could tarnish Mao's memory. In any case, Teng's detractors did drag their feet and when they could no longer prevent his reinstatement they extracted concessions from him.

On the other hand, Teng's allies and supporters in the leadership—notably Hsu Shih-yu and Wei Kuo-ch'ing, two powerful regional leaders in the Politburo—and many provincial leaders who had been brought back to power by Teng fought hard for his political revival. They criticized the delaying tactics used by Teng's critics and applied great political pressure against Hua Kuo-feng to speed up Teng's rehabilitation. Eventually a compromise was reached in a central work conference in March 1977. Teng was compelled to make an important concession: he wrote a letter to the party leadership in April in which he formally pledged his support to Chairman Hua and conceded that he had committed political errors in 1975. With this arrangement, the CC Plenum in July officially approved Teng's return to China's leadership lineup.

Meanwhile, the realignment of political forces and the vicissitudes of many political actors since the ouster of the Gang also found clear expressions in the Eleventh Party Congress, which was held in August 1977 to approve a new leadership team and a new policy line. The Party Congress, which sanctified the shift from revolutionary radicalism to pragmatic policies, represents a major victory both for China's conservative political forces and for Vice-Chairman Teng Hsiao-p'ing himself. Leaders who have in recent years pushed for modernization of China's economy and national defense, including a large group of Teng's supporters in the party and PLA who were victimized by the GPCR, are strongly represented in the new CC and Politburo.

The Congress was also an important occasion for Hua Kuo-feng. It ratified Hua's succession to the party chairmanship, which he acquired in October 1976 under circumstances of political exigency and by means of a Politburo resolution, thereby conferring legitimacy and a seeming vote of confidence to his leadership over the party. This was only symbolic but nonetheless very crucial for Hua's hold on power. He also delivered a four hour Political Report to the Congress, spelling out the policy priorities of the post-Mao leadership (a subject which will be discussed further in the next section).

The most important item on the agenda of the Congress was the election of a new CC, which in turn chose the Politburo. The composition of the new CC and Politburo has in many respects reversed trends of the 1969 and 1973 congresses and repudiated precepts and policies favored by Chairman Mao. The following are some outstanding characteristics of the new leadership lineup.

Old is favored over young. Instead of promoting more young cadres in accordance with the Maoist principle of "combining the old, middle-aged, and the young," as was done during the Ninth and Tenth Party Congresses in 1969 and 1973, this congress downgraded the young and favored the old, although it continued to pay lip service to the principle. The most outstanding examples of honoring seniority are the promotion to the Politburo of the two aged marshals Hsu Hsiang-chien (who was seventy-five) and Nieh Jung-chen (seventy-eight); in fact among the five other new Politburo members, Ulanfu is seventy-three and Keng Piao is seventy-four, and the remaining three are in their sixties. The same situation is true for the Central Committee.

Another obvious change is the heavy influx of new officials. There is a large turnover in the two leading party bodies—in the Politburo, eight new members and two new alternates have been added, bringing the total membership to 23 plus three alternates, and in the Central Committee, 73 of the 201 members and 75 of the 132 alternate members are newly elected; the new members account for 44 percent of the total membership. Most of these new members and alternates members are veteran party and military officials who were rehabilitated during the 1970s. Teng personifies and derives support from these victims of the cultural revolution. In the Politburo, Ulanfu and Air Force Commander Chang Ting-hua experienced the same fate as Teng did, while Hsu Hsiang-ch'ien and Nieh Jung-chen were also victims (although to a lesser degree). In the Central Committee, there are approximately 85 out of 201 who suffered varying degrees of disgrace during the cultural revolution. Among these, at least 40 are either close associates of Teng or were restored to positions of importance by him in 1974–75; hence they are his staunch supporters.

Another sign that the Eleventh Congress repudiated the GPCR and Mao's revolutionary values can be seen in the wholesale ouster of the Gang of Four and their followers from the new leadership lineup: out of the 195 Central Committee members elected at the Tenth Party Congress in 1973, approximately 65 have been dropped; among the 124 alternate members elected in 1973, 55 have been dropped. In total, approximately 38 percent of the members and alternate members elected in 1973 have been excluded. Many of these were young, in charge of trade unions, urban militia units, youth leagues, and women's federations, and they were supporters of the Gang of Four in the provinces.

In addition, the Central Committee is being packed with "establishment" figures. Without exception, the first secretaries of 29 provincial units are CC members. The first secretaries of Peking, Shanghai, and Kwangtung also are Politburo members, and the first secretaries of Szechuan and Sinkiang are

Politburo alternate members. Moreover, Ni Chih-fu and P'eng Ch'ung, second secretary of Peking and third secretary of Shanghai, respectively, are also Politburo members. Possibly P'eng will become the first secretary of Shanghai, replacing General Su Chen-hua, who is concurrently the Navy's first political commissar. Other than the first party secretaries, most provinces also have two or three additional provincial secretaries represented in the Central Committee as full or alternate members. In Peking, the leading functionaries of all the Central Committee departments and two-thirds of approximately 40 ministries are also represented on the Central Committee and the Politburo. The economic ministries, in particular, are strongly represented, reflecting the regime's stress on economic development.

Another characteristic is that the military is heavily represented. While the representatives of the military constitute 43 percent (10 out of 23) of the Politburo, their representation in the Central Committee is less than 30 percent (approximately 62 of the 201 members and 32 of 132 alternate members), two percentage points below the figure for the Tenth Party Congress. As in the case of the civilian cadres, the military members of the Central Committee are also "establishment" figures. Without exception, the commanders and political commissars of all 11 military regions are members of the Central Committee. More than half of these regions are also represented by additional members or alternate members. In the central military headquarters, the chiefs and deputy chiefs of the general staff department, the deputy directors of the general political department, and leading officers of the general rear service department are in the Central Committee as full or alternate members. This is also true for the leading officers of the service arms. It seems that the Air Force has enhanced its influence, for it has a few more Central Committee members than other service arms do, and its commander, Chang Ting-hua, has been elevated to the Politburo. It is also noteworthy that approximately ten combat heroes or division-level military officers who were elected to the Central Committee in 1973 have been dropped in favor of their seniors. Moreover, two-thirds of the military men who are now in the Central Committee currently work in the regions and the provinces.

Adding together the local military men, the provincial party leaders, and representatives of the mass organizations, those Central Committee members who work in the provinces constitute close to 70 percent of the entire membership. The overwhelming representation of the provincial forces in the party's major decision-making body, which is a reversal of the situation in the 1950s and 1960s, could have important implications for future Chinese politics. For one thing, the trend toward decentralization and regional autonomy could increase, and the local leaders could become more assertive, especially after such towering figures in the center as Yeh Chien-ying and Teng pass from the scene.

Other characteristics of new leadership also deserve comment. There is a discernible emphasis on cooptation of the minority nationalities, as reflected by an increase of minority representatives in the Central Committee and in the Politburo and the appointment of a Mongol, Ulanfu, to head the party's United Front Department. Second, in place of most of the mass organization leaders who supported the Gang and who were dropped from the Central Committee, there is a new (but smaller) cast of model workers, model peasants, and mass representatives. Most of them seem to be older, are expected to be more supportive of the "establishment," and can be regarded as "docile tools" of the powerholders.

Veteran party and military leaders have been favored in the new leadership lineup, while the younger elements have been slighted. It is true that several leaders in their fifties are holding major leadership positions today and will play even more important roles hereafter: Hua Kuo-feng (fifty-seven) and Vice-Premier Chi Teng-k'uei (fifty-six) in Peking, Chao Tzu-yang in Szechuan, Ch'iao Hsiao-kuang in Kwangsi, and Mai Li in Kweichow are outstanding examples. However, these and a few others are really exceptions to the overall elite structure which continues to be dominated by the "Old Guard." Teng's restoration to power has, in fact, legitimated their hold on major positions of importance and blocked opportunities for upward mobility for younger and probably more talented elements in the leadership who have been waiting in the wings for years. The inability or unwillingness of the Chinese high command to infuse new blood into the leadership is bound to alienate a large number of middle-aged and young officials.

Finally, we ought to take note of what is potentially the most significant development in the Congress, the rise of Wang Tung-hsing to China's pinnacle of power. In recognition of Wang's role in the succession struggle following Mao's death, the Congress elected him one of the party's four vice-chairmen, making him the fifth ranking leader after Chairman Hua and Vice-Chairmen Yeh Chien-ying, Teng Hsiao-p'ing, and Li Hsien-nien. In fact, even before Wang was formally elected a party vice-chairman, his functions and influence had already expanded far beyond the scope of security work with which he has been associated to date. In April 1977, for example, he accompanied Chairman Hua on a three-day inspection tour of the Taching Oil Field and was given prominent publicity in the Chinese media. Later that month he received a visiting delegation from North Korea. In May he presided over the closing ceremony of the "National Conference on Learning from Taching in Industry." When the party congress was in session he served as the secretary-general of its presidium and was also in charge of examining credentials of the delegates; this suggests that currently he may also perform the functions of the party's general-secretary (Teng occupied that position until 1966) and is responsible for personnel matters.

In the past several months, efforts were made to improve and enhance Wang's public image. The prominent publication of a sixteen-year-old letter by Mao to the Kiangsi Communist Labor University (with which Wang was associated) in *Hungch'i* in August 1977 is one example. An unusually long article by the "theoretical study group" of the CC General Office (which was headed by Wang since 1966) and published in the *People's Daily* on 8 September 1977 to commemorate the first anniversary of Mao's death is another example. It claimed credits for the 8341 unit for having saved Mao's life in a moment of danger in 1971 and depicted "the comrade [Wang] attending him [Mao]" as highly loyal and devoted to the late Chairman, and one who had enjoyed his confidence. The article also strongly defended the GPCR and extolled Mao's memory.

Obviously, Wang is a formidable figure in China's political landscape today. He appears to have been feared by other leaders not only because he controls the "palace guards" and the regime's secret police system, but also because he knows too much about the skeletons in everyone's closets. Furthermore, in recent months, the scope of his influence and functions have expanded far beyond security work and extended to, among other things, party administration and personnel matters. (Stalin, too, used the organizational power derived from his control of these same functions to enlist support and defeat Trotsky and other leadership contenders in the post-Lenin succession struggle in the Soviet Union in the 1920s.)

Other Chinese leaders seem keenly aware of the powerful cards Wang holds, and they have adopted a number of countervailing measures. The appointment of both Chao Ts'ang-pi (a longtime associate of Teng) to the top post in MPS and of Lo Jui-ch'ing (an old hand in the security system) to the party's MAC Standing Committee can be seen as attempts by Teng to dilute Wang's control over the secret police apparatus and to checkmate Wang. On 7 October 1977 an article on the cadre policy, published in the *People's Daily*, obliquely attacked Wang. It criticized those cadres in charge of personnel matters for suffering from the pernicious influence of the Gang of Four and accused them for at once being unwilling to rehabilitate the victims of the leftist purges and failing to "deal with some bad elements who wormed their way into the cadre ranks." Moreover, in several signed articles published in the *People's Daily*, such veteran leaders as Marshal Nieh Jung-chen, Hsu Hsiang-ch'ien, Lo Jui-ch'ing and Ch'en Yun also took issue with Wang and those who defended the GPCR. In sharp contrast with Wang's strong defense of Mao and the GPCR, these "old guards" bemoaned the damages wrought by the GPCR and called for the "restoration" of the party's good traditions and working style.

An attack on Wang is, by extension, an attack on Hua. Since October 1976 Hua and Wang have been close political allies and Hua has relied heavily

on Wang to back up his leadership position and consolidate his power.
Indeed, both Hua and Wang and most of their supporters, such as Wu Teh,
Ch'en Hsi-lien and Li Teh-sheng, have much in common: all of them are
relatively young when compared with most other Politburo members; all
are beneficiaries of the GPCR, rising as a result of purges of the "old guards"
like Teng, and have a political stake in the legitimacy of the GPCR and in
affirming Mao's legacy. Moreover, despite the fact that they turned against
the Gang of Four in October 1976, they had also collaborated with the
Gang for many years prior to Mao's death, and they voted for Teng's ouster
in April 1976 and tried to block his subsequent rehabilitation.

Thus, while China's post-Mao leadership basically agrees on the need to
stress law and order and to push a set of modernization programs, it is also
divided. The division, however, is based neither on institutions (such as the
party or army) nor exclusively on historical associations (e.g., field army
ties).[25] Hua Kuo-feng's group, for example, draws support from party
officials (such as Chi Teng-k'uei and Wu Teh), elements of the PLA (e.g.,
Ch'en Hsi-lien and Li Teh-sheng), and the security apparatus (Wang Tung-
hsing). Ch'en and Li are former associates of Teng Hsiao-p'ing in the Second
Field Army, but they are now in opposing political camps. Hua may also
derive support from a large number of younger cadres who have risen since
the GPCR, including former followers of the Gang of Four, probably because Hua has defended the legacy of the GPCR and thereby affirmed their
political future.

Similarly, the supporters of Teng are also based in the party and the PLA,
and they include such PLA figures as Hsu Shih-yu and Su Chen-hua, such
party officials as Teng, Wei Kuo-ching, Ulanfu, Keng Piao, Li Ching-ch'uan,
and many provincial leaders. Most members of this group were victimized
by the GPCR purge and are now advanced in age. Hence their conflict with
the Hua group has the overtone of generational differences.

The de facto de-Maoization

Since the death of Chairman Mao and the purge of the Gang of Four in the
autumn of 1976, the rulers of China have lost no time in stepping up efforts
to implement the modernization program which were proclaimed to the
NPC meeting of January 1975 by Premier Chou En-lai and pushed hard by
Teng Hsiao-p'ing throughout that year. In spite of the differences between
Hua Kuo-feng and Teng over such important issues as distribution of power
in the leadership, they agree on the urgent need for China to boost its national

economy and to improve people's living standards. This broad consensus has underlain a new "general line" which is vastly different from Mao's revolutionary radicalism.

Thus the post-Mao leadership has repudiated excessive emphasis on the primary importance of politics and ideology, revolution, class struggle, egalitarianism, subjective human factors, self-reliance, and "mass democracy" —values that were closely identified with the GPCR and strongly reasserted by Mao and the radicals in recent years. Instead, China's new leaders now stress stability and unity, enforce stern discipline in society, allow a freer use of material incentives, assign a greater role to expertise, rules and regulations for factory and enterprise management, and imports of foreign equipment and technology, and go all out to speed up the modernization of China's agriculture, industry, national defense, and science and technology (the so-called four modernizations).

One very striking task undertaken by China's post-Mao leadership to boost the national economy lies in the efforts to remove ideological constraints. In its first fifteen months, the new Chinese leadership has drastically redefined various Maoist concepts so as to legitimize what it is doing.

Consider Mao's saying "grasping revolution, promoting production," for example. It is well known to everyone that Mao placed a great emphasis on politics: he said that "ideology and politics are the commander, the soul," and that "political work is the lifeblood of all economic work"; accordingly, for Mao, the relationship between revolution and production and between politics and economics was one between the key link and the subordinate links, between the commander and the commanded. It is on the basis of this Maoist principle that the radicals attacked Teng for preaching "taking the three directives as the key link" (which means downgrading the importance of the class struggle) and for using "four modernizations" to fan up an "economic gale" (which means promoting economic growth at the expense of political-ideological values). In his eagerness to promote production and boost the national economy, a pragmatic Teng easily lent himself to the radicals' charge of practicing the "theory of productive forces."

While continuing to uphold the commanding role of revolution, the new leadership now asserts that opposing the theory of productive forces does not mean giving up production, that people need food and drink, clothing and housing, and must engage in productive activities "before they can engage in political, scientific, art and other activities," and that "man's activity in production is the most fundamental practical activity and the determinant of all his other activities."[26] The radicals are denounced for having "deliberately equated the theory of productive forces with efforts to promote production [and] brought insolent charges against other people so that no one would dare or be able to promote production." "Striving for the expansion of socialist production" is now termed a "basic task of the dictatorship of the proletariat and a glorious duty of the working class and all other labouring people."[27]

Furthermore, refuting a statement made by the radicals that "once a good job is done in revolution, production naturally will go up" (which is really no different from the Maoist quotation "Once the class struggle is grasped, miracles are possible"), China's media now emphatically and specifically call on cadres and the people to "establish and improve rational rules and regulations, do a better job in economic accounting, lower production costs, increase the accumulation of funds, carry out technical innovations and technical revolution, launch socialist emulation in work, raise labor productivity."[28]

In the same vein, the radicals' explication and interpretation of other Maoist tenets has also been modified. For example, whereas the Gang of Four attacked Teng for using "four modernizations" as a "big stick" to justify his policies, now to speed up the modernization of industry, agriculture, and science and technology is termed the necessary condition of building "a powerful material foundation for the triumph of socialism over capitalism and for the future transition to communism."[29]

Whereas the radicals previously denounced China's exports of oil and other raw materials as "selling out her natural resources" and her imports of technology and equipment as "worshiping things foreign and fawning upon foreigners," "begging from foreign countries," and "turning China into the imperialists' dumping ground," these transactions are now defended through the manipulation of Mao's authority symbols. Exporting petroleum is hailed as a victory for Mao's policy of independence and self-reliance. Through foreign trade, it is now claimed, China has acquired needed materials and introduced some necessary equipment and technology to enhance her ability to "build socialism independently and self-reliantly and quicken the tempo of socialist construction." All of these are said to fully conform to Mao's teaching to "make foreign things serve China" and with the principle he advanced in his speech *On the Ten Major Relationships*: "Learn from the strong points of all nations and all countries, learn all that is genuinely good in the political, economic, scientific and technological fields and in literature and art."[30]

On the issue of material incentives, the prescription has also changed. When the campaign against the "bourgeois Right" and against the capitalist-roaders was in full swing in 1975–76, it was a political taboo to do anything about raising the income and improving the living conditions of the people. However, the publication of Mao's *On the Ten Major Relationships* at the beginning of 1977 legitimized the discussions about adjusting the wages of the workers and raising the income of the peasants, inasmuch as he was in favor of these measures to encourage the people's "zeal for hard work."[31] The Gang of Four was specifically criticized for closing the rural markets, forbidding peasants to engage in sideline occupations, undermining the party's rural policy, and causing much hardship to people's livelihood.[32] In the summer of 1977, the Chinese government announced a wage increase of 10 to 15 percent for approximately 46 percent of China's workers who were at the lowest pay scale. What the Chinese leadership will do to improve the livelihood of the peasants who constitute more than 80 percent of China's population remains to be seen.

It should be obvious from this discussion that the post-Mao leaders of China have moved away from the precepts and values that had been closely identified with the deceased Chairman in the preceding decade. In policy matters—material incentives, literature and art, education, and other issue areas (with the probable exception of foreign relations)—China's current leaders have resurrected (or are in the process of reviving) pragmatic measures which Mao sought to do away with during the GPCR. In this connection we can speak of de facto de-Maoization, "de facto" because Chinese leaders today do not openly and *totally* repudiate Mao's ideological legacy; they merely redefine various Maoist concepts, using his own words to justify the modification of the radical measures he favored, but they continue to uphold his authority. To negate Mao's authority entirely could create serious problems for the polity and particularly for Hua Kuo-feng, whose legitimacy and power rest heavily on Mao's personal imprimatur. Indeed, to defend his claim to the position of China's supreme leader, Hua has to defend Mao's memory and ideological authority; the construction of Mao's memorial hall, the publicity given to the publication of Mao's writings, and other activities to honor Mao's memory should be seen in this light.

It is true that Maoist principles can be manipulated and reinterpreted to suit the political exigencies and sanction the new line, but there is a limit beyond which various Maoist tenets cannot be stretched. For example, Mao was on record as opposing measures such as "*san tzu yi pao*" (three freedoms and one guarantee) and dividing collective land among peasants for private farming to boost the economy; however much China's leadership today wishes to stimulate the peasants' incentives, it will not be able to invoke Mao to endorse such policies. As a matter of fact, these measures are explicitly forbidden and other "capitalist tendencies" in the rural areas have continued to be criticized by the regime in recent months.[33] Thus it seems certain that some Maoist values will continue to structure the policy alternatives mapped out by Mao's successors and to affect the parameters within which they solve problems.

Moreover, with the continuing division in the CCP leadership and with differing policy preferences and priorities entertained by various leaders and groupings, individual leaders and groups are likely to take what they need from the body of Mao's writings for their own purpose. The publication in the August 1977 issue of *Red Flag* of a letter written by Mao on 30 July 1961 to affirm and praise the Kiangsi Communist Labor University is an outstanding example. This university is depicted as having embodied Mao's philosophy of education and having been a forerunner of the educational reform put through during the GPCR—it is an "irregular" work-study educational institution which embraces primary school, middle school, and college-level courses, and which enrolls both youth and middle-aged cadres who are engaged in part-time study and part-time land reclamation and other farming activities.[34] Apparently Hua Kuo-feng and Wang Tung-hsing have resurrected this sixteen-year-old letter of Mao to slow down the wholesale changes in China's higher education, which Teng Hsiao-p'ing and other pragmatic officials are pushing and which Hua and Wang consider to have gone too far.

Concluding Remarks

In many important ways, the GPCR represents a major watershed of post-1949 Chinese politics. The enormous upheaval generated by Mao's crusade starting in 1966 has shaped the course of events in China for more than a decade and has left behind a legacy which will continue to affect Chinese politics for many years to come. Moreover, the GPCR wrought a number of significant changes in the norm of leadership conflict and in the Communist political system itself.

While Chinese politics since the second half of the 1960s continues to be a "politics of conflict" (see pp. 176–78 above), the high command of the party in the post-GPCR era displayed an outstanding new feature—it was split into two polarized, rival factions. One faction consisted of the radicals who promoted the GPCR and rose to power because of it; they were ardent defenders of Mao's revolutionary values and, during the 1970s, operated much like an "opposition party" within the CCP seeking to capture control of the supreme leadership. The other faction was composed of the conservative veteran officials who were targets of GPCR political assaults, which took a heavy toll; after the early 1970s, however, they gradually staged a political comeback and managed to retain control over many of the policy-making functions. These two major rival groups were not only divided over basic national priorities, but there was also deep personal animosity between them. It remains to be seen whether the ouster of the radicals would reduce and remove the polarization and the atmosphere of personal antagonism and recrimination from the leadership.

Since the second half of the 1960s, the Chinese leadership has had a crisis of authority, and this seems to have deepened in the past few years. The wild charges, both political and personal, leveled against large numbers of disgraced officials during the Cultural Revolution in 1966–69 and during the anti-Lin Piao campaign in 1972–74 as well as those made against the radicals since October 1976 must have severely tarnished the image of the Chinese leadership and undermined Chinese people's respect for and confidence in their leaders. As the Chinese leadership has rewritten history and changed its line so frequently and so blatantly, it cannot but suffer from a severe credibility gap; consequently, its authority and power to persuade have been eroded further.

More important, Mao's exhortation that "rebellion is justified" and his mobilization of the Red Guards in 1966–67 to attack the party organizations, as well as the radicals' open instigation of the revolutionaries "to go against the tide" (i.e., to fight the Establishment)—a sanction explicitly inscribed in the 1973 Party Constitution as a Marxist principle—have had the effect of inculcating defiance against and contempt for authority in China and of further undermining the regime's ability to command compliance from the population. The numerous reports of breakdowns in law and order, bank robberies, crimes, labor strikes, lax labor discipline, and widespread executions of criminals, not to mention the riots in Peking and other Chinese cities in 1976, are indicative of the deepening authority crisis and erosion of discipline and order in Chinese society.

Furthermore, due to the GPCR, the balance of power between the central and provincial authorities has shifted in favor of the latter and the degree of provincial independence has grown considerably, as the political turmoil impaired much of China's central control mechanism and substantially weakened the capability of Peking to elicit compliance from provincial authorities (most of which were dominated by military men). In the first half of the 1970s, Mao, Chou, and Teng tried hard to dislodge the military from the provincial administration and to reassert central control, and their efforts had considerable success. However, the intensified leadership conflicts in 1975–76 may have halted the trend toward recentralization. The radicals' attempt to enlist local support appears to have given at least some provincial authorities greater room to maneuver and undercut the ability of the center to provide unified and coherent guidance.[35]

The passing of towering figures like Mao and Chou and the fact that Chairman Hua Kuo-feng still lacks real national stature inevitably reduce the authority and prestige of the central leadership in the eyes of provincial powerholders. True, Teng Hsiao-p'ing commands wide support and respect among the provincial rulers and PLA leaders and, since his rehabilitation in July 1977, has actively reorganized leadership organs at all levels to tighten control. But how long will Teng, who is over seventy-four years old, stay in the political picture?

The GPCR has also resulted in extensive military participation in politics and may have thus opened the floodgate to further military involvement in resolution of leadership conflicts in the future. The participation of PLA units in the coup of October 1976 shows that the military can easily thrust itself into the political arena again. In the last decade, the Chinese political system has begun to display incipient tendencies of a praetorian regime.[36] If the current leadership fails to arrest and remove the trend toward praetorian politics, the military is likely to intervene again in future political conflicts, for the system does not maintain strict civil-military institutional boundaries and, as Ellis Joffe correctly points out, "the precedent has been set for military intervention in a political struggle."[37]

Appendix A
Major Positions Held by
Chinese Communist Officials

Chang Ch'un-ch'iao* Director of Literary Work Department (1956–63), director of Propaganda Department (1963–66), secretary (1965–66) of the Shanghai CCP Committee, deputy director of the CRG (1966–68); currently member of the Politburo Standing Committee, first secretary of the Shanghai CCP Committee, and director of the Shanghai Revolutionary Committee; since 1975, vice-premier and director of the PLA General Political Department. He was purged in October 1976.

Chang Chung-liang† First secretary of the Kansu CCP Committee until his purge in 1961; rehabilitated and appointed vice-chairman of Kiangsu RC in 1977.

Chang P'ing-hua†* First secretary of Hunan (1959–66); purged in 1966 but rehabilitated after 1971; second party secretary of Hunan 1973–76; appointed director of CC Propaganda Department in 1977.

Chang T'ing-hua (general)* Veteran PLA officer; inactive during the GPCR; appointed commander of Air Force in 1976; elected member of the Politburo in August 1977.

Chang Wen-t'ien‡ Until his political disgrace in 1959, alternate member of the Politburo and the senior vice-minister of foreign affairs.

Ch'en Cheng-jen† Deputy director of the State Council Seventh Agriculture and Forestry Staff Office (1955–66), deputy director of the CC Rural Work Department of the CCP (1956–64), minister of agricultural machinery

---

*Member of the Tenth CC of the CCP elected in August 1973.
†Alternate member of the Eight CC of the CCP elected in 1956 and 1958.
‡Member of the Eight CC of the CCP elected in 1956.
§Alternate member of the Tenth CC elected in August 1973.
★Elected to the Eleventh CC in August 1977.

(1959–65), minister of the Eighth Ministry of Machine Building (1965–66); suspended during the GPCR; deceased in 1973.

Ch'en Hsi-lien (general)★   Commander of Shenyang MR (1959–73); commander of Peking MR since December 1973; vice-premier since January 1975; member of the Politburo since 1969.

Ch'en Huang-mei   Vice-minister of culture (1963–65); purged in 1965.

Ch'en Mang-yuan†   Dismissed as first secretary of the Kwangsi-Chuang CCP Committee in 1957; appointed vice-minister of state farms and land reclamation in 1963.

Ch'en Mu-hua (f)★   Elected alternate Politburo member in August 1977; a ranking official of Commission for Economic Relations with Foreign Countries for two decades, named its minister in 1977; appointed vice-premier in 1978.

Ch'en Po-ta‡   Alternate member of the Politburo (1956–66), editor-in-chief of *Hung Ch'i* (1958–67), member of the Politburo Standing Committee (1966–70), director of the CRG (1966–69); until his purge in 1970 was Mao's brain-truster and ghost-writer.

Ch'en yi (marshal)‡   Vice-premier (1954–72), minister of foreign affairs (1958–67), member of the Politburo (1956–69); in political eclipse during the GPCR; deceased in 1972.

Ch'en Yun*‡★   Currently vice-chairman of NPC; vice-premier (1949–74); member of the Politburo (1945–69), vice-chairman of the CC and Politburo (1956–66); politically inactive since 1962.

Ch'en Yung-kuei★   A model peasant from the model Tachai Brigade; member of the Politburo since 1973 and vice-premier since January 1975.

Chi Teng-kuei★   Provincial official of Honan until 1969; elected alternate Politburo member in 1969, elevated to full member in 1973 and reelected 1977; appointed vice-premier in 1975.

Chia T'o-fu‡   Deputy director of State Council Fourth Staff Office and minister of light industry (1954–59); purged in 1959.

Chiang Ch'ing (wife of Mao Tse-tung)★   First deputy director of the CRG (1966–69), member of the Politburo after 1969. She was purged in October 1976.

Chou En-lai*‡   Premier since 1949; vice-chairman of the party (1956–66, 1973–76). He died in January 1976.

Chou Hsiao-chou†   Purged as first secretary of the Hunan CCP Committee in 1959.

Chou Yang   Deputy director of the CC Propaganda Department until 1966—widely regarded as China's "cultural czar"; purged during the GPCR and reappeared in public in 1977.

Chu Teh (marshal)*‡ "Father" of the Red Army, vice-chairman of the Republic (1949–59), chairman of the Standing Committee of the NPC since 1959, vice-chairman of the party (1956–66; 1973–76); died in 1976.

Fang Yi★ Minister of Commission for Economic Relations With Foreign Countries 1964–77; appointed vice-president of the Chinese Academy of Science and elevated to member of the Politburo in 1977; named vice-premier and director of State Scientific and Technological Commission in 1978.

Fu Ts'ung-pi (general)★ Commander of the Peking garrison (1966–68); purged in 1968; partially rehabilitated in 1974; reappointed commander of Peking garrison in 1977.

Hsi Chung-hsun‡ Secretary-general of the State Council (1954–62), vice-premier (1959–62); purged in 1962.

Hsia Yen★ Vice-chairman, All-China Federation of Literary and Art circles (1960–65), vice-minister of culture (1954–65); purged in 1965.

Hsiao Hua (general)‡★ Director of the PLA General Political Department (1964–67); purged in 1967; currently political commissar of the Lanchow MR.

Hsiao K'o (general)‡§★ Vice-minister of defense (1954–59), vice-minister of the Ministry of State Farms and Land Reclamation (1959–66); in eclipse during the GPCR, but partially rehabilitated in 1973.

Hsu Hsiang-ch'ien (marshal)*‡★ Vice-chairman of the NPC since 1965, also concurrently vice-chairman of the Military Affairs Committee of the CCP; elected Politburo member in 1977; named vice-premier and minister of defense in 1978.

Hsu Li-ch'un Deputy editor-in-chief of *Hung Chi* (1958–66), deputy director of the party's Propaganda Department (1961–66), P'eng Ch'en's brain-truster; purged in 1966; rehabilitated in 1975.

Hsu Shih-yu (general)★ Commander of Nanking MR until 1973; commander of Canton MR since December 1973; member of the Politburo since 1969.

Hsueh Mu-ch'iao Economist, vice-chairman of the State Planning Commission (1954–66), chairman of the National Commodity Price Commission (1963–66); purged in 1966; rehabilitated in 1977.

Hu Ch'iao-mu‡ Party theoretician, alternate secretary of the CC Secretariat (1956–66); purged in 1966 but partially rehabilitated in 1974; named president of the Academy of Social Sciences in 1977.

Hu Yao-pang★ First secretary of Communist Youth League until 1966; purged during the GPCR; currently director of the CC Organization Department and vice-president of the CC Party School.

Hua Kuo-feng* Provincial official of Hunan in the 1950s and 1960s; elected first secretary of Hunan in 1970; elected member of Politburo in 1973; appointed vice-premier and concurrently Minister of Public Security in January 1975; appointed acting premier February 1976; appointed premier and first vice-chairman of the party in April 1976; elected chairman of the party and of its MAC in October 1976.

Huang Huo-ch'ing† Mayor of Tientsin (1955–58), first secretary of the Liaoning CCP Committee (1958–67); purged in 1967; rehabilitated and appointed chief procurator in 1978.

Huang K'o-cheng (general) PLA chief of staff (1958–59), secretary of Secretariat (1956–59); relieved of these positions in 1959; appointed vice-governor of Shansi in 1964; in eclipse during GPCR; rehabilitated in 1977.

Hung Hsueh-chih (general)† Korean War veteran, director of General Rear Service Department (1956–59); purged in 1959; reappeared in 1974.

Jao Shu-shih First secretary of the CCP East China Bureau (1949–54), director of the CCP Organization Department (1952–54); purged in 1954.

K'ang Sheng*‡ Member of the Politburo (1945–56), alternate member of the Politburo (1956–66), secretary of the CC Secretariat (1962–66), member of the Politburo Standing Committee since 1966, vice-chairman of the party 1973–75; died December 1975.

Kao Kang Vice-chairman of the Central People's Government and member of the Politburo (1949–54), chairman of the Northeast People's Government (1949–54), first secretary of the CCP Northeast Bureau (1949–54), chairman of the State Planning Commission (1952–54); purged in 1954 and committed suicide.

Keng Piao* Longtime foreign service worker and once China's ambassador to Burma; director of CC International Liaison Department since 1969; elected to the Politburo in 1977; named vice-premier in 1978.

K'o Ch'ing-shih‡ First secretary of the Shanghai CCP Committee (1955–65), member of the Politburo (1958–65), first secretary of the CCP East China Bureau (1960–65), vice-premier (1965); died in 1965.

K'uai Ta-fu Maoist Red Guard leader in Tsinghua University.

Kuan Feng Writer on Chinese philosophy, member of the CRG (1966–67), deputy director of the All-PLA Cultural Revolution Group (1966–67); purged in 1967.

Kuo Liang Secretary-general (1958) and alternate secretary of the Fukien CCP Committee.

Li Ching-ch'üan*‡* First secretary of the Szechuan CCP Committee (1953–65), member of the Politburo (1958–67), first secretary of the party's

Southwest China Bureau (1960–67); purged during the GPCR but partially rehabilitated in 1973, appointed vice-chairman of NPC in 1975.

Li Fu-ch'un*‡ Vice-premier (1954–74), chairman of the State Planning Commission of the State Council (1954–67), member of the Politburo (1956–69), secretary of the CCP Secretariat (1958–66), politically inactive since 1967; died in 1975.

Li Hsien-nien* Vice-premier and minister of finance since 1954, member of the Politburo since 1956, secretary of the CCP Secretariat (1958–66), reappointed vice-premier in 1975. Elected party vice-chairman in August 1977.

Li Hsueh-feng‡ Member of the CCP Secretariat (1956–66), first secretary of the CCP North China Bureau (1960–66), first secretary of the Peking CCP Committee (1966–67), director of Hopeh RC (1968–70), alternate member of the Politburo (1969–70); purged in 1970.

Li Teh-sheng (general)* Commander of the Twelfth Army in the mid-1960s; chairman of Anhwei Revolutionary Committee 1967–72; elected alternate member of Politburo in 1969 and elevated to full Politburo member in 1973; director of PLA General Political Department 1970–73; commander of Shenyang MR since December 1973.

Liao Lu-yen† Deputy director of the party's Rural Work Department (1953–64), minister of agriculture (1954–66); purged during the GPCR; reappeared in 1977.

Liao Mo-sha Director of the United Front Work Department of the Peking CCP Committee (1961–66); purged in 1966.

Lin Piao (marshal)‡ Vice-premier (1954–71), member of the Politburo (1955–71), vice-chairman of the party (1958–71), minister of defense (1959–71), senior vice-chairman of the Military Affairs Committee of the party (1959–71), designated Mao's successor in 1966; purged and allegedly died in an airplane crash in 1971.

Lin Po-ch'u‡ Member of the Politburo (1956–60); died in 1960.

Liu Chien-hsun*†* First secretary of the Kwangsi CCP Committee (1956–61), first secretary of the Honan CCP Committee (1961–66), secretary of the Peking CCP Committee (1966–67), director of the Honan RC since 1968, first secretary of the Honan CCP Committee since 1971.

Liu Po-cheng (marshal)* Member of the Politburo since 1956; politically inactive due to poor health.

Liu Shao-ch'i‡ Vice-chairman of the Central People's Government (1949–54), chairman of the Standing Committee of the NPC (1954–59), chairman of the Republic (1959–66), senior vice-chairman of the party (1956–66); purged in 1966; died in 1972.

Lo Jui-ch'ing (general)‡★   Minister of public security (1949–59), vice-premier (1959–66), PLA chief of staff (1959–66), secretary of CCP Secretariat (1962–66); purged in 1965–66; rehabilitated in 1975; currently a member of the MAC Standing Committee.

Lu P'ing   President of Peking University (1960–66); purged in 1966 for suppressing student movement in GPCR; partially rehabilitated in 1975.

Lu Ting-yi‡   Alternate member of the Politburo (1956–66), director of the CCP Propaganda Department (1956–66), vice-premier (1959–66), minister of culture (1965–66), secretary of the CCP Secretariat (1962–66), member of the Five-Man Cultural Revolution Group under P'eng Ch'en; purged in 1966.

Mao Tse-tung*‡   Chairman of the party 1945–76, chairman of the Military Affairs Committee of the party 1935–76, chairman of the Central People's Government (1949–54), chairman of the Republic (1954–59). He died in September 1976.

Mao Tun (Shen Yen-ping)   Minister of culture (1949–65), chairman of the Union of Chinese Writers (1953–65).

Ni Chih-fu★   Director of the Peking Trade Union Federation since 1973; alternate member of the Politburo in 1973, elevated to a full member in 1977; concurrently second party secretary of Peking.

Nieh Jung-chen (marshal)*‡★   Vice-premier 1956–66, chairman of National Scientific-Technological Commission 1958–67, vice-chairman of the CCP Military Affairs Committee since the 1950s; elected Politburo member in 1977.

Nieh Yuan-tzu   Instructor at Peking University, her big-character poster on 25 May 1966 kindled the fire of GPCR at Peking University, deputy director of Peking RC (1967–70), alternate member of the CC (1969–70); purged in 1970.

P'an Fu-sheng†   First secretary of the Honan CCP Committee (1953–58); purged in 1958 for rightist deviations; first secretary of the Heilunkiang CCP Committee (1966–67), director of the Heilunkiang RC (1967–70); purged in late 1970.

P'eng Chen‡   First (ranking) secretary of the Peking CCP Committee (1949–66), mayor of Peking (1951–66), member of the Politburo (1949–66), secretary of the CCP Secretariat (1956–66), head of the Five-Man Cultural Revolution Group (1964–66); purged in 1966.

P'eng Chung★   First party secretary of Nanking until 1966; elevated to first party secretary of Kiangsu in 1974; transferred to Shanghai as its third party secretary in November 1976; elected to Politburo in August 1977.

P'eng Teh-huai (marshal)‡   Commander of the Chinese People's Volunteers in Korea (1950–54), member of the Politburo (1954–66), vice-premier (1954–65), minister of defense (1954–59); in political disgrace since August 1959.

Po I-po   Chairman of State Construction Commission (1954–56), chairman of State Economic Commission (1956–66), vice-premier (1956–66), alternate member of the Politburo (1956–66), director of the State Council Industry and Communications Staff Office (1961–66); purged in 1966.

Saifudin★   Top provincial official of Sinkiang since 1949; promoted to first party secretary of Sinkiang in 1973; alternate Politburo member since 1973; dismissed from Sinkiang provincial post in 1978.

Shao Ch'uan-lin   Writer, vice-chairman of the Union of Chinese Writers (1960–65); purged in 1965.

Su Chen-hua (general)★   First political commissar of the Navy in 1966; disgraced during the GPCR but reinstated to the Navy post in 1972 and elected alternate Politburo member in 1973; appointed first party secretary of Shanghai in November 1976; elected member of the Politburo in August 1977.

Sung Jen-chiung (general)‡   Minister of Third—Second Ministry of Machine Building (1956–60), first secretary of CCP Northeast China Bureau (1960–67); purged in 1968; partially rehabilitated in 1974; appointed minister of Seventh Ministry of Machine Building in 1978.

Sung Shao-wen   Vice-chairman of the State Planning Commission (1962–66).

T'an Cheng (general)‡   Director of the PLA General Political Department (GPD) (1956–60), secretary of the CCP Secretariat (1956–62), deputy director of the PLA GPD (1960–64), vice-minister of defense (1956–65), vice-governor of Fukien (1965–66); public appearance in 1975 was first in nine years.

T'an Chen-lin*‡★   Governor of Chekiang (1951–52), governor of Kiangsu (1952–54), secretary of CCP Secretariat (1956–66), member of the Politburo (1958–67), vice-premier (1959–67), director of State Council Agriculture and Forestry Staff Office (1962–67); purged in 1967 but partially rehabilitated in 1973 and appointed vice-chairman of NPC in 1975.

T'ao Chu‡   Ranking (first) secretary of the Kwangtung CCP Committee (1955–65), first secretary of CCP Central-South China Bureau (1960–66); vice-premier (1965–66), member of Politburo Standing Committee and a secretary of CCP Secretariat (1966); purged in December 1966; died in 1974.

Teng Hsiao-p'ing*‡★   Vice-premier (1952–66), member of the Politburo (1955–66), general secretary of CCP and member of Politburo Standing

Committee (1956–66); purged in 1966 but rehabilitated in 1973; dismissed from posts of vice-premier, vice-chairman of the party, and PLA chief of staff in April 1976 but reinstated in July 1977.

Teng Hua (general)‡§   Commander of Chinese People's Volunteers in Korea (1954), commander of the Shenyang MR (1955–59); implicated in the 1959 P'eng Teh-huai anti-party incident and demoted to vice-governor of Szechuan (1960–66); partial rehabilitation in 1972.

Teng Li-ch'un   Deputy editor-in-chief of *Hung Chi* (1962–66), Liu Shao-ch'i's political secretary.

T'eng Tai-yuan‡   Minister of Railways (1949–65), implicated in the 1959 P'eng Teh-huai anti-party incident, was vice-chairman of Chinese People's Political Consultative Conference until his death in 1974.

Teng T'o   Editor-in-chief of *Jen-min Jih-pao* (1954–57), secretary of the Peking CCP Committee (1959–66), published articles in 1961–62 attacking Mao's policies; purged in 1966.

Teng Tzu-hui‡   Vice-premier (1954–65), director of the State Council Seventh (Agriculture and Forestry) Staff Office (1954–62), director of the CCP Rural Work Department (1954–62); opposed Mao's rural policies and politically inactive since 1962; died in 1972.

T'ien Han   Playwright, chairman of the All-China Dramatic Association (1949–65), vice-chairman of the All-China Federation of Literary and Art Circles (1960–65); in political disgrace after 1966.

Ulanfu★   Alternate Politburo member and vice-premier in 1966; purged during the GPCR but rehabilitated in 1973; appointed director of the party's CC United Front Department and elected Politburo member in 1977.

Wang Hung-wen   Low-level security cadre in a Shanghai factory in 1966; vice-chairman of the Shanghai Revolutionary Committee 1967–73; elected vice-chairman of the party 1973; purged in October 1976.

Wang Li   A section chief in both the International Liaison Department and Propaganda Department of the CCP prior to 1964, deputy director of the CCP International Liaison Department (1964–66), deputy editor-in-chief of *Hung Chi* (1964–67), acting director of the CCP Propaganda Department (1967); purged and dismissed from all posts in October 1967.

Wang T'ing-tung   Deputy secretary-general of the Honan CCP Committee (1955–58), deputy director of Shansi RC since 1972.

Wang Tung-hsing★   Served as Mao's bodyguard in the 1930s; top security official of the regime after 1949; named vice-minister of public security in 1955; head of the Security Bureau of the MAC and commander/commissar of 8341 Unit (Central Security Regiment) since 1950s; director of the CC

General Office since 1966; elected an alternate Politburo member 1969 and elevated to full member 1973; elected vice-chairman of the party August 1977.

Wei Kuo-ch'ing★ First party secretary of Kwangsi-chuang Autonomous Region 1961–74; first party secretary of Kwangtung since 1974; concurrently director of the PLA General Political Department in 1977; member of the Politburo since 1973.

Wu Han Playwright and historian, vice-mayor of Peking (1949–66); purged in 1966 for having authored an anti-Maoist play "The Dismissal of Hai Jui."

Wu Leng-hsi Director of New China News Agency (1952–66), editor-in-chief of *Jen-min Jih-pao* (1957–66); purged in 1966; reinstated editor-in-chief of *Jen-min Jih-pao* in 1973.

Wu Chih-p'u‡ Second secretary of the Honan CCP Committee (1949–58, 1961–62), first secretary (1958–61), governor of Honan (1949–62), secretary of the CCP Central-South China Bureau (1962–66); disappeared from public view in 1966.

Yang Cheng-wu (general)†★ Commander of the Peking MR (1954–59), deputy PLA chief of staff (1959–66), acting PLA chief of staff (1966–68); purged in 1968; partial rehabilitation in 1974; currently commander of Fuchow MR.

Yang Chueh Secretary of the Honan CCP Committee (1958–65).

Yang Han-sheng Vice-chairman of the All-China Federation of Literary and Art Circles (1960–66); branded an anti-party element in 1966.

Yang Hsien-chen† Marxist theorist, president of the Higher Party School (1955–61), promoted to a full CC member in 1958; purged in 1964–1965.

Yang Shang-k'un‡ Director of the CCP CC Staff Office (1945–65), alternate secretary of the CCP Secretariat (1956–65); in political disgrace since 1965.

Yang Ying-chieh Vice-chairman of the State Planning Commission (1954–59, 1962–65).

Yao Wen-yuan★ Editor-in-chief of the *Shanghai Chieh-fang Jih-pao* (1965–66), member of the CRG (1966–68), currently member of the Politburo, editor-in-chief of *Hung Ch'i*, and second secretary of the Shanghai CCP Committee; purged in October 1976.

Yeh Chien-ying (marshal)★‡★ Member of the Politburo since 1966, minister of defense 1975–78, currently vice-chairman of the party and of its MAC and chairman of the NPC Standing Committee.

Yeh Fei†§★ First secretary of the Fukien CCP Committee (1955–66), promoted to full CC member in 1958; purged in 1966; partially rehabilitated in 1972 and appointed minister of communications in January 1975.

Yü Ch'iu-li★   Minister of Petroleum Industry 1958–66; appointed vice-premier and concurrently director of State Planning Committee in January 1975; member of the Politburo since August 1977.

Appendix B
Members of the CC Politburo

Seventh Central Committee (1945–56)

Elected in 1945

Mao Tse-tung*
Liu Shao-ch'i*
Chou En-lai*
Chu Teh*
Jen Pi-shih (died in 1950)*
Ch'en Yun*
Chang Wen-t'ien
K'ang Sheng
Lin Po-chü
Tung Pi-wu

Elected in 1949

Kao Kang (purged in 1954)
P'eng Chen

Elected in 1954

P'eng Teh-huai

Elected in 1955

Lin Piao
Teng Hsiao-p'ing

*Also members of the Central Committee Secretariat.

†Also members of the Politburo Standing Committee; concurrently, Mao was the chairman, Teng was the general secretary, and the rest of the Standing Committee were the vice-chairmen of the CC.

‡Concurrently members of the Politburo Standing Committee; Mao retained the chairmanship of the CC and Lin Piao was the only vice-chairman of the CC.

§Concurrently members of the Politburo Standing Committee; Chou, Wang, K'ang, Yeh, and Teng are also vice-chairmen of the CC. Teng was elected to the Politburo in January 1974 and elevated to the Politburo SC and vice-chairman at the January 1975 CC Plenum; Li Teh-sheng, elected a Politburo SC member and vice-chairman in August 1973, was demoted to an ordinary member of the Politburo in January 1975.

Eighth Central Committee (1956–69)

1956–66

Full Members (elected in 1956)

Mao Tse-tung†
Liu Shao-ch'i†
Chou En-lai†
Chu Teh†
Ch'en Yun†
Teng Hsiao-p'ing†
Lin Piao†
Lin Po-chü (died in 1960)
Tung Pi-wu
P'eng Chen
Lo Jung-huan (died in 1963)
Ch'en yi
Li Fu-ch'un
P'eng Teh-huai (purged in 1959)
Liu Po-cheng
Ho Lung
Li Hsien-nien

Full Members (elected in 1958)

K'o Ch'ing-shih
Li Ching-ch'üan
T'an Chen-lin

Alternate Members (elected in 1956)

Ulanfu
Chang Wen-t'ien (purged in 1959)
Lu Ting-Yi
Ch'en Po-ta
K'ang Sheng
Po I-po

1966–69

Full Members (elected in 1966)

Mao Tse-tung‡
Lin Piao‡

Chou En-lai‡
T'ao Chu (removed in December 1966)‡
Ch'en Po-ta‡
Teng Hsiao-p'ing (removed in December 1966)‡
K'ang Sheng‡
Liu Shao-ch'i (removed in November 1966)‡
Li Fu-ch'un‡
Ch'en Yun
Tung Pi-wu
Ch'en Yi
Liu Po-cheng
Ho Lung (removed in December 1966)
Li Hsien-nien
T'an Ch'en-lin (removed in June 1967)
Li Ching-ch'uan (removed in May 1967)
Hsu Hsiang-ch'ien
Nieh Jung-chen
Yeh Chien-ying

Alternate Members (elected in 1966)

Ulanfu (removed in December 1966)
Po I-po (removed in January 1967)
Li Hsueh-feng
Sung Jen-chiung (removed in 1968)
Liu Lan-t'ao (removed in December 1966)
Hsieh Fu-chih

Ninth Central Committee (1969–73)

Full Members

Mao Tse-tung‡
Lin Piao (purged and died in 1971)‡
Chou En-lai‡
Ch'en Po-ta (purged in 1970)‡
K'ang Sheng‡
Chu Teh
Tung Pi-wu
Chiang Ch'ing

Chang Ch'un-ch'iao
Huang Yung-sheng (purged in 1971)
Yeh Chun (purged and died in 1971)
Yeh Chien-ying
Yao Wen-yuan
Liu Po-cheng
Li Hsien-nien
Hsieh Fu-chih (died in 1972)
Wu Fa-hsien (purged in 1971)
Li Tso-p'eng (purged in 1971)
Ch'iu Hui-tso (purged in 1971)
Hsu shih-yu
Ch'en Hsi-lien

Alternate Members

Chi Teng-kuei
Li Teh-sheng
Wang Tung-hsing
Li Hsueh-feng (purged in 1970)

Tenth Central Committee (1973–1977)

Full Members

Mao Tse-tung§
Chou En-lai§
Wang Hung-wen§
K'ang Sheng§
Yeh Chien-ying§
Teng Hsiao-p'ing§
Tung Pi-wu§ (died in 1975)
Chu Teh§
Chang Ch'un-ch'iao§
Chiang Ch'ing
Yao Wen-yuan
Liu Po-cheng
Li Hsien-nien
Ch'en Hsi-lien
Hsu Shih-yu

Chi Teng-kuei
Wang Tung-hsing
Hua Kuo-feng
Wu Teh
Ch'en Yung-kuei
Wei Kuo-ch'ing
Li Teh-sheng§

Alternate Members

Su Cheng-hua
Saifudin
Ni Chih-fu
Wu Kuei-hsien

Politburo of the Eleventh Central Committee

(1977-   )

Full Members

Hua Kuo-feng
Yeh Chien-ying
Teng Hsiao-p'ing
Li Hsien-nien
Wang Tung-hsing
Wei Kuo-ch'ing
Ulanfu
Fang Yi
Liu Po-cheng
Hsu Shin-yu
Chi Teng-kuei
Su Chen-hua
Li Teh-sheng
Wu Teh
Yu Chiu-li

Chang Ting-hua
Chen Yung-kuei
Chen Hsi-lien
Keng Piao
Nieh Jung-chen
Ni Chin-fu
Hsu Hsiang-chien
P'eng Chung

Alternate Members

Chen Mu-hua
Chao Tzu-yang
Saifudin

Appendix C

Known Party Meetings (1949–66) and their Possible Agendas*

5–13 March 1949. Second (Enlarged) Plenum of the Seventh CC held at Shih-chia-chuang and attended by thirty-four full and nineteen alternate members; Mao delivered a work report on behalf of the Politburo (reissued on 25 November 1968). [*JMJP*,† **15 September 1956.**]

6–9 June 1950. Third (Enlarged) Plenum of the Seventh CC;‡ reports by Mao on financial and economic rehabilitation, by Liu Shao-chi on land reform, by Chou En-lai on united front work and diplomatic affairs, by Ch'en Yun on financial and economic work, and by Nieh Jung-chen on military affairs were discussed and approved; a decision on the rectification of the party's working style and organization was adopted. [*JMJP*, **13 June and 1 July 1950.**]

March 1951. National Conference on Organizational Work; resolution on tidying up the party's organization at basic units and the "eight qualifications" for party membership adopted. [*Hsin-Hua Yeh-pao*, **no. 3 (1953): 23;** *Hsin-hua Jih-pao* **(Chungkeng), 23 October 1952; and** *Thoroughly Destroy the Counter-revolutionary Revisionist Organizational Line of Big Traitors Liu Shao ch'i and An Tzu-wen* **(a phamphlet distributed by a rebel group of the CC Organization Department in April 1967).**]

May 1951. National Conference on Propaganda Work; on 7 May Liu Shao-chi made a speech attacking "utopian agricultural socialism," which sought to realize agricultural collectivization before mechanization. [*PR*, **no. 49, (1967): 14;** *SCMM*, **no. 633, p. 8.**]

*I am grateful to Mr. Ting Wang, of the Contemporary China Research Institute in Hong Kong, for valuable assistance on certain technical points, and to Professor Michael Oksenberg of the University of Michigan, who generously made available to me a list of party meetings which he compiled. Chinese official and Red Guard sources as well as circumstantial evidence were also used.

†See Notes for key to abbreviations.

‡Unless specified otherwise, all meetings were held in Peking.

Early December 1951. Politburo conference; decision made to carry out a nation-wide "three-anti" campaign. [*JMJP*, 10 January 1952.]

15 December 1951. Politburo conference; the "Decision on Mutual Aid and Cooperation in Agricultural Production" adopted. [*JMJP*, 26 March 1953; *JMST 1955*, p. 477.]

15 February 1953. Politburo conference; formation of mutual-aid teams and elementary APC's discussed and the 15 December 1951 "Decision on Mutual Aid and Cooperation in Agricultural Production" revised. [*JMJP*, 26 March 1953.]

13 June–11 August 1953. National Conference on Financial and Economic Work; devoted to a review of the economic work of the preceding years and preparation for the First Five-Year Plan. [*JMST 1957*, p. 31, and *Thoroughly Destroy....*]

September–October 1953. National Conference on Organizational Work. [*JMST 1957*, p. 33.]

10–12 October 1953. National Conference on Planned Purchasing and Marketing of Grain; a system of "planned purchase and planned supply" of grain instituted. [*JMST 1957*, p. 31.]

October 1953. Politburo conference; the "General Line in the Period of Transition to Socialism" adopted. [Communique of the Fourth Plenum of the Seventh CC in *JMST 1955*, p. 343.]

October 1953. National Conference on Agricultural Mutual Aid and Co-operation Work; Mao asserted in the meeting "If socialism does not occupy the rural front, capitalism will inevitably do so." [*JMST 1956*, p. 93.]

16 December 1953. Politburo conference; a CCP "Decision on the Development of APC's" adopted. [*JMST 1955*, p. 343.]

24 December 1953. Politburo conference; deviations of Kao Kang and Jao Shu-shih exposed; Mao proposed "Resolution on Strengthening Party Unity" (which was approved by the subsequent CC Plenum in February 1954). [*JMST 1955*, pp. 342–43.]

6–10 February 1954. Fourth (Enlarged) Plenum of the Seventh CC, attended by thirty-five full and twenty-six alternate members with Mao absent (fifty-two non-CC party officials were also present); Liu Shao-chi delivered a report on behalf of the Politburo attacking Kao Kang and Jao Shu-shih. [*JMST 1955*, pp. 342–43.]

February 1954 (following the Plenum). Politburo conference; disciplinary actions taken against Kao and Jao and their followers. [*JMST 1957*, p. 32.]

October 1954. Politburo conference; a decision to speed up collectivization made (i.e., to set up half a million new APC's). **[*JMST 1956*, p. 81.]**

21–31 March 1955. National Party Conference; attended by 62 full and alternate CC members and 257 representatives elected from party organizations at all levels; resolutions on the "Kao Kang–Jao Shu-shih Anti-Party Alliance," on the draft "First Five-Year Plan" and on the Establishment of the CCP Central and Local Control Committees" adopted. **[*JMST 1956*, p. 77.]**

4 April 1955. Fifth CC Plenum; the three resolutions of the National Party Conference approved; Lin Piao and Teng Hsiao-P'ing elected to the Politburo. **[*JMST 1956*, p. 77.]**

May 1955. Central Working Conference (presided by Liu Shao-ch'i); a plan to cut back 200,000 APC's, reportedly submitted by Teng Tzu-hui, was approved. **[Liu Shao-ch'i, "Confession," *MS*, 28–29 January 1967.]**

May 1955. National Conference on Rural Work in which Teng Tzu-hui carried out the decision authorizing the dissolution of the APC's. **[Liu, "Confession."]**

31 July–1 August 1955. Conference of Secretaries of Provincial and Municipal Party Committees; Mao spoke on "The Question of Agricultural Cooperation," seeking the support of provincial-level leaders to speed up collectivization. **[*JMST 1956*, pp. 80, 87, 92.]**

4–11 October 1955. Sixth (Enlarged) Plenum of the Seventh CC, attended by 38 full and 25 alternate members (388 non-CC party officials were also present); "Decision on Agricultural Cooperation," proposed by Mao, adopted; measures related to the Eighth National Party Congress in 1956 discussed and approved. **[*JMST 1956*, p. 87.]**

16–24 November 1955. Conference on the Transformation of Capitalist Industry and Commerce; decision to increase the pace of socialist transformation of capitalist industry and commerce. **[*JMST 1957*, p. 31.]**

December 1955–January 1956. Politburo conference; discussions on questions of intellectuals and Twelve-Year Agricultural Program. **[Circumstantial evidence.]**

14–20 January 1956. Conference on the Question of Intellectuals, attended by 1279 party officials; Chou En-lai spoke on "The Question of Intellectuals" and Liao Lu-yen explained the Twelve-Year Agricultural Program. **[*JMJP*, 30 January 1956.]**

23 January 1956. Politburo conference; Mao's draft 1956–1957 National Program for Agricultural Development approved. **[*JMST 1956*, p. 64.]**

Late March–early April 1956. (Enlarged) Politburo conference; decision to slow down the economic drive; deliberation on China's response to the "de-Stalinization" movement which resulted in the publication of "On the Historical Experience of the Dictatorship of the Proletariat" in *JMJP* (5 April). [*JMJP*, 5 April 1956, and circumstantial evidence.]

25 April 1956. (Enlarged) Politburo conference; Mao spoke on "Ten Great Relationships." [*HCS*, no. 6 (1960) : 4.]

25–28 April 1956. Conference of the Secretaries of Provincial and Municipal Party Committees; questions of the forthcoming party congress, "de-Stalinization," and major problems outlined in Mao's speech discussed. [*JMST 1957*, p. 31; *NCNA* (Peking), 14 September 1956, in *CB*, no. 411, p. 3.]

6 July 1956. Politburo conference; the opening date (15 September 1956) and major items on the agenda of the forthcoming Eighth Party Congress decided. [*NCNA* (Peking), 6 July 1956, in *CB*, no. 411, p. 2.]

Late August–6 September 1956. Seventh Plenum of the Seventh CC attended by forty-four members and twenty-three alternates; devoted to the preparation of the Eighth Party Congress—the political report and other documents to be submitted to the congress examined and approved. [*NCNA* (Peking), 14 September 1956, in *CB*, no. 411, p. 5.]

15–27 September 1956. Eighth National Party Congress, attended by 1026 delegates; New Party Constitution, the Political Report, and the Second Five-Year Plan adopted; 97 full and 73 alternate CC members elected. [*JMST 1957*.]

28 September 1956. First Plenum of the Eighth CC, attended by ninety-six full and seventy alternate members; a twenty-three-man Politburo (seventeen full members and six candidates), a ten-man Secretariat (seven secretaries and three alternate secretaries), and a six-man Standing Committee of the Politburo (Mao [chairman of the CC and Politburo], Liu, Chou, Chu Teh, and Ch'en Yun [vice-chairman of the CC and the Politburo] and Teng Hsiao-P'ing [general-secretary of the CC]) were elected. [*JMST 1957*, p. 69.]

10–15 November 1956. Second Plenum of the Eighth CC, attended by 84 full and 65 alternate members (147 non-CC party officials were also present); three Politburo reports were presented by Liu on international situations (the Suez and the Polish and Hungarian crises), by Chou on national economy in 1956 and 1957, and by Ch'en Yun on the grain problem; summing up the conference, Mao called for all party members to "struggle, through rectification of work style, against the tendencies toward subjectivism, sectarianism, and bureaucratism." [*JMST 1957*, p. 147.]

Late December 1956. Enlarged Politburo conference; crises in Poland and Hungary and the international Communist movement discussed. [*JMJP*, **29 December 1956, and circumstantial evidence.**]

January 1957. Conference of the Secretaries of Provincial and Municipal Party Committees; questions of inflation, of balance of payments, of "reckless advance" in economic construction and international situation discussed. [*MTTT* (1969), pp. 73–90; *Pei-ching Kung-she* [*Peking Commune*], no. 5, 28 January 1967.]

March 1957. National Conference on Propaganda Work; Mao made a speech (on 12 March) persuading the party's propaganda workers to support his "hundred flowers" campaign. [*NCNA* (Peking), 1 September 1968, in *SCMP*, no. 4253, p. 22.]

25 May 1957. Politburo Standing Committee Conference(?); Mao spoke on "Things are Undergoing a Change," which marked the beginning of the reversal of the party rectification campaign. [*SCMP*, no. 4253, pp. 22–23.]

Late July 1957. Tsingtao Conference, attended by provincial-level party secretaries and some CC members; Mao promoted a radical line in economy; Mao spoke on "The Situation in the Summer of 1957," which reassessed the state of the nation. [*JMJP*, 19 October 1957; *Chung-kuo Shui-li*, no. 1 (1958): 7; *SCMP*, no. 4000, p. 18.]

(First half of September 1957). National Conference on Rural Work; discussion on the reorganization of APC system and ways to increase agricultural production which probably formed the basis of the three CC directives on the APC's on 14 September. [*JMST 1958*, p. 520.]

Mid-September 1957. Politburo conference(?) with Mao absent; preparation for the forthcoming CC Plenum and the approval or three Politburo reports to be submitted to the Plenum.

21 September–9 October 1957. Third (Enlarged) Plenum of the Eighth CC, attended by 91 members and 62 alternates (416 other party officials were also present); three Politburo reports by Teng Hsiao-p'ing on party rectification, by Ch'en Yun on administrative decentralization and agricultural production, and by Chou En-lai on wages and welfare were presented; revised draft Twelve-Year Agricultural Program, draft regulation on wages and welfare, and three other draft regulations for improving the system of industrial management, of commercial management, and of financial management were "basically" approved. [*JMST 1958*, p. 182.]

January–March 1958. The Hangchow Conference (early January), the Nanning Conference (11–12 January), and the Chengtu Conference (10–22 March), all attended by provincial-level party secretaries and some Politburo members including Mao; in these meetings Mao actively promotes the Great Leap Forward programs; "Sixty-articles on Method of Work" were formulated as a result of discussions in the Hangchow and Nanning Conferences; Mao proposed the merger of small APC's into larger units in the Chengtu Conference. [*CB*, no. 509, p. 6; *CB*, no. 892, p. 1; *JMST* 1959, p. 25; *JMJP*, 29 August 1959; *SCMP*, 1929, p. 34; *MTTT* (1969), pp. 145–54, 159–80.]

April and June 1958. Conferences on educational work. [**Lu Ting-yi's article in** *Hung ch'i*, 1 July 1958.]

2 May 1958. Fourth Plenum of the Eighth CC; preparation of the forthcoming Party Congress. [*JMST 1959*, p. 32.]

5–23 May 1958. Second Session of the Eighth Party Congress; Liu Shao-chi delivered a political report on behalf of the CC; Teng Hsiao-p'ing reported on the November 1957 Moscow Meetings of the Communist and Workers' Parties; second revised Twelve-Year Agricultural Program approved; provincial purges reviewed; additional twenty-five alternate members of the CC elected. [*JMST 1959*, p. 16.]

25 May 1958. Fifth Plenum of the Eighth CC; Lin Piao elected vice-chairman of the CC and the Politburo, and member of the Politburo Standing Committee; K'o Ching-shih, Li Ching-chuan, and T'an Chen lin elected to Politburo, surpassing six Politburo candidates; Li Fu-chun and Li Hsien-nien elected secretaries of the Secretariat. [*JMST 1959*, p. 32.]

May 1958. The CC Secretariat convened a conference to study work of Party School (e.g., educational materials). [*SCMM*, no. 639, p. 3.]

30 May 1958. (Enlarged) Politburo meeting; educational work discussed. [*SCMM*, no. 653, pp. 22, 29.]

27 May–22 July 1958. (Enlarged) Military Affairs Commission (MAC) Conference; current PLA line of military construction (e.g., emulation of Soviet experiences) criticized. [**Mao's 28 June speech to MAC in** *Mao Chu-hsi tui P'eng-Huang-Chang-Chen Fan-tang Chi-tuan ti P'i-p'an.*]

June 1958. Politburo Conference on Wage Problems. [*JPRS*, **1 August 1967.**]

August 1958. National telephone conference of provincial party secretaries; reform of farm tools discussed. [*SCMM*, no. 633, p. 12.]

17–30 August 1958. Enlarged Politburo conference (first secretaries of the provincial-level party committees and other party officials in the center who were not in the Politburo were also present); "Revolution of the Establishment of People's Communes in the Rural Areas" adopted. [*JMST 1959*, p. 32.]

2–10 November 1958. The Chengchow Conference; attended by some Politburo members and some provincial party secretaries. [*JMST 1959*, p. 37.]

21–27 November 1958. The Wuchang Conference, attended by first party secretaries of the provincial-level party committees and some Politburo members; problems arising from the establishment of communes were among the topics discussed in this and the Changchow Conference. [*JMST 1959*, p. 37.]

28 November–10 December 1958. Sixth Plenum of the CC at Wuchang, attended by eighty-five full and eighty-two alternate members (unspecified number of non-CC members were also present); "Resolution on Some Questions Concerning the People's Communes (Wuhan Resolution)" adopted; Mao's decision to step down as chairman of the Republic approved. [*JMST 1959*, pp. 37, 39.]

January 1959. (Enlarged) Politburo conference (also identified as the Peking Conference); the 1959 economic tasks and the candidate to succeed Mao as Chairman of the PRC discussed. **[CLG, 1, no. 4 (1968–69): 45 and information supplied by Roderick MacFarquhar.]**

Late February–Early March 1959. Second Chengchow (Enlarged) Politburo Conference; changes in the original commune system—the three-level ownership system in communes—introduced. **[JMJP, 28 and 29 August 1959; CLG, 1, no. 4 (1968–69): 22–23.]**

Late March–early April 1959. (Enlarged) Politburo conference at Shanghai; continual discussions on problems arising from excesses in the Great Leap and commune programs; preparation for the forthcoming CC Plenum. [*JMST 1959*, p. 45.]

2–5 April 1959. Seventh Plenum of the Eighth CC held at Shanghai; attended by eighty-one full and eighty alternate CC members; checkups of the problems in the communes reviewed; the 1959 draft National Economic Plan adopted; candidates for government posts nominated. [*JMST 1959*, p. 45.]

2 July–1 August 1959. (Enlarged) Politburo conference at Lushan; P'eng Teh-huai, in his "Letter of Opinion" (14 July) and subsequent speeches, attacked Mao's Great Leap and commune policies—a fierce intra-party struggle between P'eng and his supporters and Mao occurred. **[PR, no. 34 (1967): 8.]**

2–16 August 1959. Eighth Plenum of the Eighth CC at Lushan, attended by seventy-five full and seventy-four alternate members (fourteen non-CC members were also present); P'eng Teh-huai and his "anti-party" clique disgraced; exaggeration of 1958 production figures admitted; the three-level ownership system in communes reaffirmed. Lin Piao and Lo Jui-ch'ing became minister of defense and PLA chief of staff, respectively, after the Plenum. [*JMST 1960*, p. 159; *PR*, no. 34 (1967): 8–10.]

September 1959. (Enlarged) Military Affairs Commission Conference; P'eng Teh-huai and his followers in the PLA and their leadership in the PLA affairs repudiated. [*CLG*, 1, no. 4 (1968–69): 79; *CB*, no. 834, p. 18.]

July–August 1960. Central Working Conference at Peitaiho; decision to reestablish six CC regional bureaus made (formally announced in the CC Plenum in January 1961); problems of national economy and possibly the withdrawal of Soviet technicians discussed. [*Chih-k'an Nan-yueh* (Canton: Proletarian Revolutionary Rebels of Literary and Articles in the Canton Area), no. 3, 1 October 1967.]

September–October 1960. (Enlarged) Military Affairs Commission Conference; Lin Piao launched an intensive campaign of political indoctrination in the PLA; "Resolution on the Strengthening of Indoctrination Work in Troop Units" adopted. [J. Chester Chang, ed., *The Politics of the Chinese Red Army* (Stanford: Hoover Institution, 1966), p. 64.]

November 1960. Politburo conference; a twelve-article "Urgent Directive on the Rural Work" issued. [Cheng, *Chinese Red Army*, p. 137.]

14–18 January 1961. Ninth Plenum of the Eighth CC, attended by eighty-three full and eighty-seven alternate CC members (twenty-three other party officials were also present); a basic change in economic development strategy —agriculture as the foundation and industry as the leading factor—announced; establishment of six CC regional bureaus made public. [*JMST 1961*, p. 11.]

March 1961. Central Work Conference at Canton; a sixty-article "Draft Regulations on the Rural People's Communes" adopted; a new work style— "investigation and study" by party officials—stressed. [Cheng, *Chinese Red Army*, pp. 405–6, 466–67.]

May–June 1961. Central Work Conference and possibly a Politburo conference; the state of the economy reviewed. [*PR*, no. 34 (1967): 17–18; *CCP* (Peking), no. 12 (1967).]

August–September 1961. Central Work Conference held at Lushan (the Second Lushan Conference); further reorganization of the commune system decided. [*CCP* (Peking), no. 12 (1967); *SCMM*, no. 640, p. 19.]

December 1961. Conference of party secretaries in charge of industrial work [*Kung-Yeh Shu-chi Hui-yi*]; the seventy-article Regulations on Industry discussed. **[*CCP* (Peking), no. 12 (1967).]**

January–February 1962. (Enlarged) CC Work Conference, attended by 7000 party officials; a comprehensive reappraisal of the state of the nation—more measures of economic liberalization introduced; guidelines for "reversal of verdict" established. **[*PR*, no. 34 (1967): 18, 20.]**

21–26 February 1962. Central Work Conference (an Enlarged Politburo Standing Committee Conference, also called Hsi-lou or West Chamber Conference); Ch'en Yun presents a report diagnosing the economic problems in the aftermath of the Great Leap and prescribing solutions. **[Liu, "Confession"**; *Pei-ching Kung-she* (Peking), no. 19 (1967); *CB*, no. 884, p. 20.]

August–September 1962. Central Work Conference held first at Peitaiho then in Peking; Mao called a halt to further retreat, disputes among the CCP leaders over future course of action on China's economic development; several top economic officials (Ch'en Yun, Li Fu-chun, Li Hsien-nien, Poi-Po, and Teng Tzu-hui) criticized by Mao; Teng Tzu-hui dismissed as director of both the party's Rural Work Department and the Staff Office of Agriculture and Forestry of the State Council. **[Liu, "Confession"**; *Pei-ching Kung-she* **(Peking), no. 19 (1967); *CB*, no. 884, p. 21.]**

24–27 September 1962. Tenth Plenum of the Eighth CC, attended by eighty-two full and eighty-eight alternate members (thirty-three other party officials were also present); Mao spoke on "class struggle" in China; resolutions on "Further Consolidations of the Collective Economy of the People's Communes and the Development of Agricultural Production" and on "commercial work" adopted; the revised sixty-article "Draft Regulations on the Rural People's Communes" approved; problems related to industry and economic planning also discussed; the decision to launch the socialist education campaign adopted; K'ang Sheng, Lu Ting-yi, and Lo Jui-ch'ing elected secretaries of CC Secretariat. **[*JMST 1963*, p. 1; Richard Baum and Frederick C. Teiwes, *Ssu-Ch'ing: The Socialist Education Movement of 1962–1966* (Berkeley: Center for Chinese Studies, University of California, 1968), app. B.]**

September 1962. Meeting of Secretariat. **[*SCMP* (supplement), no. 208, p. 22.]**

November 1962. Central Work Conference. **[*SCMP* (supplement), no. 208.]**

February 1963. Central Work Conference; the SEC of the preceding five months reviewed; Mao introduced the "successful" experience of the campaign attained in Hunan and Hopei and urged other provinces to emulate that experience. **[Baum and Teiwes, *Ssu-Ch'ing*, p. 63; *CB*, no. 884, p. 23.]**

May 1963. Central Work Conference at Hangchow, experiences of conducting the socialist education campaign formalized and codified in "Draft Resolution of the Central Committee on Some Problems in Current Rural Work" (the so-called First Ten Points), a document reportedly drafted under Mao's supervision. **[Baum and Teiwes,** *Ssu-Ch'ing,* **app. B.;** *MTTT* **(1969), pp. 440–46.]**

June 1963. Politburo conference at Hangchow; the twenty-five-point "Proposal Concerning the General Line of the International Communist Movement" formulated by Mao, P'eng Chen, Ch'en po-ta, and K'ang Sheng. **[*SCMM*, no. 651, p. 5, and circumstantial evidence.]**

September 1963. Central Work Conference; reform of the education system and rectification of art, literature, and drama discussed. **[*CB*, no. 842, p. 10.]**

3 January 1964. Symposium on Literature and Art convened by Liu in the name of the CC. **[*CB*, no. 842, p. 11.]**

May 1964. Central Work Conference at Peitaiho; the system of temporary and contract workers discussed. **[*SCMM*, no. 616, p. 24.]**

June 1964. Central Work Conference and Politburo Standing Committee Conference; among the issues discussed were the socialist education campaign—"Organizational Rules of Poor and Lower-Middle Peasants Association" adopted and Mao put forth six criteria for measuring the success of the campaign—the campaign to rectify art and literature and to reform Peking Opera, and the question of cultivating revolutionary successors. **[Baum and Teiwes,** *Ssu-Ch'ing,* **p. 120;** *JMJP,* **18 June 1969;** *CB,* **no. 884, p. 24.]**

October 1964. Politburo conference; the ouster of Khrushchev discussed—Liu Shao-ch'i allegedly stated that the new CPSU leadership would be 30 degrees different from the old leadership. **[*Ching-kang shan* (Peking Ching-kang Shan Corps, Tsinghua University), no. 16 (1967): 6.]**

December 1964–January 1965. Central Work Conference; Liu Shao-ch'i's administration of the socialist education campaign criticized—"Some Problems Currently Arising in the Course of the Rural Socialist Education Campaign" (the so-called Twenty-Three-Points) formulated under Mao's leadership. **[Baum and Teiwes,** *Ssu-Ch'ing,* **p. 118;** *CB,* **no. 884, p. 24.]**

September–October 1965. Central Work Conference (Politburo Standing Committee session attended by the first secretaries of the regional party bureaus); rectification of art and literature discussed—Mao issued a call to criticize Wu Han and "bourgeois reactionary thinking" in the party. **[16 May "CC Circular" in** *PR*, **no. 21 (1967): 6.]**

November 1965. (Enlarged) Politburo Conference presided over by Liu Shao-ch'i; the questions of education reform discussed. **[*Ching-kang Shan*, no. 16, p. 5;** *SCMM*, **no. 653, p. 28.]**

December 1965. Politburo Standing Committee meeting at Shanghai; Lo Jui-ch'ing came under attack by Lin Piao, a CC "Work Group" was subsequently set up to investigate Lo's "crimes." **[CB, no. 894, p. 22.]**

5 February 1966. Politburo Standing Committee meeting presided over by Liu in Mao's absence; the "February Outline Report" drafted by P'eng Chen's five-man "Cultural Revolution Group" approved on 5 February and issued on 12 February. **[SCMM, no. 640, p. 7.]**

17–20 March 1966. Politburo Standing Committee (at Hangchow) chaired by Mao; Mao spoke on the question of the GPCR, expressed misgivings on China's intellectuals, and criticized the CC Propaganda Department. **[JPRS, no. 42,349, p. 9.]**

30 March 1966. MAC meeting; a summary of the "Forum on the Literary and Art Work in the Armed Forces" (which Lin Piao entrusted Chiang Ch'ing to convene in February 1966)—a document that spelled out the Maoist position, policy, and intentions on the GPCR—approved. **[JPRS, no. 42,349, p. 9; JMJP, 29 May 1967.**

9–12 April 1966. CC Secretariat meeting, also attended by Chou En-lai; K'ang Sheng and Ch'en Po-ta repudiated a series of mistakes committed by P'eng Chen on the GPCR and other issues, and K'ang conveyed Mao's criticism of P'eng. The meeting resolved to revoke the "February Outline Report" and to set up a new Cultural Revolution Group. **[SCMM, no. 640, p. 12.]**

16–20 April 1966. Politburo Standing Committee Meeting convened at Hangchow to wage struggle against P'eng Chen; on 20 April, Mao endorsed seven documents repudiating P'eng's "crimes." **[SCMM, no. 640, pp. 13–14.]**

4–18 May 1966. Enlarged Politburo Standing Committee Conference in Hangchow; on 16 May the meeting approved the "May 16 Circular," which countermanded the "February Outline Report," dissolved the "Five-Man Cultural Revolutionary Group," and set up a new "Cultural Revolutionary Group" under the Politburo Standing Committee; the fate of P'eng Chen was sealed; on the same date, the meeting also endorsed an investigation report submitted by the CC "Work Group" on Lo Jui-ch'ing's mistakes and problems and decided to dismiss Lo from all posts he held; Lin Piao delivered a speech on 18 May warning against a counterrevolutionary coup. **[JPRS, no. 42, 349, p. 10; CB, no. 884, p. 27; CLG, 2, no. 4 (1969–70): 43–62.]**

Early June 1966. Central Work Conference presided over by Liu; decisions were made to dispatch "work teams" to educational institutions to direct the Cultural Revolution, and an eight-point directive was adopted. **[Liu, "Confession"; CB, no. 834, pp. 26–27.]**

9 June 1966. Politburo Standing Committee at Hangchow; Mao cautioned against wanton dispatch of "work teams." **[*JPRS*, no. 42,349, p. 16.]**

20–31 July 1966. Central Work Conference chaired by Mao; the leadership of Liu and Teng Hsiao-p'ing in the Cultural Revolution attacked by Mao, and "work teams" recalled. **[*CB*, no. 891, pp. 58–60.]**

1–12 August 1966. Eleventh Plenum of the Eighth CC; the sixteen-article "Decisions Concerning the Great Proletarian Cultural Revolution" adopted on 8 August; the Politburo reshuffled—Lin Piao elevated, T'ao Chu, Ch'en Po-ta, and Kang Sheng promoted while Liu, Teng, and others were demoted. **[*CB*, no. 884, pp. 28–29; *SCMP*, nos. 3761, 3762.]**

23 August 1966. Central Work Conference; approaches to implementing the Cultural Revolution discussed; on 23 August Mao made a speech in which he rejected a suggestion to reorganize the leadership of the Communist Youth League. **[*CB*, no. 891, p. 68.]**

8–25 October 1966. Central Work Conference; policies of, and problems arising from the Cultural Revolution in the two preceding months reviewed; Liu made a self-criticism on 23 October. **[*CB*, no. 891, pp. 70–75; *SCMM*, no. 651, pp. 2, 4–6.]**

Notes

Abbreviations

BFPC	*Birth of the First People's Communes in Shanghai* (Shanghai: Jen-min Ch'u-p'an-she, 1958)
CB	*Current Background* (Hongkong: U.S. Consulate-General)
CCP	*Chin-Chun Pao*
CCYC	*Ching-chi Yen-chiu (Economic Research)*
CFCP	*Chieh-fang-chun Pao (Liberation Army Daily)*
CFJP	*Chieh-fang Jih-pao (Liberation Daily)*
CHCC	*Chi-hua Ching-chi (Planned Economy)*
Chairman Mao's Repudiations	*Mao Chu-hsi Tui P'eng-Huang-Chang-Chou Fang-tang Chi-tuan Ti P'i-p'am (Chairman Mao's Repudiations of the P'eng-Huang-Chang-Chou Anti-Party Group)* (Photoduplicated; presumably published in Mainland China and released in 1968 by the U.S. Department of State, Office of External Research, Center for Chinese Research Materials, Association of Research Libraries [group 11, reel 2, part 9]; English translation in *CLG*, 1, no. 4 (1968–69).
CJP	*Chekiang Jih-pao*
CKCN	*Chung-kuo Ch'ing-nien (China Youth)*
CKCNP	*Chung-kuo Ch'ien-nien Pao (China Youth Daily)*
CLG	*Chinese Law and Government: A Journal of Translations* (White Plains, N.Y.: International Arts and Sciences Press)
Compendium	*Compendium of Laws and Ordinances of the Central Government* (Peking: Jen-min Ch'u-pan-she)
Compendium (PRC)	*Compendium of the Laws and Regulations of the People's Republic of China* (Peking: Fa-lu ch'u-pan-she, 1958)
CQ	*China Quarterly*

Down with P'eng	*Down with Big Conspirator, Big Ambitionist, Big Warlord P'eng Teh-huai* (Peking: Tsinghua University Chingkang-shan Corps Under the Capital Red Guard Congress, November 1967; *CB*, no. 851)
ECMM	*Extracts from China Mainland Magazines* (Hongkong: U.S. Consulate-General)
8NCCPC	*Eighth National Congress of the Communist Party of China* (Peking: FLP, 1956, 2 vols.)
FLP	Foreign Language Press
HC	*Hung Ch'i (Red Flag)*
HCS	*Hsien Chien-she (New Constructions)*
HH	*Hsueh Hsi (Study)*
HHPYK	*Hsin-hua P'an-yueh-k'an (New China Semi-monthly)*
JMJP	*Jen-min Jih-pao (People's Daily)*
JMST	*Jen-min Shou-ts'e (People's Handbook)*
JPRS	Joint Publication Research Service (Washington, D.C.: U.S. Department of Commerce)
KJP	*Kiangsi Jih-pao*
KMJP	*Kwang-ming Jih-pao (Illumination Daily)*
LJP	*Liaoning Jih-pao*
Lienchiang Documents	*Fan-kung Yu-chi Tui T'u-chi Fukien Lienchiang Lu-huo Fei-Fang Wen-chien Hui-pien (Collected Documents Captured During an Anti-Communist Commando Raid on Lienchiang County, Fukien)* (Taipei: Ministry of National Defense, 1964; English translation: C.S. Chen, ed., *Rural People's Communes in Lien-Chiang* [Stanford, Cal.: Hoover Institution, 1967])
MS	*Mainichi Shimbun* (Tokyo)
MTTT	*Mao Tse'tung Ssu-hsiang Wan-sui (Long Live Mao Tse-tung's Thought)* (Peking, 1969)
NCAS	*New China Advances to Socialism* (Peking: FLP, 1956)
NCNA	*New China News Agency* (Peking)
NFJP	*Nan-fang Jih-pao (Southern Daily)*
PJP	*Peking Jih-pao*
PKS	*Peiching Kung-she (Peking Commune)* (Peking: Central Finance and Monetary Institute, Peking Commune August 8 Fighting Detachment)

PLA Bull.	*PLA Bulletin of Activities,* in J. Chester Cheng, ed., *The Politics of the Chinese Red Army* (Stanford, Cal.: Hoover Institution, 1966)
PR	*Peking Review*
"Resolution concerning Peng"	"Resolution of the 8th Plenary Session of the 8th Central Committee of the CCP Concerning the Anti-Party Clique Headed by P'eng Teh-huai" (16 August 1959) (First published in *PR,* no. 34 [1967])
SCMM	*Selections from China Mainland Magazines* (Hongkong: U.S. Consulate-General)
SCMP	*Survey of China Mainland Press* (Hongkong: U.S. Consulate-General)
SUCC	*Socialist Upsurge in China's Countryside* (Peking: FLP, 1956)
TC	*Ts'ai Cheng (Finance)*
TFHP	*Tung-fang-hung pao* (Peking: Editorial Department of the Peking Institute of Geology)
TKP	*Ta-kung Pao (Impartial Daily)*
TMHC	*Ts'ai-mao Hung Ch'i* (Peking: The Finance and Trade System Rebels Liaison Committee)
URS	Union Research Service (Hongkong: Union General Research Institute)
WHP	*Wen-hui Pao*

Introduction

1. This tradition includes works such as Harold Lasswell and Daniel Lerner, eds., *The Policy Science* (Stanford: Stanford University Press, 1951), Robert Dahl and Charles E. Lindblom, *Politics, Economy and Welfare* (New York: Harper & Row, 1953), and D. Braybrooke and C.E. Lindblom, *A Strategy of Decision* (New York: Free Press, 1963). These works, however, also are in the tradition of so-called normative decision theory, which is concerned with how people *should* act to achieve better (or best) results, inasmuch as they intend to provide a basis for improving rational, efficient methods of policy formulation to maximize the outputs of public policy in accordance with the values of democratic society. See Enid B. Schoettle, "The State of the Art in Policy Studies," in *The Study of Policy Formulation* eds. Raymond A. Bauer and Kenneth J. Gergen (New York: Free Press, 1968), for a discussion of the evolution of methodology on policy formulation in the public arena.

2. These are the major deficiencies of both local community studies such as Floyd Hunter's

Community Power Structure: A Study of Decision Makers (Chapel Hill: University of North Carolina Press, 1953) and national community studies such as C. Wright Mills' *The Power Elite* (New York: Oxford University Press, 1956), which identified elites solely by associational role or socioeconomic status. In *Who Governs?* (New Haven: Yale University Press, 1961), Robert A. Dahl offers a different model of the elite in which there is no singular interlocking elite but several elites, each exerting power over a specific issue area.

3. For an analysis of the CC members, see Donald W. Klein, "The 'Next Generation' of Chinese Communist Leaders," *CQ*, no. 12 (1962).

4. This figure was revealed by "a man very high in the Party" in an interview with Edgar Snow (*The Other Side of the River* [New York: Random House, 1962], p. 331).

5. Robert A. Dahl, "Critique of the Ruling Elite Model," *American Political Science Review* 52, no. 2 (1958): 464.

6. Michael Oksenberg, "Occupational Groups in Chinese Society and the Cultural Revolution," in *The Cultural Revolution: 1967 in Review* (Ann Arbor: Center for Chinese Studies, University of Michigan, 1968), p. 1.

7. Harold D. Lasswell, *The Decision Process: Seven Categories of Functional Analysis* (College Park: Bureau of Government Research, University of Maryland, 1956), as discussed in James A. Robinson, *Congress and Foreign Policy-making* (Homewood, Ill.: Dorsey, 1962), p. 6.

8. See Dorwin Cartwright, ed., *Studies in Social Power* (Ann Arbor: Institute for Social Research, University of Michigan, 1959), p. 186, and Robinson, p. 4.

9. Robinson, p. 4.

10. H. D. Lasswell and A. Kaplan, *Power and Society: A Framework of Political Inquiry* (New Haven: Yale University Press, 1950), pp. 76–77.

11. These are borrowed from Robinson, pp. 2–3.

12. Teng Hsiao-p'ing, "Report on the Revision of the Constitution of the Communist Party of China," *8NCCPC*, 2: 188–89.

13. Richard Snyder, "A Decision-making Approach to the Study of Political Phenomena," in *Approaches to the Study of Politics*, ed. Roland Young (Evanston, Ill.: Northwestern University Press, 1958), p. 17.

14. It is no secret that "all the news that is fit to print" is decided by the party, and many "news reports" are supplied by the party committees at various levels. Those in charge of newspapers are constantly informed of the party's policies and the leadership's intentions, and their work is primarily to promote the party's goals. Mao once instructed two provincial secretaries as follows: "It is necessary for the first secretary to take command and to personally revise major editorials." See Liu Chien-hsun, "Seriously Carry out Chairman Mao's Instruction on the Newspaper Work," *HHPYK*, no. 24 (1958).

15. These papers were analyzed by John W. Lewis, "China's Secret Military Papers: 'Continuities' and 'Revelations,'" *CQ*, no. 18 (1964), and Alice L. Hsieh, "China's Secret Military Papers: Military Doctrine and Strategy," ibid. An English translation is edited by J. Chester Cheng, *The Politics of the Chinese Red Army: A Translation of the Bulletin of Activities of the People's Liberation Army* (Stanford: Hoover Institution, 1966).

16. For example, the essence of the twelve-article "Urgent Directive on the Rural Work" was summarized in an editorial in *JMJP*, 20 November 1960.

17. For an example of this kind, see editorials in *HC* and *JMJP*, "Along the Socialist or the Capitalist Road?"; *PR*, no. 34, 18 August 1967.

18. These Red Guard groups included the Chingkang-shan Corps of Tsinghua University, the Hung Ch'i Fighting Detachment of the Peking Aeronautical Engineering Institute, the Third Headquarters of the Capital Red Guards, which consisted of radical Red Guard groups in the Peking area. Most of the Red Guard materials used in this study have come from the publications of these groups.

Chapter 1

1. Mao Tse-tung, "The Question of Agricultural Cooperation," *JMJP*, 17 October 1955; *CB*, no. 364.

2. For analyses of the advances and retreats in collectivization in the 1950s, see "Agricultural cooperativization in Communist China," *CB*, no. 373, and Kenneth R. Walker, "Collectivization in Retrospect: The 'Socialist High Tide' of Autumn 1955-Spring 1956," *CQ*, no. 26 (1966).

3. For a comparative study of the Chinese and Soviet collectivization, see Thomas Bernstein, "Leadership and Mass Mobilization in the Soviet and Chinese Collectivization Campaign of 1929–1930 and 1955–1956; A Comparison," *CQ*, no. 31 (1967).

4. Teng Tzu-hui, "Speech at the National Democratic Youth League Work Conference" (15 July 1954), *CKCN*, 1 September 1954; *CB*, no. 306.

5. "State Council Directive on 1955 Spring Farming and Production" (3 March 1955), *NCNA* (Peking), 9 March 1955; *CB*, no. 318.

6. *JMST 1956* (Tientsin: Ta-kung Pao, 1956).

7. For a more detailed treatment of the dependence of China's economy on agriculture, see Choh-ming Li, *Economic Development of Communist China* (Berkeley: University of California Press, 1960), pp. 196–223.

8. Section numbers in this discussion from Mao, "Agricultural Cooperation."

9. Apparently Mao was equating himself with the "Party Center," although properly he was not.

10. This quotation and the following one from "Struggle in China's Countryside Between the Two Roads," *JMJP*, 23 November 1967; English version as released by *NCNA* is reprinted in *SCMP*, no. 4068.

11. Liu Shao-ch'i, "Confession," *MS*, 28 and 29 January 1967. Liu was reported to have made a self-criticism in a CC Work Conference on 23 October 1966; the text was made public in Red Guard wall posters and was subsequently acquired by Japanese reporters in Peking at that time. In general, the contents of Liu's confession seem to accord with events and other sources sufficiently to warrant general acceptance, especially when corroborated by other sources.

12. Teng Tzu-hui, "Speech at the National Democratic Youth League," and a speech of June 1956, "Changes in China's Rural Economy and Problems in the Agricultural Cooperative movement," in *NCAS*.

13. Li Hsien-nien, "Financial-Economic Work and Agricultural Cooperation," *TKP* (Tientsin), 8 November 1955; *SCMP*, no. 1183.

14. See two speeches he made in 1955 and 1956 in *CB*, no. 339, and *NCAS*.

15. See reports from Shantung and Hopei in *JMJP*, 23 August and 8 September 1955.

16. For a detailed study of the Central Work Conference, see Parris H. Chang, "Research Notes on the Changing Loci of Decision in the CCP," *CQ*, no. 44 (1970).

17. See "Struggle in China's Countryside Between the Two Roads," *JMJP*, 23 November 1967; *SCMP*, no. 4068.

18. Mao, "Agricultural Cooperation," section II. In a lower APC each peasant would hand over his land, draft animals, and implements to the APC but receive payment for these as well as for the labor he contributed; in a higher APC, like the Soviet Kolkhoz, he would only receive income for his labor. His land and the means of production that he contributed reverted to the collective ownership.

19. Data on Kiangsu and Shantung from *CFJP*, 21 October 1955.

20. *NFJP* (Canton), 24 September 1955.

21. *JMJP*, 19 October 1955.

22. I have treated Ch'en's career and his relations with Mao at length in *Radicals and Radical Ideology in China's Cultural Revolution* (New York: Research Institute on Communist Affairs, Columbia University, 1973), pp. 63–70.

23. "Decision on Agricultural Cooperation," *JMJP*, 18 October 1955; *SCMP*, no. 1151.

24. *MTTT*, p. 12.

25. Twenty-six provincial secretaries were promoted to the CC in the Eighth Party Congress in September 1956; most of them had been provincial first party secretaries.

26. *JMJP*, 13 November 1955; *SCMP*, no. 1177. Ch'en Yi's primary responsibility has not been in the economic field; that he had to make a self-criticism seems to suggest that the "go-slow" policy on collectivization also had the backing of officials in other sectors.

27. *SCMP*, no. 1183.

28. *MTTT*, p. 21. In addition, Mao said: "Comrade Teng Tzu-hui did a great deal of work in the past during the long-term struggle and was meritorious. However he should not allow his merits to become a burden. He needs only be a little bit more modest, not showing off his seniority, then he will be able to correct his mistakes." Mao might have had Teng in mind when he wrote these words in the Preface to a collection of essays in December 1955: "The problem today is that rightist conservativism is still causing trouble in many fields and preventing the work in these fields from keeping pace with the development of the objective situation." *SUCC*.

29. The contents of the program were reported in *NCNA* (Peking), 25 January 1956, and reproduced in *SCMP*, no. 1219.

30. If the targets were fulfilled, the grain production would increase from 183 million tons in 1956 to 450 million tons in 1967. The output for 1967, according to the estimate of an expert, was between 205 and 215 million tons.

31. "Explanations on the Draft 1956–1967 National Program for Agricultural Development," *NCNA* (Peking), 25 January 1956; *SCMP*, no. 1219.

32. This discussion is based on information from *NCNA* (Peking), 30 January 1956.

33. This discussion is based on information from Liao Lu-yen, "Explanations."

34. *NCNA* (Peking), 29 January 1956; *CB*, no. 376.

35. Liao Lu-yen, "Explanations."

36. "Democratic" personages, according to the Chinese Communists, are non-Communists who (1) supported the CCP either during the Civil War or soon after the 1949 takeover, and (2) did not occupy formal government positions after 1949.

37. The chairman of the Republic is empowered to convene and preside over the Supreme State Conference (SSC) whenever he deems necessary. The participants of this conference include the vice-chairman of the Republic, the chairman of the National People's Congress (NPC) Standing Committee, the premier, and "other persons concerned." Constitutionally, the SSC is not a decision-making body since it has no independent powers, although it can "submit" its views on important affairs of state to the NPC or its Standing Committee, the State Council, or to other bodies concerned for "their consideration and decision" (article 43).

38. For example, *KMJP* and *TKP* (Tientsin), 27 January 1956, and *CKCNP*, 28 January 1956.

39. *TKP* (Tientsin), 29 January 1956.

40. A few examples are "Struggle for a Better, Happy Life," *Szechuan Jih-pao*, 29 January 1956; "Starting a Tidal Wave Campaign for National Program for Agricultural Development," *Inner Mongolia Jih-pao*, 31 January 1956; "Diligently Study and Propagandize the National Program for Agricultural Development," *Ta-chung Jih-pao*, 2 February 1956; "Extensively Launching the Study and Discussion of the National Program for Agricultural Development," *Kiangsi Jih-pao*, 4 February 1956; "March Boldly on the Great Development of Agricultural Production," *Yunnan Jih-pao*, 6 February 1956.

41. *Shensi Jih-pao*, 24 February 1956.

42. *NFJP*, 8 April 1956.

43. *Shen-yang Jih-pao*, 17 February 1956.

44. *CKCNP*, 7 March 1956.

45. *TKP* (Tientsin), 9 March 1956.

46. Tung Ta-lin, *Agricultural Cooperation in China* (Peking: FLP, 1959), pp. 7–8.

47. *NCNA* (Peking), 19 June 1956.

48. *JMJP*, 18 December 1955; *NCNA* (Peking), 26 December 1955.

49. *JMJP*, 19 April 1957.

50. Ibid., and *JMJP*, 17 May 1956.

51. *NCNA* (Peking), 19 June 1956.

52. Speech by Teng Tzu-hui at the National Conference of Outstanding Workers, 7 May 1956, *NCNA* (Peking), 7 May 1956.

53. *TKP* (Tientsin), 2 May 1956.

54. "Changes in China's Rural Economy and Problems in the Agricultural Cooperative Movement," *NCAS*, p. 125.

55. The Seventh CC Plenum did not meet until late August; it then devoted its efforts to preparatory work for the Eighth CCP Congress and did not approve the draft program.

56. CCP Central Committee and the State Council, "Joint Directive on Running of the APC's Industriously and Economically" (4 April 1956), *NCNA* (Peking), 4 April 1956; *SCMP*, no. 1286.

57. Ibid.

58. *NCNA* (Peking), 26 June 1957; *JMJP*, 30 June 1957.

59. "Why do Double-wheel Double-share Plows Become Dull in Sale and Suspended in Production," *CHCS*, no. 9.

60. The public was not told about the meeting until five moths later. It is doubtful that the meeting merely discussed "the important questions for submission to and discussion by the Eighth Party Congress, as claimed in an *NCNA* dispatch (14 September 1956). There would have been no need to withhold the news of the conference from the public for such a long time if the April meeting of the regional secretaries had merely been to prepare for the Eighth Party Congress.

61. For an excellent analysis of the motivations behind the publication of the 5 April editorial by the Chinese leadership, see Donald S. Zagoria, *The Sino-Soviet Conflict: 1956–1961* (Princeton: Princeton University Press, 1962), pp. 42–49.

62. The 1945 version reads: "The CCP guides its entire work by the teachings which unite the theories of Marxism-Leninism with the actual practice of the Chinese revolution—the thought of Mao Tse-tung."

63. "The Reactionary Antecedents of P'eng Teh-huai," in *Down with P'eng*, pp. 12, 17.

64. It was Liu Shao-ch'i who first revealed the contents of Mao's speech in his Political Report to the Second Session of the CCP Eighth Party Congress in May 1958, *PR*, 3 June 1958. According to another party official, Wu Chih-p'u, the meeting was held on 25 April 1956 (*Hsin Chien-she*, no. 6, p. 4). If so, it must have been a different meeting from the one in early April which produced the 4 April joint directive and the 5 April *People's Daily* editorial. The full text of Mao's speech became available only during the Cultural Revolution; it is translated into English in Jerome Ch'en, ed., *Mao* (Englewood Cliffs, N.J.; Prentice-Hall, 1969), pp. 66–85.

65. It is true that the draft program was already being implemented even before the approval by the CC. However, since the CC did not approve the draft program in April 1956 as Mao envisioned, and in light of the fact that Mao resubmitted it for the CC approval in September 1957, one is led to conclude that Mao suffered a setback in 1956. After spring 1956, the draft program was rarely mentioned in the public, and press references to it were always in an unfavorable context.

66. *SUCC*, Preface. In this connection, it is interesting to note the personal charges leveled against Mao by Ch'en Ming-shu, a former KMT official, during the period of free criticism in 1957, that Mao was "very confident about the false reports and dogmatic analysis presented him by his cadres," and that Mao was "impetuous in making decisions without first making a careful study of the facts." *CB*, no. 475, p. 45.

67. See Wu Leng-hsi's "Confession" during the Cultural Revolution, translated with notes by Parris H. Chang, *CLG*, 2, no. 4, p. 72.

68. See *MTTT*, pp. 145–54, particularly pp. 151–52. In the light of this speech, Mao's "new" posture shown in his "Ten Great Relationships" was more of a tactical move under pressure than a change of heart.

69. Liu, as noted earlier, favored or at least went along with those who promoted a "go-slow" policy in collectivization, but available evidence suggests, as we shall have occasion to note later, that Liu, as an organization man, was opposed to a policy of "thaw" detrimental to the interests of the party apparatus. As far as Teng T'o, Lu Ting-yi, and Hu Chiao-mu are concerned, they, as propaganda officials, did not initiate such policy but merely articulated the leadership consensus as they perceived it.

70. NCNA (Peking), 29 January 1956; CB, no. 376. At the same meeting, Mao, too, urged the party cadres to cooperate with the non-party intellectuals, but little publicity was given to Mao's speech. It is fair to assume that at that time it was Chou, rather than Mao, who took the lead to promote the cause of the intellectuals.

71. According to a Red Guard report, which was apparently based on high-level sources, Ch'en Yun played a leading role against Mao's radical policies; see TMHC, 15 February 1967; SCMP supplement, no. 175, p. 27.

72. Mao's 2 May speech was never published, but Lu Ting-yi, director of the CC Propaganda Department, referred to it and interpreted it in a speech (JMJP, 13 June 1956). The new themes, as reflected in Lu's statement, represented a distinctly more liberal policy toward the intellectuals than was implied in Chou En-lai's speech of January.

73. Kung-jen Jih-pao (Worker's Daily), 9 May 1956.

74. Chia T'o-fu, "Problems of Light Industry in China," NCNA (Peking), 19 June 1956; CB, no. 407; JMJP, 9 July 1956.

75. Information on these economic reports from NCAS, pp. 61, 88, 97, 109–10, 112, 128–31.

76. NCNA (Peking), 18 June 1956.

77. NCNA (Peking), 25 June 1956.

78. Two examples are "Bright Future for Landlords, Rich Peasants Who Labor and Abide by Law," Editorial, KMJP, 15 May 1956 and "We Must Treat Correctly the Youth of Landlords Rich Peasant Family," Editorial, CKCNP, 26 May 1956.

79. Merely three months earlier, the Model Regulations for an APC made it clear that "during its first few years the APC shall not accept former landlords and rich peasants as members," Tung Ta-lin, Agricultural Cooperation, p. 101.

80. Information on the congress from 8NCCPC, 1:274–75; 279; 2:45–62, 157–98, 206–24.

81. In the early 1960s, as we shall see later, after the collapse of Mao's Great Leap and commune program, he encountered another setback and faced severe criticism, but the criticism again was directed ostensibly against cadres' errors in implementation.

82. "On Strengthening Production Leadership and Organizational Construction of Agricultural Producers' Cooperatives," NCNA (Peking), 12 September 1956.

83. 8NCCPC, 1: 13–111.

84. For a detailed analysis of the field army factions, see William W. Whitson with Huang Chen-Hsia, The Chinese High Command (New York: Praeger, 1972). Andrew Nathan, "A Factionalism Model for CCP Politics," CQ, no. 53 (1973): 34–66, has provided a perceptive analysis of factionalism in Chinese Politics.

85. Franz Schurmann, Ideology and Organization in Communist China, 2d ed. (Berkeley: University of California Press, 1968), pp. 55–57, 196.

86. Mao Tse-tung, "On the Correct Handling of Contradictions Among the People," 27 February 1957, Supplement to People's China, 1 July 1957, Section 3 (on agricultural cooperation).

87. See JMJP, 18 June 1957.

88. In Kwangtung alone, during the winter of 1956, some 160,000 peasant households applied for withdrawal and 80,000 of them succeeded (JMJP, 22 March 1957). Numerous desertions from APC's were also reported in Honan, which will be discussed later.

89. For a detailed treatment of this subject, see Roderick MacFarquhar, The Hundred Flowers Campaign and the Chinese Intellectuals (New York: Praeger, 1960).

90. JMJP, 1 October 1957, p. 1.

91. By mid-1957, 97 percent of the total households had joined the APC's, and 93.3 percent

of these were of the advanced type (*JMJP*, 5 July 1957).

92. Teng Tzu-hui, "On the Contradictions Among People in the Countryside and the Principles and Methods of Correctly Handling these Contradictions," *CKCNP*, 1 November 1957.

93. See *JMST 1958*, p. 520.

94. See Mao's editorial remarks on an article, "The Superiority of Large Co-ops," in *SUCC*, p. 460.

95. The "three-guarantee" system refers to the production brigades' contractual arrangements with the APC's by which the brigades would fulfill certain targets and receive rewards in proportion to overfulfillment. The brigade would in turn contract with individual households which would be responsible for certain areas of work or the production of a piece of land. This kind of arrangement was called "guarantee production down to households," or individual farming within the collective framework.

96. Similar measures, as we shall see later, were readopted in the aftermath of the disastrous Great Leap Forward rural policies.

97. On 7 January 1957 the *People's Daily* published a letter from three relatively senior officials of the General Political Department of the PLA criticizing the "hundred flowers" policy. Their criticisms were not refuted until three months later by an editorial of *JMJP* (10 April 1957).

98. See speeches by K'o Ch'ing-shih, T'ao Chu, Shu Tung, and Huang Ou-tung, first party secretaries of Shanghai, Kwangtung, Shantung, and Liaoning, respectively, in *SCMP*, nos. 1694, 1682, 1700, and 1708.

99. Ch'ien Wei-ch'ang, a vice-president of Tsinghua University, was attacked by Wang Wei, another vice-president of that university, for having allegedly said "the blooming and contending was unsatisfactory because the line of Liu Shao-ch'i and P'eng Chen is against this policy" (*JMJP*, 17 July 1957). Yuan Jung-hsi, former first secretary of the Tsing-hua University Party Committee, allegedly declared: "Chairman Mao is under heavy pressure. A large number of telegrams has flowed in calling for a halt to the movement" (*JMJP*, 22 July 1957).

100. If this analysis is correct, then Mao's change of mind probably came in late May 1957, when he denounced the press in a secret speech, "Things are Undergoing a Change," which was revealed for the first time in a major article in *HC*, no. 2 (1968): 12–13.

101. Mao had been absent from Peking since June and returned to Peking from Shanghai only on 19 September for the opening of the Third Plenum the following day; see *JMJP*, 21 September 1957, on Mao's tour.

102. In this connection, it is useful to recall that it was Ch'en Po-ta, a spokesman of the "radical" collectivization policy, who in October 1955 delivered a speech on behalf of the Politburo to the CC Plenum, which subsequently passed a resolution to speed up the pace of collectivization.

103. *JMJP*, 19 October 1957. The original report of Teng may not have dealt with the draft program; it may have been rewritten for publication after the Plenum with a few passages concerning the draft program then inserted.

104. *JMST 1958*, pp. 520–24.

105. Based on his research, Michael Oksenberg suggested to me that the decision to revive the draft program was made at the Tsingtao Conference in July 1957. It is most likely that Mao made such a proposal there; the proposal, however, apparently was not accepted by his central colleagues, judging by the fact that after the conference directives underlying a moderate policy were issued, as noted before.

106. According to Teng Hsiao-p'ing, Mao called a meeting in July 1957 at Tsingtao attended by the secretaries of some of the provincial and municipal party committees (*JMJP*, 19 October 1957); Mao traveled to Honan and other provinces in August (*HJP* [Kaifeng], 4 July 1958; *CB*, no. 515, p. 11); he was in Shanghai on 17 and 18 September and returned to Peking from Shanghai the following day (*JMJP*, 21 September 1957).

107. Schurmann, *Ideology and Organization*, p. 205.

108. See *JMJP*, 25 October 1957. Teng Hsiao-p'ing, in his report to the Third CC Plenum, stated that the revised draft would be discussed by the National Party Congress toward the end

of 1957. The plan to convene a National Party Congress in 1957 did not materialize.

109. See Leo A. Orleans, "Birth Control; Reversal or Postponement?," *CQ*, no. 3 (1960), about the dispute within the party over birth control. Health officials in China began to intensify birth control propaganda at the end of 1954, and Chou En-lai had spoken in favor of it in his report on the Second Five-Year Plan in September 1956. Throughout most of 1957 birth control was official policy, but a few months after the Third Plenum, the party reversed its position.

110. Wu Chih-p'u, "From Agricultural Producers' Cooperatives to the People's Communes," *HC*, no. 8 (1958): 7.

111. *HJP*, 4 July 1958; *CB*, no. 515, p. 4.

112. The central government sent 81 million catties of grain to Honan as relief (*NCNA* [Chengchow], 30 November 1956).

113. Editorial, *HJP*, 4 July 1958; *CB*, no. 515, p. 25.

114. This discussion is based on CCP Honan Provincial Party Committee reports to the CC about the incidents in the villages, mentioned in passing in an article in *HJP*, 4 July 1958; *CB*, no. 515, p. 3.

115. Wu, "Producers' Cooperatives."

116. *HJP*, 4 July 1958; *CB*, no. 515, p. 10.

117. During the Cultural Revolution, Red Guard sources charged that Li Chang-ch'uan and T'ao Chu, formerly first secretary of the Southwest Bureau and Central-South Bureau of the CCP, respectively, each maintained a Szechuanese and Cantonese restaurant in Peking to gather information on central politics. The charge, which may or may not be false, is suggestive of the "game" played by the provincial leaders to keep themselves well informed.

118. *HJP*, 4 July 1958; *CB*, no. 515, pp. 7–8.

119. "Instructions of the Jungyang Hsien Committee of the CCP to arouse Masses to Unmask and Attack Bourgeois Rightists," reprinted in *HHPYK*, no. 15 (1958).

120. CCP Honan Committee, "Instructions to Cease Struggle Against the Rightist Elements in *Hsien* Organizations and Below, 13 July 1957," ibid.; *CB*, no. 515, pp. 48–49.

121. *HJP*, 4 July 1958; *CB*, no. 515, p. 11.

122. Wu Chih-p'u, "Right Opportunism is Principal Danger in the Party Now," *HJP*, 4 July 1958; *CB*, no. 515, pp. 18–25. See also *NCNA* (Chengchow), 4 December 1957; *SCMP*, no. 1671, p. 31.

123. P'an Fu-sheng, "Survey Report on the Rural Situation in Honan," *HJP*, 20 September 1957; *SCMP*, no. 1647.

124. *HJP*, 4 July 1957; *CB*, no. 515, p. 11.

125. *NCNA* (Chengchow), 4 December 1957, *SCMP*, no. 1671, p. 31.

126. Ibid.

127. Editorial, *HJP*, 4 July 1958; *CB*, no. 515, p. 26.

128. From the fall of 1957 to the summer of 1958, P'an was again on sick leave and stayed in Peking; he may have actually been suspended, see ibid., p. 14. Since the second part of October 1957, several important conferences in Honan were presided over for the most part by Wu Chih-p'u—a fact that suggests Wu may have taken over P'an's job by that time (Roy Hofheinz, "Rural Administration in Communist China," *CQ*, no. 11 [1962]).

Chapter 2

1. Organic Regulations of the People's Government (or the Military and Administrative Committee) of the Great Administrative Areas, approved by the Government Administrative

Council (GAC) on 16 December 1949. *Compendium (1949–50)*, pp. 117–20.

2. "Decision of the 19th Meeting of the Central People's Government Council" (15 November 1952), *Compendium (1952)*, p. 38. The names of the working departments of the Administrative Committees were redesignated *Chu* [bureau] or *Ch'u* [division], instead of *Pu* [ministry] as under the Military and Administrative Committee (the same name as that of the ministry under the GAC).

3. "Decision of the 32nd Meeting of the CPGC" (19 June 1954), *Compendium (1954)*, pp. 3–4.

4. Teng Hsiao-p'ing, "Report on the Revision of the Constitution of the Communist Party of China," *8NCCPC*, 1: 204.

5. Available evidence suggests that the target of the Kao-Jao "anti-party alliance" was not Mao, but rather his top associates, Liu and Chou. According to a party resolution, the "alliance" attempted to "overthrow the long-tested nucleus of leadership of the Central Committee of the Party headed by comrade Mao Tse-tung." Moreover, Kao allegedly demanded the party's Vice-Chairmanship for himself and advocated a system of "leadership by rotation." See "Resolution on the Kao Kang-Jao Shu-shih Anti-Party Alliance" (adopted by the CCP National Conference, 31 March 1955), *JMJP*, 5 April 1955.

6. Teng, "Revision of the Constitution," pp. 204–5.

7. See "Organic Law of Local People's Congress and Local People's Councils" (adopted by the NPC, 21 September 1954), *NCNA* (Peking), 28 September 1954; *CB*, no. 302.

8. *8NCCPC*, 1: 77.

9. The supreme economic planning and coordinating agency in the government, the State Planning Commission, was swamped with the work entailed in the direct planning and coordination of all the state's economic activities; therefore, in 1956, a new planning organ, the State Economic Commission, was set up to take over the responsibility of short-term (yearly) economic planning from the State Planning Commission. See Li Fu-ch'un's speech to the Eighth National Congress of the CCP (*8NCCPC*, 2: 293–94).

10. Audrey Donnithorne, *China's Economic System* (London: George Allen and Unwin, 1967), p. 460.

11. *8NCCPC*, 1: 52.

12. Yang Ying-chieh (vice-chairman, State Planning Commission), "On Unified Planning and Decentralized Control," *CHCS*, no. 11 (1958): 3–4.

13. Jerome Ch'en, ed., *Mao* (Englewood Cliffs, N.J.: Prentice-Hall, 1969), p. 75.

14. *Ideology and Organization in Communist China*, 2d ed. (Berkeley: University of California Press, 1970), pp. 85–88.

15. The English text of Chou's speech is in *CB*, no. 398.

16. Chou En-lai, "Report on the Proposals for the Second Five-Year Plan for Development of the National Economy," *8NCCPC*, 1: 310–11.

17. Ibid.

18. For example, Ch'en Hsueh, "Further Strengthening Local Responsibility for Financial Management," *TC*, no. 1 (1956); Hu Tze-ming, "A Consideration of Certain Problems in Local Budget," *TC*, no. 8 (1957); Mao Chun-yi, "Further Discussion on Improving the Working Methods of Local Planning Organs," *CHCC*, no. 3 (1957); Yang Ching-wen, "Two Problems in the Industrial Location," *CHCC*, no. 8 (1957); Liu Jui-hua, "An Exploratory Discussion of the Problem of Decentralizing Authority for Planning the Market Supplies of Goods Subject to Unified Distribution and to Ministry Control," ibid.; Hsueh Mu-ch'iao, "A Preliminary Opinion on the Present System of Planning Control," *CHCC*, no. 9 (1957).

19. Hsueh, "Strengthening Local Responsibility."

20. Schurmann, *Ideology and Organization*, p. 198.

21. This was revealed in an editorial in *JMJP*, 18 November 1957.

22. Both Liu Shao-ch'i and Teng Hsiao-p'ing articulated this view during the Eighth Party Congress; see *8NCCPC*, 1: 76, 202–3.

23. *JMJP*, 18 November 1957. The English text of these three directives is in *SCMP*, no. 1665.

24. A State Council Staff Office constitutes, in Barnett's term, a "general system" which oversees one broad functional field of government activities involving many ministries and agencies whose work is closely related; see A. Doak Barnett, *Cadres, Bureaucracy and Political Power in Communist China* (New York: Columbia University Press, 1967), pp. 6–9.

25. Ibid.

26. Donnithorne, *China's Economic System*, p. 152; Schurmann, *Ideology and Organization*, pp. 88–90, 188 ff.

27. The Ministry of Commerce headed by Ch'en Yun since 1956 became known as the First Ministry of Commerce in February 1958, when the Second Ministry of Commerce was established. In September 1958 the two ministries were merged into a single Ministry of Commerce and Ch'en was transferred to the post of chairman of the State Construction Commission.

28. See *Compendium (PRC)*, 7: 223–25.

29. Ibid., pp. 221, 223–25.

30. Hsu Fei-ching, "Centralized Leadership and Decentralized Administration is the Correct Policy for the National Budgetary Management," *TC*, no. 19 (1959): 13, 15.

31. *Compendium (PRC)*, 7: 266; *JMJP*, 6 June 1958. In Honan, funds collected by special districts, *hsien*, and *Hsiang* were said to have amounted to four times the sum allotted to that province by the central government—a good illustration of local initiative at work; see *CHCC*, no. 5 (1958): 10–11.

32. Jung Tzu-ho, "Several Problems in the Reform of the Financial Administrative System," *TC*, no. 1 (1958).

33. For a more detailed treatment of the sources and expenditure of the extrabudgetary funds, see Donnithorne, *China's Economic System*, pp. 389–93; also see Choh-ming Li, "China's Industrial Development," *CQ*, no. 17 (1964).

34. *Compendium (PRC)*, 8: 146.

35. Huan Wen, "Some Problems in Local Budgetary Management after the Implementation of the New Financial System," *TC*, no. 1 (1958). In the nation as a whole, according to Li Hsien-nien, whereas the investment funds outside the state plan totaled 4.65 billion *yuan* in 1957, they amounted to 5.26 billion in 1958, 5 billion in 1959, and 6 billion expected for 1960; these figures represented nearly 4 percent of budgetary capital investment in 1957, 23 percent in 1958, 19 percent in 1959, and an expected 18 percent in 1960. See Donnithorne, *China's Economic System*, pp. 390–91, and Choh-ming Li, "Industrial Development."

36. See a report by the Investigation Group of Shansi Provincial Finance Department, *TC*, no. 22 (1959).

37. Ko Chih-ta and Ling Han, "Outline Discussion of Comprehensive Financial Plan," *CCYC*, no. 2 (1960).

38. "The Central Committee-State Council Directive on the Reform of the Planning Administrative System" (24 September 1958), *Compendium (PRC)*, 8: 96–99.

39. Wang Kuei-wu, "An Important Change in the Method of Drawing up Annual Plans," *CHCC*, no. 9 (1958).

40. Liao Chi-li, "The Double Track System," *CHCC*, no. 3 (1953).

41. Wang, "Important Change," p. 13.

42. *Compendium (PRC)*, 8: 97–98.

43. "The Central Committee-State Council Directive," pp. 100–101.

44. Wu Hsia, "Enhance the Nature of Organization and Planning for Inter-Provincial Economic Cooperation," *Chi-hua yu T'ung-chi*, no. 6 (1959).

45. Liang Chih et al., "A Study in the Development of Comprehensive Financial Planning at the *Hsien* Level," *CCYC*, no. 1 (1961).

46. See "Fengling *Hsien* Resolutely Implements the Correct Policy in Developing Local Industries," *JMJP*, 9 May 1958, and a report on the development of local industries in Hsin *Hsine* of Shensi, *TKP* (Peking), 25 April 1958.

47. Liang Ying-yuan, "Which is the Correct Road for China's Industrial Leap Forward," *HH*, no. 8 (1958).

48. *8NCCPC*, 1 : 311; *CB*, no. 1615.

49. Liu Shao-ch'i, "The Work Report of the CC to the 2nd Session of the 8th Party Congress," *PR*, no. 14 (1958).

50. For this point, see Schurmann, *Ideology and Organization*, pp. 209–10.

51. Donnithorne, *China's Economic System*, p. 154.

52. For example, the First and Second Ministries of Machine Building and the Ministry of Electric Machine Building were combined into the First Ministry of Machine Building; the Ministries of the Building Materials Industry, Building Construction, and Urban Construction were merged into one Ministry of Building Construction; the First and Second Ministries of Commerce were incorporated into a single ministry. For a more detailed study, see Chang Wang-shan, *The State Council in Communist China: A Structural and Functional Analysis, 1954–1965* (M.A. thesis, Columbia University, 1968).

53. Ch'en Yun, "Some Important Problems in the Current Capital Construction," *HC*, no. 5 (1959), and Wu Hsia, "Inter-Provincial Economic Cooperation."

54. Liao Chi-li, "Double Track System," p. 14. "Departmentalism" refers to the principle of putting the interests of one's own unit—province, city, ministry, or any other—above the interests of all others, the national or collective interests in particular.

55. Ibid.

56. See, for example, a report on a national conference on industry, *JMJP*, 10 April 1958.

57. For example, Liu Chieh-t'ing, "Li Ching-Ch'uan is the Khrushchev of the Great Southwest China," Radio Kweiyang, 17 June 1967, and "The Evil Deeds of the Anti-Party and Anti-Socialist Element and Counter-revolutionary Double-Dealer, Liu Chien-hsun," a pamphlet published by Revolutionary Rebel General Command of the Organs of the CCP Honan Provincial Committee, 12 March 1967, translated in *JPRS*, no. 43,357. Both provided interesting data on how these two local officials protected the interests of their own regions.

58. Liu Tsai-hsing, "On Problems in Establishing Complete Industrial Complexes in Economic Cooperation Regions," *HCS*, no. 10 (1958).

59. *Compendium (PRC)*, 8: 98.

60. In the fall of 1958 the press reported officials in the capacity of directors and deputy directors of these regions attending a conference, but nothing was ever said about their institutional setup (*JMJP*, 20 November 1958).

61. William W. Hollister, "Capital Formation in Communist China," *CQ*, no. 17 (1964).

Chapter 3

1. See reports from Chekiang, Kiangsu, Kiangsi, and Hunan in *JMJP*, 29 and 31 October 1957.

2. *JMJP*, 1 and 7 October 1957, had some fascinating reports on cadres of Shantung and Kwangtung, indicating their tendency to identify with local communities and the peasants.

3. Between 1950 and 1957, China had received Soviet credits totaling 5.194 billion yuan. A sizable share of these credits was used to finance Chinese imports of capital goods and industrial raw materials from the Soviet Union. In 1957, Soviet credits were completely exhausted. For a detailed treatment of Sino-Soviet economic relations, see Alexander Eckstein, *Communist China's Economic Growth and Foreign Trade* (New York: McGraw-Hill, 1966), ch. 4 and 5.

4. *NCNA* (Tsinan), 20 January 1958; *SCMP*, no. 1700. Mao was reportedly in Hangchow in December 1957 when a purge in Chekiang took place (Union Research Institute, *Communist China, 1958* [Hongkong, 1959], p. 1).

5. At least three regional conferences, the Hangchow Conference (January 1958), Nanning Conference (late January), and the Chengtu Conference (March 1958), were called by Mao. These meetings and their agendas were not publicized, but information about the decisions they reached was subsequently revealed by the Chinese Communists. See *PR*, no. 14 (1958): 14; an article by Chiang Wei-ch'ing in *JMJP*, 14 May 1958; *LJP*, 31 October 1958 (*SCMP*, no. 1925); and Wu Chih-pu's article in *HCS*, no. 6 (1960).

6. *NCNA* (Shanghai), 10 January 1958; *SCMP*, no. 1694.

7. *JMJP*, 25 January 1958; *CB*, no. 491.

8. Ibid.

9. See reports of T'ao Chu (Kwangtung), *WHP* (Hongkong), 8 December 1957 (*SCMP*, no. 1682); Shu T'ung (Shantung), *NCNA* (Tsinan), 20 January 1958 (*SCMP*, no. 1700); and Huang Ou-tung (Liao-ning), *LJP*, 30 November 1957 (*SCMP*, no. 1708).

10. *JMJP*, 19 October 1957.

11. *JMJP*, 1 and 7 October 1957.

12. *JMJP*, 1 October 1957.

13. For example, *JMJP*, 1, 5, and 7 October 1957.

14. Wu Chih-p'u, "From Agricultural Producers' Cooperatives to the People's Communes," *HC*, no. 8 (1958): 7.

15. *JMJP*, 19 November 1957. For reports of *hsia-fang* in other provinces, see *JMJP*, 10 and 29 October, 19 and 31 November, 9 December 1957, and *WHP* (Shanghai), 21 October 1957.

16. *JMJP*, 30 November 1957, and *WHP* (Shanghai), 21 October 1957.

17. In early 1958, the Standing Committee of the NPC passed a resolution authorizing the APC's to allocate a larger accumulation of funds; at that time, the fund constituted 8 to 12 percent of the APC collective income; *JMJP*, 9 January 1958.

18. Speeches by Liao Lu-yen and T'an Chen-lin, *HH*, no. 3 (1958), and no. 6 (1958).

19. See speeches by Teng Tzu-hui, Liao Lu-yen, and Ch'en Cheng-jen; *JMJP*, 10, 24, and 28 December 1957.

20. This was revealed in an article reporting the water conservancy campaign in Honan; *JMJP*, 13 March 1958.

21. T'an Chen-lin's speech to a water conservancy conference in Chengchow, Honan; *JMJP*, 31 October 1957.

22. *JMJP*, 15 November 1957.

23. For a typical example of this sort, see a report on Hsin Hsien of Shensi Province; *TKP* (Peking), 25 April 1958.

24. Editorial, *TKP* (Peking), 14 January 1958.

25. The model of balanced economic development—simultaneous development of agriculture and industry—and technological dualism were examined by various scholars dealing with the Great Leap period; for example, A. Doak Barnett, *Communist China and Asia: A Challenge to American Policy* (New York: Random House, 1960), and Eckstein, *Economic Growth*.

26. On 18 December 1957 the CC and the State Council issued a joint directive prohibiting rural people from moving into the city; *JMJP*, 19 December 1957. A *JMJP* editorial on the same subject appeared the same day.

27. Franz Schurmann, *Ideology and Organization in Communist China* (Berkeley: University of California Press, 1966), pp. 467–72. Shansi undertook a measure which turned the entire province into many huge administrative areas based on the principle of rural-urban cooperation and provided for a "reserve labor army"; *JMJP*, 16 May 1958.

28. See Roy Hofheinz, "Rural Administration in Communist China," *CQ*, no. 11 (1962): 150.

29. Discussion of the merger from Liu Kuei-hua and Huang Pi-pei, "The Amalgamation of the Three Kinds of Co-ops," *JMJP*, 7 July 1957.

30. Wu Chih-p'u, "Producers' Cooperatives."

31. Wu Chih-p'u, "Contradictions are the Motive Force for the Development of the Socialist Society," HCS, no. 6 (1960): 4.

32. In May 1958 the party issued an official directive instructing cadres to merge the APC's; this was implied by Wu Chih-p'u in "Contradictions," but it was specifically pointed out in a report from Liaoning; JMJP, 2 September 1958, p. 4. Schurmann's assertion that the decisions to amalgamate the APC's were made early in 1958 does not seem to be well founded; Ideology and Organization, pp. 142, 473, 476.

33. Chao Kuang et al., "One Red Flag—Introducing the 'Sputnik' APC of Suiping Hsien, Honan," Cheng-chih Hsueh-hsi, no. 44 (1958).

34. G.F. Hudson et al., The Chinese Communes (London: Oxford University Press, 1960).

35. These provincial secretaries were Wang Jen-chung (Hupeh), Chang Chung-liang (Kansu), T'ao Lu-chia (Shansi), Liu Chien-hsu (Kwangsi), Liu Tzu-hou (Hopei), Chou Hsiao-chou (Hunan), and Chang P'ing-hua (Hupeh). In all, twenty-five were elected alternate members of the CC in May 1958; JMJP, 26 May 1958.

36. T'an became the spokesman for the radical agricultural policy in the fall of 1957, apparently replacing Teng Tzu-hui as the top agricultural official of the regime. K'o's article in People's Daily (25 January 1958), quoted earlier, was one of the first by a top provincial leader giving all-out support to Mao's policies and, as revealed in Mao's speech at the Lushan Conference on 23 July 1959, K'o had advised Mao on many policy measures. Mao's speech, carried by a Red Guard publication, is translated in CLG, 1, no. 4 (1968–69): 27–43. Li, who hosted the important Chengtu Conference of March 1958 which discussed and possibly decided a number of Great Leap measures, may have also thrown his support to Mao; although Szechuan lagged in the collectivization campaign, it apparently became a pacesetter for other provinces during the Great Leap and was praised by Mao as one of the five model provinces in his Lushan speech of July 1959 (p. 37).

37. The elevation of Lin suggests that Mao may have already become dissatisfied with the performance of P'eng Teh-huai, then minister of defense and in overall charge of the regime's military affairs, and was laying the ground for P'eng's replacement. One month after the party congress in June 1958, an enlarged conference of the Military Affairs Commission was convened and severely criticized P'eng's wholesale adoption of Soviet military policies.

38. Liu Shao-ch'i, "The Report of the Work of the CC to the Second Session of the Eighth Party Congress of the Communist Party of China," PR, no. 14 (1958): 14–16.

39. These articles are translated into English in CB, no. 509 (1958).

40. Frederick C. Teiwes, "The Purge of Provincial Leaders 1957–1958," CQ, no. 27 (1966).

41. Roderick MacFarquhar, "Communist China's Intra-Party Dispute," Pacific Affairs, 31, no. 4 (1958). However, Chou appeared to have regained good standing in the fall of 1958, partly because of the Offshore Islands crisis in which his diplomatic skill was needed and partly because he was a man of great political resilience.

42. T'an Chen-lin, "Explanations on 1956–1967 National Program of Agricultural Development" (Second Revised Draft), NCNA (Peking), 27 May 1958; CB, no. 508.

43. "Thoroughly Purge the Towering Crimes of China's Khrushchev and His Gang in Undermining the Enterprises of Agricultural Mechanization," Nung-yeh Chi-hsieh Chi-shu (Agricultural Machine Technique), no. 5 (1967); URS, 49, no. 3 (1967).

44. NCNA (Peking), 27 May 1958; CB no. 508.

45. See Robert D. Barendsen, "The Agricultural Middle School in Communist China," no. 8 (1961).

46. See Wu Chih-p'u, "Contradictions," p. 4; JMJP, 2 September 1958, p. 4.

47. Theodore Shabad, China's Changing Map: A Political and Economic Geography of the Chinese People's Republic (New York: Praeger, 1956), pp. 99, 109–13.

48. For a detailed study of the campaign, see Michael Oksenberg, Policy Formulation in Communist China: The Case of 1957–1958 Mass Irrigation Campaign (Ph.D. dissertation, Columbia University, 1969).

49. NCNA (Peking), 24 April 1958; SCMP, no. 1760.

50. Hofheinz, "Rural Administration," p. 154.

51. *NCNA* (Chengchow), 12 May 1958; *SCMP*, no. 1781.

52. *NCNA* (Chengchow), 20 May 1958; *SCMP*, no. 1780.

53. It is plain from the press release of the Party Congress that P'an was already dismissed from his job in Honan by May 1958 (*JMJP*, 25 May 1958); in June or July 1958 the "crimes" of P'an were denounced in a plenary meeting of the Honan Provincial Party Committee (*CB*, no. 515).

54. Schurmann, *Ideology and Organization*, pp. 467–74.

55. For example, Wu Chih-pu, "On People's Communes," *CKCNP*, 16 September 1958; *CB*, no. 524.

56. The anniversary of the Paris Commune has been commemorated by the Chinese Communists; for example, the party published a two-volume collection of the writings of Marx, Engels, Lenin, and Stalin on that subject in 1961 to celebrate the ninetieth anniversary of the Paris Commune. Many Western writings on that subject have also been translated into Chinese. During the Cultural Revolution, there was also a short-lived attempt to build a new political order in the image of the Paris Commune.

57. See "Chairman Mao's Speech at the Chengtu Conference" (22 March 1958), *Selections from Chairman Mao*, in *JPRS*, no. 49,826, p. 47.

58. According to *JMJP*, 20 July 1958, T'an attended the North China Agricultural Cooperative Conference, held from 6 to 14 July in Chengchow, and T'an announced that "the administrative methods and the remunerative system of the APC's are outmoded" and that a "commune-type" organization was being set up in various areas.

59. Li Yu-chiu, "Letter from Hsinyang, Honan," *HC*, no. 7 (1958): 22.

60. The Chinese Communists have claimed, and Western observers generally have accepted, that the first commune, "Sputnik," was established in April 1958. In fact, in July 1958, the supposed commune Sputnik was still called an APC by its party secretary and other officials; see Chao Kuang, "One Red Flag," p. 18. One *NCNA* reporter categorically stated that the commune was set up in July; *JMJP*, 2 September 1958.

61. Editorial, *LJP*, 10 September 1958, and "The Processes of Establishing People's Communes," *Haian Jih-pao*, 22 August 1958.

62. *JMJP*, 12 August 1958.

63. *JMJP*, 13 August 1958.

64. Examples from *HCS*, no. 10 (1958); no. 9 (1958).

65. Wu Chih-p'u, "Producers' Cooperatives," p. 6.

66. See Chu Teh, "People's Army, People's War," *NCNA* (Peking), 31 July 1958; *CB*, no. 514, pp. 1–2.

67. See Mao's remark in Shantung (*JMJP*, 13 August 1958) and in Ch'en Po-ta's article (*HC*, no. 4 [1958]).

68. See Fu Chiu-t'ao, "Everyone is a Soldier," *HC*, no. 10 (1958).

69. P'eng Teh-huai, Ch'en Yun, Teng Tzu-hui, Liu Shao-ch'i; Teng Hsiao-p'ing and other top party officials who were attacked during the Cultural Revolution were accused of many "crimes," but none of them was ever accused of opposing the establishment of communes in 1958.

70. Targets of major commodities, such as coal and steel, reforms of the economic planning system were also discussed; see *JMJP*, 1 September 1958, and references to the Peitaiho Conference in Mao's speech at Lushan in 1959 (*CLG*, 1, no. 4 [1968–69]: 38–39). Possibly the Offshore Islands situation was also discussed.

71. When P'eng Teh-huai and others attacked the commune and other Great Leap programs in the 1959 Lushan Conference, Mao retorted by blaming his critics for having not presented their views in the 1958 Peitaiho meeting and several subsequent party conferences. Mao castigated his critics, saying: "If they had had a set of correct views that were better than ours, they would have presented them at Peitaiho!" See Mao's remarks in "Minutes of Talks Before and After the Lushan Conference," *CLG*, 1, no. 4 (1968–69): 45–46.

72. P'eng Teh-huai, "Letter of Opinion" (14 July 1959), *Ko-ming Ch'uan-lien* (Peking: Ko-ming Ch'uan-lien Editorial Board, Peking Institute of Building Engineering), 24 August 1967; also translated in *SCMP*, no. 4032.

73. The Wuhan CC Plenum held in November–December 1958 represented the first systematic effort by the CCP to provide uniform regulations on various aspects of the commune system.

74. For example, *JMJP*, 12, 18, and 21 August, 2, 3, 4, 19, and 20 September 1958; *HC*, no. 8 (1958); and *Nung-ts'un Kung-tso Tung-hsun (Rural Work Bulletin)*, no. 11 (1958).

75. *HC*, no. 8 (1958).

76. *TKP* (Hongkong), 31 August 1958.

77. *JMJP*, 3 September 1958.

78. *Chungking Jih-pao*, 3 September 1958, and *CJP*, 15 September 1958.

79. Based on reports in *CJP*, 15, 17, and 21 September 1958.

80. The procedures for organizing communes in Kirin, Anhwei, Szechuan, and Kwangtung provinces were briefly noted in *JMJP*, 2 and 3 September 1958; also see *TKP* (Hongkong), 4 September 1958, for a report on communization experiments of Fukien Province.

81. For a discussion of this work method, see Liu Tzu-chiu, "On Spot Experiment," *HH*, no. 10 (1953).

82. Liu Shao-ch'i, *On the Party*, quoted in Frederick T.C. Yu, *Mass Persuasion in Communist China* (New York: Praeger, 1964), p. 18.

83. Such ad hoc organizations were reported at least in Shensi, Shansi, and Heilungkiang; see *JMJP*, 4 and 14 September 1958, and *Heiho Jih-pao*, 29 August 1958.

84. *JMJP*, 2, 3, and 4 September 1958, on Kirin, Anhwei, and Hupei.

85. *Heiho Jih-pao*, 29 August 1958, and *BFPC*, p. 28.

86. *Chungking Jih-pao*, 13 September 1958.

87. *BFPC*, p. 28, and *Sian Jih-pao*, 22 August 1958.

88. *Heiho Jih-pao*, 27 August 1958.

89. Ibid.; *CJP*, 21 September 1958, on Yuhang Hsien of Chekiang; *JMJP*, 18 August 1958, on Honan.

90. See directives issued by the provincial authorities of Liaoning, Szechuan, Hopei, and Heilungkiang; *LJP*, 13 September 1958, *HC*, no. 8 (1958), and *Heiho Jih-pao*, 27 August 1958.

91. For examples, *JMJP*, 18 August 1958 and *LJP*, 16 September 1958.

92. Editorial, *Chieh-fang Jih-pao*, 22 September 1958; reprinted in *BFPC*.

93. For a systematic analysis of questions of popular political participation in China, see James R. Townsend, *Political Participation in Communist China* (Berkeley: University of California Press, 1967).

94. Mao Tse-tung, "On Methods of Leadership," in *Selected Works of Mao Tse-tung* (New York: International Publishers, 1956), 3: 113.

95. For example, "How to Establish People's Communes?—CCP Chiukiang Special District Committee's 'shih-tien' Experiences," *KJP*, 10 September 1958, reprinted in *HHPYK*, no. 19 (1958): 100–102; "How to Lead People's Commune Movement?" *JMJP*, 22 September 1958.

96. In reply to Edgar Snow's question of who launched the communes in China, a "Very High Official" (presumably Mao himself) reportedly stated "the peasant masses started them, the Party followed." Edgar Snow, *The Other Side of the River: Red China Today* (New York: Random House, 1962), p. 432.

Chapter 4

1. *JMJP*, 1 October 1958.

2. Editorial, *JMJP*, 10 September 1958.

3. For example, P'eng Teh-huai, "Letter of Opinion," *Ko-ming Ch'uan-lien* (*Exchange of Revolutionary Experience*) (Peking: Ko-ming Ch'uan-lien Editorial Board, Peking Institute of Building Engineering), 24 August 1967; *SCMP*, no. 4032, p. 4.

4. *JMJP*, 1 October 1958, p. 1.

5. Fukushima Masao, "Problems Confronting the Communes in Communist China," *Ajia Keizai Jum Po* (Tokyo), no. 411, 20 October 1959; translated in *JPRS*, no. 2604, p. 8. Information contained in the article was from a report made to visiting Japanese jurists by Wang Lu, director of the Bureau of Agricultural Producers' Cooperatives, Seventh Staff Office of the State Council.

6. *JMJP*, 1 October 1958.

7. Audrey Donnithorne, *China's Economic System* (London: George Allen and Unwin, 1967), p. 47; G.W. Skinner, "Marketing and Social Structure in Rural China," part 3, *Journal of Asian Studies*, May 1965.

8. "On Big Communes and Small Officials," *HC*, no. 11 (1958): 23–24.

9. "Tentative Regulations (Draft) of the Weihsing People's Commune," Articles 4 and 5, *JMJP*, 4 September 1958.

10. For example, "An Investigation and Study of the Problems of Transition from higher APC's to the People's Communes," *HCS*, no. 9 (1958); *NCNA* (Chengtu), 14 September 1958; "To Crush Mercilessly Sabotage Activities of Landlords, Rich Peasants, Counter-Revolutionaries and Wicked Elements," editorial, *Sinkiang Jih-pao*, 25 September 1958; and *JMJP*, 19 September 1958.

11. See a report from Honan, *JMJP*, 19 September 1958.

12. *TKP* (Peking), 20 February 1959; *SCMP*, no. 1980.

13. For example, *NCNA* (Tsinan), 11 October 1958; *JMJP*, 18 September 1958; Hunan Provincial Party Committee, "Plant the Red Flag," *HC*, no. 12 (1958); and *CJP*, 17 September 1958.

14. Editorial, *JMJP*, 4 September 1958.

15. See Mao Tse-tung, "Speech at the Lushan Conference" (23 July 1959), *Chairman Mao's Repudiations*, p. 7.

16. Li Hsien-nien, "What I have Seen in the People's Communes," *HC*, no. 10 (1958).

17. See reports from Honan, Anhwei, Hopei, and Shansi in *JMJP*, 19 September 1958, and *HHPYK*, no. 20 (1958): 25–26, 108–9.

18. *Anhwei Jih-pao*, 29 September 1958; reprinted in *HHPYK*, no. 20 (1958): 25–27.

19. Many peasants showed genuine enthusiasm toward the commune system, largely because they equated the system with free supply of food and other items of daily necessity. This misunderstanding partly explained the seeming smoothness with which the peasants were organized into communes in the fall of 1958. A Swedish writer who was in China at that time gives a vivid picture of the Chinese peasants' reactions to the communes; see Sven Lindqvist, *China in Crisis* (New York: Thomas Y. Crowell, 1965), pp. 89–91.

20. For example, "The Distribution Problems in the Rural Communes (Honan)," *Lun Jen-min Kung-she* (*On the People's Communes*) (Peking: Chung-kuo Ch'upan-she, 1958), p. 117.

21. Chang Ch'un-ch'iao, "Destroy the Ideas of Bourgeois Legal Ownership," reproduced in *JMJP*, 13 October 1958. Chang rose to great political prominence during the Cultural Revolution; for his career background, see Paris H. Chang, "Shanghai's Cultural Czar," *Far Eastern Economic Review*, no. 33 (1968): 307.

22. Wu Leng-hsi "Confession," *Hung-se Hsin-hua* (a publication of an *NCNA* "rebel" group), no. 43 (1968). An English translation of Wu's "Confession" is in *CLG*, 2, no. 4 (1969–70).

23. In essence, the "Editor's Note" stated "This problem needs discussion because it is an im-

portant issue at the present. We consider Chang's article basically correct, but somewhat one-sided, namely, it does not fully explain the historical processes. But he clearly presents the problem, and attracts people's attention." *JMJP*, 13 October 1958.

24. See *HC*, no. 12 (1958), and *CB*, no. 537, which translated a number of articles published in *JMJP*. Several radicals who achieved great political prominence during the Cultural Revolution such as Kuan Feng, Wang Li, Wu Ch'uan-chi, in addition to Chang Ch'un-ch'iao, already showed their "true colors" in 1958.

25. Wu Leng-hsi, "Confession"; Teng Hsiao-p'ing and Hu Ch'iao-mu were said to have opposed the abolition of the wage system, and Hu was said to have characterized Chang's theses as "petty bourgeois egalitarian illusions."

26. For example, reports on Kansu, Hopei, and Shansi in *HHPYK*, no. 20 (1958): 103–5, 108–11.

27. "Distribution Problems," p. 118.

28. Masao, "Problems."

29. See "Distribution Problems," p. 119.

30. For example, *Ta-chung Jih-pao*, 12 January 1959.

31. The frantic intensity with which the entire population was regimented and goaded by cadres to meet the regime's goals can be measured by a CC recommendation of December 1958 that provision should be made for the peasants to have eight hours of sleep a night. *JMJP*, 20 December 1958, p. 1.

32. *JMJP*, 11 November 1958.

33. "Communique," *Sixth Plenary Session of the Eighth Central Committee of Communist Party of China* (Peking: FLP, 1958).

34. Ibid.

35. See The Rural Work Department of the CCP Liaoning Committee, "The Structure and Organs of the People's Communes," *JMJP*, 2 December 1958.

36. It was reported that the free supply system had led to extravagant consumption on the spot, and peasants even called in their relatives to share in the free meals. See, for example, P'eng Teh-huai, "Letter of Opinion," and Cheng Ssu, "The Supply System is a Touchstone," *CKCNP*, no. 21 (1958), translated in *ECMM*, no. 155 (1959).

37. An editorial in *JMJP* on 3 September spoke of three to four or five to six years as a reasonable target for the transition from collective ownership to ownership "by the whole people."

38. For example, *JMJP*, 16 and 28 November 1958.

39. A document drafted by Mao and Liu in early 1958 clearly indicated that Mao planned to step down as Chairman of the Republic but stay in the Chairmanship of the party and that the decision was known to the members of the CC at that time; see Article 60 of "Sixty Articles on Work Methods," *CB*, no. 892, p. 13. In January 1959 Prince Sihanouk told a Cambodian audience that Mao had revealed to him the previous August that Mao wanted to resign the Chairmanship of the Republic to work on theory and avoid ceremonial chores; I am indebted to Allen S. Whiting of the University of Michigan for this information.

40. The text of Mao's speech in October 1966 is translated in Jerome Ch'en, ed., *Mao* (Englewood Cliffs, N.J.: Prentice-Hall, 1969), p. 96.

41. In an interview with Lord Montgomery of England in 1961, Mao replied to a question regarding his succession by saying that it was clear and had been laid down—Liu Shao-ch'i was the choice; *South China Morning Post* (Hongkong), 17 October 1961.

42. Richard H. Solomon, *Mao's Revolution and the Chinese Political Culture* (Berkeley: University of California Press, 1971), pp. 374–75.

43. I am indebted to Roderick MacFarquhar, former editor of *The China Quarterly*, for this information. That Liu Shao-ch'i may not have been the unanimous choice of the CCP leaders to succeed Mao as Chairman of the Republic and that Chu Teh may have been a contender for that post was also indirectly suggested by Li Chi, director of the Propaganda Department of the Shansi Provincial Party Committee from 1960 to 1963 and Vice-Minister of Culture from 1963 to 1966,

who had read Chu Teh's 1959 written self-criticism (possibly for his support to P'eng Teh-huai's attack on the Great Leap Forward policies in July 1959) and had allegedly remarked: "After this, Liu Shao-ch'i's position is truly consolidated"; see *The Counter-revolutionary Revisionist Li Chi's Anti-Party, Anti-Socialism and Anti-Mao Tse-tung Thought Towering Crimes Exposed* (Peking: Tung-fang Hung Commune of the Peking Institute of Cinema of the Capital College Red Guard Congress, 1 April 1967), p. 8. It is interesting to note that from the fall of 1957, Chu Teh traveled to many places and attended many national conferences to campaign for Mao's Great Leap policies —political actions which he had not taken previously. Was he also "campaigning" for the Chairmanship of the Republic?

44. Anna Louise Strong, *The Rise of People's Communes in China* (New York: Marzavai and Munsell, 1960), p. 70.

45. Mao's remarks at the conference revealed that the Great Leap and commune programs had encountered criticism from within the party and resistance from the peasants; see the excerpts of Mao's two speeches in *CLG*, 1, no. 4 (1968–69): 22–24.

46. *JMJP*, 29 August 1959. The available evidence does not substantiate Franklin W. Houn's assertion that in the spring of 1959 the CCP decided, among other things, to restore the private plots of land to commune members; see his *A Short History of Chinese Communism* (Englewood Cliffs, N.J.: Prentice-Hall, 1967), p. 167.

47. "People's Communes must Establish and Consolidate the System of Production Responsibility" (editorial), *JMJP*, 17 February 1959.

48. Wu Lu, "Leave a Margin," *JMJP*, 16 May 1959; Lin I-chou, "Contracts of Production must be Practical," *HC*, no. 10 (1959).

49. The party later directed communes to take inventories of the unused materials and transfer them to factories that had the facilities to use them; editorial, *JMJP*, 26 July 1959.

50. See T'ao Chu, "The Whole Nation as a Chessboard, the Whole Provinces as a Chessboard," *NFJP*, 2 March 1959, and K'o Ch'ing-shih, "On the Whole Country as a Chessboard," *HC*, no. 4 (1959).

51. Ch'en's criticism may have been aimed at Mao for it was Mao who personally encouraged the provincial authorities to set up their own independent industrial complexes; for Mao's remarks on that subject, see *JMJP*, 16 August 1958.

52. *NCNA* (Peking), 18 April 1959; *CB*, no. 559.

53. See Mao Tse-tung, "Speech at the 8th CC Plenum" (2 August 1959), in *Chairman Mao's Repudiations*, p. 16; also in *CLG*, 1, no. 4 (1968–69): 60.

54. *Down with P'eng.*

55. P'eng Teh-huai, "Letter of Opinion."

56. This information based on Wu Leng-hsi, "Confession." Wu asserted that data collected by the *NCNA* were published in an inner-party publication "Nei-p'u Ch'an-k'ao" ("Internal References")—presumably only available to top leaders.

57. The existence of this medium was revealed by the PLA *Kung-tso T'ung-hsun* (1961); see J. Chester Cheng, ed., *The Politics of the Chinese Red Army* (Stanford, Cal.: Hoover Institution, 1966), p. 406. The date of Mao's letter, 29 April 1959, was revealed by P'eng Teh-huai's speech at the Eighth CC Plenum (*CB*, no. 851, p. 30). The text of Mao's letter is reproduced by a Red Guard publication during the Cultural Revolution and is translated in *CB*, no. 891, pp. 34–35 (erroneously dated 29 November 1959).

58. Revolutionary Rebels of CCP Southwest Bureau Offices, "From Li Ch'ing-chuan's Opposition to a Highly Important Letter of Instruction from Chairman Mao, Look at his Counter-Revolutionary Double-Dealing Features," Radio Kweiyang, 23 December 1967.

59. For example, editorials in *People's Daily*, 19 and 25 May 1959; T'ao Chu, "The Mass Line and Working Methods," *Shan Yu* (Canton, a theoretical organ of the Kwangtung Provincial Party Committee), no. 11 (1959), and Lin Tieh (first party secretary of Hopei Province), "On Increasing Production, Good Quality, and Thrift," *Tung Feng* (a theoretical organ of the Hopei Provincial Party Committee), no. 72 (1959), both reprinted in *HHPYK*, no. 13 (1959).

60. See "Resolution concerning P'eng."

61. This section draws heavily from John Gittings, *The Role of the Chinese Army* (New York: Oxford University Press, 1967); Alice L. Hsieh, *Communist China's Strategy in the Nuclear Era* (Englewood Cliffs, N.J.: Prentice-Hall, 1962); and Ellis Joffe, "The Conflict Between Old and New in the Chinese Army," *CQ*, no. 18 (1964).

62. "Hold Aloft the Banner of the Party Committee System," editorial, *CFCP*, 1 July 1958; *SCMP*, no. 1881.

63. "Opposed One-Side Emphasis on Modernization," editorial, *CFCP*, 17 August 1958.

64. PLA participation in these campaigns is to be distinguished from its own production work; the PLA has a Production and Construction Corps in Sinkiang and possibly other border provinces, and it assumes various economic tasks producing goods for the PLA's own consumption.

65. Hsiao Hua, "Participation in National Construction is a Glorious Task of the PLA," *HC*, 1 August 1959.

66. For the text, see *NCNA* (Peking), 8 February 1956; *SCMP*, no. 1234.

67. Cited in Gittings, *Chinese Army*, p. 182.

68. T'an Cheng, "Questions of Political Work at the New Stage of Army-building," *JMJP*, 24 September 1956.

69. Hsiao Hua, "Participation."

70. For the text of Mao's speech, see *CLG*, 1, no. 4 (1968–69): 15–21.

71. Summarized in Ralph L. Powell, *Politico-Military Relationships in Communist China* (Washington, D.C.: U.S. Department of State, 1965), pp. 2–3.

72. Gittings, *Chinese Army*, p. 233.

73. Ibid., pp. 225–34.

74. Ibid. The Chinese Communists claim that "in 1958 the leadership of the CPSU put forward unreasonable demands designed to bring China under military control. These unreasonable demands were rightly and firmly rejected by the Chinese government. ... On June 20, 1959, the Soviet government unilaterally tore up the agreement on new technology for national defence concluded between China and the Soviet Union on October 15, 1957, and refused to provide China with a sample of an atomic bomb and technical data concerning its manufacture." Editorial Departments of *JMJP* and *HC*, "The Origin and Development of the Differences Between the Leadership of the CPSU and Ourselves" (6 September 1963); *PR*, 13 September 1963.

75. This arrangement was revealed in P'eng Teh-huai, "Letter of Opinion," p. 1.

76. Mao, "Speech at the 8th CC Plenum" (2 August 1959), *Chairman Mao's Repudiations*, p. 16; also in *CLG*, 1, no. 4 (1968–69): 60–61.

77. Quotations from Peng appear in P'eng Teh-huai, "Letter of Opinion"; for an earlier study of the proceedings of the Lushan Conference see David A. Charles, "The Dismissal of Marshal P'eng Teh-huai," *CQ*, no. 8 (1961).

78. "Resolution concerning P'eng."

79. See "P'eng Teh-huai's Speech at the Eighth CC Plenum" (August 1959), *Down with P'eng*; *CB*, no. 851, p. 30.

80. Ibid.

81. "Chou Hsiao-chou was the Ammunition Supplier for the Attack on the Three Banners," *Repudiation against P'eng (Teh-huai)-Huang (K'e-cheng)-Chang (Wen-t'ien)-Chou (Hsiao-chou) Anti-Party Group* (The Rebelling Red Flag Regiment of the Hunan Provincial Party Committee Organs), 16 September 1967.

82. This information is revealed in *Ta P'i-p'an Tung-hsun (Mass Criticism and Repudiation Bulletin)* (Canton: Canton News Service of Shanghai T'ung-chi University Tung-fang Hung Corps), 5 October 1967. The text of Mao's speech is in *Chairman Mao's Repudiations*, pp. 6–11; also *CLG*, 1, no. 4, (1968–69): 27–43; all quotations from Mao's speech can be found here.

83. Mao figured at least 30 percent of the rural population were "activists" who actively supported the Great Leap and commune programs; another 30 percent were landlords, rich peasants, counterrevolutionaries, bad elements, bureaucrats, middle peasants, and poor peasants

who were against these programs; the remaining 40 percent were neutral but could be persuaded to follow the mainstream.

84. "Was he not without posterity who first made wooden images to bury with the dead," said Confucius as he thought that this invention gave rise to the practice of burying living persons with the dead.

85. *Down with P'eng*; *CB*, no. 851, p. 30.

86. See the Chinese text of P'eng Teh-huai's Confession to the 8th CC Plenum, *Tzu Kuo* (Hongkong), no. 50 (1968): 39. The specific remark by P'eng quoted here is not accurately translated in *CB*, no. 851, p. 30.

87. "Resolution Concerning P'eng." There were, however, several self-contradictory statements in P'eng's reported confession. At one point P'eng stated that his error "was not a mistake accidentally committed" but "a kind of action well prepared and organized," later on, he said that "no concrete plan had been mapped out" for his attack on the party. *Down with P'eng; CB*, no. 851, p. 30.

88. For example, Charles, "Dismissal of Marshal P'eng." When Khrushchev visited Peking (30 September to 5 October 1959) he allegedly produced an expensive gift for P'eng, extolled P'eng as the most promising, most courageous, most upright, and most outspoken person within the CCP, and wanted to see P'eng ("The Reactionary Antecedents of P'eng Teh-huai," in *Down with P'eng; CB*, no. 851, p. 14). At the Bucharest Conference in June 1960 Khrushchev reportedly refused to apologize for his intervention in Chinese domestic affairs and defended the right of the CPSU to communicate with members of other Communist parties.

89. This information was supplied to the author by two emigres from Communist China; one is a former cadre member who worked in the Hupei Provincial Party Committee during 1959–61 and heard intra-party briefings on the Lushan proceedings; the other is a non-Communist cadre member whose father was once a vice-chairman of the National Defense Council.

90. Charles, "Dismissal of Marshal Peng," p. 67.

91. See *Tung-fang Hung* (Peking: Capital College Red Guard Revolutionary Rebels Liaision Station), 11 February 1967; also translated in *SCMP* supplement, no. 172, p. 21. Another Red Guard publication asserted that Chu Teh made a written self-criticism in 1959, probably after the Lushan Conference, and the text was disseminated to the provincial-level cadres; see *The Counter-Revolutionary Revisionist Li Chi's Towering Crimes Anti-Party, Anti-Socialism and Anti-Mao Tse-tung Thought Towering Crimes Exposed* (Peking: Pek Tung-fang Hung Commune of the Peking Institute of Cinema of the Capital Red Guard Congress, 1 April 1967), p. 8.

92. In a letter said to have been sent by Mao to Chang Wen-t'ien on 2 August 1959, Mao chided Chang for having joined the "military club" and formed a "civilian-military alliance." Commenting on a "report" concerning the dissolution of mess halls in Anhwei, Mao wrote "There are right opportunists in the Central Committee, namely, those comrades of the Military Club, and in the provincial-level organizations. . . . " Both Mao's letter and comments are reprinted in *Chairman Mao's Repudiations*, pp. 14–15, 18; also translated in *CLG*, 1, no. 4 (1968–69): 34, 67.

93. *CLG*, 1, no. 4 (1968–69): 26; also see "P'eng Teh-huai's statements made under detention," *Down with P'eng; CB*, no. 851, p. 18.

94. In June 1957 Khrushchev, first secretary of the CPSU, was outvoted seven to four in the presidium by an "anti-party" group composed of Malenkov, Kaganovich, Molotov, Saburov, Pervukhin, Bulganin, and Voroshilov; Khrushchev and his supporters managed to convene a Central Committee Plenary session in which the presidium decision to unseat Khrushchev was reversed, and the first members of the anti-party group were expelled from the presidium (see Merle Fainsod, *How Russia is Ruled* [Cambridge: Harvard University Press, 1963], pp. 327–28).

95. The fact that an unspecified number of the CC members who did not take part in the enlarged Lushan Politburo Conference during July were later summoned to attend the CC Plenum was indicated by Mao's "Speech at the 8th CC plenum" (2 August 1959), *Chairman Mao's Repudiations*, p. 16; also translated in *CLG*, 1, no. 4 (1968–69): 61.

96. "Reactionary Antecedents of P'eng Teh-huai."

97. Mao, "Speech at the 8th CC Plenum" (2 August 1959), p. 17; trans. *CLG*, 1, no. 4 (1968–69): 63.

98. "From the Defeat of P'eng Teh-huai to the Bankruptcy of China's Khrushchev," *HC*, no. 13 (1967); *PR*, no. 34 (1967): 20.

99. Since the Cultural Revolution, the Chinese official sources have accused Liu of being P'eng Teh-huai's "behind-the-scene boss" and for using P'eng as his stalking horse in opposition to Mao at the Lushan Conference; see, for instance, editorial, *JMJP*, 16 August 1969, also *PR*, no. 34, 25 August 1967. A Red Guard publication, however, has revealed that Liu denounced P'eng Teh-huai during the Lushan showdown; see *CB*, no. 834, p. 18.

100. "Down with Ch'en Yun—An Old Hand at Opposing Chairman Mao," *Ts'ai-mao Hung Chi* (Peking), 15 February 1967; translated in *SCMP* supplement no. 175, 12 April 1967, p. 27. Ch'en's absence from the Lushan Conference was also confirmed by a more official source which reported Ch'en's inspection of the Chang Ch'un Film Studio in Manchuria on 27 July 1959; see *Ta-Chung T'ien-ying*, no. 6 (1961).

101. See Mao's speech at the Lushan Conference on 23 July 1959, in *CLG*, 1, no. 4 (1968–69): 34.

102. "P'eng Teh-huai's Speech at the 8th Plenum of the 8th CCP Central Committee," *CB*, no. 851.

103. The text of P'eng's letter is reprinted in *Down with P'eng*, translated in *CB*, no. 851, p. 16. One writer later reported that P'eng at one stage was a superintendent or deputy superintendent in a State Farm in Heilungkiang; see Charles, "Dismissal of Marshal Peng," p. 69. But a Red Guard source indicated that during 1960–62 P'eng frequently visited communes in Hunan, Kiangsu, and other provinces and that P'eng also studied in the Higher Party School; "Reactionary Antecedents of P'eng Teh-huai," pp. 14–15.

104. "Resolution concerning P'eng."

105. *Eighth Plenary Session of the Eighth Central Committee of the Communist Party of China* (Peking: FLP, 1959), p. 9.

106. For a detailed and excellent analysis of the campaign, see Charles, "Dismissal of Marshal Peng," pp. 69–73.

107. On reports of meetings in Kansu and Kiangsi, see *Kansu Jih-pao* (Lanchow), 28 November 1959; *SCMP*, no. 2184, pp. 28–32, and *Kiangsi Jih-pao* (Nanchang), 2 January 1960; *SCMP*, no. 2226, pp. 24–28.

108. Editorial, *JMJP*, 2 November 1959.

109. Editorial, *JMJP*, 6 August 1959.

110. This conclusion is also deduced from a nation-wide campaign in 1962 for the "reversal of verdicts" [*fan an*] in which victims of the "anti-rightist opportunist campaign" sought their rehabilitation.

111. A source in the early 1960s had identified Hsiao K'o, Hung Hsueh-chih, Li Ta, and Yang Cheng-wu as connected with the P'eng affair; see Charles, "Dismissal of Marshal Peng," p. 73. The information that has become available since has confirmed the dismissals of these officials (except Yang) and further revealed the identity of others who were adversely affected by the P'eng affair.

112. To the best of my knowledge, these men were never formally accused of joining the "anti-party" group in the Lushan showdown, but they were specifically charged with executing the bourgeois military line of the P'eng-Huang group and defects in their work; see *PLA Bull.*, pp. 51–53, 76–77, and 44–45, on T'an and Hung, and a Red Guard publication *Chan Pao* (Peking), no. 6 (1967) on Hsiao.

113. See *Fei-chun Fan-Mao Chi-t'uan* (The Anti-Mao Groups in the Chinese Communist Army) (Taipei: The Sixth Department of the Central Committee of the Chinese Nationalist Party, 1967), pp. 69–73, 76–80. The downfall of Hsi only came after April 1962, so his disgrace was not exclusively related to the P'eng affair and may have also been due to his support of the "three reconciliation and one reduction" policy, as claimed by a defected Chinese diplomat,

quoted on p. 72; Chang's disgrace also came only in 1961.

114. A few outstanding examples were Chia T'o-fu, a member of the CC, who was dismissed as director of the State Council Fourth Staff Office in September 1959 and lost other government posts in the early 1960s, Hsueh Mu-ch'iao, director of the State Statistical Bureau, and Yang Ying-chieh, vice-chairman of the State Planning Commission, who were dismissed in September 1959. Also see Hannspeter Hellbeck, "The 'Rightist' Movement in 1959," in *Contemporary China: 1959–1960* (Hongkong University Press, 1960), for the purges in 1959.

115. Chang Hsi-t'ing, "Defend Chairman Mao to the Death," Radio Kweiyang, 29 November 1967, and Liu Chieh-t'ing, "Li Ch'ing-chuan is the Khrushchev of the Great Southwest China," Radio Kweiyang, 17 June 1967.

116. Editorial, *JMJP*, 9 August 1960; *TKP* (Hongkong), 30 December 1960.

117. *China News Service* (Peking), 27 December 1960.

118. *TKP* (Hongkong), 30 December 1960.

119. The serious peasant uprisings in Honan in 1960–61 were not publicly reported in any known source, but they were reported in a classified PLA journal; see *PLA Bull.*, pp. 118–19, 138, 561.

Chapter 5

1. The text of the program is in *JMJP*, 12 April 1960; *CB*, no. 616, pp. 1–17.

2. *NCNA* (Peking), 6 April 1960; *CB*, no. 616, pp. 18–28.

3. Peking has not made public the figures on grain production since 1959, but Lord Mont-gomery was told in an interview with Mao that the grain output in 1960 was 150 million tons and that in 1959 it was probably no better; see *South China Morning Post* (Hongkong), 17 October 1961. In 1957, a year of unsatisfactory harvest, the grain output is estimated by some outside ob-servers to have been 185 million tons.

4. Per *mou* annual rice yields in Ch'aochou and Swatou areas in Kwangtung in and before 1957 averaged over 1000 catties, and per *mou* wheat yields in Laiyang area of Shantung were over 500 catties; these areas had the longest record of using a large amount of chemical fertilizer. See *JMJP*, editorial, 16 November 1957.

5. *JMJP*, 12 April 1960; *CB*, no. 616.

6. See Senator Hubert H. Humphrey, "My Marathon Talk With Russia's Boss," *Life*, 12 January 1959, pp. 80–91, and *The New York Times*, 18 July 1959. There are indications that Mao was informed of Khrushchev's attack and that he sought to refute Khrushchev's criticism by proving the "superiority" of the people's communes; see Mao's "Remarks Concerning the Printing and Distribution of Three Articles" (29 July 1959) and "Letter to Wang Chia-hsiang" (1 August 1959), *CLG*, 1, no. 4 (1968–69): 52–53.

7. For example, Mao reportedly put forth in early 1960 "The Constitution of the Anshan Iron and Steel Company" as a substitute for the Soviet "Constitution of the Magnitorgorsk Iron and Steel Combine" as a guide for managing industry; see *JMJP*, 25 August 1967.

8. "Thoroughly Reckon with Big Renegade Liao Lu-yen's Towering Crimes in the Minis-try of Agriculture," in a Red Guard pamphlet translated in *SCMP*, no. 4001, p. 11.

9. "Speech at the 10th Plenum of the 8th Central Committee," *CLG*, 1, no. 4 (1968–69): 88.

10. Not until early 1966, after a lapse of almost four years, were references again made to the program. On 27 January 1966, *People's Daily* reported that Chekiang and Hunan had organized cadres and members of communes to study the program; an accompanying editorial on the same

day, however, cautioned cadres not to set the production tasks and targets beyond "practical possibility" not to "blindly pursue high targets" or indiscriminately popularize production-increasing measures in their efforts to achieve the goals of the program.

11. See T'an Chen-lin's speech in *CB*, no. 616, p. 21. The eight points were soil improvement, increased application of fertilizer, water conservancy, seed improvement, rational close planting, plant protection, field management, and improvement of farm tools. In fact, Ma Yin-ch'u, president of Peking University and an economist, claimed in 1959 that the original idea of the "eight-point charter for agriculture" was his, adopted by Mao; see his article, "My Philosophical Thoughts and Economic Theories," *HCS*, no. 11 (1959): 22, 35, 46–47.

12. See Alexander Eckstein, *Communist China's Economic Growth and Foreign Trade* (New York: McGraw-Hill, 1966), pp. 29–37.

13. See "Nan Pa-t'ien Hsi-yu Chi" [The Story of the Southern Emperor's Western Trip], *Chih-k'an Nan-Yueh* (Canton: Editorial Department, Proletarian Revolutionary Rebels of Literary and Art Circles in the Canton Area), no. 3, 1 October 1967, as reprinted in *Hsingtao Jih-pao* (Hong-kong). This essay, while abusing and attacking Tao Chu, provided useful information on the CC Work Conference of July 1960 and the decision to set up the CC regional bureaus. Other sources that indicated the existence of the CC regional bureaus since 1960 include Li Shih-fei, "The Party's Middlemen: The Role of Regional Bureaus in the Chinese Communist Party," *Current Scene*, 3, no. 15.

14. Liao Lu-yen, "Participate in the Large-scale Development of Agriculture by the Whole Party and the Whole People," *HC*, no. 17 (1960); Editorial, *NFJP* (Canton), 16 September 1960.

15. See, for examples, Li Fu-ch'un's article in *HC*, no. 1 (1960), and T'an Chen-lin's speech to the NPC in April 1960 in *CB*, no. 616.

16. *NFJP* (Canton), 13 May 1960.

17. *NFJP*, 2 September 1960.

18. "Carry out Thoroughly the Party's Distribution Policy after the Autumn Harvest," *PJP*, 12 December 1960.

19. *NFJP* (Canton), 25 October 1960.

20. Huang Huo-ch'ing, "Factory-commune Coordination—A New Form of Strengthening the Worker-peasant Alliance," *HC*, no. 13 (1960).

21. "Industrial Enterprises must Adopt the Idea of Taking Agriculture as the Foundation," *JMJP* editorial, 17 July 1960.

22. The issuance of this directive is also mentioned in *PLA Bull.*, p. 137. The full text of this directive is not available, though a brief one-page summary of the twelve points was made available to me by Nationalist Chinese authorities.

23. In what was called "Communist styles" [*kung-ch'an feng*], cadres' excessive attempts at equalizing peasants income, in disregard of their skill, labor power, and contribution, and transferring workers and means of production from the better-off brigades or teams to the poor ones without compensation, created much conflict within the communes and adversely affected peasants' morale and incentives; *PLA Bull.*, pp. 117, 138.

24. "Communique of the 9th Plenary Session of the 8th Central Committee of the Communist Party of China," *PR*, no. 4 (1961).

25. These regional bureaus were headed by tested loyal provincial party officials or by officials sent down from Peking; for their background, see Li Shih-fei, "The Party's Middlemen."

26. For instance, under the East China Bureau, there were departments for propaganda and for finance and trade, offices for agriculture and forestry, water conservancy, finance, and policy research, and committees for planning, economic affairs, and science and technology. A. Doak Barnett, *Cadres, Bureaucracy and Political Power in Communist China* (New York: Columbia University Press, 1967), p. 112.

27. Frederick C. Teiwes, *Provincial Party Personnel in Mainland China: 1956–1966* (New York: East Asian Institute, Columbia University, 1967), pp. 42, 86.

28. A former PLA lieutenant claimed that Chang was implicated in the activities of the P'eng

Teh-huai "anti-party group"; see *Chung-kung Jen-ming-lu (Who's Who in Communist China)* (Taipei: Institute of International Relations, 1967), p. 353. If this is true, his involvement in the P'eng affair was uncovered more than one year after the 1959 Lushan meeting, as he was active throughout 1960.

29. See, for instance, Liu Shao-ch'i's "Confession" in *MS*, 28 and 29 January 1967, and Mao's speech of October 1966 as translated in Jerome Ch'en, ed., *Mao* (Englewood Cliffs, N.J.: Prentice-Hall, 1969), p. 94.

30. "Ten Crimes of Teng Hsiao-p'ing," *Pa-erh-wu Chan Pao* (Canton), 24 February 1967; *SCMM*, no. 574, p. 15; and "Uncover the Black Mask of Teng Hsiao-p'ing's 'Petofi Club,'" *Tung-fang-hung* (Peking: Capital Colleges & Universities Red Guard Revolutionary Rebel Liaison Center), 18 February 1967; *SCMP*, no. 3903, p. 2.

31. Ch'en Po-ta, "Speech to the Central Committee Work Conference, October 25, 1966" (excerpts), *Ko-ming Kung-jen Pao* (Peking: Revolutionary Rebel Headquarters of Workers from the Capital), 12 January 1967; *SCMP Supplement*, no. 167, p. 2.

32. See *PLA Bull.*, p. 405.

33. *PLA Bull.*, p. 467.

34. Ibid. "Five styles" or "Five winds" refer to cadres' "communistic" style (indiscriminately pushing egalitarian measures), commandist style (commanding by force rather than persuasion), the style of giving blind commands, the style of exaggeration (raising targets and giving false harvest reports), and the style of being special (refusal to participate in physical labor and demanding special privileges).

35. Ibid.

36. *PLA Bull.*, pp. 406, 466–67.

37. Reflecting and articulating the new mood was Foreign Minister Ch'en Yi's "Speech to the Graduates of High Institutes of Learning" (July 1961), *JMST 1961*, pp. 319–21.

38. Two notable examples are Hsueh Mu-ch'iao and P'an Fu-sheng. Hsueh was removed from the directorship of the State Statistical Bureau and other posts in September 1959, but he was reinstated as a vice-chairman of the State Planning Commission (headed by Li Fu-ch'un) in December 1960; see Cho-ming Li, *The Statistical System of Communist China* (Berkeley: University of California Press, 1962), pp. 11, 113, 114, 118. P'an Fu-sheng was purged as first party secretary of Honan in 1958 but became the acting chairman and later chairman of the All China Federation of Supply and Marketing Cooperatives in 1962.

39. "Uncover Liu Shao-ch'i's Counter-revolutionary Words and Deeds; Comments on Liu Shao-ch'i's 1961 Hunan Visit," *TFHP*, 9 March 1967.

40. "Uncover the Black Mask."

41. "Ch'en Yun is the Vanguard for the Capitalist Restoration," *TMHC*, no. 4 (1967); *SCMP*, no. 3899, p. 4.

42. P'eng visited Hunan in November 1961 and compiled several reports on the basis of his findings which he later distributed to various provincial party committees ("The Reactionary Antecedents of P'eng Teh-huai," *CB*, no. 851, p. 15). Allegedly Ch'ang Wen-t'ien obtained the approval of Liu Shao-ch'i to visit Shanghai, Chekiang, and Hunan "in the capacity of an alternate Politburo member" from April to June 1962; see "Resolutely Strike Down the Anti-Party Element Chang Wen-t'ien," *CCP* (Peking), no. 22–23 (1967); *JPRS*, no. 41,898.

43. See *PLA Bull.*, p. 405.

44. Ibid. This article has not been included in official lists of Mao's works available to the outside world.

45. Ch'en's political eclipse during the Great Leap period has generally been known to outside observers, but his reentry to the political picture since 1961 has not. Ch'en lost his influence after he was criticized by Mao at a party meeting in August 1962 and apparently ceased to participate in the deliberations of the party thereafter. Moreover, Ch'en often chose to work behind the scenes and rarely appeared in public. One of Ch'en's rare public appearances in 1961 was the Ninth CC Plenum in which he presided with other members of the Politburo Standing Committee; see the

photograph in *JMJP*, 21 January 1961, p. 1.

46. Liu was believed to have opposed the "hundred flowers" movement in 1957; see the remarks of Ch'ien Wei-ch'ang, *JMJP*, 17 July 1957.

47. Roderick MacFarquhar, "Communist China's Intra-Party Dispute," *Pacific Affairs*, December 1958. Liu's two speeches are in *JMJP*, 7 November 1957 and 25 May 1958.

48. See Mao's remarks at the 1962 Tenth CC Plenum; *CLG*, 1, no. 4 (1968–69): 92.

49. This information is deduced from a Red Guard article's references to Liu's denunciation of P'eng at Lushan; see the translation of "Down with Liu Shao-ch'i—Life of Counter-revolutionary Liu Shao-ch'i," *CB*, no. 834, p. 18.

50. "From Defeat of P'eng Teh-huai to the Bankruptcy of China's Khrushchev," editorial, *HC*, no. 13 (1967), and "P'eng Teh-huai and His Behind-the-Scenes Boss Cannot Shirk Responsibility for Their Crimes," editorial, *JMJP*, 16 August 1967; both articles are also in *PR*, no. 34 (1967).

51. See "To Take the Socialist Road or the Capitalist Road," joint editorial of *HC* and *JMJP*, 14 August 1967.

52. See the remarks of Ch'en Wei-ch'ang (vice-chancellor of Tsinghua University), *JMJP*, 17 July 1957.

53. Ma Nan-tun [Teng T'o], *Yen-shan Yeh-hua* (Peking: Peking Ch'u-pan-she, 1961); *Teng T'o Shih-wen Hsuan-chi* (Taipei: Freedom Press, 1966).

54. "The Exposé of the Plot to Usurp the Party and the State's Power Comments on the Counter-Revolutionary Incident of 'Ch'ang Kuan Lou,'" *PJP*, 7 August 1967.

55. Ibid. See also "Before and After the Counter-Revolutionary Incident of 'Ch'ang Kuan Lou,'" *Tung-fang-hung* (Peking: Peking Mining Institute Tung-fang Hung of the Capital College Red Guard Congress), 20 April 1967; *SCMP*, no. 4001.

56. Presumably the revisions were worked out in a CC Work Conference at Lushan in September 1961; see "The True Counter-revolutionary Revisionist Face of Teng Hsiao-p'ing," *CCP* (Peking), no. 12 (1967).

57. Editorial, *JMJP*, 1 January 1962; Liao Lu-yen, minister of agriculture, was quoted by a Japanese source as saying that in 1961 there were 50,000 communes (24,000 in 1959), 700,000 brigades (500,000 in 1959) and 4,600,000 teams (3,000,000 in 1959), "Observations on the Failure of the People's Communes," *Nihon Sekai Shuho* (Tokyo), 43, no. 36 (1962).

58. The excerpts of this document were made available to this writer by the Bureau of Intelligence, Ministry of National Defenses of the Nationalist Chinese government in Tapei.

59. "Down with Sung Jen-chiung—Top Capitalist-Roader in the Party in Northeast China," *Hung Ch'i T'ung-hsun* (Chiangmen Kwangtung), no. 14 (1968); *SCMP*, no. 4201, p. 11; see also "The Ten Crimes of the Counter-Revolutionary Revisionist Po I-po, *Ching-kang-shan* (Peking: Ching-kang-shan Corps, Tsinghua University), 1 January 1967.

60. Reportedly, a conference of party secretaries in charge of industry [*kung-yeh shu-chi hui-yi*] was convened in December 1961 by Teng Hsiao-p'ing to discuss and implement the new policy; see "The True Counter-revolutionary Revisionist Face of Teng Hsiao-p'ing."

61. "From the Defeat of P'eng Teh-huai."

62. See an article by the CCP CC Party School Red Flag Fighting Regiment in *JMJP*, 12 April 1967.

63. "Before and After the Counter-Revolutionary Incident of Ch'iang Kuang Lou," in *Tung-fang hung* (Peking: Peking Mining Institute Tung-fang Hung of the Capital College Red Guard Congress), 20 April 1967; *SCMP*, no. 4001.

64. "Resolutely Strike Down the Anti-Party Element Chang Wen-tien," *CCP* (Peking), nos. 22–23 (1967); *JPRS*, no. 41,890.

65. Procedures and disputes over "reversing verdicts" in Szechuan province were described by Chang Hsi-t'ing, "Defend Chairman Mao to the Death," Radio Kweiyang, 29 November 1967, and Liu Chieh-t'ing, "Li Ch'ing-chuan is the Khrushchev of the Great Southwest China," Radio Kweiyang, 17 June 1967.

66. Liu Shao-ch'i, *How to be a Good Communist*, 4th ed. (Peking: FLP, 1964), pp. 88–89. The English translation is from the Chinese text which appeared in the double issue of Red Flag, no. 15–16 (1962), in which Liu made a number of revisions, particularly in the section dealing with inner-party struggle.

67. For a sample of articles attacking Liu's book, see *JMJP*, 8 May 1967, *PJP*, 4 April 1967, and *Kwangming Jih-pao*, 8 April 1967.

68. Wu Han, *Hai Jui Pa Kuan* (Peking: Peking Ch'u-pan-she, 1961), Yao Wen-yuan, "A Criticism of the New Historical Play 'The Dismissal of Hai Jui,'" *WHP* (Shanghai), 10 November 1965, reprinted in *JMJP*, 30 November 1965.

69. "From the Defeat of P'eng Teh-huai," p. 20.

70. "Open Fire at the Black Anti-Party and Anti-Socialist Line," "Teng T'o's 'Evening Chats at Yenshan' is Anti-Party and Anti-Socialist Double-talk," *KMJP*, 8 May 1966. Key articles attacking these Maoist critics are published in *The Great Socialist Cultural Revolution in China*, 2 vols. (Peking: FLP, 1966). For a good discussion of this subject see Philip Bridgham, "Mao's 'Cultural Revolution': Origin and Development," *CQ*, no. 29 (1967); Harry Gelman, "Mao and the Permanent Purge," *Problems of Communism*, November-December 1966; Stephen Uhally, Jr., "The Cultural Revolution and the Attack on the 'Three Family Village,'" *CQ*, no. 27 (1966).

71. In 1962 when Mao's popularity declined, publication of his writing reportedly used only 0.5 percent (that is 70 tons) of the paper used for printing books in China, while books like *The Dream of the Red Chamber* and *Romance of Three Kingdoms* consumed 750 tons; see *JMJP*, 15 July 1966, p. 3. It is said that from 1962 to 1966, only 4.4 million copies of Mao's work were printed, while 17.8 million copies of Liu Shao-ch'i's *How To Be A Good Communist* were printed in the same period (see *JMJP*, 5 June 1967).

72. "From the Defeat of P'eng Teh-huai," p. 20. Allegedly, P'eng took two years to prepare the "petition," which included five "investigation reports" compiled in 1961 and 1962 when he visited communes in various provinces. "The Reactionary Antecedents of P'eng Teh-huai," *CB*, no. 851, pp. 14–15.

73. Information in this section is based on the following sources: "Thoroughly Settling Accounts with Ch'en Yun's Towering Crimes in Opposing Chairman Mao," *PKS*, 4 March 1967; "Manifold Sins of Ch'en Yun," *PKS*, 28 January 1967; Liu Shao-ch'i, "Confession," *MS*, 28 and 29 January 1967; *Ts'ai-mao Hung Ch'i* (Peking: The Finance and Trade System Rebels Liaison Committee), no. 4 (1967), also in *SCMP*, no. 3899, p. 6.

74. Joint Editorial, *People's Daily, Red Flag*, and *Liberation Army Daily*, 23 November 1967. English text is translated in *SCMP*, no. 4068.

75. Ibid.

76. *PLA Bull.*, pp. 118–19, 138, 561.

77. Information in this paragraph and the next from "How the Evil Wind of 'Going in Alone' is stirred up in Honan," *Wei Tung* (Tientsin: Nank'ai University Wei Tung Red Guards Headquarters), 20 May 1967.

78. *The Evil Deeds of the Anti-Party and Anti-Socialist Element and Counter-Revolutionary Double-Dealer, Liu Chien-hsun* (Revolutionary Rebel General Command of Organs of the Honan CCP Provincial Committee, March 12, 1967), translated in *JPRS*, no. 43,357, p. 21.

79. Ibid., pp. 21–22.

80. Ibid. This kind of measure was also implemented in other places; in June and July 1962 T'ao Chu allegedly popularized *pao-ch'an tao-hu* in Kwangtung and other Central-South provinces; see "T'ao Chu is the Vanguard in Promoting 'Production Quotas Set at Household Level' of China's Khrushchev," *NFJP*, 26 July 1967; *SCMP*, no. 4011, pp. 14–23.

81. "Selections of Li Hsien-nien's Anti-Mao Tse-tung Thought Black Remarks," *PKS*, 27 April 1967; reprinted in *Hsing-tao Jih-pao* (Hongkong), 24 and 25 January 1968.

82. Ibid.

83. Liu Shao-ch'i, "Confession."

84. Ibid.

85. "Li Hsien-nien's Anti-Mao Tse-tung Thought Black Remarks."

86. See Mao Tse-tung, "Speech to the 10th Plenum of the 8th Central Committee" (24 September 1962), *Chairman Mao's Repudiations*, pp. 24–25; also in *CLG*, 1, no. 4 (1968–69): 85–93.

87. Li Ching-ch'uan was alleged to have said: "Only talking about class struggle is really fruitless, let us keep our energy"; "If we can settle work points every day and month, settle account every month, then we are grasping well the class struggle"; and "It is also class struggle if we check our discrepancies"; Radio Kweiyang, 29 November 1967. Ch'en Yun's reaction was reportedly similar; he allegedly said "Political and ideological work is important, but insufficient by itself'"; see "Ch'en Yun is the Vanguard of the Capitalist Restoration," *TMHC*, 23 February 1967; *SCMP*, no. 3899, p. 6.

88. Communique of the Tenth Plenum, *JMJP*, 29 September 1962.

89. See "Further Consolidation of the Collective Economy and Development of Agricultural Production" (a speech by Wang Hung-shih, first party secretary of Lienchiang Hsien), *Lienchiang Documents*.

90. Some observers have reached a different conclusion, namely that "the 10th Plenum of the Central Committee brought the period of relaxation to an abrupt end"; see Charles Neuhauser, "The Chinese Communist Party in the 1960's: Prelude to the Cultural Revolution," *CQ*, no. 32 (1967): 10.

91. See *Lienchiang Documents*.

92. Ibid.

93. *Revised 60-Article Draft Regulations on Rural People's Commune* (September 1962) (Taipei: Ministry of National Defense, 1964).

94. For an excellent study of the campaign, see Richard Baum and Frederick C. Teiwes, *Ssu Ch'ing: The Socialist Education Movement of 1962–1966* (Berkeley: Center for Chinese Studies, University of California, 1968).

95. According to Mao, the important issues "solved" in these meetings were the problems of agriculture and commerce, industry and planning, the unity within the party (in that order); Mao, "Speech to the 10th Plenum of the 8th Central Committee" (24 September 1962), *CLG*, 1, no. 4 (1968–69): 85.

96. Li Tse-wen, "From the Principle of Repayment of Credits to a Discussion of the Supervisory Functions of the Banks," *HC*, no. 6 (1962).

97. Fan Yen-chun et al., "The Centralization and Unification of Financial Work," *TKP* (Peking), 25 June 1962, p. 3.

98. Ibid.; see also Ko Chih-ta and Wang Chao, "Some Inter-Relationships between Finance and Currency Work," *TKP*, 17 November 1961.

99. Franz Schurmann, *Ideology and Organization in Communist China* (Berkeley: University of California Press, 1966), p. 219, and Audrey Donnithorne, *China's Economic System* (London: George Allen and Unwin, 1967), p. 505.

100. Schurmann, *Ideology and Organization*, pp. 219, 297; also Donnithorne, *China's Economic System*, pp. 499, 505.

101. For an analysis of this important decision-making body and the shift in the locus of authority in the CCP, see Parris H. Chang, "Research Notes on the Changing Loci of Decision in the CCP," *CQ*, no. 44 (1970).

Chapter 6

1. I have dealt with the GPCR purge and its impact on China's political system in Parris H. Chang, "Mao's Great Purge: A Political Balance Sheet," *Problems of Communism*, March–April 1969.

2. All of these problems were revealed in a set of Chinese Communist materials, the *Lienchiang Documents*.

3. In the following analysis of the SEC, I have drawn heavily from Richard Baum and Frederick C. Teiwes, *Ssu-ch'ing: The Socialist Education Movement of 1962–1966* (Berkeley: Center for Chinese Studies, University of California, 1968), pp. 59–94 passim, and Charles Neuhauser, "The Chinese Communist Party in the 1960's: Prelude to the Cultural Revolution," *CQ*, no. 32 (1967).

4. This was indicated by "Draft Resolution of the Central Committee of the Chinese Communist Party on some problems in current Rural Work" (also known as the First Ten Points), Articles IV and V; an English translation of this document is in Baum and Teiwes, *Ssu-ch'ing*, Appendix II. Much of the information here is from his source.

5. Ibid., p. 73.

6. An English translation of this document is in Baum and Teiwes, *Ssu-ch'ing*, pp. 72–94.

7. Editorial Departments of *JMJP*, *HC*, and *CFCP*. "Struggle Between the Two Roads in China's Countryside," *PR*, no. 49 (1967): 17. But Liu Shao-ch'i claimed that the Second Ten Points were written by "some leading comrades at the center" on the basis of a report submitted to Mao by P'eng Chen; see Liu's reported "Confession," *MS*, 29 January 1967.

8. "Struggle Between the Two Roads in China's Countryside," *PR*, no. 49 (1967): 17.

9. Wang Kuang-mei (Madame Liu Shao-chi) allegedly claimed that Mao initially stipulated only four criteria but added two more as a result of her suggestion; she did not specify which two were her "brainchild." See "An Investigation Report of the Crimes of Liu Shao-chi and Wang Kuang-mei in the Ssu-ch'ing Movement in Pao-t'ing Special District," *Tung-fang hung* (Peking: Peking Mining Institute Tung-fang Hung of the Capital Colleges and Universities Red Guard Congress), no. 27–28 (1967).

10. Both the timing of the conference and the contents of the six criteria were disclosed in a twenty-three point directive, "Some Problems Currently Arising in the Course of the Rural Socialist Education Movement," enacted in January 1965. The English text is in Baum and Teiwes, *Ssu-ch'ing*

11. An English translation of the document is in Baum and Teiwes, *Ssu-ch'ing*.

12. Article II of the "Organizational Rules of Poor and Lower-Middle Peasant Associations," Baum and Teiwes, *Ssu-ch'ing*, p. 96.

13. Wang Kuang-mei took part in a work team to conduct the SEC in T'aoyuan Brigade of Funin Hsien in Hopei from November 1963 to April 1964, and produced a report entitled "The Summary Experience of the Socialist Education Movement in a Brigade" in July 1964; the report, known as the "T'aoyuan Experience," was praised by Liu Shao-ch'i as having "universal significance" and became required reading for party officials and the work teams. See "The 'T'aoyuan Experience' of Wang Kuang-mei is an Anti-Mao Tse-tung Thought Poisonous Weed," *Tsao-fan Yu-li Pao* (Peking: Capital Four Clearances Revolutionary Rebel Detachment), 12 February 1967.

14. Ibid.

15. "The Line of Liu Shao-ch'i and Wang Kuang-mei in Ssu-ch'ing: Left in form but Right in Essence," *Tsao-fan Yu-li Pao* (Peking: Capital Four Clearances Revolutionary Rebel Detachment), 10 June 1967.

16. Article III of the "Revised Second Ten Points," Baum and Teiwes, *Ssu-ch'ing*, p. 108.

17. Richard Baum and Frederick C. Teiwes, "Liu Shao-ch'i and the Cadre Question," *Asian Survey*, 7, no. 4 (1969).

18. For an interesting interpretation of Liu's drastic disciplinary actions against cadres at lower

levels, see Tang Tsou, "The Cultural Revolution and the Chinese Political System," *CQ*, no. 38 (1969): 73.

19. The dispatch of "work teams" by Liu and Teng Hsiao-P'ing in June 1966 to control the Cultural Revolution in Peking's colleges and universities, we shall see later, reflected the same kind of consideration.

20. Liu Shao-ch'i, "Confession."

21. This represented a shift of emphasis away from the solution of nonantagonistic contradictions in the SEC which Liu advocated; as late as 1 October 1964 Liu's line was still affirmed by the *People's Daily* when its editorial stated that "the great historical significance of the (Socialist Education) Movement lies in the following fact—it is a movement for educating the cadres and masses in the revolutionary spirit of the general line and for correctly handling contradictions among the people."

22. For examples, compare the provisions in Article II (Section 2.3) and Article IV (Section 4.C) of the Revised Second Ten Points with those in Articles VII, and XIV, and IX (Section 5) of the Twenty-Three Points concerning squatting at points, work teams, and economic indemnities. For a more detailed comparison of the differences between the two documents, see "The Line of Liu Shao-ch'i and Wang Kuang-mei."

23. In a talk to a Central Work Conference on 25 October 1966, Mao recalled that it was during the time when the Twenty-Three Points were formulated that he became aware of the fact that those party leaders in the "first line" had assumed too much power and formed many "independent kingdoms" and that his vigilance was heightened; see Jerome Ch'en, ed., *Mao* (Englewood Cliffs, N. J.: Prentice-Hall, 1969), p. 96, for the text of Mao's talk. Chou En-lai also asserted that Mao lost confidence in Liu in the course of drafting the Twenty-Three Points; see a Tokyo dispatch of *Agence France-Presse* on 13 April 1969, quoting reports by an *NHK* reporter in Peking, *Ming Pao* (Hongkong), 14 April 1967. "A very responsible person" in China told an American writer the same thing in 1970; see Edgar Snow, "Aftermath of the Cultural Revolution," *The New Republic*, 10 April 1971, p. 19.

24. Philip Bridgham, "Mao's Cultural Revolution: Origin and Development," *CQ*, no. 29 (1967): 14–15.

25. For a more detailed treatment of this subject, see Merle Goldman, "The Unique Blooming and Contending 1961–1962," *CQ*, no. 37 (1969).

26. The full text of Mao's speech, which became available through Red Guard sources, is translated in *CLG*, 1, no. 4 (1968–69). This quotation has been repeatedly quoted by the Chinese official sources, described as part of Mao's speech to the Tenth Plenum.

27. Yao Wen-yuan, "Criticize Chou Yang, Two-faced Counter-Revolutionary Element," *HC*, no. 1 (1967).

28. For a detailed and excellent study of Chiang Ch'ing's involvement in the theatrical reform and her struggle with P'eng Chen, Lu Ting-yi, and Chou Yang, see Chung Hua-min and Arthur C. Miller, *Madame Mao: A Profile of Chiang Ch'ing* (Hongkong: Union Research Institute, 1968), chapters 8, 9, and 10.

29. See Chung and Miller, *Madame Mao*, pp. 98, 108, 127, for examples. The ill feelings she harbored against P'eng, Lu, and Chou would explain at least in part the rough treatment they got in the hands of the Red Guards at the end of 1966.

30. Yao Wen-yuan, "Criticize Chou Yang."

31. A speech by K'o at the East China Drama Festival in the end of 1963 was reproduced only in *JMJP*, 14 August 1964.

32. Quoted in Yao Wen-yun, "Criticize Chou Yang."

33. All quotations from "The Tempestuous Combat on the Literary and Art Front: A Chronicle of the Struggle Between the Two Lines on the Literary and Art Front 1949–1966," *Shou-tu Hung-wei-p'ing* (Peking: Congress of Red Guards of Universities and Colleges in Peking), nos. 34 and 35, 7 June 1967; *CB*, no. 842, 8 December 1967, pp. 17–18.

34. The speeches of Lu and P'eng were published in *JMJP*, 6 June 1964, and *HC*, no. 14, 31 July 1964, respectively.

35. It was almost three years later that Chiang Ch'ing's speech of June 1964 was finally published in *JMJP*, 10 May 1967.

36. *JMJP*, 6 June 1964.

37. "The Tempestuous Combat on the Literary and Art Front," *CB*, no. 842, p. 22.

38. Ibid.; also Yao Wen-yuan, "Criticize Chou Yang."

39. The exact date of the formation of the Five-Man Cultural Revolutionary Group is not known; judging from an article in *JMJP*, 14 May 1967, and other Red Guard sourses, the group was set up in the summer of 1964.

40. *CB*, no. 842, p. 22.

41. Chao Ts'ung, "Literature and Art in 1965 in Communist China," *Communist China 1965*, Vol. 2 (Hongkong: Union Research Institute, 1967).

42. Ibid.

43. *CB*, no. 842, p. 30.

44. Ibid., p. 26.

45. "Uncover the Black Mask of the 'Petofi Club' of Teng Hsiao-P'ing," *Tung-fang Hung* (Peking: Capital Colleges and Universities Red Guard Revolutionary Rebel Liaison Center), no. 20 (1967); *SCMP*, no. 3903, pp. 3–4.

46. Mao Tse-tung, "A Talk at the Work Conference of the Center October 25, 1966" in Ch'en, *Mao*, p. 96.

47. See the remarks of Yao Wen-yuan and Ch'i Pen-yu in *JMJP*, 24 May 1967.

48. Information in this paragraph and the next from *Counter-Revolutionary Revisionist P'eng Ch'ien's Towering Crimes of Opposing the Party, Socialism and the Thought of Mao Tse-tung* (Peking: Liaison Center for Repudiating Liu-Teng-T'ao, Tung-fang Hung Commune, China Science and Technology University, Red Guard Congress, 10 June 1967); translated in *SCMM*, no. 639, p. 2.

49. *JMJP*, 30 November 1965; the note and the article were printed on page 5, which often carried articles of "academic" nature.

50. Mao was quoted to have said "The crux of 'Hai Jui Dismissed from Office' is the question of dismissal from office. The Emperor Chia Ching (of the Ming Dynasty, 1522–1566) dismissed Hai Jui from office. In 1959 we dismissed P'eng Teh-huai from office. And P'eng Teh-huai is 'Hai Jui' too." "From the Defeat of P'eng Teh-huai to the Bankruptcy of China's Khrushchev," *PR*, no. 34 (1964): 20.

51. For example, *JMJP*, 15 and 25 December 1964, 19 January and 10 February 1966; *KMJP*, 15 December 1965, 9, 13, 19, and 29 January 1966, and *WHP* (Shanghai), 13 February 1965.

52. Also reproduced in *JMJP*, 30 December 1965. The final form of the article was allegedly examined and approved by the Secretariat of the Peking Party Committee.

53. See "Circular of the Central Committee of the Chinese Communist Party" (16 May 1966), *PR*, no. 21 (1967). The text of the "February Outline Report" is published by a Red Guard publication, *Hsin Kang-yuan* (Peking: Revolutionary Rebel Commune, Peking Iron and Steel Institute), no. 18 (1957).

54. *P'eng Chen's Towering Crimes*, in *SCMM*, no. 640, pp. 7–8.

55. *NCNA* (Peking), 28 May 1967; *SCMP*, no. 3951, p. 10.

56. Editorial, *CFCP*, 29 May 1967; *SCMP*, no. 3951, p. 21.

57. "Summary of the Forum on Literature and Art in the Armed Forces," *NCNA* (Peking), 28 May 1967; *SCMP*, no. 3951.

58. Editorial, *JMJP*, 29 May 1967; also "Two Diametrically Opposed Documents," editorial, *HC*, no. 9 (1967).

59. Uri Ra'anan, "Peking's Foreign Policy 'Debate,' 1965–1966," and Donald S. Zagoria, "The Strategic Debate in Peking," in Tang Tsou, ed., *China in Crisis*, vol. II: *China's Policies in Asia and America's Alternatives* (Chicago: The University of Chicago Press, 1968), pp. 23–71, 237–68; also

Stanley Karnow, *Mao and China: From Revolution to Revolution* (New York: Viking Press, 1972), pp. 148–51. For a somewhat different interpretation, see Harry Harding and Melvin Gurtov, *The Purge of Lo Jui-Ch'ing: The Politics of Chinese Strategic Planning* (Santa Monica, Cal.: The Rand Corporation, 1971).

60. See Karnow, *Mao and China*, pp. 150–51, and Ra'anan, "Peking's Foreign Policy 'Debate,'" p. 26 and passim.

61. *Collection of Documents concerning the Great Proletarian Cultural Revolution*, vol. I (Peking: Propagandists of Mao Tse-tung's Thought, Peking College of Chemical Engineering, May 1967); *CB*, no. 852, p. 7.

62. Ra'anan, "Peking's Foreign Policy 'Debate,'" pp. 27, 34, and passim.

63. "Reply to Red Guards' False Accusation," *Akahata* (Tokyo), 24 January 1967 (this newspaper is the daily organ of the Japanese Communist Party). Here I differ from the interpretation of Ra'anan ("Peking's Foreign Policy 'Debate,'" pp. 52, 62), who has argued that P'eng Chen consistently opposed unity of action with Moscow. The *Akahata* article indicates that several Chinese negotiators, including P'eng, consented to a communique which, among other things, called for the "broadest international united front" and only Mao was against it subsequently and scrapped the points of agreement already reached.

64. *P'eng Chen's Towering Crimes*, *SCMM*, p. 15.

65. Cf. Karnow, *Mao and China*, p. 152.

66. See speeches of Liu and Teng in *JMJP*, 29 April, 7 May, and 22 July 1966; also *PR*, 6 and 13 May and 29 July 1966.

67. Karnow, *Mao and China*, p. 153.

68. *P'eng Chen's Towering Crimes*, p. 9.

69. *SCMM*, no. 640, p. 10. Bowing to pressure, P'eng authorized the *Peking Daily* and *Ch'ien-hsien* to publish an "Editor's Note" on 16 April sternly criticizing the writings of T'eng T'o. This move was termed by the Maoists as "sham criticism," intended to "protect the commander through sacrificing the knights."

70. *SCMM*, no. 640, p. 12.

71. Ibid., p. 13.

72. *CFCP*, 18 April 1966; reprinted in *JMJP* in the following day.

73. The itinerary of Liu, as reported in *JMJP* in March and April 1966, was rather strange and puzzling. The delegation he led arrived in Pakistan on 26 March and returned to Hotien of Sinkiang on 31 March; it arrived in Afghanistan on 4 April and returned to Urumuchi on 8 April; it arrived in East Pakistan on 15 April, left East Pakistan and arrived Burma on 18 April; it left Rangoon, Burma, on 19 April and arrived in Kunming of Yunan province on 19 April. *JMJP* on 21 April published an editorial to welcome Liu home but gave no indication on what date Liu returned to Peking; he may have gone to Hangchow directly from Kunming.

74. "Circular of the Central Committee of Chinese Communist Party" (16 May 1966), *PR*, no. 21 (1967).

75. "The Terrifying Counter-Revolutionary Incident," *Ch'uan Wu-ti* (Peking: The Yenan Commune of *Chien-k'iang Pao* and the capital Medical Revolutionary Committee), no. 9 (1967). Although policy differences and failures to carry out Mao's instructions were undoubtedly responsible for Lu's downfall, certain personal factors may be equally important. As intimated by this Red Guard source, Lu's wife, Yen Wei-ping, had over a period of time written several malicious anonymous letters to Lin Piao insulting and attacking Lin and his wife; after the identity of the author was discovered, Lu allegedly got the assistance of P'eng Chen to have medical specialists declare Yen insane in order to absolve her "counter-revolutionary" offenses.

76. The text of the poster is in *JMJP*, 2 June 1966.

77. "How Lu P'ing and Company Have Undermined the Great Cultural Revolution in Pei Ta," *Kung-jen Jih-pao*, 4 June 1966. According to the paper, the article is supplied by *CFCP*.

78. "The Great Strategic Plan," editorial, *JMJP*, 6 June 1967.

79. Liu Shao-ch'i, "Confession." The full contents of this eight-article directive remain un-

known. According to one Red Guard source, it contained provisions such as "differentiating the inside from the outside," "guarding against the leakage of secrets," and "firmly holding the fort." See "Down with Liu Shao-ch'i—Life of Counter-revolutionary Liu Shao-ch'i" in *CB*, no. 834, p. 27. It is reasonable to infer that the directive tried to limit the students' scope of activities confining them to their schools.

80. Liu Shao-ch'i, "Confession."

81. An incomplete tabulation shows that thirteen such officials in eleven universities were dismissed and publicly humiliated during June and July 1966. The more notable ones included Lu P'ing, president and party secretary of Peking University, K'uang Ya-ming, president and party secretary of Nanking University; Li ta, president of Wuhan University and a founder of the CCP in 1921; Ho Lu-ting, president of Shanghai Musical College and composer of the current national anthem "East is Red"; and K'o Lin, president and party secretary of Chungshan Medical College in Canton.

82. Liu Shao-ch'i and Teng Hsiao-ping reportedly assured members of the work teams that "Dispatching the work teams embodies the leadership of the Party. You are sent by us; to oppose you is to oppose us." "Excerpts of Teng Hsiao-Ping's Self-criticism," carried in a Canton Red Guard publication and reproduced in *Ming Pao* (Hongkong), 20 May 1968. The Sixteen-Point Decision on the GPCR also criticized those who equated opposition to work teams with opposition to the party center. See *JMJP*, 9 August 1966 (also *PR*, no. 33 [1966]).

83. Information here and in the next paragraph from "Down With Liu Shao-ch'i," p. 27.

84. Mao Tse-tung, "My First Big Character Poster" (5 August 1966), *JMJP*, 31 July 1967; also in *PR*, no. 33 (1967).

85. In several respects, the Eleventh Plenum deviated from previous practices. In addition to the presence of large numbers of "revolutionary teachers and students," no mention was made in the Plenum Communique of the number of the members and alternate members of the CC who attended the Plenum. A Japanese source reported that only forty-six members and thirty-three alternate members of the CC, or approximately 46 percent of the total membership, actually attended the Plenum; see *Seikai Shuho (World Weekly)* (Tokyo), no. 37 (1966).

86. The text of the Sixteen-Point Decision on the GPCR is in *JMJP*, 9 August 1966. An English text is in *PR*, no. 33 (1966).

87. Mao Tse-tung, "Big Character Poster."

88. For a detailed treatment of the tug-of-war between the Maoists and the provincial officials, see Parris H. Chang, "Provincial Party Leaders' Strategies for Survival during the Cultural Revolution," in *Elites in Communist China*, ed. Robert A. Scalapino (Seattle: University of Washington Press, 1972).

89. Ch'en, *Mao*, p. 96.

90. Richard M. Pfeffer, "The Pursuit of Purity: Mao's Cultural Revolution," *Problems of Communism*, November–December 1969, p. 19.

91. Tang Tsou, "The Cultural Revolution and The Chinese Political System," *CQ*, no. 38 (1969): 79.

92. *PR*, 17 July 1964.

93. Cf. Richard H. Solomon, *Mao's Revolution and the Chinese Political Culture* (Berkeley: University of California Press, 1971), pp. 458–60.

94. A Red Guard source quotes Chou En-lai as saying that prior to 1964 Mao had criticized Liu on several occasions; see *Wen-k'o T-ung-hsun* (Canton: Canton Municipal Organ's Red Headquarters), no. 1 (1967). Various other Red Guard sources have indicated that many policies which Liu sponsored from 1960 to 1962 had displeased Mao and that in the Peitaiho Conference in the summer of 1962 Mao openly rebuked Liu for his "rightist-leaning" stand.

95. For example, editorials, *CFCP*, 18 April, 4 May, and 20 May 1966. During April and May, the PLA paper also actively promoted Mao's GPCR and violently attacked those who obstructed it, while *JMJP* maintained silence on that matter editorially.

Chapter 7

1. See G. William Skinner and Edwin A. Winckler, "Compliance Succession in Rural Communist China: A Cyclical Theory," in Amitai Etzioni, ed., *Complex Organizations: A Sociological Reader*, 2nd ed. (New York: Holt, Rinehart and Winston, 1969), p. 426.

2. See Richard H. Solomon, *Mao's Revolution and the Chinese Political Culture* (Berkeley: University of California Press, 1971), pp. 377ff.

3. In his self-criticism, P'eng attributed the motivation of his attack on Mao to his emnity and prejudice against Mao; see *CB*, no. 851.

4. See Wu Leng-hsi, "Confession," *Hung-se Hsin-hua*, no. 43 (1968); the text of the confession is translated with notes by Parris H. Chang, *CLG*, 2, no. 4 (1969–70).

5. See "Selections of Li Hsien-nien's Anti-Mao Tse-tung Thought Black Remarks," *Peking Commune*, reprinted in *Hsing-tao Jih-pao* (Hongkong), 24 and 25 January 1968.

6. The moving force behind the regime's campaign to revolutionalize Chinese drama and theatre in 1963–64, for instance, was Chiang Ch'ing, and she played a pivotal role in it. Chang Ch'un-chiao contributed, directly or indirectly, to the experiment of the free supply system in the communes in 1958 (see ch. 4).

7. For an interesting discussion of the roles of the presidential aides in the American policy process, see Patrick Anderson, *The Presidents' Men: White House Assistants of Franklin D. Roosevelt, Harry Truman, Dwight D. Eisenhower, John F. Kennedy and Lyndon B. Johnson* (New York: Doubleday, 1968).

8. See A. Doak Barnett, *Cadres, Bureaucracy, and Political Power in Communist China* (New York: Columbia University Press, 1967).

9. Ibid., pp. 437–38.

10. See Merle Fainsod, *Smolensk Under Soviet Rule* (New York: Vintage Books, 1963), pp. 142, 180–82, 246–47.

11. For example, "How to Run the People's Communes: In Reference to the Draft Regulations of the Weihsing Commune," *JMJP*, 4 September 1958.

12. See E.E. Shattschneider, *The Semi-Sovereign People* (New York: Holt, Rinehart and Winston, 1960) for an analysis of the application of the same tactic, which he calls "socialization of conflict," in American politics.

13. Samuel P. Huntington, "Political Development and Political Decay," *World Politics*, 12, no. 3 (1956): 386–430.

14. See Parris H. Chang, "China'a Military in the Aftermath of Lin Piao's Purge," *Current History*, September 1974.

15. It is interesting to note that both Plenums, in October 1955 and September 1957, were enlarged sessions in which provincial party secretaries who were not members of the CC participated in the deliberations.

16. Written directives were often vague and ambiguous and could be subject to diverse interpretations, thus word of mouth may have helped clarify and expound the leadership's specific policy intentions and goals.

17. For instance, see reports on Mao's various trips in the provinces in *JMJP*, 21 September 1957, 14 and 27 April and 12 and 13 August 1958, *Shensi Jih-pao*, 6 and 7 April 1958, and *Kung-jen Jih-pao*, 10 April 1958.

18. "Uncover Liu Shao-ch'i's 1961 Hunan Visit," *TFHP* (Peking: Peking Institute of Geology), 9 March 1967.

19. Ibid.

20. For a "Mao in Command" model, see Michael Oksenberg, "Policy-making Under Mao, 1949–68: An Overview," in John M.H. Lindbeck, ed., *China: Management of a Revolutionary Society* (Seattle: University of Washington Press, 1971), pp. 79–115.

21. Shattschneider, *Semi-Sovereign People*, p. 68.

22. Compare the observation of Edgar Snow: "This (Central Committee) is not a faceless rubber-stamp committee packed with yes-men, but is made of strong personalities many of whom have commanded troops in battles and have at times held discretionary power over forces that could have destroyed or overthrown Mao" (*The Other Side of the River* [New York: Random House, 1961], p. 332).

23. For a discussion of "routinized charisma" see Amitai Etzioni, *A Comparative Analysis of Complex Organization* (Glencoe, Ill.: Free Press, 1961), pp. 26 ff.

24. See Articles 19 and 37 of the 1956 CCP Constitution and Teng Hsiao-P'ing's discussion of collective leadership in his "Report on the Revision of the Constitution of the Communist Party of China" (*8NCCPC*, vol. 2, pp. 192–99).

25. See A. Doak Barnett, *China After Mao* (Princeton: Princeton University Press, 1967), pp. 91–92.

26. Based on the position(s) held by these leaders, and judging from their activities, one can draw a picture of roughly who was responsible over what in the 1950s and early 1960s: political and legal affairs: Tung P'i-wu, P'eng Chen, Lo Jui-ch'ing; foreign affairs: Ch'en yi, Chang Wen-tien, Wang Chia-hsiang; intrabloc affairs: P'eng Chen, K'ang Shang; ideology and propaganda: P'eng Chen, Lu Ting-yi, Ch'en Po-ta, Hu Ch'iao-mu; military affairs: P'eng Teh-huai (until summer 1959), Ho Lung, Lo Jung-huan, Lo Jui-ch'ing; economic affairs: Li Fu-chun, Li Hsien-nien, Po I-po, T'an Chen-lin; party administration: Yang shang-k'un.

27. See Parris H. Chang, "Mao's Great Purge" A Political Balance Sheet," *Problems of Communism*, 18, no. 2 (1969): 8.

28. The text of Mao's letter was obtained by the Chinese Nationalist authorities, and reproduced in *Central Daily News* (Taipei), 18 April 1973.

Postscript I

1. Wang's elevation undoubtedly embodied the policy to cultivate revolutionary successors and to select "outstanding persons from among the workers and poor and lower-middle class peasants and place them in leading posts at all levels." However, if a story circulated within China is to be believed, Wang was instrumental in nullifying Lin Piao's assassination plot against Mao and was credited with saving Mao's life at a moment of danger in September 1971.

2. Editorial, *JMJP*, 1 January 1976; many such statements were made during the 1970s by the radicals.

3. Editorial, *JMJP*, 1 July 1971.

4. Wang Hung-wen, "Report to the Central Study Class" (14 January 1974), as published in *Chung-kung Yen-chiu (Studies on Chinese Communism—Taipei)*, 10 December 1974, pp. 95–96.

5. See Parris H. Chang, "The Anti-Lin Piao and Confucius Campaign: Its Meaning and Purposes," *Asian Survey*, October 1974, pp. 871–86. Since the fall of 1976, Peking has also publicly acknowledged the radicals' sinister scheme; see, for example, *JMJP*, 14 January and 8 February 1977, and *KMJP*, 17 March 1977.

6. See, for example, Shih Lun, "On Worshiping Confucianism and Opposing Legalism," *Hsueh-hsi yu P'i-p'an (Study and Criticism)*, no. 1, September 1973, and "In Defense of Burning of Classics and Burying Alive Scholars," *JMJP*, 28 September 1973.

7. "A Record of Defeat in the Attempt by the 'Gang of Four' to Usurp the Party and

Seize Power," *JMJP*, 14 November 1976, and an expose of Wang Hung-wen's activities in *JMJP*, 3 June 1977.

8. Ibid. Also an article by Ch'en Chung in *Li-ssu Yen-chiu* (*Historical Research*), no. 1, February 1977, p. 34.

9. This can be inferred from the statement "Chairman Mao saved him and gave him a chance to resume work," in *JMJP*, editorial, 10 April 1976.

10. See Articles 7 and 9 of the PRC Constitution (adopted 17 January 1975), published in *PR*, 24 January 1975, p. 14. For an analysis of salient provisions of the constitution, see Chün-tu Hsüeh, "The New Constitution," *Problems of Communism*, May-June 1975, pp. 11–19.

11. The call for the campaign came in a *JMJP* editorial of 9 February 1975, "Study Well the Theory of the Dictatorship of the Proletariat." In a follow-up article on 22 February the same paper devoted three and a half pages to quotations from Marx, Engels, and Lenin on the dictatorship of the proletariat.

12. Editorial, *JMJP*, 9 February 1975. It is interesting to note that Mao's complaints were made in December 1974, before the CC and NPC meetings of January 1975 which finally approved the new state constitution. This suggests that Mao tried to persuade his colleagues to curb the "bourgeois right," evidently without success.

13. Kuei Chih, "The Rightist Wind to Reverse Correct Verdicts and Bourgeois Right," *HC*, no. 3 (1 March 1976): 20–21.

14. The charges were repeated in numerous articles in the press. The most informative and authoritative exposé of the issue was provided by Liang Hsiao and Jen Ming, who are known to speak for the radical group in the leadership, in an article entitled "Criticism of 'Taking the Three Directives as the Key Link,'" *JMJP*, 29 February 1976.

15. Ibid. Exactly when Mao made the comment is not known, but he must have done so sometime before 1 January 1976—that is, while Premier Chou was still alive. This is clear from the fact that the 1976 New Year's Day editorial in *JMJP* had already quoted the last sentence of Mao's remarks, calling it the Chairman's "latest instruction," but had omitted the first sentence.

16. Chou En-lai, "Report on the Work of the Government" (delivered on 13 January 1975), in *PR*, no. 4 (24 January 1975): 23.

17. According to the Chinese media and to wall posters in Peking, Teng attended at least six national conferences in 1975: the conference of representatives of iron and steel industries on 29 May; the enlarged MAC meeting on 14 July; the national "learn from Tachai" conference on 15 September; a conference on Academy of Sciences Work Plan on 26 September; a conference of national defense industry keypoint enterprises; and a conference of party secretaries from twelve south China provinces. The dates of the last conferences are not known.

18. Liang and Jen, "Criticism." The "four modernizations" refer to the modernization of agriculture, industry, national defense, and science and technology.

19. Tso (Chai) Ch'ing, "Read an Unpublished Document," *Study and Criticism*, no. 4 (14 April 1976): 11.

20. Ibid., pp. 18, 29.

21. Kang Li and Yen Feng, "Before and After the Appearance of 'The Outline Report,'" ibid., pp. 20–27. The capitalist-roader in question was Hu Yao-pang, Teng's protégé, who was the secretary of the Communist Youth League before the GPCR, purged in 1966, and appointed party secretary and vice-president of the Academy in July 1975. In 1977, Hu moved up to higher positions of responsibility and now holds the post of director of the CC Organization Department, among others.

22. Liang and Jen, "Criticism."

23. These quotations are from wall posters seen at Peking University and reported by foreign newsmen. See Ross Munro's dispatch in *The Globe and Mail* (Toronto), 29 March 1976, and reports in *Asahi Shimbun* (Tokyo), 7 and 11 March 1976.

24. Liang and Jen, "Criticism."

25. Ibid.

26. Ibid.

27. This account was provided to foreign diplomats in Peking by Chinese officials in the fall of 1975 and has been implicitly confirmed by the Chinese press one year later after Chiang Ch'ing's ouster. Parts of Chiang's interviews are now available in Roxane Witke, *Comrade Chiang Ch'ing* (Boston: Little, Brown, 1977).

28. Ch'en Shih-chih, "The Second Comment on Liang Hsiao—the Spokesman of the 'Gang of Four,'" *Historical Research*, no. 5 (October 1977): 77, 78–79.

29. Tso (Chai), "Unpublished Documents," pp. 12–13; also Liang and Jen, "Criticism."

30. The seven appointed provincial party first secretaries were Chiang Wei-ch'ing (Kiangsi), Liao Chih-kao (Fukien), and P'ai Ju-ping (Shantung), all appointed in January 1975; Chao Hsin-ch'u (Hupeh), appointed in May 1975; Chia Chi-yun (Yunnan), appointed in October 1975; Chao Chih-yang (Szechwan) and An P'ing-sheng (Kwangsi), appointed in December 1975.

31. The 1975 personnel changes in the PLA included a large-scale reshuffling of the top officers in at least seventeen of China's twenty-nine province-level military districts (MD's), involving the replacement of the commander in at least ten MD's and of the Political Commissar in at least eight MD's. Among the rehabilitated PLA cadres who received new appointments in 1975 were Lo Jui-ch'ing (previously PLA chief of staff), T'an Chen (previously director of the PLA General Political Department), Hsiao Hua (previously director of the PLA General Political Department), Wang En-mao (previously commander of the Sinkiang Military Region), to name only a few.

32. "Unfold Criticism of *Water Margin*," editorial, *JMJP*, 4 September 1975.

33. Ch'en, "The Second Comment," pp. 77–78.

34. Ibid.

35. See note 15 above.

36. Editorial, *JMJP*, 18 April 1976.

37. "Counter-Revolutionary Political Incident at T'ienanmen Square," *PR*, no. 15 (9 April 1976): 4–5. As noted previously, many Chinese equated Mao with the unpopular Ch'in emperor.

38. *PR*, 9 April 1976.

39. It is true that Hua, as a provincial official of Hunan in the 1950s and 1960s, did display fine leadership qualities and was personally known to Chairman Mao, Premier Chou, and other central leaders—factors which probably accounted for his entry into the top national leadership in the early 1970s; for an analysis of Hua's career, see Michael Oksenberg and Sai-cheung Yeung, "Hua Kuo-feng's Pre-Cultural Revolution Hunan Years, 1949–66: The Making of a Political Generalist," *CQ*, no. 69 (1977): 3–53. In spite of this, Hua was thrust into the post of acting premier as a "compromise candidate," after the two rival factions were unable to push through their respective candidates.

40. Apparently many Chinese leaders considered Hua nonpartisan and unlikely to grab power, a perception which may also explain Hua's appointment as Minister of Public Security in January 1975. Moreover, until October 1976, Hua was not taken too seriously by China's powerholders—this was implicitly suggested by Wang Tung-hsing, who quoted Mao as praising Hua as "not stupid."

41. Ch'en, "The Second Comment," p. 80.

42. Editorial, *JMJP*, 11 August 1976.

43. *JMJP*, 14 August 1976.

Postscript II

1. These include Kuo Hung-chieh (Anhwei), Chu K'o-chia (Yunnan), Lu Yu-lan (Hopei), Hua Lin-shen (Kiangsu), Wang Hsiu-chen (Shanghai), and Chang Fu-heng (Tientsin), all provincial party secretaries; P'an Shih-kao and Tu Lieh (both from Kiangsi), T'ang Ch'i-shan (Honan), T'ang Chung-fu (Hunan), and Tung Ming-hui (Hupeh), provincial party Standing Committee members; and Ch'en Chia-chung, vice-chairman of the Fukien RC, and Weng Sen-ho, member of the Chekiang RC Standing Committee. All of them have been ousted.

2. *PR*, nos. 35–36 (7 September 1973): 31.

3. During the early stage of the GPCR, conservative powerholders manipulated the flow of information and managed news for their own purposes; see Parris H. Chang, "Provincial Leaders' Strategies of Survival During the Cultural Revolution," in Robert A. Scalapino, ed., *Elites in the People's Republic of China* (Seattle: University of Washington Press, 1972), pp. 512–13.

4. See "A Record of Defeat in the Attempt by the 'Gang of Four' to Usurp the Party and Seize Power," *JMJP*, 14 November 1976.

5. *JMJP*, 14 January 1977.

6. Ibid.

7. Ting Wang, *Biographies of Wang Hung-wen and Chang Ch'un-ch'iao* (Hong Kong: Ming Pao Month Publishing House, 1977), pp. 15–17; also see related articles in *Li-ssu Yen-chiu* (*Historical Research*), no. 1 (20 February 1977): 29–39, and *Ta-kung Pao* (Hong Kong), 30 January 1977.

8. Ting Wang, *Biographies*, pp. 25–43.

9. Among the most outstanding examples were Chang T'ieh-sheng, The "heroic flunker," who flunked a college entrance examination in August 1973 but was made a member of the Standing Committee of the National People's Congress in January 1975, Chu K'o-chia, a rusticated youth from Shanghai who rose to secretary of the Yunnan CCP Committee. These young cadres are found at all levels, but considerable numbers of them are at the subprovincial levels, particularly at the county, as they were rusticated youths.

10. *KMJP*, 30 January 1977.

11. To cite only a few: Liu Hsiang-p'ing, former Minister of Public Health; Ch'en Shao-k'un, former Minister of Metallurgy Industry; Chia Ch'i-yun, former first secretary of Yunnan; Hsien Heng-han, former first secretary of Kansu; Sung P'ei-chang, former first secretary of Anhwei; Wang Huai-hsiang, former first secretary of Kirin.

12. See note 1 above.

13. Outstanding examples of men placed in power by the radicals include Mao Yuan-hsin, political commissar of the Shenyang Military Region (MR), and Sun Yu-kuo, deputy commander of the same unit, both in their late thirties. Many radical followers appeared to have been promoted to leadership positions at the company and regiment levels. Ting Sheng, commander of Nanking MR, and Ma Ling, commander of the Air Force, are two PLA officials coopted by the radicals; they and many others have since been ousted.

14. See Wang Hung-wen, "Report to the Central Study Class" (14 January 1974), in *Chung-kung Yen-chiu* (*Studies on Chinese Communism*), 10 December 1974, pp. 95–96.

15. *JMJP*, 3 June 1977.

16. See Parris H. Chang, "The Anti-Lin Piao and Confucius Campaign: Its Meaning and Purposes," *Asian Survey*, October 1974, pp. 871–86.

17. See article by Fan Shih-chih in *KMJP*, 14 January 1977.

18. Theoretic Study Group of the CCP CC General Office, "Forever Remember Chairman Mao's Teachings and Persist in Continuing Revolution under the Dictatorship of the Proletariat," *JMJP*, 8 September 1977.

19. In the summer of 1972, Chiang Ch'ing spoke of Wang in glowing terms; she also disclosed that Wang was responsible for organizing the military record she narrated for Roxane Witke and that six maps were specially prepared under Wang's guidance for her for that occasion. See Roxane Witke, *Comrade Chiang Ch'ing* (Boston: Little, Brown, 1977), p. 193.

20. See note 18 above and an account in *Ming Pao* (Hongkong), 31 October 1976, which was based on a highly reliable source inside China.

21. *Ming Pao*, 31 October 1976.

22. Ibid., 1 November 1976. The quote came from an authoritative source inside China.

23. See notes 11 and 13 above.

24. See note 1 above.

25. In light of such potent developments, one needs to take a more critical view of the "field army theory" expounded in William W. Whitson, *The Chinese High Command: A History of Communist Military Politics 1927–71* (New York: Praeger, 1973), which sought to explain CCP leadership factionalism in terms of former field army ties.

26. "How the 'Gang of Four' Opposed Socialist Modernization," *PR*, 20, no. 11 (11 March 1977): 8.

27. "The 'Gang of Four': A Scourge of the Nation," *PR*, 19, no. 48 (28 November 1976): 12, 13.

28. Ibid., p. 13.

29. *PR*, 20, no. 11 (11 March 1977): 7.

30. Kuo Chi, "Foreign Trade: Why the 'Gang of Four' Created Confusion," *PR*, 20, no. 9 (25 February 1977): 18.

31. *PR*, 20, no. 1 (1 January 1977): 14–16.

32. "It Is Not Permissible to Undermine the Party's Rural Policy," *JMJP*, 30 November 1976.

33. *HC*, no. 1 (7 January 1977): 65.

34. "Hold Aloft the Great Banner of the 'July 30 Directive' and March On: The Kiangsi Communist Labor University Grows Amid Struggle," *KMJP*, 26 July 1977, and *HC*, no. 8 (8 August 1977): 3–4.

35. See *PR*, 19, no. 48 (26 November 1976): 14, and *PR*, 20, no. 9 (25 February 1977): 17.

36. These tendencies may be defined as follows: political participation is "not moderated and channeled toward common goals by the reliable functioning of political institutions"; political institutions "are weak, lacking in the moral authority to work out binding, allocative decisions that will be regarded as legitimate by the society as a whole"; and there is a "tendency for the military to intervene in the political arena." See Claude E. Welch, Jr., and Arthur K. Smith, *Military Role and Rule* (North Scituate, Mass.: Duxbury Press, 1974), p. 52. Also see Samuel Huntington, *Political Order in Changing Societies* (New Haven: Yale University Press, 1968), pp. 196–97, for a similar definition.

37. Ellis Joffe, "The PLA in Internal Politics," *Problems of Communism*, November–December 1975, p. 12.

Works Cited or Consulted

Non-Communist Sources in English

Articles and Books

Barnett, A. Doak. *Communist China and Asia: A Challenge to American Policy*. New York: Random House, 1960.

———. *Communist China: The Early Years 1949–1955*. New York: Praeger, 1964.

———. *China After Mao*. Princeton: Princeton University Press, 1967.

———, with a contribution by Ezra Vogel. *Cadres, Bureaucracy and Political Power in Communist China*. New York: Columbia University Press, 1967.

Bauer, Raymond A., and Gergen, Kenneth J., eds. *The Study of Policy Formulation*. New York: Free Press, 1968.

Baum, Richard, and Teiwes, Frederick C. "Liu Shao-ch'i and the Cadre Question," *Asian Survey* 8, no. 4 (1968).

———. *Ssu-Ch'ing: The Socialist Education Movement of 1962–1966*. Berkeley: Center for Chinese Studies, University of California, 1968.

Bennett, Gordon A., and Montaperto, Ronald N. *Red Guard: Political Biography of Dai Hsiao-ai*. New York: Doubleday, 1971.

Bernstein, Thomas P. "Leadership and Mass Mobilization in the Soviet and Chinese Collectivization Campaign of 1929–1930 and 1955–1956: A Comparison." *CQ*, no. 31 (1967).

Bridgham, Philip. "Mao's Cultural Revolution: Origins and Development." *CQ*, no. 29 (1967).

Brzezinski, Zbigniew. *Permanent Purge*. Cambridge, Mass.: Harvard University Press, 1956.

———, and Hungtington, Samuel P. *Political Power: USA/USSR*. New York: Viking Press, 1964.

Chang, Parris H. "Chang Ch'un-ch'iao: Shanghai's Cultural Czar." *Far Eastern Economic Review*, no. 33 (1968).

———. "The Struggle Between the Two Roads in China's Countryside." *Current Scene* 6, no. 3 (1968).

————. "Mao's Great Purge: A Political Balance Sheet." *Problems of Communism*, March–April 1969.

————. "Research Notes on the Changing Loci of Decision in the CCP." *CQ*, no. 44 (1970).

————. *Radicals and Radical Ideology in China's Cultural Revolution*. New York: Research Institute on Communist Affairs, Columbia University, 1973.

————. "China's Military." *Current History*, September 1974.

Chang, Wan-shan. *The State Council in Communist China: A Structural and Functional Analysis 1954–1965*. M.A. thesis, Columbia University, 1968.

Charles, David A. "The Dismissal of Marshal P'eng Teh-huai." *CQ*, no. 8 (1961).

Ch'en, Jerome. *Mao and the Chinese Revolution*. New York: Oxford University Press, 1965.

————, ed. *Mao*. Englewood Cliffs, N.J.: Prentice-Hall, 1969.

Ch'en, S.C., ed. *Rural People's Communes in Lien-chiang*. Stanford: Hoover Institution, 1969.

Ch'en, Theodore H.E. *Thought Reform of the Chinese Intellectuals*. Hongkong: Hongkong University Press, 1960.

Clubb, O. Edmund. *Twentieth-Century China*. New York: Columbia University Press, 1964.

Communist China 1955–1959. Policy Documents with Analysis. Cambridge, Mass.: Harvard University Press, 1965.

Dahl, Robert A. "Critique of the Ruling Elite Model." *American Political Science Review* 52, no. 2 (1958).

Donnithorne, Audrey. *China's Economic System*. London: George Allen and Unwin, 1967.

Eckstein, Alexander. *Communist China's Economic Growth and Foreign Trade*. New York: McGraw-Hill, 1966.

Etzioni, Amitai. *A Comparative Analysis of Complex Organizations*. Glencoe, Ill.: Free Press, 1961.

————, ed. *Complex Organizations: A Sociological Reader*. 2d. ed. New York: Holt, Rinehart and Winston, 1969.

Gelman, Harry. "Mao and the Permanent Purge." *Problems of Communism*, no. 6 (1966).

Gittings, John. *The Role of the Chinese Army*. New York: Oxford University Press, 1967.

Halperin, Morton H. *China and the Bomb*. New York: Praeger, 1965.

Hilsman, Roger. *To Move a Nation: The Politics of Foreign Policy in the Administration of John F. Kennedy.* New York: Doubleday, 1967.

Hofheinz, Roy. "Rural Administration in Communist China." *CQ*, no. 71 (1962).

Houn, Franklin W. *A Short History of Chinese Communism.* Englewood Cliffs, N.J.: Prentice-Hall, 1967.

Hsieh, Alice L. *Communist China's Strategy in the Nuclear Era.* Englewood Cliffs, N.J.: Prentice-Hall, 1962.

———. "China's Secret Military Papers: Military Doctrine and Strategy." *CQ*, no. 18 (1964).

Hudson, G.F., et al. *The Chinese Communes.* London: Oxford University Press, 1960.

Hughes, T.J., and Luard, D.E.T. *Economic Development of Communist China.* London: Oxford University Press, 1959.

Institute of International Relations. *Chinese Communist Who's Who.* Taipei: Institute of International Relations, 1970.

Joffe, Ellis. "The Conflict Between Old and New in the Chinese Army." *CQ*, no. 18 (1964).

Johnson, Chalmers A. *Peasant Nationalism and Communist Power: The Emergence of Revolutionary China.* Stanford, Cal.: Stanford University Press, 1962.

Karnow, Stanley. *Mao and China: From Revolution to Revolution.* New York: Viking Press, 1972.

Klein, Donald W. "The 'Next Generation' of Chinese Communist Leaders." *CQ*, no. 12 (1962).

———, and Clark, Anne B. *Biographical Dictionary of Chinese Communism 1921–1965.* Cambridge: Harvard University Press, 1971.

Lasswell, Harold. *Politics: Who Gets What, When, How.* Cleveland: World, 1958.

———. *The Decision Process: Seven Categories of Functional Analysis.* College Park: Bureau of Government Research, University of Maryland, 1956.

———, and Kaplan, A. *Power and Society: A Framework of Political Inquiry.* New Haven: Yale University Press, 1950.

Lewis, John W. *Major Doctrines of the Chinese Communist Leadership.* Ithaca, N.Y.: Cornell University Press, 1961.

———. *Leadership in Communist China.* Ithaca, N.Y.: Cornell University Press, 1963.

———. "China's Secret Military Papers: 'Continuities' and 'Revelations.'" *CQ*, no. 18 (1964).

Li, Choh-ming. *Economic Development of Communist China*. Berkeley: University of California Press, 1959.

―――. *The Statistical System of Communist China*. Berkeley: University of California Press, 1962.

―――. "China's Industrial Development." *CQ*, no. 17 (1964).

Lindbeck, John M.H., ed. *China: Management of A Revolutionary Society*. Seattle: University of Washington Press, 1971.

Lindblom, Charles E. "The Science of 'Muddling Through.'" *Public Administration Review* 19 (1959).

―――, and Braybrooke, David. *A Strategy of Decisions*. New York: Free Press, 1963.

MacFarquhar, Roderick. *The Hundred Flowers Campaign and the Chinese Intellectuals*. New York: Praeger, 1960.

―――. "Communist China's Intra-Party Dispute." *Pacific Affairs* 31, no. 4 (1958).

Nathan, Andrew. "A Factional Model for CCP Politics." *CQ*, no. 53 (1973).

Neuhauser, Charles. "The Chinese Communist Party in the 1960's: Prelude to the Cultural Revolution." *CQ*, no. 32 (1967).

Oksenberg, Michael. "Occupational Groups in Chinese Society and the Cultural Revolution." In *The Cultural Revolution: 1967 in Review*. Ann Arbor: Center for Chinese Studies, University of Michigan, 1968.

―――. *Policy Formulation in Communist China: The Case of the 1957–1958 Mass Irrigation Campaign*. Ph.D. dissertation, Columbia University, 1969.

Orleans, Leo A. "Birth Control: Reversal or Postponement?" *CQ*, no. 3 (1960).

Ploss, Sidney. *Conflict and Decision-making in Soviet Russia: A Case Study of Agricultural Policy 1953–1963*. Princeton: Princeton University Press, 1965.

Powell, Ralph L. *Politico-Military Relationships in Communist China*. Washington, D.C.: External Research Bureau, U.S. Department of State, 1963.

Prybyla, Jan S. *The Political Economy of Communist China*. Scranton, Pa.: International, 1970.

Pye, Lucian W. *The Spirit of Chinese Politics*. Cambridge: MIT Press, 1968.

Rice, Edward. *Mao's Way*. Berkeley: University of California Press, 1972.

Robinson, James A. *Congress and Foreign Policy-making*. Homewood, Ill. Dorsey, 1962.

Robinson, Thomas, ed. *The Cultural Revolution in China*. Berkeley: University of California Press, 1971.

Scalapino, Robert A., ed. *Elites in the People's Republic of China*. Seattle: University of Washington Press, 1972.

Schram, Stuart R. *The Political Thought of Mao Tse-tung.* New York: Praeger, 1963.

———. *Mao Tse-tung.* New York: Simon and Shuster, 1967.

Schurmann, Franz. *Ideology and Organization in Communist China.* 2d ed. Berkeley: University of California Press, 1968.

Shattschneider, E.E. *The Semi-Sovereign People.* New York: Holt, Rinehart and Winston, 1961.

Skinner, G. William. "Marketing and Social Structure in Rural China," 3 parts. *Journal of Asian Studies* 24, no. 1 (1964), nos. 2, 3 (1965).

———, and Winckler, Edwin A. "Compliance Succession in Rural Communist China: A Cyclical Theory." In *Complex Organizations: A Sociological Reader,* 2d ed., Amitai Etzioni, ed. New York: Holt, Rinehart and Winston, 1969.

Snow, Edgar. *The Other Side of the River: Red China Today.* New York: Random House, 1961.

Snyder, Richard. "A Decision-making Approach to the Study of Political Phenomena." In *Approaches to the Study of Politics,* Roland Young, ed. Evanston, Ill.: Northwestern University Press, 1958.

Solomon, Richard. "One Party and 'One Hundred Schools': Leadership, Lethargy, or Luan?" *Current Scene* 7, nos. 19–20 (1969).

———. *Mao's Revolution and the Chinese Political Culture.* Berkeley: University of California Press, 1971.

Strong, Anna Louise. *The Rise of People's Communes in China.* New York: Marzavai and Munsell, 1960.

Tang, Peter S.H. *Domestic and Foreign Policies.* 2d ed. Communist China Today, vol. 4. Washington, D.C.: Research Institute on the Sino-Soviet Bloc, 1961.

Teiwes, Frederick C. "The Purge of Provincial Leaders 1957–1958." *CQ,* no. 27 (1966).

———. *Provincial Party Personnel in Mainland China: 1956–1966.* New York: East Asian Institute, Columbia University, 1967.

Townsend, James R. *Political Participation in Communist China.* Berkeley: University of California Press, 1967.

Tsou, Tang. "The Cultural Revolution and the Chinese Political System." *CQ,* no. 38 (1969).

———, ed. *China's Policies in Asia and America's Alternatives.* China in Crisis, vol. 2. Chicago: University of Chicago Press, 1968.

Uhalley, Stephen, Jr. "The Cultural Revolution and the Attack on the 'Three Family Village.'" *CQ,* no. 27 (1966).

Vogel, Ezra. *Canton Under Communism*. Cambridge: Harvard University Press, 1969.

Walker, Kenneth R. "Collectivization in Retrospect: The 'Socialist High Tide' of Autumn 1955–Spring 1956." *CQ*, no. 26 (1966).

Whiting, Allen S. "China." In *Modern Political Systems: Asia*, Robert E. Ward and Roy C. Macridis, eds. Englewood Cliffs, N.J.: Prentice-Hall, 1963, pp. 117–97.

Whitson, William W., with Huang Chen-hsia. *The Chinese High Command*. New York: Praeger, 1972.

Yu, Frederick T.C. *Mass Persuasion in Communist China*. New York: Praeger, 1964.

Zagoria, Donald S. *The Sino-Soviet Conflict 1956–1961*. Princeton: Princeton University Press, 1962.

Translations from People's Republic Sources

Current Background. Collections of articles or documents grouped according to subject, issued several times a month. (Translation: U.S. Consulate-General, Hongkong).

Daily Reports of the Foreign Broadcast Information Service. (Translation: U.S. Department of Commerce, Washington, D.C.).

Extracts (Selections) from China Mainland Magazines. Translations from periodicials, issued several times a month. (Translation: U.S. Consulate-General, Hongkong).

Joint Publication Research Service. (Translation: U.S. Department of Commerce, Washington D.C.)

Survey of the China Mainland Press. A daily collection of translations from important articles. (Translation: U.S. Consulate-General, Hongkong).

Chinese Communist Sources (in Chinese and English)

Speeches and Statements by Chinese Communists Officials;
Other Relevant Materials

Ch'en Po-ta. "Explanations of the Draft Decision on the Question of Agricultural Cooperativization." *JMJP*, 19 October 1955.

————. "New Society, New People." *HC*, no. 3, 1 July 1958.

————. "Under the Banner of Chairman Mao Tse-tung." *HC*, no. 4, 16 July 1958.

Ch'en Yi. "Comrade Mao Tse-tung's Report on the Question of Agricultural Cooperation is a Model Combination of Theory and Practice." *JMJP*, 13 November 1955; *SCMP*, no. 1177, 24–25 November 1955.

Ch'en Yun. "Speech to the 2nd Session of the 1st NPC (July 1955)." *JMST*, 1956, *CB*, no. 339, 27 July 1955.

————. "Speech to the 3rd Session of the 1st NPC" (June 1956). *NCAS*, 1956.

————. "Several Major Problems in the Current Capital Construction Work." *HC*, no. 5, 1 March 1959.

Chou En-lai. "On the Question of Intellectuals" (14 January 1956). *NCNA*, 29 January 1956: *CB*, no. 376, 7 February 1956.

————. "Report on the Work of the Government" (26 June 1957). *JMST*, 1958.

————. "Report on the Proposals for the Second Five-year Plan" (16 September 1956). *8NCCPC*, 1: 261–328.

Chou Fang. *Wo-kuo Kuo-chia Chi-kou (The State Structure of Our Country)*. Peking: Chung-kuo Ch'ing-nien Ch'u-pau-she, 1957.

Chu Teh. "People's Army, People's War." *NCNA*, 31 July 1958; *CB*, no. 514, 6 August 1958.

Hsueh Mu-ch'iao. "A Preliminary Opinion on the Present System of Planning Control." *CHCS*, no. 9, September 1957.

Kao Chu Jen-min Kung-she Ti Hung-ch'i Sheng-li Ch'ien-chin (Hold Aloft the Red Flag of the People's Communes and Victoriously March on). Peking: Fa-lu Ch'u-pan-she, 1960. 2 vols.

Li Hsien-nien. "Financial-Economic Work and Agricultural Cooperation." *TKP* (Tientsin), 8 November 1955; *SCMP*, no. 1183, 7 December 1955.

————. "What I Have Seen in the People's Communes." *HC*, no. 10, 16 October 1958.

Liao Lu-yen. "Explanations on the Draft 1956–1967 National Program for Agricultural Development," *NCNA*, 25 January 1956; *SCMP*, no. 1219, 31 January 1956.

Liu Shao-ch'i. *On Inner Party Struggle*. New York: New Century Publishers, 1952.

————. *On the Party*. Peking: FLP, 1950.

————. *How to be a Good Communist*. Peking: FLP, 1962.

————. "Political Report of the Central Committee of the Communist Party of China to the Eighth Party Congress" (15 September 1956). *8NCCPC*, 1: 13–111.

———. "The Significance of the October Revolution" (6 November 1957). *JMJP*, 7 November 1957.

———. "Report on the Work of the Central Committee of the Communist Party of China to the Second Session of the Eighth National Congress." *JMJP*, 25 May 1958; *PR*, no. 14, 3 June 1958.

Lu Ting-yi. "Let a Hundred Flowers Blossom, a Hundred Schools of Thought Contend" (26 May 1956). *JMJP*, 13 June 1956.

Lun Jen-min Kung-she (On the People's Communes). Peking: Chung-kuo Ch'ing-nien Ch'u-pan-she, 1958.

Lun Jen-min Kung-she Yu Kung-ch'an Ch-i (On the People's Communes and Communism). Peking: People's University, 1958.

Ma Nan-tun [Teng T'o]. *Yen-shan Yeh-hua (Evening Chats at Yenshan)*. Peking: Peiching Ch'u-pan-she, 1961.

Mao Tse-tung. "The Question of Agricultural Cooperation." *JMJP*, 17 October 1955; *CB*, no. 364.

———. "On the Correct Handling of Contradictions Among the People." *People's China*, 1 July 1957. (Supplement)

———. *Selected Works*, vol. 2. Peking: FLP, 1961.

People's Communes in China. Peking: FLP, 1960.

Po I-po. "Agricultural Cooperation Should be Closely Linked Up With Technical Reform of Agriculture." *JMJP*, 17 November 1955; *SCMP*, no. 1179, 1 December 1955.

Shanghai Ti-yi-kou Jen-min Kung-she Ti T'ang-sheng (The Birth of the First People's Commune in Shanghai). Shanghai: Jen-min Ch'u-pan-she, 1958.

Socialist Upsurge in China's Countryside. Peking: FLP, 1956.

T'an Chen-lin. "Explanations on the 1956–1957 Program of Agricultural Development (Second Revised Draft)." *JMJP*, 27 May 1958.

T'ao Chu. "The Investigation Report of the Humeng Commune." *JMJP*, 25 February 1959.

———. "The Whole Nation as a Chessboard, the Whole Province as a Chessboard." *NFJP*, 2 March 1959.

Teng Tzu-hui. "Speech at the National Democratic Youth League Rural Work Conference" (15 July 1954). *CKCNP*, 1 September 1954; *CB*, no. 306, 22 November 1954.

———. "Speech at the National Conference of Outstanding Workers" (7 May 1956). *NCNA*, 7 May 1956.

————. "On the Contradictions Among the People in the Countryside and the Principles and Methods of Correctly Handling these Contradictions." *CKCNP*, no. 21, November 1957.

Tung Ta-lin. *Agricultural Cooperation in China*. Peking: FLP, 1959.

Wei Kung-ku Fa-chan Jen-min Kung-she Erh Tou-cheng (Struggle for the Consolidation and Development of the People's Commune). Honan: CCP Hsinyang Special District Party Committee, 1958.

Wu Chih-p'u. "From Agricultural Producers' Cooperatives to the People's Communes." *HC*, no. 8, 16 September 1958.

————. "Contradictions are the Motive Force for the Development of the Socialist Society." *HCS*, no. 6, June 1960.

Wu Han. *Hai Jui Pa Kuan (The Dismissal of Hai Jui)*. Peking: Peiching Ch'u-pan-she, 1961.

Yang Ying-chieh. "On Unified Planning and Decentralized Control." *CHCS*, no. 11, November 1958.

Yao Wen-yuan. "A Criticism of the New Historical Play 'The Dismissal of Hai Jui.'" *WHP* (Shanghai), 10 November 1965.

Newspapers and Periodicals

News items cited and consulted in this study but not listed individually are from the following publications:

Chekiang Jih-pao (Chekiang Daily)
Chi-hua Ching-shi (Planned Economy)
Ching-chi Yen-chin (Economic Research)
Chung-kuo Ch'ien-nien Pao (China Youth Daily)
Hsin-hua Pan-yueh-kan (New China Semi-Monthly)
Hsueh Hsi (Study)
Hung Ch'i (Red Flag)
Jen-min Jih-pao (People's Daily)
Nan-fang Jih-pao (Southern Daily)
New China News Agency
Peking Review
Ta-kung Pao (Impartial Daily)
Ts'ai Cheng (Finance)

Official Documents

The best sources for laws, regulations, directives, resolutions, and "normative enactments" are the following:

Jen-min Kung-hokuo Fa-kuer Hui-pien (The Compendium of the Laws and Regu-lations of the People's Republic of China) and *Jen-min shou-ts'e (People's Hand-book)*, both of which are published annually, and *Hsin-jua Pan-yueh-kan (New China Semi-Monthly)*

Documents of CCP Central Committee 1956–1969. Hongkong: Union Research Institute, 1971, vol. 1.

The following major documents are used in this study:

CCP Central Committee and the State Council. "Joint Directive on Running of the APC's Industriously and Economically" (4 April 1956). *NCNA*, 4 April 1956; *SCMP*, no. 1286, 16 April 1956.

CCP Central Committee and the State Council. "Joint Directive on Strength-ening Production Leadership and Organizational Construction of Agri-cultural Producers' Cooperatives." *NCNA*, 12 September 1956.

"Decision on Agricultural Cooperation" (adopted at the Enlarged Sixth Plenary Session of the Seventh CC of the CCP, 11 October 1955). *JMJP*, 18 October 1955; *SCMP*, no. 1151, 15–18 October 1955.

Eighth National Congress of the Communist Party of China. Peking: FLP, 1956, 3 vols.

"1956–1967 National Program for Agricultural Development" (adopted by the NPC in April 1960). *JMJP*, 12 April 1960; *CB*, no. 616.

"Resolution of the 8th Plenary Session of the 8th Central Committee of the CCP Concerning the Anti-Party Clique Headed by P'eng Teh-huai" (excerpts), 16 August 1959. *JMJP*, 16 August 1967; *PR*, no. 34, 18 August 1967.

"Resolution on the Establishment of People's Communes in the Rural Areas" (adopted by the CCP Politburo on 29 August 1958). *JMJP*, 10 September 1958.

"Resolution on Some Questions Concerning the People's Communes" (adopted by the Sixth CC Plenum of the CCP on 10 December 1958). *Sixth Plenary Session of the Eighth Central Committee of the Communist Party of China.* Peking: FLP, 1958, pp. 12–49.

"State Council's Directive Concerning Improvement of Commercial Man-agement Systems" (November 1957). *JMJP*, 18 November 1957. (English translation: *SCMP*, no. 1665, 5 December 1957).

"State Council's Directive Concerning Improvement of Financial Manage-ment Systems" (November 1957). *JMJP*, 18 November 1957. (English translation: *SCMP*, no. 1665, 5 December 1957.)

"State Council's Directive Concerning Improvement of Industrial Management System" (November 1957). *JMJP*, 18 November 1957. (English translation: *SCMP*, no. 1665, 5 December 1957.)

Secret Chinese Communist Documents

PLA Kung-tso T'ung-hsun (Bulletin of Activities). In J. Chester Cheng, ed., *The Politics of the Chinese Red Army: A Translation of the Bulletin of Activities of the People's Liberation Army*. Stanford: Hoover Institution, 1966.

Seventy-Article "Regulations on Industry, Mines and Enterprises" (December 1961). *Kung-fei Kung-yeh Cheng-ts'e Ch'i-shih T'iao Chu-yuo Nei-yung (Main Contents of the Seventy-Article Industry Policy of the Chinese Communist)*. (Note: This is a summary, not the original text of the document.)

Sixty-Article "Draft Regulations on the Rural People's Communes" (May 1961). *Fei-wei Nung-ts'un Jen-min Kung-she T'iao-li Ts'ao-an Fu-yin-pen* (1961.5 Ting-fa). *(Reprint of the Draft Regulations on Chinese Communist Rural People's Communes)* (promulgated in May 1961).

Sixty-Article "Draft Regulations on the Rural People's Communes" (revised in September 1962). *Kung-fei Nung-ts'un Jen-min Kung-she Kung-tso T'iao-li Hsiu-cheng Ts'ao-an*, September 1962 *(Revised Draft Working Regulations on the Chinese Communist Rural People's Communes, September 1962)*. Taipei: State Security Bureau, May 1964.

The "Lienchiang Documents." *Fan-kung Yu-chi-tui T'u-chi Fukien Lienchieng Lu-huo Fei-fang Wen-chien Hui-pien (Collected Documents Captured During An Anti-Communist Raid on Lienchiang Hsien, Fukien)*. Taipei: Intelligence Bureau, Ministry of Defense, March 1964. (An English translation of the documents is in C.S. Ch'en, ed., *Rural People's Communes in Lienchiang*. Stanford: Hoover Institution, 1969.)

Twelve-Article "Urgent Directive on the Rural Work" (November 1960). *Fei-tang "Chung-yang" So Pan-pu Ti "Nung-ts'un Kung-tso Chin-chi Chih-shih"* (Kiangsi Jen-min Kwang-po T'ien-tai 1960, 11.3 Kwang-po) *(The Urgent Directive on the Rural Work" issued by the "Central Committee" of the Chinese Communist Party)*. Broadcoast by the Kiangsi People's Radio on 3 November 1960. (Note: This is only a summary of the directive.)

Red Guard Sources

Ch'iao Yi-fu. *Hung-wei-ping Husan-chi*, vol. 1 *(Selections of the Red Guard Materials)*. Hongkong, Ta-lu Ch'u-pan-she, 1967.

Down With Big Conspirator, Big Ambitionist, Big Warlord P'eng Teh-huai— Collected Materials Against P'eng Teh-huai. Peking: Ching-kang-shan Corps under the Capital Red Guard Congress, Tsinghua University, November 1967. (Translated in *CB*, no. 851, 26 April 1968.)

Liu Shao-ch'i. "Confession" (made on 23 October 1966, in a CC Working Conference, made public in Red Guard posters in Peking). *Mainichi Shimbun* (Tokyo), 28–29 January 1967. (An English translation appears in *Atlas* [New York], April 1967.)

Mao Chu-hsi Tui P'eng Huang Chang Chou Fang-Tang Chi-tuan Ti p'i-p'an (*Chairman Mao's Repudiations of the P'eng* [*Teh-huai*], *Huang* [*K'o-cheng*], *Chang* [*Wen-t'ien*], *Chou* [*Hsiao-chou*] *Anti-Party Clique*). (n.d.) Among photoduplicated material presumably published in Mainland China and released in 1968 by the U.S. Department of State's Office of External Research through the Center for Chinese Research Materials, Association of Research Libraries, Group XI, reel 2, part 9. (An English translation of the pamphlet is in *Chinese Law and Government*, vol. 1, no. 4, 1968.)

Mao Tse-tung Ssu-hsiang Wan-sui (Long Live Mao Tse-tung's Thought) (April 1967) and *Collection of Statements by Mao Tse-tung 1956–1967* (n.d.). (Some of the materials of these two collections are translated in *CB*, no. 892, 21 October 1969.)

Mao Tse-tung Ssu-hsiang Wan-sui (Long Live Mao Tse-tung's Thought) (N.P. August 1969.)

P'eng Teh-huai. "Letter of Opinion" (14 July 1959). *Ko-ming Ch'uan-lien.* Peking: Ko-ming Ch'uan-lien Editorial Board, Peking Institute of Building Engineering, 24 August 1967; *SCMP*, no. 4032, 2 October 1967.

Selections from Chairman Mao. Washington, D.C.: Joint Publications Research Service, no. 49,826, 12 February 1970.

The Evil Deeds of the Anti-Party and Anti-Socialist Element and Counter-revolutionary Double-Dealer, Liu Chien-hsun (Revolutionary Rebel General Command of the organs of the CCP Honan Provincial Committee, 12 March 1967). (Translated in *JPRS*, no. 43, 357, 16 November 1967.)

Ting Wang. *Chung-kung Wen-hua Ta Ko-ming Tzu-liao Hui-pien* (*Collected Materials of Chinese Communist Great Cultural Revolution*). Hongkong: Ming Pao Monthly, 1967–70, 5 vols.

Wu Leng-hsi. "Confession." *Hung-se Hsin-hua* (the publication of a "revolutionary" organization in New China News Agency), no. 43, May 1968; as reprinted in *Hsing-tao Jih-pao* (Hongkong), 9 July 1968. (An English translation with notes is in *Chinese Law and Government*, vol. 2, no. 4, 1969–70.)

Other Red Guard materials used in this study come mostly from the following publications (most of which are available in Ting Wang):

Chin-chun Pao. Peking: Liaison Committee for Savagely Opening Fire on the Bourgeois Reactionary Line and the Red Guard Joint Unit of the Mao Tse-tung Thought Philosophy and Social Sciences Department, Chinese Academy of Sciences, nos. 22/23, 31 May 1967.

Chingkang-shan. Peking: Chingkang-shan corps of Tsinghua University, nos. 6/7, 1 January 1967.

Hung Ch'i. Peking: Hung Ch'i Fighting Detachment of Aeronautical Engineering Institute, no. 24, 4 April 1967.

Hung-wei-ping Pao. Peking: Red Guard Revolutionary Rebel Headquarters, Chinese Academy of Sciences, no. 6, 6 February 1967.

Pei-Ching Kung-she (*Peking Commune*). Peking: Central Financial and Monetary College August 8 Fighting Detachment, no. 5, 28 January; no. 12, 14 March 1967.

Shou-tu Hung-wei-ping. Peking: Congress of Red Guards of Universities and Colleges in Peking, no. 24, 21 January 1967.

Ts'ai-mao Hung Ch'i. Peking: The Rebel Liaison Committee of the Finance and Trade System, no. 3, 15 February; no. 4, 23 February 1967.

Tung-fang-hung. Peking: Peking Mining Institute Tung-fang-hung Commune of Capital Colleges Red Guard Congress, nos. 19/20, 20 April 1967.

Tung-fang-hung Pao. Peking: Peking Institute of Geology, nos. 16/17, 9 March 1967.

Index